S0-BNJ-825

Feminist Cyberscapes: Mapping Gendered Academic Spaces

New Directions in Computers & Composition Studies

Gail E. Hawisher and Cynthia L. Selfe, Series Editors

Feminist Cyberscapes: Mapping Gendered Academic Spaces
Kristine Blair and Pamela Takayoshi, editors, 1999

Electronic Writing Centers: Computing in the Field of Composition
David Coogan, 1999

Computers and the Teaching of Writing in American Higher Education, 1979–1994: A History
Gail E. Hawisher, Paul LeBlanc, Charles Moran, and Cynthia L. Selfe, 1996

The Rhetoric of Electronic Communities
Tharon Howard, 1997

Nostalgic Angels: Rearticulating Hypertext Writing
Johndan Johnson-Eilola, 1997

The Computer and the Page: Publishing, Technology, and the Classroom
James Kalmbach, 1997

Transitions: Teaching Writing in Computer-Supported and Traditional Classrooms
Mike Palmquist, Kate Kiefer, James Hartvigsen, and Barbara Goodlew, 1998

Rhetorical Ethics and Internetworked Writing
James Porter, 1998

Opening Spaces: Writing Technologies and Critical Research Practices
Patricia Sullivan and James Porter, 1997

Forthcoming:
Digital Fictions: Storytelling in a Material World
Sarah Sloane

Feminist Cyberscapes: Mapping Gendered Academic Spaces

edited by

Kristine Blair
Bowling Green State University

and

Pamela Takayoshi
University of Louisville

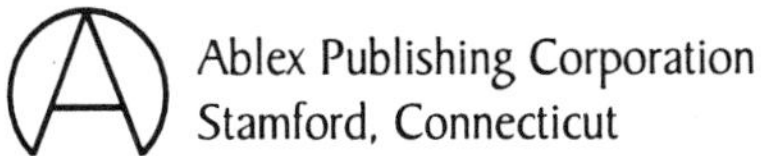
Ablex Publishing Corporation
Stamford, Connecticut

Printed in the United States of America

Publisher's Note: All e-mail extracts and postings in this book remain as they were typed. Any spelling or grammatical mistakes have been left intact.

Library of Congress Cataloguing-in-Publication Data

Feminist cyberscapes : mapping gendered academic spaces / edited by Kristine Blair and Pamela Takayoshi.
p. cm.— (New directions in computers & composition studies)
Includes bibliographical references and index.
ISBN 1-56750-438-8 (cloth) — ISBN 1-56750-439-6 (pbk.)
1. English language—Rhetoric—Study and teaching—Data processing. 2. Academic writing—Study and teaching—Data processing. 3. English language—computer-assisted instruction. 4. Internet (Computer network) in education. 5. Academic writing—Sex differences. 6. Women—Education (Higher). 7. Feminism and education. I. Blair, Kristine. II. Takayoshi, Pamela. III. Series: New Directions in computers and composition studies.
PE1404.F39 1999
808'.042'0285—dc21 98–43687
CIP

Ablex Publishing Corporation
100 Prospect Street
P.O. Box 811
Stamford, Connecticut 06904-0811

Contents

Map of Location V: The Future: To Be Mapped Later

Acknowledgments

As writing scholars, we know well that no written work springs up in isolation. Rather than a simple collection of isolated texts, this collection resonates and intersects with many other scholars' ideas and words as well as with the hard work of many other people who might not be immediately visible in the end product of this book.

First, we thank our contributors, without whose eagerness, engagement, and erudition, this book would not exist. One of the wonderful—but unforeseen—consequences of editing this collection has been getting to know these colleagues. The stimulating conversations we've been engaged in with these colleagues and friends since this project began has been very rewarding for our thinking about feminisms, technologies, gender, and power.

Additionally, we thank the many women who came before us, laying the groundwork for thinking through the problems we encounter in this book. As this text attests to many times, much of this work was invisible—but as the existence of this text also attests to—necessary and important for the building being done by the women in this collection. Chief among these role models have been Gail Hawisher and Cindy Selfe, whose unflagging support and enthusiasm for this project carried us through the many months of working in isolation.

We also thank Cynthia Haynes and Jan Rune Holmevik, administrators of Lingua MOO, for the use of the "cyberparlor." Resources such as Lingua MOO have been vital to our interests as feminist teachers and scholars.

We must also thank Tony O'Keeffe for helping us with the title.

Kris especially thanks Kevin Williams and Angela Blair, the two people who make things possible.

Pam thanks her mother, Sherry Sakowitz, for the value she placed on education, on knowledge, and on justness. Her influence has been and continues to be invaluable to Pam becoming the person she is today. Pam also thanks her family—Brian, Meghan, and Emily Huot—for encouraging her thinking about this project and her scholarly work in general while at the same time helping her remember what's really important in life.

Acknowledgments

Foreword: (Women's) Place(s)

Blair and Takayoshi, as part of their introduction to *Feminist Cyberscapes*, describe how women are already placed in cyberspace by the popular press. Some of us may be cybergrrls, but most of us are not present in the accolades given to computer gurus, not present in the discussions of social computing in workplaces, and virtually invisible in the waves of advertising aimed at accelerating the consumption of cyberspace. While there are moves to incorporate sensual appeal into websites, there are few popular stereotypes for women in cyberspace.

This absence in the popular media comes with little surprise. I worked with computers for almost 10 years before I discovered I was gendered in cyberspace as much as I am in surface life. I thought of computers innocently—as instruments, games, machines, statistics slaves, and as publishing tools. I did not seek to understand the ways in which they helped me shape certain kinds of expression and simultaneously frowned on others as not worthy. And I certainly neglected the study of *how* they were linked to class, race, or gendering. This innocence persisted in part because I was experimenting with computer writing in an environment where computers and money were plentiful but difference was not. It wasn't until I battled with the Purdue University Computing Center over computer use for writing majors that I experienced how both my use of computers and the writing technologies themselves might be constructed and seen as feminine (otherwise known as what a secretary can type and therefore a waste of technical power). I remember reading Rosemary Pringle's (1989) study of secretarial work (its chapters contrasting how female secretaries were given word processors while male managers got personal computers) at the time of one battle. When I brought the study into a meeting with some managers from the computing center they stared, paused for a while, and changed the topic. I could never get them to understand our discussions as based on class or gender; the closest I could come to open discussion of difference was an acknowledgment of disciplinary differences.

Because computers were not part of humanities budgets (or traditional instruction in humanities), our push to gain writing technology for instruction in a tight economy strained civility and brought out assumptions. The speed, efficiency, and data security needed by programmers and scientists were/are their values. Somehow in this restricted-resources environment, word processing, publishing, certain kinds of e-mail, and, more recently, personal (and perhaps even corporate) web pages became a waste of technical resources, a diversion of finds away from the real work of a (technical) university. I cannot count the number of times I heard "We have to stop students from using the labs to do their word processing" or "You have to let us train new users (read, women in humanities) to avoid computing problems (read, because you cannot without wasting resources)." Germane to this book, writing and writing technologies have been linked with both the pink collar working class and with the feminine, at least in my workplace (the technical university) they have been.

This economic situation has helped me realize that in some ways we are all likely to be labeled unwashed end users in the eyes of the technical community. Perhaps the montage of complex interactions this collection offers will help us view our positioning with fresh eyes.

TECHNOLOGY HOPES AND HABITS

Others should not be asked to shoulder all the responsibility for how we construct issues of writing technology. A statement in Walter Ong's *Interfaces of the Word* (1977) projects the technology hope we too often use to ground our issues: "The mind does not enter into the alphabet or the printed book or the computer so much as the alphabet or print or the computer enters the mind..." (p. 47). Through the years that sentiment has invited a mix of determinism and hope (amongst those in technology and writing). Consider how it resonates with discussions of emerging technologies—the waves of discovering, learning, critiquing, and abandoning discussion of writing technologies. But even as it speaks to me I recognize that some technologies no longer discussed in the computers and composition literature are still bedrock for our writing lives—technologies that form the unexplained strata of habit, the structure for cyberinteraction, and perhaps the way the computer is/was/has been entering our collective mind. Thus, I am particularly grateful that *Feminist Cyberscapes* breaks some of this cycle and does not abandon the study of more bedrock technologies (say, e-mail) in favor of emerging technologies (say, synchronous video conferencing). Such restraint in a society of technology hope shows the discipline necessary to build important issues.

With hope, too, comes the lure of exposed writing habits, and that is an elixir that feeds those of us who examine writing habits. Typically, an emerging writing technology dispossesses, at least at some level, our writing habits and urges us to make new ones. Each new program allows us to perform new actions; simultaneously it inhibits our abilities to perform other actions. Thus, the emerging technology, particularly when it disturbs our tacit patterns, lays bare our processes for examination, critique, resistance, acceptance, and/or change. Of course, this simple statement of process covers over the complex economic, political, cultural, philosophical, and poetic forces that are first exposed and later covered over in that period when we discover and examine new writing technologies. More important, focusing on processes and habits sidesteps examination of the technology hope each new technology brings us. We optimistically greet these disruptions as opportunities to remake the culture into the more egalitarian state we seek. But embracing this cycle traps our theorizing into patterns that center certain technology issues, while it decenters other more political, economic, and cultural ones. I see *Feminist Cyberscapes* challenging the technology hopes and habits cycle by addressing technology hope from vantages that allow both skepticism and respect. Such challenges certainly are needed.

GENDERED ACADEMIC SPACES

Feminist Cyberscapes explores how female teachers, students, and writers occupy many (and sometimes conflicting) writing technology spaces. I like the ways in which the writers push at both the writing technologies and the feminist conceptions of women as constructors/users of writing technologies. True, their discussions include the prominent topics of bodies and identities that are staples in previous feminist treatments of cyberspace (e.g., Balsamo, 1995; Stone, 1995; Terry & Calvert, 1997; Wakeford, 1997). But their discussions also tie those wonderfully complex discussions of gender to topics such as collaboration and discourse communities that figure more prominently in composition studies. Throughout its chapter, the collection constructs a fabric that grants women a place in the forging of academic discourse in computers and composition as sure-footedly as it delivers examinations of various genderings in cyberspace. Furthermore, both in its interstitial interviews with prominent figures in computers and composition (Helen Schwartz, Gail Hawisher, and Cynthia Selfe) as well as in Lisa Gerrard's final call for research on key issues in Chapter 13, *Feminist Cyberscapes* positions women as shapers of issues for computers and composition. Interestingly enough, Blair and Takayoshi do not end the collection with the "What next?" essay, but add a transcript from the authors' MOO and a final interview. The MOO transcript, as much as anything, disturbs the ritual closure for such theme collections in ways that remind us that tidy endings are not possible in this area; more realistically, we have a cacaphony of voices.

*****

Why read *Feminist Cyberscapes*? Since it does not purport to be the one book on women in cyberspace we need to own, why pay attention? For those of us who are women using writing technologies, these chapters enrich our possibilities for agency by weaving a more complex tapestry of being/becoming women in cyberspace and offering more than the few models popular media identifies. For us feminists, these writers are offering the serious engagement with technology that Carol Stabile (1994) argues is needed for feminist theory to confront the dominant technological society.

For those of us who are writing teachers, these chapters testify to the sensitivity needed as a teacher of digital writing. These are all important reasons to confront this volume. But there is a more compelling reason for those of us who teach writing with/in technologies: the technology elite paint all of us into the same stereotypes that the media uses for women. To them, we are all women.

Patricia Sullivan
Purdue University

REFERENCES

Balsamo, A. (1995). *Technologies of the gendered body: Reading cyborg women.* Durham, NC: Duke University Press.

Ong, W. J. (1997). *Interfaces of the word: Studies in the evolution of consciousness and culture.* Ithaca, NY: Cornell University Press.

Pringle, R. (1989). *Secretaries talk: Sexuality, power, and work.* New York: Verso.

Stabile, C. (1994). *Feminism and the technological fix.* New York: Manchester University Press.

Stone, A. R. (1995). *The war of desire at the close of the mechanical age.* Cambridge, MA: MIT Press.

Terry, J., & Calvert, M. (1997). *Processed lives: Gender and technology in everyday life.* London: Routledge.

Wakeford, N. (1997). Networking women and grrrls with information/communication technology: Surfing tales of the World Wide Web. In J. Terry and M. Calvert (Eds.), *Processed lives: Gender and technology in everyday life* (pp. 51–66). London: Routledge.

Introduction: Mapping the Terrain of Feminist Cyberscapes

Kristine Blair
Bowling Green State University

Pamela Takayoshi
University of Louisville

In February 1997, on a Tuesday night, in between segments for the evening news magazine *Dateline*, an MCI commercial for their latest networking software states: "There is no race. There are no genders. The are no infirmities. Only minds. Utopia? No. The Internet." *Dateline* returns with a segment on "Internet Addiction." Despite statistics that continue to show that most users are White, middle- to upper-class males, the focus of the *Dateline* exclusive is the addiction of women to Internet chat groups. In addition to an interview with a man who divorced his wife after discovering her online infidelity within a sexually-oriented chat group, the segment profiles a suburban wife and working mother's loss of her family through her treks into cyberspace for hours at a time. This cyber-addiction led to her alleged inattention to her children, to her job, and to her husband, who consequently divorced her for not fulfilling the duties attached to her role, such as "making the family meals." Although the commentator points out the rarity of Internet addiction, viewers are left with the image of the female addict, lamenting her losses, but starting over with a new boyfriend she recently met online. The narratives offered in the commercial and the news magazine segment tell two different stories about technology—the MCI commercial asserts a utopian vision in which we use technology to rise above our material conditions, while the story of female computer addiction suggests a rhetoric of excess in which the promised escape from our material existence positions us as victims. Together, these narratives suggest that a blanket acceptance or rejection of the Internet as an empowering site for women does not account for the complicated relationships between women and technology in their personal and professional lives.

Similarly, within the field of computers and composition studies, there exist competing narratives about computers as tools of inclusion and exclusion, the status of marginalized voices being heard in electronic writing environments, the politics of access, and the potential for community. One strand of thinking in computers and composition has fallen along the positive axis. Within this strand of scholarship, computer technologies might create shared communities of writers, democratize the classroom, create space for students marginalized by traditional classroom forums, and address inequities of gender, race, class, age, sexual orientation, and other traditionally marginalizing social forces. Cynthia Selfe (1990) has argued that "computer-based text production can help us demarginalize those individuals who have been excluded from our discussion by more traditional approaches to literacy" (p. 122). She further notes that in addition to the claims for more egalitarian participation, the "lack of face-to-face cues meant that gender, age, and social status disappeared as individuals chose to reveal themselves" (p. 122). Mary Flores (1990) suggests that computer technologies might be used in classrooms to facilitate an "interactive, diverse, and collaborative writing community in which each and every student has a voice and can engage in dialogue with each and every other member of that community" (p. 109). These positive visions of computer technologies arose out of an excitement within the field of composition studies at the changes technology seemed poised to make—changes in definitions of text, writer, and reader, changes in the nature of classroom practice, and changes in the shape of writing professionals' lives.

As writing and communication technology became more widely used in writing classes, however, it became clear that this hopeful rhetoric was not the entire picture. In 1991, Gail Hawisher and Cynthia Selfe identified the primarily optimistic, hopeful, and positive scholarship as a "rhetoric of technology." Evidenced in an enthusiasm that foregrounds positive benefits of using networked computers without acknowledging the possible negative effects, this rhetoric "...is positive in the sense that it reflects the high expectations of instructors committed to positive educational reform in their writing classes. This same rhetoric, however, may also be dangerous if we want to think critically about technology and its issues" (p. 57). Feminist scholars particularly have attempted to answer Hawisher and Selfe's call for accounts of networked classes that provide the field "with a full understanding of how the use of technology can affect the social, political, and educational environments within which we teach" (p. 64). Susan Romano (1993), interpreting her experiences as a teacher in a networked environment through the frame of feminist theory, has questioned "the egalitarianism narrative," which suggests that networked computers create egalitarian class environments where marginalized students are more likely to become "empowered." Asserting that marginalized students will not be empowered simply because the opportunity exists, nor that students will necessarily welcome the opportunity, Romano concludes that the egalitarianism narrative is nothing more than "a promise whose occasional fulfillment grants it an unexamined legitimacy" (p. 26). Takayoshi (1994) supports Romano's conclusions in her assertion that with no intervention in traditional power structures, discourse in a new, potentially more empowering forum will not necessarily be any more empowering than those traditional forums. More recently, feminist scholarship has built upon the positive rhetoric by examining the legitimacy of the positive implications of computer-mediated communications in light of the experiences of women as students and scholars. As Billie Wahlstrom (1994) has asserted, "Applying feminist theory to technology supports Foucault's claim that we must see beyond the traditional ways of organizing knowledge and identify breaks, omissions, and discontinuities in our understanding" (p. 171). Moreover, we might ask to what extent the predicted utopias of computer-mediated communications (CMC) have been realized in the personal and social needs of women in online and face-to-face contexts. Gail Hawisher and Patricia Sullivan (1998) acknowledge that technologies of literacy—writing, print, and now electronic—have traditionally excluded women from positions of power. In their study of one all-female, online community (woman@waytoofast), Hawisher and Sullivan chronicle representations of women online and their production and negotiation of electronic spaces. As the participants in this study voiced concerns about their place as women in online forums and debated a range of issues from professional, online self- representation to sexual harassment, the consensus among them was that women must persist online to be heard.

Feminist Cyberscapes builds upon both the positive and the critical scholarly traditions by recognizing that the early feminist calls for egalitarianism through technology are the basis upon which critical perspectives are founded. In exploring the next stage of feminist scholarship on technology, the contributors to *Feminist Cyberscapes* explore the varying virtual, physical, cultural, and institutional contexts influencing the nature of electronic space for women and explore the intersection of feminisms, power, authority, voice, and computer technologies. Whereas feminism has been an implicit and explicit participant in composition scholarship on technologies, articles that combine a feminist perspective with technology are often located at the margins of composition studies. They are found as the sole article within edited collections and as articles in special issues of journals. They are not found for the most part in mainstream composition journals and collections. And significantly, feminist treatments of technology are found in computers and composition, not in the work of feminist theories of composition (the notable exception, of course, is Hawisher and Sullivan (1998)—although this article, too, suffers the "sole article in the collection" status and was written by technology scholars). The authors gathered here hope this collection can bring this line of scholarship into mainstream composition studies, and in this way answer Cynthia Selfe's call that composition studies think critically about technology. In her 1998 CCCC Chair's Keynote Address, Selfe described the "piecemeal fashion" with which our professional organizations tend to deal with technology as one which has contributed to *using* technology but not *thinking about* it: "we have paid technology issues precious little focused attention over the years." Furthermore, she warns,

> Allowing ourselves this luxury, however, is not only misguided at the end of the twentieth century, it is dangerously shortsighted ... I believe we have a much larger and more complicated obligation to fulfill—that of trying to understand and make sense of, to pay attention to, how technology is now inextricably linked to literacy and literacy education in this country.

This collection pays attention to the complex relationship between women and technology as a way of understanding our own participation and resistance to systems of inequity. We think that it is important to hear these multiple and varied perspectives as a whole—although the contributors to *Feminist Cyberscapes* write from and describe different locations in cyberspace, reading the pieces as a whole suggest to composition studies themes and issues for reflection and further consideration. Using theories of materialist feminism, feminist critiques of technology design and uses, and feminist pedagogy, contributors to *Feminist Cyberscapes* examine computerized writing classrooms, Internet technologies (including e-mail, listservs, and MOOs), and professional development opportunities for women working in computers and composition. These examinations include the analysis of gendered space in virtual communities, the presence/absence of the body in virtual reality, and the collaboration and coalition-building possibilities that computer technologies offer to women. In this sense, this collection continues the ongoing conversation exploring the theoretical, pedagogical, and political implications of computer technologies for composition studies, ultimately challenging larger cultural narratives of both empowerment and victimization online.

WOMEN WEAVING THE WEB: NARRATIVES OF NEGOTIATION ONLINE AND IN CLASSROOMS

Scholars examining questions of technology for dissemination through print media face a problem of time. The machinations of print media cannot keep time with technological developments. This collection bears this imprint of time—when we first sent out our call for papers, the World Wide Web was a newly felt presence in writing classrooms and theories and, as a result, there were still very few scholarly treatments of the Web. Since that time, of course, the Web has exploded in ways in which this collection's authors were only beginning to recognize. The frameworks that the authors establish, though, are ones that carry a great deal of resonance for thinking about web culture. The Web, like most technologies, exists as a site of complex, conflicting meanings for women. Feminist media theorists have long grappled with the image of women in popular culture, critiquing print, television, and film images that construct woman as object rather than subject. Through a discussion of workout machines, Susan Willis (1991) questions technology's construction of these different subject positions for women. She is particularly interested in "the way exercise has evolved in a commodified society so as to contain or limit" the positive features that exercise for women generates (p. 65). Willis's reading of women's relationships to the Nautilus machine as existing within a capitalist framework of production and consumption is worth quoting at length:

> In the context of women's labor history, the nautilus machine is a capitalist wish-fulfillment. It gives women access to the machine but denies access to production. It requires energy and effort and negates the experience of labor. It isolates the individual from other women who work out and defines her body as an assemblage of body areas and muscle functions, each requiring a specialized machine and machine function.... Nothing is produced but the body itself. (p. 75)

Like many technologies sold to women (think of domestic technologies, which produce nothing, require energy and effort, and isolate women in their homes), the Nautilus machine relies on traditional definitions of womanhood while seeming to offer women the position of active agent of change. Unlike the Nautilus machine, however, where "nothing is produced but the body itself," the Web offers to be a site where women occupy the position of production agent. In producing positive images and representations that resist dominant patriarchal constructions of women and girls, women use the Web to carve out spaces for themselves in a culture where so many spaces (virtual and material) are uninviting and threatening. However, this position of producing agent exists within the cyberscape of the Web, alongside a position of woman as object to be consumed. These two positions—and the blurring of the boundaries between them—represent quite vividly the complexity of women's relationships to technology.

Given the Web's nature as a technology of both literate and visual representation, these concerns of image are equally realized in the Web. Questions of representation with which feminist media theorists have struggled arise anew in this new cultural site as websites for and about women develop. A brief exploration of the landscape of the Web reveals that it is again another technology of conflicted meaning for women—women on the Web exist as both objects to be consumed and as agents of production. That women exist online as objects to be consumed is no surprising revelation. Cover stories from *Time* to *USA Today* to *Glamour* have documented the pervasive nature of online pornography. These stories, often described in sensationalistic fashion,[1] are often accompanied by a narrative of online harassment. Stephanie Brail (1996), herself a victim of online harassment, argues that "these stories of online harassment are told and retold partially because of the 'car wreck fascination' factor, but more importantly because we all keenly feel our vulnerability in the new medium of computer-mediated communications" (p. 143).

The stories of harassment and pornography (which Brail is careful to distinguish as two different phenomenon) particularly involve women and children, perhaps because of one tendency for technology to replicate existing societal norms rather than constructing new ones. One site where this seems to be true is Robert Toups's *Babes on the Web* (1996). Toups collects images of women for men to consume, a wildly popular activity on the Web, as the nearly 300,000 hits to Toups's site (Gilbert & Kile, 1996, p. 147) indicate. While Toups has claimed not to be engaging in sexist behavior, he will link to a woman's site only if the site includes a picture that he can rate. His main *Babes on the Web* page provides an alphabetical list of women's names, with his own unique rating system from one to four "toupsies." Similarly, *Celeb Exposed* (1997) offers volumes of nude images of celebrities, ranging from Princess Stephanie of Monaco to Barbra Streisand and Diana Ross, all reducible to the object of the gaze for the mere $24.95 subscription fee. While *Celeb Exposed* does have a category titled "Males Exposed," only two males are in fact exposed, while 40 female celebrities are available.

What is more interesting for developing understandings of women and the Web, however, are websites written by and for women that offer women spaces for active participation in the construction of more productive, supportive, and encouraging subject positions for women and girls. Like Kaplan and Farrell (1994), we agree that "we need to know more about what attracts women to electronic environments and what features of the activities we engage in sustain us in these new spaces" (p. 3). Lisa Gerrard (1997, 1998) identifies some of the features and goals of "grrl" sites (sites that are defined as empowering to women), arguing that understanding these sites offers composition theorists and teachers important information about what attracts women to the Web. In a similar vein, Pamela Takayoshi, Emily Huot, and Meghan Huot (forthcoming), arguing that women's relationships to technology are largely depicted in the popular press and in scholarly treatments as a negative one, explore the positive and meaningful role technology plays in the everyday lives of young women who actively engage in the Web. Rather than being represented by most typical depictions of girls and the Web, these girls' experiences assert that the relationship of women to technology is neither fixed, predetermined, or stable across the categories of women's lives. As more girls and women become involved in carving out sites on the Internet, female voices are becoming established voices within the growing Internet community. In response, perhaps, to websites that construct women according to limiting cultural values and standards, there exists a network of websites that support the self-empowerment of women and girls through coalition building. These sites are explicit and vocal exclamations of female solidarity. Takayoshi, Huot, and Huot argue that in response to subject positions created for them (by men on the Web and by cultural expectations), Web grrls manipulate technology to develop their own positions: "This critical manipulation of the technology arises in the ways that girls use language in constructing their online spaces. Many adolescent girls' sites on the Web rely on 'grrl'; and while the usages vary depending on the context, for the most part, 'grrl' seems to signify an in-your-face, we're-here-and-we-won't-be-silenced-or-ignored attitude." Web grrls have carved out a position where they are in charge, where they set the definitions, and where they produce the meanings their lives and their bodies will take.

These themes can be read in sites such as *WebGrrls!* (1997) and *CyberGrrl* (1997), which suggest that as women gain more access to the knowledge necessary to produce websites, they can take control of images of women. Both sites play with and parody the concept of webgrrl and cybergrrl as virtual female counterparts to the traditionally male superheroes found in popular media through the construction of cartoon images representing WebGrrl and CyberGrrl. Although Webgrrl and Cybergrrl fall within traditional visual representations of women's material being (and in that way suggest, perhaps inadvertently, boundaries on who might identify with Cybergrrl),[2] these sites emphasize girls' strength, self-esteem, and intelligence. The women depicted are not the flesh and bone objects of desire who reveal what lies beneath their clothing; women on the grrl pages are cartoon representations who don't necessarily correspond to any actual individual woman's material body. *CyberGrrl's* creator, Aliza Sherman, is a 30-year-old woman living in New York City. Speaking of her site in Gilbert and Kile's book, *SurferGrrrls: Look Ethel! An Internet Guide For Us!* (1996), Sherman notes that "Cybergrrl was my homepage, and she was created to represent me. Now, she represents all women and girls online..." (p. 234). For Cybergrrls everywhere, the Web offers the potential for publicly rewriting oneself in resistance to the narrow proscriptions of women as the weaker sex, dependent on the kindness of strangers. Cybergrrls often flaunt their strength, their belief in themselves, and their faith that all women can fly (in their supergirl capes) above the gendered stereotypes of their culture.

Although there is a potential for women's roles to be rewritten, images of women on the Web exist along a continuum from objectification to representation. All objectifying images cannot be attributed solely to men; it is clear that women grapple with this continuum both consciously and unconsciously in their own production of electronic discourse. The Web phenomenon of Jennifer Ringley (1997) provides a good example of a website where distinctions between positions of object and subject blur.[3] A Web celebrity whose name draws hundreds of hits on Netscape (a high percentage of male Web writers have links to Ringley's pages), Ringley has created a personal web page which, in addition to her portfolio, resumé, and links to friends, includes an image map called "Name That Curve" and a gallery of video-cam images called "The Jennicam." With "Name That Curve," users link to an image of a particular part of her body and "guess that part," whether it be her earlobe, her areola, the bottom of her breast, or the nape of her neck. Successful "Curve Connoisseurs" have their names listed with the name of the part they have guessed and the week they've guessed it, suggesting the ongoing nature of the activity. This breakdown and intense scrutiny of Jennifer's body parts parallels Willis's (1991) description of the woman using the Nautilus machines who "defines her body as an assemblage of body areas and muscle functions" (p. 75). The question that arises from Ringley's use of technology, however, is whether this is an act that, like the

Nautilus machine, produces nothing but the body itself. Ringley's use of technology (digital cameras, the Web, page-layout programs) seems to put her in the position of control, although this position is complicated by the fact that what she is controlling is her position as object to be consumed. This paradox becomes even more apparent with the "Jennicam." Describing the objective of the QuickCam, which she has set up to snap a shot of her bedroom every 3 minutes and upload it to the Web, Ringley writes: "The concept of the cam is to show whatever is going on naturally...whatever you're seeing isn't staged or faked, and while I don't claim to be the most interesting person in the world, there's something compelling about real life that staging it wouldn't bring to the medium." Although the JenniCam has uploaded images of Ringley nude, doing a striptease, and engaged in sexual activities, she asserts that "This site is not pornography. Yes, it contains nudity from time to time. Real life contains nudity. Yes, it contains sexual material from time to time. Real life contains sexual material. However, this is not a site about nudity and sexual material. It is a site about real life." This peek into one 20-something woman's "real life" comes with a $15 yearly subscription fee.

Ringley's (1997) web page might be interpreted through a feminist lens as a woman taking control over the presentation of her own image online and what her male viewers are able to gaze. Ringley herself asserts an outlook that embraces womanhood: "Personally, I think any woman who says she'd prefer to be a man, or any man who says he's happier being a man, is foolish. *wink* There's nothing finer in the world than womanhood." However, this reading is complicated by the fact that the addressed and invoked audience for Ringley's website is male. Ringley's site represents a complex dialectic between woman as subject and woman as object, woman as both consumer and consumed, and woman as a "performer" of femininity through her interaction with "woman" as object of desire, a positioning that privileges the presence of women online as objects first, subjects second. As Ringley's site suggests, women attempting to re-image themselves have little encouragement from mass culture to produce resistance discourse and often are positioned as both complicit with and resistant to their traditional subject position as an object of desire.

In advocating that communication technologies such as the World Wide Web have the potential to foster empowerment, it is important to also recognize that within the virtual community, some alleys divert users into spaces that clash with this social and political objective. Some streets suggest an avenue into empowering areas, but instead lead users to feel emotionally or intellectually threatened, such as a female student who feels uncomfortable when a group of male students in her computer-based classroom access online pornography or a female user who feels disappointed when she joins an all-women's listserv in hopes of finding solidarity, but instead finds equally exclusive power relationships. The Web supports the potential for online discourse to enable an agency that, as Faigley (1992) notes, "resides in the power of connecting with others and building alliances" (p. 199). In the ways that the Web connects women, opens up a space for the rewriting of cultural norms and standards, and supports geographically dispersed coalition building, technology can become a more democratic medium where users produce textual and visual alternatives to the material and discursive status quo. This critical deconstruction and reconstruction are necessary acts for the reading practices of future consumers and producers of technology. Consider the messages sent through discursive and visual representations, for example, in a recent America Online site, *Moms On-Line*, which features only Caucasian mothers and their children, with a token reference to a "lesbian mom." As Anne Balsamo (1995) contends, "The question is how to empower technological agents so that they work on behalf of the right kind of social change" (p. 156); in our minds, the right kind of social change includes expanding representations of all minority groups, including women, so they are not made to feel as if they are virtual victims or virtual aliens.

These changes might be most effectively addressed in our scholarship as well as our classrooms. At the least, these questions that the Web brings into those classroom spaces are ones that need to be addressed. As many contributors to *Feminist Cyberscapes* stress, the multilayered, complex nature of women's relationships to technology suggests the importance of considering carefully the ways we respond to and shape environments that support our students' development. Although computers and composition scholarship has addressed the impact of electronic writing environments on teacher authority and student empowerment, fewer discussions acknowledge the differing experiences of women teaching and learning with technology, attempting to establish a liberatory and feminist pedagogy through decentered writing and learning environments, a necessary goal to women's increased presence online. Kris Blair's experience as a female teacher of a graduate seminar in electronic discourse and pedagogy suggests some of the aspects of this problem, especially in teaching students how to write and design web pages. While most men in the class possessed intermediate to expert knowledge about technology, most women possessed only novice knowledge. The resulting gender/knowledge variable often led to a redistribution of power and authority to many male students in the class, who served as the primary knowledge source for both women and men alike. In such instances, technology can complicate classrooms that decenter authority away from "the teacher." When that teacher is female, gender dynamics can reinforce traditional narratives of technology as something to be mastered and males as traditional figures of technological mastery. As one female graduate student wrote after developing her first Web document:

> In constructing the last page, I received a great deal of much appreciated help; however, I didn't learn how to make a page on my own. Therefore, in attempting this page, I found myself still dependent upon others who have even less time to tutor me. Anyway, I purchased web page software for my home computer, and I am plodding my way through and learning by making many mistakes. I already feel more confident and independent, and I almost have a page, complete with images.

Such assessments call for us to further acknowledge the narratives and literacy histories of our students, to avoid simply moving the source of power from one authority figure to another, particularly with our female students and others for whom technological access has been limited. The impact of these power relationships is indicated from another female student's narrative about the same Web-based project:

> I went into this project with meticulous notes, confident that I would have little difficulty in constructing my web page of an observation of a computerized classroom. So confident and so naive. Almost from the start of working with Pagemill [a software program that lets you create web pages], that confidence quickly diminished and I was thrown into a major meltdown. I don't think that I have ever felt so incompetent before. Luckily, I found a patient soul to teach me HTML code. My HTML mentor walked me through getting my links to work and for my images to appear on my page. After a few examples, I tried doing it myself and it worked! It really worked! I was so excited that I rushed back to the computer lab and finished my page on my own. That excitement has not faded; my confidence is anew. I feel liberated! I am now part of another discourse community!

Despite the empowering attitude behind this statement, such technological anxiety can have a direct impact on those who learn to use technology. These intersections of gender, power, and authority, along with race, class, and age, account for the continued gap between male and female comfort with technology, in that technological knowledge is defined as a product or commodity, an exact knowledge that can be mastered and somehow imparted to male and female students alike. This contrasts sharply with "technological literacy," a process that is developed, like the writing process itself, in stages involving experimentation. This process, which does not require innate abilities, is a more nonhierarchical, nonpatriarchal method through which technological knowledge and literacy is dialogically defined and negotiated. In addition, it is a process in which the distinction between expert and novice is blurred.

As students and teachers establish new narratives of negotiation in a quest for virtual voice and virtual control over their own image in electronic writing, this conception of technological literacy demands a more collaborative relationship between teachers and students and between the students themselves. Through such efforts, the social change called for by Balsamo (1995) can occur. By creating discursive electronic spaces that better account for the material experiences and diverse voices of women representing themselves online, other women in the classroom and the community can gain technological access. As women working with technology, it's important to understand how our narratives about technology may also maintain political and social borders and contribute "to a larger cultural system of differential power that has resulted in the systematic domination and marginalization of certain groups of students, including … women [and] non-whites…" (Selfe & Selfe, 1994, p. 481). We agree that as we become more familiar with electronic networks in our teaching, scholarship, and private lives, we must become, and help our students become, technology critics able to assess the ways in which any technologies (not only websites, but also MOOs, usenet groups, and listservs) all possess frameworks for exclusion as well as inclusion. The contributors to this collection take up this challenge in mapping a feminist cyberscape.

A MAP OF *FEMINIST CYBERSCAPES*

In organizing the articles in this collection, we move the reader through multiple locations in a feminist cyberscape, in this way moving readers through a range of concerns that feminist perspectives on cyberspace raise: from the place and experience of the body in virtual space, to constructions of identity negotiated online, to discourse communities, to coalitions and collaborations, and finally, to the future of scholarship on gender and technology. In this arrangement, we emphasize the movement through space from individual to systemic, from personal to collective, all the time noting the political aspects of all these different positions. In between the explorations of particular locations within the cyberscape, we pull back our perspective to reflect with women who have figured prominently in the development of computers and composition as a field of study. Through interviews with these women, we want to write into the history of computers and composition the often hidden work women scholars have undertaken in computers and composition and to articulate the role technology has played in women's personal and professional lives by including their individual narratives in the spirit of feminist dialogue.

Map of Location I: The Body in Virtual Space

A frequently cited benefit of cyberspace is that discourse in cyberspace is unhampered by the presence of physical bodies and the oppressions that often accompany them. Without informational cues about age, gender, sexual orientation, class, or race, the argument goes, discourse in cyberspace can be egalitarian. The three chapters in this section of *Feminist Cyberscapes,* however, complicate this narrative of bodiless communication and egalitarian treatment. In particular, these three chapters focus on the female body at several locations in cyberspace. For lesbians, image cues and the meaning of "body" as social, historical, and cultural construct upon which identity and community are based are radically reconceived in electronic spaces, even in so-called academic discussions as well as more informal spaces. In Chapter 1, "Technological Fronts: Lesbian Lives 'On-the-Line,'" Joanne Addison and Susan Hilligoss explore these issues as scholars, teachers, and cyberspace writers. In overlaying these subjects, the authors draw on materialist feminism and lesbian cultural studies, utilizing examples from their own participation on a women's listserv.

In Chapter 2, "Postmodernist Looks at the Body Electric: E-mail, Female, and Hijra," S. J. Sloane outlines several online locations where "maleness" or "femaleness" may be implied, ultimately calling for the breakdown of these binaries in our analysis of the format and context of electronic writing. Relying primarily upon Judith Lorber's and other postmodern feminists' links between race, class, age, sexual orientation, and contexts that destabilize the idea of a unified gender identity (Flynn, 1995), Sloane concludes that only when we explore the dynamic textual masks the computer allows us to assume will we learn more about the ways in which we might teach electronic writing.

To conclude the chapters in this first section, Barbara Monroe, in "Re-Membering Mama: The Female Body in Embodied and Disembodied Communication," explores the complex relationship between online/offline community in a peer tutoring class in which the gender distribution was 11 females and 3 males. Despite the online nature of the class as playful, thoughtful, and supportive, offline the class reverted to awkward silences and averted looks. In determining the causes behind this, Monroe explores the effects of the visual absence of the female body and the conflation of the public/private in both an electronic and face-to-face setting.

Making the Map: Interview with Helen Schwartz

In this interview, Helen Schwartz discusses the beginnings of computers and composition as a research area within composition studies, her work during that time, and the hidden work of women in this area, including struggles to fund and maintain classrooms, to encourage and support women in this area, and to provide women with mentors. Reflecting on the activities and issues scholars faced at the formation of the research area, Schwartz looks toward the future for computers and composition and the roles women are playing and will play.

Map of Location II: Constructions of Online Identities: Our Students, Our Selves

All too often, conceptions of technology's proper uses and users are constructed within traditional definitions of gender, which contributes to the gendering of technology itself, and its designs, uses, and positions in society as a male (as opposed to female) enterprise. The three chapters in this section document the struggle of forming identities online, theorizing both the processes of negotiation and the implications of those negotiations for teaching. While statistics may show that women's access to and usage of networked communications is growing within the academy and the workplace, there is often a tacit assumption about what types of women are online, an assumption that from a materialist/feminist perspective diminishes the range of women's online experiences as a result of not only gender, but also race, class, and sexual orientation. Although feminist researchers valorize the importance of a pedagogy that moves from an authoritative stance toward collaboration and gender sensitivity, computers and compositionists and feminist scholars have not yet engaged in extensive critical discussions of the many oppressions that non-white, minority female students face in a university environment, nor have they analyzed how a computer-supported pedagogy may affect these nontraditional female students who experience multiple barriers in an environment that traditionally privileges white, middle-class male discourse. In response to this situation, Chapter 4, "I, a Mestiza, Continually Walk out of One Culture into Another: Alba's Story," by Sibylle Gruber, presents a case study of a nontraditional female student, exploring how her status in a computerized classroom devoted to acknowledging differences became a source of power rather than an added burden.

Even in classroom contexts that support nonhierarchical, feminist theory and decentered pedagogy, there can exist conflicts, as Shannon Wilson's "Pedagogy, Emotion, and the Protocol of Care" (Chapter 5) chronicles. In her chapter, Wilson employs feminist and rhetorical analysis to examine the issues of gender, power, and authority in an online graduate seminar in which she was a student. In analyzing this particular electronic environment, Wilson notes the struggle between two contradictory theories of intersubjective exchange, one descending from Habermas's theory of an ideal speech community and the other a derivative of a feminist "ethic of care." While these theories clash, a protocol of care can be used to erase hierarchical positionings, which are denied in Habermas's theory of nonhierarchical exchange, but are still present in the virtual classroom. Wilson ultimately argues that feminist educators need to maintain a critical relationship with technologies that provide both exciting possibilities and the potential to reproduce existing hierarchies.

Although many researchers claim higher participation rates of students in electronic conferences, how that participation affects traditional class discussion has received far less attention. In Chapter 6, "Writing (Without) the Body: Gender and Power in Networked Discussion Groups," Donna LeCourt questions the way in which technology problematizes discursive space through the lack of a body by comparing student posting in several bulletin board discussion groups with their conventionally written responses and class discussions.

Making the Map: Interview with Gail Hawisher

An interview with Gail Hawisher addresses the difficulties she has faced as a woman administrator of computer-mediated environments, her experiences working with computers in the early 1980s, when the field was in its nascent stages, the evolution of computers and composition as a legitimate research area, and the changing social forces that have affected Hawisher's own career. Throughout this discussion, there exists an underlying concern about the ways in which these changes impact women currently working with technology.

Map of Location III: Discourse Communities Online and in Classrooms

With the increasingly ubiquitous presence of e-mail in the daily lives of scholars, teachers, and students, understanding the relationship of gender and communication technologies is a more pressing issue for exploration. In Chapter 7, "A Virtual Locker Room in Classroom Chat Spaces: The Politics of Men as 'Other,'" Christine

Boese examines the use of synchronous communications by students in two expository writing classes. Noting that each semester, two types of virtual culture appeared, one an inflammatory, abusive, racist, sexist, and homophobic environment that Boese terms "The Virtual Locker Room," and the other, more serious and focused in its discussion, Boese concludes that the differentiating factor appeared to be the known absence or presence of a woman in the group. This evidence challenges assumptions about technology's effects on feminist pedagogical practices and forces us to look at the ways existing gender norms are perpetuated in virtual cultures. Recent discussions about ethics and feminism suggest, somewhat controversially, that women focus more on "care and responsibility" than on issues of "justice and rights," with women viewing their environment contextually and subordinating traditional hierarchical issues of morality to details of relationships and narratives.

In Chapter 8, "The Use of Electronic Communication in Facilitating Feminine Modes of Discourse: An Irigaraian Heuristic," Morgan Gresham and Cecilia Hartley chronicle their own online working relationship and collaboration as teachers in different parts of the country, using communication technologies to bring together their students. In their own correspondence and in their students' communications, Gresham and Hartley noticed the fluid type of dialogue that engaged e-mail participants in several conversations, linked together by strands of thought that are neither authoritarian nor static in nature. Such strategies of discourse must be encouraged to enable students to speak and assert their own agendas, whereas the nature of the electronic communication process creates a system of checks and balances important to maintaining a dialogic, multicultural classroom. Extending these goals to the classroom, Gresham and Hartley also chronicle their collaborative effort at having their writing classes in two different states work on the same project, engaging in online invention and class discussion.

Dene Grigar's "Over the Line, Online, Gender Lines: E-mail Technology and Women in the Classroom" (Chapter 9) examines the kinds and amounts of electronic mail female and male students sent to her in both a traditional and networked literature classroom, calling for more structures that encourage women to tap into the potential of this new communication and learning tool. But while it stands to reason that a networked classroom, claimed by many to promote collaboration, sharing, and a democratic atmosphere, would be a conducive environment for women to work in, postmodern feminists construct a vision of gender that is multiple, contingent, and even transitory, a vision that is realized in the flickering and fleeting online identities assumed by computer users.

Map of Location IV: Virtual Coalitions and Collaborations

As many of the authors in this collection assert, computer technologies often serve as a bridge bringing women together in a variety of working relationships. In particular, the authors in this section emphasize the ways that technology is located at the heart of collaborations and coalitions built across space and time borders.

Chapter 10, "Designing Feminist Multimedia for the United Nations Fourth World Conference on Women," Mary Hocks stresses the importance of collaboration in the development of a multimedia project for the World Conference on Women in Beijing, China, in September 1995. Hocks overviews the goals of the conference and the way in which the development of the multimedia project fits in with those goals and the goals of feminist activism online, particularly in the representation of women, and the difference between self-representation and the objectification that tends to occur in male-designed software. The common representations of women that we find in our mass media or multimedia do not often accurately reflect the image or experiences of women in the material realm. Thus, Hocks's discussion acknowledges the ways in which such collaborative multimedia projects are empowering for women in their ability to take an active, dialogic role in creating more diverse images of and roles for women.

As Paula Gillespie, Laura Julier, and Kathleen Blake Yancey stress in Chapter 11, "Voicing the Landscape: A Discourse of Their Own," there is little work by female academics describing and examining their collective experiences on the Internet as friends, as teachers, and as scholars. What do such experiences tell us about e-mail as a medium for constructing the self? Have women found it to be a place for collaboration and voice, or is it merely a new medium, subtly replicating the hierarchies of paper? In responding to these questions, Gillespie, Julier, and Yancey construct a more complex view of e-mail, claiming it neither as utopia nor as a mere echo of offline life. Rather, e-mail is a space/place where movement is allowed, and where the female is every bit as welcome and as defining as the male.

Margaret Daisley and Susan Romano's "Thirteen Ways of Looking at an M-Word" (Chapter 12) employs a dialogic format to question the relative marginalization of women in e-spaces. Although less frequent posting and lurking on lists has been seen as a form of marginalization for women, Daisley and Romano use both their personal experiences as students in such settings in their analysis of how such empowering silence manifests itself in classes as something other than marginalization online. Such analysis includes their concerns as women for the future of their daughters, as they include their daughters' voices in their dialogue about the potential for feminist space online and the need for new metaphors to describe online participation by women.

Making the Map: Interview with Mary Lay and Elizabeth Tebeaux

In this joint interview, Mary Lay and Elizabeth Tebeaux chronicle the role computer technologies have played in their own collaboration. In a lively and thoughtful exchange, Lay and Tebeaux detail the ways computers have changed their collaborative writing process and the role technology has played in their teaching and research, and the historical and contemporary role technology has played in the professional lives of women.

Map of Location V: The Future: To Be Mapped Later

The three contributions to this final section serve as a forward vision of gendered academic spaces. In overviewing potential directions for feminist research in computers and composition, Lisa Gerrard contends in Chapter 13, "Feminist Research in Computers and Composition," that if feminist research would do for computers and composition what Elizabeth Flynn says a critique of composition studies should do for composition in general, such research should focus on four areas: 1) computer culture, the larger social context in which computer-assisted instruction takes place; 2) classroom context, the specific teaching practices and their effects on students; 3) gendered discourse, how women and men communicate on networks; and 4) the profession of computers and composition studies, how male and female academics contribute to the subdiscipline of computers and writing.

To further explore these issues in a format appropriate to feminist dialogue, we have included an MOO conversation that engages contributors to *Feminist Cyberscapes* in a discussion of access, empowerment, and voice for women online, of the processes through which the contributors have arrived at the positions they stake out in their research, and of directions for the future of technologies for women. This conclusion weaves together the voices of most of our contributors and provides a more multivocal narrative that might otherwise exist only on the margins (unspoken, unpublished) of this collection.

Mapping the Future: Interview with Cynthia Selfe

In our final interview for the collection, Cynthia Selfe talks about the ways in which her own concerns as a rhetoric, computers and composition scholar, have impacted her role as Chair as the CCCC. Selfe also comments on the way in which national future policy decisions regarding instructional technology will impact students and teachers. As she has called for elsewhere, Selfe encourages teachers and students to be both technology users and technology critics, interrogating issues of educational equity along the axis of class, race, and gender.

Ultimately, *Feminist Cyberscapes* brings together multiple feminist perspectives on computer technologies for writing, thus serving as a starting point for discussions that explore various and sometimes competing feminist responses to technology. Teachers and researchers interested in developing further theory and pedagogy that questions and enhances the role of technology in the lives of both male and female students should find in this collection arguments that complicate existing considerations of computers and composition and construct new representations upon that existing base. These political and practical considerations of computers from various feminist positions not only raise serious implications for gender and composition instruction, but also suggests a methodology from which to consider other social forces at the site of computer technologies. From this perspective, *Feminist Cyberscapes* acts as a status report on the field's thinking about women and technology at this moment in the history of computers and composition, looking critically toward the future.

NOTES

[1] For their issue on "cyberporn," *Time* magazine visually represented this sensationalism by creating a cover that depicted a young boy drop lit so that his face was extremely pale and eerily other-worldly.

[2] Although the *WebGrrls!* (1997) and *CyberGrrl* (1997) websites are meant to be a source of empowerment via their networking possibilities for women online, the representations of "grrls" on the sites remain narrowly defined. These images raise the question of who can be a cybergrrl, in their construction of WebGrrl and CyberGrrl as thin, white women with long, flowing, brown hair and smiling faces. Images like these, in their narrow (and standard) representation of "woman," exclude women from many racial, generational, and sex preferential subject positions.

[3] Recently, Ringley expanded her celebrity from the World Wide Web to television when she appeared on *Late Night with David Letterman*.

REFERENCES

Balsamo, A. (1995). *Technologies of the gendered body: Reading cyborg women.* Durham, NC: Duke University Press.

Brail, S. (1996). The price of admission: Harassment and free speech in the wild, wild West. In L. Cherny & E. R. Weise (Eds.), *Wired women: Gender and new realities in cyberspace* (pp. 141–157). Seattle, WA: Seal Press.

Celeb-Exposed [Online]. (1997, April 8). Available: http://www.celebexposed.com

The Cybergrrl webstation—Welcome [Online]. (1997, July 17). Available: http://www.cybergrrls.com

Faigley, L. (1992). *Fragments of rationality: Postmodernity and the subject of composition.* Pittsburgh, PA: University of Pittsburgh Press.

Flores, M. J. (1990). Computer conferencing: Composing a feminist community of writers. In C. Handa (Ed.), *Computers and community: Teaching composition in the twenty-first century* (pp. 106–117). Portsmouth, NH: Boynton/Cook.

Flynn, E. (1995). Feminist theories/feminist composition. *College English, 57*(2), 201–211.

Gerrard, L. (1997). *Wired women, cybersisters, netchicks, and geekgirls: The rhetoric of women's web pages.* Paper presented at the Thirteenth Computers and Writing Conference, Honolulu, HI.

Gerrard, L. (1998). *Modem butterfly, or the rhetoric of women's web sites.* Paper presented at the Conference on College Composition and Communication, Chicago.

Gilbert, L., & Kile, C. (1996). *SurferGrrrls: Look Ethel! An Internet guide for us!* Seattle, WA: Seal Press.

Hawisher, G. E., & Selfe, C. L. (1991). The rhetoric of technology and the electronic writing classroom. *College Composition and Communication, 42,* 55–65.

Hawisher, G. E., & Sullivan, P. (1998). Women on the networks: Searching for e-spaces of their own. In S. Jarratt & L. Worsham (Eds.), *Feminism and composition: In other words* (pp. 172–197). New York: Modern Language Association.

Kaplan, N., & Farrell, E. (1994, July 26). Weavers of webs: A portrait of young women on the Net. *The Arachnet Electronic Journal on Virtual Culture* [Online], *2*(3). Available: http://www.monash.edu.au/journals/evjc/kaplan.v2n3

Ringley, J. (1997, July 21). *Anatomy one-oh-one* [Online]. Available: http://jennicam.xensei.com/~jenni/tour/index.html

Romano, S. (1993). The egalitarianism narrative: Whose story? Whose yardstick? *Computers and Composition, 10*(3), 5–28.

Selfe, C. L. (1990). Technology in the English classroom: Computers through the lens of feminist theory. In C. Handa (Ed.), *Computers and community: Teaching composition in the twenty-first century* (pp. 118–139). Portsmouth, NH: Boynton/Cook.

Selfe, C. L. (1998). *Conference on College Composition and Communication 1998 Keynote Address: Technology and literacy: A story about the perils of not paying attention* [Online]. Available: http://www.ncte.org/forums/selfe/

Selfe, C. L., & Selfe, R. (1994). The politics of the interface: Power and its exercise in electronic contact zones. *College Composition and Communication, 45*, 480–505.

Takayoshi, P. (1994). Building new networks from the old: Women's experiences with electronic communications. *Computers and Composition: An International Journal for Teachers of Writing, 11*, 21–35.

Takayoshi, P., Huot, E., & Huot, M. (forthcoming). No boys allowed: The World Wide Web as a clubhouse for girls. *Computers and Composition: An International Journal for Teachers of Writing.*

Toups, R. (1996, Feb. 24). *Babes on the web* [Online]. Available: http://www.toupsie.com/BABE.html

Wahlstrom, B. (1994). Communication and technology: Defining a feminist presence in research and practice. In C. Selfe & S. Hilligoss (Eds.), *Literacy and computers: The complications of teaching and learning with technology* (pp. 171–185). New York: Modern Language Association.

Webgrrls!—Women on the web—The directory [Online]. (1997, July 17). Available: http://www.webgrrls.com/directory/html

Willis, S. (1991). *A primer for daily life.* London: Routledge.

Map of Location I

The Body in Virtual Space

chapter 1

Technological Fronts: Lesbian Lives "On-the-Line"

Joanne Addison
University of Colorado-Denver

Susan Hilligoss
Clemson University

The title of our article plays significantly on our cyberspace experiences as lesbians. The use of the word *front* in relation to technology frames our discussion within the perspective of technology as a borderland and site of struggle for many lesbians both in academic and nonacademic settings (as opposed to the democratic utopia it is often presented as in academic and popular literature). The word *front*, or the ways that we front ourselves and each other, also refers to the individual and collective behaviors, appearances, maskings, and identifyings that occur in cyberspace as we take our positions "on-the-line." Being lesbian online is, in many important ways, like being lesbian in real life. The primary similarity is that your sexual orientation or identification, and the degree to which you reveal it to others through various means, determines your subject location within a group. Furthermore, if, when, where, and how you reveal your sexual orientation or identification in relation to those around you is a delicately negotiated matter, different for different women. What is constant, perhaps, is that the act of identifying oneself as lesbian is complex, often emotionally charged, and, even in feminist or otherwise "safe" spaces, a political statement and site of potential disruption.

The premise of this chapter is that feminist theory in composition and computer-mediated communication (CMC) can be enriched by postmodern lesbian and gay theory as well as material feminist critique—especially in relation to issues of identity and identification. While there is an increasing amount of research on issues of identity and CMC, relatively little of this work is being conducted in the field of composition. Furthermore, much of the work that is being done does not account for issues of identity in terms of the real material and political conditions of online participants and instead focuses on issues of desire and play (Morton, 1995); nor does this work address the implications of the use of electronic media as a catalyst for radical shifts in identity. Relatedly, while claims for the liberatory potential of CMC have been contested, utopian visions of the potential of CMC to liberate us from discrimination based on class, race, age, and so on. still prevail in academia. Furthermore, the online industry has begun to sell the use of CMC to the media public through its advertisements based on utopian claims as played out in the theme of a recent MCI television commercial: within cyberspace, bias rooted in age, race, and disability disappear. But the work of researchers such as Janet Carey Eldred and Gail Hawisher (1995) as well as Hawisher and Patricia Sullivan (1998) clearly show that this uncritical and ahistorical utopian perspective is problematic. In addition, as Alison Reagan (1993) points out:

> Many descriptions of computer conferences laud the possibility for anonymity (or a sense of anonymity) which comes with the reduced access to social context cues. It is a mistake, however, to employ computer technology with the goal of making classrooms blind to color, class, gender, and nationality. Even if this were possible, it wouldn't be desirable; a world where everyone can "pass" for a white, male, middle-class, heterosexual, native English speaker would be no utopia; it would be neither a more intellectually stimulating nor a more liberated place. (p. 12)

The perpetuation of this disembodied rhetoric of technology[1] has also hindered discussions of the ways that technology has been designed and continues to function as a tool for the maintenance of exclusionary and oppressive cultural practices despite an individual or group's liberatory aims (Sclove, 1995).

By examining our own participation in a specific listserv group through the lens of CMC theory, postmodern gay and lesbian theory, and feminist materialism,[2] our essay will address the implications of our title outlined above in terms of what it may mean for gays and lesbians to be "on-the-line" in social and professional arenas, as well as broader potential implications for feminist theory and networked classrooms. In doing so, we will discuss the ways in which CMC was used to create a supposedly safe-space, or even momentary utopia, for a specific group of women, and the exclusionary and homogenizing practices that lead to the disenfranchisement of certain members of the group.

FIRST ENCOUNTERS

We first encountered each other in cyberspace. Our collaboration on this article began as the result of our participation in an online study of academic women and computers in 1994.[3] All of the study's participants were volunteers who were asked to join the study group because they represented women of differing ages, ethnicities, and levels of experience with computers. The participants also ranged from graduate students to full professors at a variety of educational institutions. We had two initial interviews with the researchers, participated in an online discussion that ran for 28 days with all of the members of the study group, and completed a final interview with the researchers. Many of the participants had pioneered the use of computers in their writing classrooms and conducted research on computers and writing. Some of the participants did not teach in computer labs or use the Internet extensively. All used the list to reflect on their experiences with computers and writing. Personal concerns, including incidental references to family, illness, and mood, in addition to expressions of support, sympathy, and the like, were woven into the intellectual discussion. The connections between the phenomenological and the intellectual were encouraged by the researchers' interviews and were also congruent with previous CMC research findings about the content of online messages (Sproull & Kiesler, 1986).

In response to the researchers' request for introductions, Joanne, who was a graduate student at the time, came out as a lesbian by stating that one of her research interests was lesbian studies. Providing such information is more than part of an innocent "getting to know you" exchange of statements—it is a strategic way of positioning oneself in relation to other group members. Joanne made this move for a number of reasons, prominent among them being an attempt to open the door to discussions concerning computers and writing in relation to lesbian lives. Several weeks later, in order to offer an alternative to the "negative" discussion of gender-biased experiences online being forwarded by many of the participants, she described her positive experiences with a lesbian discussion list:

> From: addisonj@MACE.CC.PURDUE.EDU (Joanne Addison)[4]
> Subject: [list] positive experiences
> Date: Tue, 15 Nov 94 19:05:50 EST
>
> So much of what we are talking about is focusing on all of the negative experiences we've had on the Internet. And while these are important and I don't want to demean them in any way—it is no wonder that so many of us are presenting a very skeptical view of the Internet and reinforcing the already negative images some of us have. But what kinds of very positive personal experiences have people been having?
>
> In my first years here at Purdue, and even now, without the Internet I would have felt even more isolated than I do at times. Being a lesbian on a very conservative campus in a state that still holds KKK rallies means that I don't have

anywhere near the social, emotional, or political outlets I had back in Chicago. And while there are many graduate students and professors in my department who are supportive and accepting, our lives are very different in many ways and it's these differences that I need to have validated by other gays and lesbians. Fortunately, I found a very active listserv group of lesbian and bisexual women which provides a much needed space to talk about our lives, ask questions, organize social events across the country, and spread political news and calls for action that directly affect our lives because we are lesbian.

Similarly, because our library is lacking in resources concerning lesbian and gay issues, I've been motivated to learn how to do things like "telnet" to other databases and use "gopher" in order to find the information I need. But more importantly, I'm motivated to learn more about the Internet just so that I can reassure myself that this kind of information is out there and accessible.

While I don't think that the internet should at all replace my f2f [face-to-face] interactions or result in isolating myself from those around me, I do know that many of the conversations I've found on the Internet have helped get me through some rough times.

Joanne Addison
addisonj@mace.cc.purdue.edu

Another participant seconded Joanne's view by mentioning the relative safety of the Net (a safety that the writer had come to appreciate, but was also skeptical of) that allowed her to come out to others as a lesbian via online communication, and in so doing came out on the list. The same afternoon, November 18, Susan posted this message, followed by a private e-mail response the next day from Joanne:

>From <@CLEMSON.CLEMSON.EDU:hillgos@HUBCAP.CLEMSON.EDU>
Fri Nov 18 13:08:00 1994
From: Susan Hilligoss <hillgos@HUBCAP.CLEMSON.EDU>
Subject: safe spaces

Unlike Joanne and [Sharon], I have not sought out lists where I might find safe spaces for discussing sexuality. I told [the researchers] in their survey that I deliberately had not joined lists on lesbian or gay issues because I was unsure that they would really be discussions. I'm not sure what I'm afraid of. Certainly I don't spend time on lists. This is the most I've contributed to any, and it has much to do with supporting [the researchers] and now supporting everyone who's writing here. Like [Sharon], I've made the computer my journal, though even that is in abeyance. I don't miss handwriting, or not much. But I do not regard the Net as a safe space or as automatically harboring safe spaces. I'm grateful to those who make others, strangers, welcome, wherever they are, and the Net is a place for that.

The Net is a powerful, powerful resource and we have to teach people to use it. Most recent major demo of that, for me: My dear friend and colleague

[Lynn] was in a car accident in July. She is recovering from a severe closed head injury. Her partner used the Net to find resources on disability, and found a recent law book. She interlibrary loaned it and found sections on sexuality in rehabilitation from head injury. She's given it to the lawyer who's representing her in a guardianship petition contested by [Lynn's] parents, who are on record as ambivalent about keeping [Lynn] in therapy and who are threatening all kinds of things because she is lesbian. I was in court yesterday. It went better than we could have hoped. There's lots more to go. If this list lasts into December, I'll let you know.

Susan

>From addisonj@mace.cc.purdue.edu Sat Nov 19 13:11:28 1994
Subject: safe spaces
To: hillgos@hubcap.clemson.edu
Date: Sat, 19 Nov 94 13:11:51 EST

Hi Susan,

I just wanted to send a note of encouragement (outside of [the list]) about you and your friend's situation—I really hope things continue to go well in court. It's just crazy that during such difficult times we have to fight these legal battles.

If your friend is interested in finding more sources let me know—I could forward a request for her to a list I'm on where these sorts of issues get discussed from time to time. She wouldn't have to join the list—I could list her address for replies to be sent to.

Joanne
addisonj@mace.cc.purdue.edu

We corresponded off the list with several very brief notes focused on finding resources both online and offline.

What was interesting about these messages? First, no one else responded on or off the list to Susan's posting. Previously, while a few people had responded to Joanne's posts related to lesbianism and technology, no one (except the other participant who had outed herself) had commented directly on these issues. While both of us noticed that there was no reply of any type to Susan's message except for Joanne's, which was done outside of the discussion group, we did not mention it to each other for five months. Joanne describes what she was thinking: "Your post and the lack of response as well as the fact that I felt like I needed to respond to you outside of the list were pivotal for me in terms of understanding what the group norms were, what was allowable." While much of the group's discussion centered on oppressive and exclusionary acts against women online, some of these same acts, albeit in subtler form, were being played out in this all-women forum as well. When working to dismantle the utopian claims of gender equity in cyberspace, we must not continue to perpetuate the white, heterosexual, liberal feminist mistake of homogenizing women's experiences and ignoring the unjust relations between women of different races, classes, and sexual orientations.[5]

Through the word play on the list, some participants made gestures that may be regarded as expressing tolerance or attempting to identify in a supportive way with the experiences of the out lesbians on the list. For example, the phrase "coming out" was part of the word play that marked many discussions, in which participants elaborated on others' metaphors and posed hypothetical questions and situations. "Coming out" was used a few times in a context other than revealing one's homosexuality, and as such was invariably put in quotation marks, presumably to indicate a secondary meaning of the term while acknowledging its primary significance. For example, one participant used "coming out" to describe a lurker on another list who suddenly posted a message; later, another participant used the phrase to describe herself as a (heterosexual) mother. Neither of us responded to these usages. Susan regarded and regards this word play as both an appropriation and a legitimate "trying on" suited to the exploratory dimension of electronic lists. But the perceived verbal freedom of electronic spaces and their intensely verbal nature may pose unexpected problems for lesbian and gay participants. The use of the phrase "coming out" by the heterosexual women on the list marked an appropriation that lessened the political and ideological significance of coming out in a homophobic culture. In this situation, the use of the phrase "coming out," a phrase that denotes a fundamental political and material site of conflict in lesbian and gay people's lives, was for us an appropriation we could not encourage.

Finally, after the list had closed, both of us had mixed feelings about the value of the discussion to the issues we had raised, feelings that were directly related to our perceptions of our lesbian "fronts" online. Upon later reflection, Joanne wrote to Susan:

> From: addisonj (Joanne Addison)
> Subject: Re: Hello
> To: hillgos@hubcap.clemson.edu (Susan Hilligoss)
> Date: Wed, 29 Mar 95 14:17:21 EST
>
> I guess I expected a lot more support for the situation you described [to the list] but it didn't happen on the list and because I didn't know to what degree you were "out," I didn't feel comfortable saying anything on the list that might "out" you more than you wanted to be. I also didn't feel like the list in general was interested in discussing the issues related to being lesbian that were raised by the three of us on the list who came out—which lead me to contact both you and [Sharon] outside of the list. Then again, it may be not that they weren't interested, but that they didn't know how to approach these issues.

Susan responded:

> From: Susan Hilligoss <hillgos@hubcap.clemson.edu>
> Subject: Re: Hello
> To: addisonj@mace.cc.purdue.edu (Joanne Addison)
> Date: Thu, 30 Mar 1995 10:23:23 -0500 (EST)
>
> I guess my coming out was subtle, imbedded in a story about someone else's lives, and indeed only because there was a tiny hook to the computing focus of [the list]. Not because I could just say this was a huge part of my life right then, a gesture that certainly seemed to fit with the list's topics and practices. I was aware of that indirection, though I was very angry. I would have edited my response even more or changed the tone if you and [Sharon] had not raised lesbian issues. I might not have mentioned [Lynn or her partner] at all. I know some of the members of [the list] from working with them or at least meeting them, and I am faculty. Still, the practices of most e-lists I have been on tend to be (I think the term is) normative and subtly exclusive, and if success is counted by being responded to, I have had little of that. [The list] was no exception in that regard, generally.
>
> So I wanted support. I was angry at the handwringing silence and lack of proactive support among my colleagues at Clemson, and I thought maybe there would be just generalized sympathy for an accident victim, a fellow academic and a woman, on [the list]. Or so I construct the situation now. But I wasn't surprised at the lack of response. My sense at the time was that my story, tacked onto a response about something else, was perceived as an outburst and so ignorable. I did not pub the question about e-resources on head injury or head injury/sexuality to the group, for example. I did not initiate a topic, as it were. I speculate that my indirection helped members ignore the whole thing, including the uncomfortable lesbian aspect. Put lesbian sexuality with head injury and the law and you have a combination that even friends, if they're academics, can hardly touch (which is why I was seeking the kindness of strangers). The lack of response hurt, but I could understand it.
>
> Thanks for your consideration about possibly outing me and for your decision to contact me outside the list. Your concern and your help got to me. Simple decency is amazingly complicated.
>
> Susan

Why is it important that we retell these experiences in this public forum? As lesbian teachers and researchers, these experiences sharply remind us of our oppositionally silenced position in society. They also raise concerns over the implications of this type of silencing for both our gay and lesbian as well as straight students. Furthermore, we are aware that neither CMC nor feminist theories have offered sufficiently textured or political readings of those silenced in electronic forums. Through our dialogue outside of the research project, Susan and I were able to build an understanding of our experiences in ways that the researchers could not because of the exclusionary practices of the community that lead to an obscuring and even disappearance of our voices. In fact, it was primarily through our individual interviews with the researchers themselves, not our contributions to the discussion list, that the researchers were able to gain our perspectives on the issues addressed. Furthermore, exploring this silencing raises some interesting questions when viewed in light of recent findings concerning CMC by researchers such as Martin Lea and Russell Spears, Hawisher and Eldred, and Takayoshi, as well as related work on classroom discourse and pedagogy. Finally, the use and design of technology will never be able to move towards its democratic potential if those of us who use that technology do not have a voice in its design and implementation (see Sclove, 1995, for a compelling discussion of this).

For example, Lea and Spears (1991) argue that according to previous research, polarization (movement toward the norm, such as a position on the political right or left of a controversial issue) in a CMC group should result in more discussion-oriented remarks, but this was not the case in their research. Where the most remarks were exchanged, there was not only the least polarization (that is, there was a depolarization away from a norm), but also the most equality of participation. This finding seems in line with the move in composition studies to engage "contact zones" in our classrooms and to ask our students to confront controversial issues. Even so, Lea and Spears found that the "equalization phenomenon" was obtained only under certain special conditions, including the members' isolation and anonymity (as cited in Eldred & Hawisher, 1995, p. 349). Above all, Lea and Spears, both in this study and subsequent research, have concluded that CMC is always social; it is at least as often reinforcing of norms as it is equalizing or depolarizing.

From our experience, we would argue that depolarization may lead to more discussion on certain topics and more equal participation for certain individuals, but that established group norms will only allow for a certain amount of depolarization to occur. The remarks that Susan and I made could be considered depolarizing in that they were an attempt to move away from the heterosexual norm in which our discussions were rooted, but they did not lead to increased discussion of the issues we raised nor more equal participation on our part (nor, we suspect, on the part of other lesbians on the list). In fact, our postings led to us removing ourselves from the group to a certain degree and establishing a separate community outside of the group. Thus, while the researchers supposed that the listserv would act as a separate community where women could articulate concerns and find support they otherwise did not have, other separate communities formed outside this community based on the need to articulate issues and find support that the list itself did not provide. This movement can be related to the concerns raised by Harriet Malinowitz (1995) when she questions the degree to which gay and lesbian students in writing classrooms are able to situate themselves openly as such due to powerful group norms—despite instructors' attempts to diversify those classrooms. Malinowitz points out: "Asking students to write and read on gay-themed topics may represent a sincere but inadequate effort to correct the situation if there is no recognition that school has traditionally been used—and is still carefully guarded—as a principle site from which to reinforce heterosexuality" (p. 40). This raises questions concerning the value of the formation of alternate communities and whether or not alternative communities serve to reinforce dominant ideologies by removing nondominant identified groups from sites of power.

Similarly, Pam Takayoshi (1994) asks: "Can we expect women to use computerized communications as a tool for empowering themselves and dismantling the 'master's house,' in this case traditional [patriarchal] classroom discourse patterns? Or are computer-mediated communication and its integration in the composition classroom merely new tools that get at the same results in a different way" (p. 21)? The same question can be asked of the relationship between our homosexual and heterosexual students and colleagues. Herring (1996) posits that one of the ways for CMC to move towards its democratic potential for women involves women participating in women-centered lists. She goes on to state that "Such lists provide supportive fora for women on-line and are frequently models of cooperative discourse whose norms can spread if subscribers participate in other lists as well" (p. 152). This kind of claim is dangerous in that is presupposes an inherent cooperative and democratic discourse among all women. As an examination of our experiences here and in other electronic forums reveals, women-centered lists are not inherently any more democratic than other types of lists and we have a responsibility as feminist teachers and researchers to recognize our own antidemocratic practices so that we can move towards transforming them as well as the technology.

LESBIANISM, FEMINISM, "QUEERS," AND TECHNOLOGIES OF THE SELF

In 1978, at the Modern Language Aassociation's annual conference in New York, French feminist writer Monique Wittig declared: "Lesbians are not women." What Wittig was arguing was that lesbians are not necessarily bound by the categorical imperative "woman" constructed in terms of heterosexual social, political, and economic conditions. Similarly, feminism as a movement by, for, and about women has seldom been about lesbians. Since at least the 1970s, lesbian theorists and researchers have argued that feminism, as a movement concerned with women's liberation, is not concerned with lesbians. But the contested relationship between feminism and lesbianism dates much further back than the emergence of an organized lesbian and gay resistance movement (often dated at the time of the Stonewall Riots in 1969).

As early feminists worked to secure a legitimate place for feminism, they had to argue specifically against the authority of the sexologists (perhaps most notably Kraft-Ebing and Havelock Ellis) who pathologized many behaviors of women that were not "feminine." As Celia Kitzinger (1990) points out:

> Kraft-Ebing described the lesbian in terms that left no doubt about the link between lesbianism and the burgeoning feminist movement of his day. Feminists attempting to

> avoid stereotypical "feminine" behaviors, or struggling for women's right to education, were slotted into his picture of pathology. (p. 34)

Because of this, many early arguments for feminism were also arguments against lesbianism (or behavior associated with lesbianism) as early feminists worked to remove the "pathologizing" aspects associated with feminism. Indeed, most feminist work today continues to ignore the difference and importance of lesbian experience.

Our experiences as and with "women" in cyberspace differ markedly with our experience as and with lesbians primarily because many issues lesbians face are not the same issues women face. Susan's post cited earlier concerned close friends in the midst of a battle simply for the right to legal standing, a situation that a number of homosexual partners have faced but that heterosexual partners must rarely confront in these terms. It is these material and political realities that have lead to the rise of separate areas of study such as queer theory and lesbian studies.

In this discussion, we're defining lesbian studies against much of what has become known as "queer studies." In defining queer studies, Sue-Ellen Case (1996) states, "Queer theory, unlike lesbian theory or gay male theory, is not gender specific" (p. 2). While this lack of gender specificity may be viewed as a resisting move, theories that actively disengage themselves from issues of gender within a society based on a gendered division of labor cannot lead to transformative action or political agency for women. Other views of what queer theory is can be understood from a 1992 issue of the journal *PRE/TEXT*. In the introduction to this issue, Margaret Morrison (1992) summarizes and comments on poet and literary critic Eve Kosofsky Sedgwick's conceptualization of "queer":

> ...what is "queer"?... It loosely connotes sexualities and genderings without pinpointing single and stable specific homo/hetero sexualities and genderings..."people whose struggle really is to experience their sexuality as normal or to experience their bodies as normal are not likely to be attracted to the term.... There are a lot of people who are gay who are not queer." Making the term as open and flexible as this allows its users to avoid both the kinds of definitional boundari[ies] and narrow one's possibilities for action and an essentialism that assumes a term's metaphysical grounding. (pp. 3–4)

Morrison goes on to equate one's wanting to experience their sexuality as normal with normalization. She states that most lesbian and gay rhetoric "has depended on a normalizing impulse" (p. 6) as a means of empowerment and definition. And that this normalizing impulse is based on a debilitating fictional sense of self.

The moves that Sedgwick and Morrison (1992) make here, and that others have made elsewhere, are problematic in many ways. Finally, this type of move is politically debilitating in its reliance on rhetorical extremes, oppositional positionings, and failure to take into account the real material and political conditions of lesbians and gays. One of the aspects of these definitions of queer theory that relates to lesbian theory is the oppositional positionings of heterosexuals and homosexuals, gays and, by omission, lesbians, as well as gays and lesbians who are queer versus those who are not. It is this last opposition that concerns us the most—not because we're invested in presenting a unified homogeneous homosexual front, although we do think a collective subjectivity is necessary for political action—but rather because we think this distinction is unfair and even counterproductive.

Part of the problem here is that fighting to have one's experiences considered a normal part of everyone's life is being equated with normalization; however, the two are not the same thing. For many, the first involves and has always involved a certain political agency and appropriation of power, while the second involves being controlled. Normalization, as defined by Celia Kitzinger (1990), is the blatant and subtle normative actions taken to preserve the social, economic, and political structure of a culture.

When examining this issue explicitly within the framework of postmodernism, this conceptualization of "queer" works as an example of the type of postmodernism Teresa Ebert (1992–93) has labeled "ludic postmodernism" (p. 8). In contrast, we are basing our work in Ebert's conceptualization of "resistance postmodernism." While we don't have space here to go into the details of Ebert's argument, we will highlight the points that relate specifically to this discussion. A simplified definition of "ludic postmodernism" involves theories that describe but do not explain and in their describing become lost in a play of rhetoric that inhibits political agency and collective subjectivity. Such is the case with a queer theory that claims no boundaries resulting in "a crisis in which texts constituted by difference can no longer provide reliable knowledge of the real because meaning itself is self-divided and undecidable; ...politics [become] a semiotic activism ... that does not so much transform practices as merely problematizes their continuation" (pp. 15–16). And while this problematizing is important, too often we become mired in the muck of signification—a miring that has led many such as Susan Wolfe and Julia Penelope (1993) to ask, "How can women, much less Lesbians, rejoice in the de(con)struction of a unified self they have never been permitted (within patriarchal structures, including discourse structures) to possess" (p. 2).

"Resistance postmodernism," on the other hand, is rooted in a materialist feminist culture critique (Ebert, 1992–93, p. 10). This strain of postmodernism insists that difference is social and historical, instead of simply discursive. Furthermore, it emphasizes the notion of individual and community identity, while foregrounding the gendered division of labor materialist feminism is based on: "In theorizing difference as always difference in relation within a system of exploitation feminism can open up new spaces for radical political action and cultural critique. Instead of merely subverting signification, resistance postmodernism seeks to critique and intervene in the systematic relations and uses of signification for exploitation" (p. 17).

Donald Morton (1995) has recently taken up the issue of ludic postmodernism as it relates to the relationship between cyberspace and queer theory: "When queer theorists envision a future, they portray an ever-expanding region of sensuous pleasure, ignoring the historical constraints need places on pleasure ... [this] ahistorical thinking [is] characteristic of queer theory and cyberspace" (pp. 375, 378). It is precisely this ahistorical view of cyberspace that has helped promote, for example, the "insistence on a simplified version of a reduced social context cues model" (Eldred & Hawisher, 1995, p. 341) of computer-mediated communication in composition studies that has recently come into question.

Morton (1995) goes on to describe current characterizations of cyberspace (and similarly "cybercized queer theory") as "a bourgeois designer space in which privileged Western or Westernized subjects fantasize that instead of being chosen by history, they chose their own histories. By manipulating the machines, the user-subjects write virtual histories according to their desires and seek to evade present historical conditions" (p. 375), or, in other words, virtually ignoring their historical bodies. But our experiences suggest that, in many ways, nowhere are we more aware of our historical bodies than in cyberspace.

IDENTITY AND IMAGE ONLINE

Identifying oneself as lesbian may actually be more complicated online than in ordinary physical spaces. One researcher and theorist who has addressed the issue of online identity in postmodern terms that engage lesbian (in)visibility is Allucquère Rosanne Stone. Using traditional social psychological theory updated with postmodern concepts of the subject, Stone (1995) theorizes how participants in online communication are able to arrive at a sense of "self" and identity for one's own communications and to extend identity to other participants' messages as well. Her formulations extend the work of Lea and Spears (and others) in online group formation and maintenance by considering not only discussion topics and the number and types of responses, but also the cultural production of identity and body.

Near-instantaneous electronic communications technology destabilizes the assumed equation of the self and the physical body. (In deconstructing the unified self and celebrating transgression, Stone [1995] tends toward ludic postmodernism, but her general formulations have implications for agency.) This destabilization is pronounced but not unique, because it is an effect of all human use of tools. (Stone, elaborating on Donna J. Haraway's [1991] image of the cyborg, calls all technology prosthetic.) Online, one's sense of identity has a spatiality but not a location and so differs from the physical body's location. Although this dissociation is problematic, it is not unique; groups adapt to it by other means of managing cohesiveness over distances. According to sociologist Anselm Strauss, human groups have long constituted themselves around common, significant symbols, so that symbolic exchanges fill in for the lack of proximity (Stone, 1995).

Online, the destabilization remains, so the need to stabilize the relationship of identity and body persists. Groups use communication technology both "to enact and stabilize a sense of *presence* in increasingly diffuse and distributed networks of electronically mediated interaction" and "to stabilize self/selves in shifting and unstable fields of power" (Stone, 1995, p. 88). In particular, according to Stone, communication technologies mediate cultural meanings and assumptions about the body: "what bodies should be or do, what form bodies should take, and what conditions relationships between bodies and selves should require" (p. 89). That is, using communication technology involves issues of power and the control of the body, as group members negotiate these questions of identity. Stone goes on to elaborate how Western conceptions of the self, post-Enlightenment classification systems of self and body, and industrial capitalism's fascination with "location technologies" for social control saturate electronic communications.

One notable effect of this actualized but delocalized self is the possibility of false or invented selves, a topic that has received much discussion, largely based on observation of MOOs and MUDs that encourage gender roleplaying. The voluntarily assumed gender roles of these spaces challenge dominant assumptions about the relationship of identity to body, as do stories of people who cross the male/female binary deliberately to deceive members of online groups. However, these selves or characters are largely apolitical, as in Morton's (1995) characterization of the Internet as "a bourgeois designer space." Even if such invented selves have political overtones, their agency outside carefully constructed spaces for such play is limited—limited to shocking groups into actions of social control against the gender transgressor, what Stone (1995) calls "warranting" the acceptable union of self and body (p. 87). What happens outside these designed spaces? What of lesbians who claim their historical bodies? We would like to explore the implications of this actualized but delocalized, destabilized self for lesbian identity in cyberspace.

Identifying oneself as lesbian is to implicate the body, in particular to make a statement about what one's body is and does and its relationship to other bodies, and so to take on the assumptions about self and body implicit in the formation of online identities. The lesbian is part of the larger cultural classification system, a legal, political, and biological entity or the "fiduciary subject" that must be fixed in space as well as terminology (Stone, 1995, p. 90). Keeping such a being "in its place" is required in virtual electronic spaces as well as geographic ones. That is, identifying oneself as lesbian is a political act online as well as face to face.

However, being online does not simply replicate the larger cultural norms, but may in some respects magnify the problem of identity. Stone, a cultural critic and herself "a transgendered academic" (1995, p. 180), argues that enacting and stabilizing the sense of presence in electronic communication creates "a deep need" in participants to describe and otherwise depict the body (p. 93). This need is particularly evident in "narrow-bandwidth" modes of communication, like the telephone, e-mail, and electronic conferences, which limit perception and thus the symbolic exchanges that characterize group formation and maintenance (p. 93). That is, coming out in a space where group members are already struggling for ways to connect self with (normative) physical images of the body and to establish (normative) relationships among the participants' online identities is yet another destabilization with which the group is faced. If the group's activities do not revolve around sexuality or gender play, the assumptions of the dominant culture may act as a powerful means of stabilizing identities.

The apparent need to describe faces, bodies, gestures, and clothing was evident in several discussions on the discussion list in which we participated. One topic early on was the difference between online and other forms of communication, chiefly the telephone and face-to-face interaction, with a discussion of gestures and expressions. In several discussions, there were occasional laments that the technology did not support visual means of identifying members (its limits as a "narrow-bandwidth" technology). In this regard, Susan mentioned the cartoon-like gestures of MOOs and MUDs as a means of giving visual identity online. Two or three weeks into the online discussion, apparently in response to one member's wish for photographs, a number of participants created online portraits of themselves using keyboard characters. Neither Joanne nor Susan did so. Three participants, including Joanne, suggested that such portraits were themselves contested sites of cultural assumptions about body image. Joanne said:

>From <@CLEMSON.CLEMSON.EDU:addisonj@MACE.CC.PURDUE.EDU>
Date: Sat Nov 26 07:40:02 1994
From: addisonj@MACE.CC.PURDUE.EDU (Joanne Addison)
Subject: faces and images

I'm catching up on messages since I've returned and am really enjoying all the images people are playing with. In some ways the list seems very different than it was about a week ago when I last logged on—as if a lot of our professional guard has been let down.

I agree with everyone as to why having an image of some sort that we create can be a positive move in this environment. But I also like not having an image associated with myself for some of the very same reasons. For example, someone said (I can't remember who) that having an image to attach to someone makes online conversations easier just because it helps us remember who said what so that we can refer back to what was said and continue the conversation....

But this is still a very linear notion of conversation—it's an easier way for us to have conversations (and write and read) because it's something that we're very familiar with (I've tried to read books that aren't linear and have a very hard time doing it—mostly I think because I'm still trying to make sense of something nonlinear in linear ways). It also locks us into certain expectations of others—if I start saying contradictory things I'll "get called on it" more readily if the contradictions can be traced through an image.

This is exactly what happens with transgendered or transsexual peoples—they're not allowed to be the contradictions that they are in our world because of our need to associate images—many don't want the ability to recreate themselves (as Foucault suggests) although they find themselves recreating themselves on a daily basis so they can survive in this world.

Joanne

Joanne's mention of transgendered people was the only such in the discussion. Soon there was another, concomitant thread on professional dress, clothing in general, and women's self-images as reflected by choices of clothing and workplace expectations. Susan responded to both threads in one posting. She did not draw an image or discuss her own clothing, but commented on the anxiety she saw in the group's need to discuss self-image and the inadequacy (for her) of the keyboard drawings. Susan also described a lesbian poet whom she assumed that some of the list members had seen at a recent writing conference and reflected on stereotypes. Another participant, one who had also commented on the contested nature of images, responded enthusiastically to Susan's posting, repeating and amplifying a phrase and extending it to other contexts, but without reference to stereotypes or lesbian identity. The list's discussions on the topics of the drawings, self-image, and clothing were lengthy and enthusiastic, prompting one participant to remark that the postings' content would be interesting to a future anthropologist.

If even a generous, supportive academic discussion list by women shows this apparent heightened need to describe bodies, images, and clothing, what of computerized classroom discussions? Not the least of the difficulty is that coming out or engaging in discussions of body image may threaten other members of the discussion by implicitly sexualizing the discussion, moving it beyond an isolated body to relationships between virtual bodies. The dominant assumption is that being homosexual means being sexual in every situation. Lesbians are well aware of this assumption. Our postings, different as they are, seem to demonstrate both an interest in maintaining a lesbian identity in these discussions and an ambivalence about participating. Susan, rather than offering a drawing of herself or discussing her own clothing, displaced her remarks to others' postings and another lesbian's image, someone not a member of the list. Joanne's response was similar, although she displaced her remarks to a context related to her own and yet very different from any that had been addressed by the group thus far (transgendered persons). Both of us mentioned negative effects of image-making, but were deferential to those who saw its advantages. Neither received a response that we saw as acknowledging our points of view as lesbians on these topics. Joanne's comment on workplace clothing, her last post to the entire list, was marked by worries as a graduate student, not as a lesbian. Later, Susan stated that these threads had made her uneasy, because she did not feel free to participate fully or feel likely to be understood; the type of responses (and general lack of response) from the list made her feel as if being lesbian somehow was threatening, and discussing clothing would have exacerbated that threat.

Both of us were interested enough to have a lengthy exchange about self-presentation and visual image as lesbians. In fact, this exchange was part of our earliest posts off the list, occurring immediately after a conference breakfast to which all the list participants were invited. Neither of us attended the breakfast, but we had met face to face for the first time at this conference. Discussion of missing the breakfast led to this exchange:

Subject: Re: Hello
To: hillgos@hubcap.clemson.edu (Susan Hilligoss)
Date: Mon, 27 Mar 95 8:29:49 EST

Hi Susan,

...

I'm not sure if this is related, but these are things I've been thinking about since [the list]. I've also been thinking a lot about why I really didn't want to go to the breakfast. It's not that I feel a hostility towards anyone on the list or the list in general in any way. I think that some of it is related to the fact that I was giving a paper on lesbian studies and pedagogy at the conference and whenever I do something like that, I feel like I'm on display, and it takes a lot of energy, support, and self-assuredness to be on display. And when you're going to meet a group of people "in person" whom you've formerly only met online, no matter who you are, you're on a physical/visual display to a certain extent.

Subject: Re: Hello
To: addisonj@mace.cc.purdue.edu (Joanne Addison)
Date: Thu, 30 Mar 1995 10:23:23 -0500 (EST)

I did want to go to the breakfast, but I have been thinking about some of the same issues. As a member of the profession I have identities constructed around almost everything but being a lesbian, but in person, ftf, I present a fair number of stereotypical lesbian features, as you probably noticed. I really understand that by presenting scholarship on lesbian studies and pedagogy you feel on display. You are. You are doing several things at once as you "deliver a paper." Taking hold of lesbian identity as a subject of study in graduate school—I admire what you are doing and how you are doing it. Conferences [4C's in particular], are parades and elaborate performances (which, if we can treat our presentations purely as performances, we undermine what we're doing). Adding being a lesbian to the nuanced display—whew. I was amused—nice, distancing word—by [the list's] discussion of representations of self, as through clothing, computer graphical images. This interest persists, if you've read the postings of the last couple of days after the breakfast. Somehow, if we'd been there—would anyone have posted anything about our appearances? I felt so conflicted about describing myself, which I did not do, and about commenting on others' representations, which I did, to no response. I felt and was awkward, although I also felt that as a lesbian I have ample experience and reflection on this aspect of everyday culture. I felt that it might be construed as unseemly for me, a lesbian, to start describing the physical features of myself or women on the list. I would have to describe myself, jokingly of course, as pretty butch. My choices of clothing have layers of meanings and I'd have to get into that. In a sense, I thought that if lesbians began to enter this strand as lesbians, we'd have a complex and interesting take (or takes, plural) on it. More complex than some of the postings, and not purely academic, in that these codes have daily impact for some of us. But I also thought that I had the capacity to threaten both the sexual identities and the conduct of discourse on the list, simply by describing myself or others from a lesbian perspective. So that strand made me nervous. My comment on [Catherine's] e-drawing was intended to poke a bit of fun at the inadequacies of such "drawings," but I had to mention breasts to do that. Did I understand my motives? I don't know. I felt I could address [Catherine's] drawing since I know her outside the list....

Susan

The charged experience of image cues online only reinforces the idea that cyberspace confronts lesbians with both risks and opportunities. Each of us revealed interest in image cues from a lesbian perspective, but also anxiety about her self-presentation and others' perceptions of her that also center on lesbian identity. However, we each think of our concerns as quite separate and inflected by our differences in age, status in the profession, relationship to cultural assumptions about lesbians, and degree of being out. As Joanne stated in a later post: "My experience of these image cues is probably different from yours—and may be part of the reason why I am very 'out' now." It is important to note that we are not trying to construct some universal lesbian experience of cyberspace through our work. The differences in age, status, and degree of outness that we forefronted at the beginning of this article continually inform the different ways that we experience and theorize cyberspace.

VIRTUAL OUTING

Received: by mace.cc.purdue.edu (5.61/Purdue_CC)
id AA00787; Tue, 11 Apr 95 10:02:18 -0500
From: addisonj (Joanne Addison)
Message-Id: <9504111502.AA00787@mace.cc.purdue.edu>
Subject: our article
To: hilgos@hubcap.clemson.edu
Date:

Hi Susan,
Along these lines I have been thinking a lot about what you said concerning images and what was going on when people started drawing images of themselves. I think this is very closely related to the issue of outing. Many people talk about one of the benefits of something like e-mail being the democratization of knowledge and more egalitarian conversations due to the fact that we don't know what color someone is or if they look like a dyke, etc. But this also closes off a lot of doors and forces people to "come out" verbally on lists like [the list] because the image cues that we might have in person are lost. And when we come out in a public way like that for whatever reason, we are putting ourselves at risk.

Joanne

Why is all of this talk of identity and identification in relation to coming out online important? Why is it important for our students, colleagues, and ourselves to be able to construct lesbian identities online if they choose to do so depending on the level of risk they are willing to assume? Why is it important that if lesbians are participating in a research project such as the one described here, that our contributions draw attention to the ways in which our experiences differ from others due to our material and political subject positions as lesbians? In the most global sense, it is because being able to construct a lesbian identity within an oppressively heterosexist culture, especially when using a technology that is still primarily designed and used in the maintenance of oppressive cultural norms, is an act of empowerment. As Mary Swigonski (1995) states:

> To claim a lesbian identity is to confront and challenge oppression. It is to become visible in the face of social institutions that are committed to rendering one invisible. The choices that lesbians make daily about their lives and relationships can be sources of creative power. Learning to claim and nurture that power are skills that lead to empowerment and social transformation. (p. 423)

Thus, to come out online is articulate an identity that our society works to render invisible. While this articulation may not always be acknowledged, because of its explicit textuality very seldom will it go unnoticed.

As mentioned earlier, coming out online as a lesbian may be harder than doing so in face-to-face interactions. One of the reasons for this is the lack of social cues related to dress/style and body image that we rely on in our face to face interactions for cues as to one's social identity and political stances. Thus, visual cues that might otherwise render verbal articulations of one's identity as a lesbian unnecessary are not present in online communications. The reduced social cues model is neither egalitarian nor likely to more liberated discourse, as we have seen. If Stone is correct, that in any electronic space participants may generate intense descriptions of the body, then lesbian students may decide not to participate, either out of fear or as a form of resistance to the reality that their lives and their online selves and interests are bounded by bodily or sexual concerns. In this situation, the process of naming oneself becomes even more discursive and dependent on group norms. It also becomes more crucial to learn to do so in ways that can lead to dialogue, negotiation, and social change. But social change can't occur if those you want to influence refuse to engage in discourse with you. From our experience, electronic discussion groups are especially well suited to this type of silencing.

TEACHING AND PROFESSIONAL IDENTITY ONLINE

In short, much of our understanding of our experiences as members of the research project, which we have used as a focal point for this discussion, was based on tensions between what we expected or perceived as professional and social needs, and our expected or perceived difference from the group's constructed norms. This tension is a good place to start with our students and colleagues in order to better understand the role of computer-mediated communication in our daily interactions with one another. Doing so is important because, as Richard Sclove (1995) points out:

> So long as their social origin, effects, and dynamics remain so badly misperceived, technologies will not suffer the same liability as would, say, functionally comparable laws or economic institutions, of being challenged on the grounds that they are politically or culturally unacceptable. Furthermore, societies will fail to develop the capacity to seek other technologies more consonant, both focally and nonfocally, with their members' ideals and aspirations. (p. 24)

For teachers, researchers, and students, this process must begin with a critical understanding of who we are as material and political subjects within our historical moment and the relationship of technology to our lives. The article that Susan and I have written is an example of an attempt to understand who we are as political subjects, the relationship of technology to our lives, and the implications of our position as political subjects within one discourse community.

NOTES

[1] We would like to thank our editors for the insights they shared with us, and specifically for their contribution of the notion of the "disembodied rhetoric of technology."

[2] We are defining feminist materialism following Leslie Roman (1992), whose approach emphasizes the material and ideological conditions of our lives and insists on an "ethical, politicized, and scientific articulation of research practice not only because it makes an explicit commitment to democratize knowledge and theory, but also because it connects research to an emancipatory and transformative vision of society" (p. 557).

[3] The initial results of this research are discussed in Sullivan and Hawisher's 1998 article "Women on the Networks: Searching for E-Spaces of Their Own."

[4] All postings remain as they were typed. Any spelling or grammatical mistakes have been left intact.

[5] In the researchers' initial report of their work, they do acknowledge the exclusion felt by the lesbians on the list who had outed themselves.

REFERENCES

Case, S.-E. (1996). The apparitional community: The apparitional lesbian. *American Quarterly, 48*(1), 161–166.

Ebert, T. (1992–93). Ludic feminism: The body, performance, and labor: Bringing *materialism* back into feminist cultural studies. *Cultural Critique*, 5–50.

Eldred, J. C., & Hawisher, G. (1995). Researching electronic networks. *Written Communication, 12*(3), 330–359.

Haraway, D. J. (1991). *Simians, cyborgs, and women: The reinvention of nature.* New York: Routledge.

Hawisher, G. E., & Sullivan, P. A. (1998). Women on the networks: Searching for E-spaces of their own. In S. Jarratt & L. Worsham (Eds.), *In other words: Feminism and composition* (pp. 172–197). New York: Modern Language Association.

Herring, S. (1996). Bringing familiar baggage to the new frontier: Gender differences in computer-mediated communication. In V. Vitanza (Ed.), *CyberReader* (pp. 144–154). Needham Heights, MA: Allyn and Bacon.

Kitzinger, C. (1990). *The social construction of lesbianism.* Thousand Oaks, CA: Sage.

Lea, M., & Spears, R. (1991). Computer-mediated communication, de-individuation and group decision making. *International Journal of Man-Machine Studies, 34*, 283–301.

Malinowitz, H. (1995). *Textual orientations.* Portsmouth, NH: Boynton/Cook.

Morrison, M. (1992). Laughing with queers in my eyes: Proposing "queer rhetoric(s)" and introducing a *QUEER ISSUE. PRE/TEXT, 13*(3-4), 11–36.

Morton, D. (1995). Birth of the cyberqueer. *PMLA, 110*, 369–381.

Reagan, A. (1993). "Type normal like the rest of us": Writing, power and homophobia in the networked composition class. *Computers and Composition, 10*, 11–23.

Roman, L. (1992). The political significance of other ways of narrating ethnography: a feminist materialist approach. In M. LeCompte, W. Millroy, & J. Preissle (Eds.), *The handbook of qualitative research in education* (pp. 555–594). San Diego, CA: Academic Press.

Sclove, R. (1995). *Democracy and technology.* New York: Guilford.

Sproull, L., & Kiesler, S. (1986). Reducing social context cues: Electronic mail in organization communication. *Management Science, 32*, 1492–1512.

Stone, A. R. (1995). *The war of desire and technology at the close of the mechanical age.* Cambridge, MA: MIT Press.

Swigonski, M. (1995). Claiming a lesbian identity as an act of empowerment. *Affilia, 10*(4), 413–425.

Takayoshi, P. (1994). Building new networks from the old: Women's experiences with electronic communications. *Computers and Composition, 11*, 21–35.

Wolfe, S., & Penelope, J. (1993). *Sexual practice/textual theory: Lesbian cultural criticism.* Cambridge, MA: Blackwell.

chapter 2

Postmodernist Looks at the Body Electric: E-mail, Female, and Hijra

S. J. Sloane
University of Puget Sound

The bodies of men and women engirth me, and I engirth them,
They will not let me off nor I them till I go with them and
respond to them and love them.
—Walt Whitman, 1983, p. 116

Moreover, the androgyne still fundamentally thinks in terms of "feminine" and "masculine." It fails to conceptualize the world and to organize phenomena in a new way that leaves "feminine" and "masculine" behind. The theoreticians of androgyny resemble poets who have been writing about two lovely beasts: winged horses and centaurs. People come to them and say, "We're tired of winged horses and centaurs. What about a new beast?"
—Catherine Stimpson, 1988, pp. 58–59

INTRODUCTION

In her complex and rich discussion of how late 20th-century conceptions of gender have been fostered by the medical technologies that enable sex changes, Hausman's (1995) important work on the phenomenon of transsexuality makes us reconsider the relationship between soma and speech, between body and its varied and lively expressions. In asking readers to measure more carefully the distance between bodies and the discourses that construct and regulate them, Hausman reverses the habitual direction of our feminist gaze. By suggesting a reversal in how we see the relations between sex and gender, by asking us to shift our attention away from theories about gender and back to the "material signifiers" (p. 74) of our sexual selves, Hausman brilliantly complicates our recent discourses about gender and sex. In the final discussion of her book, Hausman claims that "[t]he body is the horizon of medicine" and "we need to account for those points at which discourse cannot describe or regulate the body's significations, to understand how theory cannot appropriate the body as its signifiers" (p. 200). I follow Hausman here by attempting yet another reversal in our consideration of the relationships between sex, theory, and gender; I consider how our discourse might construct other gendered realities, how words might loop back and redress bodies. In this chapter, I explore how the textual conventions of an ordinary e-mail message might be composed and read as evidence of three genders speaking. Questioning current feminist theories of gender and writing thus may open up a space for new embodied behaviors—dress, conversation, ritual, and action in the real and virtual worlds.

Implicitly challenging social constructionists like Lorber (1994) and Epstein (1988), Hausman examines how contemporary medical operations and advances in endocrinology and plastic surgery transform the material signs of sexuality so they conform to our social and cultural conversations about gender. In her fascinating (and troubling) chapter on transsexual autobiographies, for example, Hausman directs us to see the body afresh, and to see the transsexual body as a subject that has yielded to cultural narratives that present the possibilities of "technological self-construction" (1995, p. 174). If, as Hausman persuasively argues, it is discourse about gender that prompts intersexuals to reconstruct themselves as members of the male or female sex, then a feminist discourse that opens the conversation to considering several genders—a computer-based discourse that acknowledges and includes the experiences of third-gendered people, for example—might help people dispense with rigid, binary ways of considering sex and gender. In other words, by following Hausman's gaze and attending to how words and bodies intersect and construct each other, and then by changing the look, shape, and sound of words presented on a computer screen, perhaps a wider spectrum of gendered behaviors might transpire. E-mail exchanges might be such a writing space in which to attempt that kind of tantalizing, reconstructive talking.

I am suggesting that we consider how we communicate at a new site (the e-mail exchange) so that we can see firsthand the implications of imposing language on bodies. In fact, each time I revise this chapter, I see more clearly that this writing is more manifesto than essay. Ultimately, I am suggesting that we play with the norms and forms of e-mail exchanges so that our linguistic practices might actually expand the range of gendered expressions our bodies can wear. More specifically, this manifesto presents a set of suggestions that might help us imagine the body in the mind as fluid, intersexual, trigendered (at least), and in reality, pliable and viable alike.

WHY FEMINISTS SHOULD STUDY E-MAIL

When feminist scholars of rhetoric and composition study the phenomenon of electronic mail (e-mail) today, we are studying a small portion of a late 20th-century culture of letters that expresses itself in a wide range of media, forms, voices, registers, and styles. In addition to studying the belletristic genres honored in an academic culture of letters—plays, short stories, poems, literary nonfiction, and novels—responsible feminist scholars must study texts (and textual ephemera) selected from a much wider compass. Personal letters, diaries, transsexual autobiographies, postcards, packet radio, junk mail, mixed-media installations of neon and granite like those cobbled together by artist Jenny Holzer, billboards, bathroom graffiti, hip-hop lyrics, autograph books, medical charts, and even Post-its, for example, are fair game for feminist theorists who wish to undertake comprehensive cultural analyses of the scenes and substances of those scribal behaviors we call "reading" and "writing." When we consider the origins of the term "literature," we are prompted to remember that at its root, literary study is the study of all lettered discourse, not just those texts that modernists deem important.[1] To understand the phenomenon of e-mail, we feminist researchers must read that phenomenon against the larger cultural and lettered backdrop against which it is composed; we need to decipher the circulation of its broken murmurs as a local form of the general cultural norms that guide discursive choices.

One task for the feminist theorist studying the phenomenon of e-mail, then, involves understanding it within the compass of a larger discursive and textual community, a multicultural community sometimes characterized as postmodern. When I see how postmodern critical practices undo modernist alignments of canon, convention, and criticism, I understand that my own late-century location requires me to assume a critical position that accounts for the shifting alignments, discursive elisions, and graphic disjunctions visible in our culture. By taking a feminist critical perspective, I can lead my readers across a particular footpath through the modernist ruins. Furthermore, my feminist perspective can map the broken terrain and grant new lines of vision across the faults and folds of a fragmented, ruptured, heteroglossic, rhetorical space we understand as the exchange of e-mail messages. Finally, by taking a postmodern stance from which to peer at the flickering pixels of textual ephemera like e-mail, feminists like myself gain an insight into how a poststructuralist critique of the subject permits a wider, more flexible understanding of gender.

As Jacques Derrida, Michel Foucault, and other poststructuralists remind us, what we write on the screen in part depends on *who spoke before* in the texts surrounding our discourse: feminist theorists like Linda Williams (1996) and Mary Jacobus (1996) have examined the dynamics of feminist transmission of ideas in literature, Williams calling those long chains of influence a kind of "chain letter" (p. 52) sent from woman writer to woman writer. However, we need to study not just the forms and voices that came before or after whatever work of literature we're studying; when we analyze e-mail exchanges, we need to look, too, at what is said above or below what we can see on the screen. Our culture's working definitions of gender roles in speaking, writing, and acting are also realized within the texts lying both under and over the e-mail message. In e-mail exchanges, what we read and write is formed and filtered through names and ideas that are literally embedded in the texts underlying the hardware and software with which our bodies and minds interact.

When we feminist researchers read the language acts that underlie e-mail's presence on a computer screen as partial acts of naming and becoming, we can see the discursive layers that underlie all computer-based writing. That is, the names of particular codes, hardware configurations, and software applications themselves depend on their cultural histories, genealogies, and contemporary contingencies of plastic and metal that are constructed and named by programmers and documentation designers, readers and writers, and ever-expanding networks of people using computer-mediated communication. Is it significant that a popular mail program is named after one of our greatest Southern writers, Eudora Welty? Does it matter that a motherboard lies within our computers? That commands are executed or aborted? That the quadrangle of the computer screen echoes the edges of paper, a page, the codex book? That disks can be "locked" and programs "opened" by secret passwords? The pasts of hardware designers haunt the present of our computers. Hardware and software programmers have a tangible presence in our keyboards, screens, and drives.

Rhetorical forms and features of electronic mail reiterate contemporary cultural patterns of idiom, content, and conversational turn-taking, patterns complicated by their layered presence within a particular information delivery system, or what Kalmbach (1997) calls the container[2] of discourse. But the matches between contemporary discourse, computer equipment, and bodies who write e-mail are not perfect. Studying e-mail messages through the lenses of feminist theories helps us understand how electronic mail commutes and transmutes the values and rhetorics of the contemporary culture within which it is embedded.

The following sections tackle the question of how the contexts of gender and technology intersect with e-mail from four perspectives—history, theory, practice, and speculation. In my explorations, I am heeding calls in the last decades for writing researchers to pay more attention to e-mail (Hawisher & Moran, 1993; Moran, 1995; Shapiro & Anderson, 1985). I explore *why* e-mail messages are composed and read as they are, as well as speculate on *how* e-mail messages might be read and written differently. As I speculate on these pages about e-mail—and its fleeting traces of online identities—I encourage readers to understand gender as multiple, contingent, and even transitory, but also as a construct of terminology that is itself changeable. As Hausman (1995) tells us, "[w]e need to take account of the significance of the body as a semiotic economy constrained by the ideology of gender, but we also need to recognize the body as a system that asserts a certain resistance to (or constraint upon) the ideological system regulating it" (p. 14). E-mail messages are a new site from which to explore how writing affects gender, and how gender affects writing. But ultimately, I admit to being persuaded by Hausman that the body has its own authority. Finally, I hope that readers will see this article as a work in progress, a sample of visible thinking that is itself fluid and tentative—writing that is moving towards understanding but that does not yet itself fully understand.

Like all discourse, this essay exists at low tide, drawn with a stick on the edge of damp sand, a soft line that will soon fade away.

HISTORIES OF ELECTRICITY AND THE MAIL

> It is impossible to read the compositions of the most celebrated writers of the present day without being startled with the electric life which burns within their words. They measure the circumference and sound the depths of human nature with a comprehensive and all-penetrating spirit, and they are themselves perhaps the most sincerely astonished at its manifestations; for it is less their spirit than the spirit of the age.
>
> —Percy Bysshe Shelley, qtd. in Birkerts, 1989, p. 13

I have recently argued elsewhere (Sloane, 1999) that the theoretical category of "genealogy," when applied to contemporary scenes of reading and writing, is essential to any comprehensive understanding of computer-mediated communication. To understand more completely the intersections of e-mail and gender, I am, therefore, taking a brief genealogical look at the histories of electricity and mail. Such "genealogical" analysis reinforces the point made recently by Cynthia and Richard Selfe in "The Politics of the Interface" (1994): "...within the virtual space represented by...interfaces, and elsewhere within computer systems, the values of our culture...are mapped both implicitly and explicitly" (p. 484). E. L. Barton (1994) and M. Flores (1990) make a similar point. By recovering the history and cultural contexts of the physical apparatus through which we send and receive electronic messages, by uncovering the language and metaphors that have been used historically to describe the patterns of use and perceived purposes of the apparatus itself, we can begin to see e-mail as a pastiche of oral- and paper-based exchanges, as an important marker in the shifting topography between speech and writing.

The history of technologies in general in this century is a history of hauntings, of new inventions being figured against the ground of a collective past. Sitting Bull assumed telephones could speak only English, the language of their inventors. Herbert Hoover banned telephones from the White House. My own grandmother, at age 82, sat at my dining room table stroking an old Texas Instruments calculator, watching curiously as the numbers flickered and changed on the digital display. Cultural critics must learn the genealogies of their subjects, including cultural responses to technological innovation, before they will fully understand them. And so must we explore the historical traces of e-mail before we will fully comprehend how we compose and read.

Genealogies of Electricity

> Traditionally the question "What is electricity?" was called unanswerable for several decades after electricity came into common use. Now it is answered with *known facts*.
> —emphasis added; *Encyclopedia Britannica*, 1959, p. 153

> Modern electric power with its host of uses extends man's mastery over the physical world.
> —*The American People's Encyclopedia*, 1955, p. 742

Currents of electricity underlie the e-mail correspondence of the late 20th century. Electricity enlivens our computer screens, enables our networks, and delivers the messages inscribed ultimately in a fleeting script of ones and zeroes, the machine language that underscores the Babel of our critical and acritical tongues coded and layered online. The primary trope of postmodernism is the oxymoron, and we can likely find no better representative of its dual gesture than the electrical current that cycles under our e-mail exchanges and underlies computer writing today.

Postmodern thinking in general relies on an associative method that is galvanized by the collision of opposites. Postmodern culture grants us the "Pope-mobile," the electric flicker of classical paintings on the walls of Bill Gates's mansion, the college president who mentions excellence and cost-cutting measures in its writing program in the same breath, the Ohio State Buckeye—heartily accessorized in scarlet and gray—who reads *Plain* magazine on his way to the Michigan game, and the woodworking craft shop in the Pentagon. Postmodernism is the signal gesture of our day, and its language is paratactic, superficial, disjointed, and often expressed in binary terms.

Dualistic thinking and Cartesian logic are nothing new, of course, and yet our postmodern culture of letters seems a particularly fertile seedbed for the paired gesture, the elision of opposites: Postmodern culture offers us a vision of sex, gender, American politics, and body-and-mind that always comes in sets of two. What would happen if we started to think in more than two, if our country had a true multiparty political system, if genders came in several flavors, if dialogues became wider conversations among whole communities of people? What would we learn about electricity if we used tropes not of "positive" or "negative" currents, but ones that described electricity in some new, tripartite metaphor? Although generating a new theory of electricity is, thankfully, well beyond the purview of this article, by acknowledging the genealogy of metaphors for electric energy in the eighteenth century, we learn something about how we speak of e-mail today.

Historically, "electricity" is a term to describe a property of "electric bodies," a property of glass, amber, and other materials that could be "excited by friction to attract light bodies placed near them" (*Oxford English Dictionary*, 1982, p. 44). The word *electricity* itself comes from the Greek word for *amber* because of that fossil resin's abilities to attract other light objects to it when rubbed. According to several traditional histories of electricity, this peculiar property of amber was first recorded by

Thales of Miletus. (Aristotle attributed to Thales the ideas that magnets have souls because they can attract iron, and that amber, too, must be full of gods because of its behavior.)[3]

In the 18th century, Benjamin Franklin synthesized the work of several Enlightenment contemporaries working with electricity, and, like many other scientists of the time, he experimented with Leyden jars (capacitors) and static electricity generators as he helped develop the dominant 18th-century theory that electricity is two fluids. Franklin popularized the terms "positive" and "negative" as words that described too much or too little of the electrical fluid in objects that attracted or repelled each other.[4] Some of Franklin's contemporaries believed "positive" and "negative" electricity to be two distinct fluids, which when combined neutralized each other, but in any case, the theories that Franklin and his contemporaries devised relied on the notion that electricity was dualistic, a pairing of positive and negative forces that resulted in energy. In time, Franklin's theory was realized as the period's best explanation of what Enlightenment figures called "the electric virtue" (Gay, 1966, p. 28). Today, the language used by Franklin and his contemporaries to describe electricity is still current.

This binary model of electrical energy is iterated throughout machine and message in contemporary computer-mediated communication. Today, electrical "current," underlies our communicative exchanges on the computer and enables electronic mail. If we trace the genealogies of machine, current, and screen, and, more particularly, deconstruct the language we use to describe these artifacts, we can see a dual impulse underlying almost every aspect of computer-mediated electronic mail. Whether we describe the current underlying the machine language as positive and negative energy, write the machine language itself in ones and zeroes, delineate the program codes in terms of machine language or higher-level program, the software in terms of code and user interface, the computing apparatus in terms of hardware and software, or the message itself as showing traces of its male or female authors, the language we use to describe most levels of the e-mail exchange is binary. And our language itself, then, in its oxymorons or elisions, may limit the ways we construe the hardware and software of computers—not to mention the e-mail messages with which we construct and support our notions of gender.

When I go into one of our campus's networked computing centers and observe an undergraduate student writing e-mail to a high school friend attending another college, I am struck by her animation as she corresponds, her soft mutterings and visible smile as she expertly types her message and sends it. How is meaning filtered when the message that conveys it speeds through the lace of a fiber optic network? When a Hawaiian student reveals that she is flying to Missouri to meet her fiancé face-to-face for the first time, I am stunned to learn that their entire courtship was initiated and pursued over the computer. How do the conventions of courtship change when conducted over computer? When I travel to Edinburgh each summer to read the primary texts of Scottish rhetoricians, I spend an hour each afternoon at a pleasant Internet café called Cyberia reading my e-mail. My hands that an hour before grasped the foxed edges of a 1798 Scottish Presbytery disciplinary record now grope for the nonexistent dollar sign on a computer keyboard. Like any postmodern feminist worth her salt, I try to keep track of all the contradictions that comprise my experiences, my settings, and even myself. I can hear the echo of the binary language of electrical terms in the words I use to describe these contradictions. Like most postmodern feminists, I realize all narrators are unreliable, but I still lack a language sufficient to encompass the range of unreliability that I know exists, especially when we talk through the keyboards, screens, fibers, and cables linking computers. I can't help thinking that we continue to miss a dimension of this writing scene by not paying more attention to how electricity literally and metaphorically underlies the postmodern discourse of e-mail. We need to learn much more about the genealogies of electricity, amber, magnets, cable, and screen before we can theorize about the genealogies of e-mail and about those subjects who send and receive its fickle missives.

Genealogies of Mail

> With all the horrors of prophetic dread,
> That rack his bosom while the mail is read.
> —Tobias Smollett, 1748, p. 160

While inhabitants of the United States are likely to use the word *mail* as a verb meaning "to send by post" or as a noun meaning "postal matter," the roots of the word itself are in the Old English words for speech, agreement, discussion, or meeting place (*The Compact Edition of the Oxford English Dictionary*, 1982, p. 44). "Post," as most readers know, referred originally to the stake or stump upon which people attached public notices. Herodotus wrote of the dispatch of letters in Persia via an intricate system of horses and riders relaying messages from one "post" to the next, and Marco Polo noted admiringly the same system operated on the roads of China. In addition to the Persians and Chinese, Aztecs, Assyrians, and Romans are believed to have established early versions of a postal system. The early universities of Europe also maintained a prototype of postal delivery. Over time, the term "post" began to be applied by English-speakers to the riders themselves and then to the bags of mail they carried. This transfer of a term used to describe communication in an oral-based culture to communication in a print-based culture is a clear example of how the past constructs the present. We can also trace the ways the past haunts the present in the terms we use to describe *icons, buttons,* and *dialogue boxes* found on the *desktop* of contemporary computers.

To continue the history lesson, the first postal system in the United States (a network of horses and riders) was established in 1639. Under the U.S. Constitution, a postal service was formally authorized by Congress in 1789. In 1838, the Postmaster General of the United States authorized the transportation of mail on the railroad. Over the next century, mail in this country was carried on wagon trains, canal boats, and railroad cars, over land, over water, and across tracks. Mail carriers traveled by horseback, stagecoach, steamboat, and rail, paid by the funds raised from the sale of postal stamps (first put on sale in New York City on July 1, 1847).

Over the last 150 years, conventions regarding what is permitted to be mailed for free (for example, official mail of the members of Congress and literature for the blind, to name two occasionally overlapping categories) and what is prohibited from being mailed (poisons, explosives, obscene matter, and so on), have been strengthened as law. If we explore the development of mail delivery over the last 360 years in this country, we can see that development guided by a desire for increased ease and speed of delivery, and shaped by the persistent hope of widening the geographic range of the public distribution of letters (a hope no doubt linked to colonial aspirations).

E-mail was first sent over the ARPAnet in the early 1970s, and today e-mail accounts for about 6% of the traffic on the NSFnet (Dern, 1994). Electronic mail has advantages over paper-based mail in its speed of delivery, its capacity to be addressed quickly and easily to multiple recipients, and its maneuverability—its property of being easily manipulated into other texts and documents by its recipients. The textual properties peculiar to e-mail include its apparent ease of erasure (of both text and identity, address and addressee), its accessibility only via the instrument of a computer, and the genealogies, range, and names of communication technologies that underlie its presentation, already discussed. Sproull and Kiesler (1993) detail six other characteristics of electronic mail technologies today: E-mail is (1) asynchronous, (2) fast, (3) text-based, and it has (4) multiple-receiver addressibility, (5) built-in external memory (the contents of e-mail can be stored and retrieved for later use), and (6) the external memory is computer processable (it can be "searched, edited, partitioned, [and] shared with others" [pp. 182–183]).

In addition, e-mail messages permit new opportunities for relocating and dislocating the identities of their senders. While we all are familiar with the tricks that can be played in conventional mail by a misleading postmark, a fake return address, or a forged signature, the set of scribal behaviors intended to disguise the identity and location of senders of e-mail is different. The recent advent of digitized watermarks to identify original ownership of clip art, the sideways carets (chevrons) indicating a piece of e-mail has been forwarded, the ability to set your "real name" as any name, and the various places to enter this information in Eudora, are all sites where new kinds of forgeries and crimes of writing are possible, even probable. The scribal gestures that disguise identity and control the presentation of *ethos* (and ethical appeals) have a new flexibility, fluidity, and range in today's postings, ground down to their binary element, transmitted through phone lines, and reconstituted as mail messages appearing on a computer screen.

When we read the words "electronic" and "mail" etymologically, and when we look at the cultural values they embody genealogically, we can understand e-mail as the latest realization of the North American culture's desires for speed, ease, visible presence, and wide range of effect. In the intersection of histories of electricity and the post, we can see a theory (in Thales's attribution of gods to amber) and a practice (in the elaborate postal systems of the great khan celebrated by Marco Polo) of bodies attracting each other and responding visibly to each other by drawing closer. That is, I see a postmodern corollary between a magnet drawing in iron filings and a Pony Express courier galloping between two points to deliver a message to a lover—on average 10½ days and 75 ponies later. Mail and electricity, the tropes we use to describe their characteristics, and their active presence as histories haunting computer networks and circuits, are cultural names that represent our desire to join bodies, link identities, play with masks, and form communities through literate acts. Posting e-mail is a cultural activity founded in anxiety, yearning, and worry, and fostered by the hope of closeness.

READING THE GENDER OF E-MAIL

When we look at the roots of electronic mail, we can see that the genre has always been gendered, in the histories of the apparatuses that allow the transmission of e-mail, in the sex of the original experimenters of electricity and the purveyors of e-mail, as well as in the cultural values e-mail embodies in its speed, the sheer *hubris* of its users, the ease of delivery, and its voracious use of natural resources. While these cursory genealogies of mail and electricity are only notes towards a longer meditation on how e-mail realizes dominant cultural values and discursive needs and practices, let me suggest the following.

If we were to look at e-mail messages with a mind to do conventional analyses of male and female gestures in language, we might look at seven sites in a typical message (see Figure 2.1 and Table 2.1). Each of these seven sites could reveal evidence of maleness and femaleness according to interpretive strategies offered by Brody (1993), Butler (1990), Haraway (1991), James and Drakich (1993), or Tannen (1990, 1993). Each of these wise feminists has theorized about ways to analyze discourse so that the speaker's gender is identified and understood. For example, we might use Tannen's (1993) observations about the amount of talking in conversational interaction between men and women, the degrees and kinds of confrontation and politeness, the questions and statements each makes, and infer from these findings gendered behaviors. Or we might look at patterns of metaphors and assume that if the message is talking about power, snakes, guns, and wrestling, that the gender of the message is probably male—as Brody does in *Manly Writing* (1993). We might examine the whole machine, as it were, and find "maleness" and "femaleness" imprinted in the software, the hardware, the box itself, as Haraway does; or we might look to the patterns of culture, power, and ideology that surround and contextualize computer-mediated communication, as Selfe and Selfe do. In each of these cases, though, we would be looking only for evidence of male or female ways of talking. In the following discussion, I speculate about interpreting reading and writing as it might assume more flexible notions of gender. I hope to move feminists from speaking in metaphors of centaurs and cyborgs (Haraway, 1991; Olson, 1995) to reconsidering the chimera—a fire-breathing, she-monster in Greek mythology, whose body is made up of the parts of a lion, a goat, and a serpent.

But none of these analyses of my e-mail correspondence would be complete because each assumes a binary system of gender. Instead, I wish to speculate about what it might be like to look for features of three genders in computer-based texts, to explore each of these seven gendered locations as though gender came in three flavors, not just two.

Date: Thu, 30 May 1996 18:01:01 -0700 (PDT)
(1) From: <xyz@edu>*
(2) To: sarah jane sloane <sloane@ups.edu>
(3) Subject: Re: Hi there!
Mime-Version: 1.0

(4) Sarah! So good to hear from you!

(5) Thanks for the congrats on the TA—I am excitedly anticipating the chance to teach on my own (to see if I can pull it off, you know!). I am glad to hear you are doing so well.

(6) I am neck-deep in trying to complete two seminar papers. The quarter is over in one and one half weeks and I am not nearly as far along as I should be on my work (as usual, I am afraid). The other night I had my quarterly breakdown where I cried myself to sleep over the fact that I'm just not going to get everything done. After I hit rock bottom emotionally, however, I have been much better. In fact, I now believe that I can write another 20 page paper in the next week and revise my existing paper I have already pounded out. The power of a cathartic cry...you just can't beat it.
(7) Love, xyz

*In this example, I have substituted "xyz@edu" for the user name to preserve his/her confidentiality and to tempt readers to make hasty judgments about the gender of the sender based on other aspects of the message.

FIGURE 2.1. Places where genders might be read or revealed in an e-mail message.

TABLE 2.1.
Key to Locations in an E-mail Message Where Gender may be Particularly Visible

(1 and 2) The to/from portions of the message (addresser and addressee)	The first cue as to the gender(s) of an e-mail message's writer and reader is found in the names given in the message header, the person's "real" name often bracketed by chevrons. In our culture, the vast majority of first names signify maleness or femaleness, and while the User ID may not signify gender, one's first name usually does.
(3) The subject line	Many researchers (McCracken & Appleby, 1992; Tannen, 1990, 1993) have found that men and women tend to talk more—and in different patterns—about different subjects. The subject line of an e-mail message may reveal a gender bias in its stated topic or in the punctuation used. (Exclamation points, questions, and parenthetical remarks have sometimes been indentified with female usage patterns.)
(4) The message shape (the "physical look" of the message on the virtual page)	The shape of particular messages may be read as gendered. Length of paragraphs, types of indentation and paragraph markers, use and pattern of "emoticons,"* and the overall "look" of the message on the virtual page may be read as gendered features of e-mail. While the present shape of e-mail messages typically echoes the familiar quadrangles of paper and screen, in time we may grow more inventive in the ways we frame messages.
(5) The message tropes	What figures of speech, commonplaces, or phrases are repeated across messages? Does the formality or informality of a salutation, for example, relate to gender, to power relationships?
(6) The message content	The general preoccupations and content of the message itself might be read as gendered. In the case of this message, the references to crying, the conventional narrative structures (conflict and resolution), and the ratio of exclamation marks to message length might be read as revealing a conventional social construction of femininity.
(7) The message context	The whole apparatus that underlies the transmission of an e-mail message—the hardware, software, and people that comprise a message's contexts and audiences—contributes to our readings of the gender of e-mail. So do the scenes of reading—the offices, homes, labs, and libraries that are the primary physical sites of e-mail exchanges.

* My informal counting of emoticons shows that women use them at least twice as often as men. In my experience, heavy users of e-mail favor reading and writing short messages that do not extend beyond what can be read on one screen. For realistic examples of the truncated language, insider's shorthand, and apostrophes of the fluent, frequent e-mail user, see the examples in Douglas Coupland's *Microserfs* (1995).

FEMINIST THEORIES OF GENDER AND ELECTRONIC WRITING

> ...may the lexicographer be derided, who...shall imagine that his dictionary can embalm his language, and secure it from corruption and decay...
> —Samuel Johnson, qtd. in Green, 1996, pp. 256–257

> ...a feminist look at the canon (the system) will reveal the petrification of the gender hierarchies that regulate the institutionalization of literature; and displace the asymmetries those hierarchies install...
> —Nancy K. Miller, qtd. in Eagleton, 1996, p. 49

Postmodernists in general have been quite good at shucking off the rigid husks of modernism, of rejecting petrified hierarchies, embalmed dogmas, and the ossificatory discourse of those who came before. Postmodern feminists in particular have constructed a vision of gender as multiple, contingent, and even transitory, a vision that is supported by the online transvestitism and variously gendered identities assumed by writers and participants in computer-mediated communications. Elizabeth Flynn (1995), in her recent taxonomy of types of feminisms, says that the postmodern feminist problematizes the categories "male" and "female" and rejects constructions of gender that depend on a binary opposition. Postmodern feminists see gender as "inextricably linked to other constructions such as race, class, and ethnicity, and to social contexts that destabilize identity, including gender identity" (p. 201). Flynn provides a perspective that accounts for the fluidity of gender constructs when they are writ on computer.

If gender is primarily a social construct, as Lorber (1994) claims in *Paradoxes of Gender,* and is a social institution "analogous to the state or the market," in the words of one reviewer, then fiddling with the conventions of e-mail might subvert binary notions of gender. Lorber extends the work of Susan Kessler, Wendy McKenna, and other American feminists of the last two decades, going beyond liberal feminism then and now to probe the dichotomies of sex, sexuality, and gender as they are built into the organization and politics of all social institutions. Lorber claims that "gender is a human invention, like language, kinship, religion, and technology." She claims that gender is "wholly constructed, symbolically loaded, and ideologically enforced" (p. 5). Lorber's insights into what constitutes the social institution of gender have been helpful in my speculative work on how genders might be reconstituted within the spaceless space of cyberspace.[5]

Alluquère Rosanne (Sandy) Stone, a professor working in the University of Texas at Austin's ACT-Lab, told a group of us over dinner 3 years ago that she was working on a performance art piece, one in which she wears a white, full-length body stocking and has slides of all different body types and genders projected on her. She off-handedly remarked that one can assume or shed different genders as easily as one can put on or take off clothes. In her recent essay, "Split Subjects, Not Atoms"

(1995), Stone uses a narrative method that parallels her proposed performance about gender. She introduces her essay with the tantalizing heading, "Increasingly, I Have Problems," and follows up by putting readers on notice that the essay at hand

> will not be so much a linear discussion ... as it will be a series of provocations, and at the end there will be not so much a summary as an attempt to thread the provocations, to point out some resonances among them and to hold them in productive tension without allowing them to collapse into anything approximating a univocal account.... (pp. 393–394)

I read Stone's meditation about her own writing strategy and her proposed performance art as linked remarks; she demonstrates a parallel movement between reconsidering writing and rethinking gender.

So, what is gender? Is Sandy Stone right? Can genders be assumed or removed as easily as a bathing suit? What if e-mail discourse came in three flavors, not two? What traces would a third gender leave in the systems of metaphors, the patterns of questions, the signatures and salutations of an e-mail message? How would we read to infer maleness, femaleness, and features of a hijra, for example? What would hijra e-mail look like?

Three Genders, Not Two

Serena Nanda's fascinating work of social anthropology, *Neither Man nor Woman: The Hijras of India* (1990), documents the lives and cultural roles of another group of people of ambiguous gender: hijras. Nanda describes hijra living in the three largest hijra households in Bastipore, and her interviews with several of the men reveal wonderful, rich, and divergent roles and identities. Zia Jaffrey's (1996) personal account of visiting the hijra echoes many of Nanda's anthropological findings of people living in a "third-gendered" state. According to Nanda, hijra are important performers at auspicious events such as birthdays or weddings. They are almost always male (and only rarely hermaphrodites, contrary to some earlier claims by anthropologists), are often castrated, and dress in women's clothing. The color photographs of hijras included in the centerfolds of Nanda's book are startling in that the people depicted look like Western stereotypes of femininity: the men wear dresses, bracelets, rings, flowers, and earrings. They often wear heavy makeup on their faces. Although Nanda repeatedly refers to the hijras as "sexually ambiguous," some of the photographs seem not ambiguous at all; they appear to be depicting conventional Hindu women. However, other photographs of the hijras in contemporary India show them performing with beards, short skirts, hairy legs, and tattoos.

If we were to speculate about what the textual features of an e-mail message revealing a hijra nature might look like, we could conjecture the seven sites I have detailed earlier as having some of the following new conditions. The text might have androgynous names in its address and signature—names like Sandy or Chris, for example. The body of the message might no longer be square; it might be circular or shaped in a spiral or a web. There might be a neutral blend of statement and question, a new set of punctuation marks and emoticons. And there might be new syntactic patterns that would approximate the songs, chants, and blessings of the hijras—or e-mail attachments of audio and visual elements that might illustrate three genders performing. In addition, the apparatus underlying the communication might be no longer a plastic monitor and keyboard. The computer might resemble the "data egg" I read about 3 years ago that was displayed at a Las Vegas computer trade show. The data egg prototype was about the size of a fist, shaped like a football, with five keys arranged along the top. Writers used these five keys in different combinations to type all the letters of the alphabet, and the message was displayed on a small monitor, 1 inch by 3 inches long, held in the palm of one's hand. The size and heft of this data egg is a precursor of the handheld and palmtop computers being developed now.

If the way we use language outside of a virtual world can be shaped by the activities and discourse of the hijra selves we use in virtual settings like e-mail messages, it is worth playing the game. If nothing else, imagining hijra discourse can alert us to the rigidity of systems of communication relying on binary distinctions alone. Imagining hijra discourse might ultimately change a world, virtual or otherwise.

Postmodern Feminism, Sex, Gender, and Writing

In mid-November of 1994, the Human Interface Technologies Laboratory in Seattle mounted a demonstration of a shared virtual environment called The Greenspace Project: Phase III. Greenspace, a virtual world that designers liken to a virtual commons, permitted researchers in Seattle to undertake a real-time VR teleconference with scientists in Tokyo who were attending the NICOGRAPH Convention (the Japanese equivalent of SIGGRAPH).[6] With some hubris, local newspaper reports equated the demonstration with Alexander Graham Bell's first long-distance telephone call. I was one of the local volunteers who participated in the demonstration.

A total of four volunteers (two on each side of the Pacific) donned a helmet and a glove and sat opposite each other in pairs at a virtual square table. Through our helmets, we saw a virtual world: We appeared to be sitting at a table in a small Japanese house. I could see Mount Fuji through a window on my left, and on my right I saw a small shrine inside the paneled room. My Japanese counterparts saw themselves sitting in a different shared space, one that contained some programmer's idea of a typical American setting (one that included log cabin walls, a view of Mount Rainier where we were seeing Mount Fuji, and so on). I looked down and saw that my hands, inexplicably, looked like ping-pong paddles. Several small, cartoonish bugs were crawling across the table. As always in my experience with virtual reality, the resolution was grainy.

The part of the encounter that was eliciting such excitement locally was the fact that in addition to the four of us Americans, four Japanese employees at Fujitsu Laboratories, near Tokyo, were simultaneously sitting at our table, two to my left and two to my right. I could see their faces and they could see mine. (Actually, we could see digitized renderings of our faces based on a set of photographs taken of each of us before we entered the virtual world.) While in actuality they were sitting at a conference thousands of miles away, in cyberspace they were sharing my table, their hands shaped like ping-pong paddles and their mouths making the same predictable motions as my own. We had voice-interaction, too, and in a muddy, fuzzy way were able to hear their voices in Tokyo. Unfortunately, the people running the experiment did not take into account that we did not speak Japanese, and the people at Fujitsu apparently did not speak English. Nonetheless, we were able to wave at our counterparts halfway around the world.

As the voices outside the world instructed us to, we collaborated with our Japanese counterparts in herding bugs with our ping-pong paddle hands off the edge of the table—most of the time. Personally, I grew far more interested in waving to my Japanese counterpart and following her ping-pong paddle through the air with my own. "Try to catch the bugs," the voice outside the world intoned impatiently. "Get the bugs." "I'd rather wave," I muttered, all the way back to Japan. The most interesting part of the experiment for me was precisely our interaction: We could speak to each other and see each other's faces—all in real-time, all across thousands of miles of ocean. The designers of Greenspace at the HIT-Lab saw this experiment as a precursor of shared-space videoconferencing. I saw this experiment as computer-mediated communication gone awry.

I read that HIT-Lab experiment as a kind of e-mail, a multimedia version of the plainer, text-based e-mail message that was likewise based on layered illusions, fractured identities, and a new capacity for lying about location and identity. Flashier, more entertaining, and with a wider band-width to allow sound and image as well as text across great distances, that cross-national, intercontinental, synchronous communication carried the traces of its cultural context more vividly than a text-based e-mail message, but its visual and audio elements were a difference in degree rather than kind. As in ordinary e-mail, the Greenspace experiment was an exercise in mediated communication, wherein every gesture and syllable was represented by computer graphics, sounds, and symbols, and through which every user must reach to grasp the meanings of his counterpart.

While computer-mediated communication obviously comes in many versions, and while our definition of e-mail can widen to such an extent that it becomes nonsensical, by reading the shared virtual world of Greenspace as a high-tech version of the lowly, text-only e-mail message, we can start to see a truth about all electronic messages. That truth is this: Although the versions of electronic mail may vary according to bandwidth and via the proportion of text, graphics, and video they convey (as well as according to the time lag and physical distances between sender and receiver), all versions of electronic mail have an inherent capacity to disguise their users and to allow writers to lie in new ways. Electronic mail offers a set of masks to its users that is peculiar to computer-mediated communication and that complicates our notions of *ethos* that are based on paper texts alone.

In making this claim, I am taking a broad view of "masks." In 1988, when I was a graduate student at Carnegie Mellon University, I took a seminar in artificial intelligence (AI) that required us to write (and program) computer-based interactive fictions. My first proposal for that course was to design an animal costume party. I imagined participants in a story typing the instructions that would allow them to enter a room, drink a glass of champagne, and then put on the mask of a raccoon, a lion, or a dragon as they interacted with other players. Five years later, at the Banff Center for the Arts, interface designer Brenda Kay Laurel invented "smart costumes" for players in her virtual world; users put on the mask of a crow, for example, and then were forced by the mask to speak and move like a crow. Participants could croak and fly. Masks like Laurel's and mine are literal examples of how computer media can provide new disguises for its users. Whether that disguise is the disembodied hand and digitized face/avatar of virtual worlds like Greenspace, or the forged signature and falsified location of a text-based e-mail message, computers expand the human capacity for play, disguise, and lying.

CONCLUSION

When we explore the electronic masks the computer allows us to assume, and when we explore those masks as dynamic, layered artifacts that have individual genealogies and that are in some ways gendered, we ultimately learn more about the ways we define ourselves at the turn of the century. The way North American people realize their roles, behaviors, and appearances in their computerized counterparts, representatives, or avatars, at the end of this century is significant for how we understand gender. One of the most interesting aspects of taking this look at gender and e-mail for me has been what I have learned about the relations between writing and identity in general. That is, I began this chapter asserting that I would take a postmodern feminist perspective, a perspective that Flynn and Lorber had persuaded me made sense. However, as I have written this article, I have found myself increasingly uncomfortable in my role as a postmodern feminist. I wonder if my discomfort about calling myself a postmodern feminist isn't related to a question about *ethos* that writing e-mail also poses. E-mail makes visible in a new way disjunctions between personal and publicly expressed identities, disjunctions that exist in paper texts, too, of course, but that in e-mail release a new capacity for disguise. I wonder if my discomfort with the postmodernist perspective derives from my dread of conformity—or my secret lust for conformity. I wonder how my own lesbian identity surfaces, appears, and disappears in e-mail exchanges, after having been forced through the layers of contrary discourse, past and present. (See Harriet Malinowitz's [1995] important work for a rich discussion of this dynamic.)

Looking at e-mail with an eye towards identifying locations in which gender may be revealed ultimately raises questions about the relationship between essential identity and the visible languages we use to express that identity. When we speak, to what extent does our voice echo within the bones and sinews of our own bodies? When we write, to what extent is each word tied to our living presence? What are the links between body and body, between partners in conversation, especially when their talk is mediated by computer? How do definitions of lying change according to medium? These questions and others are the ones that emerge whenever I use e-mail as a new site to understand gender, its behaviors, its definitions.

Although I believe that gender is largely a social construction, and I am aware of how gender roles have changed over time (both in my own country and in others), I ultimately agree with Hausman that the gulf between biological sex and socially-constructed gender might not be as wide as some feminists would have us believe—and that the relationship between the material signifiers of sex and the discursive acts used to signal gender is far more complex than we have admitted. Of course, I firmly believe in wide ranges of choices for men and women (and everyone in between) in what and how they write, who they choose as their lovers, friends, and partners, and how they choose to live. I acknowledge the very important work of feminists who have tried to unlink sex and gender so that women and men might have more choices in their employment, their housework, and their family roles. But I worry that the word *gender* erases the word *sex* in the same way that an e-mail address or a forged signature can erase the identity of a sender; and I worry that that erasure does not allow us to see clearly the relations between rhetoric and biology. Sexual orientation, gender identification, procreative roles, gender roles, and biological sex exist together in more complicated alignments than postmodern feminism may allow us to acknowledge.

I write just above the incoming tide, at the edge of the web, and on the margins of conversation in a new mode. If I achieve nothing else in this chapter but to draw your attention to e-mail as an important site for researchers in reading and writing, I will have achieved one purpose. If I further the discussion of the implications of taking a postmodern feminist stance, I will have achieved another purpose. But if, in the end, I prompt you to consider the ways in which we might play with e-mail and language to enable writers and speakers to learn new ways of speaking, speaking that dispenses with those gestures of a discourse that always sees gender in sets of two, I will be most glad. Please read this manifesto as a work-in-progress, a feminist wondering about the relations among gender, sex, and writing prompted lately by Hausman's work on transsexuals. No remark I make here is definitive in any way, shape, or form.

Just see this particular piece of writing as itself a message in a bottle, a few ideas floating through the circuit that joins you to me.

NOTES

[1] Readers might usefully recall that the privileged class of writings called "literature" is itself a cultural construction, and that the narrow definition of the term conventional today obscures the word's broader connections to "letters" and "lettered discourse" in general. A feminist definition of "culture of letters" would be one that encompasses a wide range of texts, implicitly questions modernist constructions of what comprises the forms, authors, and voices deserving of our study, and that substitutes a more elastic, fraught, flexible, and tentative understanding of letters for the neater modernist one. Such a feminist perspective allows us to consider a wide range of written ephemera—from political cartoons to detergent advertisements, from tattoo parlor business cards to online virtual worlds and MUDs—as fitting sites for our analyses of the contemporary practices of reading and writing.

[2] Kalmbach (1997) begins his intelligent discussion of publishing history with a definition of terms. He says, "A document consists of text, display space, a container, and an interface. The text is a document's contents.... The container is what holds the text (a book, a magazine, a newspaper, a brochure, or a CD-ROM). A container is usually a physical object, but in the most recent forms of distributed hypertext (such as the World-Wide Web), the container of a document is created virtually through the act of browsing..." (p. 13).

[3] For this brief discussion of the origins of electricity, I am indebted to the *Oxford English Dictionary,* the *Encyclopedia Britannica,* and *the American Heritage Dictionary of the English Language,* as well as to Peter Gay's (1966) discussion of the Enlightenment.

[4] Franklin "considered electric phenomena to be due to a subtle fluid diffused through all bodies, the excess of which above its normal quantity constituted 'positive electricity,' and its deficiency below the normal quantity 'negative electricity'" (*Oxford English Dictionary*, 1982, p. 77).

[5] As Amy Bruckman, Sherry Turkle (see Brody, 1996), and Kevin Kelly have recently explored, users of MUDs and MOOs routinely assume the indentity of the opposite sex as they participate in these online roleplaying games. Bruchman and Turkle go so far as to claim that MUDs and MOOs are really laboratories in which to explore the dimensions of personal identity. Stacy Horn, president and founder of ECHO, a thriving, New York-based "electronic salon" with over 3,000 members, calls this online cross-dressing assuming an "electronic mask." And Kevin Kelly reports in his recent book, *Out of Control* (1995), on several instances of virtual cross-dressing. Kelly explains that so many self-described "female" characters in MUDs are actually male that most savvy MUDders assume all players are male unless proven otherwise; female players are often asked questios to "prove" their gender. In these general instances of online cross-dressing, language is used to reveal or conceal social constructions of identity.

[6] The Greenspace project was conceived of by Dr. Thomas Furness of HITL and Dr. Masahiro Kawahata of the Fujitsu Research Institute in April 1993, and is funded by the two institutions. Readers interested in a fuller discussion of the shape and aims of this experiment might learn more about Greenspace through the following website: http://www.hitl.washington.edu/projects/greenspace/phaseone.html

According to the website, "The goals of the project are to to [sic] develop and demonstrate an immersive communications medium where distant participants feel a sense of presence in a shared virtual environment, a 'virtual common.'"

REFERENCES

The American People's Encyclopedia. (1955). Chicago: Spencer Press.

Barton, E. L. (1994). Interpreting the discourses of technology. In C. Y. Selfe & S. Hilligoss (Eds.), *Literacy and computers: The complications of teaching and learning with technology* (pp. 56–74). NY: Modern Language Association.

Birkerts, S. (1989). *The electric life: Essays on modern poetry.* New York: William Morrow.

Brody, H. (1996, February/March). Session with the cybershrink: An interview with Sherry Turkle. *MIT Technology Review,* 1.

Brody, M. (1993). *Manly writing: Gender, rhetoric, and the rise of composition.* Carbondale, IL: Southern Illinois University Press.

Butler, J. (1990). *Gender trouble: Feminism and the subversion of identity.* New York: Routledge.

The Compact Edition of the Oxford English Dictionary (Vol. I). (1982). New York: Oxford University Press.

Coupland, D. (1995). *Microserfs.* New York: Regan Books.

Dern, D. P. (1994). *The Internet guide for new users.* New York: McGraw-Hill.

Eagleton, M. (Ed.). (1996). *Feminist literary theory: A reader* (2nd ed.). Cambridge, MA: Blackwell.

Encyclopedia Britannica (Vol. 8). (1959). London: Encyclopedia Britannica.

Epstein, C. F. (1988). *Deceptive distinctions: Sex, gender, and the social order.* New Haven, CT: Yale University Press.

Flores, M. J. (1990). Computer conferencing: Composing a feminist community of writers. In C. Handa (Ed.), *Computers and community: Teaching composition in the twenty-first century* (pp. 106–117). Portsmouth, NH: Boynton.

Flynn, E. (1995). Feminist theories/feminist composition. *College English, 57*(2), 201–211.

Gay, P. (1966). *Age of Enlightenment.* New York: Time.

Green, J. (1996). *Chasing the sun: Dictionary-makers and the dictionaries they made.* London: Jonathan Cape.

Hawisher, G. E., and Moran, C. (1993). Electronic mail and the writing instructor. *College English, 55*(6), 627–643.

Haraway, D. (1991). *Simians, cyborgs, and women: The reinvention of nature.* New York: Routledge.

Hausman, B. (1995). *Changing sex: Transsexualism, technology, and the idea of gender.* Durham, NC, and London: Duke University Press.

Jacobus, M. (1996). Reading woman: Essays in feminist criticism. In M. Eagleton (Ed.), *Feminist literary theory* (pp. 51–52). Oxford, England: Blackwell.

Jaffrey, Z. (1996). *The invisibles: A tale of the Eunuchs of India.* New York: Vintage Books.

James, D., & Drakich, J. (1993). Understanding gender differences in amount of talk: A critical review of research. In D. Tannen (Ed.), *Gender and conversational interaction* (pp. 281–312). New York: Oxford University Press.

Kalmbach, J. (1997). *The computer and the page: Publishing, technology, and the classroom.* Norwood, NJ: Ablex.

Kelly, K. (1995). *Out of control: The rise of neo-biological civilization.* Reading, MA: Addison-Wesley.

Lorber, J. (1994). *Paradoxes of gender.* New Haven, CT: Yale University Press.

Malinowitz, H. (1995). *Textual orientations: Lesbian and gay students and the making of discourse communities.* Portsmouth, NH: Heinemann/Boynton Cook.

McCracken, N. M., & Appleby, B. (Eds.). (1992). *Gender issues in the teaching of English.* Portsmouth, NH: Heinemann/Boynton Cook.

Moran, C. (1995.) Notes toward a rhetoric of e-mail. *Computers and Composition, 12*, 15–21.

Nanda, S. (1990). *Neither man nor woman: The hijras of India.* Belmont, CA: Wadsworth.

Olson, G. A. (1995). Writing, literacy and technology: Toward a cyborg writing. In G. A. Olson & E. Hirsh (Eds.), *Women writing culture* (pp. 45–77). Albany, NY: State University of New York.

Selfe, C., & Selfe, R. (1994). The politics of the interface. *College Composition and Communication, 45*(4), 480–504.

Shapiro, N. Z., & Anderson, R. H. (1985). *Toward an ethics and etiquette for electronic mail.* Santa Monica, CA: Rand.

Sloane, S. (1999). The haunting story of J: Genealogy as a critical category in understanding how a writer composes. In G. E. Hawisher & C. Selfe (Eds.), *Passions, pedagogies, and 21st century technologies* (pp. 49–65). Logan, UT: Utah State University Press.

Smollett, T. (1748). *The adventures of Roderick Random.* London: J. Osborn.

Sproull, L., & Kiesler, S. (1991). *Connections: New ways of working in the networked organization.* Cambridge, MA: MIT Press.

Stimpson, C. (1989). *Where the meanings are: Feminism and cultural spaces.* New York: Routledge. (Original work published 1988)

Stone, S. (1995). Split subjects, not atoms; or, How I fell in love with my prosthesis. In C. H. Gray (Ed.), *The cyborg handbook* (pp. 393–406). New York and London: Routledge.

Tannen, D. (1990). *You just don't understand: Women and men in conversation.* New York: Ballantine.

Tannen, D. (Ed.). (1993). *Gender and conversational interaction.* New York: Oxford University Press.

Whitman, W. (1983). *Walt Whitman's* Leaves of Grass (M. Cowley, Ed.). New York: Penguin.

Williams, L. (1996). Happy families? Feminist reproduction and matrilineal thought. In M. Eagleton (Ed.), *Feminist literary theory* (pp. 52–56). Cambridge, MA: Blackwell.

chapter 3

Re-Membering Mama: The Female Body in Embodied and Disembodied Communication

Barbara Monroe
University of Michigan

The relative merits of computer-mediated communication (CMC) and face-to-face communication (f2f) in the classroom setting have been much discussed, both in composition scholarship and on listservs devoted to computers and writing. Briefly stated, those who would privilege CMC argue that f2f class discussion engenders a top-down teacher-student pedagogy that sets the conditions—that is, public-speaking ability, self-presentational style, and turn-taking conventions—for the instructor and a few students to dominate the conversation, while CMC tends to level this traditional hierarchy, more widely distributing the authority and broadening student participation rates in the process. But even advocates of CMC acknowledge difficulties with the medium. Students quickly learn how to be heard in online environments, typically sending short messages, using witty subject headings, typing in all caps, or "flaming," which means expressing anger online, usually directed at an individual. Student participation rates increase, but the transferability of electronic literate practices to academic discourse is questionable. And while online participation may be more democratic, it is not necessarily more equalitarian.[1]

In practice, however, most instructors use both f2f and CMC as complementary rather than competing strategies. In a discussion thread on the Alliance for Computers and Writing listserv in January-February, 1996, for example, subscribers agreed that the subject heading "f2f versus CMC" should not be seen as a matter of "either/or," but as "both/and." One subscriber wrote, "The online class discussion is an empowering activity, especially for students considered 'on the margin' of traditional class discussion, be they laconic, poor speakers, or just plain terrified. Yet I don't think its fair to 'marginalize' quick-witted, charismatic speakers who type slowly or struggle with the written word. I use online class discussions far more than oral discussions, but the spoken forum plays an oscar-caliber supporting role in my classroom" (C. Wick, personal communication, January 31, 1996). What is surprising, then, is that so little attention has been given to the effects of CMC on f2f, and vice versa, especially since they are commonly used in tandem.

The one ethnographic study by Rebecca J. Rickly (1995) on the interdependent impact of online and offline communication both confirms and complicates experience of and research on CMC. Rickly found that online discussion in her sample group resulted in more frequent and more student-to-student interaction. She also discovered that subsequent oral discussion tended to take on CMC characteristics. Her statistical analysis yielded no significant difference in the participation levels of biological males and females in either oral or online discussions, although males held the edge in both formats. Then Rickly had study participants take a psychological inventory of traditional sex-role identification, called the Bem Sex-Role Inventory, to determine the degree to which they self-identified with culturally constructed gender roles. There are four possible categorical outcomes to the test: Masculine, Feminine, Androgynous, or Undifferentiated. Overlaying gender construction as a variable instead of biological sex, Rickly found that "those who tested as Masculine and Androgynous participated more frequently [in subsequent oral discussions] than did those who tested as Undifferentiated and Feminine" (n.p.) by a difference that was statistically significant. Furthermore, those who tested Feminine actually participated less in oral discussions, although not to a statistically significant degree.

Like Rickly, I am surprised by some of the counter-intuitive outcomes of her study.[2] But what I find especially useful is her focus on the dynamic relationship between f2f and CMC, or, put another way, between embodied and disembodied communication. What I want to resurrect and put back into the discussion is the body—more precisely, the female body, both the flesh-and-blood body capable of reproduction and the virtual body, as it becomes refigured online. While women online may find the cultural space and permission to speak that they don't have in class and in public, that empowerment may actual disempower them offline. Rather than feeding a class's sense of corporal community, virtual community has the potential to bleed the life out of it.

Such was my experience in my peer tutor training seminar in the Winter of 1994. While Rickly (1995) observed that the style and content of online discussion fed into oral discussion, our online relationships delayed—and threatened to displace altogether—our offline class community. Admittedly, this was an extreme case, for a variety of reasons. I want to first describe the class dynamic that produced this extreme case and isolate some of those reasons. My analysis aims not only to critique my own pedagogy and to make some practical recommendations on using CMC and f2f in the classroom, but also to explore the theoretical implications of faceless, disembodied communication, especially for young women.

THE TWO WORLDS OF F2F AND CMC

"I...feel like I exist in two worlds in this class."
—Laurie

My peer-tutoring seminar that semester had 14 members: 11 female students and 3 male students. Although the class was scheduled to meet in a traditional seminar room, I decided to add an electronic component to the syllabus after the first month. I improvised my original syllabus for a couple of reasons. This group of tutor trainees would be piloting our Online Writing and Learning (OWL) the following semester, and only after the seminar started did I realize that many of these trainees had very little experience with communicating in electronic environments. Because a networked classroom was only available for the first 30 minutes of our class period, their assigned task was to workshop their papers for the course, online, in small groups of three and four, with an eye towards transforming the principles of f2f peer tutoring to the electronic medium. We also used our electronic forum as a kind of database for sharing our observations of instructors and tutors doing one-on-one conferencing, another required component of the seminar. Another less specific but nonetheless important objective, I told the class, was that they become comfortable with the medium and to make this virtual space their own, explicitly giving them permission to explore topics of their choosin—in a word, play.[3] In the traditional classroom for the last hour of each class period, we did many of the same tasks: We workshopped other versions of their papers and students distributed copies of their field notes. We did one activity orally that we did not do electronically: students circulated copies of their responses to the assigned reading for the day. These responses were used to set the day's agenda for oral discussion.

For our electronic discussion, we used an asynchronous conferencing program called Confer, which is basically an electronic bulletin board system. I seeded most of the 42 discussion threads; all my "seeds" dealt with issues in writing and tutoring. But "discussion drift" immediately set in and eventually marked almost all 42 threads, as students quickly diverged onto multiple tangents that, initially at least, seemed relevant. For example, their first paper assignment was a personal narrative, an autoethnography of their development as writers, which lent themselves to personal disclosures that, at the same time, became ever more personal and playful. That assignment seemed to set the pattern for our subsequent online conversation. For 2 months, our class met in the networked classroom for the first 30 minutes of each class period; after which, we would vacate the room and move to a small, well-lit seminar room. All told, we spent approximately 8 hours online as a class—although five students regularly accessed the conference outside of class, usually late at night from their dorm rooms—producing 212 pages of transcript.

The class immediately developed something of a split personality.

During the first third of each class period, the electronic segment, the class was personal and social, playful and thoughtful, supportive and meditative. Sitting in a darkened room with just the glow of computer screens eerily illuminating their silhouettes, students talked about a wide range of topics: from childhood reading habits and adult legal problems, to Kramer's sex appeal and their favorite *Seinfeld* episode ("Can You Spare a Square?," the toilet paper episode, won, with "Master of My Domain," the masturbation episode, a close second). They helped one student plan her wedding, did a discourse analysis of Seinfeld scripts and started their own about "nothing," as well as weighed their personal tastes in junk food, fat-free diets, sushi, and coffee.

But as soon as they left the computer room, they would fall into an awkward silence, like strangers in the street. In class, two of the three males dominated the conversation. (The third male rarely spoke in either format, in class or online; even in private conference with me, he would mutter and avoid eye contact.) The female students I simply could not engage in class discussion; my efforts to include them almost invariably fell flat. Typically, the women students (and the third male) would greet my opening questions with averted eyes and much body-shifting. Eventually, someone would raise her hand and wait to be recognized to respond (I would say, "You don't have to raise your hand," but the practice persisted). The response was always directed at me, and that discussion thread dropped, students rarely responding to one another.

Actually, it was this class personality—the insecure, reticient, polite one—that dominated the first month of the semester before we even started our electronic forum. What surprised me is that this personality lingered side-by-side with the social, intimate class we had all come to know online. I raised these issues in class on more than one occasion and got no response. But in the electronic conference, students had much to say about their sense of community in both settings.[4]

> Feb09/94 17:47
> 18:14) Ruth:
> ...none of us really know each other in class. If only we could say to each other, "Damn it, tell me what you think" or just "Tell me exactly what you are feeling at this very moment" I think we could have some fun (and get to know each other some more). Maybe we could do this someday....

> Mar03/94 13:40
> 25:11) Amy:
> ...I feel like we are really getting to know each other. In fact, this class seems really open on the conference. Everyone has the chance to establish closer relationships with classmates.

Mar06/94 18:48
1:24) Amaria:
...i don't know if anyone has noticed but i'm not the most outspoken or talkative person. i prefer communicating—when possible—on paper so I'm excited about the opportunity to communicate with everyone [in a] somewhat intimate and more removed setting.

Mar14/94 00:35
25:39) Emma:
I think it's easier to be ignored in real life rather than in writing. No one can write louder than me and drown me out.

Mar15/94 13:56
25:45) Maneesha:
Ya know, sorry to break the flow, but a thought just came to me, just sitting here. I mean, here we are in this classroom, all together in one room, typing on our little computers. And we're talking to each other, about personal things, about personal opinions, about our personal thoughts, and yet, when we all stand up, and leave our terminals, some of us act like we don't know any of the things about other people that we have just read. What I mean is, our verbal communication with each other hasn't changed drastically, in the same way that our electric communication has changed. I don't know, this just struck me just now, because I realized that I wasn't "talking" to the person sitting 1 centimeter away from me, but rather pressing buttons on a cold medium.
- - - - -

Mar17/94 11:20
25:48) Ruth:
...Even if I am having a really great conversation with someone on the conference, I may see that person on campus and just say hi as if we have never spoken in our lives but just know each other as acquaintances. It's funny but we really aren't much more than acquaintances to each other in person, but on the computer, we are like old friends almost.

Mar19/94 11:40
25:49) Amaria:
...It's really creepy to have carried on conversations with people via electronic communication that I haven't talked to face to face yet. I've learned a lot about [Stephen] and how he feels about writing, etc. but yet we've never sat down and talked. It kinda makes you wonder what direction we're heading in as a civilization.

Mar19/94 22:24
25:51) Emma:
I personally understand that it's difficult to explain something verbally sometimes. Maybe that the distance of the confer is a good idea.... [You] might be disappointed if you talked to me in person and found that I didn't have anything interesting to say....

Mar22/94 13:12
25:55) Laurie:
I also feel like I exist in two worlds in this class. On one level, I feel very comfortable talking to all of you over the computer. On a second level, I feel like it is an illusion and find myself less able to open up in person.

Mar22/94 13:36
25:59) Susan:
I think that computer conferencing has really let me get to know people better. I don't think I would know most people in this class as well as I think I do now. It's easier for me to open up more on paper (and conferencing) than verbally. Now that I have said more and more through conferencing, I could talk to most of you about personal things.

Mar31/94 02:53
25:75) Amaria:
...I feel that confer created a level of comfort that made talking and sharing feel a little more natural and safe...

After 2 months of working online at the beginning of the period, I asked the class if they wanted to stop going to the networked classroom after we workshopped our last papers. They agreed that the electronic segment had served its general purpose—to become comfortable online—and that it had outlived its usefulness. As it turned out, on our last day in the computer classroom, I happened to arrive late and entered the room to find students turned around in their chairs, animatedly and loudly talking to each other. When I expressed surprise, one student explained that they had begun the class online, as usual, but then someone spoke up and suggested they just turn around and actually talk to one another. So they did.

Thus, our time online ended as unexpectedly as it had begun. Only after we shed our virtual selves did the class emerge as a physical community. At the end of the semester, the students collected their writings in portfolios and reflected on their experience of the class. In her self-reflective piece that fronted her portfolio, Ruth summed up what seemed to be the inverse relationship between our online and offline sense of community:

> In a way, the conference acted as another existence for our class. We would leave our busy schedules and enter a quiet, dark room. We would sit down, relax, and then become part of a virtual community. In this community we were able to expand on whatever was on our minds, from the most meaningless of things to our own personal obsessions.... We were curious, honest, and uninhibited. However, the most striking part was that we were complete strangers outside of this virtuality. Inside and outside of cyberspace were like two different worlds. It was even difficult, at times, for individuals to recognize the relation between the two worlds.... As our computer experience was evolving and growing, our classroom interaction remained stagnant....

THE MISSING BODY

"[You] might be disappointed if you talked to me in person."
—Emma

The more intimate we became online, the more distant we became offline. Why? Our class's offline reticence would have been understandable if students' online experience had been agonistic, as is often the case with electronic discussion groups. Turkle (1995) has noted that "most computer bulletin boards and discussion groups are not collaborative but hostile environments, characterized by 'flaming'" (p. 217). An avid MUDder interviewed by Turkle suggests why: "There is a premium on saying something new, which is typically something that disagrees to some extent with what somebody else has said. And that in itself provides an atmosphere that's ripe for conflict" (p. 218).

On the contrary, the group's online intimacy became almost oppressively consensual, disagreements routinely dissipating into acknowledgement and apology. A key factor in this dynamic was the gender ratio of the class, as I mentioned earlier: 11 females; 3 males. Faigley (1992) has noted in his examination of two of his classes that the predominately female class (17 women; 4 men) never engaged in flaming; whereas the predominately male class (13 men; 7 women) quickly moved into disagreement, aggression, and open hostility online—and stayed there. This experience, he footnotes, confirms Kathleen Murphy's work on gendered stances in traditional classroom conversation: "all-male groups tend to be more declarative and prescriptive while comments in all-female groups tend to more affirming" (Faigley, 1992, p. 254). Other studies have noted gendered linguistic markings in public discussion: women tend to use hedges and modals, overexplain feelings, and make empathetic inquiries; while men tend to challenge premises and control topics of conversation (K. Butler, personal communication, May 29, 1996).[5] While the gender ratio explains the dominating feminine ethos of our online community, it doesn't explain why that all-embracing intimacy did not hold sway in our f2f classroom setting.

A more important factor than gender ratio seems to have been the visual absence of the physical body—specifically in this case, the female body. What generally makes talking-in-writing[6] easier than talking in person is "the illusion of privacy afforded by online communication," one subscriber on the Alliance for Computers and Writing listserv wrote, to which another replied that "it's not just the illusion of privacy but ... the freedom from being stared at, the freedom from being obviously tied to visual characteristics (and judged by them, which us uglier folks feel more than you good looking ones)" (F. Kemp, personal communication, January 27, 1996). Many studies support this view: because factors such as "appearance, paralinguistic behavior, and the gaze of others" are absent in faceless, disembodied communication, participants feel less inhibited and more confident (Faigley, 1992, p. 182). As one student in Faigley's class explained, "Clearly the main advantage of using [electronic] discussion is that it allows you to be both anonymous and public at the same time.... However, you are not put in the spot by having everyone look at you when you speak" (p. 182). The public, disembodied anonymity of CMC probably accounts for the increased participation rates among women that Selfe (1990) and Bump (1990), among others, have reported.

VIRTUAL BODY-SNATCHING

"No one can write louder than me and drown me out."
—Emma

But cyberspace doesn't just disembody; it also re-embodies (Stone, 1992), endowing its inhabitants with idealized cyberbodies. In psychoanalytical terms, the medium is fertile ground for projection: "the lack of information about the real person to whom one is talking, the silence into which one types, the absence of visual cues, all these encourage projection. This situation leads to exaggerated likes and dislikes, to idealization and demonization" (Turkle, 1995, p. 207). In a sense, the computer becomes a prosthesis, "the technology we use to communicate with...[becoming] an integral part of us, and the body, when not there physically, is still there as a social construct" (Cherny, 1996a). In less obvious ways, other forms of faceless communication, such as the telephone, engender alternative bodies as well. A. R. Stone (1992) has pointed out that phone sex workers endow the physical body with just a few verbal cues, and the caller decompresses these cues to conjure up a full-blown, eroticized body (p. 103). Ironically, after all this encoding and decoding, according to one phone sex worker, these bodies "all look white, 5'4", and have red hair" (p. 105).

The ease with which the electronic medium lends itself to this kind of body-snatching might be seen as yet another feature of the dark, wet side of technology. Idealization of the female body, eroticized by a masculine hegemonic standard, erases and homogenizes the visible evidence of origin and difference. Lost is our grounding in "our materialities: our cultural, ethnic, sexual, regional, physical situatedness" (Madden, 1992, p. 9). But that loss, for some groups—in this case, young women—is also the gain, as Emma's comment suggests: "[I]t's easier to be ignored in real life rather than in writing. No one can write louder than me and drown me out." The multiple illusions of privacy, equalitarianism, and homogenity afforded by the electronic medium helps us idealize not just new bodies, but also new selves to inhabit them. CMC literalizes Lacan's notion of the self as textual, as "a realm of discourse rather than as a real thing or a permanent structure of the mind" (Turkle, 1995, p. 178). One's self and sense thereof becomes what Hayles (1993) calls a "flickering signifier" (p. 69); and the electronic medium, a field of play, free if not always fair.

RE-MEMBERING MAMA

"[Online] I feel…a little more natural and safe…."
—Amaria

This capacity for fluidity holds pregnant possibilities not only for identity politics, but also for gender politics—not because the medium is gender-blind, but precisely because it isn't. While users might intentionally gender-cross in MOOs, for example, speech itself may become cross-dressed in electronic environments, in part, because of the public/private nature of the medium. Susan Herring (1995) has pointed out that because communicative styles are gendered, "then gender differences, along with their social consequences, are likely to persist on computer-mediated networks." While I agree with Herring's statement, I would also argue that these gender differences do not naturally attach themselves to biological bodies, as they do in a face-to-face classroom setting, where auditors *see* the body of a speaker, who then expect certain behaviors, both verbal and nonverbal. In like manner, in faceless communication, a new identity is spun out not unilaterally, but multilaterally, like the phone sex worker who plays to the phone sex customer's idealization, catering to the caller's construct, a strategic rather than static identity, replicated rather than original. As a female student in my class wrote, "[This electronic conference] is neat because each person gets to talk uninterrupted for however long they want and everyone listens. [O]f course this can be accomplished in a classroom but the feeling is different it doesn't seem like everyone is watching [in the electronic classroom]." Talking uninterrupted without being seen reverses the parenting dictum, "Children should be seen and not heard," an old saw that seems to hold residual force for adult women in mixed-gendered groups.

Such reversals came into play in reconfiguring gender in the electronic community of my seminar. While only 9 of the 11 females in the seminar were white and upper-middle-class, the self-presentation style of all of the women offline, including the two women of color, was marked by a kind of reserve I think of as Midwestern. They engaged in very little social interaction with each other before class started, during class, or as they left class. But online, although my students were still physically very much middle-class and the majority were white, their virtual personas were animated with uncharacteristic liveliness, one measure of which was a marked change in their humor practices. Totally absent when they were physically present in class, their humor emerged, infused with self-disclosure and self-deprecation, comic strategies that tend to veil humor's subtly aggressive, other-disparaging intent. What made the humor of my female students funny is difficult to document and dissect, because their jokes were exclusively situational ("you had to have been there"), marked by dramatic improvisation and word play, sometimes exploiting a comic moment to deflate pretension or defuse the tension of a potentially embarrassing disclosure. (In the next section, I will try to capture one comic situation in their online conversation.) Their humor wasn't funny in a falling-down-laughing kind of way, but in a witty, clever, subtle way.

These descriptors are all hallmarks of women's humor generally but more especially in private, all-women's groups than in the public domain in the presence of men (Monroe, 1992).[7] In public and in mixed company, "respectable" women in their reproductive years—mothers or potential mothers, at least visibly—are most constrained in their speech as well as in their sexuality. Joking behavior is seen as either masculine behavior or promiscuous behavior,[8] both of which threaten cultural definitions of bourgeois femininity. This blanket statement needs to be qualified, most especially in regard to socioeconomic class. Working-class women (for example, the Roseanne persona) historically have had more license to speak their mind, because they wield a measure of economic power in the family structure. The constraint on women's joking behavior tightens on its way up the socioeconomic ladder, with upper-class women most restricted of all. Patrilineal inheritance seems to be the driving cultural logic of this constraint. The more property there is at stake, the more prohibited is a woman's speech and sexuality, to insure paternity and property inheritance.

Of course, this pattern is yielding to historical pressure, as women have become more economically independent and as cultural definitions of womanhood are contested and renegotiated. One such site of negotiation is the public/private space of the electronic frontier, an unregulated nobody's land that allows for freedom of speech and of play heretofore only accorded to men and "loose" women in public settings.[9] One of Mae West's famous one-liners was "I used to be Snow White ... but I drifted." And she had to have drifted to make it on the public stage.[10] A Snow White can't joke around if she wants to maintain her marriageable and mothering image. Taking on idealized bodies in electronic environments becomes not an issue of eroticism, but of empowerment—for the female body eroticized has categorical permission to speak and to play publicly.[11]

Perhaps what makes the public place of electronic space feel private and therefore safe for women online is that such behavior is stripped of its physical consequences, the threat of violence and rape losing its force online. The issue of netrape aside,[12] the relative security of cyberspace increases women's participation (Grint, 1989). Even though Amaria, a black, middle-class, student in my class, came from a very different expressive tradition, a tradition that has more highly valued women's speech in public settings and in mixed groups (Monroe, 1994), she nonetheless felt constrained by white, middle-class standards of decorum for women talking in class—but not online. In her words, our electronic forum was an enabling place, a "somewhat intimate and more removed setting" that made talking feel "more natural and safe." In the electronic domain, biological women in their childbearing years are freed from the gaze that would fix their identities as potential mothers, and they are freed from the physical and social consequences of being perceived as loose women. Rather than replaying hegemonic images of mother, young women online can digitally re-member mama—at turns, cute and cutting, charming and sarcastic—shape-shifting across class and age lines, conflating cultural categories of womenhood at a flick of the finger on a keyboard.

RE-MEMBERING PAPA

"Yes, guys do cry..."
—Adam

In like manner, online conferences can also afford spaces for transgressing traditional gender lines for biological males as well. Cherny (1996b) observed in her study of emotive behavior in MOOs that "women's use of physically aggressive emotes with male characters is an example of women adapting to the different discourse style in male-dominated groups"[13] The reverse is also possible, especially when females outnumber males and dominate online discussion, as was the case in my seminar, where the three males in the class came to adopt the topics and the tone of the eleven females in the class. Of the three, one seemed an especially unlikely candidate for online intimacy. Adam was a self-described jock. Majoring in sports management, he aspired to become a sports columnist. He always wore a baseball cap[14] and was always late in arriving to class and handing in assignments.[15] Given this profile, one might expect a very different interactive style than the one this student presented. Let me illustrate.

In one discussion thread on the topic of using personal narrative in academic writing, Adam had much to say: "I like to use personal narrative in my papers. I find it to be therapeutic. When I am having a rough time with something in my life I try to incorporate it into a paper. I think that you have to be able to go out on a limb to do it. You have to lose something to gain something. Do you kind of understand? Ok, here's an example." He then explained that, just 2 weeks earlier, he had been arrested for driving while intoxicated on his way home from a topless bar, spent the night in jail, and was going to pretrial the upcoming week. He detailed the probable terms of his punishment and related how he was going to use this experience for a paper in another class on the meaning of freedom. He went on, in a kind of free-fall association, to tell us about family members who had fought for freedom in the military. Ultimately, he returned to his original theory of personal narrative:

> Is it personal narrative? yes. Do I go out on a limb? yes, I don't really know any of you but I basically just told you (if you didn't know me better) that I am a drunk, a pervert, a criminal, and two of my uncles were shot in Vietnam. One could consider this out on a limb. But that would only matter depending upon whom you are writing for. Personally, I am writing that essay for myself. If you all read it, so what, I don't know you anyway.... At least then it is off my chest, I have thought and discussed it and I feel better.

The class responded, expressing surprise at his self-disclosures, complimenting his honesty, and offering suggestions on how to use this narrative for his paper on freedom in another class. Then he talked about a possible opening for the piece: "lying on my back looking at the stars at my family's cabin. It is my favorite place in the world as well as my father's (it is about the only thing that we have in common)." When Susan supported his idea about writing to get something off his chest, giving her own example of fighting with her boyfriend, the male author replied that he wouldn't write about a fight with his girlfriend—"I am to [sic] impulsive for that. It has to be something that is just eating the shit out of me. Something that down deep is bugging me, something that makes me fall asleep with tears in my eyes. Yes, guys do cry themselves to sleep occasionally, too. But, it is not the manly thing to do."

Amid a profusion of support from the class as a whole, a few female students dared to dissent, apparently deprecating themselves but transparently making fun of Adam—a rhetorical move typical of women's humor that allows women to deny aggressive intent. In the following example, notice how Amy starts with an apology and ends with a zinger. When Adam quipped, "Hell, maybe I can start my first novel behind bars," Amy responded, "Sorry, this made me laugh although it's not funny. Now, I picture you behind bars, writing away. I can see the news article now. [Adam] turns his life around and becomes the next Danielle Steele. (Smiley face) [sic]. Well, since you are destined to become a famous author don't forget us little people...." Maneesha also poked fun, donning the comic mask of a dumb Valley Girl, an especially funny move, given that Maneesha was Filipina: "Boy [Adam], I gotta hand it to ya, for making [this discussion thread] all yours. I hope that all of this feedback is helping you, as for the idea of looking up at the stars ... I think that idea is just awesome, not ditz-like, ya know, like, like, TOTALLY AWESOME DUDE, I mean just large and impressively awesome in the magnitude of its symbolism."

Only Ruth was openly agonistic, challenging the male author's self-construction as a sensitive New Age guy, skewering him for his unexamined values. She reminded him that he had revealed in an earlier paper that he was a racist and now he was admitting he was a drunk, listing "your punishment as if it were a grocery list." She went on to question his glamorization of the military and the Vietnam War. She closed with the admonition that he had the potential to succeed in life and "the potential to really fuck up. I know that was a little harsh, but I just want you to think about your options, because, ultimately, the choice is yours." Three days later, Ruth apologized online for her seemingly judgmental comments and reassured us—and Adam—that she was simply "admiring how honest [Adam] was being and reflecting on that trait."

In some ways, the male author's topic conforms to the subgenre of male adolescent narratives, the "delinquency narrative" (Tobin, 1996, p. 165), but departs from that norm in its gestures at self-reflection and self-disclosure (Conners, 1996). And while the one female student quickly realigns herself with the supportive majority of the class and apologizes for attacking the male student's gestures as just male posturing—a la Papa Hemingway, she did venture far enough from the flock to challenge his positions. This was the only instance the whole semester where a female student openly challenged anyone, online or off, and invited conflict. Both the male author and the female respondent transgress traditional gender boundaries. The difference is that, in subsequent oral discussions, this female student retreated to the culturally prescribed norm of the supportive, nurturing woman, but the young man's verbal behavior continued to be self-reflective and frankly personal.

Such discursive behavior is generally associated with real-time environments like MUDs. "People are making a world together. You got no prestige from being abusive," one MUD player interviewed by Turkle (1995) suggested (p. 218). This same MUD dweller reported that he had played a woman character for so long that when he decided to drop his female persona and assume his male identity, his behavior seemed out of place: "It would be like going to an interview for a job and acting like I do at a party or a volleyball game. Which is not the way you behave at an interview. And so it is sort of the same thing. [As a male on the MUD] I'm behaving in a way that doesn't feel right for the context, although it is still as much me as it ever was" (p. 218). Another male player developed the persona of "Julia," an older, single, disabled woman who typed with a headstick.[16] This character originated when the male player logged on and struck up a conversation with a woman who mistook him for a woman. "I was stunned at the conversational mode. I hadn't known that women talked among themselves that way. There was so much vulnerability, so much more depth and complexity. Men's conversations on the nets were much more guarded and superficial, even among intimates" (qtd. in Stone, 1992, p. 83). Similarly, in her study on the emoted interactions between male- and female-identified characters in one MOO, Cherny (1996b) "found that indeed there are differences in how men interact versus how women interact: men use more physically violent imagery during conversation, and women are more physically affectionate towards other characters than men are."[17]

But I would add that the tendency to flock and gently mock is not just a function of real-time MUDs, but also a matter of gender- and class-marked behavior. Gendered modes of communication have remained "relatively stable," Stone maintains, but who uses those modes has become more "plastic" (1992, p. 84). In electronic spaces, then, gendered identity is no longer structured by the usual polarity of public and private, male and female (Haraway, 1985; Stone, 1992). Such boundaries are blurred, leaky, polluted (as Haraway might say), turning sites of social practice into amusement parks, carnivalizing the usual hierarchies and dominations.

VIRTUAL REHEARSAL FOR REAL LIFE

> "I'm just hoping that face-to-face I can find a way to spend some time being the online me."
> —woman in Turkle's study

But so what? Turkle asks the question another way: "What are the social implications of spinning off virtual personae that can run around with names and genders of our choosing, unhindered by the weight and physicality of embodiment?" (1995, p. 249). If men can act like women, or assume female identities as they often do in MOOs—in a sense, appropriating the female body—that experience is not the same as being a flesh-and-blood woman, who feels the pain of monthly cramps or the hot flashes of menopause, and who must face the psychological and social consequences if she is tagged with a "bad reputation." Science fiction writers often portray the body as just meat that can be left behind once consciousness is uploaded into the network (Stone, 1992). Stone continues: "But it is important to remember that virtual community originates in, and must return to, the physical.... Even in the age of the technosocial subject, life is lived through bodies" (p. 113). In like manner, the virtual experience of feeling free of the cultural constraints that bind women's speech does not necessarily leak over into Real Life. Electronic environments, where emoting and action have only cartoon consequences to the typist's textual body, may actually exacerbate the flattening of affect in postmodern Real Life, where emotion and expression are more muted and nuanced and where the consequences of our actions can mean pleasure or pain—physical, psychological, political—for flesh-and-blood bodies, ours and others'.

For the female students in my peer tutoring seminar, the return to the body—to the non-idealized, culturally-contrained, biologically-female body—proved to be awkward and embarrassing. For the three male students, that return seemed natural enough, because their verbal behavior online and offline wasn't wildly inconsistent. For young men, being heard (either online or in class) is more important than being seen; put another way, their words are valued more than their bodies. As a teacher in a networked classroom, I have often heard students say, usually by way of complaint, that they can't match names with faces and bodies. Anonymity in a networked classroom is a short-lived possibility; before long, an online persona will be fitted with a Real Life body. That is a key difference between the electronic environments of the classroom and the Internet. "On the Internet, no one knows you're a dog," reads the caption of a cartoon from *The New Yorker* of a dog sitting in front of a computer with a paw on the keyboard. In a patriarchal world where a woman's physical appearance is more important than a man's in the dating and mating game, in a patriarchal world where a woman's subjectivity is defined by her body and where a woman's image and worth are judged by how well that body fits the ideal, that dog in the cartoon is more likely female than male. I wasn't surprised to see how often the young women in my seminar in 1994 returned to the topic of dieting. It was the one topic about which the three young men in the class had nothing to say.

For that particular class, then, online intimacy almost destroyed our class community. Perhaps what made the two segments of this class so difficult to negotiate was that our electronic world denaturalized the culture of our offline world, rematerializing and refiguring the body politic. The class did ultimately come together and cohere as a community—and perhaps even more strongly than any other seminar I have led before or since—but it almost didn't, and that is the risk I have become less willing to take and, in fact, have less need to take. Because our tutoring program is predominately female and because a solid sense of group affiliation is necessary to our student-run program—where students work together onsite sometimes for 2 years—I have revised my pedagogy for this course. My training seminars are now scheduled in a networked classroom (so no longer do we physically vacate the room, as my 1994 seminar did, the move heightening the differences, I think, between classroom settings). We use computers mainly for their text-sharing capabilities, students posting all their work, prewritten, creating a database for ideas and examples that we use for ideas and examples for our written work and for our oral discussion. I created an e-mail group, which students typically use to broadcast information to the whole class, sometimes playfully, but never predominately so; never has a flame war broken out nor has anyone made sensitive personal disclosures in that format. Our peer tutoring program has successfully expanded to include an online tutoring service, OWL, but, unlike the trainees in 1994, students coming into the program now are comfortable with e-mail, to varying degrees. Trainees still tend to be resistent to OWL ("it's too impersonal") until they see how trained cybertutors create personas—not imaginary ones, but ones that attempt to project their personalities in Real Life—warming up the medium and approximating a f2f writing conference. Our OWL has become a kind of living textbook for trainees, which is a more productive, less risky method for training tutors than practicing with each other online, as we did in 1994. In another tutoring seminar a year later (notedly, where the gender ratio was evenly balanced), a flame war undermined our class community to an unrecoverable degree. That experience, coupled with that of my predominately female 1994 seminar, has convinced me that CMC can too easily become the site for agonistic display or intimate disclosure, and the discomfort of either experience can bleed over into and adversely affect a class's sense of corporal community. For these reasons, I rarely use computers for whole-class discussion in tutor training.

For precisely the same reasons, I do use CMC extensively in all my other courses, especially basic writing classes for incoming students, often international students or students from inner-cities or small towns. For such classes, students' developing a sense of physical community (which only lasts a semester after all) is less important than their developing a sense of themselves as acting, speaking subjects. CMC can provide a cultural space that gives them that permission, a permission often denied especially to young women. Computers mediate experience, in both senses of the word: they can act as a barrier to change, but they can also serve as a carrier of change. In the latter regard, virtuality might be likened to a transitional object in play, used to move the human subject from one stage of development to another (Winnicott, 1971). Such is the hope of one woman in Turkle's (1995) study who expressed her anxiety of physically meeting her electronic lover for the first time: "I didn't exactly lie to him about anything specific, but I feel very different online. I am a lot more outgoing, less inhibited. I would say I feel more like myself. But that's a contradiction. I feel more like who I wish I was. I'm just hoping that face-to-face I can find a way to spend some time being the online me" (p. 179). Electronic spaces can give us a place to play and co-op the cultural script, rehearsing new roles against the day when we incorporate these virtual selves into Real Life.

NOTES

[1] These summary arguments for and against CMC and f2f are indicative rather than inclusive. For more comprehensive and detailed discussions, see Graddol (1989) for an early comparison; Duin and Hansen (1994) for a more recent overview of the issues; Regan (1993), Romano (1992), and Warshauer (1995) for discussions of the overly optimistic and undercritical claims for CMC in the classroom. See Butler (1992) for an ethnographic examination of how, in the power vacuum created by a teacher's dispersed authority in a networked classroom, dominant students assume the role of the teacher and reconstitute a top-down hierarchy. I borrow the semantic distinction between "democratic" and "equalitarian" from Rickly (1995).

[2] "Research seems to indicate that females are 'silenced' as a part of their cultural education (see Gilligan, 1982; Zimmerman & West, 1975), and many females never regain their voice. Other studies have found that women are treated differently than men in a classroom situation, being called on and acknowledged less frequently (see Caywood & Overing, 1987; Coates, 1986; Lakoff, 1994; Rich, 1979; Spender, 1985; West & Zimmerman, 1983)" (Rickly, 1995, p. 124).

[3] On the importance of play in computer-assisted classrooms, see Daisley (1994). In his dissertation on the role of play in developing digital literacy, Rouzie (1996) shows that play signals student ownership of online class discussion as well as functions as an emergent system of interaction.

[4] I've selected only a few examples dating from early to later postings to demonstrate the class's ongoing preoccupation with their relationships as a class community. I could have included many more.

[5] The titles of two recent articles sum up the gendered distinction in conflict management online: Herring's "Politeness in Computer Culture: Why Women Thank and Men Flame" (1996) and Evard's "'So Please Stop, Thank You': Girls Online" (1996).

[6] See Daisley (1994) for a discussion of orality versus the written word. For a history of the "Great Divide" between orality and writing, see Walters (1990).

[7] In my dissertation (1992), I show how women's humor itself is differentiated by distinctions grounded in race, ethnicity, marital status, regionalism, age, sexual orientation, and class.

[8] Regina Berraca, a scholar on women's humor, has quipped, "Telling a joke is like making a pass."

[9] Miss Manners is especially chagrined by the lack of manners in the online world, as she explains in her new book, *Miss Manners Rescues Civilization.* "The sanctions of etiquette only have force because if you behave badly, you get a bad reputation." The problem, she continues, is that "there are no sanctions" in cyberspace, as there are in society at large (qtd. in Rothstein, 1996, pp. C1, C2).

[10] Interestingly enough, Mae West started her career at the turn of the century as a male impersonator in vaudeville; ironically, the rumor was widely circulated, both before and after her death, that she was a *female* impersonator. The same has often been said of Phyllis Diller. My point is that a witty woman often inhabits a gender-bending, ambiguous cultural catego-

ry. Notice, too, that most female comic performers had blonde or red hair up until the 1960s—hair colors associated with sexiness.

[11] Other "categories" of women with cultural permission to speak are the prepubescent girl and the postmenopausal woman—in other words, females on either side of their reproductive years, or nonmothers. The behavior of the tomboy or the old crony is stygmatized as nonladylike or masculine; whereas the "loose" woman suffers the sanction of a "bad reputation," which generally devalues her worth on the marriage market. Thus, "mouthy" women in all categories are stygmatized and policed in some way.

[12] MOOs are not a totally safe place to play, as the male-identified characters sometimes perpetrate "netrape." One typist takes control of another's character, making that character participate in sexual activities—an action only possible in an object-oriented domain. Rape in any form—either physical or online—is an act of violence which always exacts psychological damage. For an insightful discussion of netrape seen in terms of Catherine Mackinnon's argument that words are always social acts, see Cherny (1996b).

[13] But Cherny (1996b) does conclude that "women on the whole seem to prefer using less violent imagery than men use."

[14] In his analysis of this fashion statement among adolescent males, Tobin (1996) explains that the male student wearing a baseball cap in class disguises his desire to both conceal and connect: the cap conceals a student's face; at the same time, the student connects with his peers who are also wearing caps, often marked by logos of powerful organizations, thereby declaring his group identification and allegiance beyond the classroom.

[15] Adam was also technophobic, in a clinical sense of the word, displaying physical distress throughout our online time. He didn't word-process his papers, much less use e-mail. Despite being technologically disadvantaged, after a classmate or I helped him log on, Adam would type away, monologically, rarely participating in anyone else's conversaton, only conversing within his own discussion thread—largely, I think, because he didn't know how to navigate the program.

[16] I find it interesting that this male would assume a persona with a disabled, unidealized woman's body. In his choice of personas, he may have been externalizing and embodying his internal view of women as physically vulnerable and confined; or, Julia may be a coded mask for his own masculinity: Julia's age and disability suggests she is unable to bear children, and using a headstick to type is like using a penis for a pen ("pen is penis").

[17] The emoted actions of hugs and whuggles [roughly, a cross between a hug and a wave] occurred "mainly during greetings but also during other interactions, often as a sign of affection or support," and, statistically, "a hug/whuggle event was almost [four] times as likely to be initiated by a female character." Cherny (1996b) also found gendered distinctions between hugging and whuggling, though: "Women are three times as likely to whuggle men as they are to hug them, but they are equally likely to hug as to whuggle other women. Why? It may be that the whuggle is seen as a 'safe' form of affection in the MOO, while a hug has real-life significance. Men get whuggled, therefore, rather than hugged; other women, 'safer' objects of affection who won't 'take it the wrong way,' can receive hugs." Emoting affection toward another character was a touchier issue in this MOO than using violent imagery toward another character. "I don't have any cases recorded of anyone asking anyone to stop setting fire to another character, or stop cutting someone up into little bloody pieces," Cherney reports (1996b).

REFERENCES

Bump, J. (1990). Radical changes in class discussion using networked computers. *Computers and the Humanities, 24*, 49–65.

Butler, W. (1992). *The social construction of knowledge in an electronic discourse community*. Unpublished doctoral dissertation, University of Texas at Austin.

Caywood, C. L., & Overing, G. R. (1987). *Teaching writing: Pedagogy, gender, and equity*. Albany, NY: State University of New York Press.

Cherny, L. (1996a, July 7). Objectifying the body in the discourse of an object-oriented MUD [Online]. Available: http://bhasha.stanford.edu/~cherny/charley.txt

Cherny, L. (1996b, July 27). Gender differences in text-based virtual reality [Online]. Available: http://bhasha.stanford.edu/~cherny/genderMOO.html

Coates, J. (1986). *Women, men, and language: A sociolinguistic account of sex differences in language*. New York: Longman.

Conners, R. J. (1996). Teaching and learning as a man. *College English, 58*, 137–157.

Daisley, M. (1994). The game of literacy: The meaning of play in computer-mediated communication. *Computers and Composition, 11*, 107–119.

Duin, A. H., & Hansen, C. (1994). Reading and writing on computer networks as social construction and social interaction. In C. Selfe & S. Hilligoss (Eds.), *Literacy and computers: The complications of teaching and learning with technology* (pp. 89–112). New York: Modern Language Association.

Evard, M. (1996, July 5) "So please stop, thank you": Girls online [Online]. Available: http://www.media.mit.edu/~mevard/papers/please_stop.html

Faigley, L. (1992). *Fragments of rationality: Postmodernity and the subject of composition*. Pittsburgh, PA: University of Pittsburgh Press.

Gilligan, C. (1982). *In a different voice: Psychological theory and women's development*. Cambridge, MA: Harvard University Press.

Graddol, D. (1989). Some CMC discourse properties and their educational significance. In R. Mason (Ed.), *Mindweave: Communication, computers, and distance education* (pp. 236–241). Oxford, England: Pergamon Press.

Grint, K. (1989). Accounting for failure: Participation and non-participation in CMC. In R. Mason (Ed.), *Mindweave: Communication, computers, and distance education* (pp. 189–192). Oxford, England: Pergamon Press.

Haraway, D. (1985). A manifesto for cyborgs: Science, technology, and socialist feminism in the 1980s. *Socialist Review, 80*, 65–107.

Hayles, N. K. (1993). Virtual bodies and flickering signifiers. *October, 66*, 69–91.

Herring, S. (1995, May 15). Gender differences in CMC: Bringing familiar baggage to the new frontier [Online]. Available: http://www.umass.edu/english/women.html

Herring, S. (1996). Politeness in computer culture: Why women thank and men flame. In M. Bucholtz, A. Liang, & L. Sutton (Eds.), *Communicating in, thru, and across cultures: Proceedings of the Third Berkeley Women and Language Conference* (n.p.). Unpublished manuscript.

Lakoff, R. (1994). Language and a woman's place. In C. Roman, S. Juhasz, & C. Miller (Eds.), *The women and language debate: A sourcebook* (pp. 280–291). New Brunswick, NJ: Rutgers University Press.

Madden, E. (1992, Spring). Pseudonyms and interchange: The case of the disappearing body. *Wings, 1*, 9.

Monroe, B. (1992). *Mother wit: American women's literary humor.* Unpublished doctoral dissertation, University of Texas at Austin.

Monroe, B. (1994). Courtship, comedy, and African-American expressive culture in Zora Neale Hurston's fiction. In G. Finney (Ed.), *Look who's laughing: Studies in comedy and gender* (pp. 173–188). New York: Gordon and Breach.

Regan, A. (1993). "Type normal like the rest of us": Writing, power, and homophobia in the networked composition classroom. *Computers and Composition, 10,* 11–23.

Rich, A. (1979). *On lies, secrets, and silence: Selected prose 1966–1978.* New York: Norton.

Rickly, R. (1995). *Exploring the dimensions of discourse: A multi-modal analysis of electronic and oral discussions in developmental English.* Unpublished doctoral dissertation, Ball State University, Muncie, IN.

Romano, S. (1992). The egalitarianism narrative: Whose story? Which yardstick? *Computers and Composition, 10,* 5–28.

Rothstein, E. (1996, January 15). Netiquette: Miss Manners keeps an eye on cyberspace, and *is not amused. The Ann Arbor News,* pp. C1, C2.

Rouzie, A. (1996). *At play in the fields of writing: Play and digital literacy in a college-level computers and writing course.* Unpublished doctoral dissertation, University of Texas at Austin.

Selfe, C. (1990). Technology in the English classroom: Computers through the lens of feminist theory. In C. Handa (Ed.), *Computers and community: Teaching composition in the twenty-first century* (pp. 118–139). Portsmouth, NH: Boynton/Cook.

Spender, D. (1985). *Man made language.* London: Routledge.

Stone, A. (1992). Will the real body please stand up? Boundary stories about virtual cultures. In M. Benedikt (Ed.), *Cyberspace: First steps* (pp. 8–118). Cambridge, MA: MIT Press.

Tobin, L. (1996). Car wrecks, baseball caps, and man-to-man defense: The personal narratives of adolescent males. *College English, 58,* 158–175.

Turkle, S. (1995). *Life on the screen: Identity in the age of the Internet.* New York: Simon & Schuster.

Walters, K. (1990). Language, logic, and literacy. In A. Lunsford, H. Moglen, & J. Slevin (Eds.), *The right to literacy* (pp. 173–188). New York: Modern Language Association.

Warshauer, S. (1995). Rethinking teacher authority to counteract homophobic prejudice in the networked classroom. *Computers and Composition, 12,* 97–112.

West, C., & Zimmerman, D. (1983). Small insults: A study of interruptions in cross-sex conversations between unacquainted persons. In B. Thorne, C. Kramare, & N. Henley (Eds.), *Language, gender, and society.* Rowley, MA: Newbury House.

Winnicott, D. (1971). *Playing and reality.* New York: Basic Books.

Zimmerman, D., & West, C. (1975). Sex roles, interruptions and silences in conversation. In B. Thorne & N. Henley (Eds.), *Language and sex: Difference and dominance* (pp. 52–75). Rowley, MA: Newberry House.

Making the Map: An Interview with Helen Schwartz

Kristine Blair
Bowling Green State University

Pamela Takayoshi
University of Louisville

In an interview we conducted at the 1995 National Council of Teachers of English in San Diego, California, Helen Schwartz, Professor of English at Indiana University/Purdue University Indianapolis, discusses the beginnings of computers and composition as a research area within composition studies, her work during that time, and the hidden work of women in the field, including struggles to fund and maintain classrooms, to encourage and support women in this area, and to provide women with mentors. Reflecting on the activities and issues scholars faced at the formation of the research area, Schwartz looks toward the future for computers and composition and the roles women are playing and will play.

Pamela Takayoshi: The reason that we wanted to do interviews with women was that one of the feelings that we had in the beginning of this project was that the beginnings of computers and composition had a lot of women working in the area, and now there are many more men coming into this area. If you look back over what's been published, it seems that a lot of the work that women did in establishing this area didn't get into the articles that get cited all the time, so like the work that you did getting the lab set up, and the program with the loaner computers, and the work with Cindy Selfe and Kate Kiefer did in establishing *Computers and Composition*. And we saw the interviews as a way to get into the print literature the things that haven't gotten there, because particularly computers seem the area where a lot of this type of work has gone on.

Helen Schwartz: Yes, in a way, this is starting with what is the most polemical question, because certainly now I would say that the leaders in the field are if not predominantly male, at least 50/50, and that was not true at the beginning. And yet when I think of men who I think of as prominent, they don't seem to be male chauvinist pig types.

Kristine Blair: Turn off the tape recorder.

HS: It's interesting, because I see Cindy as so central because she had a very good vision, and I think it was she and Kate Kiefer, who by giving us a place to talk did a great deal to start us as a field. Another person I think was important in this way was Mike Spitzer, who's now gone on to administration, but he had a Ford or one of those big grants, and he started the [listserv] Fifth C, which was the forerunner to [the listserv] Megabyte University, and all these people who are so excited about Megabyte University—you know I'm tired of Megabyte University—I haven't been on there for years, and I remember, I clearly wasn't used to the way Megabyte University worked, because I was used to reading every message and so one time, I put out there the question that "It's clear that there's too much to read, so how do you decide what to read or what not to read? Is it that you're too busy and that you erase everything, or that you just not read certain people? And nobody answered me."

Because I think if I answered that honestly, I would see someone's name and delete everything by this person. I never want to read anything by this person again.

KB: But it also could be really political, and I'm thinking back to that study Cindy Selfe did a few years ago with Paul Meyer, with Megabyte, with the idea that certain people post, and certain people get responded to more than others.

HS: Well, I did an early study, which failed, and was much more complex than I realized, and it was on Fifth C. So what I wanted to do was to see how and why people got responded to. And so what I did was that I got a list of everybody who was on the list, and everybody who ever had posted to the list, and I put the name of anybody who ever had posted to the list, and I asked current list members several questions: First, who did people say were influential. Then, independently, I tried to develop an internal, text-based way of saying these people were influential through discourse analysis. Second, I asked people to break down their responses to the "who was influential" questions: I asked them to name the two people who were the most intelligent and by that I meant they weren't necessary knowledgeable, but they asked excellent questions, and then the next question was who was the most knowledgeable? And the third was who was the most helpful? And I think the fourth was who was the nicest? The thing I was trying to get at is what makes people authoritative, what gives them authority and what gives them influence. And so what happened was that the name people put down almost first on the list was Hugh Burns [co-founder of the Daedalus Group].

PT: For every category?

HS: Not for every category, and Hugh hadn't said more than about three or four postings. And then I realized that first of all people had come in at different times, and they were judging on the basis of different segments. I wasn't as smart as Cindy at setting up a small section. And the second thing was that after a while, they couldn't remember who had said what. Especially if they didn't know the people to begin with. And that seemed to be kind of bogus, what it showed was that reputation really was more important than what people actually said.

KB: So that his offline personality influenced how he was regarded online.

HS: Absolutely, it was clearest with him, but they also said me, which was absolutely justified, of course. :-) But I had been active on the 5th C, and Hugh hadn't. He had only posted about three postings.

KB: What was the Fifth C like? Smaller than Megabyte?

HS: Much smaller than Megabyte. It was the people who were kind of pioneers at the beginning. There were a lot of people from NYIT, which was Mike Spitzer's place, Valerie Arms. Hugh got on and then he got off, because it was fairly active, but nowhere near as active as Megabyte. You know, occasionally you'd get on and maybe 20 messages were waiting for you.

KB: Rather than 50 to 70 a day now.

HS: You could go away for a weekend and forget it. But the thing that I looked at on the basis of the transcripts themselves was first of all, an authoritative voice, someone seeming to speak not necessarily with knowledge, but with declarative statements. And the person who was the king of this was Mike Cohen, who was at UCLA at the time. And it turns out in terms of credentials, I don't even think he had a Ph.D. He was very knowledgeable, and thoughtful, but he always spoke *ex cathedra*—he would just give this big talk. Plus the fact that he had figured out how to upload and download, and he always composed on a word processor and then uploaded. So the set-up for responding (online or offline) was another confounding variable that I had, so I didn't try to publish this.

But the way I judged influence through discourse analysis was how long a "tail" did each note have. So if you responded to mine, and Kris responded to yours, I'd have the biggest tail, you got the second biggest tail, and Kris got the third biggest tail. And when you looked at it that way, the women had much more influence than the men, and partly, it was that they tended to engage people in conversation. They would put things forward sometimes even saying something like: "Pam, this sounds like something you have done. Would you tell us about that?" So I called this "soliciting response," and the women did that, and they were much less likely to do grandstanding, the kind of thing that, in bulletin boards that are not academic, you'll see all the time. In fact, I had a student who wrote a paper about how on a regular, largely male bulletin board, essentially, you'll have two rams going at each other, and that one of them would get stunned. Discussion was not an evolving thing. Somebody won, which I don't think is the way things happen a lot of times, when women are heavily involved. In fact, my student developed his description of a public bulletin board in contrast to the style of exchange on a class listserv made up mostly of women.

PT: Were women more heavily involved in the 5th C?

HS: Oh yeah, it was predominantly women, I think because it was low status at the beginning. And you were taking a risk getting into this field. I was not, because I had tenure. I know women always say they get places through luck. I also got there through hard work and good ideas. Essentially, I was in a protected position when I started getting heavily into this area because I had tenure and I was at a school that was generous in their policy, unlike UCLA. UCLA wanted all the money from the project with WANDAH [writing software]; they were heavily financially interested in the money, even though they had come up with an Exxon grant to support the project director, Ruth Von Blum. WANDAH was later published as HBJ Writer.

PT: So how did you get started in all of this, then?

HS: A couple of things. I was angry that people were talking about computer literacy, and there wasn't a lot of writing and reading literacy that was being paid much attention to. And so I wanted to get interested in it, and I think partly, it was curiosity, but I sort of went in with a chip on my shoulder, and I saw some things that I felt were awful, and some things that were quite promising.

KB: What were the awful things?

HS: Readability formulas. I did some work with that. The people who were really at the top of the field knew the limitations of it, but the problems were people were coming up with the formula for enforcing laws, and that policy had to be fought against. But I got my feet wet in that, and I started programming, and I had a sabbatical in Pittsburgh, working with a guy in the Math/Computer Science Department, a very interesting guy named Tom Dwyer. His idea was really the foundation for SEEN, the software program that I wrote. He had a project called Solo/Net/Works, and he wanted to work with simulations. People had flight simulations, like landing a plane or taking off, but then he wanted to have an air traffic controller with the flight simulator, so that if you were the pilot, and I was the air traffic controller, what I did depended on you.

KB: So it would be much more interactive.

HS: Much more interactive, so that you were working alone, but you were also being influenced by other people. And what that wound up with in the work that I did was a tutorial where you were working alone but then there was a bulletin board. Then of course I had seen Hugh's programs and I disagreed with him from the first on the kind of feedback you wanted. He was always interested in the AI stuff, that it should simulate a human being. And I always thought that was dishonest, and it was hubristic to try to do that. And he agreed with that, he never thought that what he did was perfect, but then he continued in the AI [artificial intelligence] direction, whereas I was never interested in AI. I really saw it more as a tool of communication.

PT: What happened with all of that? Around that time there were a lot of composition people writing software. It doesn't seem that there are many people doing that anymore.

HS: First of all, the only person who ever made any money, the only programs that I know that were really commercially viable were Bill Wresch's Writer's Helper and to a much lesser extent, SEEN. And I think that the grammar programs were essentially not useful because they were drill and practice, or they were decontextualized. And another program that's made money, though they were from a different organization, was Bob Bater's Blue Pencil, which Prentice Hall put out with their stuff. And that I think is fairly reasonable but it's within the context of a paragraph. But I think people turned away from drill and practice and I think Daedalus filled a need that was a good one, and went more in the direction of learning how to use tools, and that's the direction that the field is going in, and then adding things that support collaborative work.

PT: So you teamed up with this person who knew the programming part or did you know computer programming.

HS: I learned computer programming, and I did the first version of SEEN, and then I realized that life was short, and that was not the way I should go. And I was very happy with Conduit. I thought Conduit was an excellent company. They did high quality work, they gave good support for their product, and they did excellent programming. I'm sorry they went out of business.

But let me follow up on Cindy [Selfe]; the more I think about it, the more central I think that Cindy and Gail [Hawisher] and others like them have been. That for a long time, people felt very ghettoized in computers and composition, and one of the things when I was on the CCCC [Conference for College Composition and Communication] computer committee that I wanted to do was to mainstream and I think that was important. The journal *Computers and Composition* was important, and the fact that people then started getting into more discipline-wide journals, people who were writing dissertations on this stuff, and that was highlighted by the Hugh Burns dissertation award.

All of these things gave—I just taught *Midsummer's Nights Dream*: "The poet's eye in a fine frenzy rolling gives to airy nothing a local habitation and a name"—and a lot of the stuff Cindy has done gave people a "local habitation." And that's only one great thing that Cindy has done; she's done a lot of great work. But she and those who have collaborated with her, have really worked to set up an infrastructure. And the fact that she and Gail then took over the bibliography pushed them more to the center, and the fact that she's now elected as the president of CCCC. Cindy has been interested in computers from the beginning, and for her to get elected is a vindication of the centrality of this, and a tribute to her, that's she's not just become a technical person. I think once the journal just gave people a place to publish; then they worked hard on raising the level of contribution. Lillian Bridwell Bowles is another important person.

I just got interested in it, and couldn't stop being intertested in it. I also had a strong math/science background which I had not used at all. I don't think that programming is especially scientific but I wasn't afraid of it, and I had colleagues in that area who I was very comfortable with, whereas I think other people may be more diffident around people are in science and math.

KB: What reaction did you have from your colleagues when you announced that you were going to learn programming, that you were taking this up?

HS: Well, I was at Oakland University then. And that was a fabulous place for me. It was a school that had started as an honors college campus for Michigan State, and I thought my colleagues there were really extraordinary, and I won't say that they were saints, but I never experienced the kind of factionalism and mean-mindedness that I hear people talking about at other places. And I think that I was so naive, and I learned to use that in a good way, that is, I think I was also able to argue on principle rather than *ad hominem*. In a different place where things were not as aboveboard, I think that I would have been hurt by my forthrightness. Oakland gave me the sense that if you just were reasonable and fair-minded that people would come to your side.

But at the point I became interested in computers, as I say, I did have tenure, and no one ever came to me and said don't do this, but I had the feeling that they figured that Helen has gone off on another one of her crazies, and she'll come to her senses or she'll come back and tell us about it. And when I went up for full professor, one of the things I had in my documentation was a list of all the correspondence that I had done in the last few years—who it was, where they were, what the correspondence was about—this kind of documentation seemed to be in a funny way, dumb, certainly unusual, but what I wanted to show was that in an emerging field, I had become an expert. That here I may be doing four or five different sorts of things, and people all over the world were writing to me: they wanted off-prints, they wanted advice, whatever.

And I think people at Oakland were impressed by that, and I was doing a lot of consulting. And so I think they just didn't want to argue with success, though I felt very much at the time that the department, if anything, was benefiting from the work I was doing, and it wasn't the English department, it was the writing department. And they were good to me, and I was not on their faculty. I was an adjunct, and they would ask me for input on people they were hiring and so on.

But one of the reasons I moved to IUPUI was because I wanted to be in a "big concept" English department, that had both writing and literature, because I had feet in both camps. First of all, I published *Interactive Writing* and then published SEEN and organized a short-lived program, ORGANIZE, published by a book publisher. Another reason I think there hasn't been a lot of spread of software is that there hasn't been a need for that. Book publishers have a very ambivalent attitude toward software, I think they despise it.

KB: The end of the print literacy, the end of the book.

HS: I don't think they know what to make of it, but they've done some fairly intelligent things. I've heard of some software projects, for example Turbo Dog, which is like Common Space, that seems pretty sensible. I hope that works but it may not. But aside from Conduit, there really hasn't been a really good publisher. And another thing is that the software hits what they call a vertical market. That means it is used for both college and high school, and that's anathema to book publishers. Their whole structure is that there's the college level and there's the high school level, and if you try to market to both, it ruins the product's reputation in the college market. And so there's no incentive for high school and college divisions working together. If you go with a publisher, you have to decide that you're gonna go for high school or you're going to go for college.

PT: I'm interested in something you were saying a little bit ago, and if you have any more to say about this, or if there's more to say. But as somebody new to computers and composition, I'm increasingly aware of how I'll have this interpretation of something, and then I'll talk to somebody who understands what the context of the early 80s, the late 80s was, and how I'm just becoming more and more aware of how the politics of those eras and those times is not really clear to me, and I look back and I say, "Oh, look at what people were interested in, and look at what people were doing," and one example of what you were talking about forging into new areas and that you were taking a chance at doing this.

I'm just becoming aware of the politics, that everybody's arguing against this enthusiasm characterizing the 80s discourse, and I'm wondering if a lot of that was because of administrative concerns, to be able to argue positively for this, to get it in at all. Anyway, this is really long-winded, and I'm having a hard time articulating it all, but you were talking about how Cindy's being elected president really indicates moving into the mainstream, and I'm wondering if you could talk more about that, because this is one of those things that I look at the discourse, and I think I understand, but I don't think I really do because these two fields were inside composition, and we reflected a lot of the same kinds of changes composition has gone through. I'm thinking about the future of computers and composition and where it's going to fit in relation to composition in general.

HS: There was sort of a Scylla and Charybdis for people who were interested in composition in the initial stages, because on the one hand you had to get someone who believed enough in computers to get you a lab, and then almost all the research studies at first compared composition with computers and composition without computers, which is silly, because they weren't the same, and what I came to feel was that was not the question. One question was: Does writing with computers ruin your writing? That was one thing to establish, that you weren't writing worse, but because of the way of computerization discourse and academics and economics, there's no longer any question of whether you write with computers or not. If you don't know how to use a computer, you're up the creek, so unless you can prove that you hurt people by having them write with computers, it simply is no longer argued. But at first, you had to try to say, well gee, there's something going on here. And I think people who were already good writers got a tremendous surge in power from that, and that people who weren't good writers just could write badly easier. And so people would say the computer doesn't make them better writers. That's right, and that's why I wrote my textbook. You still have to teach people to write. It's not like you touch a computer and bingo, you become Norman Mailer.

PT: That's really helpful, because the implications in those two questions is do you write better with computers or do you write worse are really, would lead you to different conclusions.

HS: No, I think that do you write better, or, yes you're right, is it at least as good as without computers. and I think you can show clearly that there are certain types of errors that have crept into writing because of using word processors. Some more serious than others, but it's no longer a question now of whether you're gonna write with computers. So one thing was how did you get the labs. I happened to have a Dean who was crazy about computers. So if I hadn't been there, he would have invented me, or someone like me. So I went in and I was hanging around with people in engineering and learning about how to write grants, so I was going to ask for three computers. And they said, no, if you want three computers, ask for six computers. So I thought, well, why stop there, so I asked for 12 computers.

KB: Ask for a WHOLE LAB!

HS: No, no, no. I wouldn't want to go that far. This was before anyone was using this stuff. And I asked for 12 computers, and I got it.

PT: From the university?

HS: Yes. And then I taught this class, and all my students hated it. And then years later, one of the students said, "You know, you really taught me this stuff. You really got me into this," and I said "You're still talking to me," and she said "Yeah." It was wonderful. And I of course was learning as much as my students were. I was really feeling my way, and for example with my book, *Interactive Writing*, I had the world's best readers on that. I had Ruth Von Blum, Hugh Burns, I think Valerie Arms, and maybe Lillian Bridwell, I don't remember. I know certainly Ruth Von Blum. And all this stuff about how you never know who your readers are with manuscripts for publishers. Bullshit! I knew who they were, they knew who I was, and we wrote back and forth, because they were helping me. It wasn't this send it to the publisher, then the publisher sends it to you, it's all anonymous. Bullshit. They were pushing me and I was pushing them, in a very, very good way. And that was really exciting.

So on the one hand, there was the need to drum up support for what you were doing. On the other, there were the deans who gifted you with the lab you didn't want, and what the hell do you do with 30 computers and you don't have the slightest idea of what to do with them. And what do you say to the dean, no thank you? And those were really the two dangers, and I did a lot of work initially consulting with faculty who were either hostile to the dean and were bemused by it all, figuring out what the hell to do with stuff. In a way the Daedalus Group was like that. They got this lab, and fortunately, [composition theorist] Maxine Hairston was in there, and said you've got to base all of your work on composition theory. At that time I think Hugh was teaching there and with his excellent military experience he got a group going, and that turned into the Daedalus Group. And I was trying to think that men have come to the fore, and it's not that they're awful, exploitive people or anything, it's just that Hugh's military experience was really, really useful. And I remember reading a book by Hennig and Jardin called *The Managerial Woman*. And they made the point, I always thought before I read this that it was a big brouhaha that women didn't do team sports; it's important for women to play team sports because what you realize is with a baseball team you need nine players, or is it eight players?

KB: Nine players.

HS *(laughter)*: You can tell what I didn't play. But women tend to go into things like tennis where you're competing against yourself or it's one on one. And men are used to working in groups, so while women are seen as more collaborative naturally, they're not collaborative in a team way. And I think the things that men have accomplished in the field, one of them I think is that the Daedalus Group is a wonderful model for people in the field getting into business, and as far as I can tell doing a pretty good job of it.

Another thing is the Association for Computers and Writing, which I think Trent Batson has spearheaded, and that's mostly male, not completely. And I think that's because Trent has experience as a trainer, and I think he really had an idea, and that he was effective in pushing that idea. Originally it was the ENFI [Electronic Networks for Interaction] thing, with the networked labs. And then he saw the need for a larger attempt to influence not even the field, but the field having an influence in the larger world. And I think that, I don't know if that's male, I would hate to admit that is male. But I think that, when I look back at myself, when I speak for myself, I've had committee assignments, CCCCs, I was chair of the Computer Committee, and I worked first for other people as chair and I worked for myself and by the time I got to be chair, I asked what can this committee do, and what can we do well. By the time I left we had a full array of things that we did in the profession but they were limited things, such as setting up a structure for continuing the Computers and Writing Conference. I think the things that have come after, certainly the things that Trent thought about, were more grandiose and were more like the ACW thing.

PT: You mention the student who said to you that in the course of the semester you thought your students hated you, and she said, "No, you mentored me," and I thought you were talking about me, because I took your class because I was told "You can't take classes here and not take Helen Schwartz's computer class; you just can't do it." And I went "Oh God, I hate computers, I don't want to go," and I really credit you for a lot of my interest in this. And I don't know what exactly clicked, but when I came into that class, I was very resistant. I didn't want to have anything to do with computers, and this interest has been very sustaining in me. And I think about that a lot; Pat Sullivan at Purdue was also a mentor for me the way that you were. I did my first NCTE presentation because Helen had already done something else that had gotten me involved with the 7th graders that I taught, the "I Have A Dream" unit; and so we went to Indiana Teachers of Writing and presented that, and I think about that a lot, particularly as a woman and being a mentor myself to women. Was that a conscious thing for you?

HS: That came to me late in life. Because remember I started when I was about 38, I got interested in this stuff, and at first, it was such a rush, I had never written that much before, and now I really had something to write about, and I was fascinated by this stuff, I really got into it, much more than anything I had ever studied, and maybe because there weren't models. They say that women always want to know what the rules are, and then they follow them. There were no rules. And so we really made it up as we went along. For example, I applied for a Fulbright. I had talked to somebody in the Netherlands, Thea van der Geest. And I wrote to her and said "I would like to apply for a Fulbright, and it would help me if you would invite me, and don't worry if I don't get the invitation, I won't go, and it won't cost you any money. And you could ask me to do stuff, but this is what I would propose, and can I hear from you by such and such a date." And they knocked themselves out. Apparently nobody does that. I didn't know how things were done.

KB: But that didn't hold you back.

HS: It didn't hold me back, and I got different models, like with the computers. People said if you want six, ask for 12, if you want three ask for six. You want something from the dean, get your department to anti-up. They'll do it if they see the department's behind you. These were fabulous ideas, but these weren't from people in my department. There was no model; everything in English, in literature, which is where my background was, is so individualistic that at first I was really the Lone Ranger. And what happened to me was that I went through a crisis. I had never been as successful as I was initially in this field and what happened was that I got a lot of opportunity. I think it went to my head. First of all, I thought I was really "hot shit," and have since come to feel that yes, objectively speaking, I'm not the dumbest person I know.

But I'm not the "hot shit" I thought I was. I think I have a sense of my strengths and my weaknesses. And I'm not ashamed to say these are my strengths and these are my weaknesses. But before, I was going around collecting merit badges and the more opportunity I had, the crazier it made me because I had to do everything. So I really went crazy, and then I knew that I had to sort out, and I did. And I became much more collaborative; I recognized the joy of working with other people. I mean, I got so much out of working with you, Pam, and it made me look good. Because I had showed up at NCTE, I had never been able to get accepted. I had this bet on with a colleague, Peter Adams, and neither of us had ever been able to get anything accepted at NCTE, and we had presented at CCCCs.

KB: It's hard to get accepted at the NCTE.

HS: It is because it's not skewed toward college. And so here I was, I had my stuff at the college level, Pam's stuff at the seventh grade level, Sue Blackwell's stuff with the after-school community center, and I think Susan Shepherd was with us also. And when I learned I got on the NCTE program, I called up Peter, who had got on the year before, and I said, "I got on," and he went "Arrgh," and I said, "I lost my NCTE virginity." But really it wasn't just that. It was a thrill for me, my first taste of the joy of mentoring. You did a fabulous job, I learned from you, and to the extent that I was in some way associated with what you did, it extended my range.

That's what Cindy knew from the beginning, that by helping other people, she was helping herself. She doesn't need to do it all, that's why I think she's really a tremendous model. And the two things I've learned as I've gotten older is to work with other people and to know what I want to do. When I did the computers and writing conference in Indianapolis, that was the year I was also Bat Mitzvahed as an adult. It was roughly about the same time, too, and decided partly in my meditations with that, and partly with computers and writing, that I would never do anything for a merit badge again.

KB: What do you think about this emphasis on inclusion and collaboration? One thing that's interesting to me is that I always think how "open" the computers and composition community is. I always think they're much more open than just composition in its entirety. And I'm wondering if you agree with that type of characterization of our subdiscipline?

HS: I was coming from the Modern Language Association, and the MLA was the first convention I went to, and that was for the job interview, which is of course a nightmare. I mean you went through that, didn't you?

KB: Oh, yeah.

HS: I mean Prozac City, right?

KB: It's a Prozac moment, all right.

HS: And I couldn't understand why people liked conferences, such a horrible experience, and then I went to CCCCs and met a wonderful man from Boston University whose name I just got out of my head, and he was so welcoming, and everybody seemed to be so friendly. And then I applied to present a paper and got in, and it seemed very homey to me. And I think there was a kind of cohesiveness to the computers and composition crowd at first because we were an embattled minority. As Debbie Holdstein [of Governor's State University] has said, "If composition people were the scum of the earth in university pecking order, computers and composition people were the 'creme de la scum' or the 'scum de la scum.'" Too bad; it's a wonderful quote and I've loused it up.

But we were pariahs to some extent in the writing community. And there's some sense to it. I think there was a fear that we were more interested in the computers than we were in the writing. And that's a way to go, but I think by and large people haven't gone that way. But lately I have not felt, maybe because I've drawn back a bit, maybe because I'm no longer thrilled being on a listserv, getting 30 messages a day. I just feel overwhelmed by that. I work on my stuff, and I've had a renewed sense of joy in teaching. And so once I got in place what I really wanted to do, I was more focused. I have about 10 or 12 more years of teaching, and I've been teaching 30 years. So I have little to do and yet so much I can do. I mean that you in some ways start people along a path in thinking or interest, and that you know it's really going to be important to them.

So in that way, I have a lot of chances to be important in ways that are important to me. Because there's so little you can accomplish as a single person. But what I would really like to do is push forward, not so much the status. One of the things when I was chair of the MLA committee, one of the things I'm most proud that we did was that we came up with guidelines. And in some ways they're much more watered down than I think for example I would have liked to have seen. But MLA is a different beast than CCCCs, and I think it's become more responsive and much more open to composition people under Phyllis Franklin [president, MLA]. For one thing, Phyllis Franklin is here at this conference. I know that. And most people in the secondary and elementary wouldn't know who Phyllis Franklin is. But I've seen her come to CCCCs when people were badmouthing MLA, and I stood up and said, you know, you're badmouthing MLA, but there have been a lot of changes, and how many of you can recognize that Phyllis Franklin is sitting here at our meeting.

At this point in my own career I think what can I do that's unique? And I think what I can do that's unique is to have a standard. I think I've always had some say in setting standards. I don't think it was completely enthusiastic and completely negative. The things that I've done that I'm proud of have been pioneering, and I'm interested in bringing other people along. And now rather than saying there's too much to do, I can't do it all. Instead, I say isn't it wonderful that there are so many people around who are capable of doing the work. So much to be done. And so, it's not I have to do it or it doesn't get done.

For me it's been transforming personally, or it's been the backdrop to what I hope I would have experienced anyway. But I think that without the computer work, I wouldn't have experienced the success because I would have followed the paradigms with the sense that I couldn't meet them, with the sense that I wasn't good enough. And in a field where there was nobody there, I went in for my own curiosity, and it was a wonderful discovery to find out that when I looked around, people were modeling me. I hope she knows where she's going; I don't know where I'm going.

And sometimes you learn good things about yourself and sometimes you learn bad things, and one of the good things I learned was that when there was nothing to gain, when there were no merit badges to be passed out, I went with what was intellectually interesting to me, and made it into something that attracted the interest of other people as well.

PT: Do you think that notion of merit badges might explain the gender shift that we see in computers and composition that we started off talking about today? That now there are more merit badges available, and more people willing to go into this.

HS: Absolutely.

PT: Were men not willing to do this in the beginning of computers and composition as much as women?

HS: It was certainly dangerous at first. But most of the people were either already safe or they were too stupid to realize that this was really dangerous. They were naive,

I should say, instead of stupid. And some of them didn't care. And that's why, and many of the men didn't get tenure, so they went into the technical area. And you see people who are head of computer labs or computer centers all over the country who have degrees in Classics, English, and French.

KB: But they don't have tenure?

HS: Maybe they have more than tenure. But the point is either they made a decision not to go for tenure because it was dangerous and now it's not dangerous because it's become central.

PT: Susan Miller argued at CCCCs that, what was the argument?

KB: Now that computers are a legitimate as a discipline, men jump in?

PT: Susan Miller was saying people seem to be using technology as a way to legitimize composition.

HS: Well, I think in a way that was part of the merit badge, hoopla that you talked about in the 80s. And in a sense, that's the false side of it. The true side of it is that technology is changing writing, that it's changing our society, and we are absolutely in the center of this. If we don't take the opportunity to investigate this, then we're damned fools. But what's come together is the technology and the theory, which is really important, and it's clearly central. Look at the books that are being published on this, and the trade press. People are coming to realize that something very deep and very important is happening, and it has do with communication. And what's the other thing, oh yes, that the other thing that's involved, I won't say that it's false, but it's not intrinsically rewarding, is that there's a lot of money involved. You're talking big budgets.

KB: For labs and such.

HS: Absolutely, absolutely. And many times the English department is that place that has the lion's share of introducing students who are computer illiterate to computer use. And many times not the best machines, but the most machines are available within English. Another thing that's coming up, I'm on the advisory board of something called Academic Systems. What they're trying to do is to get courseware to support writing, so that it's multimedia, it's course-long, it's not Writer's Helper, it's not Comma Catcher, it's not SEEN, it's a coursewide, course-long software and management system that doesn't replace the teacher, but supports the teacher, supports writing groups, and supports the distribution and management of text. Which is really an extension of the type of stuff that Common Space is doing. And I think that they're doing a good job. I'm on the advisory board, so I'm probably prejudiced.

But the other thing that's happening that I see as a trend in higher education is that colleges are becoming so expensive and if that trend continues, cutback and support of higher education, that college will become an elitist or a financially disastrous proposition. And so that there has to be a way of cutting cost. And two very good places to cut cost are in courses that are labor intensive, mainly remedial math and remedial English. And these are the two courses that this company is creating computer software to support. Now some people could say oh, that's getting at our jobs, but is it? I was sitting with someone, in ESL, and she said, I really admire the way composition has raised its status, and certainly there has been a tremendous professionalization within composition and rhetoric studies. But as long as you have first-year English with multiple sections which you cannot afford to staff with Ph.Ds, you're going to have low status, and that's going to be a target for cutting, the way it's been a target in a lot of schools, i.e., "we don't need that, we don't need first-year English." I think we do. What we have out there may not be 100 percent effective, and there may be some very bad programs, but it sure beats not having first-year English.

PT: That cost issue raises the whole access issue. That universities are becoming potentially positioned to become elitist. And I think computers, that's been an issue in computers, too, that computers are so expensive, and they're elitist. And I wonder if you could talk about your work in opening access, because I know you've done a lot of interesting work aimed at that.

HS: What we tried to do was to set up a model, it was built on the assumption that eventually computers would become an integral part of all education, certainly at the college level. I know some people who decided to try to develop a pedagogy said that in order to get into this section, you have to have a computer. I felt that was going to be skewed because the people who would come into the class at that point with computers were not gonna be a true cross section. And so partly through informal ties, with Integrated Technologies, and support from the vice-chancellor for undergraduate education, I got an IBM grant, we got 30 computers and we would loan them to people in the course of the semester and then collect them at the end of the semester and we developed the use of essentially listservs in support of face-to-face education.

And we had no losses from theft by the people they were given to, that is, nobody refused to return them. We did have a couple of thefts but they were by outside people and we had some repairs that we had to take care of. And I think that we really got to understand the strengths and the weaknesses of that and that certainly has helped me in my subsequent work.

We wrote a $750,000 grant for Eli Lilly saying we have a way what with selling old computers and getting donations from the community, and selling new computers, we have a way by the year 2000 of having *x* number of students with computers. So that it would have been fairly widespread at IUPUI. And I think what's gonna happen is that it's gonna be fairly widespread anyway. The costs have come down, and you can get a reasonable system for $1,000 or under $1,000. And computer ownership is becoming so pervasive. So I think that I was really concerned about this, and remained concerned about this, and as you know, your work with the "I Have A Dream" students was a part of that, cause even if you gave a computer to people that doesn't mean they're going to learn how to use it.

The Buddy System in Indiana was an attempt, they had a suburban school, an inner-city school, and a rural school, and they gave all the students in these classes and the teachers either IBM, or Apple, and encouraged them to develop curriculum, because I don't think it's enough to say everybody's using computers. It takes a long time to understand what you should do with them or what you shouldn't do with them. And I think there's almost a dangerous situation now that the students are pushing the faculty, the faculty are never going to be able to keep up with this. I worry about it because the faculty, I don't know what the support system is that's gonna get faculty to learn fast enough. I just did a course "Shakespeare Online"; I developed hypertexts which the students used in a lab and one of my students came up and said "Well, it's nice, but it's a little old fashioned." And I said, "Oh." And he said, "Yeah, you should be using the Web."

KB: You know, that's really interesting, because I'm having my students do the exact same thing, so they have all the links to "Shakespeare Online" and we're using HyperCard and when I first envisioned it, I thought wow, this is going to be so great, and then within the last year, with the Web, I thought, they should be doing this on the Web, the whole catch-up sort of thing. The issue of access isn't just an economic issue. I heard a talk this morning where the speaker said computers used to be $3,000 and now they're $1,000 and soon lower, and everybody will be able to afford one. And I thought that was a real oversimplification of the issue. It's the access to keeping up, both for students and for teachers to keep up in the field, to be able to do those kinds of projects that help students in their knowledge-making and in that economic sense does help them in their careers.

HS: The other thing that's really disturbing is the fact that women don't seem to take to computers, it almost seems to be acknowledged as a male domain among elementary school kids, and I find a certain resistance with my college students. Like with my "Shakespeare Online" class, for which word processing is helpful, but no computer experience is required, and that class was slightly more than 50 percent male, which is unusual, my other class is not, it's maybe a quarter male, or a third but nothing like a half. The women in the "Shakespeare Online" class, a number come in with an attitude I find typical of women: I'm afraid of this but I'm determined to learn this. And the men feel the same way; they just don't admit to feeling scared. What difference does it make in my reaction? I think I tend to spoonfeed the women more because they announce they're fearful and in a funny way that holds them back, because I don't challenge them to do more.

KB: Part of the problem too, and I don't know whether you see this as a problem, is that sometimes they sort of internalize that as something innate, something biological. I mean I've had students say to me…

HS: Boys are good at computers.

KB: Yes, boys are good at computers. They just get it. And I'm trying to get it, but you have to be patient with me. I need lots of help. And I had that sort of situation with a woman in the class, where she was constantly…

HS: Older?

KB: Yes, and any time she needed help with something, she'd go to some guy in the class, and didn't even ask me, and finally I felt I had to sit down with her and say, try to at least do some hands-on, the minute you run into problems, don't just ask some guy for help. That's part of the learning process, acknowledging that you don't know everything, and that you're gonna try through some individualized learning process to figure something out. It's a difficult emotional and intellectual barrier to overcome, I think, with women and men, but particularly women.

HS: I wonder, and I don't know the background on this, but I think that women, I know that I like to understand everything as I go along, and if I don't understand something, I'll stop and say excuse me, would you go over that again? I think that that's not the way you learn about computers. That to a much greater extent you have to learn to float.

PT: Play around with it.

KB: Hit and miss. Make mistakes.

HS: Or I set up a preconvention workshop at CCCCs about using the Net, hoping that I would learn about it. So I invited all these wonderful people, who knew a great deal about it, which I studiously tried out myself. But I introduced them by saying if you could take a picture of the Internet today, and you then worked to understand every part of it, by the time you mastered that, half of the stuff would be gone. And so you can't think in terms of mastery, yet that's what I like to do. You have to think of it like you're a frog on a lily pad, you sort of have to build a nest. I don't think frogs build nests, I'm mixing my metaphors. And then you're an expert, if you can build a nest on a lily pad, see if there are more lily pads out there, and have the confidence to jump to a new one, and build a nest again. So it's a different sense of what an expert is.

KB: Do you see that as having something to do with technology in general, that technology for some people is something to know versus technology as something to help solve problems?

HS: I don't think you can know technology in that sense. Maybe you never could know English literature in that sense. But I always thought you could. You know, when I had my Ph.D. exams, I had a list of books that I had to know, and when I knew those books or thought I could fool someone into thinking I knew those books, that's when I took my exams. But I don't think mastery is possible in any field of endeavor in that sense. But with technology it's so much clearer that you'll never know it.

KB: I don't know if students come to us though with that perception. I'm thinking of software, where they say I'm going to learn this program. I'm not going to learn how to use it, and I think there's a distinction, that they think they can learn it absolutely, and that this creates all sorts of problems and frustrations in the classroom that aren't really necessary.

HS: Well, I had one student who refused to learn this program because she said "I'm going back to Bloomington, and we don't use that program there." And I thought, no, no. One of the things I think education now means is that you can move from one platform to another, and it's terribly frustrating to learn this.

PT: I think a lot of it is a mindset, too, if my students know how to use WordPerfect, they have a certain mindset about the ways to examine it and to know how to find information. But this has been great.

KB: We've talked for over an hour, and our tape is winding down.

PT: I'm thinking I might want to come see you at IUPUI, the types of technology that's there, the way that people are using it, the kinds of software, I'm thinking it would be a good idea to go see what other programs are doing.

HS: Let me suggest a couple of things. One is try to get a computer crazy administrator as high as you can get them and cultivate them. I think that IUPUI is a very top-down place, but it's also a very networked place because of the IU and the PU, so if you do things "the right way" you have to go up and over and down, so you have to get used to going right to the provost, so don't be afraid of doing that, if there's receptivity to that. Another thing I would recommend to both of you is something called the Bryn Mawr Summer Program, an institute for women in academic administration, and they always write me and say who would you recommend, and I would recommend to both of you that you drop them a line. Because some of my understanding of how the university works comes from there. And I decided not to go into administration, but I think it's useful to have faculty who understand it.

KB: Yes, we should become the administrators. Thank you so much.

Map of Location II

Constructions of Online Identities: Our Students, Our Selves

chapter 4

"I, a Mestiza, Continually Walk Out of One Culture into Another": Alba's Story

Sibylle Gruber
Northern Arizona University

It's really sheltered down here [at the University]; you see how other people, like the middle class, live, and I see the differences if I ask somebody on their background; they'll tell me, well, you know, they already had exposure to computers and I didn't, I didn't in school. (Alba, personal communication, May 8, 1995)

Alba's comment is typical among many students who come from a nontraditional background to an alienating university campus. They do not bring with them the "cultural capital" (Erickson, 1988; Giroux, 1992) expected for academic success in an environment that upholds traditional values and belief systems. As a consequence, these students are placed in first-year writing courses that are intended to provide them with the skills necessary to "master" academic discourse and to eliminate the perceived "lack" of mainstream writing and thinking abilities. They are given various designations that change over the years and are different from college to college, including among them the labels "basic," "developmental," and "underprepared." All of them, however, express the same underlying assumption: these writers need additional instruction if they want to succeed in academic life.

Researchers interested in basic writers have pointed to the need for a more inclusive look at students' experiences in the classroom (Bizzell, 1986; Hourigan, 1994; Hull, Rose, Fraser, & Castellano, 1991), but they have not yet discussed the many oppressions that non-white, non-middle-class female students face in a university environment; nor have they analyzed how a computer-supported pedagogy may affect these nontraditional female students[1] who experience multiple barriers in an environment that privileges white, middle-class male discourse. Furthermore, "basic" writers have often been seen as a universal group that encounters similar problems regardless of the university setting and regardless of the technologies used. As Hourigan points out, "the basic writing field is building generalizations about basic writers upon experiences with isolated individual programs" (p. 35). Instead, she suggests, "basic writers differ from college to college and may even differ from year to year within a single college or university" (p. 36). And, I would add, basic writers also differ from each other, making it problematic to talk about essential characteristics of these students without acknowledging the diversity among them. Just as research in the fields of gender studies and computers and composition studies must acknowledge this diversity, so must research on basic writers. To neglect this call is to ignore the highly diverse population in basic writing classes.

To move away from seeing basic writers as a uniform mass of students and to explore how the use of computer-mediated communication (CMC) and a rethinking of feminist and liberatory pedagogies can help establish the complex identity of a woman who has to juggle "interlocking identities" and "interlocking oppressions" (Houston, 1992, pp. 48–49), I analyze Alba's position in a first-year computer writing class at the University of Illinois. Alba,[2] a Latina student from inner-city Chicago, was enrolled[3] in the course because she did not exhibit what is often termed "mainstream" skills; she was therefore classified as "lacking" the necessary tools for a successful performance in an academic environment. Of course, her "lack" of mainstream skills does not come as a surprise since Alba does not fit the picture of the average college student; instead, as a woman who grew up in a neighborhood that is far removed from the world known to college students, she brings to the university all the attributes of what Bizzell has termed "'outlandishness'—their appearance to many teachers and to themselves as the students who are most alien in the college community" (1986, p. 294). Also, Alba's economic and social status—Alba ranks herself as "underclass" based on her money constraints, her neighborhood, and her lifetime experiences—reinforces her classification as "Other" by the academic community.

In this chapter, I am especially concerned with how Alba appropriates PacerForum, an electronic communication tool, to position herself in terms of her gender, ethnic and racial background, and economic situation. The various subject positions she occupies during the online interactions call for an inclusionary research agenda that values her various experiences online as well as offline. A close analysis of Alba's use of an electronic forum reveals that researchers interested in how basic writers and women use online discourse strategies need to move away from an undifferentiated and generalized view of students and technology. They need, instead, to look at the situated and multilayered nature of discourse created by the communication tools used and influenced by the intersection of gender, ethnicity, race, class, and cultural and social backgrounds of the participants. What follows, then, is the story of Alba, a narrative of a young Latina woman who became a college student on a technologically privileged campus.

A NONTRADITIONAL WOMAN'S COMING OF AGE

Gloria Anzaldúa (1987) might have had Alba in mind when she describes life in the borderlands:

> To live in the Borderlands means you
> are neither *hispana india negra española*
> *ni gabacha*, *eres mestiza*, *mulata*, half-breed
> caught in the crossfire between camps
> while carrying all five races on your back
> not knowing which side to turn to, run from. (p. 194)

Alba's coming-of-age story is breathtaking, a story that sounds more like fiction, a story that doesn't connect with real life. But Alba's story is only too real, and her experiences are not confined to a book that can be read from cover to cover and, once the last page has been turned, put back on the shelf. Alba's life can't be put on the shelf; it's still in progress, and no final sentence is written.

Alba's mother, of Nicaraguan descent, grew up in the United States. Describing her mother's childhood, Alba says:

> My grandfather, he was from Nicaragua, and you would [think] he is a real macho man, but I think he had a hard childhood, because he was an orphan, at such a young age, and he made it all the way to the US when he was 8 years old by himself, from Nicaragua, so, I mean, he wanted his kids to have like, everything that he didn't have, so my mom,...she traveled, and her dad, he showered them in gifts, and you know, he took them everywhere, and, he took my grandmother everywhere, he treated her like a queen, he was different, cause he really...valued his family, because he didn't have one.[4]

When her mother married a Mexican at a fairly young age, Alba describes her mother as being "caught between two worlds," partly because her mother wanted to live in the States and her father wanted to go back to Mexico. The job situation was unstable and didn't bring the expected monetary relief. Another reason for the difficulties in her mother's life was her husband's attitudes towards women. Alba's father came to the States in his 20s and, according to Alba, had a "different" childhood and a "different" view towards life. She attributes these differences to the influence her father's family had over him:

> My dad's father used to beat on my grandmother, so, and he used to see that a lot and so he used to beat my mom too. That was like his biggest influence in that my grandfather is really domineering, I guess. You know, he didn't believe in education, so my dad was the one to be, you know, he was the first born, and he is the one to go out in the fields and help his father, and, like his father, his dad was kind of a role model to him, like this macho man, so that's where he picked it up.

Alba's mother made some concessions and went to Mexico for a short period of time, during which Alba was born. However, the different lifestyle and the unrealistic expectations imposed on her by her husband's family brought them back to the States, and for 14 years, the family lived in Chicago. Her mother worked as a teacher's aid and school clerk, her father as a steelworker at Indiana Steelworks, where he was laid off from time to time. The pressures of his sporadic unemployment, in connection with different attitudes towards monetary issues—her father took her mother's paycheck and sent it back to Mexico instead of using it for their own needs—finally resulted in a divorce. Alba's father went back to Mexico; her mother stayed in the States because "she wanted us to get an education and she knew we'd be like illiterates, illiterate farmhands in Mexico."

Her mother's insistence on a good education seems to be one of the major reasons for Alba's positive attitude towards school. Alba attended bilingual education classes for the first two years, but, as she points out, "mom really was against it, because a lot of it is tracking, so she knew that they wanted to put us in bilingual education forever." Thus, instead of staying in bilingual education, Alba was switched to regular classes and attended high school with a population of mainly African Americans (65%) and Latinos (25–30%).[5] During her senior year, she applied to the University of Illinois, and was accepted for the Fall of 1994. Alba is now a first-generation college student, which she says is a "big deal" with her family.

Of course, Alba's move away from home and her intentions to attend college caused different reactions. She points out that her grandmother wasn't too enthusiastic about the decision:

> She used to say, "well it doesn't look like you really wanna go to college, why don't you stay home and learn how to cook and, I teach you, and you get a job downtown, make five dollars an hour, and then get married after a while."

Her grandmother's misgivings were counter-balanced by her mother's support and her wish for a "better life" for her children:

> My mom, she just wants us to get a college degree, cause she says, she says that she doesn't want us to be like her, she wants us to be like her boss, she doesn't want us to be the ones to be taking orders, she wants us to be the ones to be giving orders, because, I guess she knows, she knows that, ... she coulda done better.... She's always going, "Oh, I wished I was in your place, I wished I was in your place, I wished I had gone to college."

Now, Alba is in college, and, similar to her mother's expectations, she also wants to be successful in college and "do better" than her family in terms of academic achievement:

> I hope I get accepted to a medical school.... So hopefully after four years I'll be accepted into medical school somewhere.... If I accomplish that, get into a medical school, I'll be like the first doctor in my whole family, and it's real big, it's real big.

ALBA'S STATUS AT THE UNIVERSITY

Alba's move from her home environment to a college campus was probably more challenging than it was for students considered "mainstream," whose training at home and previous schooling is geared toward a college education. Alba was different. She was "outlandish." She was "Other." She didn't fit. She stuck out—for various reasons. One of them was her class status. Although a number of students with lower economic means insist that they are middle class[6]—demonstrating their belief in a classless and individualistic society—Alba does not consider herself middle class. She designates herself as "underclass," based on her parents' (mother's) yearly income of around $20,000 and the family's living in an inner-city Chicago community. She sees her underclass status as having an impact on her status at the university. On this campus, she points out, "we are not catered to"; instead, it is the middle-class students who by default receive more attention and thus have an easier transition:

> There is a very big difference [between middle and underclass], because my, the underclass, what I consider myself to be, it's kind of harder, you don't see that many people that I grew up with or that I went to school with or of my ethnicity going to school, and going to college.

Alba's class-based feelings of exclusion have been shared by others coming to the university from lower economic income levels. We can recall Rose's (1989) and Rodriguez's (1978) struggles to come to terms with the difficulties they experienced as students from a working class background. bell hooks's (1989) lower-class background also had an impact on her life: She felt out of place in an academic environment not geared toward lower-class students, and particularly, not toward black students.

Alba's feelings of exclusion are not only class-based. Similar to hooks, Alba faces additional challenges. Not only is her economic and social background different from the majority of students at the university, her ethnic background and her position as a first-generation female college attendee are also part of her "outlandish" status. The effects of these influences make it difficult for Alba to adjust to the university and to see any similarities between her life at home and her life in school. However, unlike Rodriguez (1978), who tried to assimilate middle-class values at the expense of his cultural heritage, Alba takes a different position. Instead of accepting the sheltered life of a college campus and forgetting the world outside of it, Alba wants to make sure that she doesn't forget:

> I just don't wanna fall into that mentality or that way of thinking that this is how everyday life is, and you know, this is how it is for everybody cause it's not, you know. I don't wanna fall into that mentality, because I know, when I go back home … it's gonna be different, I'm not gonna be able to go out after 9:00 as much, or walk alone or, transportation is not gonna be that punctual all the time, it's not gonna be, it's not gonna take you to your front door, and I'm gonna see different kinds of people walking around. I'm gonna see a lot of gang members, a lot of the people I grew up with, actually, walking around different, with babies, and people my age with babies, you know, two or three, and they have been in jail and, I'm gonna see a lot [of them] on drugs.

Drugs, babies, jail, gangs, this is life outside campus-town, which is definitely not the experience of the majority of college students at the university. In order for Alba to succeed in a new setting, she has to perform according to the standards set by a white, middle-class society. To fulfill her dream of going to medical school and to remain a part of her inner-city Chicago community, Alba needs to "be on both shores at once" (Anzaldúa, 1987, p. 78) and become adept in juggling multiple identities and oppressions. Her "home language," as Deborah Brandt (1990) calls it, is different from the language used in school, a language that she needs to acquire if she wants to be successful in a competitive society. According to Brandt, "the school, a middle-class, majority-run institution" (p. 107) disadvantages students who are "deemed to be at risk in school literacy performance to the extent to which their home language is at odds with the so-called explicit, decontextualized language of the school" (p. 106). Alba, therefore not only has to digest new information, but she also has to acquire new and unfamiliar literacies in order to be accepted in the academic discourse community.

Alba tells me that "I guess it's more of a struggle for someone of my class to make it to the university than it is for, say, someone from the middle class." But Alba doesn't think that the additional burdens will deter her from succeeding. She is convinced that "if you study, and you do, then you can get by, so you can get that degree." Alba wants to succeed in a community that does not fully embrace her. And despite her acknowledgment that she is going to face more difficulties than white, middle-class students, she is convinced that she can overcome these difficulties and achieve the "American Dream."

Alba's placement into a basic writing course and her designation as "lacking" literacy skills should not come as a surprise. Her background sets her apart; it enables her to see things differently, to move outside the prescribed standards, to be critical of oppressive forces. But it also enables others to view her differently and disadvantages her in a university setting. Alba's real-life experiences are discounted in a setting that values decontextualized and abstract literacy and at the same time brands "groups who emphasize the concrete and contextualized" as deficient (Brandt, 1990,

p. 109). Additionally, as de Castell and Luke (1988) point out, the "social, cultural, and political consequences of a national literacy which is based on imposed, rather than derived, culturally significant information" exclude those members of the community whose background is not specifically based on "American language, culture, and economic life" (pp. 173–174).

Alba started college full of positive attitudes. Nevertheless, she didn't think that she was a good writer, since her writing in high school had never received any positive feedback: "I don't think I knew how to write well, I mean I was taking an English course at Chicago State University … for writing skills before I got here, because I was scared, I was like, in high school, my papers really weren't that well, and I was just really criticized." Her placement into a two-semester course at the university reinforced her perceptions of being a "basic" writer, needing extra help. It broadcasts to her and the university community that regardless of her college admission, she does not fit in.

CONTEXTUALIZING ALBA'S CASE

For an indepth study of Alba's use of various communication modes in Rhetoric 103, a composition course which I taught in the Fall of 1994 in the department's computer classroom, I used qualitative research methods and situation-based evaluation to study specific interactions in a specific setting and to account for the multiple and interwoven discourse activities used by individual participants in the exchange of ideas. Acknowledging the differences in individuals' communication strategies and acknowledging that communication does not follow a well-worn path, but changes depending on the situation does not take away from the inequalities and oppressions faced by nontraditional students, and especially women, in an academic setting, the workplace, or at home. Instead, it provides researchers with the opportunity to look at discourse strategies not as fixed entities, but instead as "plural, local, and immanent" (Fraser & Nicholson, 1990, p. 23). This approach problematizes dichotomous traits that, for example, define women's roles in the communication process as distinct from—and often subordinate to—men's roles. Such a binary conception of gendered discourse leads to what Flynn (1995) calls a "reductive conception of identification," which implies that "gender can be detached from other factors such as race, class, and ethnicity" (p. 355). Harding (1990) also points out very clearly that such a conception contributes to a reduction of women's experiences into one "master" perspective. She ascertains that this would not account for the many "subjugated knowledges" of women and the varied forms of male domination. Harding's insistence that the female subject is "a site of differences" (p. 188) resonates with her words in the Introduction to *Feminism and Methodology* (1987) that "not only do our gender experiences vary across the cultural categories; they also are often in conflict in any one individual's experience" (p. 7).

If we apply Flynn's (1995) and Harding's (1987, 1990) insights to interactive behavior, we need to concede that whether a person favors aggressive, assertive, or questioning behavior, cooperation, collaboration, or a nurturing environment depends on many factors, each of which will lead to a different realization of discourse strategies.[7]

As Figure 4.1 shows, gender is only one, albeit important, part of the realization process; however, ethnic background, interaction with peers, expectations brought to the academic setting, parents' expectations, and other factors influence communication as well. This conception of the communication process as complex and multilayered problematizes research that is based in essentialized and universalized conceptions of discourse. The fluidity and ambiguity of discourse conventions employed by specific participants in specific situations defies notions of fixed boundaries that can be applied to all communication.[8] The dismissal of a stable and coherent self and of a transparent language undermines the notion of exclusively gendered discourse and takes into account that communication necessitates the appropriation of multiple discourse strategies, changing according to the situation at hand, the discourse partners, and the perceived benefits of an interaction.

Thus, reflecting the diverse backgrounds of communication partners, the discourse practices are similarly varied. According to Figure 4.2, interactive practices are fluid and changeable, and much less distinct from each other than assumed by scholars such as West and Zimmerman (1983) and Fishman (1983). Acknowledging the shifting boundaries allows researchers to look at participants as complex and individualized human beings who appropriate a diversity of rhetorical strategies for their

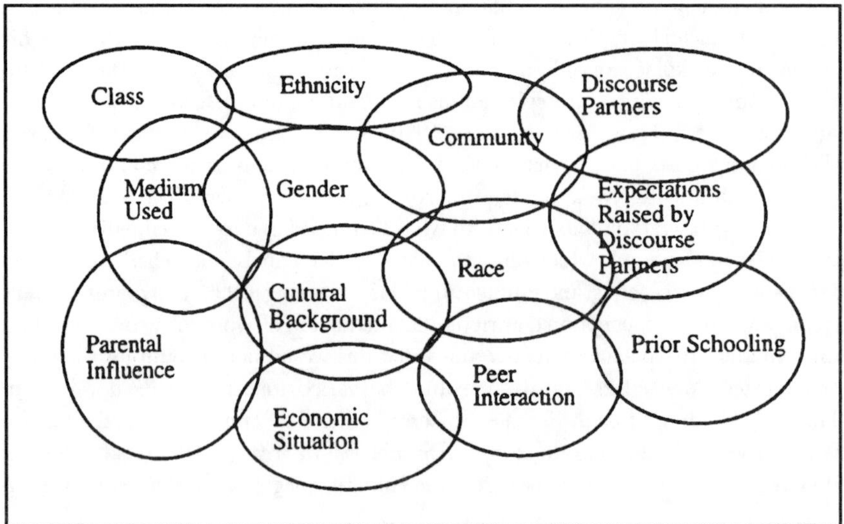

FIGURE 4.1. Influences on discourse practices.

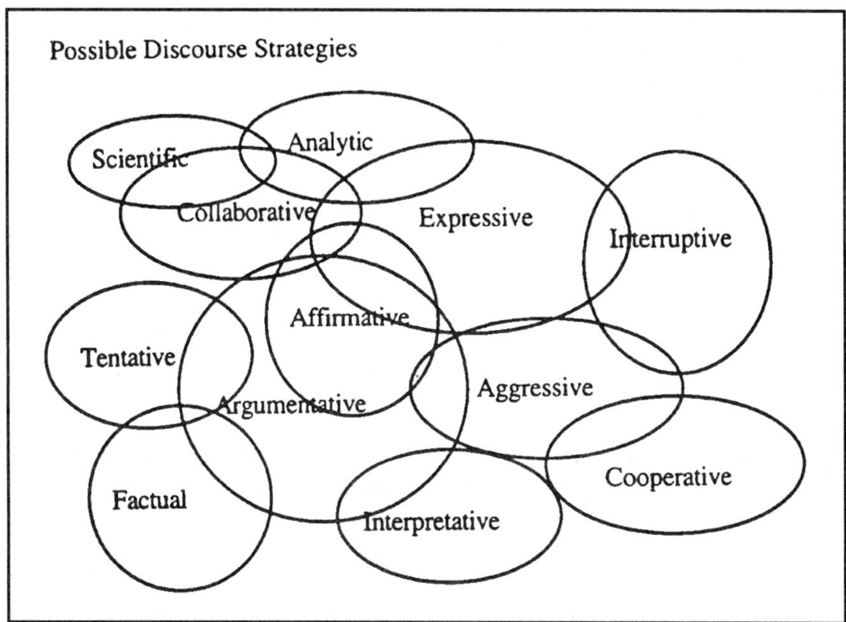

FIGURE 4.2. Varied discourse practices.

specific purposes. Although discourse cannot be divided into easily recognizable strategies, there is no elimination of hierarchies and patriarchal structures, only diverse appropriations of interactive strategies for a variety of purposes. For example, aggressive strategies can be used either to express frustrations with one's position in society, stay in power and profit from the status quo, gain a voice, express resistance, or undermine existing social and political belief systems.

The need for a differentiated approach to communication is not only necessary for face-to-face encounters, but is also apparent when exploring CMC and its implication on the user. The various concerns and individual personalities that users bring to CMC make it necessary to look for new ways of explaining interactive behavior. This is in accord with Jan Zimmerman's (1983) position that "technology is not neutral or value-free" and instead "reflects the values, thoughts, ideologies, beliefs, and biases of its creators" (p. 3). Thus, to use Smith's (1983) words, "there is no monolith called 'technology'" (p. 65). Zimmerman and Smith explore technology from the perspective of the designer, asking for less male-oriented productions of technologies and for more attention to different needs, especially the needs of women.

Looking at the same technology from a different perspective, namely that of the person who uses it, it becomes clear that any design takes on different functions, depending on the specific user of the innovation. Haas and Neuwirth, for example, point out that "conceptions about what technology *is*, and how it comes to be, profoundly shape specific acts of computer-based reading and writing; they influence as well the construction of our individual and collective selves in *relation* to that technology" (original emphasis, 1994, p. 319). To ignore the construction of our own realities and adapt a philosophy that assumes that technology is value free would discourage "any examination of how computers shape discourse and, consequently, does not authorize us to take an active role in shaping technology" (p. 323). Most important, in this context, is Haas and Neuwirth's assertion that

> the effects of any technology are the result of certain cultural and cognitive ways of reasoning about and using that technology.... That is, in a very real way, technologies are "made" through our thinking and talking about them. Consequently, technologies are continually evolving; they are not static but shaped subtly and constantly by the uses to which they are put and by the discourse that accompanies those uses. (p. 324)

This reflects Bertram Bruce's (1993) insistance on the situatedness of interactions and innovations. He points out that "innovations themselves are never fixed; they are active elements in the organization of relationships among people. As such, they are continually interpreted and evaluated with respect to the way they express these relationships" (p. 28).

The multiple realities created by users and the ambiguous and constructed nature of interactive reality online and face-to-face call for a research agenda that avoids generalizations and that looks at the individual's approach to computer technology, her interpretations of specific interactions, and her appropriation of computers to aid or restrict successful interaction. To account for the complexity in meaning making, we have to contextualize knowledge acquisition and foreground differences without ignoring commonalities arising from collective struggles against discrimination based in gender, race, ethnicity, social class, and cultural differences. Thus, acknowledging heterogeneity in the classroom does not negate shared attempts to work against continued exploitation and discrimination of disenfranchised groups; instead, it enables us to study specific situations in detail without neglecting the social and political disadvantages that disenfranchised people and students similar to Alba hold in common.

ALBA'S RHETORICAL STRATEGIES IN CLASS AND ON PACERFORUM

Rhetoric 103, the class that Alba had signed up for, included 16 students who, because of the perceived "lack" of literacy skills,were required to take a two-semester writing course in the Academic Writing Program (AWP) instead of the usual one-semester course.[9] The course was taught twice a week and was 75 minutes in duration.[10] The students in the class came from a variety of racial and ethnic backgrounds:

African American	3 men;	3 women
Anglo American	2 men;	2 women
Asian American	2 men	
Hispanic	1 man;	1 woman
Indian	1 man	
Persian American	1 man	

Additionally, students' cultural, social, and economic backgrounds varied: while they mainly came from the midwest, they were from rural towns, suburbs, and the inner city; parents worked in factories, in offices, as nurses, or as schoolteachers; and their family incomes were generally below the average income of students on this campus.[11]

At the beginning of the semester, Alba blends in with the rest of the students, being quieter than most of them. She usually sits at the far end of the U-shaped room, next to another Hispanic student with whom she speaks in Spanish. She looks at her peers and sometimes looks at the instructor. She turns slightly on the swivel chair, but she hardly ever participates in class discussions. It is difficult to figure out whether she is paying attention or thinking of something else, something unrelated to the discussion at hand. Did she do the readings? Does it not matter to her? What *does* she think? These questions are not just ones that apply to Alba; many students in classes across the disciplines do not participate extensively in class activities, and the reasons for their reluctance vary widely. The easiest assumption is that they are bored or didn't do the readings and therefore have nothing to contribute to the discussion. However, these conclusions sometimes wrongly brand students as disinterested and even agonistic toward the instructor or their classmates, especially when attending a class that they are required to take. If instructors do not give these students a chance to show otherwise, they can internalize their status as "the quiet ones," even if the reasons for their nonparticipation stemmed from a different source in the beginning, such as being unaccustomed to academic discourse, feeling out of place, being shy, having no self-confidence, or not being used to participatory classrooms. In Alba's case, it turns out that she is not at all disinterested in the topics discussed in class, but that the classroom environment, especially at the beginning of the semester,[12] does not provide the needed space for her to express her opinions without feeling intimidated and out of place.

Alba's behavior is in accord with studies on nontraditional students' behavior in classroom discourse. According to Bizzell (1986), students who have not been trained in white, middle-class values have more difficulties adapting to academic requirements. A similar argument is made by Shaughnessy (1977), who discusses the split between literacies acknowledged at home versus those acknowledged in a school setting. Bartholomae (1987) concurs with Shaughnessy and calls for providing students with tools for success in academic life. Additionally, feminist researchers have pointed out the increased vulnerability that women associate with being outspoken in a classroom setting. To provide a more congenial learning environment for women, scholars have repeatedly called for less adversarial classroom discourses, especially for women students whose socialization process has conditioned them in ways often associated with passivity, an unwillingness to speak up, and a tendency to be conciliatory (see, for example, Kramarae & Treichler, 1990; McCracken, 1992).

Alba, however, overcame these barriers, and she was able to speak up, but it was not face-to-face in the classroom. Instead, she chose to speak out on PacerForum,[13] where she could take time to formulate and organize her thoughts. Her participation on the various PacerForum discussions remained consistent throughout the semester. Compared to other class members, Alba was by no means the most vocal participant; instead, she tended to be at the lower end of the spectrum. In the synchronous discussions, for example, Alba responded between 8 to 12 times (3 to 4 percent of the total postings), while the other participants posted between 27 to 40 messages (10 to 13 percent).[14] Looking at the numbers, however, does not tell the whole story; instead, we need to account for the effects that the entries had for Alba and the other participants. Thus, we need to look more closely at how Alba situates herself within electronic discourse and how she uses rhetorical strategies and discourse conventions to define her position as an underprivileged Hispanic woman on a mainly white, middle-class college campus.

SOCIALIZATION ON PACERFORUM: "CRITICAL THINKING" AND IDENTITY POLITICS

To provide students with a means to present their opinions outside the classroom, they could contribute on PacerForum to "Critical Thinking," a tile created for asynchronous communication. To familiarize them with the concept of critical thinking, they were given a handout which read:

> To increase your critical thinking and writing skills, you will be writing responses to issues that we either discussed in class or that are otherwise connected to our overall theme in Rhet. 103P. This will provide you with an opportunity to express your ideas without being graded on them. You will post your responses on PacerForum which will give others in the class an opportunity to be exposed to as many different opinions as possible. Class participants are also encouraged to respond to the comments of others in the class.

Students were encouraged to reflect on their own experiences and to explore and share their "living literacy" with class participants.[15]

By drawing on students' knowledges and experiences, this socialization process provided a fuller and more complex picture of the participants than usually achieved in a classroom where time constraints and curricular activities do not allow for extended explorations of students' backgrounds, their struggles with university requirements, or their activities outside the classroom. Alba, like other participants on PacerForum, was able to use the "Critical Thinking" tile to inform classmates about her concerns and to let them know her position on issues of immediate concern to her. After reading an article on Hispanics in higher education, Alba acknowledges her "otherness," and uses it to define her position as a nontraditional student. She shows that she identifies herself with other Hispanic students whose situation on college campuses is mainly characterized by an exclusion from mainstream culture.[16] She writes:

> There are approximately six percent of the Latinos in the state of Illinois who pursue a higher education each year. The population of Latinos out of forty-thousand who attend the University of Illinois is only four to six percent. The article which we read only reflects the reasoning behind the sad statistics. Strong family ties, homesickness, guilt because you feel as though you are abandoning your family. All this aside from the fact that minorities in general are consistently confined to attending public schools with low funding and over-crowding. Thus Latinos are unprepared to attend the universities of their choice without being a step behind. True there is the old saying "no one is going to hand you anything, you have to earn what you want in life, and work hard for it." But isn't a shame that some should have to work harder than others because of a biased injustice-ethnicity. No one can help who they are, what there [sic] ethnic background is, the only thing you can do to help better your-self is get an education. This is especially pertinent to those of us who have no other outlet or don't come from wealth. An education is all we have but it is unfair when being who you are or believing in your culture and how you were raised becomes an obstacle. I as a Latina can not help who I am, God gave me this gift and thank him for it everyday. I will never try to hide or deny who I am, if I ever did I believe it would be impossible. It is in my name, my speech and my golden brown skin. I love my family and my culture, but I've posed a goal to become a doctor and I know there are many hurdles in before me. But I like my forefathers want to achieve something and maybe; in the process, try to make it a little easier for Latinos in the future to go to college. I am a first generation university attendee, so is my brother before me who will graduate next year. There were none before us, but there will be many in my family to come.

This comment shows acute awareness of her status as a minority student who, despite the supposedly equal opportunities at the university, has to work harder and fight against stereotypes associated with Latinos. She clearly sees education as a means "to make it," to be successful in a white-dominated world by aspiring to the goals upheld by the majority in this society. However, despite these aspirations, she did not want to sacrifice parts of her identity and deny her background. Instead, she emphasizes her position as a Latina student and uses this to show her determination at gaining access to educational goals usually denied to people from nontraditional backgrounds.

The idea of succeeding by "claiming an education" (Rich, 1977) runs throughout Alba's entries on "Critical Thinking." Her concern with the effects of unequal opportunities in education, which are based on unequal opportunities on a larger scale, provoke her to post another entry, geared towards making others aware that nonmainstream students have to work harder to achieve the same goals as mainstream students:

> I seriously feel if we had the opportunities that everyone else did (like attending private and or schools in the suburbs which have up to date educational curriculums and equipment) we wouldn't be so behind in comparison thus terminating the unfair advantages and supposed segregation because of it according to the so-called scholars.

In addition to identifying herself as a disadvantaged minority student, Alba also identifies herself as a woman who still doesn't have the same opportunities as men. Like her rhetorical strategies in her entries on her ethnic and economic status, she is assertive when discussing the role of women in American society.

> I think it's about time someone is finally addressing the issue of equality of the sexes, particularly in the school system. Males are constantly being granted more funding and support for activities and academics when women have as much right to it as they do.

Her interest in the school system is also expressed in an entry on the status of bilingual education in the United States:

> Sink or swim, that is the school system without a bilingual education curriculum.... Bilingual education aids in the preservation of the already existing native culture and the formation of the new medium of the new societal standards.

This comment relates to Richard Rodriguez's (1978) article on bilingualism in the United States, which participants read for class discussion. This sophisticated entry leaves little room for doubt about Alba's position on the American educational system and her tendency to value school literacy over home literacy. Her opposition to Rodriguez's idea that acquiring a public identity necessitates losing one's private identity becomes even more distinct during an earlier in-class synchronous discussion on that topic. During this discussion, Alba concludes by stating:

> prefiero murir parada de que vivir de rodillas
> I rather die standing than LIVE ON MY KNEES—Zapata
> I rather die living the way I choose; with freedom, than live out my life by someone else's standards!!!!!!!!

Alba is competent in conversing in Spanish—her home language—and English—the language associated with the "public" identity Rodriguez discusses in his article. However, instead of denying her private identity, she defines herself as a Hispanic woman whose identities are inseparable.

Alba's repeated emphasis on her background is quite different from a group of Hispanic students about whom Susan Romano (1993) writes. Romano points out that when exploring Los Vendidos, a play about Mexican-American farm workers, none of her students with Hispanic surnames "identify with any of the Mexican-Americans in the text" (p. 12). She argues that "evasion of experience encountered now, here, at this university, constitutes a decided disinclination on the part of the marginalized to occupy that subject position and a disinclination on the part of the dominant to respond to such a move" (p. 19). However, she finds that one of her students, Elena, although not publicly defending her identity, acknowledges her ethnicity: "What I feel is that it's worth losing your 'Hispanic identity' to society, just remember, you'll never lose it within you" (p. 26). Alba, on the other hand, not only remembers her "Hispanic identity," but also is quite confident to announce her ideologies on PacerForum. She is living proof of Houston's (1992) argument that nontraditional women's experiences are the result of the interlocking oppressions and identities that they bring to the academic setting. In her entries, she shows an ability to draw on her experiences and to include information on aspects of her life that influenced her development as a nontraditional female student.

Alba also draws on her experiences in a discussion on the use of negative stereotypes in commercials. During this exchange, students voiced a variety of opinions, mainly defending the freedom of advertisers to produce any commercial they wanted. Eric, for example, did not see the negativity of the ads, and even after an extended discussion, he is unwilling to concede that stereotypes are perpetuated by advertisers. Thus, after the synchronous discussion on PacerForum, Eric posts an entry in "Critical Thinking" that reinforces his belief in the freedom of advertisers:

> 137. Eric
> I feel the use of "Fritto Bandito" and the tall Mexican guy in commercials was not discriminating. This is because they were not negative figures. The advertisers even commented that they were try to add humor to the commercial. Maybe the advertisers chose to use the tall Mexican guy because corn chips were originated in Mexico. This would add to the viewers that these are authentic and that makes them better than other corn chips sold by other companies. Personally I think it works because right now I'm going back to my room to crunch on some "Fritto's."

Alba's opposition to Eric was carried over from the preceding synchronous discussion and from his comment on "Critical Thinking." She writes a detailed response to Eric's position on minority issues and stereotyping:

> 141. Alba
> Eric, I guess it's easy for someone who has never experienced negative stereotypes to not see how one can find the Fritto Bandito ad offensive. It is very easy to say it shouldn't bother you when you haven't experienced it. You can't possibly know how it feels for some one to say or imply negative things about you if it never happened to you.
>
> Eric, I never asked to be born who I am, just like you never asked to be born who you are. You see we didn't have a choice. But I'm proud of who I am, and fortunately and sometimes unfortunately we do have the choice of thought

> and perception and how we express it. It is too bad that in this society someone can use that choice and power to publicly try to demean someone else. Latinos aren't all Bandito's or as it means in English-thiefs. How someone could use that as a ploy to try to entertain and then sway humorously to buy a product is not funny. It is the abuse of negative perceptions like that that make it hard for someone like me to believe those who try to say you and I are equals. I know better and know that we are, because my family instilled equality and positively reinforced my self perception. Unfortunately not everyone was raised like myself, and therefore not everyone is going to dispell the advertisement as a fallacy. There will be children who will believe, there have been children who have believed.
>
> I am your equal, therefore I deserve the same respect you do. I am entitled to not be the object of one's failed attempt at comedic advertisement, that really shouldn't be funny to anyone!

Alba's emphatic statement is based on personal experience, and she makes it clear that she considers Eric's attitude as part of his ignorance and his position as a male student whose cultural, social, and ethnic background do not lead to experiences of discrimination faced by Alba. Alba, however, shows that she is willing to fight for equality, despite all the hurdles put in her way by school administrators, teachers, peers, advertisers, and politicians. Her emphatic statement, "I am your equal, therefore I deserve the same respect you do," is testimony to the many times that she has suffered from unequal treatment, oftentimes because of her ethnicity, economic status, and gender.[17]

Alba does not only emphasize her own struggles as a nontraditional student; she also uses her knowledge and personal encounters to make her classmates aware of the unjust American social and political system. Her entry on violence in Chicago—a topic that is of immediate concern to her—shows her identification with, but also removal from, life in the ghetto:

> 85. Alba
>
> I am the product of an environment you could call the Ghetto. Or in politically correct terms an underprivileged area. I was on a day to day basis surrounded by violence I grew up with many of those who committed such violent acts as murder and if I were to go home at any time and encounter any of my old "kick the can" partners I would politely carry on a conversation with some of them who haven't died or aren't in jail. Violence to me was just an everyday life occurence. I think about it sometimes and see the irony of it all, how my life has just grown accustomed to witnessing death and violence. My ears have grown numb to the gun shots, the names of the day's fatalities. Somehow one tends to just tune it out until you witness it personally and you contemplate how maybe it could of been you. On the night of April 15, 1994, two friends of mine were nearly fatally shot. I even held one in my arms as he lay shedding blood and passing out from the loss. I didn't here the screams at the time and still it all feels like just a bad nightmare. I remember trying to hold my boyfriend back from going out and trying to find those who had shot our friends. I remember the blood on my shoes, the ones I threw away. I

> remember the leather jacket I carried with a bullet hole the size of a compact, the one that would never again be used. I remember almost fainting in church the next day. I remember the phone call to my friend's mom, "I'm sorry your son's been shot." I don't remember being scared for myself but for my boyfriend's safety. These are things I vaguely remember. But, I know I'll always vividly remember the cold sweat nightmares I had of seeing my own violent death—but then again how could I ever forget I sleep with them every night.
>
> This is the experience of witnessing violence everday and occasionally first hand. There are no real ways to describe it so one who hasn't lived it could understand. I don't really try to understand myself. I guess those who haven't should just be fortunate and thank God we're alive and pray for the safety of those we love. Because I know this isn't isolated to where I live, Violevce is everywhere it sees no color, wealth, poverty, it has no religion, it just exists and we all should be wary.

Alba's ironic use of the phrase "politically correct terms" shows her disillusionment with politicians who call a part of the city "underprivileged" without trying to create an environment that would make the term obsolete. It also shows her awareness of double standards employed by people in power who talk about those "on the other side of the fence" but who do not want to work on really understanding the problems faced by this underprivileged, and oftentimes powerless, part of society.

Alba cannot be understood without acknowledging her experiences and without seeing her in terms of the literacies and knowledges that constitute her identity. Similarly, her use of discourse strategies have to be seen in connection with her background, the purpose of her entries, and the medium that she used. Thus, in her entry on violence in Chicago, Alba uses PacerForum to make her readers aware of the inequality in American society; she uses sarcasm and repetition to establish rapport with her audience, and to make them aware of what her life is like once she leaves campus. Of course, some researchers would disagree with calling Alba's entry a conscious rhetorical strategy based on conscious choices. If we look at Ong's ideas in *Orality and Literacy* (1982), Alba might be considered closer to the stage of orality and thus less analytic, abstract, and proficient in literate excursions since she is using repetition and parallel constructions to get her point across. Ong also uses this argument to refer to Black English, a language that he considers not as highly developed as Anglo-American English and which is, by implication, inferior. However, instead of relying on Ong's dichotomous view, which upholds the "great divide" between literacy and orality, it is more productive to see Alba's use of language in terms of Bleich's (1988) and Brandt's (1990) situation-based interpretation of literacy, in which attention is placed on the process of literacy acquisition, making it necessary to look at what Brandt calls the intersubjectivity of "interpretation and meaning in literate as well as oral exchanges" (p. 30).

Thus, Alba's entries begin to show that it is important to counter Ong's (1982) arguments and to also move away from the "great divide" entertained by researchers of gender-specific discourse strategies (Fishman, 1983; Gray, 1992; Tannen, 1990;

West & Zimmerman, 1983). Instead, we need to look at the situation in which discourse takes place and at how the discourse act is realized, depending on the setting and the participants, as well as on the medium used. Alba's use of lengthy messages, her tendency to make "statements," her assertive communication style, and her aggressiveness when defending her background have to be seen in connection with her appropriation of PacerForum to inform participants about herself—they must be viewed in light of her need to explain and defend the status of marginalized students.

CAN ALBA HAPPEN AGAIN?

For Alba, PacerForum took on the role of making other class participants aware of who she was, what her status at the university was, and how her situation was the result of her position as a nontraditional female student. The use of CMC allowed Alba—whose gender, ethnicity, and class background traditionally exclude her from those who are accepted in the college classroom setting—to gain a voice critical of discriminatory academic standards and critical of the dominant power structures. The appropriation of feminist and liberatory practices and the use of PacerForum in a classroom that stressed the importance of acknowledging differences and heterogeneity provided a space for Alba to be heard. In this nonthreatening environment, she was able to increase her classmates' awareness of a nonaffluent Hispanic woman's struggles in a largely hostile academic context. Her entries and the entries of other participants led to an environment that provided additional learning opportunities, a space where students learned from each other, and the instructor learned from them. Two students, Jay and Miriam, expressed their appreciation of being able to acquire a better understanding of other cultures and other people's struggles on "Critical Thinking":

> 16. Jay
> [...] I am glad that I am in this class because I can receive different opinions from all types of people. At my school everybody had the same opinion or just didn't care about going into great detail if they did conflict. [...]
>
> 18. Miriam
> [...] I found out a lot of information that I never knew before. I feel like I am much more informed on the idea of being a minority, and the ideas that go behind it. [...]

Similarly, Alba considered the PacerForum exchanges a "wonderful experience" because they "presented different perspectives" and prompted everybody to "speak up more." For Alba, discussions on PacerForum encouraged her to engage in critical thought and academic learning, thereby increasing her chances to cross boundaries and participate in academic discourse. And, as Jay's and Miriam's comments show, students' interactions online allowed them to gain insights into each other's cultural and ethnic backgrounds, thus helping them to understand different value and belief systems.[18] Alba's comments on her nontraditional background became a source of power—not an added burden—within a small segment of the university community.

Of course, Alba's case is situation-specific, and it is not possible to articulate all the features that led to her responses or the class atmosphere. What is important about telling Alba's story is the realization that to do justice to the diversity of students in our classes, scholars and teachers must avoid generalizations and instead work at exploring specific cases. We must also acknowledge the context-based nature of literacy and knowledge acquisition. Thus, students—basic writers or others—have to be seen as complex individuals whose actions are influenced by their environment, and whose home language must be taken into consideration when trying to construct environments conducive to learning. Instead of insisting on a universal "basic" writer, or a universal "woman" writer, it is necessary to be more specific when talking about students who are classified as underprepared by the academic institution or who are seen exclusively in terms of their gender. Cultivating an awareness of our differences will make it possible for each of us to teach those who most need our attention. Alba's interactions on PacerForum, for example, show that it is important to consider the many factors that shape a student's responses in specific situations. Alba's upbringing, her grandmother's insistence on her getting a job, her mother's emphasis on education, her growing up in an economically underprivileged area, her father's machismo, her desire to become a doctor, her position as a Hispanic female student—all influenced her use of discourse strategies. Only an awareness of these multiple influences on student behavior can challenge the dichotomous descriptions of interactive behavior and move beyond the easy binaries of early research on communication styles.

Accounting for the complexities involved in communication provides a new and challenging approach to looking at CMC. Instead of accepting too readily research from other fields,[19] computers and compositionists can become involved in critical studies that look at the multilayered nature of the communication process. Thus, electronic communication, by providing a forum for asserting multiple subject positions, allows researchers to move away from scholarship that emphasizes essentialist positions and instead moves toward a research agenda that promotes diversity and heterogeneity. Seeing Alba only as a woman voicing her opinions would neglect her position as a minority as well as her status as an "underclass" student; it would defy Houston's (1992) important insights concerning the multiple and interlocking oppressions faced by women of nontraditional backgrounds. Thus, instead of perceiving Alba as an easily definable and categorizable entity, we need to acknowledge that she will "continually walk out of one culture into another."

To help Alba, and all students, walk proudly and confidently is a challenge to all teachers that necessitates changes in teaching approaches. When we look critically at Alba and her interactions online, it is clear that a uniform and unchanging educational model needs to be replaced by a model that allows us to rethink our responsibilities to all our students and that uses new technologies for constructive interaction. Instead of favoring authoritarian teaching strategies and unequal power relations, we need to work toward a pedagogy that takes seriously changing notions of authority and emphasizes students' diverse viewpoints. How instructors and students arrive at sharing authority and learn to engage in dialogic action in their classrooms and online will differ from situation to situation; however, students and teachers can exercise responsible interactive behavior that disperses authority among all members in the class. For this reason, it is necessary to engage in critical reflections about our own roles in the oppression of others in the class and how we can contribute to creating a conducive learning environment. Students and instructors need to discuss how authority can become an instrument for reciprocal gain and how situations of abuse can be avoided. Students and instructors can learn, to use Giroux's (1992) words, "how representations and practices that name, marginalize, and define difference as the devalued Other are actively learned, internalized, challenged, or transformed" (p. 103). As Giroux points out,

> Power is multifaceted, and we need a better understanding of how it works not simply as a force for oppression but also as a basis for resistance and self and social empowerment. Educators need to fashion a critical postmodern notion of authority, one that decenters essentialist claims to power while simultaneously fighting for relations of authority and power that allow many voices to speak so as to initiate students into a culture that multiplies rather than restricts democratic practices and social relations as part of a wider struggle for democratic public life. (p. 139)

Power and authority—and the abuse of it—do not disappear in electronic environments. If we want to diminish the potential for abuse, students and instructors, for one, need to be made accountable for their actions online. Accountability, in turn, necessitates an integration of online discourse into classroom discussions, enabling students and instructor to discuss the usefulness of the online interactions and to look for strategies that would increase successful communication and decrease communication that is interruptive and unproductive. Students can take on the role of mediators online, assuming responsibilities that encourage them to develop a critical awareness of their own tendencies to engage in activities condoned by those in power and condemned by those oppressed. The classroom can serve as a place for reflection on the larger social and political system that defines authority in terms of unequal power relations.

Opening up the classroom to celebrate diversity among students—and the multiple identities within students—calls for a rethinking of current pedagogies to accommodate a "confusion of boundaries" and to fuse theoretical knowledge of postmodern, feminist, and cyborgian theories with a pedagogy which, like the cyborg, changes shape and meaning with the diverse and often conflicting components of a polyvocal and multicultural classroom. A pedagogy informed by these theoretical frameworks can help us to arrive at a more inclusionary approach to teaching that profits nontraditional women and all students enrolled in our classes.[20]

APPENDIX

FIGURE A.1. PacerForum interface for Rhetoric 103.

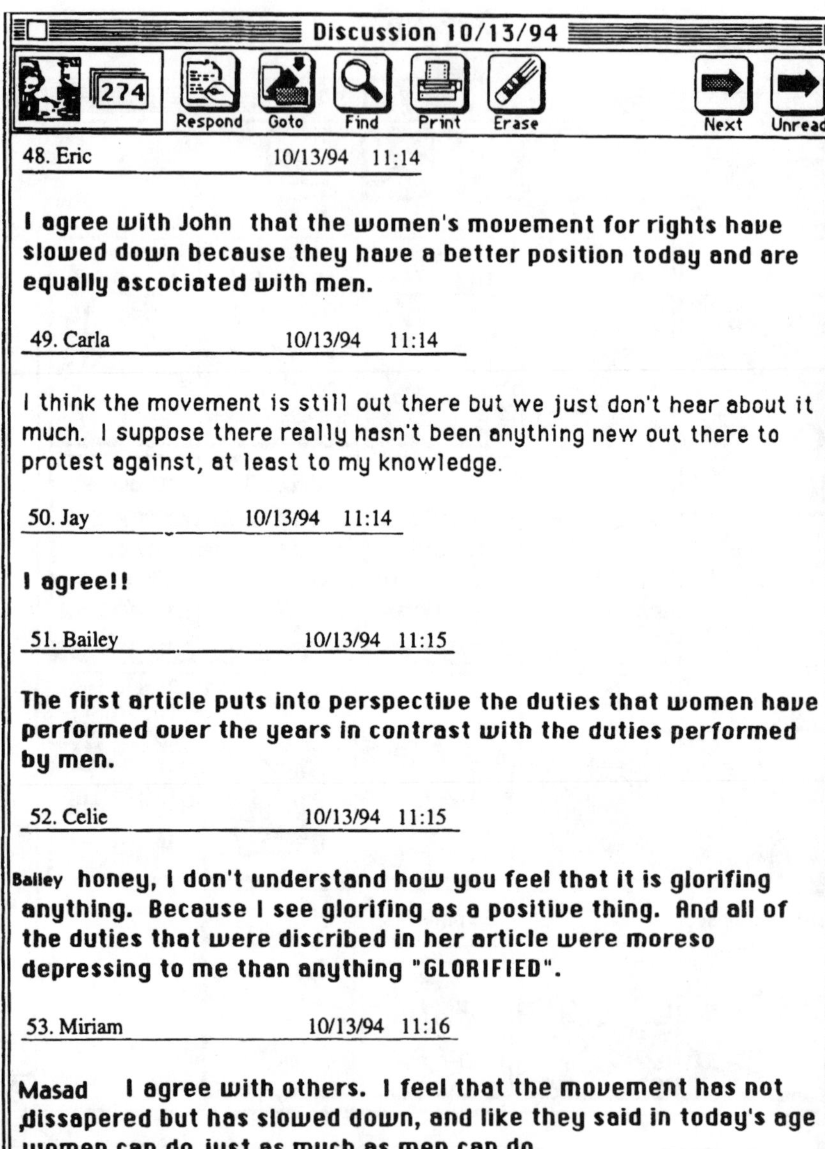
Discussion 10/13/94

274

Respond Goto Find Print Erase Next Unread

48. Eric 10/13/94 11:14

I agree with John that the women's movement for rights have slowed down because they have a better position today and are equally ascociated with men.

49. Carla 10/13/94 11:14

I think the movement is still out there but we just don't hear about it much. I suppose there really hasn't been anything new out there to protest against, at least to my knowledge.

50. Jay 10/13/94 11:14

I agree!!

51. Bailey 10/13/94 11:15

The first article puts into perspective the duties that women have performed over the years in contrast with the duties performed by men.

52. Celie 10/13/94 11:15

Bailey honey, I don't understand how you feel that it is glorifing anything. Because I see glorifing as a positive thing. And all of the duties that were discribed in her article were moreso depressing to me than anything "GLORIFIED".

53. Miriam 10/13/94 11:16

Masad I agree with others. I feel that the movement has not dissapered but has slowed down, and like they said in today's age women can do just as much as men can do.

FIGURE A.2. PacerForum discussion (excerpted).

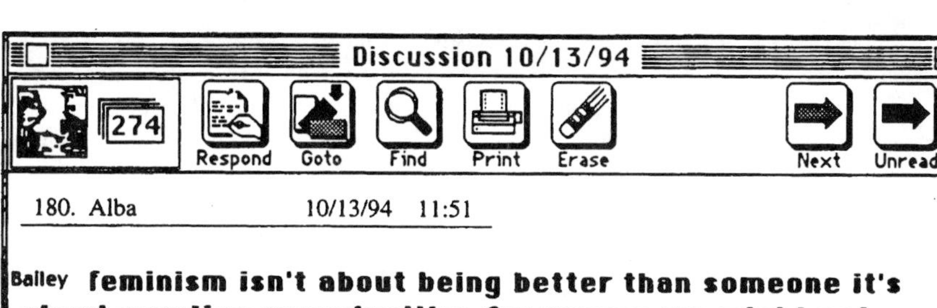

180. Alba 10/13/94 11:51

Bailey feminism isn't about being better than someone it's about creating opportunities for women we might not have otherwise.

181. Langston 10/13/94 11:51

Then, is the real question "can women play the game?" or is it "are they allowed to play the game?"

182. Josi 10/13/94 11:52

I don't think that there would be a great amount of difference if the roles were reversed.

183. Miriam 10/13/94 11:52

Good point Langston Us girls can if we want, but it is rarely offered.

184. Alex 10/13/94 11:52

I give women support in anything and everything they do. I wouldn't want a woman to risk hurting herself just to prove how hard you are or to prove that women are equal. Women shouldn't feel that all men are against them because most of the times women are our backbone.

FIGURE A.2. (cont'd.)

NOTES

[1] I use "nontraditional" to refer to students whose various backgrounds—ethnic, racial, cultural, economic, or gender—relegate them to the periphery of academic discourse communities. Thus, "nontraditional" does not refer to a homogeneous group of students, but to students who—because of various reasons—are less prepared to succeed in an academic environment than "traditional" students. For example, I consider a black female student who went

to an inner-city high school with few resources, and a white male student who grew up in an isolated rural area without adequate preparation for college, as nontraditional students. These two students, like all our students, are most likely considered traditional members in their respective communities, thus confirming the shifting realities and shifting positions emphasized by scholars such as Marsha Houston (1992), Gloria Anzaldúa (1987), and Donna Haraway (1990).

[2] To ensure privacy, students' names used in this paper have been changed to pseudonyms.

[3] I use passive voice deliberately to show that all agency is removed from Alba—she did not have the option to enroll in this class but instead "is enrolled" because of her placement scores on the ACT and essay test.

[4] If not otherwise noted, Alba's comments are taken from an interview I conducted with her at the end of the semester.

[5] Alba provided these statistics on a questionnaire concerning her high school experiences. The questionnaires were distributed at the beginning of the semester to each student in the class.

[6] According to Hourigan (1994), "class structure is an especially uncomfortable idea for first-year college students.... When they are confronted with its existence, they will deny its existence, retreating into 'unique individualism' postures" (pp. 44–45). Similarly, Villanueva (1993) points out that although American society denies clear class distinctions, they exist.

[7] The following figures are my attempt at visualizing the many influences on discourse practices and the interrelated nature of discourse strategies. The static nature of the printed page does not allow for representing the fluidity among these forces and permanently freezes the relationship of various discourse practices. However, while class and prior schooling, for example, are on opposite sides of Figure 4.1 and do not intersect, the ideal representation would be a freely moving structure in which interactions are in constant motion.

[8] Gloria Anzaldúa (1987) stresses the need to avoid binaries and "cross over":

> kicking a hole out of the old boundaries of the self and slipping under or over, dragging the old skin along, stumbling over it.... It is only when she is on the other side and the shell cracks open and the lid from her eyes lifts that she sees things in a different perspective. It is only then that she makes connections, formulates the insights. It is only then that her consciousness expands a tiny notch, another rattle appears on the rattlesnake tail and the added growth slightly alters the sounds she makes. (p. 49)

[9] "Students are placed into the Academic Writing Program (AWP) according to their Rhetoric Scores, a combination of the English ACT score and the Placement Essay score.... Students with Rhetoric Scores of 25 or 26 (and a Placement Essay Score of 6 or less) will take ... Rhetoric 103 and 104" (in handout explaining the Academic Writing Program).

[10] As a teacher interested in her students' successful completion of the course and their successful continuation of their academic studies, and as a researcher interested in students' appropriation of academic discourse and their use of computer-mediated communication, I do not exist apart from the community described in this paper but, like every researcher and teacher, my roles contribute to and partly shape the outcome of the course and the study.

[11] To gather information about the students in the class, I used questionnaires at the beginning and end of the semester, conducted interviews, analyzed the PacerForum transcripts, as

well as the research papers that they wrote for class. I also observed them in class and noted their participation and general attitudes towards the students and the class.

[12] Alba started to be more confident as the semester progressed, and she became one of the most ardent participants in class discussions. This can be related to feeling increasingly confident and "safe" in the classroom as well as to her realization that her contributions on PacerForum, and in class discussions, were highly valued.

[13] PacerForum is an electronic communication tool that allows students to post at any time from a campus location that has networked computer equipment. It is organized into tiles (see Figure A.1 in the Appendix) to which all students have access and to which they can contribute as frequently or infrequently as they desire. The opinions on how these individual tiles should be used vary according to the goals established by the instructor or the students. For example, a new tile can include an assignment and the questions that students have. A tile can be used as a "virtual office hour," during which students can log on and ask questions about assignments, paper topics, problem solutions, and so on. It can also be a forum for students and the instructor to lead discussions in the classroom or in a "virtual classroom" with students logging on at the same time from different locations. Also, it can provide a forum for feedback on papers, for extended writing exercises that are shared with the group, or, if a tile is created for each student, as a virtual portfolio of papers, assignments, and various exercises that can be included in the evaluation process at the end of the semester.

[14] During the synchronous discussion, students participated from different locations on campus. The overall participation during these four discussions ranged from 272 to 313 entries. Figure A.2 in the Appendix shows an excerpt of a synchronous discussion.

[15] Postings in this forum were by students only; I, as the instructor, did not participate in discussions posted there.

[16] To do justice to Alba's role in this study, I will reprint her postings in full. Leaving information out would not give full credit to Alba's involvement, and it would also render her partly voiceless, putting her in a position that is traditionally prescribed for a nontraditional woman on a college campus. Here I am relying on feminist approaches to research, acknowledging that "feminist inquiry joins other 'underclass' approaches in insisting on the importance of studying ourselves and 'studying up,' instead of 'studying down'" (Harding, 1987, p. 8).

[17] As Eric's and Alba's entries show, opening up space for a variety of opinions may lead to conflict. However, conflict can increase learning if students and the instructor discuss conflict resolution. Because PacerForum, and other CMC tools, is a forum for expressing ideas that might not find everybody's approval, conflict resolution is especially important. Online discussions will work only if students know how to respect each other's opinions, to criticize without insulting, and to be open-minded. Students need to work from the premise that people can hold conflicting viewpoints, but that it is possible to talk and argue about them.

[18] In this context, Alba and other students "depolarized" discussions and focused them on issues important to them. However, as Addison and Hilligoss (Chapter 1, in this volume) point out, we have to be aware that in many cases "established group norms will only allow for a certain amount of depolarization to occur."

[19] Jessup (1991), for example, draws heavily on research by Belenky, Clinchy, Goldberger, and Tarule's *Women's Ways of Knowing* (1986) to point out the contrast between "separate knowing" and "connected knowing," one employed by men, the other by women. Wahlstrom (1994) also bases her conclusions on the gendered discourse conventions found by Belenky, Clinchy, Goldberger, and Tarule, as well as Gilligan and Kramarae, and accepts their premise

that "dissimilarities exist in the way men and women approach collaboration, consensus, and conflict" (p. 183).

[20] For Alba's reaction to this article—which she read before I submitted it for publication—see Gruber, 1997.

REFERENCES

Anzaldúa, G. (1987). *Borderlands/la frontera: The new mestiza.* San Francisco: Aunt Lute Books.

Bartholomae, D. (1987). Writing on the margins: The concept of literacy in higher education. In T. Enos (Ed.), *A sourcebook for basic writing teachers* (pp. 66–83). New York: Random House.

Belenky, M. F., Clinchy, B. M., Goldberger, N. R., & Tarule, J. R. (1986). *Women's ways of knowing: The development of self, voice, and mind.* New York: Basic Books.

Bizzell, P. (1986, October). What happens when basic writers come to college? *College Composition and Communication, 37,* 294–301.

Bleich, D. (1988). *The double perspective: Language, literacy, and social relations.* New York: Oxford University Press.

Brandt, D. (1990). *Literacy as involvement: The acts of writers, readers, and texts.* Carbondale, IL: Southern Illinois University Press.

Bruce, B. C. (1993). Innovation and social change. In B. C. Bruce, J. K. Peyton, & T. Batson (Eds.), *Network-based classrooms: Promises and realities* (pp. 9–32). New York: Cambridge University Press.

De Castell, S., & Luke, A. (1988). Defining "literacy" in North American schools: Social and historical conditions and consequences. In E. R. Kintgon, B. M. Kroll, & M. Rose (Eds.), *Perspectives on literacy* (pp. 159–174). Carbondale, IL: Southern Illinois University Press.

Erickson, F. (1988). School literacy, reasoning, and civility: An anthropologist's perspective. In E. R. Kintgon, B. M. Kroll, & M. Rose (Eds.), *Perspectives on literacy* (pp. 205–226). Carbondale, IL: Southern Illinois University Press.

Fishman, P. M. (1983). Interaction: The work women do. In B. Thorne, C. Kramarae, & N. Henley (Eds.), *Language, gender, and society* (pp. 89–102). Rowley, MA: Newbury House.

Flynn, E. A. (1995, October). Feminism and scientism. *College Composition and Communication, 46*(3), 353–368.

Fraser, N., & Nicholson, L. J. (1990). Social criticism without philosoophy: An encounter between feminism and postmodernism. In L. J. Nicholson (Ed.), *Feminism/Postmodernism* (pp. 19–38). New York: Routledge.

Giroux, H. (1992). *Border crossings: Cultural workers and the politics of education.* New York: Routledge.

Gray, J. (1992). *Men are from Mars, women are from Venus: A practical guide for improving communication and getting what you want in your relationship.* New York: HarperCollins.

Gruber, S. (1997, March). *Writing it up: A dialogic reflection on the construction of meaning in language.* Paper presented at the Conference on College Composition and Communication, Phoenix, AZ.

Haas, C., & Neuwirth, C. (1994). Writing the technology that writes us: Research on literacy and the shape of technology. In C. L. Selfe & S. Hilligoss (Eds.), *Literacy and computers: The complications of teaching and learning with technology* (pp. 319–335). New York: Modern Language Association.

Haraway, D. (1990). A manifesto for cyborgs: Science, technology, and socialist feminism in the 1980s. In L. J. Nicholson (Ed.), *Feminism/postmodernism* (pp. 190–232). New York: Routledge.

Harding, S. (1987). Introduction: Is there a feminist method? In S. Harding (Ed.), *Feminism and methodology: Social sciences issues* (pp. 1–14). Bloomington, IN: Indiana University Press.

Harding, S. (1990). Feminism, science, and the anti-Enlightenment critiques. In L. J. Nicholson (Ed.), *Feminism/postmodernism* (pp. 83–106). New York: Routledge.

Hooks, B. (1989). *Talking back: Thinking feminist, thinking black.* Boston, MA: Southend Press.

Hourigan, M. M. (1994). *Literacy as social exchange: Intersections of class, gender, and culture.* Albany, NY: State University of New York Press.

Houston, M. (1992). The politics of difference: Race, class, and women's communication. In L. F. Rakow (Ed.), *Women making meaning: New feminist directions in communication* (pp. 45–59). New York: Routledge.

Hull, G., Rose, M., Fraser, K. L., & Castellano, M. (1991). Remediation as social construct: Perspectives from an analysis of classroom discourse. *College Composition and Communication, 42*(3), 299–329.

Jessup, E. (1991). Feminism and computers in composition instruction. In G. Hawisher & C. L. Selfe (Eds.), *Evolving perspectives on computers and composition studies: Questions for the 1990s* (pp. 336–355). Urbana, IL: National Council of Teachers of English.

Kramarae, C., & Treichler, P. (1990). Power relations in the classroom. In S. L. Gabriel & I. Smithson (Eds.), *Gender in the classroom: Power and pedagogy* (pp. 41–59). Urbana, IL: University of Illinois Press.

McCracken, N. M. (1992). Gender issues and the teaching of writing. In N. M. McCracken & B. C. Appleby (Eds.), *Gender isues in the teaching of English* (pp. 115–125). Portsmouth, NH: Boynton/Cook.

Ong, W. J. (1982). *Orality and literacy: The technologizing of the word.* New York: Methuen.

Rich, A. (1977). *Claiming an education.* Speech presented at Douglass College, Rutgers University, New Brunswick, NJ.

Rodriguez, R. (1978, November). The achievement of desire: Personal reflections on learning "basics." *College English, 40*, 239–254.

Romano, S. (1993). The egalitarianism narrative: Whose story? Which yardstick? *Computers and Composition, 10*(3), 5–28.

Rose, M. (1989). *Lives on the boundary: The struggles and achievements of America's underprepared.* New York: The Free Press.

Shaughnessy, M. P. (1977). *Errors and expectations: A guide for the teacher of basic writing.* New York: Oxford University Press.

Smith, J. (1983). Women and appropriate tecnology: A feminist assessment. In J. Zimmerman (Ed.), *The technological woman: Interfacing with tomorrow* (pp. 65–74). New York: Praeger.

Tannen, D. (1990). *You just don't understand: Women and men in conversation.* New York: William Morrow.

Villanueva, V. (1993). *Bootstraps: From an American academic of color.* Urbana, IL: National Council of Teachers of English.

Wahlstrom, B. J. (1994). Communication and technology: Defining a feminist presence in research and practice. In C. L. Selfe & S. Hilligoss (Eds.), *Literacy and computers: The complications of teaching and learning with technology* (pp. 171–185). New York: Modern Language Association.

West, C., & Zimmerman, D. H. (1983). Small insults: A study of interruptions in cross-sex conversations between unacquainted persons. In B. Thorne, C. Kramarae, & N. Henley (Eds.), *Language, gender, and society* (pp. 103–118). Rowley, MA: Newbury House.

Zimmerman, J. (1983). Introduction. In J. Zimmerman (Ed.), *The technological woman: Interfacing with tomorrow* (pp. 3–6). New York: Praeger.

chapter 5

Pedagogy, Emotion, and the Protocol of Care

Shannon Wilson
Miami University

The new space of electronic environments is often taken for "neutral ground" on which to build more equitable and productive communities. Numerous articles have been written citing the potential of what Hawisher and Sullivan (1997) call "e-spaces"—MOOs, listservs, e-mail, the World Wide Web, the information highway. I, too, have been caught up in this discourse of potential, advocating the integration of electronic communication in first-year writing courses. In response to the numerous accounts of the utopian potential of these e-spaces, the number of writing courses using interactive electronic discourse at the university where I work has grown exponentially in the last 3 years, forcing me to continuously question the impact of this technology on social and pedagogical configurations. To say that I suffer from either technophobia or technomania, the tidy binary delineated by Carole Stabile (1994), would be inaccurate. My position in relation to technology, and feminism, is much more complicated than either of these terms will allow.

Technophobia, as defined by Stabile (1994), consists of the "reactionary essentialist formations" of feminists who deny the possibility of positive change for women through technology (p. 1). Technomania, Stabile's opposing term, critiques feminist "political strategies framed around fragmentary and destabilized theories of identity" (p. 1). These theories, she argues, continue to reproduce privilege and partiality by producing a "new and reformed" subject who continues to support hegemonic interests (p. 135). Although Stabile's work deals primarily with reproductive technologies and genetic engineering, I believe her critique can be read for what it has to say about other forms of technology, particularly forms that shift the ways in which we imagine community and communication. Stabile's term "technomania," while useful in pointing to some of the tensions postmodern feminism needs to continually address, does not acknowledge the material analyses that these theories can facilitate. Her argument that those who embrace technology and postmodern theories ignore material reality denies the significant connections between discursive practice and material circumstances. The simple opposition of technophobia, a condition that can be seen as subsumed in the organic or material, seems to exclude many theories and practitioners from Stabile's reality. And so, as a good postmodern girl is bound to do, I problematize the binary. While I am a willing user and advocate of communications technology (and the postmodern theories that describe it), I strive to heed my frequent ambivalence about the actual practices that take place in electronic spaces, interrogating the ways in which these practices relate to the material positionings of participating (and absent) subjects. As a feminist educator, I want to maintain a critical relationship with technologies—technologies that both provide exciting possibilities for positive change and contain the tendency to reinscribe existing hierarchies.

This chapter recalls my first experience in an online educational environment and serves as a reminder to myself and others that when we ask our students to enter electronic spaces, we cannot ignore the hierarchies carried into and transplanted in new landscapes or cyberscapes. Sustaining a critical feminist evaluation of the pedagogical strategies utilized in "online" classrooms is necessary if the claimed potential of computer technology is to be realized. Using feminist rhetorical analysis to examine the issues of gender, power, and authority in an online English graduate seminar, I will look at the ways in which visions of online utopia inadvertently contributed to the reproduction of institutional hierarchies in an educational space where teachers of writing were introduced to the possibility of using electronic technology in their own classrooms.

On one level, this account is an addition to a number of cautionary tales about the reproduction of oppressive practices through potentially liberating technology, but I also aim to contribute an examination of the theoretical contradictions that can complicate any pedagogical project. I argue that my experience as a student in Alpha University, the environment I discuss, can be analyzed as a struggle between two contradictory theories of intersubjective exchange—one descending from Habermas's (1993) theory of an ideal speech community, and the other derived from a feminist "ethic of care" (Gilligan, 1982; Schweickart, 1990). These theoretical lenses help me to make sense of the dynamics that structured the electronic environment that introduced me to both the possibilities and dangers offered by the "new" public spheres that can be constructed in cyberspace. I use Habermas's theory of the public sphere and his understanding of an ideal speech community, along with feminist theories of the ethic of care, to identify underlying and unintentional forces in an environment where a protocol of care (Downing & Sosnoski, 1993) is proposed as a way to secure the nonhierarchical positionings that are desired as a means to radically revise what it means to participate in an academic community.

In 1993, Jim Sosnoski and David Downing invited graduate students to participate in Alpha University, an online project intended as a space in which traditional academic regimens would be deliberately set aside in order to cultivate a more caring, egalitarian community. An early experiment in online pedagogy, the course would take place, except for organizational and orientative meetings, solely in cyberspace, allowing students in two different states to interact in a graduate seminar. This new space provided the opportunity to reimagine what might take place in an educational environment. Most importantly, Sosnoski and Downing desired a community of equals who would work towards truth, reaching concurrence in order to solve problems—a system I read as consistent with Jurgen Habermas's (1993) theory of ideal discourse. Habermas's theory depends upon the "universal symmetry requirement"—exchange must take place between individuals in an environment where no "internal or external structures impose non-reciprocal obligations on participants or allow some to dominate others" (see Schweickart, 1990, p. 85). This description of an ideal speech situation is reflected in Downing and Sosnoski's description of power relations in Alpha University:

> Since [Alpha U.] is founded as an alternative to the modern American university system, its projects are not structured in the hierarchical, competitive ways upon which traditional academic endeavors are based....
>
> No one person [in Alpha U.] can or should have his or her say dominate. (pp. 2–3)[1]

Downing and Sosnoski recognize that we are "enculturated to behave aggressively and individualistically" and that this tendency will be an impediment to realizing their utopian community (p. 3). But there was not extended articulation and reflection about the ways people retain certain hierarchical positionings. As most of us find when teaching a course, there is little time for prolonged discussions with our students about the theories informing our pedagogical decisions. Sosnoski and Downing moved to disrupt hierarchies by instituting the protocol of care. But this protocol, I argue, although attractive in its gestures and descriptions of humane and productive interaction, also allowed for the reproduction of gendered hierarchies within the seminar.

Although Habermas was not the theoretical basis for Sosnoski and Downing's protocol or their vision of the electronic classroom, his description of noncoercive argument resonates with the kind of exchanges sanctioned by the protocol of care.

> [Alpha U.] communications are understood to be personal not impersonal. Quarreling is not encouraged.... [Alpha U.] makes no pretense to objectivity. Rather, intuitions and judgments based on personal experiences are encouraged except when they target other persons hurtfully. Refutations are discouraged. (Downing & Sosnoski, 1993, p. 2)

> Alpha U. has as its aim the creation of an environment conducive to the understanding of other human beings.... [A]ll of its projects ... are organized on the principle of care for others.... To share intellectual passion and excitement is to care for one another.... If we are to build an environment that is interpersonally healthy and vital, then joys and pains must be shared and negotiated. (p. 3)

By interrogating the implications of the competing theories I see in Alpha U.'s protocols and by examining my experience as a student in the electronic university of two dedicated and skilled cyberprofs, I want to illustrate the complex relationship between technology, gender, and power in a space where writing teachers were learning how to negotiate and structure electronic environments.

Alpha U. is the occasion for this analysis, but it is not my objective to merely critique the structure of this course or the pedagogy of Sosnoski and Downing. Indeed, these two scholars have produced and continue to produce extremely valuable perspectives on teaching, both in and out of cyberspace. My project is to use my experiences in this course as a way to more fully understand and reflect upon what informs my own pedagogical decisions, especially in moments that appear to be particularly promising in their potential for change.

UTOPIAN VISIONS: ALPHA UNIVERSITY AND THE PROTOCOL OF CARE

When Sosnoski and Downing introduced the Alpha University project, the term "protocol of care" was used frequently in talks and discussions about Alpha U. protocols that took place among seminar participants as well as in the more public academic space of departmental forums. This protocol became a major part of my understanding of how Alpha U. would transform academic exchange. Although the "protocol of care" is not explicitly defined in any of the remaining documents that I have from the course, a definition can be found in the journal *PRE/TEXT* that carries on many of the goals and projects of Alpha U. In a section of *PRE/TEXT* that delineates the ongoing Alpha U. project, five protocols are mentioned: reflection, care, concurrence, format, and professional courtesy (Vitanza, 1993, pp. 10–11). Care is defined here as a prohibition on responses that are "inflammatory or personal attack." The other protocol central in the Alpha U. seminar, and evoked as a part of the protocol of care, is concurrence, described in the seminar as "agreement to agree." Although concurrence is not a forced consensus, as a protocol it privileges common ground, utilizing difference in order to solve problems.[2] A central premise of the seminar was that we would "refrain from the rhetoric of rebuttal or refutation, if at all possible, and work in a more collaborative spirit" (p. 11).[3]

The objective of Sosnoski and Downing was to utilize the "new space" offered by the technology of electronic communication as a place to deploy a radical pedagogy that would remake old systems of academic exchange. I found these very attractive and admirable goals—and still do, but I have come to realize, as Billie Wahlstrom (1994) advises, the importance of interrogating the unacknowledged connections between the technology and the cultural hegemony from which it comes (p. 171). Recognizing that academic space is overwritten by destructive discursive and ideological structures, Sosnoski and Downing proposed a decolonization of academic space (and academic subjects) that would begin by colonizing cyberspace with a utopic pedagogical vision. By instituting a radical protocol and instructing graduate students (and other students of cyberspace) in this pedagogy, they imagined a counterhegemonic practice that could undo existing academic hierarchies. But as Lynn Worsham (1993) argues, "the work of decolonization cannot consist simply in a struggle for the recognition and legitimacy of an alternative pedagogy in terms of the dominant pedagogy, for such a struggle would inevitably neutralize the radical change promised by the alternative" (p. 126). As the Alpha U. experiment shows, without continuous, fundamental consideration of the ways alternative educational spaces are already written by dominant paradigms, radical re-vision of the ways we experience and reproduce the academic community is co-opted by existing systems of power. In the case of Alpha U., this co-optation occurred in spite of the expertise and sincerity of Sosnoski and Downing. Like any of us employed and constituted through institutional structures, Sosnoski and Downing faced residual hegemonic forces that continued to shape pedagogical practices intended to undermine existing hierarchies. By reading two contradictory theoretical legacies—one descending from Habermas and the other a relative of the feminist "ethic of care"—as part of a larger social and historical scene of this course, I work to recognize the ways pedagogy is implicated in larger institutional systems.[4]

Habermas (1993) theorized a public space, separate from spheres of state and economic interest, where subjects could engage in discursive political participation about common concerns. As feminist scholar Nancy Fraser (1993) has argued, however, Habermas's utopic vision of public discourse, while useful, is flawed by its failure to acknowledge that participants in public exchange are limited (in access and effectiveness) by stratified social positions or identities. In theory, the participants of the ideal speech community or public sphere enter as equals and their discourse is heard objectively by other participants. This community of symmetrically positioned participants, however, cannot be fully realized in the context of a society structured already by asymmetrical power relations. Fraser contends that theories of the public should be modified to "render visible the ways in which social inequality taints deliberation within publics" and to "show how inequality affects relations among publics…, how publics are differently empowered or segmented, and how some are involuntarily enclaved or subordinated to others" (p. 27). A theory such as this would make demands on pedagogies that attempt to achieve an ideal environment for academic exchange by imagining a space where hierarchy and privilege could be suspended or transcended. Although bodies "disappear" when academic work moves online, the ways gender, race, class, and academic position (to name the obvious) shape discursive exchange cannot simply be overcome or put aside. The ways we speak/write and hear/read are thoroughly shaped by our experiences as embodied subjects. In addition, the degree of someone's power/voice in cyberspace is determined in part by the degree of technical skill a person possesses and even more so by access to the technology itself. Obviously, the various ways members of the Alpha U. seminar were socially and technologically located, beyond and within the boundaries of the electronic environment, had an impact on the shape and outcome of conversations—no matter how sincere the desire to correct or erase inequitable positions. In the following section, I will look specifically at gendered power relations and the ways the legacy of institutionalized hierarchies was retained and reenacted in a theoretically neutral space.[5] As Takayoshi (1994) has argued, "in moving away from traditional discourse forms that oppress and marginalize women without analyzing the ideologies that inform their formation and staying power, we run the risk of those ideologies becoming dominant once again in another forum" (p. 21). Reading the "we" in Takayoshi's argument as instructors, potential instructors, and student participants, it is important to emphasize that we all need to reflect upon and learn from pedagogical experiences and the mechanisms that resist our efforts to develop more equitable environments.

Although 10 of the 27 members of the Alpha U. seminar were women, the power to organize, move, or delete discourse within the overarching system was held by men (the instructor/editors and two graduate-student assistants).[6] As the following description of the feminism forum (one of several discussion clusters in the Alpha U. seminar) will show, within certain conversations the power to define terms and judge whether or not discourse was appropriate within the Alpha U. community reflected traditional academic hierarchies. Contrary to the intentions of Sosnoski and Downing, the protocol of care inadvertently evoked gendered behavior expectations that can be read through a feminist ethic of care. The call to "care" reinscribed asymmetrical power relations by positioning members in the two required locations—the "caregivers" and the "cared-for." This configuration undermined the goal of eliminating hierarchy and, therefore, compromised the entire utopic vision of Alpha U.

THE FEMINISM FORUM

To attempt a more concrete demonstration of the maintenance of asymmetrical relationships along gender lines, I want to look at a particular segment of the Alpha U. seminar, the feminism forum.[7] The feminism forum was an offshoot of a discussion about feminism and cultural studies. It took place over several weeks; defining feminisms and feminist agendas was the overt subject matter. It was in this forum that the protocol of care was put to the test—a test it ultimately failed when the discussion reached a point of crisis that resulted in a decision by the instructor/editors to remove several messages from the Alpha U. space.[8]

The feminism forum was initiated by Dan, one of the graduate student editors, who thought there had been so much good discussion about feminism in other areas of the seminar that it deserved its own forum.[9] Dan begins the forum with a post from Matt, a post extracted from another forum. The dynamics of the feminism forum are shaped by the nature of its beginnings, as well as by discourse about feminism that takes place before its inception. In a prefeminism forum discussion, Dan, the initiator of the feminism forum, defends Matt in a post where he corrects another seminar member, Sarah, for her "unjustified" response to Matt's definition of feminism/feminists. Dan instructs Sarah to read previous posts by Matt that demonstrate that he is not antifeminist. The post Sarah initially responds to construes feminism as an obsession with a simple binary understanding of gender and describes feminists as those with a desire to merely invert gender hierarchies. In this post, Matt avoids responsibility for these claims by attributing them to the feminists he knows and by citing his relative ignorance of feminism at large. He ends by asking others in the seminar to suggest readings that would complicate (and possibly correct) his understanding of feminism. Sarah responds with the requested suggestions for reading, commenting that she is happy to help him expand his knowledge of feminism because she finds his current definition "scary." Her entry can be read as conversational and friendly, but her use of the word *scary* seems to trigger a defensive mode of exchange, hence Dan's defense of Matt. Following up on Dan's correction of Sarah, Matt writes what is to become the feminism forum's inaugural post in order to "clarify" his position vis-à-vis feminism for Sarah.

While Dan decides to begin the feminism forum with Matt's response to Sarah, Sarah's original post is not included in the forum—a purely editorial decision. Because of the absence of Sarah's first message, Matt has to quote her "from memory" (which he does incorrectly), even though there is an accessible textual record of what she has said in another section of Alpha U.'s electronic space. Matt ends his post with a barrage of questions and the request that Sarah and "others"—meaning women—help him understand. In some ways this exchange (and the pattern of much of the feminism forum) reminds me of a platonic dialogue with the men in the position of Socrates, relaying their experiences and asking questions that they feel they know the answers to in order to manipulate the terms and outcome of the dialogue and the status of truth. Looking at the dialogue in these terms makes the power relations clear; those answering the questions, following the lead of those questioning, are the ones being schooled.

The men in the forum continued to ask for "dialogue" with the women specifically, reinforcing a binary, hierarchical arrangement. The dialogue was set up in such a way that the men were asking the questions and defining the problems, and women were asked to supply the answers. What constituted an acceptable answer, however, was an important indication of the power relations inherent in this exchange. The men compared, "innocently," the oppression of women with child/parent relationships and with being short or bald, and continued to look only at a simple man/woman dichotomy. Women in the forum tried to complicate the conversation by introducing the importance of differences in the situations of various groups of women, but these responses were not taken up. In addition, one of the men uploaded (a technological feat that was impossible for most members of the seminar) an entire seminar paper about the "female writing voice" and asked for feedback on his project. The incredible amount of time and work required by this kind of feedback was not acknowledged, nor was there serious engagement of questions that challenged this participant to consider the politics of his academic use of female student writing or his choice of this topic in the absence of serious study of feminist scholarship.

From the initiation of the feminism forum, Matt's post emphasizing his need to engage in discourse about feminism (and a male position in general) was privileged as the concerns of the women participants (and the material conditions of women in general) were manipulated, erased, and/or ignored. In terms of space alone, the men in the forum generated 21 entries and the women 12. The posts of the men were sometimes in support of other men in the forum, but usually directed at women. In general, the entries of the men were substantially longer. There was little if any exchange among the women. (In fact, the only place in the feminism forum where a woman comes to the defense of another woman is in the portion of the forum that is removed.) In addition, the women were asked to answer the men's questions about feminism while being invited to support "post-feminism," a concept as nebulous as feminism, but seemingly less threatening to some of the men. The men asked for academic guidance explicitly, emotional support and validation implicitly. While on the surface the male participants produced a rhetorical ethos that positioned them as benevolent, willing-to-learn members of a community interested in ending gender bias, the actual exchange demonstrated that these men ultimately sought authorization of the positions they already held and felt comfortable in. What was the significance of the men constantly asking the women for definitions, responses, evaluations, and validation? This, I believe, put women into the traditional role of "caregiver," while the men were soliciting care, replicating traditional hierarchies.

The women in the forum were positioned simultaneously as the caregivers and the maternal authorities, and it became clear that the conversation was not about the ways men could be involved in projects, politics, and practices that could produce more equitable gender relations. In what ways does this kind of caring keep the women in service of the men? How do we intervene in such gendered patterns? Sosnoski and Downing set up protocols they felt would create a more democratic, less painful, and more productive academic environment; however, because of the ways "care" is gendered in our histories and everyday lives, the protocol of care itself contradicted their goal for nonhierarchical exchange. As Schweickart (1990) recognizes, valuing care in any systematic way, setting up a protocol or ethic of care does not eliminate asymmetrical relationships. In fact, it insures inequitable relationships between participants because "the caring relationship is essentially an asymmetrical relation between two modalities of subjectivity—between the one caring and the one cared-for" (p. 88). When women are socialized to be the "caregivers" and men to be the "cared-for," at least on an emotional level, we need to ask what are the outcomes for students in educational environments such as Alpha University.

Now I don't propose that the role of "caregiver" is a powerless or a useless one, but it does reproduce many of the problems that women have faced in the academy. It is, for the most part, a service role and one that can inhibit women from furthering their own goals and pursuing their own questions. According to the ethic of care, the cared-for is "free to pursue [his] own projects freely and vigorously and share accounts of them spontaneously" with the caregiver (Schweickart, 1990, p. 89). What the caregiver receives in return for her caring is the engagement of the cared-for, more knowledge about what he is striving for so that she can better contribute to his needs (Schweickart, 1990, pronouns my own). This situation is not necessarily negative if the relationship is between a student and a teacher. A teacher in the role of caregiver, with a responsive student as cared-for, should be continually "sustained and invigorated" by the exchange. In addition, a teacher should be involved in other relationships where she is also receiving care from others to enable her to carry out her own projects. But when the cared-for and the caregivers are supposed to be in symmetrical relationships, both pursuing their own questions and projects, an asymmetrical caregiver/cared-for relationship breaks down and it therefore becomes a burden for the ones who are put in the caregiver role. Even if the care-giver role is initially accepted, there is a point at which the caregiver will feel trapped. Plus, as in any caring relationship, if the cared-for does not utilize or acknowledge the care given, the caring is likely to deteriorate (Schweickart, 1990). *Deterioration* is a pleasant word for what eventually happened in the feminism forum.

I want to suggest that the "problems" that occurred in the feminism forum happened when the women in the seminar attempted to break out of the role of caregiver. During the exchanges in this forum, the men, as was pointed out by more than one participant, continued to shape the discussion only in terms of their own needs—to further their own projects, to make them better teachers, to fend off any varieties of feminism that seemed too threatening or dangerous. For the most part, the women in the conversation entertained the questions of the men, listening and giving responses and positive encouragement. This broke down, however, when some of the women began to acknowledge their frustration with the men's seemingly self-centered explorations. Despite some clear signs that the women in the Alpha U. seminar were not satisfied with the exchange in the feminism forum—only 5 of the 10 women participated at all and of these 5, two eventually dropped out—the conversation continued in this frustrating pattern.[10] At several points, the women pointed out that the men were reducing complicated issues, refusing to deal with the difficult questions themselves, and feigning ignorance in order to remain in the questioning mode. When the men continued to push for answers not being given, one woman suggested that the men's examination of feminism had more to do with self-serving interests than with an interest in ending oppression, and another remarked that the discussion seemed an attempt by the men to control feminism through definition and, by extension, to control women. The responses of the men did not change except to get increasingly defensive. Finally, when a woman, obviously fed-up, acknowledged her own questions and frustrations in language that was no longer patient, instructive, and nurturing, the forum became explosive and eventually no "caring" was evident.

The explosive exchanges that followed, marked by their overt anger and volatile language, were deleted from the conversation. The decision to extract the messages was made by Downing and Sosnoski, the instructor/editors, who had been monitoring but not participating in the feminism forum. Although Sosnoski and Downing removed the posts after consultation with the authors (meetings in which the authors expressed embarrassment and regret about the entries), some members of the seminar contested this decision—questioning both the overt reinstatement of hierarchy and the appropriateness of deleting a portion of our collaborative textual environment. Ultimately, an informal vote was taken and it was decided that the posts would be taken from the "public" seminar record but be distributed to all seminar members.

Although the editors did not say as much, I suppose the entries were construed as rhetorically violent, emotional, and irrational. Significantly, four of these posts were written by women, two by men. The messages did contain exchanges that might qualify as "personal attack" or as "inflammatory," and it is understandable that those involved would desire to have the exchange stricken from the record. But with this censure, both self-imposed and supported by institutionalized authorities, a significant element of the discourse was erased. The pain and anger felt and written by a woman no longer willing to maintain the role of caregiver and the appropriate emotional decorum is denied a place in the record. Even in the absence of her words, it is important to ask whether the entries that prompted her response—tempered, "reasonable" entries steeped in skepticism and self-serving short-sightedness—were less violent. Were emotions experienced as a result of a replicated and unacknowledged system of domination expected to remain silent beneath the surface? What did this "breakdown" demonstrate about the protocol of care and its ability to reduce the symbolic violence in academic exchange?

IDEAL SPEECH COMMUNITIES AND A PROTOCOL OF CARE

The desire to eliminate violence in our academic lives was an important component of Downing and Sosnoski's conception of Alpha U. And it is not hard to understand their discomfort, disappointment, and decision to erase the painful entries that were the culmination of the feminism forum. This erasure, however, brought to the surface hierarchical positions that had remained latent for much of the semester, revealing that the attempt to promote productive and caring communities within electronic environments was more complicated that any of us had realized. In this moment, the difficulty of simultaneously using and abdicating authority in order to create more equitable conditions for intellectual work became painfully clear.

Like Habermas, Downing and Sosnoski imagine, even posit, an ideal situation for the exchange of ideas and the solving of problems. Habermas's plan to achieve consensus through an Ideal speech situation is unconsciously echoed in the design of Alpha University. Habermas (1993) describes argument that does not involve coercion, intimidation, deception, or suppression of contrary points of view (see Schweickart, 1990). Downing and Sosnoski propose the use of concurrence, integral to a system of collaboration, compassion, and commitment, as opposed to refutation, the type of exchange they believe maintains the hierarchical and oppressive traditional academy. Participants in Alpha U. were expected to exchange ideas and put forth propositions without the type of aggressive, domineering discourse demonstrated and encouraged by existing academic structures, thus eliminating domination. While the goal of "universal symmetry" is desirable, the denial or erasure of the real social relations that shape any discourse undermines the possibility of achieving such a community, unless admission is limited to an already select group. Habermas, for example, does not consider a very diverse group of participants in his work on the public sphere, and his formulations of ideal speech communities reproduced the marginalization of voices not sanctioned by traditional positions of power (i.e., women, the poor). As Joan Landes (1988) points out, the work of Habermas is valuable, but in need of reconsideration, a re-vision that would acknowledge the significance of groups not originally figured as participants in public discourse. If we want, as I believe Downing and Sosnoski do, a conversation between people of various social positionings, and not simply a different kind of conversation among the same narrow group, our theories and our protocols must be examined for the remnant inequities that impede our goals.

An attempt to transform academic work by placing it within a system structured by an ethic of care is understandable and appealing. But as Schweickart (1990) articulates, any theory or environment attempting to institute an ethic of care cannot ignore power relations. Although Downing and Sosnoski acknowledge the difficulties of pre-existing hierarchies in ways that Habermas originally did not, the protocol of care obscures these inequities by mandating care and villainizing refutation without careful explanation as to what constitutes each. It is implicit, therefore, that refutation and caring be mutually recognized by all members of the community, but this is ultimately not possible, as different social positionings generate different definitions. Did the participants in the Alpha U. environment expect that men and women, for example, would demonstrate care in different ways? Is a blunt note posted by a woman seen as more aggressive or uncaring than the same note entered by a man? Were women's responses more nurturing, qualified, tentative, and probing, than those entered by men? And are women sanctioned when they break out of this mold? Measuring the emotional content and impact of discourse is a very complicated process. If convention is not constantly called into question, the condescension and aggression in a "low key" message is left uncensored, while more obviously "emotional" entries are sanctioned for breaking protocol.

SCHOOLING EMOTION

In her article, "Emotion and Pedagogic Violence," Lynn Worsham (1993) examines the symbolic violence implied in any teaching and learning situation. She argues that we are educated emotionally by violence embedded in institutions such as school, the workplace, and the family. Worsham also says that violences occurring in these sites are pedagogies of emotion that structure an individual's relation to the social order as much as or more than the "factual" information communicated. My experience in Alpha U. instructed me through emotions from the first time I entered a reply. Although the theory of Alpha U. taught me that the space would be nonhierarchical and caring, my emotional education taught a contradictory lesson. It became apparent that even though we had been encouraged to break dichotomies such as emotion/rationality and personal/professional, these dichotomies remained implicit in our conversations and were overtly reasserted when the tension broke into admissions of anger. Not only were exchanges an emotional experience, but the kinds of emotion allowed (and not allowed) to be openly expressed in the Alpha U. forums were equally pedagogical.

Worsham's (1993) examination of emotion and pedagogy is especially concerned with the inclination of contemporary theoretical discourse to erase the category of violence by focusing exclusively on forms of pleasure and consent. The theory structuring Alpha University participated in this erasure. Alpha U. proposed to heal pain through nonhierarchical exchange and care. Rhetorical violence was allegedly staved off by a caring protocol, and participants were invited to bring suffering experience *elsewhere* to a forum where a collaborative remedy could be found. The description of the Alpha U. project states that "because suffering cannot wait for theory, many painful interpersonal situations related to the current institutional and professional practices need to be addressed" (Downing & Sosnoski, 1993, p. 3). However, suffering that existed as a result of the dynamics of the Alpha U. environment itself was not acknowledged. The violence in any pedagogical situation may not be as obvious as the daily "real-world" occurrences of violence that we are subjected to, but the emotions entailed in such violence are very real and related to the pedagogy of emotion that educates subjects in every area of life. In spaces outside the actual Alpha U. seminar, some participants discussed the reproduction and reinforcement of an invisible emotional regimen.

> Ever since I got [involved with Alpha U.] I have found it painful to know that there is one more space in my life, a huge space, even eternal space if Jim and David save those voices forever, where I cannot talk about what is important to me, feelings. My past is not allowed there. My anger at not fitting in the conversation is not allowed there....

This quote comes from an e-mail exchange I had with one of the participants following the Alpha U. seminar. The male speaker of this quote demonstrates the damaging effect of reinscribed hierarchies even for those in a traditionally privileged position (white male). This person, although a member of the seminar, did not participate in the feminism forum but was aware of the conversation, and his comment is, in part, a response to the decision of the editors to censor the entries. This person's anger and frustration at not feeling able to acknowledge and discuss his own emotions reveals that the issue of symbolic violence is one to be considered, even if it remains silent. As teachers and participants, we need to consider the emotional impact of the pedagogical situations we sanction and enforce through various protocols. In Alpha U., the protocol of care only sanctioned the confessions of pain experienced elsewhere and safely relayed in carefully controlled prose. The protocol broke down when the emotions shaping the immediate pedagogical experience finally surfaced. The feigned separation between emotion and intellect, a remnant of traditional academic exchange, was lost; silent violence was replaced by online confrontations. Because these violent exchanges were extracted, it became clear that certain kinds of emotion were permissible and others were not.

Worsham's (1993) warning about the traps of radical pedagogy seems especially salient when considering the potential of electronic spaces like Alpha U.: "The new commitment to pedagogy may redeploy key distinctions that mystify the work of decolonization—in particular, the distinctions between public and private and between reason and emotion"—and the gendered authority of these distinctions (p.123). The role of emotion in our pedagogical decisions and experiences remains underexamined and therefore susceptible to judgments based in traditional ways of validating or denying certain affective scripts. How to negotiate between the immediate needs of various students and the long-term goals of a pedagogical project is an issue that most of us face in our own classrooms. The situation faced by Sosnoski and Downing, and the members of the seminar, was exceedingly difficult, and I cannot say that I would not have made the same decisions had I been in their place. The potential to break down boundaries and create more egalitarian communities exists, but we must continuously resist the temptation to fall back on established dichotomies and convenient blind spots when tensions arise. As difficult as it is to work through the conditioning of academic structures, attempts to rethink the relationships between intellect and emotion, especially "outlaw" emotions such as anger, are crucial in our efforts to remake public spaces.

Even though our experiences within the academy instruct us to maintain the distinction between rational and emotional, is it really to our benefit to maintain this false distinction? Sosnoski and Downing continue work that moves towards more widespread recognition of this dichotomy as unproductive, and their efforts have opened up spaces for people such as myself to ask further questions about our own experiences. Aren't all of our "rational" thoughts and arguments produced as a result of or in service of our desires and emotions? And what emotions are allowed and for whom? Emotions such as anger, rage, and bitterness are still seen as inappropriate. They are not sanctioned/are penalized in a number of ways: they can be ignored, responded to with carefully rational entries that do not acknowledge the emotion or experience, or they can be taken out of the forum entirely. All of these responses serve to school emotion and reproduce current hierarchies as the dominant pedagogy "refuses the expression of anger by subordinates [i.e., students, women, minorities], and it refuses to acknowledge that sometimes and in some contexts active bitterness might be a move away from self-deception and hence a moral achievement. [The pedagogy of emotion] schools anger to turn inward to become silent rage or passive bitterness where the energy for political insight can be consumed in the pathos of the personal" (Worsham, 1993, p. 129).

Anger, specifically, is devalued by the dominant social codes, but sometimes anger cuts to the core of the matter and reveals the connections between the "rational" and the "emotional." Although responses that are overtly angry can be more inflammatory than those steeped in anger but couched in "objective" rhetoric, I am not convinced that feigning to be "rational" or neutral always facilitates the most effective communication—or erases the emotional impact of a response. In the feminism forum, frustration and anger—important aspects of the issue being discussed—were suppressed from the beginning. Instead of the forum acknowledging and working through these emotions, acknowledging the relevance of remaining hierarchies, and negotiating the pain of the collaborative experience, we sustained a polite and reserved conversation, enacting the roles of cared-for and caregiver. The protocol of care maintained a benevolent veneer that left issues festering beneath the surface. When one of the women in the forum came out with her anger—in language so obviously angry that it could not be ignored—the legitimacy of these entries was questioned by herself and others. I believe the justification for the deletion of her voice relied in part upon the old distinction between emotion and rationality, even though the angry participant was not irrational or illogical in the content or occasion of her expression. She admitted that the responses of another writer had made her angry and attempted to explain why. She qualified her anger by stating that it was not meant to declare her general hatred of the people involved, but to inform them of her feelings and how the actions they had taken provoked those feelings. She was still responding to the continual requests of the men in the forum for advice on how not to offend anyone with their rhetoric. In fact, you could say that this writer was still in the "caregiver" role; she was still attempting to give instruction and guidance to those who had positioned themselves as in need. But by acknowledging her own stake, her own needs, and by breaking out of the benevolent persona that the caregiver is supposed to maintain, she disrupted the dominant social codes. Viewed as a breech of contract, a violation of the protocol of care, the ensuing exchanges were eradicated from the forum.

Because it became a place where emotion was regulated, Alpha U. replicated the dominant pedagogy that deals with emotion as something to be "educated, reeducated, or miseducated according to what pedagogy expressly establishes as appropriate, reasonable, and justifiable" (Worsham, 1993, p. 128). This system was unable to dismantle the traditional university set up where "in class" the discussion must remain in the "academic mode" in order for ideas to be recognized as productive and legitimate. Only in the halls can personal experience and the emotions that go along with it be recognized as relevant to the material at hand. The false separation between the discussions that take place in and out of the classroom is replicated by a system that delegates an "appropriate" space for emotion and personal connections to the material. This is unfortunate because I know that there have been many times when it has taken a discussion in the hall to help me fully understand the implications of the readings being "covered" in class. It may not be as efficient to acknowledge and allow for the combination of the personal/emotional and the academic/rational, but maintaining these as dichotomies reproduces a system that Alpha U.'s goals claimed to want to undermine. Because the same protocols of "appropriateness" found in the traditional academy carried over into Alpha U., it was difficult not to reproduce the types of academic discussions and existing hierarchies.

CONCLUSION

> This is a moment in history when we need to act collectively before the electronic revolution we are undergoing invisibly reinstitutionalizes us and reshapes our professional conduct. (Sosnoski, 1995, p. 174)

I want to reiterate that the intent of this paper is *not* to dismiss or demolish the valuable work accomplished in Alpha U. or the admirable goals of the protocol of care. Even though Sosnoski and Downing no longer employ the protocol of care that I discuss here, their attempt to create a space in which people could interact carefully and collaboratively is a move that creates possibility.[11] In fact, the seminar I have discussed launched my interest in cyberspace and prompted me to begin incorporating online exchange into my own classrooms in an attempt to create discursive exchange in a forum unlike, although related to, the classroom. And without dismissing the pain that the seminar caused for many involved, I would say that the conflict I experienced in Alpha U. allowed me to formulate questions about the usefulness of utopian visions that I can carry into cyberspaces where I hold a more dominant position. We all desire that our classrooms can facilitate the visions we have of a more perfect world, but it is important to question to what extent we can assert an environment that is empowering and democratic for all participants and whether utopia by definition must be nonhierarchical and free of conflict. What are alternatives to ideals that can only prompt the suppression of conflict in order to sustain the utopic illusion?

Foucault's (1986) essay, "Of Other Spaces," delineates a utopia/heterotopia distinction that may be one way to rethink the gap between imagined perfection and the material complexities of working for change. As Hawisher and Sullivan (1997) demonstrate, the application of Foucault's terms has interesting possibilities for consideration of electronic spaces. Foucault defines utopias as "sites with no real place... present[ing] society itself in a perfected form" (p. 24). "Sites with no real place" is a phrase that echoes the way cyberspaces are often described, with these placeless spaces offered as the sites where we can live in a perfected state. This description also evokes the kind of postmodern theorizing that Stabile (1994) is concerned about when she describes the technomanics' heteroglossia, "feminist pluralism's public face—the mythic and dematerialized belief that subjects can speak in very different languages, from entirely different social and cultural positions, yet somehow work together" (152). Although "perfected forms" and perfected spaces are tempting in their utopic promise, to imagine such sites—cyberspaces or e-spaces, in this case—as disconnected from the various locations from which they are accessed and created is to maintain a dangerous fiction. Possibilities for change are negated by the denial of material circumstances. Foucault's heterotopia, therefore, may provide a more useful metaphor for describing the active struggle that takes place in and shapes cyberspaces.

Heterotopias are countersites, "places that do exist and that are formed in the very founding of society"; they are places where a variety of other sites can be "represented, contested, and inverted" (Foucault, 1986, p. 24). To describe or imagine a heterotopic space is to acknowledge the "simultaneously mythic and real contestation of the space[s] in which we live" (p. 24), allowing for both idealized visions and the acknowledgment of conflict and crisis that arises in attempts to subvert dominant power structures. If we cannot acknowledge conflict and imperfection, the ideologies that inform our practices can go unscrutinized. Spaces for public exchange must be understood and reshaped through constant negotiation of tensions, tensions that when acknowledged and utilized can lead to positive action. The idea that society (or even the classroom) can take a single perfected form leads to the denial of difference; attempting to form this kind of space requires "making discursive assimilation a condition for participation in public debate" (Fraser, 1993, p. 17). Instead of striving for such a utopia, it seems more politically advantageous to legitimize what Fraser calls a "multiplicity of publics," in which various groups can come together, negotiate meaning, and form temporary strategic alliances with other publics in order to counter hegemonic systems.

Multiple publics cannot be described as "utopias" in Foucault's sense of the word. Rather, they are more like heterotopias, found in every culture but in various and multiple forms, shifting in form and function according to the historical moment, capable of bringing together several sites that are in themselves incompatible, and able to expose the illusory nature of other real spaces (Foucault, 1986). The idea of heterotopias resists denials of difference and conflict because it acknowledges that a "heterotopic site is not freely accessible like a [theoretically] public space" (p. 26); in order to enter, one must have permission, make certain gestures, and/or submit to specific rites or purifications. Heterotopias that seem to have pure and simple admission often hide their exclusions. "Everyone can enter into these heterotopic sites, but in fact that is only an illusion: we think we enter where we are, by the very fact that we enter, excluded" (p. 26). This description, although difficult in its turns to grasp, points to the illusions of inclusion that structured the Alpha U. experiment. Exposing the illusions is a necessary element of working for communities that resist traditional exclusions and hierarchies.

Without continual reflection upon the theories that we use to sustain our utopian visions, efforts to subvert dominant systems can end up reinforcing them. Feminist pedagogies of nurturance such as the ethic of care receive their authority from dominant discourse and its ideology of nurturing that keeps gender dualities in place (Worsham, 1993). Because it is not possible to "insulate special discursive arenas from the effects of societal inequality" (Fraser, 1993, p. 14), Habermas (1993), and in turn Downing and Sosnoski (1993), can be seen as complicit in the reproduction of domination. As we work within institutions, we are all complicit in their reproduction, yet we do not need to give up the idea of care or throw out Habermas's theory for an ideal speech community and desire for a reconstituted public sphere. Instead, we need to deal with the flaws and contradictions in these theories, constantly working and adjusting to meet the needs of particular persons and projects. The reproduction of dominant ideology that occurred in the Alpha U. seminar (and that likely occurs in my own attempts at online pedagogy) was not done maliciously or even consciously, but as an effect of the ever present difficulty of recognizing privilege in situations we want to see as equitable. Although I embrace the potential of electronic environments, I want to remind myself, as a feminist teacher and a member of these communities, of the complexities of the systems and of the baggage that I bring with me when I enter and consequently shape electronic spaces.

NOTES

[1] The document I quote from here and throughout was a "work in progress" for Sosnoski and Downing. More finalized thoughts on these matters can be found in their many publications and ongoing work. I quote this document only in order to demonstrate the pedagogical scene that students of the seminar encountered. This document was significant in the expectations and terms of participation that it set up for the course.

[2] For a more extensive discussion of concurrence, see Sosnoski's Chapter 14, "Critical Concurrence," in *Modern Skeletons in Postmodern Closets* (1995).

[3] A more elaborate description of the protocol of care and a discussion of its origins can be found in Sosnoski & Downing, 1994.

[4] I want to make clear that neither Habermas nor a feminist ethic of care is explicitly cited by Sosnoski and Downing as a theoretical basis for their proposed protocol. As mentioned earlier, at the time of the seminar there was no discussion of the theoretical underpinning of their pedagogy. In my discussions with Sosnoski and Downing, I have found that the protocol of care was developed, in large part, from Milton Mayeroff's *On Caring* (1971) and influenced by German philosopher Martin Heidegger. In addition, both Downing and Sosnoski are critical of Habermas's theories.

[5] Although the focus of this paper is gender, I don't intend that this is the only social category that would yield useful and needed analysis.

[6] In theory, all students were supposed to be able to manipulate and arrange certain aspects of the electronic environment. This was, however, a new medium for many students and the uneven technical abilities of participants contributed to gendered distribution of power.

[7] My arguments here are indebted to a collaborative final project Cari Allyn Brooks and I wrote to fulfill part of the requirements of the Alpha U. seminar. I would like to acknowledge Cari for her important role in the initial version of this paper, specifically for her detailed empirical examination of the feminism forum.

[8] Because participants in the seminar being discussed made an agreement not to directly quote the online exchanges, the following account of Alpha U. forums must be given without direct quotes. I will, therefore, attempt to paraphrase exchanges with as much accuracy as possible.

[9] "Dan" is a pseudonym, as are subsequent names of seminar participants.

[10] It should also be noted that less than half of the men in the seminar participated in this exchange.

[11] Sosnoski and Downing also continue to work and reflect on the complexities of on-line pedagogy. Sosnoski is currently managing the TicToc Project, conceived to "explore and perhaps defuse tensions and anxieties created by online learning situations" (see Dorwick, 1996). In addition, a forthcoming edition of *Works and Days*, a journal edited by Downing, will discuss this project extensively.

REFERENCES

Dorwick, K. (1996, July 1). *The TicToc Project* [Online]. Available: http://www.uic.edu/kdworwick/dissertation/tictoc.htm

Downing, D., & Sosnoski, J. (1993). *Teaching in electronic schools: The CYCLES Project.* Unpublished manuscript.

Foucault, M. (1986). Of other spaces. *Diacritics*, *16*(2), 22–27.

Fraser, N. (1993). Rethinking the public sphere: A contribution to the critique of actually existing democracy. In B. Robbins (Ed.), *The phantom public sphere* (pp. 1–32). Minneapolis, MN: University of Minnesota Press.

Habermas, J. (1993). *The structural transformation of the public sphere: An inquiry into a category of bourgeois society* (T. Burger, Trans.). Cambridge, MA: MIT Press.

Hawisher, G. E., & Sullivan P. (1997). Women on the networks: Searching for e-spaces of their own. In S. C. Jarratt & L. Worsham (Eds.), *In other words: Feminism and composition* (pp. 172–197). New York: Modern Language Association.

Landes, J. B. (1988). *Women and the public sphere in the age of the French Revolution.* New York: Cornell University Press.

Mayeroff, M. (1971). *On caring.* New York: Harper and Row.

Sosnoski, J. J. (1995). *Modern skeletons in postmodern closets: A cultural studies alternative.* Charlottesville, VA: University of Press of Virginia.

Sosnoski, J. J., & Downing D. (1994). The Protocol of Care in the Cycles Project. *JMMLA*, *27*(1), 75–84.

Schweickart, P. P. (1990). Reading, teaching, and the ethic of care. In S. L. Gabriel & I. Smithson (Eds.), *Gender in the classroom: Power and pedagogy* (pp. 78–95). Chicago: University of Illinois Press.

Stabile, C. A. (1994). *Feminism and the technological fix.* Manchester, England, and New York: Manchester University Press.

Takayoshi, P. (1994). Building new networks from the old: Women's experiences with electronic communications. *Computers and Composition: An International Journal for Teachers of Writing, 11*, 21–36.

Vitanza, V. J. (Ed.). (1993). Introduction. *PRE/TEXT, 14*(1-2), 7–13.

Wahlstrom, B. J. (1994). Communication and technology: Defining a feminist presence in research and practice. In C. L. Selfe & S. Hilligoss (Eds.), *Literacy and computers: The complications of teaching and learning with technology* (pp.171–185). New York: Modern Language Association.

Worsham, L. (1993). Emotion and pedagogical violence. *Discourse, 15*(2), 119–148.

chapter 6

Writing (Without) the Body: Gender and Power in Networked Discussion Groups

Donna LeCourt
Colorado State University

> On the computer you can't tell who I am (well, most of you anyway) and so does this anonymity mean that we are equal in this discourse?... is there anyone here who has more Power? Is power important???? Just wondering. (Socks, personal communication, November 16, 1994)

The question my student poses above gets at the heart of my concern in this essay: Do online discussion groups alter the power relationships of the classroom and society? As a feminist teacher concerned with providing my female students alternatives to potentially oppressive discourses, this question is particularly pertinent. Given the analyses of the ways in which classroom discourse (West & Zimmerman, 1983), academic writing (Flynn, 1988; Lamb, 1991), and linguistic practice itself (Lakoff, 1975; Spender, 1985; Tannen, 1990) serve either to silence women and/or create subject positions for them that are accorded less power in society, I can't help but wonder whether online classroom discussions are simply more of the same. In describing online discussions to my students as "open" and "less controlled" spaces for dialogue, am I simply providing another way for my female students' voices and ideas to be silenced or ridiculed? Do online discussions create any possibility for resisting the ideological forces that seem consistently to position women's contributions as "lesser" in both my classroom and society?

Unfortunately, current research provides little insight into these questions of how gender and power might play themselves out in the use of online discussions in the classroom. For some, online discussion groups create more egalitarian contexts in which marginalized voices can be given equal space (see, for example, Butler & Kinneavy, 1991; Cooper & Selfe, 1990), while for others this new textual space merely reproduces the ideological, discursive spaces present within society (see, for example, Hawisher & Selfe, 1991; Janangelo, 1991). The disparity between these positions emerges in feminist analyses as well. Relying on what Eldred and Hawisher (1995) label the "equalization phenomenon," many feminist arguments assert that the ability for all participants to post equally in an environment that "eliminates social differences" allows for previously silenced voices to be heard (p. 347). These silenced voices bring with them alternative forms of knowledge and perspectives that have the potential to not only resist, but also alter traditional power hierarchies (see, for example, Flores, 1990; Selfe, 1990). Such presumptions about the ability for the presence of women's voices to be a site of resistance, however, have also been questioned. Because of the way discussion technologies provide explicit markings of gender through names or more subtle content-cues in anonymous postings, these critiques point out that women's voices may be subjected to the same hierarchical positioning they are accorded in other realms, or even in some cases, in sexual harassment online (see, for example, Matheson, 1991; Takayoshi, 1994). Similarly, speculations that networked discussions provide a connective, collaborative, and personalized environment amenable to women's preferred way of knowing and communicating (see, for example, Flores, 1990; Jessup, 1991) have been directly contradicted by research in other disciplines, which point to how the reduced social context of such groups actually have the effect of depersonalizing the communication process (Takayoshi, 1994; see also Forman, 1994).

The contradictory positions and research findings in these feminist discussions are admittedly frustrating to those of us concerned with providing our women students with a space in which they can potentially subvert the power relationships that silence them. I want to suggest in this essay, however, that one reason we are presented with such contradictory results may be because we are asking the wrong questions. Such contradictions are not surprising if we look closely at the assumptions about gender and discourse with which these analyses begin. In general, the analyses summarized above rely on either essentialist (that is, the "voice" of biological women) or social constructivist (that is, women's ways of knowing) perspectives on gender and discourse, which presume that the feminine is already constituted as a site of resistance to power. That is, more essential arguments rely on how physically recognizable women contribute online, while constructivist models assert the reality of both a masculine and feminine mode of being in culture inscribed by historical relations. While the constructivist models do not link the masculine and feminine to "body" like essentialists, the assertion that masculine and feminine qualities exist, no matter what body they are written on, makes the historical process of gendering a "presence" within culture that can be aptly labeled masculine or feminine (see Showalter, 1989). In so doing, such examinations reproduce a masculine/feminine or man/woman binary, which presumes students only construct voices online that can be described in such either/or terms. As a result, the questions asked lock us into searching for a unified, textual voice that can be characterized only in terms of the subject positions already provided by culture. Yet, asking questions about gender in such reified terms may tell us very little about power because of the ways in which culture becomes replicated in such discussions. That is, if online discussions do nothing more than provide equal access to women's voices and "feminine" ways of knowing, then they could also be seen as providing the means through which gendered hierarchies can be asserted.

The ways in which power can easily reassert itself, despite the increased possibility of the "feminine" to emerge can be seen most clearly in arguments relying on "voice" as a site of resistance. Voice arguments assume that reduced social context cues result in a discussion space that occludes the issues of status and hierarchy usually associated with the visible cue of gender (see, for example, Dubrovsky, Kiesler, & Sethna, 1991). As a result, online discussions create an environment characterized by "reduced risk" for "traditionally silenced and marginalized students" (Selfe, 1990, p. 132). Such a changed environment is seen in itself as a subversion of "traditional hierarchies" (Jessup, 1991, p. 345). Furthermore, it is speculated that such altered environments might create "communities that value revision and reinterpretation of traditional educational structures" (Selfe, 1990, p. 123). Yet, whether increasing women's access will result in a resistant voice is highly questionable. As Takayoshi (1994) puts it, "just because women are offered a 'safe' space in which to speak does not mean they will know how to do so" (p. 32). Rather than using the possibility of "voice" to speak difference, it is just as likely that women students will reinforce the phallocentric means for achieving authority learned in the contexts of academic and other cultural discourses. As Ellsworth (1992) points out in her critique of critical pedagogy, creating a space in which "voice" could be heard in her class actually "exacerbated the very conditions we were trying to work against" (p. 91). Focusing on the "authenticity" of voice only led to taking oppositional positions against the discourses created within the classroom context, merely reinstantiating already available power hierarchies.

Ellsworth's (1992) experiences leads to a key question "voice" analyses are unable to answer. Even if we assume that networked discussion groups allow students to be "free" of the traditions of academic writing and classroom discourse, from what discursive realms are they left to choose a voice? Will they construct a voice that is "authentic" to their experience, or, in a more poststructural sense, are they left to choose among subject positions constructed in other discourses that might similarly reify oppressive power relationships? The constructivist perspective seemingly provides an answer to this question by arguing that the type of voice women would use in such a space would, in fact, be resistant because it would reflect not only the unique experience of women silenced in many other public realms, but also introduce an alternative way of knowing based on women's experience of the world (Flores, 1990). In much the same way that the "voice" arguments presume that women, by their very presence in the conversation, will disrupt power hierarchies, the assumption within the epistemological argument is that speaking women's experience or a women's epistemology is an alternative that challenges the masculine forms of discourse that construct such power hierarchies. Yet, there is little guarantee that speaking the feminine will necessarily lead to a change in power relationships. It seems just as likely that "feminine" modes of expression and ways of knowing would be discounted as less powerful online, much as they are in other public realms. Similarly, the discourse forms might themselves "mark" the gender even of anonymous participants, again creating the grounds for gendered hierarchies to re-emerge. In short, focusing on a knowable feminine writing and epistemology preserves gendered definitions created by the patriarchy. As such, feminine forms open themselves up to continuing marginalization as the lesser term of the male/female binary.

Thus, while essentialist and constructivist concepts of gender provide a useful way to examine whether online discussions might help equalize gendered hierarchies, such analyses also look for a feminine presence that could just as easily replicate power relationships. Given the ways in which the feminine is easily reincorporated within current economies of power, I suggest here that the more vital question about power relationships online, particularly in terms of gender, seems to be whether such discussions provide *alternatives* to culture. In short, do online discussion groups provide my female students with any alternatives to culturally available subject positions? How might such new forms of textuality create the opportunity for my female students to literally refashion their voice such that they are accorded more power not only online, but also in classroom discussion?

In order to get at these questions, I suggest turning our analytical lens away from reified concepts of gender to the discursive and linguistic grounds through which these positions are created. By examining how discourse itself creates the ideological positions from which women speak in culture, I hope to illustrate what role textual forms might play in resisting and, indeed, refashioning these positions in ways that might resist current gendered hierarchies online and in the classroom. Specifically, I first turn to the theories of Luce Irigaray (1977/1985) to gain a perspective on feminine resistance not locked into current binary positions. I then consider how Irigaray's theories might suggest forms of textuality amenable to creating alternative subject positions and explore whether these forms might be encouraged by online discussion groups. Finally, I demonstrate how these alternatives realize themselves in a discussion group from one of my classes and discuss the implications of this realization for changing classroom discourse.

REDEFINING FEMININE RESISTANCE: THE QUESTION OF TEXTUALITY

Arriving at a theory of feminine resistance that avoids the problems noted earlier necessitates first considering the role discourse plays in constructing gender. By examining closely how discourse and language create the possibility for women's contributions to be accorded less power, hopefully a form of textual resistance can be located in online discussion groups that avoids current hierarchies. This is where Irigaray is particularly helpful. Because Irigaray (1977/1985) begins with the premise that gender is learned primarily through language, the forms of resistance she suggests are linguistic and performative. As such, textuality becomes almost more important than the material realities of biological women. That is, if discourse itself is gendered in such a way that the material effects of language silence and/or marginalize women, any possibilities for resistance must be similarly grounded in the linguistic realm of textual practice. From Irigaray's perspective, then, the feminine is not voiced through text; instead, it becomes a form of textuality itself.

To begin to look for such a textual resistance, we must first examine the ways in which language and gender interact for Irigaray. Following Lacan, French feminism begins with the premise that language and meaning are structured by paternal law (that is, the Law of the Father) based on the symbolic morphology of the phallus. Butler (1990) provides one of the most succinct summaries of this premise:

> According to Lacan, the paternal law structures all linguistic signification, termed "the Symbolic," and so becomes a universal organizing principle of culture itself. This law creates the possibility of meaningful language and, hence, meaningful experience through the repression of primary libidinal drives, including the radical dependency of the child on the maternal body.... This language, in turn, structures the world by suppressing multiple meanings (which always recall the libidinal multiplicity which characterized the primary relation to the maternal body) and instating univocal and discrete meanings in their place. (p. 79)

Within such a symbolic order, "instating univocal and discrete meanings" is one of the primary ways in which paternal law circumscribes meaning such that it always benefits the masculine subject. The masculine subject—always a unified subject who speaks in *one* voice producing *one* meaning—becomes the organizing principle for all discourse.

As Butler (1990) explains, for Irigaray, "the relations between masculine and feminine cannot be represented in a signifying economy in which the masculine constitutes the closed circle of signifier and signified" (p. 11). In short, the realm of discourse is a homogeneous one that does not allow for sexual difference because the only symbolizing morphology present is male. Seemingly alternative concepts of the feminine (for example, women's ways of knowing) are similarly circumscribed within this logic, since concepts of the feminine can only be constituted in opposition to what is masculine. As Irigaray (1977/1985) puts it, "to claim that the feminine can be expressed in the form of a concept is to allow oneself to be caught up again in a system of 'masculine' representations, in which women are trapped in a system of meaning which serves the auto-affection of the (masculine) subject" (p. 122–123). That is, to give the feminine *a* meaning is to engage in the very forms of univocality that can only refer back to the male subject as the organizing principle of such a meaning. To speak univocally, in definable concepts or with a unified voice, is always to speak within a masculine signifying economy, ensuring that language use will not threaten the sovereignty of a unified (masculine) subject. In this view, discourse oppresses women because the "feminine" cannot be defined within a binary system that refers back to the singularity of subjectivity and meaning.

Thus, Irigaray (1977/1985) asserts that the "feminine" does not yet exist. Rather, it is the very condition of difference that must be repressed in order for language to speak univocally. If discourse contains difference (the feminine) primarily by linking meaning to univocality, then the only possibility for resistance to current power relationships lies in disrupting such ways of making meaning and the unified voices that speak them. As Irigaray puts it, changing the way power is orchestrated must begin with "jamming the theoretical machinery itself, suspending its pretension to the production of a truth and meaning that are excessively univocal" (p. 78). Resisting power and creating new ways to imagine gender, then, is essentially a linguistic project. Changing the way power is orchestrated through language involves, for Irigaray, working toward a discourse in which no *Master* signifier (the phallus) exists. It involves speaking the multiplicity that would be silenced in order to disrupt univocality. Although Irigaray proposes multiple meanings and the fluidity of subjectivity as the keys to resistance, it is important to note that such "fluid" language does not itself become a new woman's writing. Instead, such fluidity and multiplicity are mechanisms for interrupting phallocentric power such that alternatives to culture might be imagined. Although Irigaray is primarily interested in the discourse of philosophy, seeing such disruptions as a more effective way for women to resist oppressive power relationships need not rest only in such an abstract realm. What is so useful about Irigaray for my purposes here is that she also proposes concrete strategies through which we might examine how power can be orchestrated differently in text. Such strategies can be found in her concepts of speaking (as) woman (*parler femme*) and mimicry.

Speaking (as) woman is a significant move because it limits the ability to speak to a particular moment. Unlike concepts of *ecriture feminine* employed by theorists such as Cixous (1976), there is no metalanguage of speaking (as) woman; it is a moment of enunciation within a particular context (Whitford, 1991). Much like recent composition theory, Irigaray (1977/1985) presumes that any given context creates a subject position out of which the writer must operate. Whether it be a position created through the limitation imposed by the topic, context, and audience, or one circumscribed within a given discourse community, any writing context creates *a* position from which the "I" must speak. Such contexts are part of the way in which a phallocentric discourse ensures that the speaking subject will be a unified one, writing/speaking in a single voice presumed to refer back to an authentic subject—what Susan Miller (1989) has called the writing subject's "fictional" stability. Given how context creates a unified position from which women must speak, thus subjecting her voice to the mechanisms of phallocentric power, speaking (as) woman seeks to disrupt the unity of such a position. Irigaray proposes that women deliberately assume the role inscribed for them within particular discursive contexts in order to "convert a form of subordination into an affirmation, and thus begin to subvert it ... it means to resubmit herself... to ideas about herself that are elaborated in/by a masculine logic, but so as to make 'visible' by an effect of playful repetition, what was supposed to remain invisible" (p. 76). It is in this way that different subject positions, not already circumscribed within the current discursive order, might be created.

What such mimicry and speaking (as) woman might mean in terms of textuality, particularly the localized contexts of academic discourse, is making visible the multiplicity of meaning that the discourse and the subject positions it creates seeks to repress. More specifically, such a "jamming of the machinery" would interrupt the univocality of the subject. In the simplest of terms, it would deconstruct the idea of authentic and singular voice. Thus, a resistant form of textual feminism would create a space for speaking multiple and contradictory subject positions within a single voice. For the very practical terms of analysis essential to us here, a feminized textual space would include single postings by one author that speak multivocally. Examining the possibilities that such textuality is taking place would also include looking closely at the way individuals might turn "subordination into affirmation" in response to both the discursive contexts set up by other postings and the contexts of academic discourse within which the discussion group is embedded. Furthermore, because such strategies are linked to discourse, speaking the difference that is the feminine need not have any correlation to biological sex. Instead, the category of the feminine is linguistic and textual, able to be employed by men and women alike to change how power is orchestrated in a given context.[1]

A RETURN TO THE MATERIAL: NEWSGROUP DISCUSSIONS AND THE FEMININE

If we define feminine resistance in these terms, then the key question for feminist analyses of networked discussions becomes one of textual space: Is there anything about the space of networked discussion groups that suggests a form of textuality in which multiplicity might be spoken more easily than in other discursive realms? Ironically, some of the research findings I critiqued in the introduction suggest just such a possibility for multivocality. What this research points to is how many of the ways we traditionally locate ourselves in oral and written discourse are removed and/or changed in networked discussion groups.

In terms of conversational corollaries, the most obvious change is the impossibility of relying on the physical context, which frequently orders oral communication, resulting in the claims of reduced social context cues discussed earlier. By creating a public space for classroom discourse that takes place outside of the classroom, much of the influence of the physical space of chairs, blackboard, other students' expressions and comments, and teacher mediation is removed. Perhaps the most significant change discussion groups bring about, though, is a form of conversational discourse that removes the body as a site of organization. As much feminist theory suggests, the body of a biological woman frequently serves as the organizational principle through which all her discourse is interpreted. By being seen as physically female, her discourse is thus interpreted via the visual cue of the body as "feminine," no matter the specific content or purpose of what she actually speaks. By removing the body and the physical context of discourse, discussion groups disturb the conventional means of locating oneself in oral conversation.

Written discursive norms are similarly interrupted. By providing students with a space in which to write without any specific purpose, there is no "exigence," to use Bitzer's (1968) term, created by a rhetorical context through which students can order their discourse, except the more localized contexts, which change from posting to posting (and even these can be ignored without disrupting any discursive norms). Similarly, through the mechanism of pseudonyms, concerns about ethos and audience become almost moot. Finally, the ability to construct a unified persona for a piece of written discourse (the monologic "I" of most academic writing) is disturbed by the reality of multiple postings written at many different times. As Faigley (1992) argues, the authority of the text, and thus the authorial voice, becomes decentered in these discussions as students are forced to realize that other students are interpreting their discourse in ways they thought impossible. For Faigley, the reality of many voices in networked discussion groups and the lack of closure they encourage results in a dispersion of the writer's subjectivity wherein the rational, autonomous subject is difficult to preserve.

The ways in which many of the "givens" of both oral and written discourse are disturbed through networked discussions suggests encouraging possibilities for a disruption of the field of semiosis in the ways Irigaray (1977/1985) describes. Such a disruption of the traditional organizing principles of discourse—physical and rhetorical context, an invoked or addressed audience, the internalized assumption of monitoring by "authorities" of the discourse community, the authority of text, the univocality of the author, and the lack of a physical body—makes it much harder to position ourselves along the discursive norms to which we are accustomed. Although online discursive norms are quickly emerging, their effect on our students, I suspect, are not yet as normalizing as those in other contexts, since our students, in my experience, engage in online discussions far less frequently than we do. As a result, they are left unsure how to construct a position from which to speak in this space, making it much less likely that they will invoke the already constituted subject positions usually created within other discursive realms, particularly those of educational discourse. In sum, the difficulty of accessing familiar subject positions makes it much more likely that new subject positions, which can speak difference, might be constructed.

THE ENGLISH 501 DISCUSSION GROUP

Although the discursive nature of networked discussion groups discussed earlier suggests that resistance to a phallologocentric symbolic order might more easily be orchestrated in these spaces, the question remains: does it happen? By way of testing out some of these assumptions, I offer an analysis of one of my course's discussion groups based on a close reading of the text of the entire newsgroup as well as individual interviews with the students involved.[2] Before describing the results of such an analysis, however, a few contextual factors are important to situate this discussion group.

The students enrolled in E501, "Writing Theories," are typically first-semester M.A. students. The course, which attempts to introduce students to the multiple possibilities for approaches to writing (from classical rhetoric to cognitive theories to critical pedagogy), required the use of a newsgroup as a course assignment. Minimally, students were asked to post 16 times to the group over the course of a 16-week semester; when each entry was posted was left to their discretion. Instructions for the group were included in the course syllabus and asked students to respond to the class readings and discussion or to "bring up issues related to [the reading] from your teaching, life, or other reading." As such, these instructions clearly set up an expectation that the newsgroup discussion fall, at least partially, within the realm of academic discourse. Although orally I prompted students to go beyond the class if they wished, class discussions most likely contradicted this encouragement, since they were almost exclusively centered on the readings for that day.

I left the choice of anonymity up to the class, and they chose the use of pseudonyms. Without any prompting from me, almost all the class members chose either gender-neutral pseudonyms (for example, "Hatless Cat" or "Skiing Naked") or ones that suggested their opposite sex. They also decided that I could participate in the group as long as I used a pseudonym as well. The only "monitoring" function I played was to count the number of posts made by each class member on the last day of class when they revealed their pseudonyms. Although I am sure knowing that I would eventually know who wrote what influenced some of the entries, the students interviewed claimed that this monitoring function had no influence on them. Perhaps because they are graduate students (and thus more likely to complete assignments no matter the obstacles), gender also seemed to play no role in how often students participated (see Table 6.1). Similarly, those students with the highest amount of computer experience (Usul and Skiing Naked) were not, in fact, the people who participated the most often. Overall, this group was not only very active—at the end of the semester, students had contributed over 300 individual postings—but also seemed to provide the types of egalitarian access many claim for such groups.

TABLE 6.1.

Pseudonym	Total Number of Substantial Posts*	Sex
Dorothy's Ruby Slippers	34	M
Max E.	28	F
Usul	27	M
Snoopy	26	F
Andromeda	24	F
Skiing Naked	23	F
KDP	22	F
Peter Rabbit with Blue Shoes	22	F
Socks	20	F
Guppy	19	F
Tasman	19	M
Theo	18	F
Cold Debt	17	M
Lothar of the Hills	16	M
Hatless Cat	12	F
Sylvester the Cat (the instructor)	5	F

*A substantial post was anything that contributed new content to the discussion. Posts such as "Thanks for the comment" or "I think I know who you are, Andromeda" were not counted as substantial.

PERFORMING THE FEMININE ONLINE: RESISTING DISCOURSE

In performing the textual analysis, I looked for three factors that might indicate the forms of feminine textuality Irigaray's (1977/1985) work points to: (1) whether students speak outside of the discursive positions created for them in other realms of academic discourse (that is, the classroom and academic writing); (2) indications of mimicry through a deliberate subversion of the positions created for an author by the local context of a particular exchange; and, (3) postings by a single author that speak multiplicity through indications of contradictory positions within a single voice. Before describing how these three forms of textuality emerged in the newsgroup, however, I turn first to an analysis of the other types of posts in which such forms of resistance were embedded.

Authority and Subordination

My initial look at the early postings of the group seemed to indicate that I would find, like other such analyses, only indications of taking up different positions regarding educational discourse. By and large, the early postings were replications of the type of discourse we expect in response papers or journals. These entries are lengthy, include an authorial voice that speaks monologically, and engage in sustained argumentation with either the readings or a previous comment. In short, little except the informal language and a few jokes indicates anything other than acceptable academic discourse. As Andromeda notes in one of the last entries of the semester, the academic nature of early posts set up a context to which others respond throughout the discussion: "Have you ever noticed that although it has never been mandatory, almost every single newsgroup entry has had something to do with what we've discussed in class? Personally, I don't always feel like writing about something related to class discussion, but a lot of times feel pressured to" (personal communication, November 30, 1994). Academic norms of textual authority and monologic voice show up in the more connected entries as well. Although many responded more directly to other people in the type of dialogue we expect on such groups, the ways they did served only to validate the idea that each individual post was representative of a monologic voice that must be recognized. For example, many begin their posts with phrases such as "In response to Lothar's question" (Guppy, personal communication, September 13, 1994), or "In response to Guppy, I believe" (Andromeda, personal communication, September 13, 1994). Some connections to other posts were even embedded within the text as support (almost like a citation) of the writer's position.

Those entries out of the first 100 posts that did not speak from subject positions firmly grounded in academic discourse wrote from a position more indicative of the personal, contingent, open forms that are associated with women's conversational styles. For example, in the following post, KDP *does* have an idea about what Flower and Hayes (1981) propose, as indicated by her statements about audience and organization. Rather than put forth her interpretation as fact, however, KDP begins with a false claim to complete confusion, framing the post such that her interpretation seems tenuous, much like hedges serve to undercut assertions in women's speech (see Lakoff, 1975).

> Aaagh! Somebody please explain that Flowers article that I just finished reading. My head really hit the desk this time and stayed there.//Her article with Hayes wasn't that great either, but at least I could follow it—somewhat.//I think I understand this cognitive stuff because it seems this is how I've been writing most of my life. Most of the time I have directed my writing toward a certain audience: the teacher. That usually occurs when I have to write something that I don't give a damn about. I put my facts in order, say what I have to say and turn the paper in.//Any thoughts on these articles from anyone?//Anyone think that I'm just confused? I'm starting to feel that way. (personal communication, September 20, 1994)

More clearly than any other example, this response points to how KDP becomes "silenced" as a result of her more "feminine" way of writing in ways that those writing within the realm of academic discourse do not. By creating a more invitational form of rhetoric that seeks response and connection, rather than a monologic statement that speaks only onto itself, KDP's post is evocative of the consensual and "web-like" relationships that have been associated with "women's" ways of knowing (see Belenky, Clinchy, Goldberger, & Tarule, 1986; Gilligan, 1982). Yet, invoking such a "feminine" version of preferred knowledge-making strategies provides an opportunity for KDP's discourse to be positioned as "lesser." Rather than responding to her reading of Flower and Hayes (1981), the replies KDP received respond only to her claims of confusion, composed in a tone of explanation from a position of greater authority than hers. After four such replies, KDP responds with "Thank you for a summary I could actually understand. *Maybe I wasn't confused after all. / / I have nothing else of importance to say* for this entry. I'm still pondering that Bereiter and Scardamalia article" (emphasis added; personal communication, September 22, 1994).

Learning to Disrupt Discursive Norms

At the same time most of the posts were replicating academic discourse norms or engaging in more invitational forms of discourse, others were indicating an awareness of how the group seemed to disrupt normal discourse patterns. Such indications of the difficulty in finding a secure subject position from which to speak came up in both the articles posted and the interviews conducted after the course had ended. In the interviews, I was intrigued by Hatless Cat's relatively low participation; in class, she was one of the most vocal participants. As a result, I asked her why she had contributed so few times to the discussion, failing to meet the minimum requirement. Her response is telling: "In the beginning, I waited quite a while to post because I wanted to see what other people had posted first; see what was okay to say."

Such insecurity about what is "okay" in this textual space is also exhibited in the posts themselves, particularly in the early entries. Theo's is perhaps the most overt about the problems such a space poses for knowing how to position oneself:

> I could respond to someone, but since everyone's using a pseudonym I won't know who it is. This makes me uneasy! What if I get really vehement in my disagreement and then I find out that person I disagreed with is someone who, in person, intimidates me? And then what if they found out who I was? Our relationship would change in a way it wouldn't otherwise. (personal communication, September 14, 1994)

The responses to Theo's post are just as intriguing:

> —I hope that Theo was just suggesting the scenario of being worried about conflict within E501 & intimidation; let's all send <<<HUGS>>> to Theo so that s/he knows that most? some? of us *like* vehement disagreement and hope that Theo vehemently disagrees with all sorts of stuff. (Skiing Naked, personal communication, September 14, 1994)

> —Disagreement—the spice of life! Violence isn't necessary, but wasn't perceived anyway ... thanks for telling it like it is <<hugs>>. (Usul, personal communication, September 14, 1994)

In both Skiing Naked and Usul's replies, we get a strange mix of validation and connection (hugs) for Theo. At the same time, the writers express a desire for disagreement that they characterize as "vehement" and "violent." Such contradictions seem, like Theo's original comment, to mark the ambiguity surrounding what positions should be taken in this space. The contradictory positions such comments suggest also effectively foreshadow later entries that begin to engage in the three types of feminine resistance I analyzed.

Subject Positions which Resist Academic Discourse

The earliest indication in the E501 group of these forms of resistance are, not surprisingly, those in which students take on positions of authority usually granted only to the teacher. Since so much has already been said about the ways in which students resist educational authority in networked discussion groups, I will only briefly characterize the nature of this resistance. By and large, much of the resistance to educational norms came in the form of direct challenges to the premises of the class (for example, "Why are we spending sooooooooo much time debating on how to write, what to write, when to write, where to write, and to whom to write?" [KDP, personal communication, September 14, 1994]), a resistance to the idea of theorizing about writing itself (for example, "Why don't we see how many times we can kill the art of writing by applying supposed objectivity to something that is by definition subjective and personal?" [Tasman, personal communication, September 14, 1994]) or direct challenges to the course design (for example, after Dorothy's Ruby Slippers entered a post questioning the assigning of short papers and oral reports, ten other people responded, resulting in a change in course requirements).

What was more interesting in this category of analysis were the ways in which students took up positions from which to speak that they would never have used in class. Some of these were empowering; others were not. The most obvious example of empowerment is Snoopy. Snoopy never spoke in large group discussions and only rarely in small groups, yet on the newsgroup she is the fourth most frequent participant. Most intriguing is that Snoopy's impetus for such activity on the board was, according to her interview, a response to a class interaction in which one of the male students quipped "You sure are quiet, aren't you?" at the end of a class period, leaving before she could reply. In her own words, Snoopy saw the newsgroup as a chance to "respond to a situation where I was silenced by his leaving the room." In fact, she further pointed out that she chose the pseudonym, Snoopy, because the character is silent in the Charlie Brown television specials. On the other hand, Hatless Cat found the newsgroup silencing. An active class participant, she found the newsgroup "intimidating because everyone sounded so smart."

While occupying subject positions different than those provided by the classroom does disrupt how academic discourse traditionally works for particular students, these positions offered little resistance to other discursive contexts. Students most often took up oppositional positions to teacher authority or responded in textual forms that mirror academic discourse, both positions already available within other discursive realms, if not the classroom context. What became the most fruitful categories of analysis were those that looked at contextual positioning through mimicry and multivocality within a single post.

Subversion in Local Contexts (Mimicry)

The second category of analysis presumes that feminine resistance includes a seemingly deliberate subversion of the subject positions created for a writer within the local context set up by other postings. Furthermore, such subversion would be orchestrated through deliberately playing with the positions created for the writer through this particular context for enunciation. While this category is perhaps the most difficult to illustrate without being able to ask the writer at the moment of writing how she/he is assessing the context, there do appear to be multiple examples of this taking place in the E501 newsgroup. These examples tend to take place in response to varying levels of context: (1) the local context of other posts in the newsgroup, (2) the context of the class in which the newsgroup is situated, and (3) the larger social realm in which the other two are embedded.

Skiing Naked provides one of the most obvious examples of how a subject position created through the local context of other students' posts might be resisted through "mimicry" (that is, the deliberate and playful invocation of the subject position that subordinates in order to subvert). The following post is the first to appear since Skiing Naked's response to another writer's question about the appropriateness of the word *organic* as a description for writing. Skiing Naked's response quite seriously took up this question, in a monologic and academic form, yet the responses she received questioned the value of the topic (for example, "All this 'organic talk' is causing me to flashback to the 60's and the early 70's!... When I think of organic the first thing that pops into my mind (flashback) is a compost pile" [Guppy, personal communication, September 20, 1994]). In what I see as a direct response to the disdain with which her earlier comment was met, Skiing Naked's next post deliberately uses humor to make yet another serious point. In other words, she takes on the position created for her as someone who introduces topics that may not warrant serious discussion and uses that position to introduce yet another topic, while playing with the position created for her. She calls attention to her need for validation, but plays with that as well by invoking a position usually seen as outside the context of academic conversations—her lower, middle-class upbringing. In Irigaray's (1977/1985) terms, she turns a form of "subordination into affirmation":

> Oh, I just about had little cognitive orgasmic spasms in my brain when I got to page 25 of Chapter One of Bereiter and Scardamalia.//I dig this stuff, and did anyone else find themselves wondering, "Oh, my, which one am I? Telling or Transforming?" It's so hard to tell since so many of the papers we write, and all the ones we assign, involve lots of telling and less transforming than we should probably be shooting for...sigh...it's my lower middle class upbringing

> which makes me seek this kind of external validation (that which would come from being a knowledge transformer—hey! we could print t-shirts!)...and I have a feeling that Carl and Marlene's parents are awful proud...//Anyways since everything I seem to say tends to rhyme anyway://To the cognitivists:
> I could dig you in a ditch.
> I could read you in a pinch.
> I could love you while I'm poor.
> Rich, I'd treasure you e'en more//
> Bereiter and Scardamalia are my friends
> They draw charts and diagrams
> I could dig them in the snow
> Skiing Naked! Off we go!! (personal communication, September 23, 1994)

In this example, Skiing Naked primarily responds to the context set up by the immediate responses preceding this post. In another instance of mimicry, however, Snoopy seems to respond not only to such an immediate context, but also to the silenced position she feels in the classroom. In this post, Snoopy responds directly to the position of silence created for her within the group when no one responds to an earlier posting. In this earlier post, Snoopy uses a conversational style that Tannen (1990) associates with women's attempts to create symmetrical power relationships in conversation. While Snoopy writes herself into a clear position here on her initial question, she poses her position in a seemingly tentative way, thus inviting revisions from other participants. She further ends her post with a question, another clear way of creating a conversational space that invites connection. In this post, then, Snoopy employs a style of discourse evocative of women's ways of making knowledge and, as in class, is silenced as a result:

> I think the worksheets are helpful [a reference to an in-class assignment]. A few very basic things keep confusing me, though. This thing about material reality in relation to the writer. Have any of the theorists explicitly (or implicitly) stated that writing changes MR? How concretely should I be thinking about MR? Sure, a piece of writing can change over time, after it's affected an audience. But, is there a theorist who flat out says: "Once someone writes their thoughts, it is a given that he/she has altered material reality?"//Okay, wait a minute. I'm starting to believe the quotation I just wrote. If a text is produced, materiality has changed, but I don't think that's what MR means in the context of E501.//Will some higher authority, or at least someone less confused than Snoopy, please help me out? (personal communication, September 29, 1994)

In her attempt to change the silent subject position created by the lack of response to this post, Snoopy again employs a "feminine" style of communicating by making explicit connections to another participant's text, even picking up the other writer's terminology and style. In this post, however, she turns such an attempt at connection back in on itself by calling attention to the silencing she received the last time she posted in this manner:

> Dear Andromeda, I'm with you on combining expressivist theory with cognitive. They could complement each other so well! Elbow could tell Moffet to stop being so anal and Moffet could tell Elbow to lay off the hash [both anal and hash are direct uses of Andromeda's language]. Until this happens, writing theory is doomed and so is the world and our children. //So, it looks like no one took me seriously about the material reality thing. Thanks for the support, SNOOPY. (personal communication, September 30, 1994)

By deliberately maintaining a "feminine" emphasis on connection while simultaneously undercutting it with sarcasm, Snoopy seems to deliberately subvert the silenced position created for her within the recent newsgroup posts as well as in our classroom discourse. Significantly, Snoopy also draws attention to her name and voice through the use of capitals in her sign off. Not surprisingly, after this post, she does receive a response to the "material reality thing."

In the third manifestation of subversion in local contexts, Usul, a male student, responds to his sense that he is being read through the lens of gender, perhaps because his earlier comments were all positioned by the others as direct challenges and arguments. In his interview, Usul was one of the few people who remembered why he wrote what he did. As he describes it, "I felt as if people were reacting to the things I said as a gendered position. I wanted them to think that it might not be so." In this post, then, he deliberately plays with the gendered position created by the local context set up by other students' responses to his earlier comments. Furthermore, I would argue, he also tries to play with the reading of the male body he seems to feel in other discursive contexts. Usul accomplishes this subversion of the subject position created for him by employing a more fragmented style that stands in contradistinction to his earlier, monologic posts. Significantly, his first line calls attention to the momentariness of such a text as well. Most importantly, however, Usul directly challenges, through a question about gender, how other students might read his text. By denying any attempt at univocality either in his writing or how he is read, Usul comes close to engaging in the types of multiplicity seen more clearly in the following section.

> A quote from Borges that seems approPoe to my mood of the moment, "Writing is nothing more than a guided dream." from _Dr. Brodie's Report_//I'm having a lot of trouble incorporating most of the cognitivist ideas into my own gradually coalescing (sp?) theory of writing (to skip to the end—I get the sense that the conclusion of this class may be that we will each have to determine our own theory of writing and that it will be most applicable to ourselves).//I'm with Dorothy that the charts in S&B seem much to static and stilted (they are too reminiscent of a computer program which isn't nearly organic enough—all do respect to the FINE machine I'm working with at the moment!)//Stemming the flow before I too become verbose,//—Usul (she, thank you very much—do you believe it?) (personal communication, September 27, 1994)

Multiplicity in a Single Voice (Parler Femme)

If we define multivocality in the ways Faigley (1992) does—as a voice which changes with each new posting created in response to other students' comments—there are many such examples in the E501 newsgroup. In fact, I would be extremely hard put to try and characterize the nature of any of the comments according to the writer's name rather than within the context of a single entry because of how often a single student occupies multiple subject positions from entry to entry. For the feminine form of multiplicity we are searching for here, however, we must go further than this type of multiple positioning to include multivocality within a single moment of enunciation. That is, a form of multiplicity that subverts both the monologic voice of text and *the author* within a single context. There are far fewer examples of this type of multiplicity in the newsgroup, although given the level of expertise graduate students have attained with academic discourse, there are more than might be expected. Generally, entries that engaged in multiple positions within a single enunciation fell into two categories: those characterized by fragmented textuality and those in which the writer (un)self-consciously contradicts him or herself within a single post, suggesting a multiplicity of voices within a single author.

The most common form of multiplicity I found are the increasingly fragmented forms of textuality the students use more and more often as the discussion group continues. At times, as in Lothar's example below, there is a "point" submerged within such fragmentation, yet the way in which such points are framed by jokes about the entire concept of writing theory itself and another seemingly irrelevant joke undercuts any attempt at a monologic expression of *a* thought or idea. Similarly, Lothar invokes contexts (that is, the "she" who told the joke) not available to his readers, further disrupting the sense of a single voice within a closed rhetorical context. Equally important is not only how Lothar's textual coherence and unity breaks down, but also how his post begins to defy the conventions of paragraphing and capitalization that the majority of entries employ:

> it seems like to me—and i'm sorry for perhaps getting too philosophical right after thanksgiving—but, wouldn't all of these theorists have a grand old time at a convention far away from this place! anyway, i was thinking about the critical pedagogicalists and what type of utopia they might have when there is no hierarchies or power structures. could this ever happen? what would it be like? politically would it be an anarchy, and socially would everybody simply get along without any violence, after all violence is just trying to gain power in most cases. i really can't see anything like this ever happening, and maybe i am just a realist or something, but anyhow. that is my deep thought for the week! by the way of my dumb joke, three tomatoes were walking along. the mama and papa were ahead and the baby tomatoe was lagging behind. so the papa tomatoe walks back to him, steps on him and yells, "ketch-up" I think she probably told it better than me! oh well! (personal communication, December 1, 1994)

While Lothar still makes a point about critical pedagogy and a Marxist utopia here, other entries do not see even this nod to the academic context as necessary. In the most fragmented example in the entire group, Usul clearly addresses other entries in their concerns about the fragmented subject and/or inscription within academic discourse, yet he also implicitly challenges the very nature of discourse itself in the ways Irigaray (1977/1985) proposes. Usul wreaks "havoc" on discursive meaning in a post that speaks with multiple voices, poses questions rather than answers, and even plays with the spacing of text to speak its fragmentation.

> series of fragments   that I am   if there is an I   to speak "of"
> buying-in selling-out   how goddamn
> frustrating!
>
> I don't want to have to be in the discourse community in order to converse with it. If I drop-out, will you all refuse to speak to me about everything? Or just certain things like "what is writing?"?
>
> angst! what language   is sufficient   to   talk across discourses
>
> One final question, if I buy-in with the purpose of causing as much havoc in the discourse as I can, is that the only way I can truly be in, and challenge the discourse?
>
> With no pardon asked for annoyed ramblings. —Usul (personal communication, November 11, 1994)

Significantly, Usul's last line that asks for "no pardon" and Lothar's apology for "getting too philosophical" is typical of almost all the entries I would classify as multiplicitous. In almost all cases where an entry is posted that speaks in a fragmented form without a clearly positioned voice, the students offer some sort of apology for the entry, including frequent claims of needing more sleep. These apologies seem to indicate that the students *know* that they are acting outside of discursive norms, that perhaps in some way they intuit that what they are doing is threatening to the nature of discursive meaning.

The second type of multiplicity I found in the newsgroup, just as significantly, offers no apologies for the contradictions spoken within their texts. Contradictory positions within a single voice seem to be acceptable in the group. Although the writer below does not reflect on her own contradictions, in this example of multiplicity Skiing Naked not only contradicts her own position on whether self-actualization can occur in the university setting, she also "pastes in" comments from another entry in a way that this person's voice becomes part of her own (the ">" symbol indicates where such pasting has taken place). Given that the newsgroup allows for the possibility of "following" an entry by posting in the same space immediately below the previous entry, it seems significant that Skiing Naked does not choose this format of response, nor does she choose to respond by creating another posting as most of the class members do. Equally telling in terms of characterizing this entry as resistant is that it is the only entry in over 300 in which the writer identifies herself as a woman.

>Donna asks, Can or Should self-actualization be the goal of the university? And that's justification, as far as I'm concerned, for her to be paid to hang around!!!

Unidentified flying student wrote: >It's probably a better goal than we have now. Maybe.

I think that we'd need to clarify the express and implicit goals of the university in order to answer this question. I think that I'm becoming more self-actualized with every thing I do in life, and university has surely been a huge part of my life, especially lately. But I have achieved more self-actualization in settings far from the U. Self actualization happens for different people in different ways; most people who choose to come to the U. could probably self-actualize if they thought it was important...No?

>That university would have to be a very different place in a very different>world for self-actualization to be happening for more than a few out of >hundreds.

Depends how you define SA, right? maybe all the football players are pretty righteously self actualized after the huge win last weekend—we should ask them.

>Note: self-actualization is more fun than Freshman Composition.

Oh, in that case, I'm not sure I've ever self-actualized, since I've NEVER ONCE had more fun than I had in Freshman Composition. (does she mean taking it? Teaching it? She's not saying!!!)

She's, Skiing Naked (personal communication, September 19, 1994)

Although even clearer examples of internal contradictions exist in single posts, I cite Skiing Naked's here not only because of how it reinterprets another person's voice as one's own, but also because of how early it occurs in the discussion. While it took some time for the fragmentation described above to begin, the possibility of simultaneously speaking from multiple positions began very early, although it is admittedly more common in later entries. Such early speaking of multiplicity seems to indicate how the discursive space of networked discussions almost immediately provides a forum for differently ordered forms of textuality—perhaps the very forms that might move us closer to Irigaray's (1977/1985) signifying morphology of the woman's body wherein gendered binaries become moot.

CONCLUSION

I began this essay with the question of whether electronic discussion groups provide our women students with a space in which they can subvert and/or resist the power relationships that silence them in other realms. The analysis above suggests that electronic discussions provide both our male and female students with such a possibility, at least within the space of the newsgroup itself. That is, employing feminine forms of resistance *did* disrupt discourse such that power relationships were altered, and more importantly, subverted. Yet, such disruptions were not linked to a student's sex, but rather to the potentially oppressive positions he or she occupied within the discourse of the newsgroup, some of which resulted from gender relations and others from the power relationships inscribed by academic discourse. Despite the success of the newsgroup in providing a space for both male and female students to subvert such power relations, such empowerment did not make its way into the classroom. In fact, the online reality seemed to have little, if any, effect on classroom discussion.

As my analysis indicates, there are many indications in the E501 newsgroup of textual forms that provided students with a way to disrupt the "normal" workings of discourse. More importantly, such a disruption seemingly has material benefits for the student in terms of how power is orchestrated over her. Whenever students accessed alternative subject positions outside of academic discourse, particularly those associated with more "feminine" conversational forms, they were quickly silenced. Responses to such forms reinvoked academic norms, effectively repositioning the original comment as "lesser" and thus silencing the writer (for example, KDP: "Maybe I wasn't confused after all. I have nothing else of importance to say"). In contrast, the use of the forms of multiplicity I discussed earlier had a radically different effect. Snoopy's mimicry of her previous comment resulted in her comment being attended to by the others: a subversion of the silence created by the lack of "voice" she was forced into by the lack of response to the earlier post. Usul's fragmented posting resulted in replies to various "phrases," yet no reply seemed able to "contain" his entire comment within academic discourse, nor reposition it as monologic or univocal. By calling attention to the humor with which her earlier seriousness was met, Skiing Naked effectively creates a new subject position in response to a local context. This repositioning successfully subverted the silence earlier created within that context, reasserting her right to speak. In sum, attempting to speak the multiplicity of the feminine *did* result in material benefits for students: their voices were heard, their discourse resisted reincorporation and silencing within already constituted discourses, and "new" subject positions were momentarily created that granted students power over how others had positioned them. Although such a feminized textual space did not make power "disappear" into a form of egalitarianism, its potential to disrupt such power hierarchies is promising. By opening possibilities for both male and female students to seek out discursive positions not offered them in other realms, perhaps alternatives to culture can be more readily imagined.

If speaking fragmentation and multiplicity do interrupt the mechanisms of power in the electronic space, then it would seem that students would be less likely to be subject to the discursive power that silences and marginalizes them in other contexts. Such a "crossover" from the new positions created in the newsgroup to the classroom, however, did not take place. In class, students continued to place each other into "roles" in oral discussion, resulting in a seemingly monologic "voice" for each student, which was subjected to the same hierarchical mechanisms of power associated with academic and societal discourses. As Max E. put it in one of the later entries: "I don't think that this computerized community benefits the classroom commune that much. I think the class hierarchy is established and negotiated strictly in the classroom.... The reference to anything posted on the newsgroup in class has never really made much of an issue in class, even I think, when Donna has photocopied entries from the newsgroup" (personal communication, November 14, 1994). Max E.'s comment clearly indicates how the discussion group seemed limited to the space provided by the computer. While the electronic space may have given students a place to "rehearse new roles," as Barbara Monroe suggests (see Chapter 3, in this volume), there seems to be little indication that such rehearsals are preparation for the day they "incorporate this virtual self into real life."

There are many ways to read the way in which feminine textual resistance is contained within the electronic space without leaking out into other realms. If we see electronic spaces as supported by programs that are patriarchal in nature (Wahlstrom, 1994), then such containment might point to yet another example wherein what seems alternative is controlled by a phallocentric discourse to ensure that a threat is not posed to the material realms of culture. Or, the problem may lie in my analysis, which could be seen as exactly the type of "technomania" that Stabile (1994) critiques as "dematerialized, idealist theorizing" (p. 4). Neither of these options seems to explain Max E.'s comment, however. What seems more likely is that the problem lies with the classroom space itself rather than with the electronic one or an overreliance on theory. What Max E.'s comment points to are the ways in which the classroom space reinvokes all the conventional ways of locating oneself in discourse that the electronic space seemed to disrupt: the physical and rhetorical context, the reactions of others, a reading of the physical body, and so on. Given the immersion in school of these students (or any undergraduate or graduate student), they no doubt long ago internalized the panoptical gaze of teachers, the institution, and other students such that acting differently upon context cues must seem inconceivable in a classroom, while it may be less so in a newsgroup.

The implication for the classroom, then, might be to seek ways of disrupting discursive norms in ways similar to those that seemed to occur somewhat "naturally" in the electronic space. Learning to disrupt these norms seems necessary if students are to be given the opportunity to incorporate virtual selves into real life in the ways Monroe suggests. A closer examination, with students, of how classroom discourse intersects with other discursive positions to create inequitable hierarchies, much like the strategies employed in critical pedagogy and cultural studies, might provide a similar "interruption" of the semiotic field of the classroom. Making students metacognitive of their discursive positions and how those already constructed embody different relations of power would create a context in which the forms of textual resistance so productive in the electronic space could become consciously employed, and perhaps more importantly, equally possible in the classroom space. In other words, disrupting the facile access to the subject positions created in the classroom necessitates developing a critical awareness with students about how such discourses position all of us. Only through such awareness can we then begin to consider with our students the different positions allowed them in all our classroom spaces—electronic or traditional—in order to develop the meta-awareness of positioning that seems necessary, lest forms of feminine textual resistance remain simply "dematerialized theorizing."

NOTES

[1] I must note that Irigaray (1977/1985) is also interested in women-as-subjects and sees the "feminine" writing of male philosophers, like Derrida, as an appropriation of women's space. Because they still have socioeconomic power, men writing "differently" is a writing of the Other of the Same, rather than the Other of the Other of women's writing (Whitford, 1991). Whitford cogently distinguishes between these two movements in Irigaray: "the unheard feminine in the patriarchy," the multiplicity that serves as a constructing absence in the current symbolic order (i.e., the Other of the Same); and the "'femininity' of *parler femme*—the rights of women as epistemological subjects (the Other of the Other)" (p. 51).

[2] I make no claims of objectivity in this analysis. The reading was conducted only by myself, and as such, is probably open to "researcher bias." However, I would argue that the perspective I'm taking here would discount any possibility of an objective analysis, even if the text of the group had been coded by multiple readers. My hope is that the earlier parts of the article make my own position clear such that other readers can assess how much my own positioning might have affected my reading of the group.

REFERENCES

Belenky, M. F., Clinchy, B. M., Goldberger, N. R., & Tarule, J. M. (1986). *Women's ways of knowing: The development of self, voice, and mind.* New York: Basic Books.

Bitzer, L. (1968). The rhetorical situation. *Philosophy and Rhetoric, 1,* 1–14.

Butler, J. (1990). *Gender trouble: Feminism and the subversion of identity.* New York: Routledge.

Butler, W. M., & Kinneavy, J. L. (1991). The electronic discourse community: God, meet Donald Duck. *Focuses, 4,* 91–108.

Cixous, H. (1976). Laugh of the medusa. *Signs, 1,* 875–893.

Cooper, M., & Selfe, C. L. (1990). Computer conferences and learning: Authority, resistance, and internally persuasive discourse. *College English, 8,* 847–869.

Dubrovsky, B. J., Kiesler, S., & Sethna, B. (1991). The equalization phenomenon: Status effects in computer-mediated and face-to-face decision-making groups. *Human-Computer Interaction, 6,* 119–136.

Eldred, J. C., & Hawisher, G. E. (1995). Researching electronic networks. *Written Communication, 12,* 333–359.

Ellsworth, E. (1992). Why doesn't this feel empowering?: Working through the repressive myths of critical pedagogy. In C. Luke & J. Gore (Eds.), *Feminism and critical pedagogy* (pp. 90–112). New York: Routledge.

Faigley, L. (1992). *Fragments of rationality: Postmodernity and the subject of composition.* Pittsburgh, PA: University of Pittsburgh Press.

Flores, M. J. (1990). Computer conferencing: Composing a feminist community of writers. In C. Handa (Ed.), *Computers and community: Teaching composition in the twenty-first century* (pp. 106–117). Portsmouth, NH: Boynton/Cook.

Flower, L., & Hayes, J. (1981). A cognitive process theory of writing. *College Composition and Communication, 32,* 365–387.

Flynn, E. (1988). Composing as a woman. *College Composition and Communication, 39,* 423–435.

Forman, J. (1994). Literacy, collaboration, and technology: New connections and challenges. In C. L. Selfe & S. Hilligoss (Eds.), *Literacy and computers: The complications of teaching and learning with technology* (pp. 130–143). New York: Modern Language Association.

Gilligan, C. (1982). *In a different voice: Psychological theory and women's development.* Cambridge, MA: Harvard University Press.

Hawisher, G. E., & Selfe, C. L. (1991). The rhetoric of technology and the electronic writing class. *College Composition and Communication, 42,* 55–65.

Irigaray, L. (1985). *This sex which is not one* (C. Porter & C. Burke, Trans.). Ithaca, NY: Cornell University Press. (Original work published 1977)

Janangelo, J. (1991). Technopower and technoppression: Some abuses of power and control in computer-assisted writing environments. *Computers and Composition, 9,* 47–64.

Jessup, E. (1991). Feminism and computers in composition instruction. In G. E. Hawisher & C. L. Selfe (Eds.), *Evolving perspectives on computers and composition studies: Questions for the 1990s* (pp. 336–355). Urbana, IL: National Council of Teachers of English.

Lakoff, R. (1975). *Language and women's place.* New York: Harper & Row.

Lamb, C. (1991). Beyond argument in feminist composition. *College Composition and Communication, 42,* 11–24.

Matheson, K. (1991). Social cues in computer-mediated negotiations: Gender makes a difference. *Computers in Human Behavior, 7,* 137–145.

Miller, S. (1989). *Rescuing the subject: A critical introduction to rhetoric and the writer.* Carbondale, IL: Southern Illinois University Press.

Selfe, C. L. (1990). Technology in the English classroom: Computers through the lens of feminist theory. In C. Handa (Ed.), *Computers and community: Teaching composition in the twenty-first century* (pp. 118–139). Portsmouth, NH: Boynton/Cook.

Showalter, E. (1989). *Speaking of gender.* New York: Routledge.

Spender, D. (1985). *Man-made language.* London: Methuen.

Stabile, C. (1994). *Feminism and the technological fix.* New York: Manchester University Press.

Takayoshi, P. (1994). Building new networks from the old: Women's experiences with electronic communications. *Computers and Composition, 11,* 21–35.

Tannen, D. (1990). *You just don't understand: Women and men in conversation.* New York: Ballantine.

Wahlstrom, B. J. (1994). Communication and technology: Defining a feminist presence in research and practice. In C. L. Selfe & S. Hilligoss (Eds.), *Literacy and computers: The complications of teaching and learning with technology* (pp. 171–185). New York: Modern Language Association.

West, C., & Zimmerman, D. (1983). Small insults: A study of interruptions in cross-sex conversations between unacquainted persons. In B. Thorne, C. Kramarae, & N. Henley (Eds.), *Language, gender and society* (pp. 102–117). Rowley, MA: Newbury House.

Whitford, M. (1991). *Luce Irigaray: Philosophy in the feminine.* New York: Routledge.

Making the Map: An Interview with Gail Hawisher

Kristine Blair
Bowling Green State University

Pamela Takayoshi
University of Louisville

Our interview with Gail Hawisher, Professor of English at the University of Illinois, Urbana-Champaigne, at the 1996 Conference for College Composition and Communication in Milwaukee profiles the difficulties she has faced as a woman administrator of computer-mediated environments, her experiences working with computers in the early 1980s, when the field was in its nascent stages, the evolution of computers and composition as a legitimate research area, and changing social forces that have affected Hawisher's own career.

Pamela Takayoshi: We thought that if we started talking about the first question, then probably we wouldn't have to go back to the rest of the questions: it would just sort of evolve. And the first question that we have here is if you just could tell us about how you got interested in computers, or how you got involved in this area, and what it was like starting out in that area, and the changes that you've seen?

Gail Hawisher: Sometimes when I talk to graduate students I'll say something like "I have a really checkered past," because I think women my age often do have a checkered past. We finish school, perhaps get married and raise children, and then go back to school. So although I was in graduate school for a long time, I didn't go back to school for the Ph.D. until the early 80s. Before then I was a department head in a large high school in Columbus, Ohio. At that time I took lots of graduate courses with Ed Corbett and others at Ohio State, and then when we moved to Champaign [Illinois], I taught for one year at Urbana High School, and was riffed—they were just cutting back with numbers, and I thought, okay, a perfect opportunity for me to go back full-time to graduate school. So I talked to Professor Corbett, and we were talking about who was at the University of Illinois that I could possibly study with, and he pondered the whole thing, and he said "You've got to do word processing." And I said, "What?" He said, "You've got to do something with computers." I know that sounds weird, but Ed really said that.

Kristine Blair: I think that's good.

GH: So I began graduate school again—now at the University of Illinois. I was first in the Department of Linguistics, but then I started with computers. I took my first course in computers, I don't know, it was in 1982 or something. And it was on PASCAL. And I quickly decided I wasn't going to be a computer programmer in any sense of the term. We were working with Apple IIEs or IIGs. The Apples had a 40-column screen, and if you wanted to see the other side of the paper, so to speak, you had to toggle back and forth. And that was a time when the word processors, like the Bank Street Writer, were much more primitive. You could enter text, but if you wanted to revise that text, you had to go out of the insert mode and into the revise mode. So word processing was not particularly transparent, but I was determined to use it to teach writing. The first course that I taught at the University of Illinois was rhetoric for engineers, and I decided it was the perfect class for us all to get up on computers. Forget about those Apples, I reasoned, we were in engineering, and we were going to use the mainframe. So we used an old line editor, ICE, where you enter text, then if you want to change it, you have to enter commands; it's like the VI online text editor we first used with UNIX e-mail.

KB: I wanted to ask you about this, because we both taught technical writing to engineers, and as women being in those kinds of environments with technology. I mean how did you feel about that, and what kinds of reactions did you have from your mostly men students.

GH: They were mostly men—you're right. I had only four women in the class. I honestly don't remember any unusual reactions from the men. In my mind and theirs I think, I was their teacher. But by that time I had also been teaching for 13 years. What I remember best about the class is that I took them over to the mainframe lab, introduced them to word processing, which as I mentioned was called ICE. Very good name for it—it really stood for something like Interactive Computer Editor. To make a long story short, those guys—four women and all—learned the editor, but I'm afraid it always remained something of a mystery to me!

What happened then, to give you a better picture of my early years as a graduate student and teacher: In the English Department, where I was doing my teaching assistantship, we got an EXCEL grant, and I find this really interesting, because at that time there was nobody doing much at the University of Illinois in rhetoric and composition. The EXCEL grant meant that 50 IBM computers arrived, and we set them up in two classrooms. We had one of the earliest networks for teaching writing in the country. That was in 1984, and we began teaching about 10 first-year classes on computers. What fascinates me is that a year later Texas also got an EXCEL grant, and out of that grant, came the whole Daedalus Group. The difference was that they had a graduate program in rhetoric and composition. (Cindy [Selfe] and Hugh Burns [co-founder, the Daedalus Group], of course, had come out of that program a few years earlier.) And how those grad students were able to use the technology! All guys initially. In contrast, I was really the only one to come out of the program at Illinois, but Texas was able to spawn a great many scholars in computers and composition primarily, I think, because of having a rhet/comp graduate program already in place.

At that time I also remember running into problems at the University and I see this primarily as a problem of my being a graduate student. One of your questions concerned nontraditional students. While I was a graduate student, the University started a Bridge program for those students who score lowest on the ACTs but are admitted to the University because of their promise. The students were required to take summer classes. They arrived in June, and their coursework was intensive writing, math, study skills, etc. I wanted the Bridge students to be able to use the new computers. Apparently, this idea was pretty radical in 1984. I wanted them up writing with computers so that in September they would have an advantage over the other students—would already know the technology. But the administration closed down the two labs in the summertime because they didn't want the computers to get ruined. Honestly! So that was my first battle to get computers used equitably at the University, and I failed.

KB: Was there anyone who was supporting you though? Because you're talking about being alone, and I think that the portrait you paint of yourself and compare that to the Texas situation, where there's clearly that kind of network, I think we see that network now, across the country. But how do you think that you worked to form it locally?

GH: I felt pretty much alone at the University at that time, but fortunately things changed. But before things really changed, there was this dissertation I needed to do. Remember I was this graduate student who had virtually no power. The dissertation was on the revising processes of students using computers for writing, and I was very much influenced by Lilly Bridwell-Bowles's work. So I finished and defended my dissertation, and then there was a job open at the University as visiting assistant professor to coordinate what came to be known as the Writing Outreach Program. We invited teachers from all over the state, about 40 came, and I taught a course on reading and writing connections and computers. Dennis Baron taught a course on issues in language and the program was set up so that teachers came in for 4 weeks. This was a superb summer program—I think it really had an impact on teachers. And I finally felt I was doing something worthwhile with the technology. We also taught many first-year students with word processing during those early years, but the classes were always targeted at the brightest of the new students. I never did get to teach basic writers in the computer classrooms.

PT: That's the way it is in some high schools. The advanced people get to use the computers.

KB: Or get to use it for grammar skills.

GH: When I started using computers, CAI was also very prevalent. Back when I was taking that PASCAL course, my project was a sentence-combining program—it was absolutely awful, and it took me hours to do this thing. So one of the things that I tried to introduce to our program in the English Department was an emphasis on writing—if teachers were going to write, they needed to use word processing rather than CAI. They didn't need to be experimenting with CAI programs that were no better than workbooks in electronic form. I was a visiting assistant professor at the University of Illinois for one year. Then the next year I was hired by Illinois State University as an assistant professor in a tenure line. And Illinois State University was the first school in the country that used computers for all its first-year writing classes. In many respects, it was a very equitable approach to teaching writing with computers.

PT: And when was this?

GH: It was 1986.

PT: And all of the courses were using computers then.

GH: Yes, it was interesting because at the time those of us doing research were still involved with quantitative studies, and you couldn't find a control group—no student was not being taught on computers in a writing class. It was really interesting to me to see how Illinois State could do things to make the technology available for everyone. At the time this was much harder to do at the University of Illinois. But a lot of it has to do with the people who are running the programs. One of the reasons Texas just did such a fantastic job back in the 80s is directly attributable to the superb people heading up the various programs. And that's also true of the program at Purdue, which you both came out of.

KB: I think it is related very much to those administrative structures. Because having been there at Purdue, we know in a case like that, even accessing the technology in the beginning. All the work that Pat [Sullivan] had to do to make technology available, to get all of, in our case, the tech writing classes in computer labs, and the idea that Purdue is so rigidly controlled by the Computer Center, that to get access to the labs themselves. I think that's changed a lot in the last 7 or 8 years, but initially it was very difficult.

GH: Yes, I think you're right. I had a great three years at Illinois State, and then I was offered the job at Purdue. But when I got to Purdue, the first thing I wanted to do was get e-mail, and I said something to Pat, and she said no and frowned. I said "Why not?" She frowned some more—she's funny you know. Her response was "No, I'm not standing in those lines. I'm not going through that with PUCC [the computer center]." And I said, "Don't be silly. We can't not have e-mail." So anyway, I found Victor Raskin, a linguist, who was extraordinarily helpful. And we made Pat get an address too, so she got an address, and we used to go to that little linguistics lab on the third floor in Heavilon Hall to access our mail. Of course, we used UNIX and that awful vi editor. At that time Helen Schwartz was teaching a class over at IUPUI, and we were able to talk back and forth with her class, and that was back in 1989. It seems like it was back in the dark ages. [The listserv] PURtopoi grew out of Pat's and my getting e-mail at that time. We were then able to get the listserv up with Tharon Howard working with it. I like to say that we took on PUCC a little bit there—the computer forces—and we succeeded. But you're absolutely right about the infrastructure constraining us and preventing us from doing things easily and effectively. Pat's early attitude about getting e-mail reflects the hurdles we had to jump. It was sheer persistence on our part that got us online.

PT: Lisa Gerrard [of UCLA] has talked about being doubly marginalized, a number of people have, but I can think most clearly of Lisa's argument, where she talks about being doubly marginalized about being a woman working with technology and then being a humanist working with technology. And I see a lot of that in dealings with this big monster we have at the University of Louisville called IT (Instructional Technology). And I see a lot of that with Pat and PUCC. One time we talked about this, and it seemed to be she was not really clear about whether she was being treated the way she was because she was a woman or because she was an English person, because English people didn't have any need for this technology.

GH: I was actually amazed in getting to Purdue in 1989 and seeing that the English Department only had one computer classroom, which was equipped with National Cash Register computers, the NCRs. Pat had worked like a trooper to get even this lab. Other departments on campus at the time were doing somewhat better. I don't know when you all started your programs.

KB: I came in '89.

GH: What struck me the most was that Purdue was still buying into the mainframe mentality. Having come from a school like Illinois where there is so much technology available, I found it unusual for Purdue not to have a ready supply of PCs. The Math Department did have a wonderful classroom filled with Macintoshes, though, and we often had to rely on Math's generosity for teaching space.

Hmmm. Another thing I actually forgot about happened at Illinois while I was there. Illinois had the Plato system—it's one of the oldest systems for instructional technology. Plato came about 1960 and was used at one time all over the world. A lot of it was CAI stuff, but there was also something called Notesfiles that was like e-mail. It was much better than, say, UNIX mail and the mainframe because the editor was easy. I wanted my students to have the Notesfiles so they could write to one another. There were different levels of access to the Plato system. But the computer people didn't see any reason why English students should be talking with each other, so they wouldn't give us this privilege. And I was unable to pull it off. This was the sort of attitude we frequently encountered at Purdue too. In the case of Plato, I don't know whether it was the graduate student, the woman, or the humanist who was denied—I suspect it was the combination of the three.

But back to your question. I don't agree with the notion that we in computers and composition are marginalized within writing programs or even within English departments. At one time we may have been seen as the CAI people, sort of tinkering with technology, but I think we're seen very differently today. Information technology has become critical to our society, and we're often viewed as being out in front with these communication technologies—at least that's my perception. And at no time have we been entirely the sort of typical male techie who just happens to teach writing.

In fact, one of the things that is so exciting about our field is that it's a field that has been shaped by women. We just finished our history book (Cindy, Charlie [Moran], Paul [LeBlanc], and I), *Computers and the Teaching of Writing in American Higher Education: 1979–1994*, and the people who reviewed it acknowledged the importance of women to the field. Joe Amato wrote something to the effect that computers and composition studies is a field in which women have played crucial roles and I think that's true. You asked me, Kris, if I felt alone working at Illinois for awhile. When I started not feeling alone was really when our community began. In 1984, Lilly Bridwell held the second Computers and Writing Conference in Minnesota, and many of us who are still in the field came together there. The conference was one example of women taking hold and making our field into more of a community than it might have been otherwise. The women have been a potent force—Lilly, Helen, Cindy, and Lisa have all made tremendous contributions. And there's also Glynda Hull, Chris Haas, Chris Neuwirth—and many of the women you're featuring in this book.

PT: That's really fascinating to me because I've often thought of the parallels between composition and computers and composition. I think that computers and composition history has sort of followed the history of composition in general. And I'm really fascinated by that. It's also fascinating to me though that so many feminists have theorized the masculinity of technology, but at the beginning of technology's entrance into composition, it was women's work that was crucial, and it doesn't seem to fit with what women feminist theorists say about technology being alienating to women. How is it that, when women brought computers into composition.

GH: We did a very strange thing with it, and I'm not quite sure how it happened, but we saw that when we introduced computers into our classes, suddenly students started to talk to one another more. The teacher was not the primary expert with technology so students took over some of the teaching and seemed to create more of a community within the class. At least this is how it seemed. This is at the same time, of course, that social constructionist views were entering the profession.

Instead of fearing computers, we began to embrace the technology a bit too much and lost our critical perspective. As humanists, we began saying that the computers were all too wonderful—that they help create community and to institute a collaborative pedagogy. But that's not the whole answer either. Truly the technology carries with it an infrastructure saturated with the values of those who developed it and that's very male. We are excluded by it, but I also think that oftentimes we've been able to bend it to our needs. We need to constantly acknowledge, however, that we're shaped by the technology as much as we ourselves influence its use—maybe more.

PT: That's an interesting way to think about it, that technology was, that women were able to use the technology toward their goals, and I think that's one thing that feminists have theorized. Who do you remember when you began working in computers and composition, at that first conference, what are your first memories of that?

GH: I remember Lilly perhaps more than anyone at the time. She was just wonderful. Here you have this gracious Southern woman welcoming everyone to Minnesota, and we had Alfred Bork from UC-Irvine as keynote speaker, and he was a very well known computer person in science and instructional technology. I remember Cindy from that conference, that's where we met, and Cindy with all her energy, pulling all these people together and saying "What projects do you all want to do, well you go do that and for next year…" I evaluated that conference as part of a project for graduate work and really got to see all these wonderful personalities coming together. I remember a little bit of Don Ross. He had great fun in bringing us all together socially. I guess I remember the women better than the men. Elizabeth Sommers was there, Glynda Hull, Ellen McDaniel.…

KB: Do you think computers and composition is sort of a microcosm of the field in that women played a major role in legitimizing the profession, the major profession and then the subprofession, and then once that happened, you saw more and more men getting involved?

GH: Perhaps. Except the difference is that the men were always already in composition, people like Ed Corbett, Frank D'Angelo, Jim Kinneavy, Jix Lloyd Jones. It's really the women who came the second round in composition studies, Andrea [Lunsford], who was Corbett's student, Janice [Lauer] who was Richard Young's student. I do see parallels between the two fields though, but I'm not always sure that computers and composition followed composition. I think there's a synergy there in that both fields feed one another. Lester [Faigley], for example, has used the synchronous computer writing class to represent the instability of the student subject in postmodern times while at the same time talking about how learning might take place among competing discourses.

PT: I am wondering if there isn't just sort of certain structures that fields follow when they're in the formation stages. One thing I wanted to ask you, to go back to 1984, the conference. I remember when I first went to NCTE, Helen Schwartz played a major role in my being where I am right now.

GH: I remember reading that. Where did I read that? In the MOO for the history book? I think you mention Helen there.

PT: Yeah, I took a course with her because I remember Brian [Huot] telling me I could not take a course with Helen Schwartz. And I thought, computers, I never want to touch them. In fact, my brother did something to a computer in her course, and I had to take it back and say, "Helen, my brother stuck something in the disk drive." But anyway, she was really important in getting me involved with computers and one of the things she did that really stood out, a small thing, but it really stood out for me was that she was at CCCCs, and I was at home, and we got on-line, and she put Lillian Bridwell online.

GH: I remember that—she and Lilly were sharing a room at CCCC. That was probably in 1989 or 1990 when Pat and I had our go round with e-mail.

PT: I was like, "Oh my God, Lillian Bridwell just sent me a note." And I was this person who was brand new to the field and I knew her, her importance as a scholar.

GH: That's exactly the same set-up Helen arranged with her INDY 100s listserv or something like that. With Pat and me at Purdue, she taught a graduate course and the book that Cindy and I did in 1989 had just come out, and she was using *Critical Perspectives* in her class. I talked to her class about the book and how we put it together.

PT: We used that book in that class. Was that 1989? I don't remember that. Maybe I wasn't in that section.

GH: That's okay.

PT: I would have remembered talking to you. I think about the people who have been mentors for me, and they've all been women. I don't know exactly why that happened, but it's been a fact in my professional development.

GH: One of the reasons I think I persisted so with the technology is that it's not something that comes naturally to a middle-aged woman. And I'm more middle-aged now than I was then. Thank God the technology has become more transparent rather than more difficult. I wanted to be able to say to my women students, if I can do this, then you my students can do this too. I have worked with a lot of the English education students who to this day often stand back from technology and really don't want to get involved. Certainly, men have done some important mentoring along the way too, but maybe having as many women involved in the field as we have, we've been able to do more. There have been times when Cindy and I have asked one another whether we were doing enough for women in the field. We've consciously tried to support women. We're absolutely thrilled, by the way, to have your book in our series. When we look down the list of upcoming books in the series, we see lots of men. We also have Sarah Sloane's book, *Computing Fictions*, under contract, though, and it's a great book.

KB: You just said you're happy that technology is easier, and I guess my thought, was...

GH: Is it really easier?

KB: Well, for me it seems easier, but I guess the question is that it may be easier, but is it necessarily more accessible, and I think this comes out of some of the stuff we talked about on Waytoofast because the fact that any time I get on e-mail or get on an MOO, though on an MOO you can't really tell, it can be so gendered. When we're working with our graduate students, to get them on MOOs, to get them on listservs, so that the same sort of structures, as Pam's talked about in her work, simply don't get replicated online, because that can so easily happen. Do you see any kind of schism with that, that as much as the field, especially the founding field of CMC, has been women...

GH: Well, the interesting thing is that remember on Waytoofast, when we were trying to come up with what constitutes feminist action—what can we do? And we were so frustrated by it, deciding that silence was not action in cyberspace since it goes undetected. And remember that time when Susan Romano simply took from the Georgia Tech web page the statistics of how many men and how many women were on the Internet, and it was something like 94 percent men. Do you remember how her statistics were challenged? And that was the Computers and Writing listserv for the conference. If I had been she, I would have wanted to quit very quickly, and she hung in there. But also remember what a difference it made when I then posted a message, challenging the challengers, and then SOS'd Waytoofast, and Pam immediately jumped in, and a couple of other women jumped in, and as soon as we got our voices in there, we could begin to change the conversation. We weren't rude—nobody said anything obnoxious—but we were able to change that culture. It's not always that easy.

One of your questions concerned what I've been able to do to make technology more accessible to more people, and you've seen that I wasn't very effective as a graduate student. I think I do better today, but even now, when I go to meetings—I'm usually invited because several feel there should be some representation from technological people in the humanities—they want women too. Sometimes because you're a woman, you're asked to sit on so many committees. We need to be on these committees, we need to have our voices heard, and we need to make a difference. Yet the more we're put on these committees, the more it pulls us away from our scholarship. It can be a real bind, but nevertheless when I go to these meetings, and I'm talking to men, and I stand there, they're talking about computers and most of them are tall, I don't know why they're tall but they're way up there, and here I am down here trying to get my word in edgewise. Even if I could talk "techie talk," which I only do minimally, they can barely hear me.

This year, however, we have managed to have three women on the Educational Technologies Board at the University. Several of the men suggested we make a "technology kit" available to new users. But another woman and I said, "We don't want a kit, we want training, and we want a hotline, we want somebody to call, somebody to come over and work with the new people." Some of the men, the technology leaders on campus, need very little help with this technology—they play with it constantly and spend hours at it. But we have been able to get them to think that a training program will make a difference for those with less expertise. We're hoping to create in the colleges computer learning centers where students and faculty members can get help in a nonthreatening environment.

KB: That's really interesting. I recently did a survey of all the women employees in the Corpus Christi system. I was replicating a study about e-mail in university settings, and I just wanted to get some data for a presentation I was doing. It was really interesting because the one issue that came up was the issue of online help, or help in general, human help. Most of the reactions of the women toward e-mail and toward networks in general was very positive, and there wasn't very much where they said they had been harassed, no instances of that. But when it came to online help, there was just this vociferous anger, so that was about the only significant thing I got out of it.

GH: The technology experts often make women feel stupid, and we already feel pretty stupid about computers. Training could really make a difference. Cindy and Dickie [Selfe] have done such a wonderful job with training in the computers and writing workshop they do at Michigan Tech. When the teachers from around the country come for the two-week workshop in June, they go back saying they want to take their consultants home. The consultants all dress in these red kimonos, and how threatening can you be when you have a kimono on?

KB: You know, I'm looking at this list, realistically we've covered almost every question, and the one question maybe we haven't covered is the fourth one, because we've gone through the history to where we are now, and I think it would be a good way to end, to sum it up by considering what possibilities and constraints do you see for women currently? I mean, there's always that thing: "We've come a long way, baby?" Where do you think we're at now?

GH: Well, I'm not sure we have come a long way. We have to be careful not to delude ourselves. Dale Spender has written about women's predicament with writing technologies. Women were kept out of the print culture for a long time. In her *Nattering on the Net* she writes that early women scholars, nuns, began to make a difference in the scribal culture. But when society turned to print, these gains were lost. She argues that it took us 400 years to finally make our mark in print. We finally developed feminist presses in the 70s so that many women could publish. Now that we're finally making our mark in this area, print is becoming less important as the arena in which we need to achieve. It's now the electronic context that's becoming important, and you see very few women as heads of software companies, very few women who have a say as to how the technology gets developed and used. We just have to keep persisting in trying to get our students, many of whom are women, online and urge them to be just as active as they can possibly be.

KB: Well, and there are economic consequences to that as well. I knew that I wanted to look for another job this year, for example. So in early January, I was like "Oh, my God. I have got to learn HTML right now. I have got to get a home page. I have got to get a resumé," because everybody was raving about HTML. I'm like, I don't even know how to do it, and so it became my New Year's resolution, and all during the summer, I just did all this stuff. And finally when I had all those little codes memorized in my head.

GH: Then they came out with the new stuff.

KB: Where you could just save it out as an HTML source file in WordPerfect 3.5 for the Mac. I nearly died, but I learned it all.

GH: But that's like UNIX, and learning that older VI editor. It never hurts, though, because you'll be able to jump in the conversation when the guys are talking and say "Do you remember when?" You can be one of them and say, "Yeah."

KB: It's true, because knowing that I wanted a position that involved technology, and the way things were going, if I didn't have something on the Web, I just wouldn't look as good. Knowing some of the people in the community I was competing with who were doing work with hypertext and MOOs.

GH: That's a good point about getting up to speed with HTML this summer. What resources did you have to do that?

KB: Like some book, "HTML in a Week."

GH: But did you have anyone to ask?

KB: Actually I had one systems administrator who helped me put my resumé online preformatted. He did that for me, he just said, "Oh just let me do that," so in many ways, it was very paternal. Quite honestly I needed that, so then I did it myself. I was able to print the source and see exactly what he did to my resumé, and I think that's the way a lot of people learn HTML these days, they just rip off the code from someone else.

GH: That's what I've been told. You have to take what's out there, and insert what you want.

KB: That's exactly what I started doing, and now I do pages right and left. I do way too many pages.

PT: We have a really good person I found who was actually a part of IT. And he is a really wonderful person. I have six women in a women's studies class right now, women and technology. I asked him if he would come to one of the periods and run a session on setting up home pages. And before he came, I realized that any time I had questions in this lab, people would come and take over my keyboard, the basic rule that you never do that.

GH: Right.

PT: So I wrote to Adam [the IT person], and I said you might think about the implications of people taking over keyboards or whatever. The next day I went in and asked a question of somebody, and this person who has always taken the mouse, stood behind me and told me how to do it. And I was really impressed by that because I could have just let that pass thinking oh, he won't do anything about it or that won't have any effect. His willingness to think about that, and then he came in with my students and he was just wonderful.

GH: We have a faculty member, Bob Jones, I don't know if you remember him, but he started the hypermedia lab at the University of Illinois. It was featured in *Academic Computing* sometime back. He's been so wonderful and supportive. He has an advanced information technology group and I'm on the advisory committee as is Cheris Kramarae and a couple of other women. We also have what we call our WITS group that Cheris started, the Women, Information Technology, and Scholarship. And the idea behind it is to provide a safe place where women can meet and learn about the latest technologies. It was started in 1992 when lots of women at the University weren't even up on e-mail at the time. We meet on Wednesday a couple of times a month, and we have speakers talk on some of the most pressing issues regarding the new technologies. Dale Spender has come. I had Cindy down to speak to us all. Pat came to our meeting once. And, as a group, we're no longer way behind. A lot of the women are working with the National Super Computing Center (NCSA). Many of the women had these jobs before, but now they're more aware of some of the practices that exclude women. These "techie" women have become much more proactive as a result of this group. And the other neat thing is that when we go to these various meetings—all of those committees we serve on—invariably we'll run into one another. So WITS is also an example of feminist action. Other campuses can also form something like WITS. We're all available through e-mail, etc., to tell you how we did it too.

PT: Sort of like women on Waytoofast, and I wonder if you could talk about that a little bit. I read an interesting article recently where this woman talked about she feels like calls for special protection for women and children are being made in the popular media and that's why you hear stories of pedaphilia on the net, and stories of children being abducted by people they meet on the Net, and women being harassed online. One of the implications that she suggests comes out of that is that women are special class in need of paternal protection.

GH: That we shouldn't be victimized.

PT: The paternal fathers should set in place these ways to protect us.

GH: Some women argue for guidelines regarding what you can say or not say on a particular listserv. I'm leery of censorship though. I would much rather be proactive, getting more and more women to participate online, rather than painting ourselves, constructing ourselves as victims. Pat and I mention this issue in the chapter that we did on Waytoofast—there's so much out there about women being victimized online (I'm thinking of Julian Dibbell's article "A Rape in Cyberspace" or Lindsay Van Gelder's article "The Strange Case of the Electronic Lover") that we now need very powerful stories to counteract these notions of the victim. And some of these experiences happened to you all too—I'm thinking about what we wrote about on Waytoofast. So what do we do? We need to keep trying to come up with concrete actions that don't border on curbing people's free speech—and we need to continue to speak out both online and in print. There are no easy answers, but as always we can persist…

PT: I have this student in this women's studies course who's really impressed me, and a really exciting person for me to be around. Because she's 19 years old, and she's graduating *summa cum laude*, so she's a very bright and motivated person. But she came into this course, and I asked them to define technology, and she defined it as masculine and divisive, not personal. And she really didn't want to have anything to do with it. And now at this point in the semester, she's really active on the MOO, and she's on the MOO every Tuesday and Thursday, and then they talk during the rest of the week on e-mail. She's discovered different MOOs, and sends me info about them. She's on Daedalus MOO talking about me. She has a web page, and she talks to other people with web pages, and she has really grown with this technology. And she's not victimized. She goes to the MOOs, especially Lambda MOO, that if you first walk in and identify yourself as female, she'll have 10 people come up and ask if she'd like to go have sex. And she says no, but it's not a big deal to her in the way that some of the depictions of women suggest that it could be.

GH: You know there's a study Nancy Kaplan did with her daughter, Eva Farrell, and the participants were young adolescent women. And they did the exact same thing. All right, so this is no big deal, let me just go on with it, and I guess it's again the word "persistence," that we have to be active, we have to persist, and sometimes we get hurt.

PT: I wonder if it also has to do with what you said earlier that women get asked to be on a lot of committees because they're women and how to balance that with your scholarship. And I wonder if that's the reason there are fewer women active on listservs. Because it does take a lot of time to be a presence on listservs.

GH: One of the things we learned from the Waytoofast study was just how busy we all are. Women that participated in the study, yourselves included, were just so gracious. We know it was taking a couple of hours a day, and there were a few messages from women who really resented it. Fortunately, they let us know they resented it, too.

PT: I really liked that experience, though, because I knew enough of the people on there and I liked enough of them. One of my experiences on listservs is that I find myself getting in these big discussions, arguments that take a lot of time with people I really don't even like sometimes. And I think what is this all about. I'm spending so much time with this person that I don't like, and there are people I do like I'd like to talk with and conversations that I get something out of.

GH: And why is it someone like Susan [Romano] whose remarks get attacked? She did absolutely nothing unusual. There was nothing inflammatory about her putting those statistics out there.

KB: Perhaps because they're fairly accurate statistics.

GH: Aha. You're probably right. The men then started making the argument that the statistics might be true for the Internet as a whole, but that in the field of writing there were so many women that it didn't hold true for our field at all. Which doesn't sit very well.

PT: Recently that happened on my campus, in our department. We have a listserv in our department and somebody wrote on there that there were more men than women. A man then wrote back and said, well no that isn't true and he reported some statistic, and I wrote back and quoted the statistic that you all gave in your article. And it was interesting, because it was almost the same argument, word for word, as the one that Susan encountered. So I wonder how many times that argument has been played out across the country.

KB: In a lot of cases, men don't seem to want to acknowledge that this new transformative medium has that same ability to disenfranchise. Because when I was at NCTE in November, I went to a panel where a male made the argument that "Oh no, women have no problems online." And the women on the panel were arguing that these can be alienating spaces, and the refusal to acknowledge that alienation merely enforces it.

GH: Yes, you've got to examine the whole context carefully. You've got to be a critic of this technology. You can't just accept it wholesale.

KB: Maybe this is a good place to end.

GH: Thanks so much to you both!

Map of Location III

Discourse Communities Online and in Classrooms

chapter 7

The Virtual Locker Room in Classroom Electronic Chat Spaces: The Politics of Men as "Other"

Christine Boese
Clemson University

With the increased use of electronic classrooms, collaborative software tools, and the Internet with its interactive forums, a great deal of scholarly speculation has turned to new social contexts this technology may create. Many have suggested that electronic tools and forums have a democratizing influence, at least for those granted access (Bolter, 1991; Flores, 1990; Selfe, 1990; Selfe & Selfe, 1994a, 1994b). Some feminist theorists have recently examined this assumption, in light of the ways women and men participate in news groups on the Internet, and have found subtle effects of "silencing," a *de facto* kind of censorship that seems to reinforce inequalities of power and influence based on gender (Herring, 1992; Herring, 1993; Herring, Johnson, & Dibenedetto, 1992). While many teachers of introductory writing classes are turning to feminist pedagogies (Eichhorn et al., 1992; Hollis, 1992), others are incorporating features of feminist and radical pedagogies into computer versions of writing classes (Selfe, 1990; Selfe & Selfe, 1994).

At issue then is whether these computer forums can serve the goals of various feminist pedagogical practices in writing classrooms. Is this technology fair and democratizing, or is it simply a forum that reproduces and perhaps amplifies the biases and inequalities of the dominant society, despite anonymity and equal access to the "conversational floor"? And if the answer is the latter, does it mean that the technology is unsuitable for use by teachers employing feminist pedagogies? Should feminist teachers be using a computer tool that allows men to continue to dominate and oppress women?

To examine these questions, I brought synchronous conferences or chat rooms[1] into my electronic classroom, incorporating the forums into prewriting activities and peer review sessions. Due to unusual circumstances of registration in 1994, I was able to compare variables of gender in electronic chats for pedagogical purposes, with interesting results for rhetoric and composition research as well.

I held four comparative real-time electronic conferences, two simultaneously in the same class in the Spring semester of 1994, and two simultaneously in the same class in the Fall semester of 1994. Each conference occurred in connection with the same assignment in an electronic classroom section of "Expository Writing: Language and Culture" at Rensselaer Polytechnic Institute. Each semester, the class was divided into conference groups of approximately six to seven members. One group used their real first names and one group used anonymous nicknames.

Because Rensselaer is an 80 percent male engineering school, there was only one woman regularly attending my class both in the spring and the fall semesters. In the Spring of 1994, the woman participated in the Real Name Group. In the Fall of 1994, the woman participated in the Nickname Group.

Each semester, two distinct types of virtual cultures emerged, independent of a condition of anonymity. One became an inflammatory, abusive, sexist, racist, and homophobic environment, the Virtual Locker Room, while the other remained serious and focused in its discussion. Each semester, the differentiating factor appeared to be the known absence or presence of a woman in the group.

Captured texts of the conferences and student journal responses afterward reveal how the Virtual Locker Room culture was created, and show how gendered communication was affected by the absence or presence of one woman, who became a "normalizing" force in the online culture. For a feminist frame to examine these texts, I want to look at this electronic communication by men as something "Other," putting a reverse spin on conventional assumptions of alterity.

I also want to consider whether such an exercise has any classroom value, and whether the electronic forums can be productively integrated with the ideals of feminist pedagogies. In this class, the discussion and introspection generated from an oppressive locker room atmosphere provided a gateway to a higher understanding of the politicized contexts of language and culture. Particularly interesting was how nearly all-male classes responded to their own debate texts as course readings, analyzing the culture space they had created in ways that are consistent with the goals of most feminist pedagogies. My research, then, validates a contradiction between the egalitarian ideals for CMC and the effects of conflict in computer-mediated spaces, and uses this contradiction directly, for feminist, consciousness-raising purposes.

TEACHERS AS TECHNOLOGY CRITICS

In the journal *College Composition and Communication*, Cynthia and Richard Selfe call for teachers to step back from "overoptimistic ways" of embracing computer-assisted pedagogy, to the end of helping "teachers identify some of the effects of domination and colonialism associated with computer use so that they can establish a new discursive territory with which to understand the relationships between technology and education" (1994a, p. 482). In bringing teachers into a role of technology critics, the Selfes point to a growing understanding that while teachers may have high-minded, liberal democratic goals, they may be promoting racism, sexism, and colonialism inadvertently along with the technology. One may even speculate that there is something intrinsically imperializing about the technology (Winner, 1977). Indeed, many teachers such as Lester Faigley (1992) and others have commented on how online discourse degenerates into juvenile gibberish and obscenity in student-centered chat spaces; but I wasn't ready to dismiss this discourse so easily. In the interests of greater intellectual reflection and understanding of the "cultural and ideological characteristic of technology" (Selfe & Selfe, 1994a, p. 484), I decided to explore the Virtual Locker Room when it appeared in my classes.

In other research, Cynthia and Richard Selfe have noted an oppressive presence of the State, or the military-industrial complex, in shaping computer culture-spaces, and have suggested that democratic social action in these virtual spaces is actually a subversive activity, one possibly best undertaken by "nomadic, feminist, cyborg, guerrillas" (Selfe & Selfe, 1994b, pp. 346–354) to work against "the logics and practices of domination" (Haraway, 1991, p. 177). But most of the rhetoric surrounding electronic discourse communities is closer to utopian optimism, looking to the advantages of information sharing, networking, egalitarian access to forums and conversations (although access to the technology itself is unfolding in ways which perpetuate an elitism of computer haves against have-nots), higher levels of literacy and semiotic thought (Bolter, 1991), the overthrow of traditional and textual authorities, and nonlinear or nonhierarchial relationships. In Bolter's "network culture," disintegrating hierarchies lead to "greater and greater freedom of action" in accord with "the goals of liberal democracy" (p. 232) where "[o]ur whole society is taking on the provisional character of a hypertext: it is rewriting itself for each individual member" (p. 233).

Meanwhile, some significant doubts have been raised by Susan Herring and her collaborators in an analysis of gendered discourse in Internet newsgroups. These studies seem to show that gender domination and sexist bias perpetuate themselves in these supposedly egalitarian cyberspaces (Herring, 1992; Herring, 1993; Herring, Johnson, & Dibenedetto, 1992). Although access to the "conversational floor" is open to all group members, Herring's more detailed look at two specific discussions in two different Internet newsgroups, LINGUIST and Megabyte University,[2] shows that domination by male group members remains consistent. At points in the discussion where women did assert themselves in greater numbers (often using qualifiers and hedge words), group backlash was immediate and silencing, with threats from some male members to unsubscribe from the list.

Without going into detail on Herring's studies here, I think we can find aspects of democratizing assumptions that relate directly to the cultural climate created in the electronic chat space by my virtually all-male class. We can do this in light of the formal "rules of reason" advocated by Habermas[3] (qtd. in Ess, 1996, pp. 209–210) as necessary qualifications for "a discourse to be truly democratic" (Herring, 1993). These rules cover "internal and external coercion" as a form of censorship which prevents a democratic exchange of ideas. If computer forum members can be internally coerced by electronic social structures not to participate even when they have access, and if we can call this censorship, then these electronic forums cannot be truly democratic. In applying this criterion, we are allowed to look past the simple matter that all members have equal opportunities to post messages to Internet newsgroups, and to begin to consider the cultural dynamics created in the virtual spaces of the group discourse.

FEMINIST FRAME FOR ANALYSIS

In order to examine the effects of gendered communication in these captured chats, I want to locate myself in the taxonomy of Spitzack and Carter's "five conceptualizations of women that are present in communications research" (1990, p. 403). Tracing the evolution of communication scholarship on women, Spitzack and Carter find "The Politics of Women as Other" and "Women as Communicators" as two of the five typical frames for study.

In the "Politics of Women as Other" category, they suggest that scholars should view Women as Other openly, allowing the alterity to become a focus for analysis. In this category, scholars acknowledge their politics and seek out the richness in women's communication styles because:

> Given the social polarization of males and females, identical communication behaviors are unlikely: thus, presumably universal principles that guide inquiry are not universally applicable. The priority placed on objectivity in research practices serves the dominant culture because registers of discourse "have been encoded by males for their own ends.... Women shall either be excluded, or made uncomfortable, or serve those ends if, and when they do participate." (Dale Spender, qtd. in Spitzack & Carter, 1990, p. 414)

Within this model, it should be noted that while "male speech is the standard against which female or 'other' speech is judged," the politics of that conception are brought into the forefront. According to Joseph Pillota, "To recognize differences it is necessary either to assume one of the cultures as a base and interpret others in terms of it or to assume common features across various cultures on the basis of which the variations are comprehensible" (qtd. in Spitzack & Carter, 1990, p. 413).

The mistake would be to allow the alterity to go unacknowledged and unanalyzed, with the risk that scholarship would unwittingly help entrench the conception of Women as Other. To guard against that risk, the political implications of the different discourse conventions must always be considered as well.

In contrast, Spitzack and Carter's (1990) more inclusive "Women as Communicators" approach allows for insights on both men and women without turning a blind eye to the special conditions women experience, for instance as both outsiders and insiders. The value here is that male communication does not have to define the standard against which women's communicative actions are judged. Moving outside the frame of alterity altogether does not mean studying communication as if women did not exist. It does allow us to view women's and men's communicative actions more flexibly as both genders move inside and outside dominant discourse conventions. As Spitzack and Carter write, "Female inclusion requires not only an understanding of women within the parameters of communication studies, but includes analyses of gender as an organizing force in social interaction" (p. 426).

The twist I'd like to put on these two categories is a simple reversal of gender in the interest of feminist politics. Since, in these captured chat texts, the single woman communicator becomes a "normalizing" force in the virtual culture, why not examine the male-only Virtual Locker Room texts as Other, as the deviation from the norm of standard rhetorical conventions? This twist may reveal for us the politics of a commonly self-censored gender and minority/ethnic prejudice. In turn, it may shed light on the majority group exercise of power behind closed doors. By adopting the inclusiveness of the "Women as Communicators" frame and placing women in the mainstream of study, perhaps we can also take a step toward examining the "Politics of Men as Other."

SETTING

I have continually played with electronic forums in an anti-authoritarian or "democratized" feminist classroom. I also wanted to go a step further in decentering the teacher than Lester Faigley did in his "Achieved Utopia of the Networked Classroom" (1992) by leaving the teacher out of the discussion while it is taking place, even as an eavesdropper or lurker. Other than in routine monitoring of software and hardware, I did not see the texts my classes created until they were captured into word-processing files.[4]

The context of the assignment that led to the online discussions was an attempt to persuade, to write a position paper. I had assigned formal topic proposals, due well before the assignment and brought to class on the day of the chat. The electronic chats were set up to give students feedback on various argumentative positions raised by their topics. This exercise took place near the middle of the term, and it was not our first foray into the chat space, although it was our most purposeful and most extended use, since students didn't have to take time to learn the software. Using the chat space for a prewriting exercise, I hoped it would help students consider their classmates as an audience for their upcoming paper. I recorded real-time electronic debates in captured transcripts, and I announced that we would be reading the transcripts in the next class period. I had seen electronic chats become chaotic when a class had no direction, but I thought the medium held promise if I set up a loose structure and gave specific instructions. Two groups were established, each with an assigned Guide and a Gadfly. One group would use real first names and the other would use anonymous nicknames. Students selected their own nicknames on private screens. The Guide would host the session and keep group members informed about which topic held the floor, various threads of the debate, and technical glitches that arose. The Gadfly would marshal the opposition, ensuring that important points were not ignored or silenced. Other group members could take and change their positions as the debates evolved. As one topic became exhausted, the Guide would ask for another topic and they could begin again.

In the old way of debating, it was rude to change direction or interrupt. Here, I encouraged students to see past old models and to try to introduce several ideas or threads at once. I pointed out that everyone could talk at once, yet no one would be interrupted. In that way, I did make an overt effort to give students enough background on the issues surrounding the technology so that they could observe their debate culture and the language it used even as it evolved. They were told (and it was explicitly repeated in an instruction handout) that we would capture the text and study it in a later class period. In both classes, however, students claimed to have forgotten that announcement. I can only surmise that in the heat of debating it slipped their minds. I did use members of each group to capture the debate texts, and many heard me working out the logistics of the text capture at the end of the hour. Perhaps they used forgetfulness as an excuse for the outrageousness of their behavior.

Of course a key factor in the two groups had to be that with one woman in class all semester, one group would be all men and one group would have one woman. Due to logistical concerns with the software linkup, I divided the groups on either side of a central aisle. In this way, it was commonly known to the group members whether the woman was present in their group or not, as much as they may have thought to pay attention. I never mentioned to the class gender or gender issues in connection with chat discourse until after the texts had been captured for discussion in the following period. I occupied myself principally with monitoring the performance of the software and preventing crashes.

Much could be made of the biases of group leadership if this were a conventional discussion or debate. But this should have been less of a factor, given the open access to chat room interaction and the technical impossibility of interruption. I selected Guides and Gadflies on the basis of their apparent ease with the UNIX interface (common at an engineering school), and included a mix of good and average writers, races and ethnic backgrounds. I did not assign a role to the lone woman, not wishing to single her out further unless it was by her own choice. I was more concerned that each group member had a grasp of chat room functionality, that each saw how to quickly send a comment, that the group knew it was not required to stick to one linear conversation thread, and that, in the ephemeral nature of electronic communication, students knew they did not have to write carefully and selectively. Instead they could write more quickly and responsively, more in the nature of a verbal exchange than a written exchange.

THE DEBATES

My first impulse is to tell about the Virtual Locker Rooms the way I would tell a story. These texts, after all, do not lend themselves to extensive quoting because they are so long and unwieldy. Yet even as they are multithreaded, nonlinear, polyvocal documents, it is very difficult to remove excerpts from their larger contexts, and purists could argue that it should not be done at all, particularly in rhetorical analysis where context is of great importance. The ideas are so interwoven and closely linked that a great deal is lost in excerpting. There is not a single excerpt with a clear beginning or end. To many readers the chat texts are dense and hard to follow without practice. I believe these texts are a new rhetorical form and a rich lode to mine for textual analysis in future research, but somehow I must solve the problem of how to even begin writing about them.

A comparison of group participation levels, similar in style to Herring's analysis, does make one distinction between the groups in my classes very clear. In both semesters, the groups without the woman participant generated considerably more text.[5] The groups that generated the most text in either semester (perhaps reflecting high energy and interest levels) were also the most broadly participatory, meaning all members were quite active evenly throughout the debate, and two or three members were not able to dominate the discussion. The percentages for the most broadly participatory groups can be compared to scores for a well-balanced basketball team when all the starters and several players on the bench score in double figures, but no one player is a big star.

On the other hand, the groups with the woman participant were also dominated by several members who each contributed more than 20 percent of the text. In these chat groups, dominant speakers, with the strength of their writing voices and attitudes, somehow kept the others from fully participating, or at least participating at the same relative level as the more dominant members. This can also be compared to the box scores of a basketball team where one or two star players alone rack up 20 to 30 points.

Yet, if more members do participate fully, the total number of comments goes up, and the percentages become more balanced. There are no external features to control who writes and who does not. The controls are cultural, social and psychological. Interestingly, broad-based participation does not appear to be contingent on whether real names or nicknames were used. But, broad-based participation does correlate with the degeneration of conversation into the Virtual Locker Room, and it correlates with the absence of the woman. In other words, the discussions in which the woman was present generated comparatively less text and tended to be dominated by two or three members (not the woman). When the classes analyzed and discussed the captured texts of both debates in a later face-to-face session, there was widespread agreement as to which group had remained serious and which group had gotten rowdy. For the sake of shorthand, then, I will refer to the two rowdy groups, the Nickname Group Spring 1994 and the Real Name Group Fall 1994 as Virtual Locker Rooms. Indeed, the discursive similarities between the two texts were so uncanny that I asked students if they had any friends from my class the previous spring. But most members of my Fall 1994 class were first-year students, new to the institution, and they hadn't met many others a year ahead of them.

Let me subjectively summarize what I read in these texts from having lived with them and the representations of the students I once knew in 1994. I will also excerpt a characteristic section from each conference group so the reader can get a feel for its tone and participants.

The Spring 1994 debates took place in a brand new electronic classroom that had just gone online at Rensselaer, and we met there every other class period. It was quiet and well-designed, with carpteting and good lighting, and students sat comfortably on swivel chairs. Even in the hushed calm, I had problems with the software, and a crash made me lose two thirds of the text for the Real Name Group (W)[6] Spring 1994. Still, according to the group members, the saved comments are representative of the group, which was focused primarily on Stephen's topic of banning smoking in public places.[7]

Excerpt: Real Name Group (W) Spring 1994—Woman named sue[8]

1. Guide Norb: So everybody, should we ban smoking??
2. Guide Jeff: I dont think so. I dont use tobacco in any form, but people should be free to do what they want with their bodies as long as it doesnt threaten someone elses rights.
3. Guide Norb: Does anybody see this???
4. sue: But smoking does...it threatens someone elses life
5. Guide Norb: I agree with Jeff, who are we, or the government, to prohibit people from doing as they please.
6. Stephen: Second hand smoke does threaten others lives
7. Guide Jeff: Only if they smoke right in front of someone else
8. Guide Norb: Smoking shouldnt be allowed in public places, such as the Union, but why not outside.
9. Guide Jeff: Or in your own home
10. Stephen: It is illegal to shoot a gun down a crowded street but one can blow smoke down the same. Is it a matter of time.
11. sue: I think the laws are fine the way they are. They dont prohibit people from smoking. They just limit where they can smoke.
12. Guide Jeff: good point
13. Stephen: The gun kills instantly, the smoke takes a while
14. Guide Norb: Smoke only kills if there is contact.

15. Guide Norb: If someone smokes outside the somek dissipates.
16. Guide Jeff: the smoke diffuses in the air, while the bullet is a projectile
17. Stephen: Yeah, but the point is, they both kill
18. Guide Norb: The smoke from one cigarette doesnt compare to they amount of pollution put out by your car.
19. Guide Jeff: If smoking is banned in public places you dont have to worry.
20. Guide Norb: Second hand smoke is only a threat if there is someone else there to recieve it.
21. Stephen: True. Pollution control standards are being formed.
22. Stephen: Yeah, in restaurants, sporting events, walking behind someone, walking out of a building in the entrance way
23. Guide Norb: Point being, the amount of smoke put out by one cigarette or a million is inconsequential when compared to the other forms and quantiier of pollution we produce
24. Guide Jeff: The amount of smoke from all the tobacco smoked in the U.S. doesnt even compare to the amount of smoke from burning the Amazon rainforest
25. Guide Norb: Smoking should not be allow at sporting events, in restuarants, or in other public places.

As we can see, Guide Norb dominates the discussion not only with his quick, fluent writing, but also with an emphatic tone, not so much debating as making pronouncements. He generated 37 percent of the text in his group. Other group members filled in with 23 percent, 19 percent, 9 percent, and 2 percent. (Also, there was some confusion in this group as to who would be the Guide and Gadfly. That is why there are two guides.) Despite its seriousness, this debate introduced two potentially ridiculous arguments, an analogy comparing secondhand smoke to shooting a bullet down a crowded street, and later another about whether tobacco companies ever mix marijuana into cigarettes. In Virtual Locker Room groups, this kind of conversational thread could have easily instigated further silliness, but this group was so serious and Guide Norb so intent on pursuing his points that the discussion remained very linear and single-threaded.

In contrast, the Nickname Group Spring 1994 (Virtual Locker Room) began silly and intensified to rudeness. Topics officially discussed were the death penalty, euthanasia and doctor-assisted suicide, and the abortion pill. Unofficial topics included sex, the Jerky Boys, modified song lyrics, and the movie *Hamlet* with Mel Gibson. As a group, there was much laughter and high spirits, and many commented in their journals that they felt the conversation was out of their control. By the same token, this discussion did elicit high levels of inventive verbal performance and creativity, even if the end result degenerated into what would be offensive to most general readers. Group participation levels were well balanced, 22 percent, 19 percent, 19 percent, 17 percent, and 15 percent, with one goof-off constantly changing names for about 4 percent each. Also notice how much shorter the lines are compared to the previous excerpt.

Excerpt: Nickname Group Spring 1994—No Woman (Virtual Locker Room)

32. Felix the cat: if somebody takes a life they should lose theirs as well
33. Tula: but at least thats one problem that could be fixed, gadfly
34. Gadfly: if the people are given a chance for rehap they may be useful
35. Guide: an eye for an eye right kitty
36. Hamlet: So the people who put the guy in the chair should die, and the ones who kill them should die
37. VanDam: what desides who is to die and who is not
38. Tula: for the most part felix
39. Tula: hamlets an idiot
40. Gadfly: that would make us no better than the murderes and rapists
41. Guide: ya whatever hamlet
42. Felix the cat: how so?
43. Hamlet: Thank you Tula...I agree
44. Gadfly: killing people for killing. Is that right?
45. Felix the cat: how else do we punish them
46. Guide: good question vandam, what do u think
47. VanDam: gadFly.. An eye for an eye?
48. Tula: eh?
49. Felix the cat: grrrr
50. Gadfly: Im glad to see someone supports my position Vandam
51. Gadfly: cats dont grrr they purrrr
52. Guide: anyway......
53. Felix the cat: do we punush someone by teaching them useful skills and giving them food?
54. Gadfly: how bout so input from the guide
55. Hamlet: New Topic?
56. Gadfly: Useful skills that may improve the society Cat
57. Guide: if u fry a criminal u dont have to worry about him repeating his crime
58. Felix the cat: speak it girl
59. VanDam: ...Guid: certain acts of criminal behavior should be punished by death and these should be known by all
60. Guide: you go kitty

This is one of the milder exchanges for this group, with fun banter easily traced between the Guide and Felix the Cat. It is also worth noting how well this group has adapted to the medium, using conversational feedback to make up for nonverbal cues. They quickly learned to attach names to their responses, which allowed multi-threaded exchanges to coexist in the same spaces.

The Fall 1994 debates took place in a crowded older lab with uneven lighting. Loud air conditioners hummed and buzzed the whole hour, and still the room was very hot. However, even with the older workstations, the software did not crash. In this semester, the Nickname Group (W) Fall 1994 remained very serious, covered everyone's topics, tolerated mild multithreadedness, and took on a volatile topic, feminism, in an even-handed manner. Other topics covered by this group included violence in the media, gun control, roleplaying games, and late night infomercials.

Nickname Group (W) Fall 1994—Woman named Clide

66. Guide: We should be on Media and Violence now everybody, why doesnt the big Ragu give us some input.
67. The Big Ragu: It is also wrong to censor the media. It is also a breach of the Constitution.
68. Clide: This sounds like the legalization of pot issue, if you make it illegal people will get it anyway.
69. Cable: meida is not the root of violence.
70. The Big Ragu: WHAT?
71. Gadfly: So if guncontrol is so hard to enforce we can have total gun control
72. Guide: Hey Clide where are you, and what the hell are you talking about?
73. The Big Ragu: Cable, Great call!
74. Kurt Cobain: I dont think we should censor violence on TV, but I think that the networks have some responsibility...
75. The Big Ragu: Who then is responsible for violence.
76. Guide: Gadfly, lets talk about the Media thing now.
77. Kurt Cobain: ....the networks have a responsibility to control what they braodcast.
78. Clide: They are only giving you what you want to see.
79. Kurt Cobain: I dont think that there is necessarily a correlation between violence and what is on TV...
80. Cable: how come Japan has the most violent television in the world but has the least violence on the street?
81. Guide: The only people responsible for violence are the people who sadly believe that everything on T.V is true.
82. Gadfly: Violence should be eliminated from the media. Because the TV tells us basically what to do
83. bob: They networks do a little, for example some shows have viewer discretion is advised every time it comes back from a commercial
84. The Big Ragu: Is it right to show Beavis and Butthead at 8:00p.m.
85. Clide: In japan, what kind of violence do they show?
86. Gadfly: most of us believe everything we see
87. Cable: hvae you ever seen japanese anamation? When they brough it here, some of it was rated NC-17.
88. The Big Ragu: They show graphic violence in cartoons. You see people getting there heads and limbs blown off.
89. Guide: Wow I didnt know that Cable.

The Big Ragu participated more than the Guide in this group, although with the Gadfly, the three dominated with 21 percent, 21 percent, and 17 percent, compared to 13 percent, 12 percent, 9 percent, and 7 percent for the rest. The Guide's comments reveal that he felt compelled to obey the constructed authority of the teacher in the classroom, even though I was not looking over his shoulder. Although this group knew a woman was present, they did not know which nickname she was using. In the class discussion the following period, several tried to guess who she was, but the woman kept her identity to herself.

On the other hand, the Real Name Group Fall 1994 (Virtual Locker Room) reads like urban street kids "playing the dozens," each trying to out-insult each other. Official topics covered very energetically by this group included racial misconceptions, nuclear power, the RU-486 abortion pill, the death penalty for Jeffery Dahmer, and the General Agreement on Trade and Tariff (GATT). Unofficial topics included sex, masturbation, one's parentage, and one's masculinity. Again, notice how much shorter the lines are compared to the previous excerpt.

Real Name Group Fall 1994—No Woman (Virtual Locker Room)

50. Guide: we are doing the death penalty
51. Gadfly: Thats right and we are starting with you
52. Eric: This is dumb
53. vic: i think that all the prisoners should be made into minced meat and the turn them to dim-sum.
54. Lin: I am doing the death penalty]
55. Gadfly: No. You are, dam it!
56. King Cobra: My topic for the final paper is that Cutco Cutlery is the finest set of kitchen Cutlery in the world
57. Hans: I say we should put more people on death row, this way we dont have to pay 500000 $ a year for tham.
58. King Cobra: Do you guys know what Cutco cutlery is?
59. Guide: lets get back to the topic
60. Lin: I support people die
61. Hans: King Cobra what the fuck are you talking about
62. Lin: who is cutco cutlery
63. vic: Dim-sum and we can start a franchise selling human meat dim-sum
64. King Cobra: Its not a who you dooff.
65. Guide: I agree with the money figure, do you know that if Dahmer was jailed Ny he would cost us 3,1 Million
66. Gadfly: Well the problem with death row is that my of the criminials go through many appeals for a number of years before they are put to death.
67. Lin: that is a lot the city can give it to me and I will be rich
68. King Cobra: Its a brand of kitchen knives. I has been around over fifty years.
69. Hans: Are you trying to say that you want to eat all the people who have been executed.
70. Gadfly: Lets get down with business.
71. vic: I think that swiss army knives are the best cutnary in the whole wide world
72. Eric: I dont think we should waste money on the electric chair or lethal injection just give them a bath with a toaster!
73. Lin: yeah
74. Guide: I dont believe in the death penalty but I also dont believe in paying tax dollars because some criminal needs housing
75. Lin: lets debate
76. Hans: No more appeals if you are suppostu be killed than be it.
77. Lin: If someone kill you do you want him/her to pay

78. Hans: Guide you are a pussy
79. Gadfly: Remember the Constitution, no cruel and usual punishment.
80. Guide: I think if someone is to be in jail for life he should work of his stay
81. Eric: do your job guide
82. Gadfly: Hey, Hans watch you lingo man
83. Eric: slacker!!!
84. Lin: what are we debating
85. Gadfly: I second that.
86. Guide: you and me later on Hans well see who is the pussy
87. Eric: Your mom

While this Virtual Locker Room lacked the level of creative performance exhibited by its predecessor in the spring semester, it more than made up for it with higher levels of sheer rudeness. In another part of the text, a group member introduced nontextual, physical information about another group member, taunting, "You have a pimple on your nose," even though the workstations blocked sightlines. The student was drawing on his real name knowledge and face-to-face memory, since he could not see his target. King Cobra unilaterally chose a nickname, even though he knew he was in the Real Name Group. In this group, all members participated in a range from 10 to 20 percent. Gadfly dominated somewhat at 20 percent, but six other members participated at 15 percent, 15 percent, 15, percent, 13 percent, 13 percent, and 10 percent.

OVERT GENDER PREJUDICE

In order to characterize what seems to be happening in these all-male groups and relate it to what I call the "Politics of Men as Other," we need to range from the obvious to the subtle, from overt examples of gender or minority/ethnic prejudice to silencing or control and subtle effects of self-erasure, in both types of groups. When someone types "The Guide is a faggot," or "You and me later—we'll see who is the pussy" or "I did my job with your mom last night," or "Peace out my nubian brothers" (when all group members but one are white), I believe we are seeing overt prejudice and bias as an unthinking impulse, despite any tongue-in-cheek intent or deliberate irony. We have an unusual opportunity within these captured texts to study the rhetorical effects when this language runs largely uncensored and becomes a social norm that stands in direct contrast to more "polite" conversation. When that happens, more subtle effects can be detected, such as when one male student called another male student a "woman" in the following extended exchange (line 266). Notice how the discussion evolves from the introduction of "mother insults" to increasingly higher and higher stakes, until the final line, where the Guide verbally enacts sexual activity.

Real Name Group Fall 1994—No Woman (Virtual Locker Room)

238. Hans: Ru486 is the answer
239. Eric: Your mom tried it
240. King Cobra: the issue is freedom to choose
241. Eric: it failed miserably
242. Hans: dont talk about my mom
243. Guide: just look at him
244. King Cobra: Keep with the topic here
245. Eric: I do more than talk with her
246. Hans: guide who are you talking about
247. Gadfly: why not she was so good last night
248. Guide: you
249. King Cobra: new topic?
250. Gadfly: no you
251. Lin: yeah
252. Hans: she, are you sure it wasnt a he
253. Gadfly: probably
254. Eric: guide do your job
255. Gadfly: maybe both
256. Lin: oh
257. King Cobra: Cutco Cutlery
258. Guide: give me a new topic
259. Lin: ha
260. Gadfly: waterfight
261. Lin: new topic
262. Eric: Ill give you a topic!1
263. Gadfly: girls
264. King Cobra: Cutco Cutlery
265. vic: Your mum is so dumb
266. Gadfly: woman
267. Hans: lets talk about your mather
268. King Cobra: girls are alright too
269. vic: Pathenon
270. Eric: they have cooties
271. vic: Atlantis
272. Guide: idid my job with your mom last night
273. King Cobra: stop callling names
274. vic: Pergamon
275. Gadfly: what woman are you
276. Lin: woman
277. Eric: your mom rides a vacum cleaner
278. Hans: you are sick, guide she is 75 years old
279. Guide: give me a topic
280. vic: Your mum is cheess
281. Gadfly: I am not
282. King Cobra: new topic
283. King Cobra: new topic
284. Hans: guide we need a topic

285. Gadfly: How your sex life
286. Gadfly: guys
287. vic: Lets talk about Guides mum
288. King Cobra: gooo
289. Guide: ooooooooooh but she was great the way she moved was unbelievable

Clearly a great deal of overt gender prejudice is revealed in the above exchange. Many may wonder what kind of teacher allows or even tolerates the above behavior in the classroom, even in the electronic spaces of the classroom. That thought has certainly gone through my mind. But the challenge of a writing classroom where students are encouraged to be independent thinkers, where authority is decentered, and where feminist pedagogies place greater value on consciousness raising and active questioning of all texts rather than dogmatically asserting authority, is that the teacher is literally riding a wild horse in a contact zone where she never knows what people will say or write next. One impulse says, "Oh my God, get this under control," while the other impulse says, "All learning is discovery. Ride the wild horse." That is why I made one of the central pedagogical tenets of the assignment the in-class reading and analysis of the printed chat texts the following class meeting. My goal was not to wag fingers, but rather, to remove the texts from their location in fast-scrolling, synchronous time in order to reflect on electronic strategies of kairos and persuasion, the prevailing ethos each group created, and some oppressive assumptions in the contrasting virtual cultures. When the class analyzed the above text as a printed class reading (an assignment written into the syllabus along with any other assigned readings), there was very little I had to do. On their own in small groups and then back as a whole class, students effectively characterized the virtual culture that had been created and noted its hostility toward women. They also commented on how this locker room culture, usually self-censored in the presence of "outsiders," seemed to enjoy a perennial existence in spite of the censorship. My students showed a common knowledge and acceptance of the politics of insiders and outsiders, and knowledge of the discourse in groups that close ranks thorough self-censorship in the presence of an outsider. While they could identify the characteristic discourse readily, their initial attitude toward it was that the locker room culture was simply the way of the world, that it was somehow off-limits to political awareness and change.

My own point of analysis centers around the seemingly innocuous (in comparison to everything else) use of the word *woman.* The word appears three times above, serving as a haunting kind of punctuation in the context of the rest of the discourse about women, mothers, and sex. Most of the time in this group, women are on the outside, spoken of derisively, "done to," until Gadfly utters that line (266). Woman as Other then comes into the group as one of their own, into the group that has no woman, and in spite of all of the other rude talk in this exchange, the lowercase word "woman" is the most supreme insult offered, and so it is picked up and echoed into the virtual culture.

Eric introduces women into this particular excerpt in line 239, but in the overall debate context, "mother insults" have been present since line 87, and the theme is mentioned in 13 different entries in this group. In the above excerpt, Eric implies that Hans's mother tried to abort him. Hans snaps back and shows sensitivity to the topic, which instigates Eric's further taunting that he has had sex with Hans's mother. King Cobra shows discomfort with this thread and tries to rein in the group, but he is ignored. Gadfly picks up the theme and claims that he had sex with Hans's mother just the night before (line 247).

Again, seemingly bristling with sensitivity, Hans lashes back with a suggestion that Gadfly had not been with his mother, but with another man (line 252). Rather unimaginatively, vic chimes in with a mundane insult about Hans's mother's intelligence. But Gadfly has been the most greatly diminished as an accused homosexual. In retaliation, he writes one word, "woman," seemingly to no one, yet ultimately directed at Hans (line 266). With that word, he tries to "one-up" the homosexual insinuation. In the world of Western prejudice against things connected with women, a gay man may be considered by some as stereotypically effeminate, but he is still a man.

Still trying to get the topic off his own mother, Hans tries to get the mob to take on Gadfly's mother. King Cobra wants to make sure no one thinks HE is effeminate, the woman, the image of the Other who has entered the chat room with Gadfly's line. King Cobra types, "Girls are alright too" (line 268). Always the bold ringleader, Eric shows he has no fear of the homophobic insults and declares that girls "have cooties" (line 270), an elementary school defense against the "enemy sex." The Guide now wants his turn in this virtual gang bang of Hans's mother. Meanwhile, "woman" is further invoked into the room by Gadfly and Lin (lines 275 and 276). But the Guide has been sparring with Hans since line 86, with "You and me later and we'll see who is a pussy," calling him out after class. In the above excerpt it is the Guide, an African-American Latino bodybuilder, who types the penultimate insult, pushing invisible boundaries of social norms within the Virtual Locker Room to the typographic imitation of sexual performance with "Oooooooooh but she was great the way she moved was unbelievable."

SILENCING AND SELF-ERASURE

These are the strong forces within the virtual culture. Now let's turn to some of the more subtle effects of silencing, verbal control, and self-erasure, which only show up within the dynamic context of the synchronous threads as they scroll up the screen. By far the most difficult question to ask has to be "How does this internal or external coercion (Habermas's censorship) occur in this environment and exert force, both for men and women, if it does?" For in this environment, if someone tries to exert control over a person or group, anyone can disregard the "herding of the stray" and flaunt rebellion to the entire group. (One such rebel in each separate Virtual Locker

Room group independently discovered that hitting the Return key over and over forced everyone to look at rows of his blank lines, immediately breaking up all conversation threads.) In a text-based synchronous culture, the group can only enforce social norms through verbal control or indifference. We have already looked at instances of verbal abuse. Now let's consider indifference.

I have written of the broad-based participation in the Virtual Locker Rooms. Yet many of the controlling effects also occur on different levels in the serious discussions as well, where two or three group members were more effectively able to dominate and possibly silence other members, and in a nonabusive fashion. For instance, it appears that the Real Name Group (W) Spring 1994's way of dealing with multiple threads when they were introduced (usually by already marginalized group members) was to choose not to respond, to ignore the tangential thread, as when Amet was the only person to bring up the addiction angle in line 37 in the debate over smoking ordinances:

Real Name Group (W) Spring 1994—Woman named sue

25. Guide Norb: Smoking should not be allow at sporting events, in restaurants, or in other public places.
26. sue: The smoke from the rainforest has nothing to do with lung cancer.
27. Guide Jeff: There should be specified smoking areas
28. Stephen: True, but we have to start somewhere. Another point, what about all the money it costs tax payers for health care?
29. sue: It might deplete our ozone, but that seems like a completely differentissue in itself.
30. David: What is wrong with smoking at sporting event if its in the open air
31. Guide Norb: I concede on the cost issue. THe government should not cover healthcare costs that result from smoking
32. Stephen: People who dont want to breath it have to
33. Guide Norb: I still smell the smoke of those around me in the open air
34. Guide Jeff: Put yourself in someone elses shoes. What if you enjoyed smoking. How would you feel if it was banned?
35. Guide Norb: Consideration for others should override someones selfishness to smoke in public
36. Stephen: So we have the streets full of people coughing, with black lung. With no health care
37. Amet: People who enjoy smoking are really addicted. Its not a question of enjoyment its just another drug
38. Guide Norb: Once again, the responsibility lies with the user.
39. Guide Jeff: Im not talking about smoking in public. I think that should be regulated. What Im arguing is smoking in the privacy of your own home or car.
40. Guide Norb: As a smoker you are making the conscious decision to harm your health.
41. Guide Jeff: That is your body, not the federal governments
42. Stephen: On the drug issue, I used to smoke. I have even tasted reefer in cigarettes. What does the manufacturers add to tobacco?
43. Guide Norb: I have no problem with smoking in private. just dont burden me with your health care costs

Several marginalized group members (see the lower percentages of participation in the Appendix) did comment on the effect of being ignored in their journal entries, often while praising the seriousness of their group's debate over the antics they saw upon re ading the transcripts of the other group. Amet, an Indian student who struggled at times with American idiom, wrote in his journal:

> My group had two guys that really took off with the topic leaving everybody behind. They were both well-informed and serious about the debate.... Consequently, I put in my two cents and had it ignored for the most part. The combination of our names being presented and moreover the fact that the "chat" was being taken over by two well informed individuals, enabled our debate on smoking to be intellectual, serious, non-circumlocution, wealthier, and mundane.

Meanwhile, the dominant members of the Real Name Group (W) Spring 1994 made no mention in their journal entries about the lack of participation by their own members. Most interestingly, no member of this group ever referred to another member by name in the debate texts. But all participants in the Real Name Group (W) Spring 1994 had a great deal to say in their journal entries about the frivolousness of the Nickname Group Spring 1994 (Virtual Locker Room), most of it disapproving. Stephen's entry captures the representative tone.

> ...I feel that 2/3 of the debates were nothing but a bunch of babble from sexually repressed immature adolescents. I was in the group that debated the topics of financial aid reform and banning tobacco. Our debate were 99% serious with 1% consisting of political jokes during the lulls in the debate. Our peers however were 1% serious and 99% jokes.

Interestingly, the one woman in that class, sue, although easily as disapproving of the Nickname Group Spring 1994, expressed regret in her journal that she wasn't allowed to switch groups in mid-class. I can't tell if she meant that she wanted to be raunchy along with that group, if she wanted to go undercover with a male-sounding nickname, or if she wanted to confront the sexist language the group was using. An outside reader of the transcript immediately noted that sue's use of lowercase letters for her name and Amet's denial of his own silencing at the hands of classmates both constitute subtle effects of self-erasure. This was a group so dominated by Guide Norb, Guide Jeff, and Stephen that sue only logged 9 percent of the posts, and Amet barely 2 percent.

Members of the Nickname Group Spring 1994 (Virtual Locker Room) even seemed to admire the other group's debate, as one remarked in his journal:

> The second debate was very different. It was a real conversation that could easily have taken place on the floor of the House of Representatives. It was simply one good point after another. There was some real discussion going on. Gadfly, Nickname Group Spring 1994

We can also consider the ways in which silencing, or attempted silencing, played a role in this Virtual Locker Room group. One group member, Tula, appeared to violate the bantering tone debating the death penalty with an argumentative point (line 64) that was longer and perhaps more suited for the ethos of the Real Name Group (W) Spring 1994 (Virtual Locker Room).

Nickname Group Spring 1994—No Woman (Virtual Locker Room)

56. Gadfly: Useful skills that may improve the society Cat
57. Guide: if u fry a criminal u dont have to worry about him repeating his crime
58. Felix the cat: speak it girl
59. VanDam: ...Guid: certain acts of criminal behavior should be punished by death and these should be known by all
60. Guide: you go kitty
61. Gadfly: Maybe so, but have you ever asked for a second chance Guide?
62. Felix the cat: good point vandam
63. Guide: sure gadfly, meanwhile he escapes rapes your mom and kills your dad
64. Tula: i went to the middle east one year...to UAE (United Arab Emirates) ...They have no crime, no homelessness, no poverty...because they are so strict with capital punishment
65. Gadfly: What would be those certian crimes Vandam?
66. Felix the cat: this topic blows goats
67. Guide: I rest my case then Tula
68. Hamlet: I agree
69. Gadfly: But is it good to live in fear of strict capitol punishment?
70. Guide: yes
71. Felix the cat: how about them Mets
72. VanDam: ...Gadfly: This is to be desided by the court
73. Guide: wer not talking about little league
74. Gadfly: The courts waste so much money with appeals for the death penalty
75. Hamlet: Oh sure...let other people decide for us vandam
76. Tula: their rules are like...if someone steals something, they chop off their hands...a murder—-off goes the head!....i dont want to know what they do for rape!
77. Felix the cat: yeah but more money is wasted suppoting these people
78. VanDam: ...Hamlet: Those other people are us, "SOCIETY"
79. Hamlet: The courts are not us...we dont even decide who the courts are vandam
80. Hamlet: excuse me the courts are not us vandam
81. VanDam: Hanlet: DO YOU VOTE?

We should note here that within this comment about the United Arab Emirates, Tula possibly also revealed to group members that his nickname was the identity of the single, non-white member of the group, from the Middle East. Tula's point and more wordy writing style were not taken up, but two exchanges later Felix the cat interjected, "This topic blows goats," and his next entry was "How bout them Mets." Felix the cat was just as unsuccessful in his attempt to pull the group off topic, so he had to rejoin the death penalty exchange. Tula, an older and more assertive member of the class, was not one to be marginalized or silenced easily. Until the above segment of the debate, he was behind the other group members in a running tally of comments made. He remained relatively quiet until the Guide's machine crashed and a new topic was introduced, and then he asserted himself, becoming the most dominant member of the group, accounting for 22 percent of the comments by the end. In his journal entry, he was glowing about his experience in virtual culture.

> The Chat Box was cool although it didn't seem like we were getting much accomplished. It was cool to learn to use this new tool. I think it could be used in a very effective manner. It was like experiencing a whole new culture.

On the issue of silencing, the Nickname Group Spring 1994 (Virtual Locker Room) members also tended to assert themselves in tantrum fashion if no one responded to their threads.

Nickname Group Spring 1994—No Woman (Virtual Locker Room)

202. Guide: nobody answered my question!!
203. Tula: what ?
204. Guide: $?
205. Hamlet: Do we really need buissinessmen anyway?
206. Felix the cat: do I look like a dictionary guide
207. Tula: buttloads of moola

The Guide in this group commented in his journal entry about being ignored, and about his (mock) frustration with unruly group members.

> ...One thing that definitely made the debate difficult was that there was so many people and it was impossible for everyone to respond to everyone else. A few times when I said something to someone it went totally unnoticed, even though I used the person's name to get their attention. I'm not sure why people did not take the debate serious. In the beginning, I tried to have a serious debate, and it went well for a while, but then people started to get silly. Reading over the transcript I found the point where the debate went downhill to be exactly where my session crashed. After I came back it was too late; they were lost forever. I just went along with the goofiness after that because there was not much I could do about it.

But in thinking about the issue of silencing and internal censorship in the context of this group, we have to consider the cultural space this group created without the presence or input of women in particular. Tula also contributed many of the overtly sexist comments. A debate culture was being created that had high levels of participation, openness, and abusive and outrageous language, often directed toward belittling women or other minority groups. The following exchange is a good example of its attitude toward women.

Nickname Group Spring 1994—No Woman

215. Hamlet: Kill Guide
216. Felix the cat: $22.95 per hour
217. Tula: 20,000,000 bucks/per death
218. Guide: kill ophelia!!
219. Tula: do her first
220. Guide: me first
221. Hamlet: Ouch!
222. Gadfly: I love they way we stick to the topic
223. Guide: she was hot!! in that movie with Mel Gibson!!!!!!
224. Tula: hell yeah
225. Felix the cat: what topic?
226. Gadfly: but she died (suicide)
227. Hamlet: What was the topic anyway?
228. Tula: what a waste
229. Gadfly: fuck her

Hypothetically we have to ask, what would have happened to a woman in this virtual space? Would her presence have modified the discourse? Would she have been swept along into the discourse of the group? sue commented aptly on this in her journal after reading the transcript of the Nickname Group Spring 1994 (Virtual Locker Room).

> As I read through the repartee of the latter group, I found myself making comments in the margins like "confusing," "obscene," and "candor superseding morality." I believe that in their aliases the members of the second group found the voices of the idiot in every one of us. He very much exists, just more curtailed in some people than in others. The entire exercise reminded me of *The Lord of the Flies*, and how quickly, when left to his own devices, man can forget all his prior teachings and regress.

Note that her unconsciously ironic use of the "universal" man, as in "…the idiot in every one of us. He very much exists" and "...when left to his own devices, man can forget all his prior teachings and regress." In many ways, sue allows us to view Men as Other, even as she subsumes her own identity into the "us" of "all of us."

To conclude that women would be silenced in such a boys' locker room virtual culture, or that they would be forced to write like the boys while wearing a sickly smile at some of the jokes, is basically impossible since there were no women in the Nickname Group Spring 1994 (Virtual Locker Room). But if a woman had been in that group, the attitudes of these men might not have been as candidly revealed. I did, however, attempt to reverse the conditions the following Fall and put a woman into the Nickname Group. What I found is that it appears to be impossible to put a woman into the Virtual Locker Room, because if a woman is known to be present, the Virtual Locker Room disappears.

Homophobia also became an integral element to the abuse in the Nickname Group Spring 1994 (Virtual Locker Room). In the class discussion on the transcripts of the Spring 1994 debates, a student who admitted to being Felix the cat protested that he was not being homophobic when he called the Guide a faggot (line 150). "I have two good friends who are gay and I'm really cool with it. I just wrote that because we were ranking on each other." I asked him if he was so cool about gay issues, why the term "faggot" was still considered a "rank," a bad thing to call someone. This student continued to protest that he was not homophobic, as did other class members.

I don't want to tell any student what or how to think. I did not have a stake in convincing that student that he was homophobic in order to call the exchange a success. He is still thinking about it, and he can work it out on his own. He responded to that class in his journal entry, rigidly holding on to his original idea, unaware of the irony of what he was writing.

> I think that we read into the debate way too much. We shouldn't make judgments of people for what they wrote. If we do this, people will be afraid to say what they mean in fear of being made [fun] of. It's not correct or fair to call a person homophobic just because they call a person a faggot. It's just joking around and it should be taken that way and none other. You can't characterize a person about what they write. We should not create an opinion about a person just from what they write. Felix the cat, Nickname Group Spring 1994 (Virtual Locker Room)

I enjoy this journal entry most of all. This student claims we read too much into the transcripts of the debates, and it is a charge worth thinking about, given the speed of the interactions as they scroll up the screen. His motive for writing above is defensive. He did not have to own up to his nickname, but he did it anyway, because he felt that we were wrongly characterizing "the guide is a fagot" (line 150) as homophobic discourse. He says it was just a joke. But between the lines of his journal entry are the seeds of its own undoing. In claiming that "We shouldn't make judgments of people for what they wrote," he remains oblivious to the fact that calling someone a faggot is making a judgment of another person, a much more harsh judgment than suggesting that a certain discourse reflects homophobic attitudes. This student is defensive over being called homophobic, yet claims that he should be able to call anyone a faggot and that person should not be defensive, rather, he should take it as a joke. Felix the cat's position on this matter seems to reflect his majority group/insider status in the Virtual Locker Room. According to the apparent rules of this group, certain name-calling is understood to be a joke, and other name-calling is not. The way to tell the difference is whether the names, in this case "faggot" or "woman," are seen as representing members of the group. They are not, thus the name-calling is okay and an acceptable joke.

But am I reading too much into these debate texts? For me, the most enlightening aspect of all of the prejudice and bias found in the two Virtual Locker Rooms is its rootedness not purely in sexism, but in the homophobia that underlies the sexism. To look at the insults and idle comments, "woman," "speak it girl," "the guide is a fagot," "he's a pufta," "a flying faggot," "ok there sweet tits," "kill ophelia!" "do her first," "me first," "fuck her," "Guide you are a pussy," "you and me later on well see who is the pussy," "if you don't want to be raped dont do the crime [referring to male rape in prison]," "I did my job with your mom last night," "she, are you sure it wasn't a he," "guide is a weiner," "suck my dick," and "you homo" as an extended list, the connection becomes clear. Suzanne Pharr, in *Homophobia: a Weapon of Sexism* (1986), suggests that homophobia gives sexism much of its power because it links sexism with heterosexism. She writes,

> Heterosexism creates the climate for homophobia with its assumption that the world is and must be heterosexual and its display of power and privilege is the norm. Heterosexism is the systemic display of homophobia in the institutions of society.... It is not by chance that when children approach puberty and increased sexual awareness they begin to taunt each other by calling these names: "queer," "faggot," "pervert." It is at puberty that the full force of society's pressure to conform to heterosexuality and prepare for marriage is brought to bear. Children know what we have taught them, and we have given clear messages that those who deviate from standard expectations are to be made to get back in line. (pp. 16–17)

To examine sexism and gender bias without making the link between sexism and homophobia is to miss half of the story, a story about misogyny so complete that even when no woman is present, her aura cast upon men in a closed group makes sexuality between men as constant a tension as sexuality between men and women. This is the political impact of a societal imbalance of power: an enforcement of the value of all things male while devaluing all things female, yet at the same time desiring them, obsessing upon them. I would venture that this is an attribute of groups that understand themselves to be something "Other," outside the norm of society, able only to define themselves in terms of that mainstream society. This is how I move to my understanding of the Virtual Locker Room as closed group communication by Men as Other. From this understanding, we can look both inside and outside of these groups and perhaps see the effects of the Politics of Men as Other.

Which leaves me to consider the Nickname Group (W) Fall 1994, as anticlimactic as it is. Three group members were able to dominate the rest somewhat (20 percent versus 7–12 percent). One group member, Cable, was a racial minority and an experienced MOO-er whose debate topic was Roleplaying Games, yet he participated the least of anyone in the group. In analyzing the transcript of this group, which held in many ways a model debate, the most notable feature is the heavy enforcement hand of the Guide, who took his role seriously and played it with the fairness of a good teacher, a benevolent despot. When I selected him for the role, I had no inkling he would do that, as this student was quiet in class. Even at the beginning of the debate, when some group members initiated silliness, testing the water, he didn't take the bait and go along, as the following exchange shows:

Nickname Group (W) Fall 1994—Woman present, Clide

1. Guide: Hello everyone
2. bob: Hey everybody.
3. Cable: present and accounted for...
4. Guide: Tell me some topics please
5. The Big Ragu: Hey, hows everyone doing? My topic deals with censorship in the media with regards to violence.
6. bob: I have not yet figured out a topic. Im open for any ideas.
7. Guide: Wheres everybody else
8. Kurt Cobain: My brain hurts...
9. Guide: sorry about that Kurt
10. The Big Ragu: Lets get this thing underway Guide.
11. Guide: I can only do what she tells me
12. The Big Ragu: No, you dont.
13. Guide: Yes I do

I should note that the "she" is the teacher, me, and the Guide's sense of my directing him was his own construction. My only direction toward the Guides of both groups concerned pace, and getting to everyone's topics at approximately 15-minute intervals so no one would be left out. I should also add that a friend was sitting in on the class to learn the software, and he participated in this group as Kurt Cobain. He was sitting in the back of the room and no one knew he had slipped in, or which nickname was his. People always drifted in and out of the back of the lab, trying to use an open machine if the teacher would let them.

The woman in this group on her own selected a man's nickname, Clide, and kept her identity to herself. The group knew she was one of them because she sat on the same side of the aisle, but they didn't know which pseudonym. Even in the following class session, the face-to-face discussion of the printed transcripts, she slyly kept her identity secret and the class argued over which nickname she had, opening a discussion on assumed characteristics of gendered communication. Half of the class thought she was Kurt Cobain. Several others guessed correctly.

A test of this group's even-handedness can be seen in its discussion of a volatile and attitude-revealing subject, feminism, a thread that ran for quite a while because it was the topic of two different group members (taking opposite positions). The following two excerpts show this group in action early in the thread, and near its end. At no time did the discussion degenerate into *ad hominem* attacks or highly charged emotional statements. Most interesting is how near the end the group explored writing issues around sexist language, all of its own instigation. Perhaps these classes don't need teachers after all.

Nickname Group (W) Fall 1994—Woman named Clide

148. The Big Ragu: Feminism, we could do without the radicals.
149. bob: What is Feminism???
150. Kurt Cobain: ...I personally think that RPGs are sort of silly, why not experience the real world and all it has to offer?
151. Gadfly: kurt every things harmless to you next to a gun (If you had one...)
152. Guide: Im against Feminism for the most part. Your right Ragu, the radicals are the worst.
153. Clide: Where do you draw the line between being over sensitive to feminist issues and bening ignorant?
154. Cable: Some time you just want to get away when the real world brings you down.
155. The Big Ragu: The problem that I have encountered is that they ask for equal rights so they get equal rights, but when it comes to being a
156. Guide: Good question Clide, I really dont know the answer?
157. Kurt Cobain: Ragu, finish your thought
158. The Big Ragu: gentleman and paying for the bill or opening a door, if we dont then we are a pig and rude and inconsiderate.
159. Clide: A feminist is someone who believes in equal rights for men and women.
160. The Big Ragu: It is a double standard that us men cannot win.
161. Gadfly: It should be equal rights all the way?
162. Guide: Is that true Clide. I wasnt aware of it.
163. Clide: Thats the basic definition
164. Kurt Cobain: Of course it should be equal rights all the way
165. The Big Ragu: It should be but it is not.
166. bob: Im for feminism but it shouldnt be called that.

[167.–192. cut for space]

192. Gadfly: I do not like to say "he or she" every time in my papers
193. Kurt Cobain: GAdfly, stick to writing "she" then.
194. Clide: No one does. Can you think of a gender neutral word?
195. The Big Ragu: "it"
196. Gadfly: thats what I thought but are we being politically correct?
197. Guide: Clide we dont have one.
198. Clide: That sounds primitive.
199. Kurt Cobain: how bout "they"? All it takes is a little thinking and reiwriting.
200. The Big Ragu: but it is gender neutral and that is all the criteria that was asked for.
201. Guide: They is plural and doenst refer to one thing.
202. Gadfly: I have to go out of my way though
203. bob: yeah, but they has he in it isnt that wrong.
204. Gadfly: good guide
205. Clide: Youd have to create a new word.

The Big Ragu and the Guide open the discussion of feminism by stating that they were against "the radicals" (lines 148 and 152). While this potentially could become an attack on feminists, bob asks what feminism is, leading a number of group members to help him work out a definition. Clide (the woman in the group) raises the issue of drawing a line between oversensitivity and ignorance. The Big Ragu shows some sensitivity to what he perceives as a double standard about equal rights and gentlemanly conduct. Kurt Cobain (the outsider) allies with Clide and uses an emphatic tone, "Of course it should be equal rights all the way" (line 164). By line 166, bob understood feminism well enough to have developed an opinion on it.

In the second part of the excerpt on feminism, the discussion had evolved to writing class papers. Gadfly objects to political correctness and says that he does not like writing "he or she in his papers." "It" and "they" are offered as alternatives. The discussion does not accept simple answers or simple contentiousness. Instead, we get a feeling that the group is wrestling with pros and cons of different alternatives. Later, they talk about possible new words and the awkward feeling of "one." As the teacher, I should add that I had mentioned the chapter in our writing handbook on gender fair language when I handed out the syllabus on the first day of class. At the time of these debates, a full-fledged class discussion of the topic had not yet taken place (I usually wait until I comment on sexist language on a paper and students bring it up when I am handing papers back).

What happened to keep this debate on track? Was it the strong hand of the Guide, the presence of the woman, or the dynamic of the entire group? Most certainly, anonymity was not a factor. And, despite my having varied the conditions over two semesters, I still cannot rule out utter chance and circumstance, or teacher influence. More research will have to be done in this area, and throughout 1995 and 1996 I have continued my work along these lines. I also look to others to conduct further studies under different conditions and variables. But my first priority remains the quality of my classroom discussions and the pedagogical value of the whole exercise, both before and after electronic chat experiences. I must put the needs of my students first and continue to strive for enlightening, interactive, and positive experiences in the classroom, both electronic and otherwise.

CONCLUSION

That said, I have to add that I look forward to using these electronic spaces in my classrooms again and again, with debates or any other topics I might think up. I will of course continue to experiment with structures and group leadership in order to tilt the experience in a more positive direction for all students, while at the same time relinquishing teacherly control and authority to my students as active learners, increasing the amount of interactive, dialogic experiences and helping them to think and analyze for themselves, without looking to an authority. But still, I must ask the following pointed questions: "Why would I want to have students participate in an activity that generates oppressive, hegemonic, sexist, racist, and homophobic atmospheres? How could this possibly align with my goals for feminist and critical pedagogies?"

However, just think of how often this locker room discourse is self-censored and thus hidden from the eyes of the people whom it would offend. Would you rather know about it or not know about it? How about your students? Would you rather protect them from it, as sheltered children unaware of the gut-level feelings of their hegemonic oppressors, or would you rather use the site of your classroom to open the door for rare dialogue and interaction with these commonly hidden and unexamined attitudes? I know my answer.

I find the electronic chat rooms to be an intriguing educational tool for feminist pedagogies, and one that my activist heart will not let me flinch from. The class discussion of the printed chat texts was the most essential and valuable part of the experience. My students had created collaborative, dialogic texts in a somewhat nonlinear form, and we were able to turn around and have an active discussion of the language and cultures created in the virtual space of those texts. Their words, their peculiar polyvocal compositions, became the highlight of the class reading list, bringing in alternative and often unprivileged texts for examination. This gave us a valuable gateway to a higher understanding of the politicized contexts of language and culture. For instance, consider an assigned class bulletin board posting one week after the Fall 1994 debates. It is from the Guide of the Real Name Group Fall 1994 (Virtual Locker Room), the student who described having sex with Hans's mother:

> Doing the chat box was pretty fun, I mean we were supposed to be doing work but it seemed like other things were on our minds. I now wish that you never printed out the results of the chat box. It is pretty evident that I have a very dirty mouth. I guess you learn something about yourself in those kind of situations.
>
> One of the things I learned was that a society can be formed by something so basic as a different name or the lack of one. There was an obvious tone difference in the writing of the real name group and the writing of the nick name group. The group with the real names seemed to be more violent and aggressive (raw even) with their speech but the writing of the nick was easy flowing and easy to comprehend. Though these differences were obvious it doesn't make one lesser than the other. Guide, Real Name Group Fall 1994 (Virtual Locker Room)

In light of this and other similar responses, I would have to conclude that seemingly oppressive electronic forums can have an important consciousness-raising function in a writing classroom, illustrating the subtle effects of sexist, racist, and homophobic language more dramatically than position papers on pronoun usage and social oppression alone. And if we assume that these forums are a simple reflection of our existing cultures, rather than some democratizing, egalitarian ideal space, then classwork analyzing how communication in these spaces can silence and empower different groups and individuals will become a valuable step in changing the existing cultures that are reflected in the electronic forums.

We can also see at times greater participation and interaction in a Chat Room debate than we might see in a face-to-face classroom discussion, particularly since there is no turn-taking and people need not queue waiting to talk or deciding that what they have to say is not worth the wait. This brings a richness to class discussions, due to the volume of ideas able to be introduced in a multithreaded discourse, a subject that in itself is worthy of more research. But we should not pretend that this effect is automatically a good thing, especially not for all students. Several students in my class commented in their journals that these debates were also biased toward fast typists and people with good vision, and that is indeed the case.

Yet after looking at these texts, we still have to ask: Isn't all this obvious? What is the big deal about the common phenomenon of adolescent banter getting out of hand?

The contrast between mainstream discourse and male-gendered discourse that emerges online can reveal for us another aspect of gendered communication in a forum where traditional nonverbal cues can be removed, and where egalitarian access and the inability to interrupt have been widely noted. These conditions eliminate often-cited variables affecting gendered communication and unfold before us a curiously distilled view of dominance and silencing. We can see how the gendered tone is set in the creation of online cultures, perhaps leading us to a better understanding of similar face-to-face cultures.

But more importantly, if we shift around to view these online male-gendered discourse conventions as deviations from the mainstream, as something Other, these texts have a great deal to reveal about attitudes toward women and minorities that only show up when the door seems to be closed, when the group is insular. In an age when prejudice and overt discriminatory practices have gone underground, these texts serve as important proof to counter those who claim that the war is over, that the battle already has been won. Without the evidence of these texts, how many of my students would have sat in a class discussion and vigorously asserted that sexism and racism were things of the past, that women and minority groups needed to "get over it"? How many of them insisted that anyway?

But beyond the immediate classroom contact zone, these texts allow us as scholars to examine the dynamics of communication in exclusive domains, both with and without the presence of an outsider, a woman who represents and brings with her mainstream values and discursive styles. To spin Spitzack and Carter's (1987) categories, "The Politics of Women as Other" and "Women as Communicators," into "The Politics of Men as Other," brings a hidden aspect of gendered communication into the open. From my analysis of the above chat texts, we can see that at times some men do view their position as one of Other, set off from the mainstream. This position of alterity can easily be characterized as resentful, hostile, and oppressive to women. If, according to Spitzack and Carter, "male speech is the standard against which female or 'other' speech is judged," exactly what is this locker room speech, mainstream or Other? If it is mainstream, why is it usually so carefully hidden?

Spitzack and Carter's "Women as Communicators" approach lets us consider political implications for men and women as both outsiders and insiders. In the Virtual Locker Room, women are outsiders, yet Virtual Locker Room discourse is outside the mainstream, affected by the controlling factor of even one woman (dare we refer to this male self-censorship as Habermas's "internal and external coercion?").

So if male communication is not the standard against which men's and women's communicative actions are judged, what is the "organizing force in social interaction?" What are the political implications of these two different positions, mainstream and Other, once we construct them to operate more flexibly, less dualistically, to allow us to consider deviant, commonly self-censored, marginal discourse from men, the very group holding the greater political power?

For instance, an all-male locker room culture may be old news, yet from the point of view of women communicators, it is a cultural attitude and space from which they are excluded, along with other traditional bastions of male privilege, the men's clubs, the good ol' boys golfing circles. While few women may want to be included or exposed to locker room discourse, a greater issue is at stake. Getting in to the Men's Club, the golfing circle, etc. may make no difference. As we see in the Virtual Locker Room, it is possible that the discourse conventions that define this exclusively male terrain may cease to manifest themselves, given the presence of even a single woman.

As many writers have already noted, power, favors, and connections are often commodities in these exclusively male groups, despite attention to other topics such as basketball or golf. Cultural precedents may be established that in effect circle the wagons of the group, defining itself as Other, to effectively exclude, even when it is forced to or seeking to include by law or social mandate. Allowing women into men's clubs may make no difference if the cultural boundaries demand self-censorship in the presence of an outsider.

Perhaps this kind of research could be done with conventional face-to-face methods (or unethical hidden tape recorders). The fact that this locker room discourse broke into the open in the medium of cyberspace should be sobering for those who make claims for greater egalitarian forums, for higher levels of democracy in this so-called "achieved utopia" of virtual reality. Rather than theorizing impossibly ideal democratic features for cyberspace classrooms, communities, and cultures, we might be better off trying to democratize our existing face-to-face cultures as they move into cyberspace, because more than anything, cyberspace culture seems to simply mirror and perhaps distort whatever we bring into it.

APPENDIX

TABLE 7.1.
Key: Gender/Minority/Ethnic Identity (self-described)

W	Woman
AA	African-American
A	Southeast Asian-born
MEA	Middle East Arabia-born
MEI	Middle East Israeli-born
L	Central American/Cuban-born
I	India-born

TABLE 7.2

Real Name Group (W) Spring 1994: 43 Comments Total *
(Computer crash destroyed some text.)

Guide Norb	37 percent	sue (W)	9 percent
Stephen (Gadfly)	23 percent	David	2 percent
Guide Jeff	19 percent	Amet (I)	2 percent

Nickname Group Spring 1994 (Virtual Locker Room): 322 Comments Total

Tula (MEA)	22 percent	Hamlet	15 percent
Felix the cat	19 percent	Van Dam (changed names)	2 percent
Gadfly	19 percent		
Guide (machine crash)	17 percent	The Beaver/Phoque/ others	2 percent

Nickname Group (W) Fall 1994: 244 Comments Total

The Big Ragu	21 percent	Clide (W)	12 percent
Guide	21 percent	bob	9 percent
Gadfly (MEI)	17 percent	Cable (AA)	7 percent
Kurt Cobain	13 percent		

Real Name Group Fall 1994 (Virtual Locker Room): 467 Comments Total

Gadfly (L)	20 percent	Eric	13 percent
Guide (AA-L)	15 percent	Lin (A)	13 percent
Hans	15 percent	vic (A)	10 percent
King Cobra (A)	15 percent		

* All percentages have been rounded to whole numbers.

NOTES

[1] These chat-based computer forums occur synchronously, scrolling lines of text in a window, where participants' comments appear immediately on a common screen with a strike of the Return key. These types of forums contrast with asynchronous systems, such as e-mail lists, where separate, longer messages can be posted at any time to a common forum or bulletin board space, and the user often reads posts individually at a different time.

[2] LINGUIST and Megabyte University (MBU) are listservs for academic discussions in linguistics and computer-assisted pedagogy, respectively. Selfe and Meyer's 1991 study of MBU comes to similiar conclusions about power relationships on this particular listserv as well.

[3] Habermas's version of these Rules of Reason (as qtd. in Ess, 1996, p. 21) are: (1) Every subject with the competence to speak and act is allowed to take part in a discourse. (2A) Everyone is allowed to question any assertion whatsoever. (2B) Everyone is allowed to introduce any assertion whatever into the discourse. (2C) Everyone is allowed to express his attitudes, desires, and needs. (3) No speaker may be prevented, by internal or external coercion, from exercising his rights as laid down in (1) and (2).

[4] The classes met in a networked UNIX classroom using chat software in NCSA Collage.

[5] For a full breakdown of percentages in list form, see the Appendix.
[6] (W) indicates a woman was present in the group.
[7] All real names have been changed. Nicknames remain as the students typed them.

REFERENCES

Bolter, J. D. (1991). *Writing space.* Hillsdale, NJ: Lawrence Erlbaum.

Eichhorn, J., Farris, S., Hayes, K., Hernandez, A., Jarrat, S. C., Powers-Stubbs, K., & Sciachitano, M. M. (1992). A symposium on feminist experiences in the composition classroom. *College Composition and Communication, 43*(3), 297–322.

Ess, C. (1996). The political computer: Democracy, CMC, and Habermas. In C. Ess (Ed.), *Philosophical perspectives on computer-mediated communication* (pp. 197–230). Albany, NY: State University of New York Press.

Faigley, L. (1992). *Fragments of rationality: Postmodernity and the subject of composition.* Pittsburgh, PA: University of Pittsburgh Press.

Flores, M. J. (1990). Computer conferencing: Composing a feminist community of writers. In C. Handa (Ed.), *Computers and community* (pp. 106–117). Portsmouth, NH: Boynton/Cook.

Haraway, D. (1991). A cyborg manifesto. In D. Haraway (Ed.), *Simians, cyborgs, and women: The reinvention of nature* (p. 177). New York: Routledge.

Herring, S. C. (1992, October). *Gender and participation in computer-mediated linguistic discourse.* (ERIC Document Reproduction Service No. ED 345 552).

Herring, S. C. (1993). Gender and democracy in computer-mediated communication [Special issue]. *Electronic Journal of Communication/La revue electronique de communication, 3*(2), 1–16.

Herring, S., Johnson, D., & Dibenedetto, T. (1992). *Participation in electronic discourse in a "feminist" field.* Paper presented at Locating Power: Proceedings of the Second Berkeley Women and Language Conference, Berkeley, CA.

Hollis, K. L. (1992). Feminism in writing workshops: A new pedagogy. *College Composition and Communication, 43*(3), 340–348.

Pharr, S. (1988). *Homophobia: A weapon of sexism.* Little Rock, AR: Chardon Press.

Selfe, C. L. (1990). Technology in the English classroom: Computers through the lens of feminist theory. In C. Handa (Ed.), *Computers and community* (pp. 118–139). Portsmouth, NH: Boynton/Cook.

Selfe, C. L., & Meyer, P. R. (1991). Testing claims for on-line conferences. *Written Communication, 8*(2), 162–192.

Selfe, C., & Selfe, R. (1994a). The politics of the interface: Power and its exercise in electronic contact zones. *College Composition and Communication, 45*(4), 480–504.

Selfe, C. L., & Selfe, R. J. (1994b). Writing as democratic social action in a technological world: Politicizing and inhabiting virtual landscapes. In A. H. Duin & C. J. Hansen (Eds.), *Nonacademic writing: Social theory and technology* (pp. 325–358). Hillsdale, NJ: Lawrence Erlbaum.

Spitzack, C., & Carter, K. (1990). Women in communication studies: A typology for revision. In B. L. Brock, R. L. Scott, & J. W. Chesebro (Eds.), *Methods of rhetorical criticism* (3rd ed., pp. 403–426). Detroit, MI: Wayne State University Press.

Winner, L. (1977). *Autonomous technology.* Cambridge, MA: MIT Press.

chapter 8

The Use of Electronic Communication in Facilitating Feminine Modes of Discourse: An Irigaraian Heuristic

Morgan Gresham
Texas Woman's University

Cecilia Hartley
University of Louisville

One would have to listen with another ear, as if hearing an "other" meaning always in the process of weaving itself, of embracing itself with words, but also of getting rid of words in order not to become fixed, congealed in them.
—Luce Irigaray (1977/1985)

CIRCLE OF DISCOURSE: "YOUR OWN NAME FIRST"[1]

Date: Thu, 16 Feb 95 10:12:02 cst[2]
From: Cissy <egcah@vm.cc.olemiss.edu>
Subject: Re: Hmm
To: Morgan "Mad Dog" Gresham

Warning: The following e-mail message may contain some actual pieces of information which could be offensive to those expecting the usual mindless e-chat.

OK, the latest on Joy. She and Pete were both accepted to Kent State, so she's pretty much walking on air. Life's good for her. As for the B'fast Club paper, I'll remind her. I can't ever remember to tell her to e-mail you when she's over here.

As for our straying far from our original topic and the possibility of a paper in there somewhere, why you are on the cutting edge of modern theory! We were talking in Dan's captivity narrative class the other day about the effect of "writing" on the narrative itself. That rather than stylized patterns being repeated over and over, the act of recording narratives led to the preservation of the particular and the concept of truth vs. fiction (I'm getting to the point here I promise). Anyway there are some theorists who are now postulating that the advent of electronic communication is returning us to an oral society and resurrecting some of the old oral traditions. What do you think?

The impetus of this chapter arises from the sometimes precarious nature of the dual roles of student and teacher. Much of what piques our interest theoretically, pedagogically, and philosophically as graduate students eventually finds its way into our own classrooms as teachers. There, it undergoes a sort of trial and error process as new ideas are either assimilated into or rejected from our pedagogy. The student/teacher dichotomy is a liminal state in which we are at once both and neither, and which affords us the ability to experiment with our conception (and construction) of each role.

The dual roles we play as both student and teacher offer a potential-laden perspective on the pressures faced by our students. They, and we as graduate students, negotiate a space in which the struggle to find a personal voice is often at odds with the desire to speak in harmony with the academy. It is an awkward stage in which our voice is changing rapidly, often speaking of a theoretical grasp that it cannot quite yet hold. In flux, it, in turns, exhibits a greater sophistication than our students, then

Date: Thu, 2 Mar 95 09:02:16 -0600
To: "Morgan Gresham"
<GRESHAM@beowulf.it-servers.louisville.edu
From: egcah@sunset.backbone.olemiss.edu
(Cissy)
Subject: Re:

>> Good morning!
>Don't need "good" when "morning" will suffice.

demonstrates our own naiveté in the face of those more experienced.

It is also this position that allows us to take risks, try out our theories, and talk with others about our ideas on both sides of the classroom. Trying out ideas in the classroom is one way we have of refining and defining our theoretical base, at the same time finessing our theories of instruction.

Such experimentation does not take place in a vacuum. We both come from programs that encourage collaboration on both the graduate and undergraduate levels. An important part of our training is learning to enlist our colleagues as fellow knowledge-makers and defend our positions or modify our ideas, often both. Through agreement and disagreement and the intercourse of conflicting theories, we learn to engage others' ideas in connection with and opposition to our own.

>> Where are you?
>here.
>> Write back.
>back.
Thank you for the succinctness lessons. They are most appreciated. I follow with some of my own.

What you wrote:

>i just sent you (well, not "just sent" cause i did
>it about 10 minutes ago, but our system is
>sluggish this morning) my additions to the
trip >plan—let me know what you think
What you said:
Sent additions. Let me know.

But we don't really _want_ to work at succinctness, do we? Irigaray would be
turning over in her grave. She _is_ dead, isn't she?

While colleagues at the same university, we therefore used one another as a resource and sounding board. When one of us moved to another university, that relationship continued. Initially, we acknowledged only the importance of maintaining communication itself and did not recognize the particular importance of the medium through which those conversations were conducted. However, over time, as e-mail was becoming our chosen form of communication, we came to recognize that the medium was shaping not only the ways in which we spoke with one another, but in many respects the thought processes behind our communication as well.

As our conversations gradually began to shift from telephone to electronic mail, we discovered several advantages to making this shift. The semi-permanent nature of electronic communication meant that we could vary the amount of time we spent responding to a comment or series of comments. By choosing the appropriate amount of time to respond more carefully to one another's drafts and ideas, we considerably increased the number of facets we could examine. Some conversations were immediate, transpiring at the same moment in time, and very nearly oral in terms of proximity and dialogue. Others were slow, meandering, allowing a day or more between replies, coming closer to traditional written response.[3] Furthermore, we discovered that by maintaining links with several different messages we could carry on multiple strands of conversations at once and thereby approach one topic from a number of different angles.[4] For example, different threads of those conversations over time incorporated literary theory, feminist theory, and composition theory, although not always in a formal sense. At times, the theoretical concepts we were grappling with were dense, and we worked to learn them by engaging them on a number of different levels. The spontaneous banter fostered by online concurrent communication allowed us to play with the language, interspersing threads of the highly theoretical with the mundane, enabling us over time to assimilate them more thoroughly. By watching those threads interweave and evolve, we began to see similarities and juxtapositions, places where those theories spoke to one another, that we had not recognized before.

> Date: Tue, 20 Feb 95 09:29:07 CST
> From:<egcah@vm.cc.olemiss.edu>
> To: Morgan Gresham
> Subject:Re: On break
>
> I'm home. I haven't read the first. What point does she make about what marriage does to women?
>
> If the Irigaray is in _This Sex_ I've read it. Do you remember the name it's under?
>
> Do you see this warping of our sexuality as necessarily a Western thing? It seems to me that most cultures I can think of (Asian, African, etc.) do similar damage to their women, only manifested in physical ways.

Though we were only two, our dialogue with each other had become multivocal, heteroglossic in a Bakhtinian sense, layered over with meanings and understandings formed from countless strands of conversation and interaction. In actuality, of course, we were not simply two. Our discourse carried the voices of theorists, writers, other colleagues, our students, as well as ourselves. We were able to experience consciously (and very neatly trace out by examining e-mail messages) Bakhtin's (1991) "living utterance," which he says "cannot fail to brush up against thousands of living dialogic threads, woven by socio-ideological consciousness around the given object of an utterance" (p. 276). We had become "knowing participant[s] in the social dialogue that constitutes all discourse" (Goleman, 1995, p. 44).

In addition, through our dialogue with others online (by way of e-mail, listserv, and IRC discussions), we perceived that electronic interaction was allowing us to approach a sort of "feminine" discourse that theorists such as Luce Irigaray had long called for—a discourse that not only rejects traditional models of linear logic and argument by dichotomy, but which breaks down the hierarchical walls between communicants.

IRIGARAIAN PEDAGOGY: "THIS IS A METAPHOR"

Many composition theorists, of course, have recognized that the application of Irigaray to composition theory has the potential to open our students to a broader definition of writing (de Beaugrande, 1988; Juncker, 1988; Looser, 1993; Mullin, 1994), writing that privileges multiplicity. "It's our good fortune," Irigaray (1977/1985) states, "that [feminine] language isn't formed of a single thread, a single strand or pattern. It comes from everywhere at once" (p. 209). However, what all of these discussions have in common is the belief that French feminist theory has the *potential* to change composition theory and the call to begin thinking of ways to incorporate that change. Clara Juncker ends her discussion of Cixous by suggesting that compositionists find ways to "allow for multiple kinds of writing … to encourage [students] to exist simultaneously in the realms of 'reason and folly'" (p. 434). Similarly, Robert de Beaugrande links the use of Irigaraian theory to a new conceptualization of writing theory: "It is time for us to listen and read in unwonted ways; to disaccustom ourselves from our facilitated certainties and our complacent literacy; to multiply meaning without an irritable grasping at closure" (p. 272). What these articles also share in common is that they stop short of practical application, of demonstrating what such theories could look like in the classroom. As Joan Mullin acknowledges, however, theory without practice is mere intellectual exercise. She notes that "[w]hile postmodern (French) feminists can unmask power and encourage us to seek self definition…unless we radically change our own classroom practices and begin to listen to students, we only play with the very words we claim to unmask" (pp. 22–23).

Given that we feel it has been well established, then, we are not arguing here for Irigaray's place in composition theory. Rather, we argue that with computers and composition, and in electronic discourse in particular, there is a way to demonstrate, to see visibly, the practical application of Irigaray's (1977/1985) theories of language to the composition classroom. Our recognition of Irigaray's applicability to electronic communication began with an e-mail conversation in which we juxtaposed her discussion of the fluidity of language against one of Margaret Atwood's poems. While in one thread of messages we were discussing the theoretical aspects of Irigaray's propositions, in another thread we were considering the more practical uses of such fluidity. As we continued the conversation and the threads grew more

From: "Morgan Gresham"
To: Cissy
Date: Thu, 23 Feb 1995
18:26:12 EST
Subject: Re: on two things

> You know, it's just a thought, but
>could you argue the premise that
>Atwood _was_ responding the
>Irigaraian call for l'ecriture >
>feminine. Not sure whether she's
>echoing it or starting a
>how-to primer, but there seems to
>be a definite attempt to
>express in words (so difficult to do)
>language grounded in the body.

Yes, i think that's a great idea (at
some point we should do a paper
on this together). Later in "When"
Irigaray states:
If we don't invent a language, if
we don't find our body's language,
it will have too few gestures to
accompany our story. We shall tire

of the same ones, and leave our desires unexpressed, unrealized.... (p 214)
check it out

interconnected, we became aware that these multiple texts enhanced our conversation as a whole. It allowed us to clarify, explore, and question some of the assumptions that are often left unstated and unexamined in traditional face-to-face linear dialogue. We began to look for ways to incorporate Irigaray into our pedagogy so that our students might similarly benefit from experiencing this type of circuitous interaction.

In particular, we felt that such a potentially heteroglossic space would encourage our students to ask questions about hierarchies, cultural divisions, and the social construction of knowledge. Indeed, Irigaray's (1977/1985) language indicates that she values many of these same questions:

> If you/I hesitate to speak, isn't it because we are afraid of not speaking well? But what is "well" or "badly"? With what are we conforming if we speak "well"? What hierarchy, what subordination lurks there, waiting to break our resistance? What claim to raise ourselves up in a worthier discourse? (p. 213)

Asking such questions, we feel, is the first step towards resistance and creating a more egalitarian space.

Grounding discourse metaphorically in the sexual body, Irigaray defines marginalized discourse as feminine.[5] In *This Sex Which Is Not One* (1977/1985), she outlines what she sees as the difference in traditional, acceptable (masculine) discourse and that which is marginalized, unacceptable (feminine) discourse:

> She is said to be whimsical, incomprehensible, agitated, capricious... not to mention her language, in which she sets off in all directions leaving him unable to discern the coherence of any meaning. Hers are contradictory words, somewhat mad from the standpoint of reason, inaudible for whoever listens to them with ready made grids, with a fully elaborated code in hand. (pp. 28–29)

Rather than creating essentialist divisions, employing such "contradictory" and "unstable" discourse in our classrooms permits us to be more inclusive. Allowing writers to experiment with nontraditional forms of writing does not exclude the traditional forms valued by the academy. Rather, it frees writers to make judgments relative to the needs of a particular audience, purpose, or situation.

Date: Fri, 24 Feb 95 13:46:14 CST
From: Cissy <EGCAH@VM.CC.OLEMISS.EDU>
Subject: Re: Did you say the Tower?
To: Morgan Gresham

And together our brilliant minds have come up with yet another publishable paper topic. "The

Irigaray (1977/1985) proposes a fluid type of dialogue that engages the communicants in multiple conversations at once. What is achieved, finally, is a web of conversations linked together by strands of thought not held rigidly in place by convention. Irigaray's discussion of "feminine discourse" echoes closely Bakhtin's (1991) heteroglossic discourse community and his explanation of what happens to words engaged in living discourse:

> Use of Cybercommunication in Facilitating Feminine Modes of Discourse: An Irigaraian Model"
>
> What'd'ya think? Don't you think we come much closer to circuitous (i.e. nonlinear) thought & speech when communication via e-mail than we do by traditional written communication where we feel compelled to follow the established rules of language?

> The word ... enters a dialogically agitated and tension-filled environment of alien words, value judgments and accents, weaves in and out of complex interrelationships, merges with some, recoils from others, intersects with yet a third group: and all this may crucially shape discourse, may leave a trace in all its semantic layers. (p. 276)

Indeed, as we stated at the beginning of this chapter, for Irigaray, feminine expression requires that "One would have to listen with another ear, as if hearing an 'other' meaning always in the process of weaving itself, of embracing itself with words, but also of getting rid of words in order not to become fixed, congealed in them" (1977/1985, p. 29). Neither of us were using Irigaray in our pedagogies the semester we discussed Atwood online, and we were only beginning to understand the implications of Irigaraian theory. We were not working together, with the exception of responding to one another's drafts. We were not collaborating. And we certainly were not using our conversations to form the basis of a publishable article. In retrospect, as our own definitions of work and play have evolved, we realize that we *were* working together, collaborating on many levels. At the time, we thought we were using e-mail for play, to pass the time when we were in the lab or when procrastinating on work to be done. What was happening, however, was that

> Date: Fri, 24 Feb 95 13:53:19 CST
> From: Cissy
> Subject: Re: Did you say the Tower?
> To: Morgan Gresham
>
> No, actually I didn't think I was kidding at all. I was going to suggest we start saving some of these back and forths in a file somewhere. Even the nonsense ones (especially the nonsense ones?) would have something to say about the formation of circular speech.

> Date: Fri, 24 Feb 95 13:56:15 CST
> From: Cissy <EGCAH@VM.CC.OLEMISS.EDU>
> Subject: Re: We have a winner
> To: Morgan Gresham
>
> I say let's go for it.
>
> Plan of action? Oh, no. Far too linear. Ideas?

the theory we were reading and working with in our classes was "in the process of weaving itself" to the point that Irigaray and other theorists were frequent players in our casual conversations. When it finally occurred to us that this play had given birth to something substantive, and because we are always looking for ways to engage our students, to help them find they have something to say, we began to speculate on what would happen if we encouraged them to play as we had. If we put our students online, encouraged them to engage one another, what ideas might weave themselves into their conversations? What meanings might they create?

In our role as composition instructors, we continually critique our classroom practice, finding ways to more closely match our theoretical grounding. Our ground, feminist social-expressivism,[6] encourages us to create a decentered classroom and to value collaboration and multiplicity of voices. Before this point, we had been encouraging multiplicity of meaning and voice in our classrooms by means of nontraditional assignments and group projects, and our efforts had been successful to a degree. But negotiating a space in which to voice that which often goes unheard does not come naturally to our students. As Irigaray notes, "we haven't been taught, nor allowed, to express multiplicity. To do that is to speak improperly" (1977/1985, p. 210). Neither have we been taught how to play with language nor that such playfulness has value in its own right. Students and teachers have been conditioned to believe than learning and play do not happen at the same time. As a result, such "play" often goes unvalued, not only by teachers, but by the students themselves. However, playing allows us to hear with the "other ear," not with the same ear that hears rules and hierarchies, that cannot hear the multiple voices of those who are usually silent. When play is devalued, the rigidity of the traditional classroom structure may encourage students to rely upon the visual cues of race, gender, and class and fall into hierarchies where those accustomed to power and privilege and being heard take the lead, the rest falling silent. Such a scenario effectively bars many from the knowledge-making process and hinders any real dialogic interaction (Ward, 1994). Unstructured or less-structured discourse, however, opens both the speakers and their words to new patterns of conversation. Because our experiences online demonstrated this fact, we suspected that communicating electronically would allow our students to experience on a practical level the multiplicity that we had only been theorizing.

FROM THEORY TO PRACTICE: "HOW DO YOU LEARN TO SPELL?"

We are not alone in our interest in incorporating electronic conversations into our classrooms, nor is it unwarranted. Indeed, the field of computers and composition is experiencing increasingly rapid expansion. The questions raised by Gail Hawisher and Charles Moran (1993), in "Electronic Mail and the Writing Instructor," are still applicable to those of us who incorporate electronic communication into our classrooms:

> How may e-mail change *what* we teach? How may it change how we teach? And how may it impact our lives, both as teachers and as scholars? Our overarching assumption is that e-mail, as a medium for exchange of the written language, is a proper subject for study in the field of composition theory. (p. 64)

We believe that by asking and answering questions such as Hawisher's and Moran's, instructors can enhance their theoretical and pedagogical approaches significantly. As we have argued, electronic communication reshaped our conversations and the ways in which we participated in and created those conversations. It is an investigation of those changes and how they continue to shape our feminist pedagogy that we undertake here.

As Cynthia Selfe (1990) explains, computers "change the nature of written communication and, thus, the nature of literacy education itself" (p. 118).[7] Intrigued by the possibilities of using electronic discourse to enhance our classroom practices, we wanted to create a system by which our students would be able to participate in electronic conversations with one another, thus opening them to the possibilities of experiencing a similar transformation.

In an effort to create an environment that would foster circles of exchange, we established a linked composition class through which our students would interact electronically with one another, debate essay topics, engage in peer conferencing, and conference with us as instructors. We defined the basic structures of the two courses, including a collaborative listserv, asking students to make the list as much a part of the class as they found useful. This move to incorporate technology was not a shift in our pedagogy, but rather a refinement of the theory behind it. In fact, this refinement invites an even greater multiplicity of voices, while creating a space in which they can be heard. Selfe (1990) notes that using computer networks in this way enables a feminist pedagogy:

> Within reading and writing intensive classrooms, computer networks, computer conferences, and computer-based text production can help us demarginalize those individuals who have been excluded from our discussions by more traditional approaches to teaching literacy. Such systems can, in a feminist sense, invite more people into active engagements with, and conversations about, texts and encourage them to participate in different, and perhaps more egalitarian, ways than might be possible using more traditional media. (p. 122)

Despite our agreement with Selfe's assertion that electronic discourse can diminish hierarchies, our experiences have demonstrated what Selfe and Selfe (1994) later conclude—technology does not of itself create egalitarian space. It can certainly, however, foster an environment that invites more voices. And if it does not remove hierarchies and barriers to communication, it brings them into sharper relief against that backdrop of voices. As feminists, we incorporated technology to further expand and enhance our existing pedagogy. Feminism has shaped our use of the technology just as certainly as the technology has shaped our feminism.

As we reflect upon our experiences with electronic communication (an ongoing process), we have come to recognize that much of the potential and many of the problems that we have encountered with electronic communication in our classrooms are visible in the joint introduction we gave our students when they joined the class listserv. That introduction falls primarily into two sections: a fairly linear first half in which each of us relates the particulars of our academic and secular backgrounds, explaining our interests in composition and rhetoric and in electronic communication in particular. Secondly, we include for our students a brief (and somewhat elementary) discussion of the pedagogical basis for our electronic class, a discussion that was conducted via e-mail and that was intended to model a dialogic approach to writing. This introduction was posted to our listserv, Comp, about two weeks after our students had composed, revised, and posted their own introductions to the list:

> Since you guys introduced yourselves on the list, we thought it was about time we did. Our introduction is still in progress, however, and we will up-date it when the mood strikes.
>
> My name is Morgan Gresham, and I am a second year Ph.D. student at the University of Louisville.[8] I am originally from Greenville, Mississippi, which is on the Mississippi River. In another semester, I will be done with my course work, and I hope to teach computer-assisted composition at the university level when I'm done. My research interests are gender theory, computers and composition, and women's literature. I did my undergraduate work at Millsaps and Hendrix Colleges and completed my master's at U of L. After a year at the University of Mississippi, I returned to U of L to complete my Ph.D. Outside of school (is there such a thing?), I like to camp, hike, cycle, sail, swim (I'm a swimming instructor on the side), watch movies, and read. Stephen King is one of my favorites.
>
> ...and here's Cissy to tell you a little about herself:
>
> I'm Cissy Hartley and I'm a perpetual Master's student here at Ole Miss. I'm finishing my thesis this year (no, really, I am) and then, Master's degree in hand, it's off to who knows where. All I know for sure is that I want to teach and I want to write. That, and that I have to live near the ocean. I keep trying to get there but somehow seem to keep moving horizontally rather than vertically. I gotta get that fixed.
>
> I'm originally from Alabama. I spent the first 20 some-odd years of my life there. I went to the University of Alabama and Athens State College for undergrad, getting my B.A. in English and History. After flipping the proverbial coin, I ended up here for my grad work. My research interests are early American literature, Southern literature (especially Southern women writers), and—big surprise—computers and composition. As all of my students know, I'm researching my thesis this semester on the effect of electronic communication upon the composition classroom.

...and here's how you got to be engaged in this research project:

C: So how did we come up with our twisted plot to connect you all online?

M: Yeah—so how did we come up with this idea? It seems that it came up in one of our many online conversations. We started talking and thinking that if online communications help us think and write better....

C: Wait. I think we need to back up here. Give a little history. (Remember, I'm the history major here). Morgan and I were office mates when she was a student here at Ole Miss. Then she moved back to Louisville, and we began to run up phone bills. Last year I finally got a modem, and the conversations began. Before long we began to realize that our online conversations were a lot more productive than our phone calls. Our e-conversations actually seemed to be improving our communication skills.

M: We started to put two and two together, but it wasn't until we started talking about theory that we really got it together...

C: Well, actually, it all started from reading a theorist who hasn't a smidge of interest in electronic communication but has a lot to say about communication in general. Luce Irigaray, a French feminist, has several theories about the different ways men and women communicate. To boil it down to a nutshell (and mix my metaphors at the same time) Irigaray says that men communicate linearly—straight forward, point to point, logically—and that women speak in a more circuitous, roundabout way, covering a lot of territory but getting there just the same. This may be telling you all far more than you want to know, but basically it occurred to us that electronic communication seems to promote what Irigaray would call "feminine" speech.

M: So the long & short of it is—we think that this electric community will help your writing and we hope that you have as much fun with e-communication as we do.

We should acknowledge the disjunctions embedded within this hopeful posting. In an effort to simplify Irigaraian theory for our students, we essentialized it, grounding masculine and feminine discourse in biology. Too, despite our claim that we would "update it when the mood strikes," our introduction remained static for two semesters. And, despite our desire to model dialogue, we did not converse publicly. Although we formulated, revised, and finessed several drafts of both the linear and conversant sections of our introduction electronically off the list, we only posted a final draft to the listserv. We failed to allow our students an opportunity to watch our engaging and drafting at work. Despite all we felt about the fluidity and playfulness of electronic communication, we created a rigid, albeit conversational, document. As Takayoshi (1996) warns, the fluid nature of electronic communication can in some ways intensify the rigidity of a final product: "As [Johndan] Johnson-Eilola acknowledged, although students may be learning and writing within explicitly process-centered pedagogies, for many student writers the end product remains the objective" (p. 248). Clearly, we too fell into this trap when creating our introduction and in so doing set a precedent for our students to follow.

Regardless, we have designed our courses to encourage collaboration and interaction on a number of levels from our students. We choose to make our students aware of the pedagogical and theoretical ideologies to which we subscribe so that they have a better sense of the kinds of critical thinking and writing we expect from them. Such honesty yields other benefits as well. Those who maintain decentered classrooms understand that at times students demonstrate a hunger for stricter limits, greater teacher-authority, and more structure. That phenomenon is not particularly eased in an electronic classroom where students are responsible for initiating and maintaining their own dialogues. We have found, however, that sharing our theoretical framework with our students and reminding them of the value of play, as well as installing them as fellow researchers, helps appease their desire to relinquish their own authority. By our making them aware of our research, in particular the project you are reading, they came to understand that their cooperation was an asset to the work we were doing. Likewise, they relied upon our cooperation in helping them with their own projects.

Though separated from each other by hundreds of miles and a number of cultural and class differences, the students in our classes debated issues, discussed paper topics, used each other as resources, critiqued and responded to each other's essays and, when the assignment called for it, collaborated on papers themselves. The composition programs at the University of Mississippi and the University of Louisville exhibit similar philosophies; both stress the importance of small writing classes (approximately 25 students per class) and social construction of knowledge. Despite these similarities, the schools display a wide variance in student demographics. The University of Louisville is an urban university in which the typical student is nontraditional, working full time, and attending school; at the University of Mississippi, a high percentage of incoming students are wealthy, white, and 18 years old. Placing them online with a group of students who are distanced not only by location, but by socioeconomic status and racial diversity provide many with their first opportunity to listen to voices that have traditionally been silent or absent in their experience. Although such factors as class and race are not immediately apparent in an online environment, our students chose to reveal themselves as defined by their relationships with sex, class, and race in conversations on interracial dating, sexual experiences, private and public education, and others.

At the beginning of the second semester, in order to ease students into speaking with one another on their own and more explicitly incorporate Irigaraian theory into our pedagogy, we devised an assignment that encouraged students to use electronic communication to open up new ways of thinking and communicating. With this assignment, e-mail became not only a message courier, but an active part of their creative processes, changing not only what they said, but how they spoke to one another. In this assignment, the classes at both universities first watched the movie

Don Juan DeMarco, after which there were face-to-face and online discussions of perception versus reality and the ways in which hearing another's story often changes the way we look at our own. They were then assigned to meet and speak with other students online, telling each other their own life stories, after which they were to write an essay, relating not only the life story of the student whom they had gotten to know electronically, but the ways in which hearing that story and getting to know this person affected the ways they view their own lives. This first major writing assignment for both classes was posted to the listserv as follows:

> For this paper, your job is to communicate with two other students via e-mail to tell one another the "story" of your lives. Following that communication (which you'll need to cc to your instructor), you will write your paper, re-telling the story that you heard, highlighting what you find interesting or important. In the course of re-telling that story you should also explain, as best you can, how their stories shape your own retelling as well as the story of your life that you tell others.
>
> Be creative with your assignment. You are not required (nor encouraged) to treat this as a simple interview or a word-for-word re-telling of what you have heard. This is a story filtered through the lens of your perception. Tell what you heard and how you were affected by what you heard.
>
> Suggestions for getting started:
>
> You have been assigned to a group of 3 or 4 students. Send an introductory message to both of them telling them a little about yourself. Once you've all "met" each other, you should decide who will tell their story to whom. That is, in your group of three you will tell your story to one partner and hear the story of another.
>
> Ask each other questions, elicit stories from one another. Be interesting, DON'T bore each other with dry repetition of facts.
>
> Questions to consider when writing your first paper:
> 1) What does it mean to tell the story of your life?
> 2) How do we know what we know? "Facts" and "memories" are highly subjective and selective.
> 3) How does hearing someone else's story shape your own?
> 4) What does it mean to tell the story of someone else's life?
> 5) How can we change our stories?
> 6) How does the act of telling and writing down stories change them?

Don Juan DeMarco is a film that shows the multiple perspectives from which one young man's life can be viewed. We specifically chose this movie because it demonstrates the importance of choosing one's own meaning among the many possible interpretations. The film, however, does not limit itself to choosing a single meaning. Rather, it asserts that there are many truths, each one appropriate to its own circumstance. For example, in the process of telling his own story, the character of Don Juan begins to relate the story he has been told of his parents' life together. After mentioning that they had met in the sunlight, he states that, immediately upon meeting, they had begun to dance under the moonlight. Upon being corrected, he shrugs off the inconsistency by replying, "That was in my mother's version. This is my father's." The casual relationship that Don Juan has with "truth" was at first frustrating to our students who felt compelled to determine *the* truth about his life. During in-class and online discussions aided by those students who "got it," who understood that the film never intended to offer a definitive explanation, we encouraged them to realize that likewise there are many voices and many stories that go into creating the person they believe themselves to be.[9] The next step in the assignment was for the students to create their own stories by telling multiple stories to multiple collaborators, listening with an "other" ear for the juxtaposition of truths. To do so, our students abandoned the rules they had previously learned about biography, recognizing that "facts" are often a matter of perception. Acknowledging the importance of many voices opens storytelling to those students who do not (or cannot) use the voice they so often believe is appropriate for the composition classroom.

As classes begin to engage not only the students who understand how to manipulate language in traditionally acceptable ways, but also those who have previously been marginalized, a heteroglossic community begins to form. Students struggle to find their voices in this community. They create identities for themselves based on their constructions of gender, class, race, and ethnicity. At the same time, the network creates a distance that grants students a new perspective on the relative importance of these constructs, encouraging voices that are typically dismissed or drowned out. Of course, with such greater opportunities to be heard comes a new set of ways to be ignored. "As Andrew Feenberg notes, 'Communicating online involves a minor but real personal risk, and a response—any response—is generally interpreted as success while silence means failure'" (qtd. in Hawisher & Moran, 1993, p. 67).

> Date: Mon, 19 Feb 1996 09:44:18 -0600
> Reply-To: comp@sunset.backbone.olemiss.edu
> From: gabe <[xxxxx]@ULKYVM.LOUISVILLE.EDU>
> Subject: riddle me this...
>
> ... Respond if you like, or don't, and I'll feel like a hopeless loser and answer it anyway in a couple days.

Importantly, however, this new competition for peer recognition has its roots in composition skills themselves. Rather than relying upon sex or social status as arbiter of whose voice is to be respected and responded to, students look to the words themselves. Posts that are creative, provocative, timely, or hostile stand the best chance of eliciting response. Eldred and Fortune (1992) note the importance of critically examining the metaphors we use to describe our pedagogy in their discussion of the common metaphors associated with computers and composition pedagogy. They note that there remains a sharp division, in many writing classes, between speaking and writing that teachers expect computer technology to bridge.

For Eldred and Fortune, a computer-assisted pedagogy in which the false dichotomy separating speech and writing is dismissed invites new metaphorical possibilities. In such a pedagogy, the computer in the composition classroom is far more than just a tool. It becomes, in effect, an extension of the human voice. In our networked classrooms, student voices are contiguous, interacting, echoing, changing each other, yet remaining distinct. Indeed, Cooper and Selfe (1990) posit that computer conferences are "powerful, non-traditional learning forums for students—not simply because they allow another opportunity for collaboration and dialogue… but also because *they encourage students to resist, dissent and explore the role that controversy and intellectual divergence play in thinking and learning*" (emphasis added; p. 849). That is, the distinctions between writing and speaking activities are recategorized into the broader definition of critical thinking skills. Furthermore, we suggest that the fluid nature of electronic language allows students more room to play with the language they are engaging. As Hawisher and Moran note, electronic communication is a hybrid of speaking and writing:

> Reply-To: comp@sunset.backbone.olemiss.edu
> From: <[xxxxx]@beowulf.it-servers.louisville.edu>
> Subject: Re: The Listserv
>
> Well, angie, my dear. It is all very simple, you see. After a long day of instigating invigorating discussions about the various uses of Sweet & Low or hamsters, and the like, one has to set aside time to sort out all the major life questions of the day. But, of course, no one does, and I left my Buddah out in the driveway, so the the rest of the night is devoted to solitare and playing in the peanutbutter jar. Finally, when we lay down to sleep, or lick the peanutbutter off our hands, our brain downloads everything we've experianced during the day for sorting and review. Humans used to start doing this during dreaming, but people of today are far to busy watching Days of Our Lives and avoiding mini-malls (vicious little suckers aren't they?) so people need MORE time to file their memories. Anyway, people always think about what is most desirable to them. You see, oh-jeep-driving-one, we all live in our fantasies and endure our realities.
>
> But, late at night, when the nightlite is broken and our teddies are sulking in the corner over what Newt Gingrich said that afternoon, we are quite alone in our own thoughts. We have the chance to second guess ourselves and fear not being good enough, or whatever. Finally, before we wake up, we all invision a bright world with puppies and pantyhose that doesn't run. This is that magical place where you can drive on driveways and park on parkways, a land where no Republican roams the Earth. I usually dream about getting some sleep. Sometimes the ocasional Dove Bar. [student post]

> [E]-mail is composed online, rapidly. Typically it is not subjected to the reflective scrutiny we usually give to the language we inscribe on paper. Indeed, researchers such as Sproull and Kiesler most often refer to online communication as "talk" or "dialogue." Some colleagues pour their hearts out on e-mail; others seem terse, almost "telegraphic." Conventions of language and style are emerging, but, as we would expect, the conventions are not universal or stable. (1993, p. 65–66)

Indeed, we contend that it is this lack of stable conventions that engages communicants and gives them freedom to try new, multifaceted conversations. For example, just as our students have used the online space to discuss the merits of bubble gum and superheroes (which they may or may not feel comfortable enough to do in our classrooms), the two of us have used our online conversations to question both the applicability of Irigaray to composition, which we could discuss in a graduate seminar and to ponder playfully its connection to sanctioned revelry, which we perhaps would not. Selfe (1990) argues that in the right environment "computer networks become human networks—electronic circles that support alternative, non-traditional dialogue and dialectic, communities that value revision and reinterpretation of traditional educational structures" (p. 123). We maintain that the possibilities offered by fewer conventions help create just such an environment for both ourselves and for our students.

> Date: Tue, 28 Feb 95 08:01:43 CST
> From: Cissy <EGCAH@VM.CC.OLEMISS.EDU>
> Subject: Re: You there?
> To: Morgan Gresham
>
> You know the problem with this country? We don't have an established period of revelry. I mean, there _is_ Mardi Gras, but it only celebrated by a few, in a limited way. Most cultures build in periods of revel & discipline; creates a sense of balance. We leave it up to the individual to decide making for people who party all the time or those who never break loose at all. Terribly out of balance.
> Well, there was my soapbox. Don't know where it came from. I know you exhausted. Been there; done that; sort of am doing that. So did you really knock? You'd wake a poor sleeping schmuck on her morning off so you could have some company?

Maintaining this community requires that students and teachers learn to define achievement in new ways. Finding success within the group dynamic propels conversants beyond the competitive individualism often sanctioned by the academy. While such group interaction is difficult, at best, to maintain in a traditional classroom setting, in a networked environment, barriers to collaboration are mitigated by the multitude of voices learning their own power to speak, power that originates not from a central figure of authority, but emanates from the group itself. In an electronic community (especially those that engage more than one class), the students engage one another, feel each other out, butt heads, and brush up against opposing value systems. They claim the forum as their own in important ways. They find and fight their own battles and establish their own rules. The elite students find they no longer have the automatic advantage of being listened to; in this forum, their audience is no longer primarily the instructor. Traditionally framed arguments are often ignored in favor of sharper prose.

LANGUAGE AT PLAY: "THERE IS NO EITHER/OR"

Incorporating feminist social-expressivism into a networked classroom is not without its share of problems. One of the more basic barriers we encounter is the reality of student computer-illiteracy. This deficit increases the workloads of both students and teachers, which in turn fosters considerable frustration in both camps. Also, many students demonstrate a desire for more central authority, resisting in subtle and unsubtle ways the feminist pedagogies we employ. Interestingly, the very latitude and flexibility encouraged in a feminist classroom opens up the space for such resistance. Students have used the listserv itself, that virtual classroom with no walls, to complain about lack of restriction, seeking solidarity in classmates who are not, in the physical sense, their classmates.

One difficulty is that our method of instruction often belied what we were expecting students to do with the technology. As Alison Regan (1993) notes, it is vital that teachers continually reassess the pedagogical implications of their use of technology. She states:

> Technology provides us with tools to turn our classroom into places where student texts are central; it is important, however, that we recognize how the strategies we use to promote intellectual liberation may actually create additional stress for some students and may limit certain kinds of expression. (p. 18)

Too often we allowed our students and ourselves to view the computer as simply a tool, abandoning the feminist framework we had so carefully articulated. In the end, this abandonment of theory forced us into positions inconsistent with our pedagogies. As George Hillocks (1995) suggests, a separation between theory and practice leads to disjunctions and autocratic methods, or at least it does not allow our students' experiences in our classrooms to impact the evolution of our pedagogy. For example, for the first third of the first semester, the listserv that we had so carefully crafted to be a place of community-building was, for all practical purposes, dead. The only activity taking place was a series of announcements from us about class activities, occasional invitations to speak on the list, and the lonely postings of one student who had previous experience with listservs. In light of this inactivity, we reexamined our classroom practices and realized that we had set a precedent early on, perhaps as early as our initial introductions, that the list would be used to make class announcements. The listserv was introduced as a loudspeaker of teacher authority, which essentially wrested ownership from the students' hands and claimed the list as our own. Upon this discovery, we rerouted classroom-specific assignments to another venue and once again opened the listserv to public discussion. The adjustment was more than successful; within the last third of the semester, we had well over 700 messages on a wide variety of topics pass through the list. Reflection, a continual assessment of both theory and the practice that arises from it, is vital for maintaining a dialogic space.

Still, as the list became utterly the students' territory, we were uncertain at times precisely what was being accomplished. Discussions ranged from the mundane to the absurd. In addition to asking for help with papers and projects and debating various "socially relevant" issues, students spent time arguing everything from bubble gum to which superheroes would win in the ultimate showdown. It was difficult not to wonder occasionally if their interaction were nearly as important as we had been convincing ourselves it was. Yet, we knew from experience that if we attempted to steer the conversation, students would, in Eldred's terms, "prefer not to" participate (pp. 64–65).

It soon became apparent, however, that the most seemingly trivial thread could reap hidden benefits, and that by allowing our students free reign to discuss whatever caught their interest they would find a way to discuss what was important/meaningful to them. An example of that distinction becomes apparent in a thread that began as a question regarding a television show:

> Date: Tue, 20 Feb 1996 11:35:30 -0600
> Reply-To: comp@sunset.backbone.olemiss.edu
> From: gabe <[xxxxx]@ULKYVM.LOUISVILLE.EDU>
> To: smgres01@homer.louisville.edu
> Subject: not a riddle, I SWEAR!
>
> I know you all are REALLY getting tired of hearing from me, but I wanted to pose a question for discussion. Does anyone here watch the show "Star Trek: Voyager?" Well, yesterday they raised an interesting question: if an individual has accomplished every goal they have ever had, seen everything, been everywhere, done everything, and their [sic] was nothing new for them to experience, would they be justified in taking their own life? They are in no pain, and are not suffering physically in anyway, they are not infermed [sic] or decrepit, they are, in fact, extremely powerful, but have lost all interest in life. An extension to this question is this: if you were in a position to grant asylum to such a person, seeking protection from those who would force him to live, would you grant him protection, knowing they would only use that protection as the opportunity to kill themselves unstopped? Pretty heady stuff and I hope to hear from someone.

The question itself was intricate and complex, yet the thread could easily have degenerated into a facile discussion of *Star Trek*. What happened instead shaped the listserv for the remainder of the semester. It also provided our students with reams of experience negotiating text and participating in the creation of knowledge. The thread that arose from this one, in fact, never ended. It evolved time and time again as students brought in new ideas and new questions and discussed personal experiences and deeply held convictions. The initial question evolved from assisted suicide to a debate on fate versus free will. That debate, in turn, yielded the question of the nature of God and whether or not religion is a historical construct, which then led to a discussion of evolution versus creation that sent students on both sides of the issue into libraries and produced some of the best writing we saw all semester, on or off the listserv.

"A WORD AFTER A WORD AFTER A WORD IS POWER"

In Margaret Atwood's poem, "Spelling" (1985), she links her daughter's play with blocks to the act of creating meaning. The child's simple play of linking letters to form words leads to the linking of word upon word, an act that becomes at once powerful and dangerous as she realizes that such play carries meaning. When we encourage our students to play with the language and engage one another in acts of spontaneous communication, they begin to explore one another's ideas as they explore their own. For students, there often seems to be an inherent danger in verbalizing conflicting views; however, when our students struggle with conflict, they recognize the power of engagement. In so doing, they move away from much of the structure that does not allow for multiplicity of voice and meaning. Our students, though perhaps not in a position to articulate the underlying reasons, make it clear to us that they sense a difference in their relationships with the various types of writing we ask of them. The same students who came to us complaining that they had "nothing to say" in a particular assigned paper would turn around and spend several pages in conversation on the listserv, arguing a point about which they felt strongly.

Conversation is the key. Through conversation, we recognized the "feminine" nature of our own online communication. Incorporating a feminist pedagogy that values conversation allows students a space to engage and communicate directly with one another. As students learn they can create knowledge and come to understandings through hearing the voices of others, they become increasingly dissatisfied with isolated writing practices that tie them to a printed text, which is difficult for them to read as dialogic. As a result, we have found ourselves adding more collaborative assignments—ones that draw upon, often emerging from, the e-mail connections our students make—to our syllabi so that the end products more accurately reflect the writing processes in which our students are engaged.

Clearly, feminine dialogism requires that instructors be attentive to the types of assignments and activities that they ask of their students. Simply incorporating listservs and other forms of electronic communication does not guarantee dialogue. Technology does not create feminine space. To create such a space, the technology must be used in ways that encourage conversation and multiplicity of meaning and voice. An electronic space, just as a traditional classroom, can become static when instructors fail to match theory with practice. Despite our strong motivation and theoretical grounding, we temporarily experienced this stasis when we lost sight of our goals of dialogue and conversation. Our online introductions and the manner in which we initially established authority on the listserv, although seemingly minor, *did* silence our students for a time. Ongoing assessment of our pedagogy, however, allowed us to make the necessary adjustments to return multivocality to the forum. Because the medium is somewhat new to our students, they watch carefully how its use is modeled for them, and the ways in which instructors conduct themselves online become magnified under their gaze. If overly rigid rules are established, the space returns to monologism, and monologism will never reflect student voices. If, however, we play to the medium's strengths by opening it to spontaneity and play, we create a dialogic space of feminine discourse. Within the cacophony of an active forum, students learn to articulate their discomfort with the "Other," to value multiplicity of meaning and to heed Irigaray's advice:

> And don't worry about the right word. There isn't any. No truth between our lips. There is room enough for everything to exist. Everything is worth exchanging, nothing is privileged, nothing is refused. (1977/1985, p. 213)

APPENDIX A

Margaret Atwood's "Spelling"

My daughter plays on the floor
with plastic letters,
red, blue & hard yellow,
learning how to spell,
spelling,
how to make spells.

.

I wonder how many women
denied themselves daughters,
closed themselves in rooms,
drew the curtains
so they could mainline words.

.

A child is not a poem,
a poem is not a child.
There is no either/or.
However.

.

I return to the story
of the woman caught in the war
& in labour, her thighs tied
together by the enemy

so she could not give birth.

Ancestress: the burning witch,
her mouth covered by leather
to strangle words.

A word after a word
after a word is power.

At the point where language falls away
from the hot bones, at the point
where the rock breaks open and darkness
flows out of it like blood, at
the melting point of granite
when the bones know
they are hollow & the word
splits & doubles & speaks
the truth & the body
itself becomes a mouth.

This is a metaphor.

How do you learn to spell?
Blood, sky & the sun,
your own name first,
your first naming, your first name,
your first word.

APPENDIX B

Date: Mon, 27 Feb 95 15:16:08 -0600
To: gresham@beowulf.it-servers.louisville.edu
From: egcah@sunset.backbone.olemiss.edu (Cissy)
Subject: Paper Piddles

Well, personally I think you got a killer paper here, though I think it would have been more fun to write if you could have concentrated on Irigaray and gone on for 10 or so more pages. Ah, well. Another paper, another time.

As for your latest draft, I have little to say—mainly a few questions. Though you know me, I did find a few piddley places to pontificate on.

1) pg 3 You say that when the constricting language of men "falls away," [oops just noticed you said "falls _w_ay"—better fix that] the body is able to speak. I have a vague tickle in the back of my mind that makes me think Irigaray said something to the effect that it is the oppression by men which _leads_ to such falling away. And, shoot, I can't find my book. It was just here. The quote said something about women and women's language being squeezed, molded, made liquid by the pressure of the law of the Father (or something to that effect—I can't find the book darn it) that is really reminiscent of those Atwood lines. I think I mentioned it the other night when we first started talking about it.

2) pg 3 - last paragraph. I hate to say this; I really do. But I hate the sentence "Yet Atwood also shows what has happened to women that have tried before to speak." I don't

As feminist literary research is particularly heterogeneous, it is important to define which aspects of theory will be employed. French feminist Luce Irigaray's theories seem an apt choice for an examination of Atwood's poem as, upon close examination, "Spelling" echoes Irigaray's call for a type of *l'ecriture feminine* that she names *parler femme*, a feminine means of communication based upon women's bodies. In "When Our Lips Speak Together," Irigaray (1977/1985) states the dangers of relying on masculine language:

> If we keep on speaking sameness, if we speak to each other as men have been doing for centuries, as we have been taught to speak, we'll miss each other, fail ourselves. Again...Words will pass through our bodies, above our heads. They'll vanish and we'll be lost. (p. 205)

Irigaray argues that women have been marginalized by language as it has been appropriated by men, and therefore, women need to create new ways through which to communicate with one another. Failure to do so, suggests Irigaray, will result in both a loss of consciousness of the female body as well as an inability to speak to one another as women. In the second stanza of "Spelling," Atwood expresses the choices that women have made when accepting the language of men, what Irigaray calls the "Law-of-the-Father." Atwood states:

> And I wonder how many women
> denied themselves daughters,
> closed themselves in rooms,
> drew the curtai
> so they could mainline words. (ll. 7–11)

These women have denied themselves "daughters," a feminine language with which

think it says what it's supposed to be saying.

3) pg 4 - 2nd full paragraph. "It is just this type of play, or adventure, that Irigaray proposes in _This Sex Which Is Not One_ in which she tries to reproduce the multiplicity of women's language."—a bit unclear

4) pg 5 - just under 1/2way down. "From this play, combining of letters with blood, sky and they (oops! fix) sun, a daughter learns how to spell first her name and then the act of spelling."—the dreaded "Awk" rears its ugly head.

5) Next sentence. I'd break paragraphs at "There remains..."

6) Parts of page 7 seem to undercut the Irigaray thesis (which is fine since it's a comp/cont, but I wonder if you should address that fact? The statements I refer to are: "...as we take on the language of another, we learn." and "This power stems from the ability to manipulate the language; that is, accepting the Word of the Father. However, learning to take on another's language is not as simple a process as it might seem."

7) same idea as #6, just on page 8 "...women...have _chosen_ this enclosure _in_ language"—do you want to remind reader(s) of Irigaray at this point?

OK, I'm done. That didn't hurt, did it? I really like it. Let me know how it turns out.

Now, as for dream analysis...surely you don't need _that_ dream explained! :)

Write back,

they may have been able to speak to one another, so that they could speak the language of the Fathers; that is, to become poets. Irigaray concurs, suggesting that, "speaking well" involves a type of conformity and "pull[ing] yourself away from the limitless realm of your body" (213). In essence, the incorporation of women into the Word of the Father means a literal distancing from the female body as Irigaray asserts that *parler femme* is a language of the body that is grounded in female sexuality. As women accept the laws of masculine language, we are divided from the language of our bodies. Atwood's poem speaks directly to this separation and calls for the body to speak once more when she explains:

> At the point where language falls away
> from the hot bones...
> ...the word
> splits & doubles & speaks
> the truth & the body
> itself becomes a mouth.
> (ll. 26–27, 32–35)

Here, the speaker in Atwood's poem addresses the ways in which a woman's language is intricately connected to the body. She suggests that when the constricting language of men "falls away," her body itself is able to speak. Further, this new language allows the word to speak the truth: "& the word/ splits & doubles & speaks/ the truth.../" (ll. 32-34). As this truth comes from the mouth of the body, it is not the "Truth" that is coveted by the Law-of-the-Father; rather, it is the truth of the body, the hidden side of truth. Irigaray explains:

> We haven't been taught, nor allowed to express multiplicity. To do that is to speak improperly.

Date: Fri, 24 Feb 95 13:40:42 CST
From: Cissy <EGCAH@VM.CC.OLEMISS.EDU>
Subject: Re: We have a winner
To: Morgan Gresham <GRESHAM@beowulf.it-servers.louisville.edu>
In-Reply-To: Your message of Fri, 24 Feb 1995 14:37:03 EST

Who said we e-mail nonsense? Blasphemy. Sheer blasphemy. So how much text would a context con if a context could con text?

Since we're on a time limit here, let me just tell you to please
e-mail me a couple more times (not now, over the weekend is fine) @egcah@sunset.backbone.olemiss.edu. Hopefully I'll be able to get it up and running soon. With the new software, I'll be able to include you text w/ my messeges & you won't have to wonder what on earth I'm talking about sometimes.
So what do you want to cover in 20 minutes? The status of women's rights in 3rd world countries? Romanian orphans? Massacres in Mexico? OJ's guilt/innocence?

APPENDIX C

Date sent: Mon, 27 Feb 95 17:00:13 -0600
To: "Morgan Gresham"
From: Cissy
Subject: Re: Paper Piddles

>> >should i use the Sunset exclusively now?
>> >
>> >Something tells me this could get really
>>>lrigaraian if we let it.
>Our words could mix in a circle of discourse
>that could continue endlessly

Oh, I hope so. More fodder for our paper. Circle of Discourse"—I sense a sub-heading!

>As i said, go easy (unless it's something easy
>to fix)—at this point, i'm just afraid of
what might be lurking in there.
>Btw, where have you been? I've been
>e-mailing my little heart out all to no
>response—i was most sad. I am much
>happier now!
>Continue to write me—i cannot think
>anymore.
>Oh, you should have several pieces of
>male/strike that/mail from me by now!
>—m confused!

Well, you should have a message to the effect now that I've been in la-la land. You are about to receive a message from me saying I got a big pile of gobble-de-goop from you. No, that is _not_ a critique of the paper. It really was gobble-de-goop. Anything to be done? I really want to read...

Date: Mon, 27 Feb 95 17:10:35 -0600
To: "Morgan Gresham" >
From: egcah@sunset.backbone.olemiss.edu
Subject: Re: I've sent you my draft

>Let me know when it arrives!
>or if it arrives.

Yon pigeon has arrived.

>say only nice things (or quickly fixable
>things) at this point—it's been printed and
>stapled.

Oh, it's wonderful. The best paper I've ever read... Perhaps I should read it first?

>I'm going to run to the library to make a copy
>of the poem for the woman who will eat my
>draft. After that, i'd like to converse, if at all
>possible. I've got a good hour to kill before
>class; i'd prefer to kill it with you :-)

>be back shortly—check your e-mail
>—m

Well, I napped briefly, but I'm up now and about to read your epic.
-Ta

Date: Mon, 27 Feb 95 17:36:36 -0600
To: "Morgan Gresham" <GRESHAM@beowulf.it-servers.louisville.edu>
From: egcah@sunset.backbone.olemiss.edu (Cissy)
Subject: Re: You really should check your e-mail

>Hey.....pay attention to me!!!

I am!

> i just finished a draft—i'm in need
>of love and sympathy and all sorts of good stuff

I love you. I sympathize. Sending lots of e-energy & good stuff.

>(my last typo was
>studd. Freudian? shoot freud while he's not looking.)
>

But if I shoot Freud with a gun, wouldn't he consider it a phallic symbol?

>what are you doing that could _possibly_ be more inviting,
>entertaining, involving...than me?

Bite your tongue!

>i've got the beginnings of a poem in my head—
>
>dance circle dance
>cirle dance circle
> wheel of time
>
>I know that it's there—it's just taking a while + it's been almost a year >exactly since i've written anything.....

So write, it sounds beautiful and elegant. It needs to be finished. Poor poem. Hanging out there in limbo, waiting for you to write it. Don't you feel sorry for it?

>well, i guess that i better pretend to work since you aren't there for me to
>kill my 45 minutes with. IF YOU GET THIS BEFORE 5:30 YOUR TIME,
>WRITE ME!!!!

Your wish...

Now, respond!!!!!!!!!!

Date: Mon, 27 Feb 95 17:31:53 -0600
To: "Morgan Gresham"
From: egcah@sunset.backbone.olemiss.edu (Cissy)
Subject: Re: My final draft! Say nice things only.

> * This message contains the file
>'E691COMP.227', which has been
> * uuencoded. If you are using Pegasus Mail,

I'm not.

> * then you can use
> * the browser's eXtract function to lift the original contents
> * out to a file,

Ergo, I can't.

>otherwise you will have to extract the message
> * and uudecode it manually.
>

One problem. Haven't a clue how to do that.

What follows is, to me, a load of symbols—kinda like one really long curse word. Any other options?

```
>begin 660 E691COMP.227
>M_U=00XX!```!"@`!`````/O_!0`R``@!```#``H
>M``P`6@````*0`````)``(```#^`````T`8&```$`!@`&T&D
>M>``L`0$``````W6OT`7@`_A4V$%@"`````!!%`
>M______^__^_____________________^
>M```````````````````````````2%!,05-%24DN4%)3`-
```

—I cut off the rest. The size was making my e-mail go goofy.

Date: Mon, 27 Feb 95 17:39:30 -0600
To: "Morgan Gresham"
From: egcah@sunset.backbone.olemiss.edu
Subject: Re: Paper Piddles

>I'm rereading Cixous for class tonight "Laugh
>of the Medusa"—i think that perhaps i should
>have included her also.
>
>AAAAAAAAAAAAAAAAAAArgh!
>—m

Repeat after me: "My paper is perfect. My paper is perfect. My paper is perfect. I do not need Cixous. My paper is perfect. My paper will receive an A. Dr. Janeway, er, G______, will be astounded at my depth of perception. She will not chew it up and spit it out. My paper is perfect."

Date: Mon, 27 Feb 95 17:43:59 -0600
To: "Morgan Gresham" <GRESHAM@beowulf.it-servers.louisville.edu>
From: egcah@sunset.backbone.olemiss.edu (Cissy
)
Subject: Re: I've sent you my draft

I see what you mean. Circles within circles.

>> >Let me know when it arrives!
>> >or if it arrives.
>>
>> Yon pigeon has arrived.
>Aha, at last the great pigeon. I bow down before him in supplication.

It's the great pigeon, Charlie Brown.

>> >say only nice things (or quickly fixable things) at this
>> >point—it's been printed and stapled.
>>
>> Oh, it's wonderful. The best paper I've ever read... Perhaps
>>I should read it first?
> well, yes, but be very careful—you might find some mistakes if
>you look too hard :-)

I didn't look hard at all, as you now know.

>> >I'm going to run to the library to make a copy of the poem >> >>
>for the woman who will eat my draft. After that, i'd like to >>
>converse, if at all possible. I've got a good hour to kill
>> >before class; i'd prefer to kill it with you :-)
>>
>> Aren't you sweet!
>well, yes, but is that necessarily a good thing?

Always.

>> >
>> >be back shortly—check your e-mail

Right back at you.

>> >
>> >
>>
>> Well, I napped briefly, but I'm up now and about to read your epic.

>I feel now that i'm turning it in no matter what. I cannot bear to think of
>—it gives me the heebie-jeebies

No doubt the wisest course of action. Sometimes you just gotta let go.

>help, my brain has fallen and it can't get up!!!
>

Nah, you'll recover. 'Tis a temporary condition at best.

Date: Mon, 27 Feb 95 17:49:02 -0600
To: "Morgan Gresham" <GRESHAM@beowulf.it-servers.louisville.edu>
From: egcah@sunset.backbone.olemiss.edu (Cissy)
Subject: Re: Paper Piddles

See the pretty triangles?

>> >>
>> >> >should i use the Sunset exclusively now?
>> >> >
>> >> >Something tells me this could get really Irigaraian if we let it.
>> >Our words could mix in a circle of discourse that could continue
>> >endlessly
>>
>> Oh, I hope so. More fodder for our paper. "Circle of Discourse"—I sense a >>sub-heading!

>Yes-yes! Are you able to save them on your end? If not, let me know so i can send
>them to myself to download.

Yeah, I can save them now. Much friendlier system now. (except for the tech people :)

>> >As i said, go easy (unless it's something easy to fix)—at this point, i'm just afraid of >> >what might be lurking in there.
>> >Btw, where have you been? I've been e-mailing my little
>> >heart out all to no response—i was most sad. I am much
>> >happier now!
>> >Continue to write me—i cannot think anymore.
>> >Oh, you should have several pieces of male/strike that/mail
>> >from me
Once again, Freud rears his ugly head.

>> >by now!
>> >—m confused!
>> >
>> >
>>
>> Well, you should have a message to the effect now that I've
>>been in la-la land. You are about to receive a message from me saying I got a big
>>pile of gobble-de-goop from you. No, that is
>>_not_ a critique of the paper. It really
>>was gobble-de-goop.
>>Anything to be done? I really want to read...
>That's an affirmative on the lalaland! gobble-de-goop? Noooooooo.
>Actually, i think i know what i did wrong—i think that i have to convert the file to ascii to >send it all the way to you. I shall ask michael about that either when he gets down
>here or after my class.
>At any rate, it _SHALL_ get to you one way (e-mail) or another
>(i can _bring_ it when we come)
>we're coming to see you!!!!

YEA!!!!!!!!!!!

>and your b'day present is still on the kitchen table; i think it
>likes it there :-0

Well, tough. It can't stay. Al Joleson not the same anymore :(It's not fair. He just looks surprised.
Well, were my responses earlier any help at all? I don't remember hearing and I demand validation.

APPENDIX D

Reply-To: comp@sunset.backbone.olemiss.edu
From: Rebecca Claire Haithcoat <[xxxxx]@sunset.backbone.olemiss.edu>
Subject: Perception as reality journal

The more I think about it, the deeper and deeper it gets. It's so strange to think that everything—truth, reality, me—is all perception. Yet, it makes sense. Who am I? I can tell you stories, descriptions, little antedotes, about myself, but you will more than likely perceive me to be at least a little different than I perceive myself. I may try to make you see me a certain way, but I can't control every facial expression and body language I have when I talk. I have had similar experiences to what Ms. Hartley described in class today. I guess I tend to overanalyze things, but it seems I always worry if things I say are misconstrued. I will feel guilty if I am kind of blunt with a friend and later ask her if she is upset with me, and she will be like, "What? I didn't even notice it."

Pertaining to how hearing others' life stories affects your life, I firmly believe someone else's recounted experience can totally change your life. Including books and movies, certain stories have made me seriously reflect on my life. Maybe because I act, or perhaps Im just introspective, I find that characters have the same effect on me that people do. When I play a role, my primary goal is to literally become that character while I am on stage, so it is necessary for me to fully understand why she behaves or reacts, what has made her the way she is—in essence, her life story. If that story did not affect me, at least as an actress, I would do a pretty poor job at convincing the audience that I was that person. Well, I guess I could fake it, but then I would not be personally satisfied. To wrap this up, I have a feeling I'll be thinking on this perception thing quite a bit. It isn't an idea that is easily dismissed. Knowing myself, I'll lose myself in thought for the next few days:).

One more thing—I thought Don Juan was faking for the judge, but I wish he would have winked or said something to Dr. Hinkler as they walked out. Do you guys think he was normal and made himself into Don Juan to escape his reality, or do you think he really was Don Juan (although now that I think about it, that seems a little far-fetched)?

Reply-To: comp@sunset.backbone.olemiss.edu
From: Jamie Vernon <[xxxxx]@sunset.backbone.olemiss.edu>
Subject: DJdM

Everyone's got their own take on reality. What may appeal to one may disgust or bore another. What may appear to one may be invisible to another. On the wall of the men's bathroom in the Hoka (for those of you who want some good philosophy, go in there—girls too, if ya really want...) there lies "Only the insane have the strength to prosper. Only the prosperous define what is sane."

The only reason that we have different periods in art, literature, music and sciences is because someone saw something differently, and too many other people were influenced by that single person to keep the change suppressed. A small group of people once thought that a king was wrong and unjust. Today the descendants and the followers...believers of those people make up what is arguably the strongest nation in the world. If a man by the name of Leonardo had been afraid to hide his thoughts, his perspective, because he was afraid of isolation, intellectual quarantine, we would have never had (or at least waited longer for!) the hot-air balloon, the helicopter, the tank (a questionable discovery) and much more. In ancient Rome and Greece, the forum was where men and women (tho' not as much for the females) could listen to ideas and voice some of their own, for no other purpose than to have feedback for what they pondered while sweeping their houses.

Perspective is everything. For a more concrete example, watch any of the many versions of People's Court. One person watching a car wreck from one angle has an almost completely different view (can you say...PERSPECTIVE? Good!!) from someone on the opposite street corner. In the same sense, it is almost inevitable to find someone with the same perspective as yourself—if you do, don't hang around because life will get real boring fast!! Different perspectives are what make the world go 'round (just look at the class discussions in about a month when people become less inhibited) and allowing other's views to impact your own is almost necessary for intellectual expansions and mutations and radiations and all the other squiggly things that make life that much more interesting inside yer own head...

NOTES

[1] All quotations in subheadings are taken from Margaret Atwood's "Spelling"; see Appendix A.

[2] The snippets of e-mail conversations found throughout the text are included to demonstrate the circuitous nature of our language at play as we move between theory and practice.

[3] See Appendix B.

[4] See Appendix C.

[5] Some argue, of course, that grounding discourse in the female body is essentialist and divisive. It is important to note here, as Irigaray does in her work, that when we say "feminine discourse" we do not define such discourse as dependent upon biology, but as metaphorically represented by the body. Both monologism and dialogism can be found in a woman's speech as well as a man's.

Nor do we wish to privilege discourse that simply supplants itself into a position of authority, privileging only one type of speech at the expense of others. Indeed, there is a danger in making such a connection, for as Gail Schwab (1991) notes, "Monologistic textuality has traditionally silenced the female voice" (p. 68). Despite the inherent dialogism of feminine discourse, Irigaray (1977/1985) warns that if the "aim were simply to reverse the order of things, even supposing this to be possible, history would repeat itself in the long run, would revert to sameness: to phallocratism" (p. 33). Offering alternatives to traditional, linear discourse, Irigaray calls for a kind of communication that promotes interaction by elimination of rigid structures where positions are strictly defined and enforced, a discourse structure in which all may participate. For a full discussion of the question of Irigaray and essentialism, see Fuss (1989).

[6] Sherrie Gradin (1995) aptly defines the ways in which social-epistemicism and expressivism can inform one another in *Romancing Rhetorics: Social Expressivist Perspectives on the Teaching of Writing.*

[7] The question of whether or not computers themselves alter literacy patterns is one which continues to be debated in professional journals and listservs. See Haas (1996) and Rickly (1998).

[8] This joint project was completed in 1996. Morgan is currently working on her dissertation prospectus, and Cissy has completed her Ph.D. coursework at the University of Louisville, finally moving vertically, but in the wrong direction.

[9] See Appendix D for examples of student voices in online discussions.

REFERENCES

Atwood, M. (1985). Spelling. In S. Gilbert & S. Gubar (Eds.), *Norton anthology of literature by women* (pp. 2298–2299). New York: Norton.

Bakhtin, M. (1991). *The dialogic imagination* (M. Holquist, Ed. & C. Emerson & M. Holquist, Trans.). Austin, TX: University of Texas Press.

Cooper, M., & Selfe, C. L. (1990, December). Computer conferences and learning: Authority, resistance, and internally persuasive discourse. *College English, 52*(8), 847–869.

De Beaugrande, Ro. (1988). In search of feminist discourse: The "difficult" case of Luce Irigaray. *College English, 50*(3), 253–272.

Eldred, J., & Fortune, R. (1992). Exploring the implications of metaphors for computer networks and hypermedia. In G. E. Hawisher & P. J. LeBlanc (Eds.), *Reimagining computers and composition: Teaching and research in the Virtual Age* (pp. 58–73). Portsmouth, NH: Boynton/Cook.

Fuss, D. (1989). *Essentially speaking: Feminism, nature, and difference.* New York: Routledge.

Goleman, J. (1995). *Working theory: Critical composition studies for students and teachers.* Westport, CT: Bergin & Garvey.

Gradin, S. (1995). *Romancing rhetorics: Social expressivist perspectives on the teaching of writing.* Portsmouth, NH: Boynton/Cook.

Haas, C. (1996). *Writing technology: Studies on the materiality of literacy.* Mahwah, NJ: Lawrence Erlbaum.

Hawisher, G., & Moran, C. (1993, October). Electronic mail and the writing instructor. *College English, 55*(6), 627–643.

Hillocks, G. (1995). *Teaching writing as reflective practice.* New York: Teacher's College Press.

Irigaray, L. (1985). *This sex which is not one.* Ithaca, NY: Cornell University Press. (Original work published 1977)

Juncker, C. (1988). Writing (with) Cixous. *College English, 50*(4), 424–436.

Looser, D. (1993). Composing as an "essentialist"?: New directions for feminist theories. *Rhetoric Review, 12*(1), 54–69.

Mullin, J. (1994). Feminist theory, feminist pedagogy: The gap between what we say and what we do. *Composition Studies/Freshman English News, 22*, 14–24.

Regan, A. (1993, November). "Type normal like the rest of us": Writing, power, and homophobia in the networked composition classroom. *Computers and Composition, 10*(4), 11–23.

Rickly, B. (1998, May 18). *Re: Paul LeBlanc on who we are.* Rhetnet-L [Internet]. Available e-mail: listserv@lists.missouri.edu. Message: GET rhetnet-1, rhetnet-1.log98Ø5d

Schwab, G. (1991). Irigarayan dialogism: Play and powerplay. In D. M. Bauer & S. J. McKinstry (Eds.), *Feminism, Bakhtin and the dialogic* (pp. 57–72). Albany, NY: State University of New York Press.

Selfe, C. (1990). Technology in the English classroom: Computers through the lens of feminist theory. In C. Handa (Ed.), *Computers and community: Teaching composition in the twenty-first century* (pp. 118–139). Portsmouth, NH: Boynton/Cook.

Selfe, R., & Selfe, C. L. (1994). The politics of the interface: power and its exercise in electronic contact zones. *College Composition and Communication, 45*, 480–504.

Takayoshi, P. (1996). The shape of electronic writing: Evaluating and assessing computer assisted writing processes and products. *Computers and Composition, 13*, 245–257.

Ward, I. (1994). *Literacy, ideology and dialogue: Towards a dialogic pedagogy.* Albany, NY: State University of New York Press.

chapter 9

Over the Line, Online, Gender Lines: E-mail and Women in the Classroom

Dene Grigar
Texas Woman's University

INTRODUCTION TO THE STUDY

From: student@utdallas.edu
To: aca102@utdallas.edu
Subject: Re: Last Night's Class (fwd)

Dene,
I am really enjoying the class and the readings. However, I am feeling real insecure about my writing skills and abilities. Please be patient.

This e-mail message, received at the beginning of the semester from one of my female students, demonstrates her willingness to communicate to me that she is nervous about her ability to be successful in my classroom. Ironically, I had actually seen this student on at least three different occasions during and outside of class, but never had she expressed to me in person this fear she had about her ability to perform. However, by using e-mail, she felt quite comfortable telling me about her insecurities. Questions I immediately asked myself in that Spring of 1995 are those I still ponder even now: Why is it that female students communicate more openly using e-mail than they do in person? Does this kind of verbal activity indicate that e-mail enhances learning in the classroom? Is forcing students to use technology counterproductive to learning? These questions lie at the heart of my research on women and technology and frame the discussion that follows.

Rationale

From: student@utdallas.edu
To: aca102@utdallas.edu
Subject: Re: Message received and comments

Dene,
I would be very interested in a little mini-seminar. This is my first experience with a modem and anything remote like this. I really don't feel like I know what I am doing at all, but this seems like it is going to be great. After installing the internet programs Saturday, I made connection easily, but then that night and all day Sunday I could not make a connection even though I could hear the modem dialing okay. I left a recorded message with the UTD Computer Center, but nobody ever called me back. However, today I was able to connect okay. Is this normal? Should I call them when I cannot make a connection for a long time like that?

Much research about e-mail technology and computer-aided instruction has emerged since the inception of computer-aided instruction, but, for the most part, those of us who teach with computers still have no clear evidence that computers actually assist students with learning—and chances are, we may never have clear-cut evidence to support this idea. Therefore, the study that I have undertaken focuses on the way that students, particularly female students, converse and express themselves more freely with their instructors with e-mail technology and asserts that this activity of electronic communication allows for a positive environment for learning, one that opens itself up to notions of community and collaboration often linked to women's ways of knowing.

Debates about Computer Technology and Learning

Hi, this is the first time that I am responding to an e-mail message this year due to the dact that the computer people have messed up my entire life as it concerns the computer world. They have, in reconfiguring the new system, lost all my stuff from last year—and I had some pretty good stuff, and it would not allow me to send mail saying that I did not have the capabilities to do so. Also due to the sorry MTS lines at the apartments, we have gotten so much line noise that the stuff that it not only looks like Greek to us but is actually the Greek alphabet in various constructions. Ha Ha.

Anyway, I am waiting for some articles to come in on the Hemingway Review for my paper, but the librarian says that they probably won't be in till Monday, I hope they get here sooner—I'm gonna look for them every day. Question: Where can I find a cheap dictionary of symbols adequate for the class? And what is considered a good price to pay? What book would you suggest if any?

I appreciate your time and effort and hope to hear what you say on the questions soon.
Thanx,

Early scholarship about using computers in the classroom centered on a debate about whether or not they augmented learning and focused on two major areas relating to students: academic improvement and personal enrichment. On one end of the spectrum, we find scholars who claimed that computers have a positive effect on student achievement and growth. Papert (qtd. in Hawisher & Selfe, 1989), for example, tells us that computers aid students in mastering writing even before they master speaking. Smith and Smith (1990) suggest that computers enable students to find "a new joy in language" (p. 140). Likewise, Eldred (1989) points to the "connectivity" that computers promote among students and the positive social interaction that results in collaboration and the sharing of information (p. 216). For these scholars, computers help students learn better and provide them with a sense of community.

Some scholars, however, reported that computers have an adverse effect upon students and learning. Pea and Kurland (1987) tell us that although computers stimulate students' desire to write, they do not improve writing skills or connect thinking and writing (pp. 277–278). In that same study, they call computer-based tools "slave technologies," implying that computers do nothing to emancipate students from the real complexities of thinking and writing (p. 285).

More recent studies have moved away from this line of inquiry and instead have focused on the political and ethical ramifications of using online resources in the classroom and in one's personal life. Specifically in studies beginning in the 1990s, feminism and queer theory have both emerged as tools for conducting research and interpreting data. For example, Boese (1995), Brail (1997), and Kramarae and Taylor (1997) indicate that online communications systems provide environments where women can be intimidated by others merely due to gender. Likewise, Gill (1997) discusses problems, such as stalking and sexual harassment, that women encounter online using e-mail. A study by Regan (1993) focuses on the way gay people can be intimidated online, while an article by Silberman (1997) suggests that gay people can find expression for their sexual difference in online communities in a way not available to them in their face-to-face experiences.

While we cannot prove students learn better with computers, we do know—as Redd (1997) suggests in her study about e-mail usage—that they certainly *write* more. And writing more is viewed as a positive outcome of computer-aided instruction. Likewise, in my study I do not set out to prove that using e-mail helps my female students learn better, but certainly they communicated their ideas and needs more. And *communicating* more had a positive effect on our classroom environment and their perceptions of themselves as successful participants in our learning community.

OVER THE LINE? LEARNING, ONLINE PEDAGOGY, AND MY STUDENTS

From: student@utdallas.edu
To: Dene Grigar <aca102@utdallas.edu>
Subject: essay

With some research under my belt, I have changed the topic of my essay. I would like to write about "A Very Old Man with Enormous Wings" as a children's tale, comparing it with "A Penny A Look" by Zemach and possibly other similar stories that attempt to teach a lesson, what that lesson might be and how children respond. Input please!!??

Women and Learning

From: student@utdallas.edu
To: aca102@utdallas.edu
Subject: Re: poetry paper

dene-

I just relized I scheduled my meeting tomorrow during one of my classes. Can I come at another time? I'd prefer to come earlier, but any time is okay. Just let me know. Thanks!

As Belenky, Clinchy, Goldberger, and Tarule (1986) demonstrate in their groundbreaking study, *Women's Way of Knowing: The Development of Self, Voice, and Mind*, women begin their intellectual development in a state of silence, a place in which they unquestioningly accept the authority of others. From here, they may progress through as many as four other stages, but more than likely few will ever arrive at the final stage, in which they perceive themselves as experts and demonstrate expertise in a field. Most women, according to Belenky, et al., are unable to assume the posture of authority and autonomy.

We can attribute women's inability to move through the five stages successfully to societal expectations of women's conduct, particularly such traits assigned to women as modesty, the denial of self, and subjugation to male authority. At some point in their education, learners must assume a position of authority over a subject, and eventually their teachers, if they are truly to progress toward independent thinking and active engagement with their work. Yet, female students come to our classrooms, many times having learned control and subjugation, traits sometimes reinforced by pedagogies and methodologies centered in masculine ways of learning: through competition, argument, and individualism—concepts that according to Belenky, Clinchy, Goldberger, and Tarule's (1986) study run counter to the notion of women and learning.

Another study that also holds great implications for women and learning is Gilligan's *In a Different Voice: Essays on Psychological Theory and Women's Development* (1982). In her study, Gilligan discovered that women perceive the world and their place in it as a complex web of connections between people and ideas. Women identify most readily with terms associated with responsibility and nurturing and generally make decisions based upon the particulars of a case rather than universal concepts relating to a problem or idea.

As Gilligan's (1982) work demonstrates, women see the world in terms of connections and responsibility to and the nurturing of others. Yet, looking at traditional classroom strategies, such as the Socratic Method with its emphasis on rigorous individual performance and the "professorial lecture," which focuses on an impersonal dissemination of knowledge from one teacher to many students, we see that women can easily be discouraged from speaking up in a classroom and from asking questions.

Understanding this basic concept about women and learning compels us to seek other ways to assist female students to gain their voices, to help them learn. Therefore, while I would never suggest that increasing the numbers of conversations we may have with students in itself is a major achievement that will miraculously result in better learners, my study indicates that the ongoing, one-on-one conversations that I had with my female students helped to forge an environment that encouraged them to speak up more regularly in class discussions, which, according to both Belenky, Clinchy, Goldberger, and Tarule (1986) and Gilligan (1982), does indeed facilitate women's intellectual development.

Online Pedagogy

From: aca102@utdallas.edu
To: 3303
Subject: Last Night's Class

Dear students,

Welcome to the virtual classroom. Here on the internet we can conduct conferences, discussions, and research without leaving the comfort of our home. As I introduce other resources to you during the semester, we will expand upon this notion of the virtual classroom—conducting a "real time" cafe where we will all meet for expresso and lively conversation. You will also gain access to scholarly lists in order to participate in discussions with other scholars in the fields you are interested in pursuing. You will also be able to conduct your basic research via the libraries and databases available to you on-line.

I am very happy you all decided to take my class. The enthusiasm you all demonstrated last night for the subject matter...energizes me.

Once we have all of your addresses, we will make them available to the class so that you can all contact each other outside of class. I encourage you all to communicate with one another via e-mail.

Please feel free to contact me whenever you wish. I normally check my mail during the following times: 1) 7-8:30 am 2) 10-10:30 am 3) noon 4) 3-4pm 5) late at night, between 9pm-2am.

Other people have noted changes in their classroom environment and structure when teaching with e-mail. In his article, "Computers and English: What Do We Make of Each Other?" (1992), Moran, indicating a positive view of using e-mail in the classroom, suggests that e-mail can create a "corporate, collaborative, collective" individual, one who is "more knowledgeable than the old" (p. 193). Thus, for him, uniting with others online provides strength and intellectual power for both the individual and the larger classroom community. Similarly, Cooper and Selfe (1990) agree with Moran's assessment that students benefit from nontraditional classroom environments where they can work together collaboratively. They tell us that when students participate in oral and written dialogues with one another, they broaden their understanding of ideas (p. 847). But besides simply communicating ideas with others, students also have the right to "initiate change" (p. 848)—that is, they should have a say in what gets discussed and written about in class. Thus, the notion of collaboration extends beyond student working with student to that of students working with teacher to ensure learning takes place in the classroom. This shift in political structure suggests that students have much to share with their teachers about how students best learn.

Trained in both the electronic and traditional classroom, I am comfortable with various types of learning environments and levels of teacher authority, and I am aware that each student has a particular learning style. The key, as I have always seen it, is to develop pedagogy that fits each student in each class during each semester *and* to find resources that meet each student's individual needs. Understanding the ways in which women learn best is part of my pedagogical approach to classroom teaching. Therefore, while many women may view the computer classroom as a masculine, highly technical place, hostile to women and unconducive to their learning experience, I see the various online technologies, such as e-mail, the World Wide Web, and the local LAN netshare program, as spaces that reflects the connectivity and collaboration women feel comfortable with in their everyday lives.

My Students

From: student@utdallas.edu
To: R M Grigar <aca102@utdallas.edu>
Subject: Literary Analysis

I did not receive my second reaction paper. Do you have it for me? Thank you.

I focused my attention on female students in my Literary Analysis course because they constituted the vast majority of students that I taught. In fact, during the fall semester, 15 of the 23 students were female; in the spring, 11 of 15 students. Most of them fit the profile of the "re-entry" student: Women with families, working full time, who have returned to school to improve their earning power. Their schedules made it difficult for them to meet with me to ask questions during office hours or before class started. They literally would rush into the classroom just in time for class to begin. Though they had read the material and, when pressed, could answer questions about the reading easily, the discussions seemed disjointed and few felt comfortable about speaking up in front of the others. Those who struggled with the literature and the accompanying writing assignments never asked for my assistance, despite the fact that I had listed both my home and office phone numbers on my syllabus. I thought e-mail would give students a more convenient way to contact me, one that allowed them to speak up without fear or embarrassment. But I was concerned that the e-mail assignments intended to assist them with learning the technology and staying in contact with one another might overwhelm them because though simple, the assignments were, indeed, time-consuming.

To encourage my students to learn e-mail effectively, I required them to contact members of their groups numerous times during the semester to share essay topics, collaborate on homework assignments, and check in on absent group members. In addition to their assignments were the frequent messages I would send to entice members of the class to talk to me about their work and ideas. For reference purposes, I archived all e-mail messages written to me and encouraged them to save their mail for future reference. Other Literary Analysis sections, taught by others in traditional classrooms, did not require the use of e-mail as I did. By talking to students in those classes, my students could easily find out that they were expected to undertake more work than their colleagues.

Following Cooper and Selfe's (1990) argument, I reasoned that if my female students were using e-mail for asking questions and making comments about the material they were reading, then they might gain more power over their learning. Since many female students indicated to me that they were nervous about discussing their ideas in front of classmates, I theorized that e-mail would give them a forum by which they could express their ideas to me and their classmates without having to be physically "in front of" their classmates. Likewise, because when I respond to e-mail messages my attention focuses on one message at a time, each student could receive individualized attention from me when it was perhaps more convenient for them to receive feedback—in addition to the attention they were already receiving from me in the classroom. Lastly, by teaching them how to use e-mail, they could master a form of technology that is rapidly becoming an integral part of communication in our society. I theorized that if they did not master technology, they would be enslaved by it.

To be honest, it was the issue of enslavement that motivated me the most to teach women about technology in the first place. Daisley (n.d.) points out that the under-representation of women online suggests "marginalization," not unlike the silencing of women that has taken place in writing and other contexts, such as politics. Marginalization is "dehumanization," tantamount to placing women in intellectual "straitjackets" (pp. 1–2). Marginalization means taking women outside the realm of authority and putting us into a position of oppression. Thus, Daisley suggests to empower female students, we must change the metaphors used for describing technology so that they are more inclusive of women.

Such change has long been underway. In "A Manifesto for Cyborg," Haraway (1985) advocates the union of female and machine, the recognition that we are already a hybrid creature—"a borg"—comprised of machine parts and flesh (p. 372). For her, the boundaries between human and machine, man and woman is "messier" and more blurred than we realize (qtd. in Kunzru, 1997, p. 157). Implied in her writings is the idea that organisms, female or otherwise, are already participating in a constant communion with the cybernetic. Awareness of this connection is our empowerment; resistance to it, futile. Haraway tells us, "Feminist concerns … are inside of technology, not a rhetorical overlay" (p. 158). Cyberfeminists following her lead believe that the relationship between woman and machine is "long-standing" and that this connection gives us great flexibility in constructing and reconstructing our world, our lives, our selves (pp. 156–157).

Believing that understanding technology results in gaining some level of control in our lives, I strove during those semesters to push all my students beyond their defined boundaries of knowledge and reconstruct themselves as students less wary of technology and more accepting of its possibilities. E-mail was but one computer resource I promoted, but because of its application to communication, I saw it as an important one.

At mid-semester, I evaluated my methodology in order to get a clearer picture of my students' views toward using e-mail. And because most of my students were women—the gender traditionally associated with discomfort with or lack of training in technology—I decided to concentrate on the way in which e-mail affected them. My study, then, was generated out of a natural curiosity about my students' needs and the effectiveness of my methodology.

ONLINE WITH MY CLASSES

From: malestudent@utdallas.edu
To: aca102@utdallas.edu
Subject: Re: Him in Weigh

On Tue, 7 Mar 1995 aca102@utdallas.edu wrote:

> I sent a message to Dr. ____________ in Arts and Humanities about your request.

Thanks bunch! I also sent so e-mail to Dr. ________ and plan on visiting him either tomorrow or the next day to discuss this.... I think it would be an honor to work with him if any of this actually goes through. Honestly, I'd be suprised if it did. Oh well, if nothing else, it'll let me know exactly what the limitations of my scholarship are. I really do appreciate your help and wish you the best of luck in Boston. I'm sure you'll knock 'em dead (in a good way, of course!).

> Good luck. I hope your spring break is productive (hint hint) and restful....

Yes, I will work on my paper over break, thanks for the reminder.
Love, S—.

The course that I was teaching, Literary Analysis, is required for all students desiring a degree in the humanities, and because critical thinking and critical reading underlies our pedagogy for this course, many nonmajors are also required to take it. In Literary Analysis, students study and analyze various forms of literary works, such as short stories, poetry, and drama, and are introduced to research techniques that will prepare them for other upper-division courses. Generally, we are expected to teach students to write long, argumentative essays requiring library research and explications of various works of fiction. Like the other literature courses at this university, Literary Analysis is normally taught in a traditional classroom. However, because few of these students had ever used computers or Internet resources, I had always offered my sections of the course in my department's Macintosh Lab so that these students could be exposed to the World Wide Web, MOOs, e-mail, hypertext programs, electronic databases, and library catalogs. Teaching in an electronic classroom gave me the opportunity to teach students how to conduct research and write using these online resources, as well as engage in online dialogues with one another—activities that, at the time, they would not have gotten in a Literary Analysis class taught in the traditional classroom.

I cannot stress enough the concern I had about the lack of computer literacy among these upper-division students. Close to graduating and many of them planning for careers in teaching, they had not learned how to use computers and were not benefiting from the electronic resources available to them. Since most jobs now require some level of computer competency and because computers are being used for communicating in both industry and the home, I feel compelled to educate students—particular those traditionally relegated to low-paying jobs or have difficulty finding work—about computer technology.

To further clarify the situation that drove me to adopt this pedagogical stance, let me detail the student population that comprised my course. Beginning as a research institution, The University of Texas at Dallas opened its doors to upper-division undergraduates in 1978 and lower-division students in the Fall of 1990. I was among five graduate students selected to teach the first freshmen composition students, so I was very involved in the early planning for curriculum and technology. Recruiting efforts targeted students interested in studying engineering and the sciences, a vast majority of which were male. In the first-year composition course, all taught in a networked computer classroom, these students were introduced to computer technology, such as e-mail, Internet resources, hypertext, and CD-ROMs. On the other hand, the upper-division students, comprised of students transferring in from community colleges or from other universities, and re-entry students who had had no such experience in the courses they had taken earlier, had little background in computers. Some did know how to use a word processor or interoffice communications, but certainly none had much experience beyond that. Humanities and education majors, especially, were matriculating through the system without ever having touched a computer. A disparity emerged in my class between the younger, mostly male engineering and science majors, who came to UTD as first-year students and received training in computer technology from their composition instructors, and the older, female nonscience majors who had transferred in to UTD from other institutions with little or no experience with computers, and who made up the bulk of the upper-division student population. Alarmed at the inability of older, female students to use computers for word processing, much less know how to conduct research with electronic databases or find information on the Internet, I had made it a point to teach my literature courses in electronic labs whenever possible.

The Fall Semester Class Profile

From: student@utdallas.edu
To: aca102@utdallas.edu
Subject: paper

Dene—
I was just wondering if you found out anything about the author of "Love Letters," Patricia Zelver. I went to the library again today to get the information for the poem, and while I was there I looked again for information on her, but I don't know what to do except for look in the computer for this specific author. If you have any ideas for finding information on her, or her writing, or anything else I can do to help my paper, please let me know.

Thanks!

The section of Literary Analysis I was assigned to teach during the Fall of 1993 was scheduled in a traditional classroom. Because students had already enrolled in the class and had not paid the lab fee required of all electronic-based classes, I did not have adequate time to move the course into the Macintosh Lab. And despite the fact that the fall class was held during the day when we have the highest rate of full-time and younger students, my class was still heavily populated with females (15 of the 23 students) who had returned to school after a long hiatus or had transferred in from the local community colleges. Accordingly, I felt like I had little contact with these commuters. Like my night students, they too were juggling a full load of classes and working full-time, on top of taking care of their families. At the end of the semester, the standardized student evaluations gave little feedback about my ability to help them or address their educational needs, and, of course, what little information I could glean from my students' comments came too late to make changes in my course that would affect them.

Even though we did not have daily access to the electronic sources I normally used when teaching Literary Analysis in the lab, I did indeed teach my students in the fall course how to use e-mail and electronic databases. I took them to the lab for instruction twice during the semester, giving them manuals and handouts on the protocols they needed to use the technology. I followed up these demonstrations with library visits to introduce the CD-ROMs, such as the MLA and Humanities Index, available for research. Additionally, I sent students e-mail messages about class assignments or forwarded them information pertinent to their work each week. Accessible at any time were several labs and multiple stations of networked computers around campus so that they could use to contact me. As I commonly do, I retained records of all correspondence with these students, logging phone calls and e-mail messages so that I could keep track of requests and special needs.

It is interesting to note that during the fall semester, I received a total of 25 e-mail messages from the 23 students taking my course. Only six messages originated from female students. Telephone conversations remained at similar levels: I received five phone calls from my female students during the course of the entire semester. In other words, there was little difference in the modes with which students communicated with me. E-mail or telephone, it was all the same, and, more importantly, communication was extremely infrequent.

The Spring Semester Class Profile

> From: student@utdallas.edu
> To: aca102@utdallas.edu
> Subject: Literay Analysis Paper Topic
>
> Just to let you know—I thought I'd do a biographical survey of Ellison in relation ship with either "The Battle Royale" or possible The Invisible Man (Sorry, I don't know how to underline yet). This is just a test message.

For the spring semester, I returned to the electronic environment, moving my course back into the Macintosh Lab equipped with full Internet connections. I should mention here that the location and the lab fee for this course were both listed in the class schedule so that students would know in advance that they were signing up for a computer-oriented class. To further ensure that students who enrolled for the course would be forewarned about the technology requirements, I created a course information sheet that outlined all of my objectives, highlighting those that centered on computers. Thus, for 16 weeks, 15 students worked in a networked classroom, using the many different forms of technology available to assist them in understanding literature and essay writing.

As I do in any course I teach in a computer environment, I arrived an hour before class to give students time to meet with me face to face outside of office hours and ask for assistance with the assignments due at class time. I do this so that they will feel comfortable with the technology and with me. Allowing extra time for conferencing makes students aware that I am committed to their learning and that I, too, am working hard in the class. It gives a sense that we are all working together to achieve the goals and objectives I lay out in the beginning of my course. Likewise, arriving early to class inspires them to show up on time and be prepared to work, since they already know I will be there waiting for them. Additionally, this protocol allows students to practice the technology I want them to master. It also makes it easy for students to check e-mail and send messages at the beginning and end of each class. As I mentioned previously about my literature classes, to encourage them to communicate with me, I send regular messages about class assignments, technology, university or departmental information, and their comments from class. Although I was not surprised that my contact with students improved from the fall semester, I was taken aback by just how much the percentages rose: In some categories, correspondence with my female students increased well over 100 percent by mid-semester.

To better understand what my students' needs and concerns were, at mid-semester I gave them an evaluation sheet to fill out, called the "Student Profile," that focused on their use of the computers in the course (see Figure 9.1). Because I did

1. Total number of students in course: 15; 11 females (73%)/4 males (27%)
2. Experience: Explain your experience with each of these technologies prior to this class:
   PC
   Macintosh
   E-mail
   Other technologies
3. Age:
4. Gender:
5. Academic level:
6. Computer access: Do you have access to a computer at home? Modem? Computer at work? Are you required to use e-mail at your job?
7. Signed up for the course because of the technology component: Yes or No?
8. Didn't know about the technology: Yes or No?
9. Have telephoned the instructor during the semester: Yes or No? Number of times?
10. Have e-mailed the instructor during the semester: Yes or No? Number of times?

FIGURE 9.1. Student Profile Sheet

not want to intimidate them, I avoided any questions that would cause them to evaluate me or their literature assignments. In this profile, I also asked about previous experience with computers, current computer access, and their use of e-mail in my course. So that I could get a fix on the way they perceived our teacher-student communications, I also asked them to estimate how many times they believed they contacted me both by telephone and by e-mail.

Their profiles indicated what I had already guessed. Only the full-time students who had entered the university as freshmen felt comfortable about using the computers in the classroom and had any experience with technology. What was interesting about these students was that each one had been exposed to computers while they were in high school. Working on the yearbooks and the school newspaper provided these students the chance to become acquainted with Macintoshes and various graphics and word-processing programs. On the other hand, those upper-division students who had transferred in or had come back to school after many years had limited experience with computers. Furthermore, older students who indeed used computers everyday in their jobs only learned a particular activity with the software they were required to use. None of the companies my students worked for made any attempt to educate their employees about the complete software package or train them in computer usage. None of my upper-division students had ever been exposed to the Internet. Also, in their comments, all but one of the female students reported that they were nervous about using computers, but were also excited at the opportunity. I was most surprised to discover from the student profiles that the female student close to graduating with a degree in education was the most resistant to using technology. She saw no reason for learning computers and assured me that she would never need it again, especially in her English classes.

This information was telling. Because only those students who had experience with computers during high school and the first year of college indicated that they felt comfortable with using technology, it demonstrated the importance of computer literacy training at an early age. Second, the student profiles suggested that students were not gaining computer experience in the home—that both high school and college teachers, particularly college composition teachers, shouldered the responsibility for teaching students about computers. The profiles also indicated that businesses were not doing enough to educate workers about computers and computer resources. Because students' experience with software was limited to a particular program and activity, they had a difficult time extrapolating from that experience. I found that students could not figure out how to turn computers on, much less understand how one software program may work like another. Most importantly, it suggested that those of us teaching with computers need to develop standards and plans for educating with technology, that these standards need to address not only decisions about which computer resources to teach, but what our pedagogical stance toward teaching with technology will be.

After I had evaluated the student profiles, I spent time in class sharing the results with my students. It was important that they had the chance to see the outcome of the student profiles in order to assess their own attitudes toward and perceptions about technology. The class discussion that resulted from this "recycling" of their comments helped my students see that they were not alone in their fears. One of the comments made by one female student was that she felt like she was the only one who didn't grasp using the computers well. When she realized that she wasn't alone and that even some of the younger students were not all that comfortable with certain electronic technologies, she became less intimidated. In addition, when the future teacher in the group recognized that the younger students had learned computers from their high school teachers, she became a little less obstinate about learning computers, admitting that she may indeed need to know how to use them after all.

GENDER LINES:
WOMEN USING E-MAIL IN THE CLASSROOM

From: student@utdallas.edu
To: R M Grigar <aca102@utdallas.edu>
Subject: the PAPER!

Dear Dene,

I hope that it's OK if my paper doesn't have all the meat that it should by tomorrow, right? I still want to incorporate some materials that I haven't yet accessed.

In other words, the contents of the paper won't be judged tomorrow, right?

See you at 3:40.

Love,
D—-

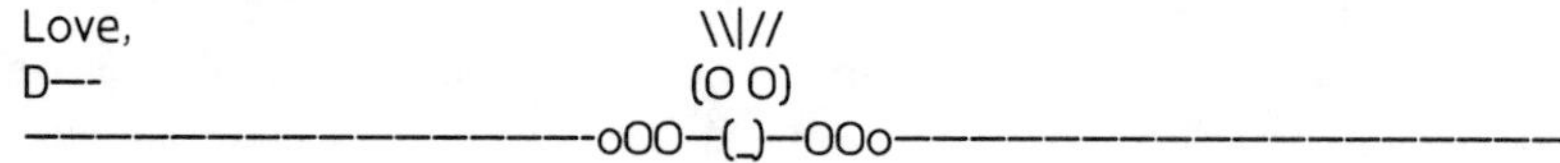

As I mentioned earlier, I archived every message my students sent me during both the fall and spring semesters. At this juncture, I should add that the e-mail package that the university uses, Pine, does this easily and that I get my students' permission to save and study their e-mail messages. It is important to forewarn students that we are, indeed, saving their messages and to get permission to use their e-mail. Like student papers, e-mail messages are private documents containing students' thoughts and ideas, musings and complaints, errors and risks. Using their mail without permission betrays the trust that we must develop with students in order to build an effective learning community. Besides asking them in advance if I can use their e-mail, I also encourage students to archive all messages from me, especially those that contain any agreements concerning grades, late papers, and absentees, in case they need to remind me of promises that I have made them.

Along with evaluating the student profiles, therefore, I also studied the archives of e-mail conversations I had with my students, organizing them into six different categories:

"General Questions about the Course and Assignments," "Assistance with University Business," "Personal Assistance," "Explanations for Missing Class or Turning in Late Work," "Personal Comments," and "Waxing Philosophical" (see Figure 9.2).

Category #1: Questions about Courses and Assignments

12 total; 9 different students: 5 females (66%)/4 males (34%)

1. Reading/Writing Assignment Assistance: 9 total; 7 different students: 3 females/4 males
55% of the responses were by female students

1/24	Paul	Class assignment
2/2	John	Paper topic
2/2	Josh	Reaction paper assistance
2/9	Carol	Paper topic
2/13	Sherry	Paper topic
2/15	Dena	Clarify assignment
2/21	Michael	Paper assistance
3/7	Dena	Question about rewrite
3/7	Dena	Question about rewrite

2. Technical Assistance: 2 total; 2 different students: 2 females/0 males
100% of the responses were by female students

2/8	Susan	Internet assistance
2/13	Sherry	Internet trouble

3. Housekeeping Chores: 1 total; 1 female/0 males
100% of the responses were by female students

2/6	Ann	Looking for graded paper

Category #2: Assistance with University Business

2 total; 1 different student: 0 females/1 male
100% of the responses were by male students

3/6	John	Help with summer study program
3/7	John	Help with summer study program

Category #3: Personal Assistance

2 total; 2 different students: 2 females/0 males
100% of the responses were by female students

2/2	Bette	Nervous about writing
2/8	Abbie	Questions about other courses

FIGURE 9.2. Categories of E-mail Messages from Students' Spring Semester

Category #4: Explanation for Missing Class or Late Work (Apologies)

0 total; 0 different students: 0 females/0 males

Category #5: Personal Comments

7 total; 5 different students: 4 females/1 male
71% of the responses were by female students

1/18	Paul	Likes class
1/23	Paul	Likes class
2/8	Sherry	Thank you
2/9	Patsy	Get well wish
2/9	Carol	Thanks for e-mail list
2/9	Dena	Thanks for the information on *Wired*
2/13	Sherry	Request to share course material

Category #6 Waxing Philosophical

1 total; 0 females/1 male
100% of the responses were by a male student

1/23	John	The literary canon

FIGURE 9.2. (continued)

The "General Questions about the Course and Assignments" Category

From: student@utdallas.edu
To: dene@utdallas.edu
Cc: aca102@utdallas.edu
Subject: extra credit

Dene:
What do you recommend I do to get extra credit in your class. I am looking for a few points of light. I am having problems understanding the hypertext assignment. Could you please help me? I placed my paper in your folder tonight.

Thanks,

The "General Questions about the Course and Assignments" category included inquiries about reading and writing assignments, how to use the computer or a particular software package, and basic housekeeping chores like setting student conference appointments or citing reasons for missing a meeting. During the fall semester, three women out of the 15 asked general questions. All three asked for assistance with their reading material and writing assignments, but none requested help with the technology or information about student conferences or missing meetings (see Figure 9.3). During the spring semester, 12 females asked general questions: Five wanted help with reading and writing assignments (up by 166 percent from the previous semester), two wanted help with the technology (up by 200 percent), and one had a question about her conference (up by 100 percent). In fact, 55 percent of all inquiries in this category came from women. Thus, it appeared that during the fall semester, few students gained any interest in learning how to use e-mail, even after my demonstrations and in spite of the incentives I concocted for them, or perhaps they had little time to devote to sending and answering e-mail. In the spring, however, students may have had more at stake because of the e-mail assignments I had given them. Five times more females used e-mail to ask questions during the spring than during the fall semester.

The "Assistance with University Business" Category

From: male student@utdallas.edu
To: Dene Grigar <aca102@utdallas.edu>
Subject: Hemingway

I've got a big question to ask.

I've received some information from the Center for Continuing education about their expedition entitled "Searching for Hemingway." The expedition will

Category	Spring	Fall	% Increase
Category #1: General Questions about Course and Assignments	12	3	400%
Reading/Writing Assignment Assistance	5	3	166%
Technical Assistance	2	0	200%
Housekeeping Chores	1	0	100%
Category #2: Assistance with University Business	0	0	0%
Category #3: Personal Assistance	2	1	100%
Category #4: Explanation for Missing Class or Late Work (Apologies)	0	0	0%
Category #5: Personal Comment	5	0	500%
Category #6: Waxing Philosophical	0	0	0%
Telephone calls	2	5	-40%
Total e-mail output by mid-semester by females/total # messages	15/24	4/25	375%
Total communications with female students	17	9	180%

FIGURE 9.3. Comparison of Fall and Spring Semester Responses by Category

be by yacht from St. Petersburg around the coast to Dry Tortugas and on to Key West. The scholar accompanying us will be Dr. ____________, a personal friend of Hemingway and accomplished writer. He is a winner of an Emmy, the Writer's Guild Award, the Peabody, an Oscar Nomination and the Christopher award. I feel that the trip would give me a fantastic basis for further literary studies, and some unique insight into Hemingway's work and 20th century history in general.

My problem is: I need to figure out some way to get credit for the trip.... [Administrator] in the CCE told me that it might be possible to get a major professor to give me the credit I need, by making it part of a lit course I am already taking this semester, or by putting it into an independent study framework.

I was hoping that you might be able to help me. Would you be either willing to give me credit for this trip as a part of literary analysis, or to supervise my work in an independent study program? I appreciate any advice you can give me.

Thanks,

Assistance with University Business centered on course advice or help with summer study programs. During both semesters, 100 percent of these messages came from male students. I suspected that male students, who were mostly lower-division students, had little experience in choosing courses and were still uncertain of their majors. My older female students who were juniors and seniors may have been fully advised about courses they needed for graduation and felt secure about the direction of their coursework, which may explain why they were not asking questions in this category. Because of family responsibilities or financial constraints, few of them were free to participate in summer study programs abroad, programs some of my younger male students were asking about.

The "Messages Pertaining to Personal Assistance" Category

From: student@utdallas.edu
To: aca102@utdallas.edu
Subject: E-mail Assignment

Dene,

The computer lab gave me UNIX login and PC login, but not Infoserv login, so I'm having to go through the CSCLASS UNIX host to send you this. I will pick up my password tomorrow before class. Good [?]ched about this class. Thanks for offering it. BTW, what are you teaching next semester?? Sorry bout the long first line, I'm just learning.

Sincerely

Although my female students may not have needed career advice, they did require much encouragement about their ability to succeed in the class. In the category I called "Messages Pertaining to Personal Assistance"—that is, nervousness about the course, recommendations on books to read, or help with another course—women participated far more frequently than they had in the previous category. During the fall, one female student asked for help with the internet. The rest of those posting e-mail of this sort were male students; during the spring semester, two female students sent messages of this kind. Although the rise in numbers is small, it is nonetheless significant: Students from the fall semester were not required to use technology in the classroom and had little reason to be nervous about it; however, spring semester students, working in a Macintosh lab and expected to use multiple kinds of computer resources daily, voiced little concern about the workload. I fully expected a deluge of requests for help from the spring semester students. But as their comments on the student profiles suggest, though they may have been nervous, they were enjoying what they learned and making steady progress. Many of them remarked to me that they liked the laid-back attitude I had set early in the semester concerning their ability to understand technology.

The "Explanations for Missing Class or Late Work" Category

From: student@utdallas.edu
To: R M Grigar <aca102@utdallas.edu>
Subject: my lit rewrite

Dear Dene,

Sorry that I haven't contacted you earlier; I realize that you are going out of town Wed night. This is hell week for me ... it seems like everything is due Friday. I have a few theses that I'd like to look over with you, but I work on Tues and Thursday all day except for Lit class, and Wed, I'm booked for the whole day for classes.

When is the rewrite due? Do you have any tips regarding how to approach forming a thesis?

When are you leaving Wed night? Is there any way to meet you at six or seven, or are you already gone by then?

Love,
D—-

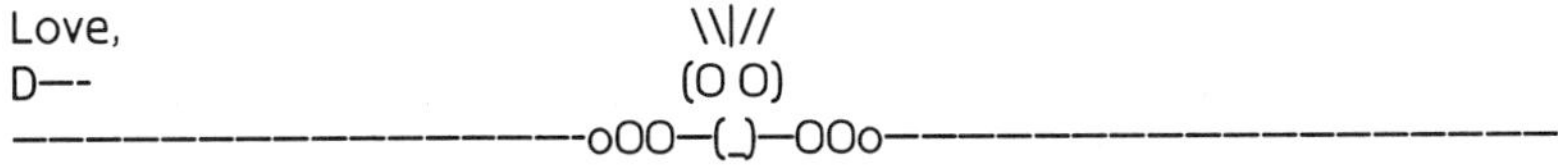

During the fall semester, one male student sent e-mail in the category of "Explanations for Missing Class or Late Work." During the spring, I received no messages of this type from any students. To be honest, my absenteeism dropped from the fall to the spring. I surmised from student comments that attendance improved during the spring because I began posting via e-mail an "agenda" containing all of the work and activities that we would be undertaking during class, days before the actual class. The agenda, long and detailed, made it clear from the long list of things to do that the class was too important to miss. Likewise, the agenda told them exactly what they needed to know about the class if, indeed, they did miss. So they did not have to contact me when and if they were absent—simply by checking e-mail they would know what we covered and what was assigned for next time. And because there was numerous ways to turn in work electronically when students missed class, they did not have to turn in work late—no apologies were required for this reason.

The "Personal Comments" Category

From: student@utdallas.edu
To: dene@utdallas.edu
Cc: aca102@utdallas.edu
Subject: PER YOUR REQUEST

SORRY, I'M JUST NOW SENDING THIS, BUT AT LEAST I GOT THROUGH THIS TIME. I HOPE YOUR HUSBAND IS DOING OK.

The category I have identified as "Personal Comments," those messages that contained compliments about the class, a thank-you for some assistance I had provided, special requests, or get well wishes, rose significantly among female students during the spring semester. In the fall, no women sent e-mail messages in this category; in the spring, five females students did. Thus, it seems that they were using e-mail as a way to connect with me in a very personal way.

The "Waxing Philosophical" Category

From: malestudent@utdallas.edu
To: aca102@utdallas.edu
Subject: Re: E-mail

Hi Dene.
QUESTION=> I was sitting at home last night listening to my very favorite Pet Shop Boys CD and drinking a nice cold root beer when it occurred to me that many of my professors have been talking to me about this literary canon thing and I'm still foggy about the whole idea. I read that little part about literary canons in our textbook, but it didn't help very much. What the heck is a literary canon? Is it the critics? Is it the foundations of Western Literature e.g. Chaucer? I am soo confused. What do you do with a literary canon? Is it something that should worry me? What if I'm a canonical critic and I do"t even know it? Help!:)

In the final category, called "Waxing Philosophical," no females responded—in fact, I only received one message in this area, and it was from a young male student. I considered this category important because it moved from questions about the daily innerworkings of the course to larger issues dealing with the reading material. And since one of my goals for using e-mail was to give students a method of discussing their insights into the material with me without the pressure of classroom performance, I was disappointed that I had so few messages. The student who did make an intellectual inquiry did so about the literary canon. He had been one of our first-year students and had studied the notion of the canon in his composition class. That so few messages fell within this category implied that neither women nor men were presenting their ideas or voicing their opinions about the reading assignments at all *and* that I was not doing enough to stimulate discussion for *either* gender. This finding prompted me to send out more inquiries about the readings during the latter part of the semester as a way to prod students into thinking more along these lines.

Despite the low participation in some categories, the overall number of messages I received from female students rose dramatically from the fall to mid-spring semester, from four to 15. When I count both e-mail messages and telephone calls, the numbers change from nine students in the fall to 17 in the spring.

Why is it that female students communicated more openly in e-mail than they do in person? Many factors may have contributed to the rise in my communications with my female students and the ease in which they communicated with me. First, because I held class in the lab and spent time helping them learn the technology, female students in the spring may have become more adept at using e-mail than their fall counterparts. Likewise, they had time to send messages before and after class, since I opened the classroom early and stayed until they were finished with their work. Second, during the spring, I devoted more activities that exposed students to e-mail and devised more ways to entice them to communicate with me and their classmates. In particular, I had developed a special hypertext group project and required them to share all research for their papers with other students. Third, so that they could understand the benefits of mastering e-mail and technology, I made information about the Internet available to them. Along these lines, I introduced them to the Internet by getting them into listservs and participating in MOOs.

Although the overall number of messages generated by female students more than doubled, the kinds of conversations male and female students were having with me broke down by gender lines. As I pointed out earlier, women were more apt to ask for help with their coursework and with computers, and they sent me over 70 percent of the compliments and thank-you messages. However, any kind of request for career advice came from men, and larger philosophical questions about literature were also generated by my male students.

These revelations guided me in the second half of the semester. From early March onward, I worked to initiate more conversations with my students about some of the ideas we discussed in class, and I inquired frequently about my female students' career goals. Likewise, I encouraged male students to talk to me about their other classes and some of the experiences they were having at school so that I could better understand their needs.

The student evaluations (see Figure 9.4) at the end of the spring semester made it clear that my students had indeed gotten over their fear of computers and enjoyed learning literature with technology. The most positive comments found in the written section of the evaluation, however, centered on my availability to my students. Some evaluations point directly to the use of e-mail as the reason why they felt good about the class. Others simply noted that I was very accessible and that they felt comfortable talking to me. Considering that I received fewer phone calls during the spring semester and the number of students showing up during my office hours did not rise, I suspect that they were referring here to communicating with me electronically and that the kind of relationship I had established via e-mail helped to reduce

1. Total numbers of students in course: 15 total; 11 females (73%)/4 men (27%)
2. Experience: Explain your experience with each of these prior to this class:
   IBM:
   Macintosh:
   E-mail:
   Other technologies:
3. Age:
4. Gender:
5. Level:
6. Computer access: Do you have access to a computer at home? Modem? Computer at work? Are you required to use e-mail at your job?
7. Signed up for the course because of the technology component: Yes or No?
8. Didn't know about the technology, but stayed in class anyway: Yes or No?
9. Have telephoned the instructor during the semester: Yes or No?
   Number of times:
10. Have e-mailed the instructor during the semester: Yes or No?
    Number of times?
11. E-mail friends on campus since learning e-mail in this class: Yes or No?
12. E-mail friends off campus since learning e-mail in this class: Yes or No?
13. What else do you use e-mail for?
14. Additional coments that would shed light on your views toward the technology

FIGURE 9.4. Student Survey: A Midsemester Evaluation of the Use of Electronic Technology in the Classroom

their discomfort with computers. Negative comments about technology were derived primarily from typical problems that occur in a lab: the network going down, computers that broke, and a poor computer projection system. No students complained about using e-mail, or any other technology for that matter. My students' views toward electronic resources we used may have been shaped by my constant reassurance—via e-mail—about their ability to use computers effectively and by my expectations for their achievement. Thus, *my* use of e-mail may have influenced *their* use of e-mail, as well as their attitudes about it and other technologies.

It goes without saying that teachers seeking to use technology in the classroom need to be aware of student needs and limitations, as well as limitations set by the environment. In the case of my students, I introduced e-mail so that nontraditional, commuting students could communicate with me easily. I wanted to build an environment where everyone felt at ease to discuss their ideas freely and comfortably and students could take control of their education by asking questions and seeking information. I sent students weekly messages to keep them informed and stir their curiosity. The mid-semester evaluation of my teaching made me aware of where my strategies were falling short of my target. Sharing that information with my students helped them to see their attitudes toward their work and abilities in a clearer light and made them feel less alone with their fears and successes. After I had completed my evaluation, I made it a point to send e-mail that encouraged more critical questions and comments about the material.

OFFLINE: EVALUATING OUR PEDAGOGY AND STUDENTS' NEEDS

From: student@utdallas.edu
To: dene grigar <aca102@utdallas.edu>

Hi, Dene. How are you doing? I'm doing fine. I'm a PA this year, and I enjoy living on campus. Last year I commuted and it was a pain. We still talk about the great gumbo we had at your house last year. I just wanted to say hi and to find out if you are going to teach a rhetoric class in the spring. A couple of freshman were asking which professors were good and I thought of you. But I didn't see your name in any of professors teaching for this spring. Is that a mistake? I really enjoyed your class and benefited from it. Plus, I got to learn how to use E-mail. See? Anyways, I must be on my way. I've got that pesky homework stuff. :-)

How can we best ensure that the use of technology is actually enhancing learning and not, in fact, undermining our students' education? Is forcing students to use technology counterproductive to learning? The answer is, of course, that there is no definitive answer. Technology as technology does not teach a subject or improve students' learning. We can no more hand our students a textbook and claim that they have mastered the course than we can say that sitting students in front of a monitor will make them better thinkers.

So naysayers of computer technology are right insofar that technology may intimidate and limit learning if we do not take the proper precautions or devise good methods for disseminating knowledge. Interactive learning can only come from interactive teaching. As facilitators in this process, we must be ever watchful of situations that could undermine our students' ability to function at their highest potential in our classrooms. Those who embrace computer-aided instruction are also correct in predicting the great potential of electronic technology to enhance learning. In the case of my own students, many stated in their student evaluations that using e-mail to clarify ideas and gain information helped them to learn the material I was trying to teach.

Practitioners of computer-aided instruction know that technology is effective only when it fits our own particular students' needs *and* when we create effective pedagogy for the use of it. Therefore, even teachers well trained in technology must always be willing to evaluate themselves and their pedagogy in terms of students' needs and course objectives. We must reflect upon our practices in order to ensure our students' achievement. Forcing students to use technology, particularly technology such as e-mail, should be appropriate to the situation and depends upon student access and incentive to participate.

Does a rise in verbal activity indicate that e-mail enhances learning in the classroom? When working with female students in particular, we should also keep in mind that recent discussions about ethics and feminism indicate that women focus more on "care and responsibility" than on issues of "justice and rights." In fact, as Gilligan's (1982) work points out, women view their environment contextually and subordinate traditional hierarchical matters of morality to "details of relationships and narratives" (qtd. in Benhabib, 1992, p. 270). Thus, it stands to reason that a networked classroom, claimed by many to promote collaboration, sharing, and a democratic atmosphere, would be a conducive environment for women to work in. As my study bears out, this *can* be the case. But to ensure that the converse does not occur, that female students will not be uneasy in the electronic environment, we must work hard to create an effective pedagogy that helps them to go over the line that frequently limits their progress when they are online.

REFERENCES

Belenky, M. F., Clinchy, B. M., Goldberger, N. R., & Tarule, J. M. (1986). *Women's ways of knowing: The development of self, voice, and mind.* New York: Basic Books.

Benhabib, S. (1992). The generalized and the concrete other. In E. Frazer, J. Hornsby, & S. Lovibond (Eds.), *Ethics: A feminist reader* (p. 270). Oxford, England: Blackwell.

Boese, C. (1995, March). *A virtual locker room: Gendered democracy in a classroom electronic chat space.* Paper presented at the Conference of College Composition and Communications, Washington DC.

Brail, S. (1997). Take back the Net! In G. Hawisher & C. Selfe (Eds.), *Literacy, technology, and society* (pp. 419–422). Upper Saddle River, NJ: Prentice-Hall.

Cooper, M., & Selfe, C. (1990). Computer conferences and learning: Authority, resistance, and internally persuasive discourse. *College English, 52*, 847–869.

Daisley, M. (n.d.). *Thirteen ways of looking at the m-word.* Unpublished manuscript.

Eldred, J. C. (1989). Computers, composition pedagogy, and the social views. In G. E. Hawisher & C. L. Selfe (Eds.), *Critical perspectives on computers and composition instruction* (pp. 201–218). New York: Teacher's College Press.

Gill, M. S. (1997). Terror on-line. In G. Hawisher & C. Selfe (Eds.), *Literacy, technology, and society* (pp. 76–85). Upper Saddle River, NJ: Prentice-Hall.

Gilligan, C. (1982). *In a different voice: Psychological theory and women's development.* Cambridge, MA: Harvard University Press.

Haraway, D. (1985). A manifesto for cyborgs: Science, technology, and socialist feminism in the 1980's. In V. Vitanza (Ed.), *CyberReader* (pp. 372–404). Boston: Allyn and Bacon.

Hawisher, G., & Selfe, C. (1989). *Critical perspectives on computers and composition instruction.* New York: Teacher's College Press.

Kramarae, C., & Taylor, H. J. (1997). Women and men on electronic networks: A conversation or a monologue? In G. Hawisher & C. Selfe (Eds.), *Literacy, technology, and society* (pp. 348–357). Upper Saddle River, NJ: Prentice-Hall.

Kunzru, H. (1997, February). You are borg. *Wired*, 154–210.

Moran, C. (1992). Computers and English: What do we make of each other? *College English, 54*, 193–198.

Pea, R. D., & Kurland, D. M. (1987). Cognitive technologies for writing. *Review of Research in Education, 14*, 227–325.

Redd, T. (1997). Accomodation and resistance on (the color) line: Black writers meet white artists on the Internet. In D. Reiss, D. Selfe, & A. Young (Eds.), *Electronic communication across the curriculum* (pp. 139–148). Urbana, IL: National Council of Teachers of English.

Regan, A. (1993). "Type normal like the rest of us": Writing, power, and homophobia in the networked composition classroom. *Computers and Composition, 10*, 11–23.

Silberman, S. (1997). We're teen, we're queer, and we've got e-mail. In G. Hawisher & C. Selfe (Eds.), *Literacy, technology, and society* (pp. 58–62). Upper Saddle River, NJ: Prentice-Hall.

Smith, J. B., & Smith, C. F. (1990). Writing, thinking, computing. *Poetics, 19*, 140.

Map of Location IV

Virtual Coalitions and Collaborations

chapter 10

Designing Feminist Multimedia for the United Nations Fourth World Conference on Women

Mary E. Hocks
Georgia State University

WHY FEMINIST MULTIMEDIA?

For those of us committed to teaching and performing academic work with technology, communication technologies and new media offer powerful opportunities for visual communication, human connection, and engaged participation. By combining video, graphics, text, and sound in electronic format, interactive multimedia appeals to multiple senses, as it tells stories with pictures and voices rather than just words. With the rich communicative possibilities of new media in mind, I designed and presented a multimedia project for an international feminist audience. With my collaborator, Anne Balsamo, I designed "Women of the World Talk Back," a multimedia presentation exhibited at the United Nations Fourth World Conference on Women, which took place near Beijing, China, in September of 1995. Our presentation documents this landmark event by incorporating interviews, footage, and statements from world leaders and activists, many of whom helped organize the forum or gave plenaries at the conference. Created with the software program Macromedia Director™, the project features the perspectives of the conference organizers and many long-time activists in global women's organizations.

Many people worked on this project using a collaborative team model that is commonplace in multimedia development.[1] Because of our institutional locations—Georgia Institute of Technology and Spelman College—we were able to garner the resources necessary for this project. Multimedia production takes an incredible amount of money, time, expertise, and coordination of resources. As is the case with most noncommercial computer projects, we worked primarily after hours, several evenings a week, to complete the initial presentation, which is really a prototype for a more extensive project. I must highlight that this prototype version was developed on a shoestring budget with donated time, university equipment, and the group's determination to make the most out of the opportunities presented by the Conference. Of course, everyday use of new technologies cannot exist outside the conditions of access and privilege that make them available in the first place. As Nancy Kaplan (1991) argues, materialist critiques of technology demonstrate that "existing ideological practices … envision, shape and control tools" (p. 22). However, "Women of the World Talk Back" did demonstrate that the machines, laboratories, production time, and talents could be deployed for other purposes than the continued accumulation of capital. We hoped this kind of multimedia project would demonstrate the benefits of deploying privilege for broader feminist goals. Our goal was to create a communication experience that brought people together to discuss the topics of the conference itself, but especially women's use of technology around the globe. This experience offered an exciting opportunity to participate in an international political arena and to draw those attending the forum into thought-provoking dialogue. Thus, rather than a predetermined message sent to a passive audience, this exhibit literally became an occasion for a conversation. I want to argue that, via multimedia technology, we created a successful, if limited, moment of feminist activism and cross-cultural connection that subverts the dominant uses of these types of technologies.

Materialist feminist critiques of technology reveal the typical cultural messages offered by technologies. Given that technological artifacts manifest cultural values, these values are marked and embedded in the design, the dissemination, and the use of technologies. The net effect of technology's relationship to cultural values, as feminist critiques of technology argue, is that technologies often reproduce traditional cultural arrangements (Balsamo, 1996; Kramarae, Ebbon, & Taylor, 1992; Perry & Greber, 1990; Rakow, 1988; Wajcman, 1991). For example, machines are traditionally coded as masculine and associated with male privilege, military power, and the masculine culture surrounding engineering (Perry & Greber, 1990). Furthermore, in their role as market commodities designed to be consumed, technologies are analogous to information, power, and access. Technologies offer greater access to a greater quantity of information that, in turn, translates into greater personal power. Feminist uses of technology can then be defined as interventions within these dominant cultural narratives about technology. A deliberately feminist design, for example, can be collaborative and open-ended, rather than fixed and prescriptive, so that technological artifacts can facilitate dialogue and exchange among people (Balsamo & Hocks, in press). Rather than simply rehearsing the "information as mastery" model, a feminist design might embody specifically feminist values of collaboration, multivocality, and open-ended possibility.

My specific role in developing this project was as co-designer, rhetorician, and educational technologist. While designed for a feminist context and a specific occasion, "Women of the World Talk Back" also exemplifies how new media can be used to make rhetorical statements that are both visual and verbal. I would suggest that this project points toward an important new area of feminist work: the development and critique of new media. This presentation moves beyond the traditional documentary style not only by being interactive media, but by offering the opportunity for others to be incorporated into the master narrative and the conversation, albeit in an imperfect way. It carries a message of cooperation while respecting difference, but without trying to exhaustively *represent* difference. Feminist projects offered via multimedia can greatly increase women's diverse presence and activism in electronic environments. New media designed by women and driven by feminist goals can also empower women by aggressively creating more diverse images of women. Furthermore, as teachers and scholars we need to use new media and communications technologies to empower our students with critical tools and more liberating knowledge about technology. Finally, the experience of designing multimedia offers a participatory and hands-on model for students that uses and enhances the processes we value both in feminist pedagogy and in the teaching of writing. Before describing the design process and the implications for teaching, I will provide the background on the occasion for this multimedia presentation.

THE FOURTH WORLD CONFERENCE ON WOMEN

The Fourth World Conference on Women in Beijing followed other recent United Nations conferences during the last two decades that focused on women, the environment, children, population, and development. The first women's conference, for example, took place in Mexico City in 1975; it raised women's awareness of how they could organize and influence policymaking globally for their own benefit (United Nations Development Fund for Women, 1995). The third women's conference, in Nairobi in 1985, resulted in a document providing strategies for the advancement of women worldwide. Governmental representatives met in Beijing to discuss and adopt a platform for action that would reinforce the resolutions outlined in the Nairobi document. Once adopted by the delegates at the conference, the final Platform for Action was then published in several places in print and on the World Wide Web ("Beijing Declaration and Platform for Action," 1996; Institute for Global Communications, 1995). This document provides the rationale and the strategies for particular countries to follow up on the ideas presented at the conference. Government delegates describe their common mission in the "Beijing Declaration" section of the Platform for Action, which was adopted at the conference:

> [We] recognize that the status of women has advanced in some important respects in the past decade but that progress has been uneven, inequalities between women and men have persisted and major obstacles remain, with serious consequences for the well-being of all people.... [We] dedicate ourselves unreservedly to addressing these constraints and obstacles and thus enhancing further the advancement and empowerment of women all over the world. (Articles 4 and 7)

The platform that follows these statements focuses on specific areas for action, or "critical areas of concern." Governmental delegations are not required, however, to include members of so-called "nongovernmental organizations," or NGOs. Government-appointed delegates and policymakers do not necessarily represent the interests of activists or the people actually working in educational system or activist organizations. The NGO Forum thus runs concurrent to the conference and gives feminist individuals and organizations from around the globe an opportunity to network and to influence their delegates at the UN conference. While those attending the NGO Forum did not necessarily attend the UN conference, they could hold demonstrations, lobby the delegates from their countries, and offer statements about an area of concern. Thus, we submitted a statement on the education of women in science and technology, and we had the opportunity to meet with several official U.S. delegates to the UN conference.

While the NGO Forum was a high profile and impressive event, it was plagued with problems for those who attended. The majority of these problems arose from the location and the oppressive nature of the Chinese state. Known for its human rights violations and oppression of women, China was a strange place to attend a women's conference that carried the message "Women's rights are human rights." To contain the activities of unofficial participants, the Chinese government moved the forum to Hairou, a resort town 35 miles outside of Beijing. Participants arrived to find unfinished buildings and inadequate facilities for lodging and forum activities. We discovered that visas had been delayed or denied, especially for known political activists. Materials on topics considered offensive, from Tibetan Independence to Lesbian Organizations, had to be smuggled into the site. Our worries about censorship and logistical nightmares came true as we witnessed the official attempts to control the activities of women and men attending the Forum. Police surrounded the town and restricted the activities and travels of visitors. Journalists, in particular, were harassed by Chinese officials and police. Several cameras and tapes were confiscated without warning. Journalists had difficulty securing lodgings and transportation in and out of the city of Beijing. At the same time, officials cautioned Chinese citizens not to interact with the visiting women activists, and spread bizarre rumors about nude demonstrations and other activities by Western feminists.

Despite these well-publicized obstacles presented by the Chinese government to NGO participants and members of the media, the NGO Forum still succeeded in providing networking, information, and thousands of workshops and presentations. These workshops, like the conference itself, fit into 12 broad themes, such as women and violence, women and the media, and the education and training of women. Typical workshop topics included violence against women in Algeria, ancient tea ceremonies in Japan, images of women in the U.S. media, and agricultural techniques pioneered by women in Kenya. The forum thus provided ample opportunity to meet and learn from others, and particularly those who shared my areas of focus: women's participation in new technology and technological education.

The Internet played a key role in many participants' preparation for Beijing and follow-up to the conference. In fact, the Internet became a key tool for access to information about the conference before it began, and a key vehicle of communication in China. For example, many people obtained the draft Platform for Action—a document of several hundred pages—from the Feminist Majority (1995) website and then prepared materials and statements to take to Beijing. The Platform educated us about key issues surrounding women and technology and allowed us to write a position paper addressed to our delegation. The website included other key information: the history of the UN women's conferences, a summary of the Nairobi document, and strategies on how to lobby the American delegates. Many American participants used the Internet to research the conference and discover the key areas where our interests intersected with official statements under discussion at the conference. These Internet sites also provided day-by-day updates on essential preparations for the conference, including how to obtain visas into China. In this instance, we see how communication technologies help people organize and share information. Online activism and collaboration can occur when electronic discussions create what Nancy Baym (1995) calls "computer-mediated communities"—people remotely connected through electronic conversation who share common interests or purpose. As both a tool for information and for communication, the Internet became a direct instrument of activism and organization for some NGO Forum participants. Those who took advantage of the Internet were empowered by the extensive information available to them.

The President's Interagency Council on Women in the United States has used the Internet extensively to follow up on the commitments made in Beijing. They published a written report in May 1996 outlining U.S. priorities such as health, domestic violence, and discrimination, and presented how agencies are implementing the commitments made during the conference (see also The Feminist Majority, 1995). The Agency also established a website with extensive policy information and opportunities for response over electronic mail (http://www.igc.org/beijing/index.html). These resources provided access to our government's efforts to put the Platform initiatives into action in this country. The Internet thus has helped many Americans gain indepth information about our own country's follow-up to the conference event.

Computer access also played a crucial role during the conference itself. Apple Computer sent representatives to the conference and established an online site for journalists and other participants with Internet and electronic mail. Computer support representatives also offered numerous workshops on using the Internet and electronic mail. All of this electronic activity was in stark contrast to the silence imposed by the Chinese government on its own people: little media coverage was disseminated to the Chinese public, though Chinese women, student translators, police, and government officials were attending the NGO Forum. Throughout the conference, foreign journalists could e-mail their articles in, and individuals could contact those at home who were monitoring the public perceptions of this event. Given how Chinese officials harassed journalists throughout the conference, some writers covering the events might very well have been cut off from their home bases without access to the Internet. Our presentation fit in nicely within this empowering technological context, while also exploring the interactive potential of new media design.

MULTIMEDIA DESIGN AND RESPONSE

When deciding on an appropriate design for "Women of the World Talk Back," Anne and I decided that a narrative composed of multiple voices would be the most provocative and effective means for presenting information about women's global situation. The concept of "Video Dialogues" became a way to use composite interviews and a documentary technique to illustrate key topics and principles of women's empowerment. Each specific video dialogue[2] follows a narrative that emerged from screening hours of interviews about several recent United Nations conferences. The resulting videos are short, 2–3 minute movies that constitute a dialogue of voices about a conference topic. Consisting of polished sound bytes from highly visible leaders and heads of state, these dialogues do not presume to represent all women in their diversity or the complexities of their local political situations. In fact, they represent the official story—the bureaucratic language of international policy and global politics. Given their "official UN-speak" style, the video dialogues still sparked interest in the conference and provoked responses from activists who were enacting solutions to the issues brought up by their own leaders in the interviews. Participants were then invited to "talk back" in a variety of ways: by leaving literature about their organizations, by recording an interview, or by giving contact information for the future, when the project might become a fully funded multimedia documentary. Because of the local follow-up to the conference and the networking of various groups, this information had multiple uses and destinations. Some of the print information our team gathered, for example, later became incorporated into databases and reports created by the Georgia Commission on Women.

The context of an international conference required a professional-looking presentation that would attract visitors in a very noisy setting. The interactive design uses a simple point-and-click navigational strategy that focuses on a main menu and a set of movies that are the heart of the project. The main menu displays the logo—the female symbol and a globe next to one another—and a simple list to access the different movies and textual information. The logo becomes an icon on later screens for navigating back to this main menu. The introduction displays a short video with dramatic music that ran continuously during the Forum to lure people out of the crowd and over to the computer. The brief, emphatic statements and complementary images were originally designed as public service announcements for CNN

International, illustrating why the women's conference deserved worldwide public support and attention. This introduction concisely conveys the essential message from a broad spectrum of political leaders that women still need to achieve equality and opportunity worldwide.

The Video Dialogues Screen serves as the access point to all of the indepth information in the project. The screen forms a visual rhetorical statement as a question with three emphatic answers: "What do Women Want? Access to Education. Economic Opportunities. Empowerment." Each graphical image is a large button that, when clicked, leads to another screen and plays a video. For example, in the "What do Women Want?" video, Irene Santiago, an activist from the Philippines and Executive Director of the 1995 NGO Forum, claims, "There is no issue that is not a women's issue!" Other voices follow that assert how women need access to the economic resources of their own countries and higher visibility in public life. As in a documentary movie, it presents a narrative crafted out of multiple voices. In this way, the multimedia format is particularly effective, because it allows the opportunity to include actual voices, facial expressions, and nuances of speech. Like any documentary, however, the story is partial and determined by the perspectives of the designers, who have the ultimate responsibility of representing a fair and accurate story. This work enabled many voices and points of view to be heard, but it could never represent the whole story or the material circumstances of participants.

Because the project was sponsored by the Georgia Institute of Technology, the booth, in a crowded exhibit hall, displayed information about educational opportunities for women at this still male-dominated university. At one side of the booth, the kiosk ran continuously to attract those who were interested by the electronic media. "We are not invitees on this planet," begins UN secretary-general Gertrude Mongella, in a low, powerful voice. "What we want is for women to be taken seriously," adds Irene Santiago. Given our relative technological privilege, this exhibit would exemplify what women can do with technology given the means and the opportunity. Accordingly, its design was aesthetically pleasing, inspiring, and straightforward. The audience's experience with multimedia was somewhat unknown, but we assumed that many may have little or no experience with a computer interface or a mouse. Because English was one of the official languages of the conference, we did not make the project multilingual. We trusted that large icons, graphics, music, and interactive elements would still offer non-English speakers an experience with multimedia. The project design highlighted original music and professional quality video interviews, all designed within a background screen that reproduced a richly colored quilt. With posted signs and verbal invitations from the faculty and students in the booth, participants could interact with the kiosk and respond to it either formally, with an interview, or informally, in conversation.

The many people who visited our booth provided us with an education about the global situation of women and technology. Many visitors, mostly women, were unfamiliar or uncomfortable with running a computer. They often sat down in chairs and asked us to demonstrate the presentation for them. We would ask which topics interested them and then click on those sections of the video dialogues. Notable exceptions were several young girls who publish a youth activist newspaper in the northwestern United States, and many of the Chinese students (male and female) who attended the conference. These younger people obviously felt comfortable interacting with computers and did not hesitate to run the program. Most people viewed different video dialogues for 10 to 15 minutes. Then, we would often sit down and discuss their own activist work in particular parts of the world. We talked with publishers of women's newsletters from Haiti, artists from Mexico, and television producers from India. In several cases, we videotaped people who had their own electronic artwork or media-oriented projects to discuss. These conversations and interviews demonstrated that women are using many types of traditional media—from video to print—to educate themselves about everything from political rights to health issues. While there remains a striking global imbalance in the distribution and access to communication technologies, such as fax machines, video players, computers, and network connections, activists from around the world were very interested in using new information technologies for grassroots organizing and educational efforts. Because of limited access to technological resources worldwide, however, some people wanted to know if the final project could be distributed on CD-ROM or even videotape so that they could share it with their local organizations. We learned that access to technology obviously remains a central issue of concern for women across the world.

By the end of our 3-week stay, we had begun a series of conversations and this project became an ongoing development project with plans to continue adding more statements and more voices. After these conversations with women at the Forum, we began to think about how we might make the project available to people after the conference ended. The initial goal of educating others had also changed: As privileged Americans, we needed to teach ourselves more about what others are doing with the resources available to them. Now, our audience has become other educators and students, especially those in institutional positions where they have access to technological resources.

IMPLICATIONS FOR TEACHING AND WRITING

In many ways, multimedia design marks a new horizon for electronic writing similar to the first decade of research and practice in computer-assisted composition, when we witnessed grassroots efforts toward creating suitable materials for college students in computer writing classrooms. The new writing technologies—software programs for composition and communication such as Daedalus Integrated Writing Environment™, Storyspace™, and Writer's Helper™—all came forth from early development efforts by *teachers*.[3] David Jay Bolter's speculative book, *Writing Space: The Computer, Hypertext and the History of Writing* (1991), predicted the impact of multimedia on writing by suggesting that hypertext would radically change the fundamental nature of writing into a spatial and nonlinear form, so that libraries, texts, and reading itself would shift into a new form that combines communication, visual writing, and interactive technology. Gary Heba (1997) confirms this assertion as he describes the elaborate collaborative processes for web page design and how hypertext projects map onto traditional compositional processes of invention, arrangement, and style. A multimedia project provides a rich communication context that requires extensive rhetorical planning, designing, scripting, writing, careful organization, and close attention to the audience of the presentation. In other words, all of the practices necessary for successful academic writing can be incorporated into hypertextual and multimedia writing projects, with the added dimensions of enhancing visual, metaphorical, and nonlinear critical thinking (Joyce, 1995).

As both a writer and a teacher of writing, I believe these technologies can transform writing practices. Multimedia, whether created for the Web or for media such as CD-ROM, is a verbal, visual, auditory, and participatory form of communication between the writers/designers and their audience. Students also need to be encouraged to engage in writing processes that involve intense collaboration among their individual strengths and interests. In a multimedia project, students learn that the whole product is much bigger than the individual parts, that each person's role is interdependent, and that graphics, words, and navigational structure must work together to create a visual argument and a message. As Lanham (1993) argues, writing in the age of digitalization has brought forth a coherent digital rhetoric of image and word. If teachers can engage students in these rhetorical designs, they will create valuable materials while internalizing processes that help them become better communicators, both verbally and visually. With the ultimate goal of developing a technologically sophisticated college curriculum, I am committed to helping students create new media that provides nontraditional research materials and pushes the horizon of creativity in the computer classroom.

Multimedia projects are valuable because they require interdisciplinary teams of people who bring different skills to the table—whether it's conceptualizing, visualizing, structuring, navigating, troubleshooting, or editing. Multimedia design also helps engender visual literacy in students. Visual literacy includes skills such as: how to read the message of an image; how to analyze film technique and video footage; how to create a consistent visual and verbal metaphor; and how to move through electronic space. Students can use multimedia tools to develop essays, documentaries, video presentations, oral presentations, information databases, and public service announcements. These collaborative projects can be presented in class, distributed over a local network, written onto a CD-ROM, published on a web page, or in whatever new forms the future will offer.

Design projects also require a fair amount of linear writing. For example, several documents resulted from our planning meetings, including written scripts for voice-overs and textual information in the project. Our core group met weekly and rewrote many drafts of a project description as well as meeting agendas and minutes that documented the evolving changes in the design and scope of the project. Along with visual storyboards of each screen's design, written scripts determine the map and plan for the multimedia project. Not surprisingly, most projects require that 40-50 percent of the total time be spent in planning a design, a script, and navigational strategies. The entire group must reach a consensus on content and develop a full-fledged design before the media-authoring can be completed. Many professional writing and publishing projects now typically include image design and planning for online delivery of the final product on electronic media or over the World Wide Web.

In the writing classroom of tomorrow, I see students regularly collaborating on intensely visual and audio compositions that never see the printed page. They become conscious of the visual message, the stories told, and the complex context for the communication. While gaining valuable experience with technology, students engage in a recursive composing process that results in a professional and powerful act of communication. Inasmuch as we accomplished these educational goals with "Women of the World Talk Back," members of our team offer it as an example of what we might accomplish with multimedia technology.

We designed "Women of the World Talk Back" to create provocative conversation: It became a starting point for more dialogue and a way to discover what women activists are doing around the world. This documentary has become a collaborative work-in-process involving the work of students, faculty, and professional media people who provided artwork, music, and video footage. We learned that our first project was only a starting point, a model and a means for developing materials about women and featuring women's issues in electronic format. We have begun the second phase of development with a new audience and expanded purpose in mind. Our design process and the responses we have received demonstrates the value of creating feminist multimedia as an opportunity for communication, collaboration, or online activism. When we also bring our students into the center of the development process, we can pass on these values, while teaching them valuable tools for the age of electronic writing.

NOTES

[1] Our original design team consisted of seven people: two professors, three graduate students in Georgia Institute of Technology's M.A. program in information, design, and technology, one professional television producer, and one professional musician. A professor and director of the Writing Program at Spelman College, I co-directed the project with Anne Balsamo, a professor in Georgia Institute of Technology's school of Literature, Communication, and Culture. We provided the basic design concept and the content for the project. Our planning team included graduate students Kelly Johnson, a multimedia designer; Mary Anne Stevens, a graphic designer; and David Balcom, a multimedia author. They all contributed to the design during the initial development process: thus, the use of "we" in the discussions about design processes and goals throughout this chapter refers to this core development team. Phil Walker, a television producer, produced the interviews, the original, award-

winning CNN public service announcements, and the music soundtracks used in the project. With the help of a local musician, Bryan Arbuckle, Phil co-wrote and produced the music used in the project. On recent modules, M.A. student Sandra Beaudin and professor Ellen Strain, both from Georgia Tech, contributed additional graphic design and multimedia authoring.

[2] Portions of these video dialogues are available online at: http://www.gsu.edu/~engmch/mmdoc.html

[3] For the history of teachers developing writing software, see LeBlanc (1993) and Hawisher, LeBlanc, Moran, and Selfe (1996).

REFERENCES

Balsamo, A. (1996). *Technology and the gendered body: Reading cyborg women.* Chapel Hill, NC: Duke University Press.

Balsamo, A., & Hocks, M. (in press). Women making multimedia: Notes toward a feminist theory of technology. In B. E. Kolko (Ed.), *Virtual publics: Policy and community in an electronic age.* New York: Columbia University Press.

Baym, N. (1995). From practice to culture on Usenet. In S. L. Star (Ed.), *The cultures of computing* (pp. 29–52). Oxford, England: Basil Blackwell.

Beijing Declaration and Platform for Action (1996, Spring/Summer). *Women's Studies Quarterly 24*, 154–289.

Bolter, D. J. (1991). *Writing space: The computer, hypertext and the history of writing.* Hillsdale, NJ: Lawrence Erlbaum.

The Feminist Majority. (1995). *Report of the Fourth World Conference On Women* [Online]. Available: http://www.feminist.org/other/beijing.html

Hawisher, G. E., LeBlanc, P., Moran, C., & Selfe, C. L. (1996). *Computers and the teaching of writing in American higher education, 1979–1994: A history.* Norwood, NJ: Ablex.

Heba, G. (1997, January). HyperRhetoric: Multimedia, literacy, and the future of composition. *Computers and Composition, 14*, 19–44.

Institute for Global Communications. (1995). *Beijing '95: Women, power and change* [Online]. Available: http://www.igc.org/beijing/index.html

Joyce, M. (1995). *Of two minds: Hypertext pedagogy and poetics.* Ann Arbor, MI: University of Michigan Press.

Kaplan, N. (1991). Ideology, technology, and the future of writing instruction. In G. E. Hawisher & C. L. Selfe (Eds.), *Evolving perspectives on computers and composition studies* (pp. 7–42). Urbana, IL: National Council of Teachers of English.

Kramarae, C., Ebbon, M., & Taylor, J. (Eds.). (1992). *Women, information technology, and scholarship.* Urbana, IL: University of Illinois Center for Advanced Study.Lanham, R. (1993). *The electronic word: Democracy, technology and the arts.* Chicago: University of Chicago Press.

Lanham, R. (1993). *The electronic word: Democracy, technology, and the arts.* Chicago: University of Chicago Press.

LeBlanc, P. (1993). *Writing teachers, writing software: Creating our place in the electronic age.* Houghton, MI: National Council of Teachers of English and *Computers and Composition* Press.

Perry, R., & Greber, L. (1990, Winter). Women and computers: An introduction. *Signs, 16*, 74–101.

The President's Interagency Council on Women. (1996, May). *U.S. follow-up to the U. N. Fourth*

World Conference on Women [Brochure]. Washington, DC: Author.

Rakow, L. (1988). Women and the telephone: The gendering of a communications technology. In C. Kramerae (Ed.), *Technology and women's voices: Keeping in touch* (pp. 86–101). New York: Routledge.

United Nations Development Fund for Women. (1995). *Putting gender on the agenda: A guide to participating in UN world conferences* [Brochure]. New York: Author.

Wajcman, J. (1991). *Feminism confronts technology*. University Park, PA: Pennsylvania State University Press.

chapter 11

Voicing the Landscape: A Discourse of Their Own

Paula Gillespie
Marquette University

Laura Julier
Michigan State University

Kathleen Blake Yancey
University of North Carolina at Charlotte

How does e-mail affect women? How/can it bring women together—to think, to talk, to laugh, to work, to understand, to become? The three authors here—Paula Gillespie, Laura Julier, and Kathleen Blake Yancey—take up this question almost self-consciously. We are long-distance colleagues, brought together initially by writing chapters for the National Council of Teachers of English essay collection entitled *Voices on Voice*. That exigence, and a face-to-face meeting to celebrate the volume's publication, led to our proposing a panel for the Conference on College Compostion and Communication, to our writing this text, to our planning to write a volume ourselves, on place.

The place that made these plans real for us: e-mail.

How did it work? What concerns did we bring here? Were those concerns strictly academic, or were there personal matters? Were our experiences here similar to those in other e-mail-based relationships? What theorizing might we be able to do about all this?

To answer these questions, we've talked variously—as scholars, as mothers and sisters and daughters, as friends, and always as women—in search of a discourse of our own. We've written the chapter much as we've experienced our relationship—in multilogue. Please feel free to enter *in medias res*.

* * *

Kathleen Blake Yancey: I have been skimming *Manly Writing* by Miriam Brody [1994]. She identifies what she calls an "in-between place" as the site for a new kind of discourse, one that is androgynous. I'm not certain I buy this—I'm not unhappy with being a woman, and I don't think I want my discourse androgynized. To a certain extent, actually, this has already happened, in that in order to succeed in academic life, one tends to work in a masculine discourse, and that has written me too. I think a masculinized discourse (the norm) has something to recommend it, but I also think a feminine discourse does too. And that is what I want to receive critical attention: the way we know in that discourse is as valid—and more important, as valuable—as what we know in the other.

Paula Gillespie: I was drawn into e-mail initially by WCENTER, the discussion group for writing center people. My office is across the campus from the English Department. Even there, I have colleagues, but their specialties are eighteenth century lit or British Modernism. I am the only person on my campus, aside from my staff, who is doing lots of thinking about writing center issues. On WCENTER, I found a group of colleagues who would think with me, brain-

KBY: How does this work for you two? Pam wants us to set up the structure of the article with some sort of narrative intro that lets readers know we're focusing on professional women's lives online…

PG: This is such a nourishing collaboration, so energy-giving, not energy-consuming. I loved doing this. The finished product, unlike a good effort at crochet, is rough. Usually when I craft something, it's finished and right. But this is like showing you the pieces of Ann's graduation dress, which at the moment is hanging, one front, two backs, no zipper, no hems, in my closet just feet away from where I sit sweating this hot evening. The difference is that I have a pattern for that project—we're going to make this one up. So here we go.

storm about problems, plan projects, vent about frustrations, offer support, become my friends.

Now I'm concerned about the writing of my CCCC paper because of experiences I've had on e-mail—and the way I seem to people. When I first met Katie Fischer, someone I met on WCENTER, she took one look at my wild hair, my leggings and my long, long silk sweater and said, "Wow! I expected to see you in one of those subdued paisley pleated skirts and a white blouse with a Peter Pan collar." When I think of e-mail as a place, I also think of it as a masking place, one where I can go all dressed up in my pleated skirt, or one where I can wear sweats and jeans. I seem to come across in two ways: passionately businesslike to those who don't know me, and like myself to those who get beyond my very thin veneer of professional competence. Well, I guess it's not so thin.

LJ: I don't know how your e-mail program handles your mail or if it shows you the address I use on my posts to you two. My name for the "alias," or mailing list that is you two is TechnoBabes. What do you think we're wearing, Paula, when we take up or move into this space?

Laura Julier: The biggest thing about e-mail for me right now is how it revolutionized my relationship with my father, and I choose that word deliberately and without exaggeration. He had the habit for 20 years of calling from his office, whenever he felt like it, often with lunch in his mouth, to talk about nothing. My sisters and I hated it. When he retired, I got him a modem and subscription to Compuserv.

He sends us messages daily, but we are now free to read them when it suits us, and to respond or not. We are also free to fume about things that drive us nuts before simmering down to compose a response. We can ignore him.

But more significantly, e-mail has created a space—a distance—wherein he has been able to say things to me in a more measured, affectionate way, and I have been able to hear them. And I have been willing to share things with him I'd never ever have done before. I have plastered my walls with things he's written that I had never heard him say, all the things I never even knew I craved to hear. It has been like being parented anew.

I speculate about why this has been enabled. He speaks with a pretty distinct New York accent; my mother the college graduate and child of immigrants constantly corrects his grammar and pronunciation. When I went to college, he used to write me letters, sometimes quite long, which *inevitably* began with apologies about his "English." They had *none* of the spontaneity and easy rapport that his e-mail messages do. He allows misspellings, without apologies, on e-mail.

On the other hand, I've just had a series of difficult exchanges with my two sisters over e-mail. Very painful. I could call, but I don't. I realize e-mail is a space/place we go to have this conversation, which is safe in some ways, but also without the inflections and deep breathing of "heard" voice. We have misunderstood humor, anger, irritation. But we have voiced love in a way that I don't think we could have over the phone. I wonder if there is a tentativeness about e-mail that is attractive, but (because you can edit and think before the words are heard) also a safety that appeals.

PG: Laura, I envy you that e-mail exchange with your father. My two daughters who live out west are online, and we exchange messages, sometimes in a three-way conversation. With my chil-

LJ: Notice that we are talking about discourse *and* gender as places we inhabit and have choices about. "I'm not unhappy about being a woman," K says. But being a woman is not as stable as we

dren, though, e-mail doesn't do it. We use e-mail for business messages: when my flight is due in, what I want for my birthday, what they want for theirs, what our sizes are. Whether the baby's new tooth is in yet. E-mail doesn't work for the important business we transact on the phone, though. Our history is one of rapid give and take, negotiation, communication through nonverbal things, laughter. A smiley face on the Internet isn't enough. There are laughs and laughs, and I need to know how my children sound, not just what their words say. I need to hear the sounds of their voices to feel in contact. If they called me every day at lunch time, though, this whole issue would shape up differently.

I feel that we create our own communities on e-mail, and that we can set boundaries, that as women we can create with others a set of rules of our own liking, and observe or break them at our own pace, in our own places. When we set out to create these communities with people we know primarily through e-mail, we can create the people too to an extent, and control the relationships in ways we can't when we're face to face. These communities, artificed though they are, are places of refuge, places where fun happens, where we can go to talk and be listened to.

I hear this Internet connection as a real playground of voices.

KBY: The research on creating online communities gives us conflicting and complex notions of how that happens. As Eldred and Hawisher call for research on CMC, so must we call for research on women and our uses of electronic media. Maybe our experiences are similar to may sometimes prefer to believe—I tend to see it as a choice, a place we choose to inhabit variously. We try on (like clothing) male discourse, and we carry it off if we are "successful" academics, but at home, I change into different clothes and live in a different place.

KBY: Well, I am going to rave about both of you!! I haven't a clue yet as to how to put it together, but your writings are wonderful. What I'm going to do is to respond to each of these, with a cc to both, and then I have written too (much more academic, I'm afraid, as you'll see) and I'll send this on.

those of other women; maybe they are way off.

PG: A striking thing happened for me when I went online. Here in Milwaukee the friendships I make are always qualified: most of them are defined not by me as a person, but by me as half of a married couple. But my good qualities are very different from Michael's good qualities; my personality is very different from his. Sometimes people who like me don't like him and vice versa. In a perfect social world that wouldn't matter, but for the most part it does. My close friends here in town tend to be based first on professional interests; then they broaden out and include the personal. But online, I am myself. I'm not a couple. Colleagues on lists can like me and we can become friends based on just me, or at least on the self I show them in writing. That was revolutionary to me after almost 20 years of marriage. Once I realized that I was free to form bonds here, I began spending too much time online, my family told me. An online friend gave me a pocket protector when we first met. At times my interest in being online seemed borderline pathological to me, but I began to recognize how deep was my need for friends. Once I began to see the dynamic, I began to make more friends in person. E-mail helped me collect a sense of myself as both singular and very collaborative, but not necessarily—and most important—not exclusively as half of a couple.

Recently, there was an intrusion into my e-mail life of a type of conflict that had never been there before. Though I'd seen flaming on lists and read about plenty of dark episodes, e-mail had been such a safe space to me that it came as a jolt that someone I cared about could get really angry at me online and express that anger there. It really rattled me. I'm pretty well over it by now, but it gave me nightmares at the time and really disturbed my universe. So I have this sad new perspective to bring to e-mail.

KBY: I like what you are both saying about e-mail as a *space* and about ourselves as a text for discussion. I think even with friends who live near me I preserve a kind of long-distance convention. The truism about me is that time with me is difficult to get (true), but worth having (sometimes, I'd say). I think I like the distance-intimacy kind of split that comes with long distance. It allows me to feel close without feeling suffocated.

I think this pattern has a lot to do with why I like e-mail; it allows me to develop and maintain friendships with folks who aren't physically available, but who can be intellectually and emotionally here. It allows me to be friends with them when I want to be—which might be at a very inconvenient time—say 2:30 a.m. or so. And largely, I think the friendship develops out of a mutual interest in something else, so that it develops in ways similar to f2f relationships. When I talk about women, then, it comes up as a "natural" topic, rather than because I joined a feminist list. And that, I think, matters to me.

The pathological part, for me, is probably that I find such relationships very satisfying. My guess is that they are like the friendships between Melville and Hawthorne, i.e., based primarily on verbal text. But since this is e-mail and the conventions aren't determined yet, we aren't reduced to/constrained by a male

PG: I just went downstairs to tell the family that I'd be tying up the phone with e-mail and said to them, "I feel so lucky that this is my *work.*" It doesn't feel like work.

model of prose, nor by ways that male friendship has historically developed or been maintained.

Deceptively, this could look like a return to letter-writing of the past via new technology. But I prefer not. That letter-writing was mostly male, was inscribed in masculine ways of knowing and of re/presenting that knowing, was merely dialogic. Our e-mailing (which is not writing nor speech, but a mixture of both) is multilogic if only because it includes more than two writers. Our e-mailing is not inscribed in masculinist discourse; this is, for me at least, a deliberate political point/agenda. It is rather inscribed (if that be the correct word) in multiple discourses. In re/presenting what we know, we again vote for plurality, for multivocality. So while we may be indebted to the letter-writers who came before, we are only indebted. In fact, we are making other kinds of work here. And even that is plural.

So this too makes e-mail a woman-friendly place, I think.

LJ: What I hear in our emerging stories is that e-mail is a *space* where there is room for moving boundaries—both moving them back to create breathing room, as in the case with my father, and moving them closer, as in the case of the friendships you've developed; and space too for standing alone, as you describe, Paula, when you say you're not a couple on e-mail, and as perhaps is the case in my new difficulties with my sisters, with whom I've perhaps been too meshed, too merged, assuming communication should just happen by osmosis, whereas e-mail makes clear the distance we have to travel in order to be heard.

I'm struck by all this. I think that what we have to say so far about this is that as women we have ourselves as the ground of study, and we ought to study and reflect on that, and theorize that, and *then* perhaps see what there is to learn about or apply to working with our students.

KBY: What we said earlier, briefly, is that we all found our experiences on e-mail different than in f2f encounters and than in print. As I recall, I was the most skeptical of the three of us; I do think electronic discourse *can be* friendlier to women than other media, but it doesn't have to be. I also think it's a kind of frontier (aged metaphor, I know), but one where words and an ability to *read into* a new situation are the assets of choice. Women are said to be intelligent about discourse, smart about interpreting subtle discursive cues, able to read at and through nuance. Situations, they understand, are variously populated, and they have learned how to read those situations just as variously. Perhaps this is why we seem reasonably adept at reading the situation of e-mail, a place that because it is new is yet without obvious markers. It requires, I think, another way of navigating.

I've learned a kind of verbal dexterity here that I am trying now to bring to the page. Looking back, I realize it was in fact a woman—a colleague here, named Boyd Davis—who introduced me to the Net. And on e-mail I talked and played and was serious sometimes and found all these other people here, who talked and played and were serious sometimes. Not unlike the real world, but *unlike* the real world, the virtual world was: the

LJ: Kathleen, I like this part a lot about how you got introduced to the Net. I want to keep it here, if it's ok with you. Because this is part of the thread about relationships and conversation. How *do* we get socialized and mentored and introduced to a community, a conversation, an identity? Who teaches us, and how? We all have stories, I think, about how we learned computers, especially those of us who did not take to it easily. Stories about how the computer geeks who teach the courses speak a language that locks out novices, and of course that most of the computer geeks are male and for most women this is just another experience of being excluded because we don't speak the language. I'm working with some students now who are trying to discover stories about how folks—undergrads as well as seasoned faculty—learned and are learning to use the Web. Our observation/hypothesis is that most people learn this in ways that replicate old pedagogies: individually and in isolation, frustrated and struggling to catch up. Their question is: can we use collaborative pedagogies to teach technology?

folks here seemed decidedly sympathetic as audience, willing and able to play things out with me, aware that this was a new way of communicating, and excited about it. The experience was more like being a child and learning to talk—with other people who applaud most everything you say and who are constructing a world with you, a self with you. But not all these people were women. In particular, there have been three men with whom I've shared this, but in different ways. So I can't say that for me it's totally a woman thing.

Does this make sense at all?

PG: It sure does. In a profound way. There are men I cavort with on the Net, but my sense is that to cavort with them we must enter into a nonmale, nonlinear discourse. For one thing, the linearity is fractured by the asynchronous nature of e-mail. For another thing, we keep multiple strands going, we keep old, old puns running month after month. And for another, especially in a group of six of us writing center people who keep in contact daily, there is no individual who can, wants to, or is willing to dominate the discourse. We talk about a lot of serious writing center things, but mostly we clown and pun and bring laughter into one another's days. We get serious, but we negotiate all serious projects without anyone taking the paternal role, and we like it that way. One of the women calls the men in that group "girls," because they are willing to enter into very emotional dialogues with the three women—and no, not "willing to," but rather, the three men will initiate that sort of discourse, carry it on, cry with us, and say so.

PG: J. Weedman [1991] describes this kind of uninhibitedness as positive, not negative in tone. But when I read this kind of research, it sounds as if it takes place in a different electronic space, not mine. The journal where it appears, *International Journal of Man-Machine Studies*, might help to explain why.

There's a way that this electronic space has made it safe to enter into that sort of dialogue: eyes watching screens, fingers tapping out a different discourse. This group tries to include the body. We started as six relative strangers planning to meet at the DC CCCC. We thought it would help if we could picture ourselves, so we all described ourselves (oh, that was hard). We thought it would help us picture one another if we started giving a fashion report—telling what we were wearing that day so we could gather a sense of what we look like. It's been almost a year since the Fashies, as we began calling ourselves, started doing that, and we still do it each day, give a fashion report. We describe the same old clothes over and over; the men, especially two of them, are much more energetic and enthusiastic about doing that than the women are—but I think we are trying to undisembody ourselves, to allow our torsos into the dialogue.

KBY: On the one hand, I think this is right, especially the disruption of the linear; there is a kind of discursive multitasking that is all too intimate to those of us familiar with the domestic sphere and children. This is easy, just e-mail style: we bring to e-mail the multiple threads of our lives, with the assumption that the idea of "our lives" will provide enough center for the discourse to hold. On the other hand, I also think that this kind of play and relational styling and discourse could take place f2f. I'm a member of an interdisciplinary teaching group whose characteristics seem in many ways to match what we've said about e-mail. "Is e-mail friendly to women? If so, what about it makes it so?"

PG: For me one of the things that makes it safe is the double sense that I have that I am responding to *a person* and to *a text*. The person may be impatiently tapping a foot, demanding a reply. The text just has to cool off, wait for me to be in the right mood, or wait for me to think of the clever or correct or judicious thing to say. We all seem so clever and correct and judicious at times on the Net. In real f2f dialogue, I have to come up with a response on the spot; e-mail allows me to incubate, to reflect, to postpone, to be silent. f2f does not allow that. I'm on the spot. If I'm fuming mad or embarrassed, it all shows. Here, I have more control over what shows—oh, I know, it leaks out around the edges, and dialogue reveals just as it conceals.

I can read into the text. I can to a certain extent read into people, if I want to and sometimes if I don't. But the text is mine to interpret, until the person or persona at the other end of it exercises some volition and says, "That's not what I meant at all." But the distance and the asynchronicity allow a kind of freedom that f2f does not.

I'm anxious for f2f with my e-mail friends, love to hear their telephone voices, visualize those telephone voices when I read their posts, hear their accents, picture their faces.

"Visualize," though, isn't the right word at all; I love to *hear* those voices as I read, hear the text dramatically in the voice of the speaker.

But there's more in it than that for me; I have the joy of creating narrative, a form that gives me pleasure. And I take joy when people tell me their stories. I like to get specific. I love to describe scenes and atmospheres, take

PG: Kathleen, you asked if we could include some of the posts I wrote about the weather, the flowers in bloom, the atmosphere. I wonder if I have any of them at all. I tend to save "business" e-mail in my folders, but I treat those other treasures like daffodils, here to enjoy today, gone tomorrow, but back in all their glory. If you see any of mine, please do include them. They're

note of the details around me and know that those I keep in close touch with care about them.

For me this comes from my mother, who was a great teller of stories. She made them up for us as bedtime stories, three a night: a Bible story, a Farmer and the Fox story she made up about the clever fox who would always outwit the farmer out of his best hams and never get caught, and a little girl story. She grew up around the turn of the century, and told stories about losing the cow, finding the woman who was killing their grape vines, about my grandfather unknowingly borrowing a race horse to pull his buggy, the first auto in town, and on and on. These were wonderful stories, full of details, stories that set my imagination spinning each bedtime.

When I moved away, we kept in touch by letter, almost every other day. And she and I would collect details to tell one another, every little detail of every sign of progress and growth and maturity of my children, but other little details, too: the color of viburnum berries, wintergreen berries growing in the mountains, underground rivers—it was like picking her a bouquet of violets and bringing them home to be put in water.

And I'd devour her letters. They were the umbilical, still pulsing, and keeping us close. When she lost her memory and her ability to narrate, it was as if she was already gone. What was she without her discourse?

But in those close friendships I have on e-mail, I find the space and time to work narrations through, polish details, embellish, reread, revise, and send—it's a way of touching. It's by no means a mother-substitute, but it's a continuation why I live here, not for the business, really.

of the tradition she started: if I love someone or care for them, I'll take the time to tell them stories. I'll save up details, horde them, then take pleasure in writing them out.

KBY: I think the story-making is important. For one thing, it represents another way of knowing, often in a discourse that some think of as nonacademic. I don't mean here that such knowing isn't valid or truthful (as Joan Didion points out, the truth and the facts are not co-identical) but another way: a way that I haven't used often in my "scholarly" writing, but a way that is familiar to many women. It's a way that hasn't had as much *public* expression, so it's a way in search of development—as a mode of inquiry. E-mail allows story-making to go public, to become collaborative in the way that public discourse is shaped by the listener as much as by the teller, especially when, as in the case of e-mail, the listener then often becomes the teller, and the single story prompts other stories that then become part of a larger narrative.

For another thing, stories require that we take a rhetorical stance—that we think about perspective—and that means that more than one point of view is not only allowed, but also encouraged. That's decidedly nonacademic, nonmasculine. As a medium, e-mail makes this difference in perspective very obvious: in part because the e-mail can be recorded (it does seem a kind of speech that is and is not writing), in part because it is initiated at each site, so that the speaker's role is apparent throughout, and in part because in e-mail we tend to repeat snippets of messages that we want to include, respond to, appropriate. The flux

PG: So what do we do now to edit this piece? How would it be if we all section out the discussion and see what our three takes on it are? Do we want to try to shoot for a deadline on this? I have a *free weekend*.

KBY: Shall we just do this over the weekend, and then post it here? or put little dribs and drabs here as we go along? (I can do either.)

PG: I like the dribs and drabs approach. It feeds me. Should we shoot for a deadline of Monday night? Is that doable for this sectioning? Laura, you did some of it already in your previous post. I need a deadline. If I just say I'll do it soon, it gets shoved aside.

LJ: Well, as you can tell from my header—YIKES!—I feel deluged. I came in today (Saturday) to work, and found a slew of messages from you both. I'm trying to sort through them. I came in to sort out all this stuff for our article, to try to assess where we are, and try to propose what to do next. We do work in interesting ways, kind of like menstrual cycles synchronizing when women live together. I too have the weekend "free" (what *does* that mean??) to work on this, I work best under deadlines, and Monday night is a good one for me, too.

between and among discourse and discoursers is built into the medium itself.

So, stories—put more academically, narrative—as *another* way of knowing, one thought of as more feminine. Yes. E-mail as hospitable to stories, yes. A *place* where a mode familiar to women is encouraged, but a place that isn't exclusive to women. A place that doesn't insist on academic modes, even if academics are the e-mailers.

Stories aren't innocent. So perhaps we should think about whose needs our stories on e-mail serve. And perhaps we should think about whose needs this story is serving. Yes?

You see, it's the dialogue that helps establish a place for women. In cyberspace, particularly in comp circles, women are part of the dialogue. Why? Hmmm. Partly because some women got there first (i.e., let's think in Foucaultian terms): Cindy and Gail and Helen Schwartz. Partly because e-mail by its very design anticipates a response, is predicated on the notion of dialogue. And it's not hierarchical; it's merely sequential. And it enables folks to reproduce what was said <snip> and pass it on and build on it—in relational ways congruent with the kinds of observations that folks like Belenky [1986] and Gilligan [1982] say is true for women. So here, unlike Nancy Sommers, we do not have to write between some manly drafts. *Ain't* no manly drafts to write between. Here, we can write to each other, develop a manner of expression that suits us, and take it f2f or in print classic as we like.

LJ: I love this idea of an e-slumber party!! Here's my drib or drab for the

OK. So I am now going to try to generate "dribs and drabs." But who is going to collect these dribs and drabs and make them into something whole?

KBY: Paula, this was a great idea to stage this marathon (or is it an extended e-slumber party?), and I love the idea of being a technobabe. We are developing a collective identity here, *ladies*, which is what *Collective Minds* suggests can happen when things work right.

afternoon. It refers to you two in third person, not second, and I'm not sure why, but it's a start. I think it goes under either the "Collaboration" thread we're developing, or the "E-mail as Space and Landscape" thread.

I've been thinking a lot about the ways in which e-mail has shaped and fostered our collaboration for this article. If we send messages to one or to both of the others in our threesome, it changes the conversation. I have felt out of touch and out of the loop a couple of times. I know I may have missed something in a message Kathi wrote to Paula separately. I notice that Paula just wrote asking for clarification about what she was supposed to hand-carry to me next week. It seems that we have to work harder, or differently, to be sure that we keep track of all the details, and that we let both others hear the relevant parts of the conversations. Doing that means attending to different things, such as who I address a message to, and how often I check in on e-mail.

I don't have my computer hooked up at home (yet), and so I can't check in online on the days I don't go into my office. I'm in a transition between one machine and a much bigger upgrade. To set it up requires me to rearrange the space in my study. Now there's an interesting notion. The technology—which is to say in this case the "furniture" that allows the conversation to take place on e-mail to begin with—requires space. Or new space. Or rearranged space.

Space matters to me. I was speaking to a friend about my need for silence, my recent inability to have or take it, and my search for a space/place where I can *hear* the silence. She said to me, "Space matters less than taking the time." But no, the space matters a great deal: there is a connection for me between the aesthetics of a space and the way silence opens up in it. So it is with writing.

To fit my new computer—larger, more bulky, with parts that stick out in different places—into my study will necessitate rearranging something that I do not want to change. My study is a masterpiece of make-do, crammed into dimensions that are far too small, but its arrangement now after 5½ years is a map of my mental, intellectual, and emotional landscape. I can't change it without losing some of that. Although I am not about to begin either of the two research projects filling the shelves on my desk, I cannot bring myself to find a new spot for them. All my barely-nascent ideas reside in that hodgepodge on the shelf, in the arrangement of them.

KBY: "Evidence already indicates that the very fabric of computer system development reflects the dominant cultural values," claims Billie Wahlstrom [1994], and in large measure I agree. But looking at e-mail, I see a medium where the dominant/masculinist (isn't this redundant?) value of interruption is made impossible and thus where such interruption cannot be used as a source of control. Like many others, I conceive of e-mail *physically*, as a place—indeed for me it has become the place that Adrienne Rich [1979] talked about when she said that women needed boundary areas in order to develop a woman's voice. Ironically, I think such a place is particularly needed by academic women, who typically have succeeded because they have demonstrated that

PG: Here are some of the comments we just got from the manuscript reviewers: "Furthermore, on page 13, one of the authors claims that dominant masculinist discourse is not allowed on e-mail. Again, I don't agree with this point. Two of my students have used e-mail to express their demands, using the masculinist discourse. Furthermore, the structure of language is inherently patriarchal so to escape from masculinist discourse, we would have to devise a new way of conveying meaning on e-mail, one that did not use the words we currently use to communicate. I would

they can *talk male*, because in so doing, they haven't spent time trying to create their own voice: women like the class of (generally "deflected") academic women described in *Women in Academe: Outsiders in the Sacred Grove* [Aisenberg & Harrington, 1988], women like Nancy Sommers, lost "Between the Drafts" [1992].

In their review of CMC research, Eldred and Hawisher [1995] take as one variable "Task Orientation." The research shows, they say, that "CMC was useful for reception of information and good for establishing contacts, but unsatisfactory for decision making, for getting to know another person, and resolving disagreements" [p. 346]. What we have here, as they say, is a "very efficient, rational model for CMC communication." You bet, I say: this model of "efficiency" is overwhelmingly masculinist in nature, and second, it makes assumptions that are questionable even on a good day. First, the assumptions: that communication without a social dimension is more efficient, that efficient has a single definition, that the system design or the network acts as an independent agent. As a distributed system, a network does not lend itself to clean decision-making. Is this bad? The assumption is yes, but the assumption here is *also* that f2f is the ideal: "In such cases, it was argued, patterns of decision making are more predictable, more rational and efficient, and perhaps even more closely aligned with face-to-face communication" [p. 346]. Given the analysis that Spender [1992] provides about patterns of discussion in classrooms, where men talk more than women and are rewarded for it, too, "closely aligned" to f2f ain't the ideal for me, nor for lots of women. As important, agree that e-mail can be used in many different ways, some of them liberatory and feminist. But I would not agree that e-mail itself is not masculinist. Look at e-mail's origins and you'll find a patriarchal story."

In other words, they tell us that's not their experience. What do you both think?

the model of efficiency touted here values a single model of efficiency: a linear, no-nonsense approach that is at odds with other approaches. I don't think what we have here is a "systems design" flaw; what we have here is a migration of the values of the dominant culture to the new one that insists on the primacy of the first. Put another way, we shouldn't be asking, How close can we get to f2f on the (apparently substandard) new medium? Instead, we should be asking, How do you work on this medium?

LJ: In this medium, space matters. The physical space houses the furniture—the computer—which gives me access to e-mail, that space in which the conversation and collaboration and elaboration of ideas takes place. It may be virtual space that we occupy in conversing, but it is grounded or connected inextricably to the physical space that I must occupy. My relationship to cyberspace is both different and the same.

KBY: Can you use this phrase, "space matters," a little more often in this segment? It sets up a kind of refrain that I like.

I haven't been able to access e-mail at home, and so Kathi and Paula have had exchanges of about a dozen messages yesterday when I stayed home to work. Had I not come in to the office today, Saturday, I would not have known until Monday about their plans to do most of the writing and conversing about our project over the weekend. I would have come in to my office on Monday to find that the slumber party and the work had happened without my voice or contribution.

As it happens, this morning I was on the phone with a friend who was complaining to me that although we have kept in touch recently in various ways, our unusually busy schedules had not allowed us to be with one another on the phone, and she was frustrated: "I have strongly felt the absence of your voice," she said. I told her about this project of ours. She reminded me that absence or silence or being out of the loop happens with any technology, and is not unique to e-mail. But it seems to me that the difference here has to do with our access to the technology that makes it happen.

KBY: Not that I don't like f2f. But I am always astounded when more contact is possible, and folks choose not to exercise it. One of my sisters has e-mail, and I e-mailed her and my mother on Thanksgiving Day. To date, and it is now February and I have told her in person that the e-mail is there, no one has read it. My best Indiana friend is on her husband's account, and she sent me the ID in her annual Christmas card with the admonition, "Maybe now I can finally hear from you." Sure, like in 5 minutes of my getting the ID. One week later: a reply. I e-mail back. That was December: quiet. But perhaps what I'm onto here is something else, too: both e-mail accounts were in the "husband's name," the computer is the husband's, the interest in e-mail is the husband's. Perhaps it's like Virginia Woolf's *A Room of One's Own.*

Yes, I do have my own e-mail, my own computer, my own room.

LJ: Boy does this hit the mark for me!! This is exactly what I'm trying to get at when I talk about the "space" that e-mail provides in some of my family relationships. And when Paula wrote about the way that e-mail doesn't allow for the "rapid give and take" which is so important with her children, I mused about

KBY: With the "Discourse of Their Own," I'm trying to invoke Woolf. But what's interesting to me is that Woolf's is a fairly individualistic argument, whereas ours is more collaborative. Which leads me to the observation that Pam made regarding our e-mailing being a modern invocation of old-timey masculinist e-mailing. I don't think so, but I haven't been able to say why. Something about the multiple readers (after all, the relationships I mentioned were all just two people, we have three, and I think that how differently that fact resonates for me. It is precisely *because* e-mail is not so "closely aligned" to f2f that it is so healthy for me. That space which interferes with the rapid give and take cuts down on the abundant misunderstandings and emotional chaos that seems to predominate in my family. We get to breathe, we get to consider, we get to choose. True, we miss the physical, the hugs. I do miss them. But in my family, the chaos is dangerous. We steamroll over one another. We are so emotionally enmeshed that we bleed all over one another. It is not good. That space allows us to remember to be kind, to acknowledge one another as separate human beings with needs and lives that are not blurred and blended together. Wow—even writing this gets me very worked up at how crucial that space is for me. Yes, that lack of immediacy feels like a loss of sorts, but there is no question in my mind that it is the best thing that ever entered our collective lives.

PG: It feels very sterile to be writing a paper for our session at the Cs, though I want to write it, because it is not part of an ongoing dialogue *in the same way* that online is. We'll invite discussion at the end, and people can answer us in print or next year, but there's no beep and message at the bottom of the screen that says, "Yeah, but...." And f2f dialogue can be sustained over distances.

I like your term "electronic proximity," Kathleen.

And here's a good word for us, one that opposes itself nicely to that need for space that you discuss, Laura. Immediate: "Absence of a mediating agent." Nothing between us. Except, of matters, for starters). So a discourse of our own, indebted in some interesting ways to what came before, but only indebted, not replicated. Ours is different. More plural, more associative, more multiple, more immediate. Yes?

course, our systems and the Internet. But it feels immediate. Presence feels present, embodiment and time.

LJ: I think this is all very interesting, because this sort of thing—embedded in the technology that allows the conversation/collaboration to happen—definitely affects the conversation. The blips in communication are, for one thing, traceable. Sort of. We can take a picture, so to speak, of the exchange, and try to untangle it. In f2f, we can't, unless we've been doing an audio recording. It seems to me that only on e-mail do we have the *visual* representation of it that is available for re-examination and scrutiny and analysis.

KBY: Perhaps more importantly, the work-related nature of e-mail that then spills over into the personal. Let me go back to real life: I have a tendency to develop acquaintance-ships, I'd call them, with people I have business with—you know, the realtor who sells you a house, the woman who cuts your hair, definitely the women who babysit. (I pretty much stick to college students.) It drives my husband crazy that I don't keep these relationships "clean," that I bring personal into the business sphere. I think what I like about e-mail is that it is both spheres.

LJ: What happens to e-conversations when the loop has a momentary difference or becomes f2f for a piece? Sometimes it's noise to me, and sometimes not. Talking with you two, in this protected, intense way is womb-like. Focused. But when I come in on a Monday morning to find a jillion nagging messages from too many people, and with a bunch of deadlines piled on my desk and three meetings scheduled for the day, it just feels like something I want to sweep out of the way. Like kids tugging on my shirt-sleeve.

My hunch is that for an e-mail conversation to develop, it also takes some work. Two people have to figure out how to be online together, how to work the communication, what to expect, etc. How do we talk online when mostly we've talked curled up with tea in my living room, or over pots and pans in the kitchen, or over drinks by the ocean? Does this mean that we have to invent a landscape for ourselves on e-mail?

PG: For me it's such a richly voiced landscape, a place I go to find my own voice, to be able to hear myself, to develop a thought without interruption. Often when I envision landscapes, I see them as silent places, visual places. E-mail is a landscape of sounds, some of them my own.

KBY: Btw, I finally have a personal e-mail story, two of them in fact. My youngest sister came online this winter, and we e-mail several times a week. It's been wonderful. And my friend in Alaska: ditto. So finally e-mail has become a place for me, also, that can be *merely* personal. But I have to say that for me this merely personal still seems academic in the best sense of the word: even in the personal exchanges, we seem to take up big questions, to disclose and talk in ways that foster intimacy. Which is what I think I've been trying to say all along—that e-mail can provide this space. I'm wondering now (this is a dan-

PG: I've spent some time with our text, trying to see the words on the page as independent of the sounds of our voices, and to an extent I can't do it. But I've tried. In a way I agree with the reviewers when they say that our voices are alike. We influence one another, I think. In good ways. We influence one another the way I want my students to be influenced by Jane Austen and Henry James and Barbara Kingsolver; I want them to absorb, through repeated exposure, the stylistic elements that make complicated thoughts more possible to them than if their only stylist is Stephen King.

ger of revision—that you see something new to add) if/how much a self-awareness of this makes it so. In other words, I don't think e-mail gets *used* as a new space—with all the opportunities that entails—unless one is aware of and uses it that way. Does this seem right to you?

LJ: The landscape on e-mail with my sister Vivian is dotted with short comments, lots of <return> hits. It's not a long rolling terrain; it's more like skipping and starting, like a hike through dense woods, where things change quickly and up close and you don't get big vistas. Her letters begin with descriptions of where she is, like, "I'm sitting here in the living room,..." but her e-mails rarely tell me where she is or when it is.

My youngest sister, Alice, will send quick short messages when we've been e-mailing frequently. It is as if she is in the next office and sticks her head in to either make a quick comment, or sit down for an extended exchange. She too is funny, plays with the keyboard marks a lot, has a better sense than Vivian of ongoing dialogue. This terrain is more like a long walk you take daily, or almost daily, over the same neighborhood, although you might vary the streets you take. Things are familiar, but they change, and noting the changes is part of the fun. I suppose that says more about how tuned in to one another's lives we are.

My father's e-mails are like a walk through the mall. Lots of detail, lots of road marks, lots of stops and starts. He checks in every day. He always says something kind and loving. He always lets me know if he hasn't heard from me in a day or two. He always refers to what I've written. But he often gets it wrong!

But on the other hand, both style and content distinguish us three. We speak of different things, and we speak of them in different ways, and we meet, listen, grow from one another's discourses.

Kathleen, you are the most likely to draw the academic world into our exchange and to use appropriate academic terminology. You are the most likely to use slashes: "...we aren't reduced to/constrained by a male model of prose...." You quote from our literature, drawing from a wide array of theorists and artists. But then after drawing your outside sources in, you analyze, speculate, question, take issue, and assert your own take on things, rather than take these printed sources as the authority. You take authority for yourself, and then you often finish with a question: "Does this make sense to you?" or "Yes?" So you quote, analyze, assert, then ask. And you pack into a tight space a lot of thought: "...I do think electronic discourse *can be* friendlier to women than other media, but it doesn't have to be. I also think it's a kind of frontier (aged metaphor, I know), but one where words and an ability to *read into* a new situation are the assets of choice."

Laura, you draw your family into our circle in ways that make my throat ache with envy: "I have plastered my walls with things he's written that I had never heard him say, all the things I never even knew I craved to hear. It has been like being parented anew." You are likely to move from the concrete (a narrative of your e-correspondence with your family) into simile ("My father's e-mails are like a walk through the mall. Lots of detail, lots of road marks, lots of stops and starts.") You are the one who plays with words.

PG: For me this whole collaboration could never have come about without/in spite of the technology. As we finished the e-mail section and switched to faxes, I felt the frustration as the immediacy of e-mail went out of the equation. I'd have to go to campus to fetch my mail; we'd have to coordinate our schedules. Scheduling has always been tricky, I think, for women. For Kathleen and me, juggling kids' schedules and needs, making that all fit with academic jobs; for Laura, fitting all that tenure-frenzy (and I think we need to have a celebratory comment about both your triumphs, since they happened in the midst of all this creativity), being able to fit writing, research, and collaboration in around our lives (and of course my family argues that I fit *them* around *it*) is what makes the e-mail connection vital for me. I *can* find or make time for it. Time and place, a space, an open space where/when I can reflect, talk, mix the personal with the professional and the political.

LJ: I passed on to Danielle, a graduate student, the article by Herring, Johnson, and DiBenedetto from *Gender Articulated*, "This Discussion is Going Too Far" [1995], and she wrote back about her experiences as a woman on a local bulletin board: "Via computer, I come across very, very strong. In a situation where there's no social risk of asserting my personal opinions, I am very open about asserting them. Tactics used against me by the men who called were varied. Some would actually respond to my posts with a well thought out counterargument, but usually I was attacked. 'You're probably fat and ugly.' 'You're

You say, "I, too, have the weekend free. (What *does* that mean??)" And you invite us to speculate about place and space in metaphors and similes.

And me: I seem to write about professional groups that invite friendship and the growth of closeness and trust, and I contrast that with what I need from my daughters: the sounds of voices at the very least, f2f in a perfect world. I seem to write in strings with odd juxtapositions: "At WCENTER, I found a group of colleagues who would think with me, brainstorm about problems, plan projects, vent about frustrations, become my friends." In my writing I found strings of adjectives, strings of verbs, lists of things, lots of specifics.

Yet we borrow from one another: Laura and I use slashes, Kathleen and I use a simile here and there, and we all write in strings of specific, concrete things. We color one another, not quite in a subtle kind of *style indirect libre,* but very close. And that comes from trust and acceptance and love. Embodiment of one another.

probably a stupid dyke lesbian.' I can't tell you how many insults and accusations (or at least their attempts at accusing me of something) I've received over the years merely for making what I consider to be mildly feminist assertations" [D. DeVoss, personal communications, October 18, 1996].

She also reported that one of the men would "constantly attempt to shut down conversation, or at least my participation in it," by refusing to address her directly. She told me that this experience "didn't bother me too terribly much—I know who I am and what my goals are," but that "it was disheartening and incredibly aggravating to be seen one moment as an aggressor and an implementer of conversation and the next as a weak, misled woman who has wandered off track."

Reading her story made me stop to contemplate the kinds of experiences we three have accumulated here. It leads me to a part of Eldred and Hawisher's article, "Researching Electronic Networks" [1995], where they report Lea and Spear's research about the connection between visual anonymity and group identity:

> "When people are physically separated, as in electronic communication, *and* when group identity is made strong or 'salient,' group norms will prevail. Conversely, when people are physically separated from one another and individual identity (rather than group identity) is made salient, social identity is reduced and group norms are less likely to be followed." (p. 340)

On the bulletin boards that Danielle speaks about, there is no group identity.

LJ: I'm feeling a bit uncertain about how to proceed with these revisions here, because I almost feel as if I'm pushing them on you two. But I know you're both trying to balance teaching and family obligations and going off to Utah for the conference, and I'm the one with the blessing of a sabbatical. If you each look at the next message and let me know if you have any additions or objections to the changes, I'll incorporate them. If not, well, I'll just make the best decision I can. You see my dilemma? The first option sounds like imposing more work on you two, while the second sounds like I'm taking over, and I don't like either of them.

PG: OK, how does this look? I think this gives enough structure to get readers going but not too much. It's a tricky balance we're striving for. But I like the mix here—the writing for print, the meeting f2f, the e-mail, the plans for the book. This suggests something about the richness, the generativity of our relationship.

LJ: You both gave me permission to move stuff, as it made sense to me. But I find I am making big changes in how the thing looks, and I'm nervous that you both won't like it.

KBY: Trust us on this, ok?

And the men (as well, she says, as some of the women) behave badly. They seem free, in her experience, to exercise the full range of locker room crap. But in our stories, either there already is a group identity (family, for instance, stands out in our stories) or there is strong impetus to form a group identity (as in Paula's fashies). And so, I speculate, we work to make the bumps in the communication smoother, or we are able to exploit and enhance the advantages of the new style of communication (as, for instance, when I write that the distance created and necessitated by e-mail becomes a plus for me with some of my family). Like any new technology or mode of communication, the social context determines the landscape. Sometimes, gender roles and expectations seem to flare up as loudly as they do anywhere/anytime else, but sometimes, we find some open spaces, some far reaches, some potential for carving a new path. We explore. We find openings.

KBY: In preparing this text—and it *is* prepared, as a kind of e-mail collage, I think—we've e-mailed hundreds of posts (quite literally), then collected them into a single multivocalic text. We've rewritten and faxed; we've examined and read and talked and analyzed and e-mailed some more and reflected upon this issue, this issue of e-mailed place. What we have learned in and through these processes isn't simple and isn't simply obvious and isn't even the same for all of us. (Which is in part the very point, no?) But....

Upon reflection, I think, some generalizations are possible.

We are academic women who find something missing on our own campus-

LJ: Well, ok, but I'm saving all the versions—and we have so many!—so if you don't, I can revert to an older one.

KBY: I think when you write something that still interests you, the end of it is always false: that is, you are still thinking about the material, but you have to bring it to some closure for some reason. Put another way, revising this text yet again has helped me articulate more of what I think I do know, if only tacitly. And that knowing has raised other questions.

es: that "something" is intellectual *and* social *and* personal, a matrix of interactions that we found online. Found? Hmm. Perhaps no, not found, but created—as you said, Laura, through the identity we created together. At the same time, the place itself was created too, and once created, mapped and landscaped—by us for us. It's not like other places we've been.

Place matters. Place matters to us, though differently: physical place to you, Laura, embodied to you, Paula, and textual to me. E-mail evokes the senses of all of these three places for us, a kind of multiplicity in the unity of the place where we could come together and be/come.

The medium, of course, constructs us as it is constructed by us, and what it constructs isn't universal either. For some, we know, it seems to provide an opportunity for relationships to flourish, while others can't find a home here at all. In other words, the medium is—of course—*rhetorical*. And as you suggest, Laura, it may therefore require new discursive conventions, new ways of behaving verbally, and as you suggest, Paula, it may never satisfy in the way f2f can. At the same time, however, it allows women in three different parts of the country to work together in ways unheard of 20 years ago, to weave into that work the lives of our families as well as our academic stories.

We don't know how our stories will develop through this medium, do we? But don't we hope that this text suggests what is possible—both in how we know and in how we represent what we know, in our case in the e-mail and in the collage that e-mail composes?

EPILOGUE

So there we are, sitting in a semi-circular, red-tapestried booth in the Russian Tea Time in downtown Chicago, over borscht and pierogies, each of us with Russian tea in a silver filigreed podstokan, wondering about editorial desire. "It's like narrative desire," explains KBY, then asks, "Is it just me? Are you two comfortable that the editors aren't telling us how they want us to respond to the reviewers' comments?" We all three intermittently glance at the male waiters, who move through the Tea Time at lunch hour with a kind of officious diffidence, seating clutches of women, some with conference badges, some with rich silk scarves, carving spaces, now in real time not virtual. "Yeah. I am," says LJ. "We get to shape it the way we want."

REFERENCES

Aisenberg, N., & Harrington, M. (1988). *Women in academe: Outsiders in the sacred grove.* Amherst, MA: University of Massachusetts Press.

Belenky, M. F., Clinchy, B. M., Goldberger, N. R., Tarule, J. M. (1986). *Women's ways of knowing: The development of self, voice, and mind.* New York: Basic Books.

Brody, M. (1994). *Manly writing: Gender, rhetoric, and the rise of composition.* Carbondale, IL: Southern Illinois University Press.

Eldred, J. C., & Hawisher, G. E. (1995, July). Researching electronic networks. *Written Communication, 12*, 330–359.

Gilligan, C. (1992). *In a different voice: Psychological theory and women's development.* Cambridge, MA: Harvard University Press.

Herring, S., Johnson, D. A., & DiBenedetto, T. (1995). "This discussion is going too far!": Male resistance to female participation on the Internet. In K. Hall & M. Bucholtz (Eds.), *Gender articulated: Language and the socially constructed self* (pp. 67–96). New York: Routledge.

Rich, A. (1979). When we dead awaken: Writing as re-vision. In *On lies, secrets, and silence: Selected prose 1966–1978* (pp. 33–49). New York: W. W. Norton.

Sommers, N. (1992, February). Between the drafts. *College Composition and Communication, 43*, 23–31.

Spender, D. (1992). Talking in class. In D. George & J. Trimbur (Eds.), *Reading culture* (pp. 131–138). New York: HarperCollins.

Wahlstrom, B. J. (1994). Communication and technology: Defining a feminist presence in research and practice. In C. Selfe & S. Hilligoss (Eds.), *Literacy and computers: The complications of teaching and learning with technology* (pp. 171–185). New York: Modern Language Association.

Weedman, J. (1991). Task and non-task functions of a computer conference used in professional education: A measure of flexibility. *International Journal of Man-Machine Studies, 34*, 303–318.

chapter 12

Thirteen Ways of Looking at an M-Word

Margaret Daisley
University of Massachusetts, Amherst

Susan Romano
University of Texas, San Antonio

When the blackbird flew out of sight,
It marked the edge
Of one of many circles[1]

"M" IS FOR...

"M" is for margins, marginalization, marginalizing, the marginalized. Numbers, for instance, say females are marginalized in electronic environments. Yet, *we* are among the numbers of females who find ourselves in electronic environments as part of our professional and private lives, and although we sometimes feel marginalized in these spaces, many times we do not. This makes us question the uses of "m-words," which seem to cast a pall of linguistic determinism over our lives, and the lives of our students. As Romano (1993) has

* Some material in this chapter is adapted from an article previously written by Daisley, "Silence. Silence! Silence? Silence... (An Ethnographic Study of 'Silence' in Computer-Mediated Communication)" (1995).

argued elsewhere, "we deceive ourselves by imagining empowerment within the terms *marginalization* and *egalitarian*, which call to mind standard categories—race/class/gender—that may well be refused by the students themselves" (p. 9).

Similarly, Deborah Cameron (1992) says that we place women, in particular, in "straitjackets" (p. 132) when we label them in a deterministic manner and place them outside a system they can never enter, which is "demoralising" (p. 130). Gayatri Chakravorty Spivak (1990) writes that we cannot deny the reality of the historical hegemonic narrative in which "certain peoples have always been asked to cathect the margins so others can be defined as central." Yet, on a personal level, Spivak says she is "tired of dining out on being an exile." "In a certain sense," she argues, "there is nothing that is central" (pp. 40–41). Pamela Takayoshi (1994) calls for more research that examines the "marginalizing patterns of discourse" in traditional classrooms, prior to the integration of virtual environments (p. 32). We need to confront these forces and "dismantle" them, Takayoshi argues, rather than assume technology will somehow do it for us.

Our argument is *not* to throw out the baby with the bathwater, to use an old wives saying. We do not argue for one interpretation of "margins," "marginalization," or "marginalized" over another. Instead, we argue for returning m-words to their more complicated origins, for contextualizing uses of these words, and for problematizing them within those contexts.

MEANWHILE, OUTSIDE THE MARGINS...

Silence in electronic environments is often seen as marginalization in terms of its being not-discourse, reflecting the absolute presence or absence of authority. On one end of the spectrum is the Big Brother-panopticon nightmare; on the other, rampant wilding. Both have a similar effect: abuses of "technopower and technoppression," as Joseph Janangelo (1991) calls them, which are used to silence or marginalize others.

However, silence does not represent half a binary, according to Foucault (1978)—words or not-words—but rather, silence is "the element that functions ... within overall strategies" (p. 27) of rhetoric. "There is not one but many silences," Foucault writes, "and they are an integral part of the strategies that underlie and permeate discourses" (p. 27). According to sociolinguist Dell Hymes (1974), "the distribution of required and preferred silence most immediately reveals in outline form a community's structure of speaking" (p. 32). Yet, as Muriel Saville-Troike (1993) and other sociolinguistics have noted, silence as a rhetorical construction has traditionally been ignored, except for its value as the "absence of discourse" and as a "boundary-marking" function (p. 145). However, silence has a wide range of rhetorical functions, she says. Because of that, "particular care is required in seeking their proper interpretation" (p. 148).

The construction of silence-as-marginalization in electronic environments can be traced to now-canonized traditions in feminist literary criticism inspired by Tillie Olsen's ground-breaking *Silences* (1965), which opened new territory in literary criticism. *Silences* drew attention to a range of constructions for women's silences: "silences because women are not speaking, silences because women are not heard, silences because their voices are not understood, and silences because their voices are not preserved" (Fishkin, 1994). *Women's Ways of Knowing* (Belenky, Clinchy, Goldberger, & Tarule, 1986) was built on the tradition founded by Olsen, with a study that framed a female epistemology in terms of "voice" and its opposite, "silence." In the study, "silence" represents "an extreme in denial of self and in dependence on external authority" (p. 24). These are the extremes, and feminist theory has given us a language for these extremes.

However, we feel that when m-words become watered-down metaphors for explaining all forms of silence in electronic environments, their weight as signifiers is diminished. Frequently overlooked in feminist constructions of silence-as-marginalization is Olsen's (1965) distinction between "unnatural" circumstances, which deprive a writer of her voice, and "natural" silences, which all humans endure and which are marked by some sense of agency—"that necessary time for renewal, lying fallow, gestation, in the natural cycle of creation" (p. 6)—pregnant pauses, liminal moments *before* another cycle of writing or discourse begins.

While these and other theoretical constructions[2] are useful references points for beginning an analysis of silence and marginalization, our concerns are more specific to studies of electronic environments. There, silence frequently is constructed as evidence of an unnatural marginalization (see, especially, Selfe, 1990), and in terms of other various "illocutionary forces."[3] Silence can signal "resistance" to playing a rhetorical "game" (Selfe & Cooper, 1990); silence can cause "communication anxiety" (Hawisher, 1990) or feelings of failure (Hawisher & Moran, 1993). "Lurking" is another way of referencing silence in electronic environments, though its meaning is ambiguous. Even in specific situations—such as electronic forums in which we have both been participants—the meaning of silence as "lurking" has been highly contested. Indeed, without specific contexts of inquiry, theoretical constructions of silence and marginalization become "only" theories after all. We also need stories, dialogue, conversation, and anecdotal evidence to help create a more thorough understanding of what we mean when we bring together ideas such as "marginalization" and electronic spaces.

BEHOLD THE EXOTIC WATERFOWL: A PERSONAL TALE OF MARGINALIZATION

While enrolled in a graduate seminar entitled "Computers and English," I, Susan, discovered electronic conferencing. Nine of us—five men and four women—met for 90 minutes twice each week. We seldom greeted each other on entering the classroom, indeed scarcely spoke face-to-face at all, instead saving the rituals of becoming "human" and "free"—in the ancient meanings of these terms—for the virtual meeting place. There, we gathered to intoxicate ourselves with words.

I found being/writing in this space compelling and clearly recall our repeated acts of self-reflexivity. Frequently, we recounted for each other how we felt about being together, fishing for real-life analogues—metaphors—for the virtual experience. I remember especially the recurrent expressions of heady pleasure regarding the text we produced each day: its volume, its intellectual depth, its spontaneity, its frivolity. Yet, the pleasure statements I contributed to our communal text were not truthful—if truth be construed as a confession of emotional state. For I perceived the screen as a river of rapids running hot and cold, into which I must plunge again and again in order to exist. My pleasure was tempered with much anxiety. My-words-and-I would dive in repeatedly, striving to keep afloat as best we could while some sober shadow-self remained ashore and watched us anxiously as we sputtered, floundered, and choked, waving our verbal arms in distress. Sometimes my-words-and-I submerged gracefully, performing a silent and unremarkable drowning. But with luck, we would catch in some small eddy of our own making and form a sideshow, a minor curiosity for our classmates to point at, as if we were a strange species of waterfowl—colorful, interesting, exotic—but not of them, not of the mainstreamers.

Quickly I learned that She Who Denies Pleasure in the Presence of Technology becomes ever after suspect of infection with the dreaded Technophobia/Luddite disease—a terminally marginal condition. The Pleasure Principal drove our communal narrative to consistently positive endings regarding the coming of technology. The mythic lines of our text were marked out strongly by those for whom talking technology felt terribly, terribly good, and for whom playing with the digital manually and playing with the digital verbally was utterly absorbing. I could persuade no one that dominance is a discursive growth, made of human language, no matter the media.

I have constructed my experience from memory, and I do so unapologetically, firm in my idiosyncrasies, unwilling to abandon my tale. It is a true story of situated experience. Yet experience, writes Donna Haraway (1991), "does not pre-exist as a kind of prior resource, ready simply to be appropriated into one or another description. What may count as 'women's experience' is structured within multiple and often inharmonious agendas" (p. 113).

OIKOS AND POLIS

The graduate seminar was entitled "Computers and English." Put before us students for rational discussion were the following topics: computers and the mind, computers and intelligence, computers and freedom, computers and equity, computers and language, computers in the workplace, computers and communication. More interested in how discourse works than how software works, I was inclined to be silent about computers and instead to consider how hierarchies were being formed and dissolved by our very own writings.

For one thing, the topical dominance of high technology was all too *familiar* to me. In my household, computers and their speed, power, prices, and promise are dinner table conversation, then and now and at all meals in between:

> The 32-bit version of Netscape not only should run faster on Windows 95 or NT but it also will interpret Java applets on the Web. That's why I would delete Winsock and move to the Win95 Dial Up Networking. Just make sure that you configure your IP address and DNS IP addresses correctly from your old Winsock configuration when you set it up.

Such talk is proper to my *oikos*, that marginalized space called home, while feminism and rhetoric—marginalized topics in my domestic space—are available to me only outside the home in the *polis* of university life.

Feminism was a weak topic that semester, and so it goes. Yet feminist understandings of subjectivity provide strong explanatory lenses for examining discourse on technology. Feminist/deconstructionist Gayatri Chakravorty Spivak (1990), for example, writes that "the use of the (historical) figure of the woman is one way to manage the crisis of phallocentrism" (p. 102), and this observation suggests to me that it is we, the successfully speaking women in online environments, who by our imagined movement from margin to center, help to legitimate all projects associated with technology. Imagining women as once marginalized but now happily centered provides an ethical justification for preferring digital to print, and the virtual to the nonvirtual.

Feminist social theorist Nancy Fraser (1993) relies upon "revisionist historiography," women's histories in particular, to critique the false utopianism often implicit in Habermasian conceptions of the bourgeois public sphere. Her insights aptly comment on the prevailing enthusiasm for public discourse in electronic public spaces. Fraser writes:

> A discourse … touting accessibility, rationality, and the suspension of status hierarchies is itself deployed as a strategy of distinction. Of course, in and of itself this irony does not fatally compromise the discourse…." (p. 115)

I draw attention, of course, to Fraser's analysis of the exclusionary mechanisms built into discourses that understand themselves as inclusionary. But I note well the last sentence, for here Fraser asserts that critique is not necessarily a devaluing gesture. Just as Fraser is committed to "theorizing the *limits* of democracy in late-capitalist societies" (emphasis added; p. 107) without dismissing democracy *per se*, so feminists online are committed to theorizing the *limits* of virtual communities in order to enhance their serviceability.

MANY BEACHES

I, Margaret, have a story to tell as well: Once upon a time, a few weeks into the semester in a first-year writing class, I opened an Interchange[4] session with the prompt: "Quick question (Socrates might ask this): How do we know what we know?" In the first four responses, students posted thoughts about parents, schooling, "our environments," and the possibility that "We really don't know anything for sure. That's what life's about." Although a lively discussion ensued, including a debate about God and faith, the fifth response was from a native-born Japanese student whose name, translated into English, was "Many Beaches." Many Beaches' first contribution to the discussion was "Who knows?" and his only other responses that day were "Who cares if you know something?" and "Whatta boring things [sic] we are talking about." After that, for a long time, he stayed out of online discussions.

I didn't know quite what to make of the situation in the case of Many Beaches. I had been teaching writing for four years, with several semesters spent in networked computer labs, but I had only recently begun to form questions about the swell of discourse on the electronic page where center and margin are figured in terms of "participation," some supposedly measurable unit for calculating grades. And though stories such as this one about Many Beaches seem to be illuminating in and of themselves about such matters, eventually (as academics, at least) we turn to theory to explain what it all means. I wound up ruminating over the words of Eldred and Fortune (1990), who say that one of the keys to judging the "successfulness" of participation in electronic environments is in examining the metaphors we use to characterize these spaces. If we conceive of electronic discourse as writing, they say, usually we will value it more than if we conceive of it as speaking. However, it is more useful to think of the rhetorical activity in these spaces in terms of "hybrids," Eldred and Fortune argue.

Using their framework, it would seem that my metaphors for online participation are very much oral-based, as my rhetoric for discussing such environments is riddled with phrases such as "dialogue," "discussion," "conversation," and—echoing Shirley Brice Heath (1990)— "learners talking and considering together." And, because even the least active online participant in that class, Many Beaches, earned a good grade for "on-line participation" by the end of the semester, it would seem (by Eldred and Fortune's standards) I must not have valued online participation all that much. It might be said that that particular course was not a successful case of using this medium for instruction. But, in truth, I'm not sure what my "participation policy" for Interchange was that semester. I only remember having to think hard about it because of Many Beaches. His very name became, for me, a metaphor for the shiftiness of m-words.

AN EXAMINATION OF MARGINS AS METAPHORICAL SPACES

"The essence of metaphor," Lakoff and Johnson (1980) write, "is understanding and experiencing one kind of thing in terms of another" (p. 5). The ways that we conceptualize electronic spaces reflect the ways we act in, and interpret, rhetorical situations. The idea of margins signifies that a territorial or container metaphor is employed, and as Lakoff and Johnson argue, "there are few human instincts more basic than territoriality" (p. 29). In fact, when we experience situations as having no boundaries, "we often project boundaries upon them" (p. 58). This presents a paradox: Prior to specific contexts, how can we even begin to conceptualize the reality of marginalized subject positions? Is it so impossible to imagine marginless space? What happens when we start with a clean canvas, *tabula rasa*? Aesthetically speaking, extreme constructions of silence and marginalization seem to represent a sort of aural *horror vacui*—a fear, repugnance, incomprehension, or assumed negative value of unfilled discourse space *per se*. In art criticism, "horror vacui" has been used traditionally to describe the art or artifacts of non-Western traditions, aesthetic styles that have "similar tendencies [to] barbarian art" (p. 299). We are quoting from a mid-1980s art history textbook (de la Croix & Tansey, 1986) that uses the term *horror vacui* to describe a style of Islamic art where decorative patterns in the foreground seem to blend into equal relationship with the background. Such "stylization" reflects an "impermanence," these critics claim. "Space" itself becomes an "arbitrary" notion, which threatens the dominance of the "design." Keeping with aesthetic theory, this filled/empty space binary is currently referred to as the *figure/ground* relationship. Cynthia Dantzic (1990) explains that traditionally the figure has been considered the "real" subject, and the ground "merely" the environment in which it is contained, a "negative" or "empty" space. In more recent artistic endeavors, however, as Dantzic points out, artists have been known to make deliberate attempts to bring figure/ground into equal relationship, in some cases even "stressing the area around the object to the point of eliminating *any* treatment of the 'figure' itself" (original emphasis; p. 35). This is not only a different approach to making art, but a different approach to interpreting art. In design theory, according to Dantzic, shape begins with the drawing of a line, or even the insertion of a dot upon a surface. As soon as the dot is large enough to become visible, we begin to see it in terms of two shapes, both the dot itself (the figure), and the enclosing area around it (the ground). So it is that we are trying to envision the discourse space of electronic mediums: as blank slate or black hole, where the first hint of designated purpose, and the first "dot" of discourse on it, implies a relationship with what is not-discourse, and what is not-the-purpose of this space. The first question we would ask, then, is what are language and rhetoric and silence in this space being used *for*?[5]

MANY BEACHES, FURTHER OBJECTIFIED

In examining her metaphors for online participation in terms of speech and writing (and "hybrids"), Margaret began to confront her own sense of *horror vacui* at the prospect of unfilled discourse space in the classroom, where Many Beaches' online silence became the *ground* that threatened to overwhelm the all-important *figures of speech*, the written and spoken discourse which are so prominently valued within the spaces of a writing class.

Many Beaches fit the category "marginalized" as it is generally constructed, Margaret reasoned, beginning with an examination of his identifying characteristics. Japanese students were a rarity at her school where the average student was from the northeastern United States and of second-generation European descent; many were the first in their families to attend college. In contrast, Many Beaches was raised in a wealthy, educated family and had attended private boarding schools in England and other parts of Europe (although he had been expelled from several of them). English was not his first language, but that itself was not the reason for his reticence in discourse—for once he started writing, Many Beaches was frequently playful, experimental, and verbose.

At first, Margaret read his behavior as "aloofness" and thought he might be spoiled and arrogant—an international playboy-type, hanging out in the margins of the class because he was too cool for school. And for quite some time, she walked a fine line between dual roles: In one, she was the authoritarian witch who forces students out of comfortable spaces and into unfamiliar subject positions called "writers"; in the other role, she was protectress of "safe houses," to use Mary Louise Pratt's phrase (1991, p. 40), leaving space for Many Beaches to lurk in the margins of the class, where he seemed to feel more comfortable, allowing him—encouraging him—to act out "resistant" behaviors in his writing, as Cooper and Selfe (1990) might characterize them. And he did.

Many Beaches turned in every paper exactly one paper behind his classmates (except the last, which was on time), but in doing so would sometimes imitate another student's style, or pick up on another's theme. It began to seem that in lurking in the margins of the class, whether online or not, he was reading, listening, and learning. He began experimenting with playful and sometimes provocative prose in his papers, and then once used the word "fuck" in an Interchange session. Margaret reacted with "patience" at this, using the occasion to offer a private lesson in rhetoric. "Don't you realize how the others in the class will react?" she asked Many Beaches, "They might—." But the look on his face stopped her. He seemed pleased to think his writing could provoke reactions, and interactions.

At the beginning of the semester, Margaret had asked students to try out a variety of metaphors and choose one that described their writing. Many Beaches chose a sports-based metaphor—writing was like running a marathon without the proper shoes; it was like spending all of one's energy before reaching the finish line. Later, he wrote that in all the schools he had attended, he had never actually been required to turn in a piece of writing that constituted a "paper." Then, in a class the previous semester, one paper had been required. He procrastinated writing. The paper haunted him, he wrote, to the extent that friends no longer greeted him without asking, "How is the paper going?" Finally, in desperation, he wrote the paper in a sleepless, 24-hour marathon two days before it was due.

When he revisited his sports-based metaphor at the end of the semester as part of a portfolio review, Many Beaches wrote that he felt like a better-equipped runner who could now pace himself. In their portfolios, students were also asked to include an argument for their grade for "participation." To Margaret's surprise, Many Beaches argued he deserved an "A" for the course. Though much of his work had been turned in late, he said, he had accomplished all of it by the final deadline, and his participation was significant because he had "broken the ice" when he used the word "fuck" online. After that, he reasoned, "everyone" opened up and began to join in. He and Margaret negotiated a "B" as a fair grade (though Margaret secretly gave him an "A+" for chutzpah). "That's all I really hoped for," Many Beaches concluded, with a smile.

Ah, closure (sigh). A happy little tale with a happy little ending, when told a certain way. When Margaret moves from center to margin as narrator, she becomes simply a teacher in the background, and Many Beaches is the central figure in the story, successfully negotiating his way towards becoming a confident user of the English language. His online silence becomes something more than simply a metaphor for the absence of writing or speech in online discourse (*the horror!*). Instead, by the end of the story, Many Beaches can be seen fully inhabiting the discursive spaces of the classroom. While for other students the online forum became a fertile space for experimenting with verbal dancing and sparring, for Many Beaches it proved to be a good perch from which to lurk and listen, and a dark stage on which to try out words, sometimes outrageous.

And yet, there is no closure for the storyteller. There are many complicating details that Margaret has left out of this story, and there are always other semesters and other students. So, she continues to think hard about the matter of participation policies, and how best to value students' online discourse, or lack thereof. She isn't even sure it is possible to begin every semester with those values already firmly established. Wouldn't that leave her unresponsive to the ebbs and flows of alluvial forces? she wonders. What are the Many Beaches she will encounter next semester? And the next?

TWO WATERFOWL ON THE SHORES OF DISCOURSE: FRACTALS

Susan and Alice, who identified themselves as feminists in the "English and Computers" seminar that semester, were both active contributors to the extensive online discussions. Both were careful readers and sharp commentators. Over the course of the semester, each woman put feminism on trial within a discourse thick and weighty with words about computers and language, computers and mind, hypertext, interactive forums, software, hardware, and programming languages. Linda Brodkey (1987) proposes that feminism is "a self-conscious and systematic attempt to remain positioned on the margins ... and [to] make positive use of that marginality" (p. 13). Yet, gender/feminism as topic and gender/feminism as tactic fared differently in each woman's hands.

Susan

On the third session of the semester, the class produced an unusually lengthy text centering on the relationship of artificial intelligence to human intelligence. Several participants expressed satisfaction with the discussion:

Joe: How do you keep a room full of grad students preoccupied?
George: Give them all keyboards? I give up, Joe.
Alfred: I would be willing to bet that we broke the 50K barrier today!

About a month later, when someone referred to that session as "excellent—the best ever," Susan wrote back she had not enjoyed it. She appended to her remarks a breakdown by gender of the messages produced: 99 messages composed by men, and 29 by women, in a class of five men and four women. Classmates were befuddled; hypotheses were presented:

Response 1: Susan,... maybe what those numbers suggest is that [George, Alfred, Joe, Billy, and I] *wanted* to participate so extensively because we were deeply engaged by the topics and by the way the discussions unfolded....
Response 2: It would be interesting to know whether the proportion still holds. I'm wondering, that is, whether continued experience with interchange has made any difference in the women's sense of freedom, etc.

Susan did not respond to the proposed explanation that participation is merely a matter of desire, nor to the suggestion that women take longer than men to adjust to freedom. Then, three open-ended requests for interpretation came her way:

Response 3: Susan—Did lengths of messages differ between women and men?
Response 4: Susan—to what do you attribute the difference in number of times men vs. women spoke?
Response 5: Susan—it is interesting—the breakdown of participation.... You should do it for every Interchange....

Susan demurred, answering with self-imposed silence.

Susan: I'm hesitant to assign causes for the discrepancies between men's and women's participation in that conversation....

Later in the semester, someone performed a quantitative analysis on a subsequent Interchange, finding no significant gender differences. Thus, the problem of gender in electronic spaces was quietly laid to rest.

Alice

Alice was markedly more successful than Susan, judging by feminism's staying power as a topic under her sponsorship and by her classmates' approval of her discourse. Although Alice's remarks often followed immediately upon Susan's more abrasive ones, the two women apparently did *not* collaborate, if collaboration implies some consciousness of its own motion. Indeed, Alice often contradicted Susan. To Susan's presentation of empirical evidence on gender and messaging, for example, Alice responded by describing a visit to an undergraduate networked classroom where the female students spoke frequently and well. On another occasion, Alice broke pointedly from Susan's skepticism in favor of an alliance with visionary computer scientists, writing "Susan, I think the arrogance of people in the computer field is part of their charm...." Eventually, Alice received an invitation to speak at greater length about feminism:

> Alice, answer your own question: Where *does* the feminist fit in? What *do* you care about, and how might this technology or some later version of it help in bringing about whatever that is?

Although the invitation was conditional, wrapping feminism tightly in the embrace of technology, and although the invitation required her to speak for all feminists everywhere, Alice accepted these constraints and responded with more "strong women" stories:

> Well, I think a feminist can fit in anywhere she puts herself.... All of my best friends are feminists, and my three closest friends are feminists who work with computer technology. My best friend from college is in a Ph.D. program in decision sciences [and] devotes her free time to working for Wages for Housework—an international feminist organization, and she writes programs (models, I guess) for food distribution to the poor in New York....

Toward the end of the semester, Alice garnered two compliments from Bill, a classmate, for her brand of feminism, which he found required no changes in his behavior:

> Alice, I am very pleased to see a feminist stance taken on grounds of difference, not superiority (moral and otherwise). Boys will be boys, I'm happy to say, and they'll have to pry the joystick from my cold, dead fingers before I'll give up being a kid at heart.

> Alice, your mode is one of careful scrutiny and powerful argument, with a dose of feminism that is neither hesitant nor abusive (sometimes hard to find)....

"Will the successful feminist please stand up?" is the wrong question to ask. This story of two women immersed in discourse constructs an alliance that was not really there. It plots the "just-barely-possible affinities, the just-barely-possible connections that might actually make a difference in local and global histories" (Haraway, 1991, p. 113).

THE OTHER F-WORD: "I'M A FEMINIST, BUT..."

Margaret: Why is it that some of us who see ourselves as feminists hold off introducing the issue of gender in the work we do? It reminds me of an article I wrote one time as a freelancer, where I interviewed a variety of professional people in the community, males and females, and asked if they thought of themselves as feminists, and why or why not. Without fail, each person said either "I'm a feminist, but..." or "I'm not a feminist, but..." Why are we always using these qualifiers?

Susan: Did you see Virginia Anderson's 1997 article, "Confrontational Teaching and Rhetorical Practice"? She argues that what a particular brand of feminism has in common with other critical practices is some pretty naive assumptions about how persuasion works. The discussion focuses on a feminist teacher who defines herself in such a way as to discourage student identification with the feminist mission. Well, I'm oversimplifying Virginia's argument, but it strikes me that "I'm a feminist but..." means these people are ambivalent about two things: first, the definition of "feminist" and second, their own willingness to identify with it. The "but" says, "I need to do some redefining before I associate with the image."

Margaret: Yes, I read the article and I also found myself drawn to Anderson's point that "activist" feminist teachers devalue and actually discount students' negotiating their own positions of identity.

Susan: Well, judging from your account of Many Beaches, you leave plenty of room for students to negotiate identity and name their own discursive practices as well. But I'd bet that if Many Beaches had introduced the other F-word—*feminism*—into the Interchange discussion, you would have had an even more lively discussion. But back to your other point—yes, it has bothered me that some of my female colleagues shy away from the f-word, and Virginia is the first to develop a well-articulated rationale for their doing so.

Margaret: Yet, she points to the idea that there are many kinds of feminisms, multiple perspectives. You know what alarms me more? My own daughter seems to be rather ambivalent about feminism.

Susan: Mine too. She says it deauthorizes and weakens her. That's the "but..."

Margaret: We should ask them about it. We're always putting our students in that position. How about if we ask for a definition of feminism, then ask why they can or can't identify. Okay?

* * * * *

Daughter #1: Let's see, I am loathe to call myself a "feminist" because, when I think of the word, I see all sorts of negative connotations that come with that word. I think of the diehard, screaming, bra-burning women who, to me, whine more about equality than actually get off their asses and do something.

Daughter #2: Okay, I hesitate to call myself a feminist because that could mean just about anything and therefore tends to mean nothing except that there exist some issues concerning women on which I have opinions that I believe support/protect/liberate/whatever women. What's your definition? Oh, you're asking the questions.

Daughter #1: I can certainly see very good reasons for the qualifiers that most of "us" give when we say we are or we aren't feminists. I don't know that much about feminist theory because the one class where I should have learned a bit about it was taught by Professor Andrews who liked to talk, but kept getting off track. Maybe if there were a definitive definition of what a feminist is it would be easier to say I am or am not one. But, like words such as "love" and "truth," I think feminism is interpreted differently by each person: I "love" it *but*... I am telling you the "truth," *but*... I'm a "feminist" *but*...

* * * * *

Margaret: Okay. Here we have it: They find the term "feminist" too specific in terms of certain behaviors associated with it (bra burning). On the other hand, they find the term too broad—it means nothing because it means everything and contains so many contradictory behaviors that, like truth and love, it always requires qualification (that's the *but*). They say it in plain English: "We need to work on this definition. Then we'll talk about ourselves."

Susan: A response that confirms Virginia's point about letting students wrestle with definitions before being asked to accept feminist proposals for action. I was particularly taken with Virginia's point that identification is not a one-time event but an ongoing *process*. Let's ask the daughters about their processes of becoming or unbecoming feminists. We'll ask for stories.

* * * * *

Daughter #2: In high school and college, I never thought of myself as primarily female in the context of academics, maybe because I was focused on learning and working toward goals and didn't associate academic interests with personal interactions. However, in grad school and at work, where academic pursuits are closely tied to interactions with other researchers, I've come to be extremely aware of gender, but I think this is primarily due to the unwelcome attention of particular men.

Daughter #1: When it's all said and done, I think that, by many definitions, I am a feminist. I believe that there is a lot of inequality in areas such as the workforce, where it's proven that men are paid more for the same work women do. I think women need to stand up more and realize that they do have a voice. If you want something changed, the only way to do it is by yourself with action. Words can be powerful and they are a large part of the action, but there is more than that.

Daughter #2: I always think about feminism as a struggle, actually. I have trouble imagining it as anything else. It's tiring to go through life being acutely aware of the many ways that one might be treated badly specifically because of gender. Ideally, you could go through life unaware of any correlation between gender and types of encounters with people, and then simply react according to the immediate situation. Unfortunately, when certain types of situations occur repeatedly, you can't help inadvertently classifying them, remembering how best to deal with them, recognizing them in their various forms, and responding to them according to some preconceived notion of how this type of "gender-related struggle" is best dealt with.

******

Susan: Here's what I hear: Feminism should move from whining to doing, from words to actions (this argument is central to rhetoric). If not, it loses force for our daughters, as well as our students. What identification they *do* have grows out of experience and necessity (harassment, for example) and/or observations of gender inequalities in and out of the workplace. They mention no role models—no Xena the Warrior Princess and no Thelma, no Louise. But finally, they find feminism a lens that should not be used as an everyday, all-occasion tool. Not everything in life is about power and gender!

Margaret: You're right—our editors say we have to get back to the idea of e-spaces and technology if we're going to be so long-winded about feminism.

Susan: Okay. Virginia cites Burke on the Marxist "mistake" of using the disempowered worker as image. What about our new, powerful, mythic, cyberfeminist image: ta da! THE CYBORG!

Margaret: You know, the very word "cyborg" conjures up images of the Terminator or Frankenstein, and stories that always begin with hopes for progress in the future through the union of man [sic] and machine, but always end with disappointment and destruction. Humans + machines = humans *versus* nature. You know what I mean?

Susan: Are you saying, "I'm a cyborg, *but*...? Actually, Haraway is pretty explicit about the erasure of distinctions between the human and the natural and the artificial. She argues that the differences between animals and humans are no longer at issue, as they were for Mary Shelley. The new site of cultural anxiety is the link (connection or disconnection) between the human being and the machine, as expressed in *Terminator*. A female cyborg, some would say, is a being who exists comfortably in her animal, human, and artificial "natures." Lynn Randolf's painting, for example, shows a woman with a digital switch for a heart, a mountain lion sewn/grown onto her head, and fingers ergodynamically fitted to the keyboard in front of her. It's an image of one very, very peaceful woman writer.

Margaret: But isn't that a myth again? A romantic myth, of some kind? I need realism, the kind you get by finding out how real people deal with their relationships with technology.

Susan: Yes, what bothers me about the Randolf painting is the absence of other writers. It's quite modernist in that sense—lone woman writer needs only her cougar and her computer. Straight out of the romantic tradition. And yet I kind of like the sense of a naturalized relationship with one's computer.

THELMA AND LOUISE IN MEXICO: FEMINIST MATERIALIST TECHNOLOGISTS

Flashback

Feminist heroes Thelma and Louise, as many women have always suspected, did not die. Instead, they crossed Texas and headed south into Mexico, as they had planned, then west toward the Sonoran Desert. Passing directly through *Like Water for Chocolate* territory, Thelma learned of the life of Gertrudis—passionate, sexual Gertrudis—commandante in the Revolución, and polka dancer par excellence. "I wouldn't mind being abducted, Louise, if it was gonna be like that," Thelma would say dreamily, thinking of naked Gertrudis, galloping Gertrudis, dancing Gertrudis, as she and Louise drove on and on across the desert, through Ojinaga, Coyame, El Morrion. "Oh, shut up, Thelma," Louise would say. "It was a movie, just a damn movie."

Thelma and Louise do not live in the past now, nor in fantasy only. In Tecalitlán, Jalisco, birthplace of El Mariachi Vargas, they own and manage the small but ever-busy Posada Cyberfeminísima, where they serve *desayuno* and *comida corrida*—the latter a one-menu-only, middle-of-the-day meal at a reasonable price. They offer Internet access as well. In short, they run a bed and breakfast *cum* cyber café. It's a popular spot for locals and *turistas* alike.

On this particular evening, however, we find the two virtually alone. Louise is busy straightening up the bar area, taking a tequila inventory, and calculating the day's profits on an Excel spreadsheet. Thelma is sitting at one of the computers in the cyber café, cruising the Net. The Pentium II she uses is equipped with CU-See-Me technology, and before long, Thelma encounters a handsome face on the screen in front of her.

Thelma: Louise! Get over here and take a look at this hunk I found online!

Louise: Uh-huh. Whadda ya think? Should we order seven cases of Herradura Añejo? Or do you think we oughta... *[Louise is now absorbed in updating the tequila database.]*

Thelma: He wants to know if I'm married. *[As the audio portion of the program isn't working, Thelma begins keying in a response, talking out loud as she types.]* Why…no…I'm…not…married. I…used…to…be…but…

Louise: *[Looking up from her task]* Who the hell are you talking to, Thelma?

Thelma: It's just some cute guy I met online. He says his name is Bjorn. I think he's from Sweden or Norway or something. *[She continues typing]* no…I'm…not. I…live…in…Mexico....

Louise: Honey, Bjorn—or whoever the hell he is—is just some guy you're never gonna see in real life. That there is nothin' but a bunch of photons. Here— *[She sweeps Thelma's hands off the keyboard]* —I want you to see this. [*Louise signs on to Womenwaytoofast, a feminist discussion group]* I found this one last week. Now, THESE women are wild! [*Thelma stares eagerly over her shoulder as the script of the online conversation scrolls across the screen in front of them.]*

Donna Haraway: [Online] Phallogocentrism was the egg ovulated by the master subject, the brooding hen to the permanent chickens of history. But into the nest with that literal-minded egg has been placed the germ of a phoenix that will speak in all the tongues of a world turned upside down [1991, p. 148].

Thelma: [Offline] Louise! What the hell is she talking about?!

Louise: Oh, honey, she's just talking about these two women in some college classroom and how some of them didn't say as much as the men. And something about technology.

Thelma: Looks to me like she's talking about sex—eggs and phalluses and stuff—right, Louise? Hey, look at this one. Sombody's writing to me!

Joan Wallach Scott: [Online] In its most recent usage, Thelma, "gender" seems to have first appeared among American feminists who wanted to insist on the fundamentally social quality of distinctions based on sex. The word denoted a rejection of the biological determinism implicit in the use of such terms as "sex" or "sexual difference." "Gender" also stressed the relational aspect of normative definitions of femininity.

Cynthia Selfe: And Thelma, pay attention to technology! When we fail to do so, we share in the responsibility for sustaining and reproducing an unfair system that…enacts social violence… [1998].

Thelma: Okay, you got my attention. We know plenty about violence. [*She gives Louise a knowing look.]* But what's this thing about sex and computers?

Louise: Here we are with a computer, and all you can think about is cybersex. Get real, Thelma. Cynthia is saying we live in a third world country where we're *extranjeros* and entrepreneurs. There's poverty here and there's guns and there's hunger and there's violence. And there's women here who work too hard for too little. And there's children who don't go to school. Life is not just some endless cyberfantasy, you know.

Thelma: Hey, I was just having some fun. *Un chiste. ¿Comprendes?* Where's Bjorn? Bjorn!

Cynthia Selfe: Pay attention, Thelma!

Louise: Yeah, pay attention. Look at what's going on all around you, not just on this screen.

Gayatri Chakravorty Spivak: Louise, if you get totally involved in political activism, you will find that you become more and more aware of the problems of the textuality of the socius. You will not go away from the text by deciding to join movements, or by deciding to stop reading books. A bullet in the chest, the fact of the death, might seem to stop textuality, but the reason why the bullet, the access to the bullet, why the bullet at all; who killed whom, why, how? Why without reason, etc.?... [I]f we are going to *do* anything about the phenomenon, we have *no* alternative but to involve ourselves and mire ourselves in what we are calling the textuality of the socius. The real task here is to displace and undo that killing opposition between the text narrowly conceived as the verbal text and activism narrowly conceived as some sort of mindless engagement [1990, pp. 120–121].

Susan Romano: Margaret, what's happening?

Margaret Daisley: Hey, what is this? Some kind of hoax? Cindy? Is that really you?

Donna Haraway: The relation of hoax and popular natural history is unnervingly close, Margaret. A reminder of this relationship is particularly salutary in approaching the political and biological science of being female. Hoax and natural history both have deep roots in democratic and populist histories, but the practice of hoax more seriously resists the closures of those hegemonic discourses on nature, in which each being finds its ordained place. Ordination has been generally bad for the health of females.... Our problem will be to find the evidence of stitchery without ripping out the patterns in the lives of females... [1989, pp. 279–280].

Thelma: Louise? Susan? Margaret? Could someone explain? This sounds serious. I know something about guns. And bullets. But that's behind me now. I wish I never had to think about it ever again.

Gayatri Chakravorty Spivak: When I think of the masses, Donna, I think of a woman belonging to that 84% of women's work in India, which is unorganized peasant labour. Now if I could speak in such a way that such a person would actually listen to me and not dismiss me as yet another of those many colonial missionaries, that would embody the project of unlearning about which I've spoken recently.... I come from a state where the illiterate—not the functionally illiterate, but the real illiterate, who can't tell the difference between one letter and another—are still possessed of a great deal of political sophistication... [1990, p. 565].

Thelma: [Offline] I think I'm getting the picture, Louise. I mean, hey—I can read, you know. It sounds to me like that woman really wants someone to listen to her. I'm trying to, but—.

Cynthia Selfe: [Online] We need not only additional examinations of the ideological systems and cultural formations currently informing the literacy-technology link, but [we also need] the historical patterns established by *other literacy* technologies.... We require multiple perspectives if we hope to construct a robust and accurate understanding of the ways in which technology functions in our culture.

Louise: [Offline] Don't you see, honey? They're just saying we oughta take a look at how we're using all this technology—computers and stuff, cars, guns. I mean, are we using them? Or are they using us?

Epilogue

Although the circumstances of their past dictate that the two can never return to the country of their birth, Thelma and Louise continue to lead rich lives. Their interactions with Tecalitlán women have enabled them to adapt their own business acumen to the local economic culture. The *posada* business thrives under Louise's management—especially after she sets up an all-women market cooperative, complete with in-house preschool, where each morning she purchases fresh produce to supply the restaurant.

On the side, Thelma has become an expert in the practical means of deconstructing *machismo,* and currently offers a series of workshops on dance, sex, safety, and sound relationships—both online and offline. As you might imagine, her Spanish is colloquially impeccable. Louise has kept up her interest in travel, although most of her travel is through the Web. She belongs to the Women's International League for Peace and Freedom (WILPF; www.wilpf.org/). One of the founding mothers of this organization, Jane Addams, was awarded the Nobel Peace Prize in 1931 and at the same time was declared to be "the most dangerous woman in America" by the FBI. Louise feels an affinity here. And, she has developed an interest in textiles, learning the ancient art of weaving from local women, whose fibers of knowledge run backward for centuries, along multiple family lines.

It wasn't long before Thelma married a local rancher, a good man, and recently they've begun producing an award-winning line of goat cheeses in conjunction with a ranching cooperative that supplies the milk for their business. Although the website for this business takes over 500 hits per month, it garners few sales at present. But because the site is maintained by local secondary students who are learning HTML and developing their own projects, the expense seems worth every penny. Thelma and her husband have two children, Marginalia and Fénix. Louise, of course, is their proud godmother and hopes to teach the children everything she knows.

IN THE BEGINNING WAS THE M-WORD…

o o o
o o o o oo o o o o
o o o o o
o o o o
o

In the beginning
was the m-word—an ur-word of some
kind that was used to denote a sense of space, and
one's—or another's— position in relation to that space.
The OED, bible of our profession, traces the genesis, genres,
and generations of the word from the archaic "margent," to its modern
descendant "margin," which encompasses a range of meanings. The most
prominent references in this genealogy are to the margins of a page, the places
for commentary upon the text, or the commentary itself. Many medieval manuscripts have beautifully shaped margins—wrapped around text shaped like
recognizable objects … such as fish. Medieval readers were expected to gloss the
printed page. Indeed, contemporary scholars find the glosses as valuable as the
text itself, as they provide social context and reader response. Speaking of literary
theory, in recent times m-words have begun to play active roles in our various disciplinary jargons. In geography and the arts, m-words point to contours, boundary
lines, or distinct borders differing in texture from the main body. Psychology considers marginal the edges of the field of consciousness. In economics, marginalization signifies a condition beyond which something ceases to be possible or
desirable—an amount of space, time, money, or material supplementary
to the strictly necessary (a profit margin, for example), or a provision
for unforeseen contingencies. On the other hand, "marginal"
applies to natural resources barely worth
developing, or to a person working
with such resources. In finance,
a margin account
affords the account holder purchasing
powers beyond her means. Political science employs
m-words to reference consti- tuencies in which an election
or an issue is likely to be closely contested. Sociology uses the
concept to refer to individuals or social groups whose
characteristics or customs differ from those of an
identifiable mainstream population. In zoology,
however, we come across a very different
meaning. In that discipline, "margins"
are the feathers on the edges
(black) bird's of a wings.

MARGINALIZED@WHEREVER.EDU

Since our stories focus on the dynamics of discourse in electronic environments within educational settings, we would classify them as "literacy narratives"—personal stories that focus on the themes of language learning, schooling, and academic careers. Eldred and Mortensen (1992) identify several recognizable motifs for these narratives. Literacy myths (such as those deconstructed by Graff and Altick) are narratives in which "literacy necessarily leads to economic development, cultural progress, and individual improvement" (p. 512). Narratives of socialization are those that "chronicle a character's attempt to enter a new social (and discursive) arena." And, "literature of the contact zone" (Pratt, 1991, p. 513) is that which studies the problems of forcing a sanctioned literacy on colonized subjects.

Although we can identify strands of the socialization narrative in our own accounts, and we do identify strands of the mythic element within those accounts, we classify our storytelling as literature of the contact zone. In doing so, we consciously take a critical look at the socializing aspects of literacy, and use language both as a way to resist and to identify with authority in the dominant circuits of literate culture, as Pratt calls them (1991), in this case electronic spaces. In particular, we think of our stories as computer literacy narratives, as Daisley (1995) puts it, personal stories that focus on the meaning of computer technologies within the larger themes of literacy in our lives. In our computer literacy narratives, we examine our positions at the margins and/or centers of electronic spaces, the quality of our access to these spaces, and how these factors help us to characterize our identities. As feminists, as cyborgs in these electronic contact zones, we not only tell our stories in ways that disrupt popular hegemonic narratives, but we disrupt our own stories as well in order to clarify larger themes and questions, asking for instance: Is a particular instance of marginalization (or silence) natural, or unnatural? And, who is doing the defining?

We would be the first to point out that our narratives do not remain the same with each telling, nor would yours, dear readers. We create and recreate our stories, rehistoricizing them over time because our personal and professional lives—the *oikos* and *polis* spaces that we inhabit—do not remain static. Second, with each telling, we try to approach our stories with fresh perspectives—sometimes purposefully using literary devices, stepping into the third-person-singular voice of an omniscient narrator, trying on the voices of "Thelma" and "Louise," and engaging in dialogue with real and imagined others. Third, referencing critical rhetorical and ethnographic theory, we recognize also that our stories might be told differently, depending upon the audiences we imagine as our readers. Here, we imagine our readers as being somewhat like us: sometimes feeling marginalized in our computer literacy narratives, and sometimes not; skeptical of numbers that cast us as marginalized within narratives in which we feel we play no part. Last, there are no endings to our stories, for as Margaret Atwood has pointed out, there is only one ending for all stories: And then they died. As yet, we have not. Like feminism, as one daughter put it, it's an ongoing struggle.

*****

In her first attempt to compose a computer literacy narrative in the Fall of 1995, Daisley wrote about the breakdown of the family's first computer, an Atari. Via the yellow pages, she found herself in a mom-and-pop-style video store in Queens, New York, where the Sylvester Stallone look-alike behind the counter, on that summer day, wore no shirt. Bare-chested! (Yo, Rocky! Can ya fix my computuh?) She concludes that chapter ("The Early Years, 1980–1990") with the tale of her first experience getting an e-mail account where she gushes forth screens of prose to everyone she knows who has e-mail, and tries to convert others who have not yet seen the light.

In Daisley's next installment, all has changed. She is whining about her access situation, and how she is feeling "left behind," not having the money, time, or support systems to keep up. "I've always been a 'nontraditional' graduate student," Daisley wrote, "but now I live three states away from my home campus, still using the same technologies I was using when I moved 3 years ago—a Zenith Z-Sport laptop from which an octopus of wires connect to an aged monitor, a printer, a full-size keyboard, a mouse, a power source, and the telephone line." Daisley's continuing narrative is inseparable from the technical problems of telnetting to her campus address, using a 2400-baud modem and a not-quite-legal local account. At the same time, she recognizes that her outdated technologies are what allow her to have any academic life at all.

The latest chapter further complicates Daisley's story. At her nonacademic temp job, she has acquired a work-based e-mail account, and feels somewhat elated about the prospect of having access to a "point-and-click" system for e-mail and the Web, and technical support when problems arise. Yet despite her excitement about this new equipment, she has become uneasy about what it means to have a particular address—to have ".gov," ".uk," ".com," or even ".harvard.edu" associated with one's name. Her new address doesn't signal her worth, she thinks. It's not an address she plans to move to permanently, nor an address she sees as constituting her "identity." Her snail-mail address has changed four times in the last 5 years, but her academic e-mail address has remained the same, giving her a sense of permanence and an affiliation of which she is proud. As she ends this cycle of her narrative, she finds that she only wants to use her employers' technology to give her access to her "real" life, her intellectual life, and wonders if in so doing she is practicing cyborg arts. At this intersection of her narrative of computers and literacy, she prefers to think that she is not marginalized, but in a liminal phase, a somewhat "natural" state, to use Tillie Olsen's (1965) framework—"that necessary time for renewal, lying fallow, gestation, in the natural cycle of creation" (p. 6).

*****

Romano, too, occupies liminal territory. She feels indignant that one of her academic privileges—ownership of a Unix-based e-mail account—was removed upon her graduation. Although she never made much use of Unix, she did feel somewhat empowered to have been able to issue the "ls" command, to manipulate her directories herself, and to moan about the "vi editor" while issuing techie commands such as "yank" or "kill." The University of Texas at Austin does not callously dump its grads off the Internet and into the streets, however, for Romano was provided a free @mail box for an indefinite amount of time. She actually prefers her "people's address"—@hotmail, that web-based, corporate-sponsored Internet residence for the truly homeless, the place where the masses (those with *some* access, that is) reside.

Romano will not linger among the marginalized for long, however. Her new academic employer has invited her to choose new computer equipment for her office, and so she is in the process of developing a new vocabulary with which to narrate her ongoing socialization into the community of the electronically literate. She prompts her friends, family members, and mere acquaintances to enter into the Macintosh versus PC debate and willingly plays audience to their persuasive rhetoric performed in the low, middle, and high styles. Pouring over spec sheets, she is now able to employ numbers to reference the speed and power that become an assistant professor of English. She has decided to order a Mac 7300/180 with a PC compatibility card and defends her decision with arguments about the 604 processor that, she claims, will afford her "sufficient power." Her willingness to conceptualize power in terms of a model of machinery makes her blush. She has begun to talk about space differently, too, and mulls over the possible features of a feminist webpage, having found no spec sheets, no models, and no numbers to assist her. She practices before a browser just how she will appear in this space—her words, her designs, her images—without actually going public just yet.

~ And so it goes...

AND FURTHER, FROM THE MARGINS...[6]

NOTES

[1] This is an excerpt from Wallace Stephens's poem "Thirteen Ways of Looking at a Blackbird" (1917), which serves as a classic example of the use of collage to decenter a single perspective. That is our main goal in writing about m-words in this fashion.

[2] See, for example, Freire's construction of a "Culture of Silence" (*The Pedagogy of the Oppressed,* 1993); Kenneth Burke's discussion of "ineffable silence" (*Rhetoric of Motives,* 1969); and George Kalamaras's argument of silence as "tacit" knowledge (*Reclaiming the Tacit Dimension: Symbolic Form in the Rhetoric of Silence,* 1994). In sociolinguistics, also, there is increasing interest in studying the values of silence in particular cultures and contexts.

[3] Saville-Troike (1993) defines certain types of silences in terms of speech acts: 1) the "prosodic dimensions of silence" would include rhythmic pauses in oral and written discourse—silences that carry "meaning but not propositional content"; and 2) silences as communicative acts that carry "illocutionary force" (p. 146) within specific contexts—signifying, for instance, anything from censorship to the act of prayer.

[4] "Interchange" is the realtime conferencing module of the Daedalus writing environment.

[5] This question—what is it being used for?—is proposed by C. H. Knoblauch (1990), as it relates to literacy in general. His question is referenced frequently in Selfe and Hilligoss's *Literacy and Computers: The Complications of Teaching and Learning with Computers* (1994).

[6] This space is intentionally left blank as an invitation for readers to articulate their own thoughts about "m-words." The reader is always in the "margins," so to speak. It takes a major conceptual leap—for students, especially—to imagine having the authority to create a critique of, much less a dialogue with, texts. So, we encourage you to write in this blank space, as well as in the margins and between the lines. We hope all our thoughts will become part of a larger, richer conversational thread.

REFERENCES

Anderson, V. (1997, May). Confrontational teaching and rhetorical practice. *College Composition and Communication, 48*(2), 197–214.

Belenky, M. F., Clinchy, B. M., Goldberger, N. R., & Tarule, J. M. (1986). *Women's ways of knowing: The development of self, voice, and mind.* New York: Basic Books.

Brodkey, L. (1987). *Academic writing as social practice.* Philadelphia: Temple University Press.

Burke, K. (1969). *A grammar of motives* (Rev ed.). Berkeley, CA: University of California Press.

Cameron, D. (1992). *Feminism and linguistic theory* (2nd ed.). New York: St. Martin's Press.

Daisley, M. (1995). *Computer literacy narrative.* Unpublished essay.

Daisley, M. (1997). Silence. Silence! Silence? Silence… (An ethnographic study of "silence" in computer-mediated communication). In B. Baldwin & T. Flood (Eds.), *The rhetorical dimensions of cyberspace* [Online]. Available: http://dewey.lc.missouri.edu/rhetnet/rdc/

Dantzic, C. M. (1990). *Design dimensions: An introduction to the visual surface.* Englewood Cliffs, NJ: Prentice-Hall.

De la Croix, H., & Tansey, R. G. (Eds.). (1986). *Gardner's art through the ages* (8th ed.). New York: Harcourt Brace Jovanovich.

Eldred, J., & Fortune, R. (1990). Exploring the implications of metaphors for computer networks and hypermedia. In G. E. Hawisher & P. LeBlanc (Eds.), *Re-imagining computers and composition: Teaching and research in the virtual age* (pp. 58–74). Portsmouth, NH: Boynton/Cook.

Eldred, J., & Mortensen, P. (1992, September). Reading literacy narratives. *College English, 54*(5), 512–539.

Fishkin, S. F. (1994). Reading, writing, and arithmetic: The lessons *Silences* has taught us. In E. Hedges & S. F. Fishkin (Eds.), *Listening to silences: New essays in feminist criticism* (pp. 23–48). New York: Oxford University Press.

Foucault, M. (1978). *The history of sexuality. Vol. I: An introduction* (R. Hurley, Trans.). New York: Vintage Books.

Fraser, N. (1993). Rethinking the public sphere: A contribution to the critique of actually existing democracy. In C. Calhoun (Ed.), *Habermas and the public sphere* (pp. 109–142). Cambridge, MA: MIT Press.

Freire, P. (1993). *Literacy and the pedagogy of the oppressed.* New York: Continuum.

Haraway, D. (1989). *Primate visions: Gender, race and nature in the world of modern science.* New York: Routledge.

Haraway, D. (1991). *Simians, cyborgs, and women: The reinvention of nature.* New York: Routledge.

Hawisher, G. E. (1990). Electronic meetings of the minds: Research, electronic conferences, and composition studies. In G. E. Hawisher & P. LeBlanc (Eds.), *Re-imagining computers and composition: Teaching and research in the virtual age* (pp. 68–88). Portsmouth, NH: Boynton/Cook.

Hawisher, G. E., & Moran, C. (1993, October). Electronic mail and the writing instructor. *College English, 55*(6), 627–643.

Heath, S. B. (1990.) The fourth vision: Literate language at work. In A. Lunsford, H. Moglen, & J. Slevin (Eds.), *The right to literacy* (pp. 289–306). New York: Modern Language Association.

Hymes, D. (1974). *Foundations in sociolinguistics: An ethnographic approach.* Philadelphia: University of Pennsylvania Press.

Janangelo, J. (1991, November). Technopower and technoppression. *Computers and Composition, 9*(1), 47–64.

Kalamaras, G. (1994). *Reclaiming the tacit dimension: Symbolic form in the rhetoric of silence.* Albany, NY: State University of New York Press.

Knoblauch, C. H. (1990). Literacy and the politics of education. In A. Lunsford, H. Moglen, & J. Slevin (Eds.), *The right to literacy* (p. 75). New York: Modern Language Association.

Lakoff, G., & Johnson, M. (1980). Metaphors we live by. Chicago: University of Chicago Press.

Olsen, T. (1965). *Silences.* New York: Delacorte Press/Seymour Lawrence.

Pratt, M. L. (1991). Arts of the contact zone. *Profession, 91,* 33–40.

Romano, S. (1993, August). The egalitarianism narrative: Whose story? Which yardstick? *Computers and Composition, 10*(3), 5–28.

Saville-Troike, M. (1993). *The ethnography of communication: An introduction* (2nd ed.). Oxford, England: Blackwell.

Scott, J. W. (1988). *Gender and the politics of history.* New York: Columbia University Press.

Selfe, C. L. (1990). Technology in the English classroom: Computers through the lens of feminist theory. In C. Handa (Ed.), *Computers and community: Teaching composition in the twenty-first century* (pp. 118–139). Portsmouth, NH: Boynton/Cook-Heinemann.

Selfe, C. L. (1998, April 6). *Technology and literacy: A story about the prils of not paying attention* [Online]. Available: http:///www.ncte.ofg/forums/selfe/

Selfe, C. L., & Cooper, M. M. (1990, December). Computer conferences and learning: Authority, resistance, and internally persuasive discourse. *College English, 52*(8), 847–869.

Selfe, C. L., & Holligoss, S. (1994). *Literacy and computers: The complications of teaching and learning with computers.* New York: Modern Language Association.

Spivak, G. C. (1990). *The postcolonial critic: Interviews, strategies, dialogue* (S. Harasym, Ed.). New York: Routledge.

Takayoshi, P. (1994). Building new networks from the old: Women's experiences with electronic communications. *Computers and Composition, 11*, 21–36.

Making the Map: An Interview with Mary Lay and Elizabeth Tebeaux

Kristine Blair
Bowling Green State University

Pamela Takayoshi
University of Louisville

In this interview, Mary Lay, Professor of English at the University of Minnesota, and Elizabeth Tebeaux, Professor of English at Texas A&M University, discuss the role computer technologies have played in their collaborative relationship, detailing the way computers have changed their collaboration and their collaborative writing processes, the role technology has played in their teaching and research interests, and the historical role technology has played in the lives of women.

Kristine Blair: One of the reasons that we wanted to interview the two of you was because of the idea of online collaborations, particularly in your work in gender and technology within the realm of professional communication. So much has been said about the positive nature of technology for women, yet when you start to talk about that and put that technology in the context of women's lives, particularly in issues of professional communication, we see that those predicted benefits don't always match up. And we wanted to get a sense of what you thought about these issues, as experts in the field.

The way that we've set the text up, we talk about issues such as subjectivity online, bodies in virtual space, and with regards to your work, the notion of collaborative relationships. So we're also very interested in hearing about how the collaborative relationship that you've had has been helped, assuming that it has been helped, by these new technologies. So with that, we can begin very generally with the question of how you got involved in professional communication and how you've shifted to technology in particular.

Mary Lay: With the two of us, I think of gender and professional writing on a very broad level. We do slightly different things than Cindy [Selfe] and Gail [Hawisher]. We focus less on the computer; we focus more on historical texts. I look more at reproductive technologies. Beth looks more at recovering women's style in a historical context. My involvement in professional communication came on a very pragmatic level. I was a technical editor for IEEE and Wiley and went to graduate school in American Literature. The job market was terrible, and I resold myself as a technical communication professor. And then in 1986 I went to Stanford for an NEH summer seminar in women's history, which inspired me to focus on the connection between gender and professional writing. When computers were available at Clarkson University, where I was teaching at the time, I teamed up with a male instructor to take the basic programming class in BASIC, so that we could understand the technology and what our students were being exposed to. We had a wonderful working relationship in taking that class, doing our homework together; students were very much encouraged to collaborate. And then when Beth and I began writing together, of course, we switched disks and it made it much easier for us to collaborate in separate states. When I went to Minnesota, we continued to collaborate. It enables us to combine our different strengths. Beth does the archival research, and I do the gender theory.

KB: Yes, you just had a piece in *Journal of Advanced Composition* a couple of issues ago.

Beth Tebeaux: We're going to do another one, based on what I'm presenting here at CCCCs. Tomorrow I'm explaining historical changes in women's writing during the 17th century. This second piece will pick up where we left off.

ML: Since that time, I've been focusing on following traditional midwives in Minnesota as they go through the public hearing process to become licensed and why that failed in Minnesota, their relationship with the medical community, how birth is defined, and how technology is defined in regards to reproduction. So I guess we bring a very broad view of gender, but at the same time, I've been interested in girls and technology and what very young females experience when they first encounter the computer.

Pamela Takayoshi: Have you started doing work on that?

ML: I guess my knowledge comes not so much through my own research, but from a forum on women, girls, and technology at the University of Minnesota.

KB: That's right.

ML: I direct the Center for Advanced Feminist Studies at the university, and we have a forum every February in which this is sort of our outreach or service to the community. We invited community members to come and talk about their experiences as females encountering technology. One of the presenters talked about starting a girl's technology club on a third grade level, and videotaped interviews with how the girls felt about learning technology in an all female setting and how the boys they interacted with in a different setting reacted to this.

PT: That's a project I'm starting to work on. I've written a research proposal to get money to survey girls at the sixth grade level in the public schools in Louisville about their attitudes toward computers and then to do a follow-up interview with a group of them. There seems to me, in my personal experience, that girls really like computers a lot, then at some point, it becomes a very gendered thing for them. So they start to turn away from it, so I'm interested in that moment, of intervening in that when that happens.

ML: Well, the girls at the third grade level were very fearful of the computer. They were convinced they would break them, and they got a lot of teasing from the boys that this is not a girl's activity. But on the other hand, they used the computer in a way that I think the boys would not do. They didn't use it for games, but they set up a penpal or keypal system. They were using the computer to communicate with somebody in a different country.

KB: I wanted to follow up on that a little bit. You were mentioning the programming class. When we interviewed Helen Schwartz last fall and Gail Hawisher on Wednesday, they talk about technology in a very similar way, taking a course where in their cases, they were the only woman in that actual class. Gail was talking about PASCAL and I can't remember what program Helen was talking about. Especially given the research you're doing now with these young girls in a female setting. What was the setting you were in?

ML: The first year course was mostly business students and very mixed gender. What was interesting I think for me in working with my male colleague is that we sort of reversed what you would consider the typical gender roles. The instructor used to call John "Micro" and I was "Macro" because I could do the programming, I saw the logic of the program, I could do the flow chart, but I was sloppy and I would type "L" instead of "1," and the program wouldn't work. Whereas John came along with the details of the program, he would fix them and then the program could run. He had a hard time working out the logic of the program.

So it was an interesting sort of gender reversal for us. We brought those two strengths, and we both got A's. So it was successful, and it was a setting that was again mixed gender, though at the University it was predominantly male, and it was taught by a male instructor. But I decided to go on and take the next class, which was COBALT. And John decided not to go on, and without that collaborative opportunity, I dropped out. And I was older than the students, I couldn't find a partner to work with, and I was unable to go on because I didn't have that sense of collaboration. I'm not sure if that would have happened to a male.

KB: One of the notions we're trying to develop is this idea of collaborative relationships, but we're also trying to get a sense of your own history in the field of professional writing and technology issues, and how you got involved in that.

BT: I went to Texas A&M to work on my Ph.D. I had already done some technical writing on my second Master's. I had helped my husband, who worked with Southwestern Bell, on some procedure manuals. Texas A&M needed a technical writing teacher, so I said I'd like to do that. I started teaching and got my Ph.D. Merrill Whitburn was in charge of technical writing at this time. Merrill launched a course called "Analysis of Business and Technical Writing" to prepare teachers. I never took it. I finished my Ph.D., left for a while and then A&M hired me back. I was the only tenured Aggie in the College of Liberal Arts. I took over the program after Merrill went to RPI, and I began teaching that class, "Analysis of Business and Technical Writing." I initially thought I would continue to work some in John Donne, but I went straight into technical communication, doing courses for the business school, teaching components for the College of Engineering. It became an all-consuming task. And that's the direction my writing has taken.

I met Mary at ATTW when she was Vice President and I was member at large. We began rooming together at CCCCs. She began exploring women's issues in technical communication. I had a background in Renaissance with two theses and a dissertation, so whenever the Short Title Catalog was available on microfilm, I would read the STC, looking for examples of technical writing and found a bunch of what we call "how-to" books. I wrote 10 papers. These cover a range of topics—audience awareness (Renaissance technical writers were aware of the reading comprehension level and the information needs of their readers), format, style, the influence of Ramus, the evolution of technical description.

Then I started noticing all the books for women, many of them "how-to" books. Mary asked me if any were written by women. As a result of that question, I check and found that there were few books by women, and these were written by educated women. There were no technical books written by women. I had just finished a paper for *Written Communication* that discussed the literacy level of Renaissance middle-class women based on the technical books written for them. Mary and I did a follow-up paper on the topic for *IEEE.* That first collaborative paper led us to the *JAC* article, which discussed changes in women's style and the problems women, as writers, confronted in the Renaissance. Now that I am completing a book on the emergence of technical writing in the English Renaissance, I am moving into the last half of the 17th-century. My paper tomorrow will sketch the changes during the 1641–1700 period. Based on this new collection of technical books *by* women, we have several papers planned. One will discuss the differences in style after 1641, as compared to women's style in the Renaissance. We also want to explore the midwives' books. I have found the first proposal written by a woman. It proposes a midwives college. Since Mary is interested in the rhetorical aspect of the midwives issues, we can again combine her knowledge of women's issues and language and my knowledge of Renaissance technical writing.

I've got a book coming out on Renaissance technical writing. So now I'm in the 1640–1700 period. And this paper I'm doing tomorrow is sketching out what happened to the women as technical writers in the last half of the 17th century and the writing books that had been written by men for women. But I looked one day and I found the first technical proposal written by a women and it's for a midwives college.

ML: And at the same time I was reading one of Londa Schiebinger's books, *The Mind has No Sex,* and I said, "I just read that section where she mentions the proposal, but she doesn't do a textual analysis."

BT: And then I found the first English midwives' book written by a English woman named Anne Sharp. I found a defense this woman wrote for the proposal. She must have caught a lot of flack from the men doctors.

ML: It was unsuccessful.

BT: She was very angry. And she published about an eight-page attack on doctors. I made copies for Mary and brought it to her, saying we'll probably write an article just describing what's happened to them as women.

ML: And then we'll do one where we talk about the midwifery texts.

BT: And then probably another one where we're really going into language, which will be a companion piece to the first one.

ML: I think what we've been looking at is inclusion and exclusion, which is what I think you talk about when you're faced with women and computers. Does the technology create this utopia for women in which you have a gender-based discourse, or do women opt out of technology and technical education because of a cultural message? Were women allowed to publish, were they encouraged to write, was this a forum in which their voices were welcome? And what we found in our *Journal of Advanced Composition* article was no. They would be very careful. They would say this is for my sons, for the education of my sons. They were only allowed to function within the narrow cultural boundary that was defined for them.

BT: But then when the Civil War began, women were left to run the family businesses, the estates, and the farm, and take care of all legal aspects. So after that, the number of books by women increased dramatically. In this explosion of women's writing, there were medical books written by women, domestic medicine books. The 17th-century midwives texts show an angry group of women who resented the fact that the male physicians were trying to prevent them from practicing midwifery. While these women admitted that they did not know the technical medical jargon, as none of them had attended medical school, they did not see that they had to have the standard medical training to be effective midwives.

ML: Of course, they didn't succeed, ultimately, because once medicine became professionalized and institutionalized, women weren't allowed access to medical education. So technology has been used a lot to exclude those without power, which have been women in most settings. For example, forceps were developed, a new technology, but midwives were not allowed to use forceps, only the physicians were. Technology is being used to create boundaries, and I think that's what Cindy [Selfe] and Gail [Hawisher] have researched, and what we've found going back to those girls opting out of computers, that technology has set up a boundary and women have been left out of that access to technology. And that attitude almost becomes our cultural history, and I think that girls absorb that attitude, without even being told they can't use technology or use computers. They opt out of it, because it's not within that cultural gender role. Girls don't use computers. Like the third graders were told, this is not something they should be using anyway. But of course, they don't use it in the same way boys use it. Boys play war games, and girls use it to communicate with their keypals.

PT: There are these two commercials I saw one afternoon. The first one was a little diary for girls, a computer that if Beth had one and I had one we could send messages to each other and we could keep a shopping list and of course, it was in pastel colors. And the next commercial was for SuperNintendo and it was a boy, and it was dark and it was really energetic and he was killing those monsters, and I thought what a perfect cultural moment right there, to see the way that children on TV after school are told what's appropriate for girls and what's appropriate for boys.

KB: And the idea that that technology gets devalued. I saw a commercial for one of those personal diaries for teenage girls and the pastels, and electronic organizers are marketed toward adults as precisely that, but they're marketed to girls as your personal diary to keep all your secrets about your boyfriends and all those frivolous kinds of things. And it occurred to me as you were talking that this notion that the minute women do become associated with a particular technology, that technology becomes deskilled and devalued both economically and socially. Shoshona Zuboff talks about the typewriter and what happens when women become typewriters when it was initially a male enterprise and then the devaluation when it becomes primarily a female technology.

BT: As you may know, I have expressed some concern about the lives of women majoring in engineering. I think there's concern that some of the women don't seem to be as comfortable with all of the computer requirements as the men. Engineers are expected to have a very sophisticated level of computer skills. I don't know, we can't figure out what the problem is, why women are not comfortable with engineering.

ML: Well, it could be learning style. If you go back to that article by Turkle and Papert, where they talk about bricoleur learning style versus top-down programming learning style, if you're only teaching computers in one way, and it's not the preferred learning style of one half of your population, that population will opt out of that profession. We worried about that at Clarkson too. We were both teaching in a setting where there are a lot of technical majors, and even though women are encouraged to go into engineering, the initial hoops you have to jump through, not only computers but also math, either don't engage women or women have received a message that this is not part of the accepted gender role and opt out of it.

PT: Somebody at a session yesterday was talking about his technical writing class. He has them in groups, there's a woman in the class who is the "best" computer person, and she knows it the best of all of them. But what happens when she comes into the group is that she becomes the typewriter person. And he was talking about how she's the smartest and most capable but lets herself be put in that position, and they continually put her in that position.

ML: I teach a course on visual rhetoric where we use three software packages. We use Excel, we use SuperPaint, and we use PageMaker. So the students develop display of data, and they're designing. And it's been a real challenge for me because I have to learn the software and the programs in order to teach design principles. I tell the students this is a course in design principles, not to learn all the ins and outs of all these programs. These are simply tools. And I find a couple things. Students want to learn the tool and not the principle. And I'll typically have someone in the class who knows the tool really well.

This quarter, we just finished the winter quarter, two of the people who knew the software really well were men. And we had a battle of authority in the classroom. A student might be doing a design and he or she couldn't get SuperPaint to do what they wanted to. And the two males would want to jump up and fix the problem. And I discovered I had a number of female students who knew the program just as well. But the male students were eager to show their authority by how much they knew about that particular software. The female students knew it as well, but kept quiet about it, and solved their own problems. They didn't feel comfortable being pseudo-instructor in the classroom and doing the problem solving.

PT: I remember at one point I was at Purdue in a class with Pat Sullivan and I knew something very well. I was thinking of two things. One time, Pat asked me to demonstrate something in a computers and composition seminar we were in. And I was really flustered by it, and I really didn't do it. And she said to me afterward, well you know, I wanted you to do that because you were a woman; there were guys in the class who knew it, but they always position themselves as knowing it, and they always offer themselves as experts. And I knew you knew it just as well as they did . She was trying to give me that space, and I just felt so odd in it, because they had so clearly established by that point, and this was only 3 or 4 weeks into the semester, that they were the authorities on it. I felt as if I were sort of talking out of turn. You know, I am a person who's been working and thinking about these issues, but had not realized how I put myself in that position.

BT: When Mary and I first started working, I sent her a draft along with a number of copies of the texts I had retrieved from my research. With each one, I added a page or two explaining the historical context.

ML: Did we do that on disk the first time?

BT: No, we did not. We didn't know what we were doing. Now, we can do file transfer, because I can do FTP from my house, and you probably can too.

PT: Has technology helped your working relationship? Was it recently you did the file transfer?

ML: We exchanged disks on the last documents. We'll probably do the documents on e-mail. We used this process with the textbook I co-edited for Irwin Publishing.

PT: Could you talk about that a little bit? I'm really interested in the way that people collaborate online. It's a hard thing to negotiate.

ML: I think my co-editor and I clearly have to define our roles and what we were looking for in each iteration of the draft. We simply exchanged documents. Sometimes we would code our remarks within the draft. Say, "Look at this. I've made this change, but I'm not sure." Or she would leave a gap in the draft, and would say, "Now Mary, you fill in."

BT: In the last draft of ours, you put material and comments in brackets. I'd look at that, then make comments and then add material.

ML: Yes. The final stage, and this is where the computer does help a lot is that you've got to reestablish one voice throughout the document. So you've got to do that by making sure you're using the same vocabulary.

BT: But she and I have similar writing styles.

ML: So the computer has helped a lot, and it helped with that textbook project, too, because we had eight people, some of whom were on different coasts. My co-editor and I were sort of the clearing house. And we would receive their documents by way of disks rather than on e-mail, and then a lot of what we did was editing, trying to establish one voice. I guess what we're doing was trying to establish an anonymous voice, because we didn't want people guessing who wrote what. So and so's an expert on audience, so obviously he wrote that chapter. The eight authors had very different writing styles.

KB: Did you get any feedback from the co-authors about how they liked that online collaboration?

ML: I think they were really pleased with what we did with their manuscripts, the editing. They were surprised at how different their documents were once we took them through the editing process. So I think they relied on us more than they would have if we had not been doing this on computer, where you can do very many drafts easily. So we would have had to go back to them and say, would you make these changes, whereas we could make the changes, and it was much easier for us. I think that's why they were surprised at how the chapters eventually looked.

PT: *Computers and Composition* has an article of mine. They're getting ready to publish it, so they sent me this e-mail recently that was very long, a big piece of mail, and every paragraph started: "On page 4, in paragraph two, sentence starts… We've changed it so that it reads…," and they would be pretty minute changes, not meaning changes, but style changes. And they would ask for my approval on every change, which I thought was an interesting sort of respect, but on the other hand, I thought just do it. I don't have time to read this 800-line message.

BT: File transfer is the way to go. Just ship it. Mary's the Mac person and I'm the IBM person, and with Word you can save it whatever way you want. If I save it as a Mac file, then I can transfer it to her. That will be the best way to do it and save on all that postage.

ML: I think the technology has made it easier for us to work, to have more projects going at the same time. We also e-mail, and use the phone too.

BT: She did the final draft of the last paper. So far, the decision of who does the final draft depends on our schedules. I did the first one, and she did the second one. However, we did the final editing by e-mail. For example, if she had questions about names, titles, etc., she would e-mail me. This is becoming a standard way of developing material. Richard Gebhardt has an anthology that's being published by

Erlbaum on composition and tenure criteria. Each author sent him a disk after each paper was accepted and revised. As he would edit our revisions, he would e-mail us queries to find out what each of us could live with and what wording we simply could not accept.

ML: I think the computer has allowed us to network in a way that may be the old boys networked functioned before, they might have dominated the conferences or the associations, exchanged ideas and created opportunities for themselves. We can network and collaborate just as easily long distance.

BT: It occurred to me, during our many phone conversations, that we can do a midwives' paper, and then a general one of changes in women's style and voices in the late 17th century. I imagine that we will approach these in the same way we have approached the first two. But collaboration will be easier now that we have established a pattern that works for us. Both of us are compartmental thinkers. We organize our writing about headings and subheadings. That enables us to exchange material and "fill in" and revise. We also use different fonts so we can see who has added what information.

KB: So then you think the computer has helped you in doing that? Particularly since you're a visual thinker, helped you in getting your drafts done, not just in actually producing them, but in using the technology to solve a rhetorical problem?

BT: I guess so. I think what's helped me more than anything is figuring out what I was doing as far as the historical research. I've learned a lot since 1990 or 1989, when I started my technical communication history projects. And working with Mary has helped. But I can now sit down, and I know what I'm doing. When we first started, I don't think we were sure what we were doing. But you still have to start somewhere. Word processing gives you a way to articulate your thoughts and change them quickly. Collaboration is a form of thinking.

ML: I think I write better now that the computer is available. Because when I first started trying to write articles in 1976, I wrote them out by hand, and then I would type them on the typewriter, and as I was typing, I would edit. I guess I write more in chunks too. Because when I write a paragraph, I'll look at it, I'll play with it, I'll rearrange it. So I'll also keep a bibliography going at the same time. So when I'm finished with the paper, I'm finished with the bibliography. So I'll have a couple files that I'm working on. I can see that finished product that I'm pretty satisfied with, even if it's just the first paragraph. And then when I come back to the manuscript and do the next section, I'll read through what I've done, and it's fairly polished and it gives me a lot of confidence to begin the next section. Whereas looking at a handwritten draft, or cut-and-paste typewriter draft, it would still look unfinished and unclear to me. With the computer, it really looks like I have a thought or an argument going on.

BT: Last time we had trouble with the introduction. And I wrote something, and you wrote something, and we had taken something out and put something in. And we just kept doing that.

ML: So I guess it helps to negotiate, whereas without the technology one voice might dominate. So it helps us negotiate on a very small level, on a sentence or word level.

BT: But she does most of the gender stuff. I know just enough to be dangerous.

ML: And I know enough to say we better not say all males, or all females. You know, this is a matter of difference; we better say this woman more clearly identified herself with the traditional gender roles assigned to females, and this one resisted that role.

BT: So what I do is work on the history, and lay that out, and I can spot certain things. And Mary articulates what's going on in terms of current theory.

ML: And again, we can bring two specialties to the project and merge them to come up with a text that represents recovering historical texts and gender theory at the same time. And it would be pretty hard for one person to do that.

ML: Beth and I only see each other once a year. It would be very hard to be collaborators without the relationship to the computer, e-mail, exchange of disks, sort of the merging of both our voices.

KB: It's really interesting to hear you talk about this, because Pam and I have been collaborating on things for a couple of years. Initially, I think our collaborations were easy because we were at Purdue together, and now we're in very different parts of the country, so we do a lot of stuff online. And I don't think because we're so new at it that we've articulated how we collaborated. It's making me think that one of the things we can address when we write the introduction for this book, and we're going to have to write a pretty weighty introduction, is how we've collaborated on this book, and how technology has fostered that collaboration. It's interesting to hear you talk about this.

BT: Technology can allow interesting forms of collaboration. Word 6.0 and Word for Windows 95 have a revision feature under "Tools." This is extremely useful in some situations. For example, I am currently working on a paper with Linda Driskill at Rice. Because we currently have very incompatible schedules, we work on the draft separately. That is, we developed a draft together, but as we complete and revise it, we have to work separately. We use the highlight and revisions feature to add and edit. Linda leaves me an e-mail that she has worked on the draft. When I turn on the computer, I can see exactly what she has done. She also leaves any comments or explanations in brackets. I then add information and my own notes to her.

Sometimes we don't see each other for two weeks, but we are nevertheless collaborating via the capabilities the software provides. Again, Linda and I have similar styles and processes, but technology enables us to work despite schedule problems. In short, technology can be useful in a number of ways—when authors are in the same school or in different regions of the country.

PT: It's interesting to think of the text growing without both of its authors there.

KB: Very virtual.

BT: But it's very neat. Because she'll put up a little sticker and say please note the strikeout and highlighted material. If you like it, let's keep it. Because you have to save or reject all changes. What I may do is move a section totally out on the hard disk, then copy and work on it, then I go back and reinsert it.

PT: It sounds like that collaboration is very similar to your collaboration with Mary. Those kinds of collaborations require a certain kind of personality who's comfortable not seeing somebody. And I wonder if you all have tried to collaborate with people with whom it was not as easy a task because they felt they needed to be face to face or whatever.

ML: To me it would be a matter of trust. When I work with Beth, I trust that she's doing her part and working.

BT: Which I always do.

ML: And if I didn't have that trust, I would be more reluctant to rely on the technology. I would be more insistent that we meet and sort of display what we've done and confirm that we're both committed to this. So maybe it's a matter of our having a relationship before we started to write. Because we were working together and we were friends before we started to write.

BT: And she knows that if I say, I'm going to do this, it's going to be done. If something comes up, I call her and let her know. If she has a problem, she lets me know. I mean, we just do it.

ML: So in a way we can use the technology because we were already connected as friends, and the technology enables us to remain connected because this manuscript is going, and the e-mail is going back and forth. Now I've had collaborative projects with men, I was thinking, now is this gendered? I'm not sure. Bill Karis and I did a collection together on collaborative writing. And I think that was a successful working relationship. I liked the product. We enjoyed working with each other. But I think we had more of a division of labor. He sort of took one half, and I had the other half of the book, and we went off and did our own editing. But when we wrote the section openings together, we actually sat in front of the computer and wrote those. He was a faster typist; for that reason he was doing the typing, and I was sitting next to him. I mean I don't sense that these two projects were different because Bill is male and Beth is female. I'm not sure that gender made any difference.

BT: But with that project, you had different chapters in the book. And it might have been easier just to say you're identifying more with A, G, and F, for example, and Bill identifying with the others. If we were doing something like, we might do it that way. You might say, okay I can work with this essay, because I'm more into this subject, and whatever.

ML: So it's a different kind of collaboration. But when we're creating one document between the two of us.

PT: I like that image of the way you describe writing the document together. It makes me think of the way I work with Kris. All the chunks, something about putting the chunks together. There's something very neat visually for me in that image.

BT: Lots of times I send Mary texts to read. I find them interesting and know that they will mean more to her because of her background in gender theory. Many of the texts I found that I knew were important—like writings by Elizabeth I when she was young girl and then when she was Queen—I did not know how to assess in terms of gender theory. However, Mary knows exactly what to do with the material. As you may have guessed, we are good friends. During our conversations, we always discuss our research. I think it's often difficult to separate our work from our friendship. I think it's the friendship that makes the work rewarding.

ML: Well, we did not place the article enough in the conversation about gender. We didn't acknowledge some of the questions and the battles being raised. So our manuscript was too discrete. So what we had to do was to sort of put it in the context of the debate about difference.

BT: Now's the first time I understand it.

PT: But do you really buy it, Beth?

(Laughter)

BT: I just read it. I'm really more interested in historical things. I had found texts written about people and by people that nobody has ever discussed. I'm really more of an archivist.

ML: And when I put in my interpretation of the text...

BT: Those people become alive. I'm interested in them as artifacts. She puts faces on them. That's probably the difference. I really like digging around finding things. Mary makes the text live.

PT: I really like the way you compliment each other.

BT: I call her and say, "Guess what I found today?" And she says, "Hey, that's really neat." We start talking about it. I remember the day I called her and said, "I have these books that have sections for men and sections for women." She asked, "Are there any differences?" The phone conversations we've had led to the rest of it.

KB: I wanted to pick back up on a point that you had made, Mary, about different learning styles of students and recognizing that when you're trying to introduce students to technology, you have to employ that. So I guess I'm wondering what strategies you might use. Because one of our questions is how you make technology and computers and the field of professional communication more accessible for students, particularly women students. Are there things you do in your classroom and in your pedagogy that help the students engage in the kind of collaborative relationship you have that seems so valuable, and to use technology as a tool in fostering that collaboration?

ML: So you want to talk about collaboration. When you first started that question, I didn't link it to collaboration.

KB: It could, but it doesn't necessarily need to.

ML: When I teach my course, Visual Rhetoric, I think what helps engage students, no matter what their preferred learning style, is that they do a lot of work in the classroom with the computers right there. So that enables me to go from student to student, and work with them and try to figure out how they're going to solve the problem I've given them in whatever way they prefer. Some students want to be left alone. I go over to them, and say, "How are you doing?" And they say, "Fine." Sort of "Go away." Other students want me to approve what they're doing so far. Other students will do a thumbnail sketch, and then transfer it to the computer. It's going to be a finished product, and the computer is just going to finish it a little bit further. And other students are sort of like those bricoleurs with lots of tiny sketches, and that's going to build up to the whole thing on the computer. So that's one way, whereas, if you want to talk about collaboration in the computer lab.

KB: Well the reason I put it in that way, just in having taught technical communication for a few years, I know that so many of the projects end up being collaborative.

BT: At Rice, in this capstone course, I have 21 students in there. And so for the white paper topics, which are quite hard, I put them in collaborative teams of two. And I have more men than I do women. I have four male/female teams out of 10, and I have one of two women, and the rest men. So there are five all-male teams. And there's one student working by himself because he's the 21st, and because of his work schedule that would work better. I don't have a problem with that.

What I told them is you have to figure out what you're going to propose as a project, and how you're going to handle it in the proposal, setting up the research, who's going to do what. And I had them turn in drafts of the proposal, and it was evident that they had figured out whose part was what. And they had figured out, with everything else that they were doing at Rice, that they were going to have to have very strict divisions of labor. And I said, "Fine, if you want to do that, that's fine. But then at some point, after you get the material, you're going to have to smooth out the difference." And those kids were very smart and said they understood. And when the proposals came in, by the final draft, you couldn't tell who had written them. Initially, I know from their drafts, they had who was going to do what, and you could see that they had sat down in the lab and they had done parts of it.

PT: And then did they do a successful job in the final document?

BT: Yes, and when it all came in, if I hadn't looked just to grade them, I wouldn't have known which were done by the male teams and which were done by the female teams. I knew one female team, because those two women are just incredible, and I have two men who work together who are just incredible. Just the way these kids, who are very bright seniors, handle their content is great. They seem to figure it out. I didn't give them that much instruction, just let them see what they could come up with.

ML: I think when we set up collaborative groups in our writing courses, they use the computer for different things, for communication via e-mail and for collaborating. Our computers are networked, and we can create a group file for them. They can drop a draft in and their collaborator can pull it out. I'm trying to think of gender differences I observe in the classroom as students collaborate. I think sometimes if you have a group of all women, they might enjoy sitting down and collaborating and printing the draft. The computer enables them to do that, not to work in isolation, to work to be connected. So if there is a difference, if you want to engage students no matter what their learning style, I think the computer makes it easier particularly if they're collaborating. I don't know if that's getting at what you were asking.

KB: It was just one of the things we're very interested in because it ties back into the earliest discussion we had about making technology accessible to women and girls. I wanted to ask Beth, because one thing we hadn't talked about is what sort of access your students at Rice have. I was wondering to what extent they were working online?

BT: I noticed what they did was they would come in at the beginning of class and one of them would say, here's the disk and it's clear what I've done and pass it to the partner. And one would say, "Okay, I'm gonna do this and I'll have this back to you." So what they're doing is that they're really doing one document. And they're working kind of like Mary and I do, deciding who does what.

PT: One of things that I think, the comment you made just a minute ago, Mary, about how women collaborate. I think there are people who will say women are more likely to collaborate, but I'm not sure that is. Because I have worked with women who I just can't collaborate with. So I don't think it's anything in women necessarily that allows them to collaborate more than men do.

One thing that I have thought quite a bit about is how computers have connected women, or have allowed women to form alliances or coalitions with people that they might not otherwise have. And I was thinking about that earlier, when you, Beth, were interested in recovering women's texts, and Mary is interested in analyzing them in terms of other social factors, and how that's such a powerful form of collaboration and alliance. And how women have been historically kept separate. Because at one time we're talking about the old boys club.

ML: I think your observation is correct in terms of empowerment. I mean Beth and I might have done one article together, and say "Boy, that was really hard. We had to retype that draft a lot of times and we spent a lot of time on the phone. And this would only work if we could sit down together and do it." But I think we've been able to produce because we could rely on the technology, again drawing on two specialties, that wouldn't be possible because of distance, or wouldn't be possible because of effort that it would take without technology.

BT: We were talking to a publisher about putting a managerial communications book together in the same way. You do a part; I do a part. And I told Mary, "I'd like you to come to College Station because in our study at home, we have two computers." She could work on one computer and I could work on another. And we could write and revise quickly.

ML: So even in a face-to-face situation we would still use the technology.

PT: Has it strengthened your personal relationship? You knew each other well, initially. Do you feel like you've become friends during this?

ML: I think so. To me, it's sort of a gift that Beth gives to me periodically. You call me up and say, "We've got another opportunity to work with each other." And it's also strengthening confidence, because you think an idea is neat, but if you've got somebody else who says I think this is a great idea, and I'm willing to make the investment, then you have the confidence to go ahead. I guess the answer to your question is yes, I think it has strengthened our friendship to be able to do these projects.

BT: And another thing, I'm into distance education, and I found this article that said that women do better in distance education. And I called Mary and I said, "My women made more A's than the men did."

ML: That's in an article she just published in *TCQ.*

BT: I didn't even think of this until then; I just went back and looked at my grades for last spring and last fall, and the women are making the better grades.

ML: We're of another generation though, and it's going to be interesting when the next generation comes along. We educated ourselves as adults to use the computer, and at that point, at least in my experience with John, the man I took the computer course with, we were both equally awed by the computer, and we were committed to learning the computer and we learned it. If you said to me, during that same year, you're going to have to learn calculus to use it, I don't think I would have overcome that barrier because I learned early on when I was in my teens, that I was not going to go into the world of calculus very easily. So I don't know what it's going to be like as the generation of young girls who may have good or bad experiences with the computer in elementary school come along, if they're going to be more or less comfortable.

BT: What I've noticed in the business schoools is that the accounting students in the 150-hour program all seem to be comfortable with the technology. They must use it in their accounting courses. If they can't, or don't want to use it, then they have to leave the program. Right now, Texas A&M's professional program in accounting has more women than men—about 60 percent are women.

KB: So in some sense the technology is necessary for their economic and social success.

BT: Yes, or you can't major in accounting. Accounting is not cookbook and paper. Accounting is technology, so you either do it, or you get out.

PT: Maybe their gendering comes before they made that decision.

ML: And we don't know how many students said, "I can't do this," even though they may have had the ability, or had gotten out of the field, or didn't elect that field.

BT: Yes. The accounting students in the professional program have to make the decision by the end of their sophomore year. If they stay on the fast track, they have to enjoy hard work and rapid learning. The accounting firms do not want to spend time training people who are not really interested in a career in accounting. However, technology is becoming more crucial to tax and auditing. Students who don't understand the role of technology and understand how to use it simply do not belong in those fields.

PT: So now that computers are part of life, you think about how do women use computers, not whether or not they do. But why are there very few women computer engineers or scientists, but a lot of women writing teachers?

BT: In public schools today, students are having to become computer literate. Then in college, in business schools, all students have required computer classes. Business computing science is required by the accrediting agency for the schools of business. For that reason, I don't think in 10 years this problem of women not being comfortable with the technology will be an issue. There are too many women majoring in business.

KB: I think one of the constraints of this fact, the impact of technology on our economic and social status, is that it gets back to that notion of students viewing technology as a commodity and not necessarily something to solve problems, to be part of that problem-solving process. In that sense, I see that as a real constraint. And I was looking at these questions really quickly, and I guess that in some sense, we've covered many of the issues. I think we'd also like to address the question of possibilities and constraints, sort of hinting at that as a sense of closure, Mary. And Beth, you just said in a few years that you think it's not going to be as big of an issue as it is now. And I wonder if we could conclude with that?

PT: And what changes have you seen since you've started and what about the future, which is sort of the same question?

BT: I see everybody getting more comfortable with technology. Technology is in everything. There's software for every profession. I just see people getting used to it. I have two sons who hate computers. But they realize if you're going to get an MBA, you have to be in the peer group. So they're doing it.

ML: I really do believe it's easier to collaborate and easier to ask students to collaborate because we have computers. That's much, much easier. I guess I remain suspicious because it's not so much a matter of gender; it's a matter of access. Technology is being used to draw that boundary between the empowered and the nonempowered so often that it doesn't look neutral ever to me. So possibilities and constraints computer technologies have for women, I guess it's a matter of how the computer is being used and if everyone has access to it, or if it becomes a limited commodity. Whenever you have a limited commodity, you have groups defining the other as not having access to that technology.

BT: But if a student is going to major in business at X school, all students in that major have the same access.

ML: But there are a limited number of seats, and who are you going to exclude and how are you going to exclude them? And who are you going to welcome, and how are you going to describe the typical user? Is it going to be a white male, or is it going to be an anonymous person?

BT: What happens is that they register online and they close the class when the class is full. And they know how many seats they have in the lab, and it's first come, first serve. And the people who get to register first are the honor students. I don't think it's any kind of deliberate exclusionary thing. Resources will be limited. It's going to be first come, first served.

ML: Well, I don't know. Here's where we may disagree slightly. As I was driving somewhere this week, I was listening to the radio. And there was an announcement that the phone company, US West, in Minneapolis, was giving free voice mail to a certain number of homeless people in the Twin Cities who were looking for jobs so that they there would be a place to leave them messages and they could have a specific announcement on that voice mail, and they could pick up their messages. And I was thinking what a wonderful thing, how difficult it is to look for a job if there's no way you can be contacted.

And at the same time, I was also wondering how they were going to decide who was going to have access to that free voice mail, how long it was going to last, and how many people wouldn't have access and be able to take advantage of that because there would only be a limited number. I guess I'm still suspicious there will be a gap between those who have access to technology and those who don't have access and how that gap is defined. Who's empowered and who isn't? I don't know. It could be along gender lines, it could be along class lines, it could be along race lines, it could be, as Beth is saying, along the lines of the more capable and the less capable, but how are capabilities established? Are they innate?

BT: You're talking about how people learn technologies, and I thought you were talking about learning technologies in school. And if someone is admitted to the business school and you want a degree in any of the business majors, you have to take these computer courses. They're offered at certain times, and you have to register by phone, and you give them your number, and when the class is full, they shut it off. And you have to do this.

ML: But how is the computer taught within those classes?

BT: It depends on who is teaching the class. The methodologies differ depending on who is teaching. And there are some excellent women teachers and excellent men teachers. I know people who have great reputations, male and female. So to me sometimes people don't do well because of none of the things that we've talked about, but because they've taken too many hours, they may be trying to work and go to school. I don't know if you can look at their grades and see that there's a difference.

ML: Well, when I was looking at collaboration and gender in general, I looked at the students' journals and how they particularly dealt with conflict, a lot of the choices they made related to how they saw themselves fitting according to gender roles. So if a female student wanted to assert herself, she might say in her journal, "I would have said that, but I didn't want to be thought of as a bitch," for example. So she didn't see as part of the accepted gender role for women to be that assertive. So I guess I see the cultural message being stronger and potentially more interfering with that type of free choice.

KB: Well, thank you so much.

ML: I hope we were coherent.

PT: We'll take the transcript and then edit and send both of you copies of it, where you'll have the opportunity to add something in or take something out.

ML: As you listen to the interviews, if you see other connections between the interviews, you can pose more questions.

KB: We could even do something like that over e-mail.

BT: The last editor at *TCQ*, Laurie Gardner, was just wonderful at using e-mail to clarify editing problems in papers. When Laurie was working on the paper that I coauthored with Jimmie Killingsworth, she would e-mail me queries. I remember asking her about sentences that didn't seem familiar. However, I could see that the edited sentence, usually Mary's version, was much better than mine. I don't worry about that. Again, my concern is analyzing the original texts. I'm entirely flexible about how we handle the final text. Sometimes Mary helps me when I'm struggling with sentences and paragraphs. I think we help each other. As you know, when you work on something long enough, you lose objectivity. Mary is a great editor.

ML: Well, that's another thing that makes it easy for us to collaborate. I don't sense ownership of words, and I don't sense sort of the competition, as in I've got to be first author or I've got to have the last draft.

BT: And a lot of people do that. They have an ego thing going on. Mary and I don't have a political agenda. We are both interested in the texts.

PT: I think that's what's happened with Kris and me. Whoever has the time at that moment when it needs to be done is the person, because we both have so many things going on. Whoever can put it on the top of the stack first is the one who gets to do it.

ML: But again, I think it's a matter of trust. I think you have to have a basis established before you rely on the technology to enhance the collaboration, before you collaborate to begin with.

BT: And I have never written anything that couldn't be better. And after I write something and it's published, I never even look at it again. When I was putting my dossier together for promotion, I went "Oh my God."

KB/PT/ML: I know!

ML: Well, it's sometimes embarrassing to go back to something you said 10 years ago, and you no longer believe that. But I like to look at Sandra Bem's, the development, first she had the Bem sex role inventory.

KB: I used that in a study once.

ML: Do you like warm fuzzy things or do you like a truck or something? And for awhile, she said here are male traits and here are female traits. Then she said, "Let's look at androgyny, we all have these traits within us, and you can bring them out," and then she took another step back, and said, no, some males buy more into that definition of masculinity than other males, and so on.

BT: But that's just knowledge, knowledge she has gone through.

ML: And you see that progression of learning, and you say, okay, nobody will hold me to what I said in the 70s.

PT: How nice though. Because I was thinking of that with the two of you when you were talking about your articles coming up. What a nice progression and how nice that everything seems to build on each other.

BT: I've figured out today that we're going to do two. We're going to do an emphasis on the midwifery, and then we are going to do one that's a continuation of what we already did. And I'm going to do one that's laying out the whole thing.

ML: Well, you know the reason we can do this is that the academy is more accepting of collaborative pieces in the field. And without that it would have been impossible.

BT: But I just realized that I've got no axe to grind. I was in a meeting because we're about to do the ninth edition to *Reporting Technical Information.* I talked to my co-author who said we have to do this, we have to do this, and I said fine.

PT: You could just drive yourself crazy if you try to hold on to every idea.

BT: We talked about the limits of it. You don't want the book to be a mismatch. We told this editor to just tell us what the research says needs to be there for this particular kind of book, and we'll just do it.

PT: I know that sometimes I have written text, and just love the introduction, fall in love with it. And I just leave it there, and refuse to let it go. And finally I cut it, and all this stuff just falls. And I'm trying to be better about letting those perfect introductions go. At some point, maybe I thought I'd write an article of all my perfect introductions, just so they could be done.

ML: Well, good luck on your presentations this afternoon.

KB: Thanks again for everything.

Map of Location V

The Future: To Be Mapped Later

chapter 13

Feminist Research in Computers and Composition

Lisa Gerrard
University of California, Los Angeles

Feminist research would do for computers and composition what Elizabeth Flynn (1991) says a feminist critique of composition studies should do for composition generally: 1) identify androcentrism, which she defines as "ignorance of women's different epistemological perspective and of women's subordinate position in society" (p. 143); and 2) introduce a female epistemological perspective. With these goals in mind, I have identified four areas within computers and writing that offer feminist researchers substantial opportunities for study. Ultimately, such studies might show us how our male and female students are learning in the computer-based writing course and teach us how to make our classrooms friendlier and more productive places for everyone. They might also clarify our professional practice outside the classroom.

The first section of this chapter begins by looking at the broader context in which computer-based writing takes place—the world of computers, which, despite a vigorous community of "net chicks" ("It's about being a grrrl with a capital R-I-O-T"; Sinclair, 1996, p. 6), is still very much a man's world. It suggests that researchers consider how students may be influenced by this association of computers with masculinity and raises questions for investigating this influence. The second section describes some of the ways computers might be fostering or undermining a feminist pedagogy—defined as a pedagogy that connects personal experience with political knowledge, reduces hierarchical relationships in the classroom, promotes collaboration, validates women's experiences, and offers a forum for women's voices. This section suggests ways researchers might study different computer-based practices and tools to determine which ones support feminist goals and which may not. The third section outlines some of the theories advanced by feminist linguists and psychologists about how men and women learn, think, write, and converse. It argues that the computerized writing classroom provides unique opportunities to test these theories, and poses questions for further study. The last section moves away from the classroom and toward the broader profession of computers and composition studies, describing how some of our scholarly interests and ways of interacting with colleagues appear to be gender-linked, and identifying issues for future research into gendered practice in the computers and writing community. In all four sections, I discuss past studies that feminist researchers might want to build on, challenge, or incorporate into their own work. As is inevitable in such a multidisciplinary field as computers and writing, these studies cover a range of interests, from boys' and girls' preferences in software design to academics' interactions on professional listservs. Feminist research in computers and writing thus offers substantial opportunities for discovery.

COMPUTER CULTURE: THE SOCIAL CONTEXT FOR OUR TEACHING

The Male Image of Computers

Computers have long been perceived as male machines, and computer culture as an exclusive boys club. This perception is not surprising, given the modern computer's origins—the largely male enterprise of warfare. The first modern computer, the British Colossus, was designed in 1943 to decode German radio transmissions; in the 1940s, the first computer in the United States, the ENIAC, calculated ballistic tables for bombing targets; and the Internet, launched by the Department of Defense in 1969, was meant to save information that would be lost if the military's computers were destroyed. In recent decades, the civilian image of the computer user has remained that of the adolescent male hacker, despite the existence of a small, but feisty, female hacker underground (Romero, 1993).[1] Since the early 1980s, studies of computers and gender have indicated that computer culture is still seen as a male preserve. An analysis of computer advertisements found images of confident male executives interpreting computer output and women as typists, computer phobics, and bimbos (Marshall & Bannon, 1988). Studies of the computer industry have portrayed a workplace hostile to female computer professionals, who, as in other technical fields, receive less pay, less responsibility, fewer opportunities to advance, and overt harassment (Frenkel, 1990; Hornig, 1984). In the computer industry, women have occupied the bottom of the hierarchy; according to a 1990 study by the U.S. Department of Labor, 91 percent of the data entry operators—the least-skilled workers in the industry—were women, whereas only 32 percent of the programmers and 30 percent of the systems analysts were women (Goff, 1990).[2] For the most part, men have designed the new technologies; women have simply "push[ed] buttons" ("Technology Jobs," 1993). In cyberspace, men outnumber women about 3 to 1 (Maier, 1995); Nancy Tamosaitis's 1995 survey, run by CompuServe, found that 92 percent of the Internet population consisted of men; a 1996 study by the Georgia Institute of Technology found that males constituted 69 percent of the users of the World Wide Web (see "On Line," 1996). Sexist jokes, pornography, stories of "cyber-cads," sexual harassment, stalking, torture and rape fantasies, and even an online rape send the message that virtual reality is a male reality.

In practice, women have always been important in the computer industry—in the 1840s, Augusta Ada Lovelace invented the algorithm and became the first programmer; in the 20th century, the "ENIAC girls" programmed the first modern computer, Admiral Grace Hopper invented COBOL, and Roberta Williams wrote the first adventure games. Women have long been computer users, a fact computer marketers have finally begun to notice. In 1992, Apple began to advertise in *Parenting, House Beautiful,* and *Sunset* magazines; in 1993, Compaq advertised in *Mirabella, Self,* and *Working Woman.* Market researchers are discovering that women have considerable buying power: In 1995, women constituted 37 percent of the buyers of computer equipment for business and made 47 percent of the buying decisions for the home market—percentages that have been growing each year (Kondo, 1995).[3] Counting on the increasing number of women buying personal computers and modems, magazines such as *Self, Woman's Day, Elle,* and *New Woman* have made themselves available in online versions. Hundreds of websites, newsgroups, and listservs cater specifically to girls and women of all tastes, interests, and attitudes—to name a handful, Women's Studies, Parent Soup, Feminist Majority, Nancy Drew, GeekGirl, Heartless Bitches International. Nevertheless, the dominant *image* of computing is masculine: "Computers are power, and power, in our world, must be the realm of men" (Coyle, 1996, p. 43).

What matters for us here is that this perception pervades the social context in which we teach. As compositionists, we might study how this cultural schema affects our students' work. Does the image of the computer as a male technology make men initially more comfortable and women less so in a computer-dominated classroom? Or does the neutral—possibly feminized—ground of composition neuter this image? Many compositionists have described composition as a feminized field. Elizabeth Flynn (1988) notes the preponderance of female researchers in the development of the discipline, as well as the image of the composition teacher as a nurturing mother, "concerned about the growth and maturity of her students, who provides feedback on ungraded drafts, reads journals, and attempts to tease out meaning from the seeming incoherence of student language" (p. 424). Similarly, Cynthia Tuell (1993) compares her job as compositionist to the midwife's, "to provide a generative atmosphere in which to assist and encourage [students] as they give birth to themselves as authors" (pp. 134–135). Susan Miller (1991) sees the image of composition instructor not only as mother and nurse, but also as a sadomasochistic disciplinarian, with "enormous capacities for untheorized attention to detail" (p. 46). When a masculinist icon like the computer (*Time* magazine's 1982 "Man of the Year") is joined with a feminist and feminized pedagogy, does it lose its masculine associations? What preconceptions of computers do students have when they enter our courses, and do these conceptions change over the academic term?

Students' Past Computer Experience

Another issue that may affect our students' performance in computer-based writing classes is prior access. Students' first sustained encounter with computers is likely to be games—games designed for boys. A game like *Night Trap*—described on the package as "five beautiful coeds ... being stalked on an eerie estate"—is not going to appeal to girls. The subject of most games is not so much violence against women, but violence in general—shoot-'em-ups of one kind or another. But it's not just the violence that repels girls, it's the design of these games. The very characteristics that attract boys repel girls, the focus on rules and winning, for example. According to game theorists, boys like rules and are energized by competition, whereas girls prefer to bend rules and generally avoid competitive games. In addition, boys find the quick, reflexive action exciting; girls like to take their time; boys like the rigid structure (if you lose, you "die"); girls find it constraining; boys are challenged by the redundancy of these games (if you fall off a cliff, you start over); girls get bored and quit (Jacobs, 1994). Not surprisingly, 75 percent of all video games are purchased for boys. One researcher argues that video games develop depth perception and spatial reasoning skills, which prepare boys to use other computer applications. Thus, video games are helping boys to become adept with computers, while girls are being left behind (Pereira, 1994).

Some game manufacturers, however, have tried to appeal to girls. Some games reinforce female stereotypes, such as *Barbie Super Model* (High Tech Entertainment), in which the user puts makeup on Barbie, follows her to the mall for a date with Ken, and walks her on a fashion show runway; or *Girls' Club* (Philips), where the user chooses her "dream date" from a set of boys' heads that pop up on a slot machine (Jacobs, 1994). Others are less stereotypical: the CD-ROM adventure *Hawaii High: Mystery of the Tiki* has two girls working together to solve a mystery (Colker, 1994); *My Computer Diary for Windows* (Stone and Associates) has players create a diary and a password to protect it; *Hello Kitty Big Fun Storymaking* (Big Top Productions) helps children tell stories (Perenson, Ehrenman, & Brown, 1994); the *Berenstein Bears* (Sega) allows the player to choose between male and female characters; and *Chop Suey* and *Smartypants* (Theresa Duncan) follow young girls on an adventure in a small town, where they explore a root cellar, watch 1930s cartoons, make jewelry, and act in the school play. But because boys won't play girls games, historically the market for these products has been small. According to Nancy Chodorow (1978), boys learn to define masculinity negatively, as that which is not feminine, and thus avoid activities noticeably earmarked for girls. Some of the earliest feminist games—*Jenny of the Prairie*, *Cave Girl Clair*, *Kristen and her Family*, and *Sara and her Friends*—were history games, intended to teach history and map-reading and note-taking skills. Developed in the mid-1980s, these products were intended as an alternative to the alien attack and war games, but they did not stay in print long. As I write, however, the market for girls' games is gaining new life. Sega of America has a Girls Task Force to develop products for girls; e-Girl Interactive is designing software with the kind of reward system they believe will appeal to girls, games in which girls play socially rather than competitively. In 1995, software developer Laura Groppe studied girls' computer use and found that girls use computers for briefer periods than boys do and prefer to do something useful as well as entertaining. She started the company Girl Games and developed the CD-ROM *Let's Talk About Me* for 8- to 14-year-olds, which departed from industry practice by having girls give their input throughout development of the product rather than testing it when completed. *Let's Talk About Me* allows players to keep a scrapbook, meet others from around the world, and hear successful women (for example, author Maya Angelou, Senator Dianne Feinstein, designer Kate Spade) talk about their teenage years (Becklund, 1996). In its first eight months on the market, *Let's Talk About Me* sold half a million copies (Corley, 1997). Believing that girls games can make a significant dent in the software market, the companies Purple Moon, Her Interactive, and Girl Tech, all founded in 1997, are developing computer adventures that focus on sharing information, resolving problems, building relationships, and competing in a friendly way—strategies they believe will appeal to girls.

Games matter because they are teaching a whole generation of children about computers. If girls don't play games, they may come into our classrooms with little prior computer experience. Several studies have shown that fewer young girls than boys use computers: parents are more likely to buy computers for their sons than their daughters, and send three times as many boys as girls to computer camp (Hess & Miura, 1985). In school, girls get less hands-on experience, less attention, and easier assignments than boys do (Levin & Gordon, 1989; Lewis, 1985). Furthermore, before fourth grade, girls and boys are equally excited about computers, but with every year after that, girls develop an increasing aversion to the technology. By high school, they are seldom found in the advanced math courses, where most computer instruction takes place (Abtan, 1993). Few women major in technological fields in college, and those who do find a cold reception (Dain, 1991; Frenkel, 1990).

Given this social context, researchers might find out what our male and female students know about computers when they enter our classes. They might survey high school and college students to find out if they have a computer at home, and, if so, if they use it; if they've had any formal computer training and if so, where and what kind; whether they play computer games; what attitudes they hold toward computers and what their experiences with the technology have been like. The research from the late 1980s and early 1990s suggested that our female students come to us with an experience deficit; is this still the case? Few female college students take the advanced math and engineering courses that require extensive computer work, so we might ask graduating students if their computer-based writing classes offered them hands-on experience they might not have had otherwise.

If the computer-based writing class is a student's first extended encounter with computers, developing control over the machine can give her confidence and a sense of belonging in a potentially alien place. When students enter a computer-equipped classroom, they confront a world that is doubly male: 1) the masculinist computer world, and 2) academia, a patriarchal institution dominated by a male professoriate and infused with competitive and hierarchical values. M. K. Cayton (1990) points out that men entering college are likely to think of themselves as apprentices "mastering a process that will allow them to contribute to a generalized body of knowledge," whereas women are more likely to perceive themselves as outsiders "with misgivings about entering the circle of the elect" (p. 333). If women are already predisposed to feel like outsiders in academia, does the computer-based writing class make them feel even more alienated? Or does it help integrate them into academic culture?

FACILITATING A FEMINIST PEDAGOGY

Connecting Personal Experience with Political Awareness

Another area to research is how we might use computers to support a feminist pedagogy and to what extent we are already doing so. Feminist pedagogy guides students to reflect on their lives and to connect personal experience with ideology and social issues. Early consciousness-raising groups emphasized the sharing of personal experience as a starting point for social analysis and action. In feminist methodology, "feeling is looked to as a guide to a deeper truth than that of abstract rationality" (Weiler, 1991, p. 463). Given that electronic discussions are by nature opportunities for sharing, might an electronic classroom encourage students to discuss personal issues? Several instructors have reported that e-mail (especially when students use pseudonyms) invites less inhibited conversation (Cooper & Selfe, 1990; Faigley, 1990; Spitzer, 1986). At the same time, one study found that anonymity does not necessarily lead to free expression. In a study of e-mail use in women's studies classes, students in an all-female class were more likely to discuss personal experiences online than students in a gender-mixed class, even though both classes posted their messages anonymously (Newton, 1995). Anonymity did not free these students from their reticence in front of members of the other sex. Thus, we might investigate how freely our students express their personal feelings on the net. Does e-mail personalize intellectual activity and thus facilitate feminist pedagogy? How can students use networks in ways that connect the ideas, language, and literature they are studying with their own and others' lived experience?

Another goal of feminist pedagogy is to make students aware that not all women are oppressed in the same way, that in addition to being female, women may be oppressed because they are lesbian, black, or poor, and that they may—by virtue of being white, heterosexual, or middle-class—be members of groups that oppress other women (Weiler, 1991). As a potential agent of consciousness-raising, can the Internet facilitate this goal? Several writing classes are conversing with their counterparts across the globe. It would seem that such cross-cultural conversations would enable students to examine their status as members of a race, ethnic group, or economic class. Does a pedagogy that uses the Internet this way help students not only understand their own experience, but also see their relationship to that of others?

Democratizing the Classroom

Compositionists might also study whether e-mail promotes another goal of feminist pedagogy: to diminish hierarchical relationships within the classroom. Feminist teachers seek to equalize power among students and, as much as possible, between the instructor and students (Weiler, 1991). While the Internet is sometimes described as a democratizing force "resist[ing] control of governments or any central authority" (Perry & Adam, 1992, p. 22), its ability to democratize the composition classroom has been contested: some instructors have argued that e-mail minimizes power inequalities based on characteristics such as race, age, or gender (Selfe, 1990), whereas others have argued that networks cannot prevent such imbalances of power (Castner, 1997). If instructors hide behind a pseudonym, do they divest their voices of greater authority? Are there ways we can use networks to democratize the classroom?

If the computer-based classroom increases collaboration among students, does it simultaneously increase interdependence among students and thus minimize the instructor's authority? Collaborative activity, a strategy of feminist pedagogy, has become routine in composition classes, and computers, in making it easy to share and send files, seem to make group work inevitable even in non-networked classrooms. Is group work more frequent in the computer-based writing classroom? Does the frequency or degree of collaboration depend on whether the classroom is a computer facility, as opposed to one with a computer or two, or a course where students meet in a traditional class, but make occasional trips to the lab?

So much collaborative activity takes place in computer-based writing classrooms that we might also investigate the nature of these collaborations. What kinds of collaborative interactions equalize power among students? Evelyn Ashton-Jones (1995) has argued that writing groups do not necessarily bring about equality in the classroom; often, they merely perpetuate conversational practices that silence women—conversations in which women's contributions are interrupted, devalued, or ignored. In a similar vein, a study of 10- and 11-year-olds doing computer-based assignments in pairs found that collaborative computer projects didn't automatically produce a feminist pedagogy. Single-sex pairs working at a computer solved problems by negotiation, but in mixed-sex pairs, the boys made the decisions and the girls typed (Underwood, McCaffrey, & Underwood, 1990).

Students come to class aware of their status relative to their classmates—status conferred not only by gender, but also by such markers as membership in campus groups, athletic skill, academic achievement, ethnicity, race, wealth, physical attractiveness, and "coolness." While no classroom activity is likely to erase this consciousness of hierarchy, computers make it especially easy to bring together students who might otherwise dismiss one another. In the same way, as long as the instructor grades students' performance and has expertise students lack, a truly democratic relationship between instructor and student is impossible; but networked discussions can give students a much more active and authoritative position than they typically hold. Instructors have debated how much the computer diminishes inequalities of power (Romano, 1993), and it is clear that considerable research remains to be done here. Researchers might observe (directly or through videotape) students working together, noting such behavior as who initiates projects, who organizes the group's work, who encourages other group members, whose opinions are taken seriously, and who speaks loudest or most often. They might require students to write narratives, describing their experiences in these groups. They could experiment with different group structures and assignments and compare students' relationships from one project to another. They might study the number and nature of contributions students make in networked discussions, compare online discussions conducted with and without pseudonyms, or compare online talk that occurs with and without the instructor's participation.

Using the Internet

One of the earliest goals of feminist pedagogy was to validate women's experiences and voices: to create a learning environment where women students would be taken seriously (Rich, 1979). Given the widespread belief that the Internet is "blind to race, age, gender, or handicap" (Perry & Adam, 1992, p. 22), does e-mail provide a forum for marginalized perspectives, as some computers and writing practitioners have claimed, and do women using e-mail feel any freer to voice their distinct concerns? Dale Spender (1980) argues that men are generally more comfortable with public discourse and the chance to exercise leadership through persuasion, while women are more comfortable with personal conversation. Given the fact that the Net is a public space, do our students use e-mail as personal conversation or as display or oratory, and does their practice vary by gender? Are women developing a public voice in response to this new form of expression? Or does the Net simply replicate the power relations that dominate other areas of their lives?

Some classes have students participating in listservs and newsgroups on the Internet, a valuable learning activity in many ways. But the Internet is not always a welcome place for women. "Online lotharios" (Shade, 1993) harass women, pornography is widely distributed over the Net, as are sexist jokes (for example, the responses to one newsgroup's query, "Why is the Internet like a vagina?"). Uninvited sexual invitations on the net have become so commonplace that in 1994, *Glamour* magazine published guidelines for fending them off (Broadhurst, 1994).[4] In 1993, a virtual rape was reported on a MOO, a form of virtual reality. The rapist impersonated another participant and had her commit degrading sexual acts (Dibbell, 1993).[5] On one campus, a student was arrested for stalking a woman after she and the police repeatedly told him to stop; on another campus, a student was arrested for posting a fantasy about torturing, raping, and murdering a female classmate (DeLoughry, 1995).

Though hostility toward women is widespread on the Net, it should not be overstated, given that there are thousands of listservs, newsgroups, MUDs (multiuser dungeons),[6] and other sites of electronic interaction, with millions of conversations taking place everyday. But where harassment is not a problem, women may still feel uncomfortable with the aggressive discourse they find online. As Lori Kendall (1996) points out, on the Net, "women encounter a social environment and behavioral norms formed largely by men" (p. 211). Researchers have argued that women are not used to the competitive and boastful language that are common in conversations between men, whereas among male users, adversarial behavior is regarded as friendly. Netiquette guides approve of "flaming," describing it as part of the game of online conversation, "part of the fun" (Sutton, 1996, p. 181).

Thus, we might study whether males in fact generate more aggression by boasting and flaming on the Net, and whether such behavior is more frequent in certain sites than others. For example, some users have found that the participants in pay services like CompuServe and America Online are more hostile to women than those on the Internet and Usenet; and that sites frequented by the hacker underground are a feminist nightmare, as are—more predictably—such sites as alt.fan.howard-stern and any of the alt.sex series (Clerc, 1996; Gilboa, 1996; Sutton, 1996). We might also consider the extent to which such behavior deters women from participating in online discussions. Finally, researchers might compare female students' experiences on mixed-sex listservs with those on the many women-only lists and services, such as WELL, ECHO, Women's Wire, Systers, and Macwomen.[7] These lists were specifically set up as alternatives to the other services, all of which—including those devoted to women's issues—are dominated by men.[8] Some, such as U.S. News Women's Forum on CompuServe, include visits from such well-known participants as Patricia Ireland, president of the National Organization of Women, and journalists Susan Faludi and Barbara Walters. Others engage in political action: In 1993, when Mattel introduced its Talking Barbie, whose mindless utterances included "Math is hard," Systers organized a protest that pressured Mattel into revising Barbie's script (Camp, 1996).

Feminist Software

Composition researchers might also consider what kinds of software might support a feminist pedagogy. Are some interfaces more appealing to students of one sex than the other?[9] One study found that educators developing a program to teach the use of the comma designed differently for male than female students. When the user's gender was not specified, the designers assumed a male user. They designed software for male students more as a game than a learning tool; it used less sound and required more aggressiveness, hand-eye coordination, and quick reflexes than the program they designed for girls. The girls' program required more typing skill, more sound, and was more like a tool than a game (Huff & Cooper, 1987). This design accords with the observations of others in the software industry: girls and women prefer software that is practical. According to Robin Abrams, general manager of Apple Asia,

> men are seduced by the technology itself and fall into the faster-race-car syndrome, bragging about the size of their "disks" and the speed of their microprocessors. [But] if the computer industry wants to put more and more machines in the hands of the masses, that means appealing to women with practical, accessible technology tools. (qtd. in Wilkinson, 1995, p. 22)

The word "tool" recurs in analyses of girls' and women's uses of software, even when the program is a game. Whereas men like to tinker and explore, women want to accomplish something: "[Women] are looking to save time, which makes them less tolerant of...messing with endless variations of modem strings or system configurations" (Wylie, 1995, p. 3).

We might also look closely at the metaphors implicit in software design, and see if they appeal principally to men or women. Karen Coyle (1996) observes that the macho image of network software is embedded in the information highway metaphor:

> The highway metaphor lends itself well to masculine images. [A] *New York Times* article that talked of computers in hot rod lingo showed a cool dude with a souped-up computer leaving tire tracks over his slower rivals.... An advertisement for software that allows a direct Internet hookup from a personal computer shows a man on a motorcycle and the caption "Pop a wheelie on the Information Highway." On closer inspection you see a pair of high heels flying off the back of the bike: His wheelie has just dumped a woman on the road. Not a friendly image for women but the guy is portrayed as having the time of his life. (p. 52)

Richard and Cynthia Selfe (1994) have suggested that we imagine a Macintosh interface with a different metaphor from that of the office—such as that of a kitchen. A change in metaphor would disrupt the masculine mythology associated with computers. What might feminist software look like? What metaphors would it use?

TESTING FEMINIST THEORIES ABOUT GENDERED LEARNING AND LANGUAGE

Learning Styles

The computer-based writing classroom offers opportunities to reconsider current theories about how men and women learn, write, and converse. Compositionists might use their observations of students writing with computers to reexamine research into gendered learning styles. Does the way students use computers in the writing classroom confirm or challenge claims that researchers have made about these patterns? Gilligan, Ward, Taylor, and Bardige (1988) argue that men are solitary and competitive learners, whereas women learn better through collaboration. Studies of children working with computers partly support this view: Girls are more attracted to technology when they work in groups rather than alone (Kantrowitz, 1994). Even before composition pedagogy began to embrace theories of socially constructed knowledge, instructors noticed that the computer itself, even a standalone machine, socialized the classroom (Payne, 1987). Now that local- and wide-area networks make sharing of drafts and long-distance discussion commonplace in the classroom, we might study what effect these collaborative practices are having on our male and female students. Classes that require students to post on e-mail or exchange work online demand considerable interdependence among class members and a sense of duty toward other students—traits that Gilligan (1982) sees as singularly suited to women. Do female students have an advantage in such classes? Does such a pedagogy conflict with the learning styles of solitary, silent students—who, according to Gilligan, are more likely to be male than female? Does it change the learning style of such students? We might use the computer-based classroom to test whether these two distinct ways of learning follow gender lines.

Gilligan (1982) also suggests that female students prefer to explore connections among disparate bits of information, whereas men are more likely to appreciate the efficient acquisition of facts. E-mail discussions in the writing classroom can be chaotic. Unlike a face-to-face discussion, the comments usually appear on the screen out of order, and the discovery of "truth," if such a discovery takes place, is likely to be messy and inefficient. Do some students find such e-mail conversations irritating, a waste of time? Are such reactions gender-linked?

The computer-based classroom can also provide an opportunity to test the claim that men tend toward linear, and women toward associational thinking. Gilligan (1982) has found that women are more likely than men to think in nonlinear ways. Sherry Turkle and Seymour Papert (1990) found a similar pattern in female computer programming students, who rejected the hierarchical algorithms of traditional progamming in favor of "bricolage," a process of constructing computer programs by moving around the elements of the program as if they were tangible objects. One way to study male and female preferences for linear or associational thinking might be to look at students' uses of hypertext. Unlike the linear, argumentative essay, which rhetorical theorists have argued is a "masculine" form—hierarchical, contentious, and competitive (Sanborn, 1992)—hypertext is a nonlinear and nonhierarchical way of accessing information. Instructors who assign students to write hypertexts rather than essays or to construct home pages on the World Wide Web might consider whether women are more comfortable with these modes of exploring and presenting ideas than men are[10] and whether men are more at ease writing a thesis-directed, single-line argument.

Hypertext can be used not just as a writing tool, a way of presenting knowledge, but also as a tool for exploring others' ideas. Madeleine Grumet (1988) defines a male epistemology as one that values either/or constructions of truth, predictability, distinct boundaries, and certainties, and devalues ambiguity, flexibility, and interconnectedness, values she ascribes to women. Such a way of thinking, gendered or not, would seem to be incompatible with hypertext. Given the way hypertext supports nonlinear exploration of ideas and nonhierarchical thinking, do men and women respond differently to hypertext documents? In addition, Kathleen McCormick (1994) argues against a writing pedagogy that pressures students to reconcile conflicting ideas in order to present a unified stance, and suggests instead that students learn to explore contradictions in an issue they are researching. Does hypertext encourage students to interrogate contradictory positions rather than rush toward reconciliation? If so, do male and female students react differently to this challenge?

If our students' responses don't follow the male/female epistemologies Gilligan and other researchers have identified, can the experience of men and women in the computer classroom help us reconsider these formulations of how men and women think? In other words, how does our students' experience contradict or support the research done in noncomputer environments?

Gendered Writing Styles

The computer classroom may also provide opportunities to test theories of gendered writing styles. Pamela Annas (1985) identifies female language as "sensual, contextual, and committed" and male language as "abstract, logical, and impersonal" (p. 360). Do these differences hold true when students write in nontraditional contexts—constructing web pages and other hypertexts or chatting on networks. These tools provide opportunities for students to play with language and to use styles and content (such as personal writing) not usually validated in academia, but that Annas sees as essential to students' gaining power there. Does the writing produced under these circumstances follow the gendered distinctions Annas defines? Furthermore, those who find, as M. K. Cayton does (1990), that women students do not see themselves as sufficiently authoritative to engage in academic discourse or even to use its "privileged language" might explore whether computerized writing tools give female students a chance to be heard.

Are women more comfortable with private writing and men, with public writing, as Cinthia Gannett (1992) has argued? If so, does the computer-based writing class, which publicizes an individual's writing in many ways, affect men and women differently? Individual work is not completely private, because in a computer lab, the monitor exposes an individual's writing to anyone walking by. And computers facilitate the public sharing of writing, so that students routinely see their words exposed to others: their instructors require them to send files to one another, co-author papers by merging files, project their work onto a large screen in front of the class, and conduct e-mail discussions with other class members or with classes across the world.

Gendered Discourse

Composition instructors using electronic mail might study online discourse for what it reveals about male and female rhetorical styles. How well does our students' conversational behavior accord with research on gendered discourse? Linguist Deborah Tannen (1990) finds that women's talk is more cooperative and intimate than men's, whereas men are more likely to report information and debate opinions. Tannen has also observed that in conversation, women try to minimize or avoid conflict, while men are more likely to be confrontational. Roxanne Missingham's 1994 survey of librarians on two library lists, FEMINIST and PACS-L, found a similar pattern in online conversation: Women used the Internet to seek information, participate in general discussion, and support others, while men posted reports about resources, gave opinions, and presented criticism. Susan Herring's 1992 study of the listserv LINGUIST came to similar conclusions and also found that the different rhetorical styles caused conflict: While women were more tolerant of newcomers who didn't know what they were doing, they also tended to ask basic questions, which annoyed men.

Sociologists Candace West and Don H. Zimmerman (1975) found that in face-to-face communication, men interrupt women three times as often as they do other men. Do women have a better chance of being heard in *online* conversations? So far, studies of academics on two listservs suggest that they don't. One study found that even open networks focusing on women's issues were dominated by men, and that topics of special concern to women were not taken seriously (Kramarae & Taylor, 1993). In their 1991 study of the computers and writing list Megabyte University, Cynthia Selfe and Paul Meyer found that men wrote twice as many messages and 40 percent more words than women. When Susan Herring analyzed Megabyte University and LINGUIST in 1993, she reported similar results: Women contributed only 30 percent of the messages and their posts were shorter than men's. Herring also found that women's messages were more likely to be ignored than men's.[11] A small male minority dominated the discussion, both in length and frequency of posts and psychologically, through self-promotion and combativeness. Men either ignored women's posts or attempted to delegitimize them. As researchers studying face-to-face conversation have found, Herring (1993) also noted that when women's participation approached 50 percent, they were perceived as dominating the discussion: During three such occasions,

> a handful of men wrote in to decry the discussion, and several threatened to cancel their subscription to the list.... At no other time during the period of observation did women participate as much as men, and at no other time did any subscriber, male or female, threaten publicly to unsubscribe from the list. (n.p.)

Herring concludes that academic lists are power-based and hierarchical, continuing the pattern of male dominance in academia and in society as a whole.[12]

Do these patterns hold true when we study *student* discourse on the Net? We need additional studies of rhetorical behavior on the Net, asking such questions as who initiates topics of discussion, and changes topics? Whose messages are ignored, who responds to requests for help? Who expresses personal feelings, who asks questions, who displays knowledge? Who agrees, argues, boasts, gives support, apologizes? Who lurks and why? Which topics interest women, which interest men, which interest both? What uses do men and women make of the Net?

If there is a gendered pattern to online talk, we might also ask if synchronous conversations show the same patterns as asynchronous ones. And if there are gender-based differences, do they correlate with other personal characteristics, such as students' ages, ethnic or economic backgrounds, or success in school? And finally, we might compare the discourse on mixed-gender lists with male-only and female-only lists.

THE PROFESSION OF COMPUTERS AND COMPOSITION STUDIES

Both men and women have been active in computers and composition from the outset, and women have been especially influential in shaping and organizing the discipline. In the early years of the field (1977–1984), roughly equal numbers of male and female compositionists developed software: Among the female software developers were Mimi Schwartz (Prewrite), Kate Kiefer (adaptation of Writer's Workbench), Helen Schwartz (SEEN), Ruth Von Blum and Lisa Gerrard (WANDAH), Christine Neuwirth (DRAFT), Lillian Bridwell-Bowles (ACCESS), Dawn Rodrigues (Creative Problem-Solving), Deborah Holdstein (Writewell), Cynthia Selfe and Billie Wahlstrom (Wordsworth II), and Nancy Kaplan (PROSE).[13] Women have been the principal organizers of all but 2 of the 13 computers and writing conferences (1982–1997). They have edited the earliest journals in the field: Kathleen Kiefer and Cynthia Selfe edited *Computers and Composition* from 1983 to 1988, and Cynthia Selfe and Gail Hawisher have edited it from 1989 to the present; the editors of *Computer-Assisted Composition Journal* were Lynn Veach Sadler and Wendy Tibbetts Greene from 1986 to 1987, and Lynn Veach Sadler from 1988 to the final issue in 1996. Nearly all the editors of anthologies on computers and writing have been female, as are approximately half of the authors of the articles within these texts.[14] Roughly equal numbers of men and women have instituted composition listservs, though men pioneered the two original ones, Participate, organized by Michael Spitzer in the mid-1980s, and shortly afterwards, Megabyte University, founded by Fred Kemp.

Those who research the work of men and women in the discipline might investigate not only the degree, but also the *nature* of men's and women's influence, both in the past and present. How do men and women conceptualize computers and composition studies? What do they write about? In a review of 17 panels at the 1989 Conference on College Composition and Communication, Emily Jessup noted that men talking about computers and writing tended to emphasize technology. They discussed hypertext, computers and text analysis, the technology of networking, and a national project on computers and writing. By contrast, the women speakers emphasized the social implications of computers in writing instruction: computers and basic writers and the "social rhetoric of empowerment in computer-supported writing communities" (qtd. in Jessup, 1991, p. 340). Is this difference in intellectual interest a recurrent pattern? Does it appear elsewhere in the profession—in publications on computer-based composition, in conversations on MOOs and listservs, or at the annual computers and writing conference? Are there other gendered patterns of inquiry?

We might also consider the relative status of men and women in computers and writing. Are men's and women's contributions equally valued? Is there such a thing as men's and women's work in computers and writing? Traditionally, academia has valued theory over classroom practice; does the subdiscipline of computers and composition replicate this value? How egalitarian are we as a community? Susan Herring's (1993) study of Megabyte University found that we are not a democratic group: Men and women recognized as experts in the list's topic posted more often, posted longer comments, and were responded to more often than nonexperts were—expertise transcended gender. But where expertise was not an issue, men still dominated women in all these ways. In short, e-mail replicated the pre-existing power relationships in academia. We need to do additional studies on male and female interactions on professional listservs. What kind of Net behavior is rewarded by others on the listserv, what is censured, and does any of it follow gender lines? In addition to analyzing transcripts of online conversations, researchers might query colleagues who have quit a listserv or ask listserv members their reactions to specific discussions. They might ask journal editors which approaches to computers and writing are regarded as publishable and which aren't and ask committees that give awards what kind of work most deserves recognition; and consider who determines the value system underlying both cases. In analyzing whether the work of the profession follows a gendered pattern, researchers could also explore the making of a computers and writing conference; who does the intellectual work (reads proposals, determines the program) and who administers (plans the budget, delegates clerical work)? We might query colleagues whose work in computers has contributed to their tenure or promotion, find out what kinds of work matters, and determine if such work is gender-linked.

FEMINIST METHODOLOGY

Counting posts on a bulletin board, interruptions in a conversation, and female software developers can reveal a great deal about male and female behavior in computers and composition. But to get fully at how men and women are using technology and responding to its culture, researchers need to go beyond statistics and look at context. If women participate less often in electronic discussions, is it because they find the topics uninteresting, they've been alienated by the prevailing netiquette, they're less technologically adept than men, or do they simply have less time? Contextualized research, such as interviews, surveys, and case studies—methods that have become staples of feminist research—help answer questions like this and provide a rich analysis of how men and women use—or why they don't use—technology. Observing students in class, considering the material and social conditions in which they work, and listening to their narratives are important ways of collecting information. In addition, these methods give researchers a chance to consider how their own expectations shade what they ask and what they see. Influenced by Sandra Harding (1986) and Evelyn Fox Keller (1984), who have shown the masculine bias in traditional scientific methodology, feminist researchers strive to consider how their own personal perspectives—their ethnicity, sex, or economic class—affect the validity of their research.[15]

Feminist scholars have focused on gender differences because traditionally, male experience has been regarded as human experience. In the social sciences as elsewhere, male behavior has been the standard against which women have been judged. Thus, it has been important for feminist scholars to address male biases in research methods, in the questions researchers consider worth posing, and in the conclusions they draw. Nancy Chodorow's work (1978) on the development of gender identification, Carol Gilligan's work (1982) on the moral development of girls and boys, and Belenky, Clinchy, Goldberger, and Tarule's (1986) research on intellectual development all emphasize gender differences in order to challenge the assumption that male behavior is the norm.

At the same time, human behavior—whether it be our colleagues' e-mail habits or our students' learning styles—is too complex and contradictory to fall consistently into categories of male or female. Not all men flame on the Net, not all women nurture, and while men may lean toward hierarchical thinking, most of us probably think in webs sometimes, and in hierarchies other times, regardless of our gender. What feminist theory gives us is an ability to recognize a multiplicity of learning styles and ways of interacting and to reconsider their usefulness. Rather than polarizing male and female experience, feminist research has the potential to extend the discussion of ways of seeing beyond gender to ethnic, cultural, and socioeconomic groups, with the goal of challenging the idea that a single way of thinking is superior to all others. Thus, we will need to go beyond gender to investigate this question: If there are differences in the way men and women learn, work with computers, talk to one another on e-mail, and interact as computers and writing professionals, how do these differences intersect with other differences—those of class, race, age, computer background, writing ability (our students), and status in the profession (us)?

POSTSCRIPT: COMPUTERS, GENDER, AND SOCIAL CLASS

The computer world is still male turf, from the video arcades crammed with adolescent boys to the over 40,000 bulletin boards on the Internet, populated mainly by men. But technology is not only a gender issue; it is a class issue as well: two factors that consistently correlate with computer use are education and income. A 1995 study of 1,000 men and women found that of those who considered themselves noncomputer users or technophobes, 42 percent had a high school education or less, whereas 9 percent had graduated college; this study concluded that it was "education, not gender, that correlated with fear or hostility toward computers" ("It's the Education, Stupid," 1995, p. 8). A 1996 study of 1,200 Southern California households connected computer ownership with both a college education and a high income; it found personal computers in only 22 percent of households with annual incomes under $25,000, compared to 69 percent of those with incomes over $50,000 (Harmon, 1996).[16]

Women with minimal education and low-paying jobs are thus at a particular disadvantage; both their gender and their social class are likely to keep them from being computer users. Women who work outside the home frequently use computers, but do so in the least interesting ways: word processing and data entry.[17] Women who work chiefly as homemakers are unlikely to have even that much exposure. If there is a computer in their home, they don't use it; a third of American families own a computer, but most of these are purchased and used by males (Kantrowitz, 1994).[18] Neither these women nor their daughters are likely to see themselves as computer users.

A 1994 survey, however, found that the more familiar women became with computers, the more likely they were to use them, and that women were especially attracted to electronic mail and online services (men preferred games or educational software) (Dholakia, Dholakia, & Pedersen, 1994). Given the vast resources and attractions of the net, will e-mail be the tool that makes computers as routine a part of women's lives as the telephone? The history of the telephone offers an analogy. Just as the computer was originally developed for the military (rather than for education or entertainment), so the telephone's original purpose was serious: it was strictly a business tool. The people who developed and marketed telephone systems came primarily from the telegraph industry and expected the telephone to be used as the telegraph was. Men used the telephone in the office, and though they often had a phone connection from home, they saw phoning one's friends for "trivial gossip" as an abuse of the technology. By the 1920s, however, their wives began using this phone connection from home to office to talk to their family and friends; confined to the home with small children, they discovered that the telephone gave them access to the outside world. In so doing, they simultaneously made the telephone a gender-inclusive tool and redefined its function (Wajcman, 1995).

Most of the female users of the Net work in the professions; others are in management, technical fields, or are students. Few are homemakers. A study of over 4,000 female subscribers by Women's Wire found that 2 percent were homemakers; similarly, homemakers made up only 1 percent of the 60,000 users surveyed by Yahoo!/Jupiter (DeBow, 1996). But will the movement of computing from the office to the home increase the participation of homemakers (and their daughters) in this technology? Like telephone users in the 1920s, a large proportion of home network users receive their network connection through their business or university, and 85 percent of them, according to the Yahoo!/Jupiter survey, have connections from home. It remains to be seen, then, as access to the Net becomes a household staple, whether it also becomes the entrée into the computer world for girls and women.

Whether logging in from home or office, women constitute the fastest-growing group of network users (Pine, 1996). Since I began researching this article, women have not only increased their participation online, but also set up hundreds of websites, listservs, and user groups of special interest to them as women. With this increased visibility of women and women's concerns on the Net, the context in which we practice computers and writing will change, and so, too, will the questions we ask.

NOTES

[1] According to Irony, "an all-around Swiss Army hacker," capable of breaking into bank accounts and police radio frequencies, women not only know their hardware, but they also have a "knack for social engineering": "If there's someone who doesn't trust anyone, and doesn't give out information, I could get it in a week, without fail. Guys could try for years and never get it" (Romero, 1995, p. E1).

[2] Another study, which broke down patterns of employment according to ethnicity as well as gender, found that white males received the highest salaries and the highest level positions, followed by black men, white women, Hispanic men, black women, and Hispanic women (Banks & Ackerman, 1990).

[3] In 1996, one analyst identified women as "the fastest growing segment of the online market," a judgment based on such statistics as this: Between 1994 and 1996, female subscribers to CompuServe more than doubled, increasing from 12 percent to 25 percent (Pine, 1996).

[4] The guidelines included these caveats: don't flirt unless you want someone to flirt back, be aware of any unintended nuances in what you post, don't post your home phone number or address, and, if someone harasses you, notify the online staff. A few months earlier, the February 1994 *Glamour* had reported the experience of a male University of Kansas student who used a female pseudonym on the Internet. He was surprised to find that male users assumed he wanted sexual come-ons ("Can I kiss you? Can I hug you? Will you kiss me back?"), that he needed the most elementary computer advice, and that he would want to hear them confess their personal problems (see Dominus, 1994).

[5] In an MOO, participants adopt a persona that interacts with other personae in the same virtual community. The perpetrator used a "voodoo doll," a subprogram that allows users to attribute actions to other participants' personae. The victim suffered considerable emotional upset in real life, and the entire community was outraged and eventually had the rapist "toaded," removed from the MOO.

[6] An MUD is also translated as multi-user "dimension" or "domain." "Multi-user dungeon" is its original name, reflecting the origins of MUDs in such role-playing games as Dungeons and Dragons.

[7] Women's Wire is an Internet service based in San Francisco; ECHO (East Coast Hang-Out) is a service directed toward women, based in New York; Systers is a mailing list for women in the technical professions; and Mac-women is a Help forum for female Macintosh users. ECHO offers three bulletin boards for female subscribers only, and one for men only. Its managers make phone checks of potential subscribers to ensure that men don't subscribe to the women's forum (Rigdon, 1994). The founders of Women's Wire believe their service to be far more supportive (they describe it as a "small town") than male-dominated services, such as America Online and CompuServe (which are 10-15 percent female, as opposed to Women's Wire, 90 percent of whose 700 participants are female). They make a special effort to reach women who are intimidated by their lack of computer experience, and their participants avoid the flame wars and one-upmanship characteristic of other services (see Ness, 1994).

[8] For example, in the Usenet newsgroup soc.women, specifically started as a place to discuss women's issues, men's posts outnumber women's (Camp, 1996). A 1993 study of the newsgroup alt.feminism found that men contributed at least 74 percent of the postings (Wylie, 1993).

[9] In 1984, in a critique of computer literacy programs, Margaret Lowe Benston, professor of computer science and women's studies at Simon Fraser University, argued that feminists needed to develop their own computerized educational tools. Only then could men and women gain some control over the technology and understand the social context in which technology is produced and consumed—her definition of computer literacy.

[10] Gilligan (1982) as well as Turkle and Papert (1990) described their female subjects' way of thinking as a "web."

[11] The direction of responses was as follows: men to men 33.4 percent, women to men 21.3 percent, men to women 15.8 percent, women to women 11.2 percent.

[12] In her essay in Chapter 5 of this volume, Shannon Wilson also notes the difficulty of erasing hierarchy in online discussion when hierarchy is already inscribed in the participants' relationship.

[13] Among the men developing writing software during this period were Hugh Burns and George Culp (Topoi), Michael Cohen (Homer and WANDAH), James Strickland (FREE), William Wresch (Writer's Helper), Michael Southwell (COMP-LAB), Stephen Marcus (Compupoem), Raymond Rodrigues (Creative Problem-Solving), Donald Ross (ACCESS), Charles Smith (adaptation of Writer's Workbench), and Stuart Davis and Joseph Martin (PROSE).

[14] For example, female authors are represented in the following percentages:

The Computer in Composition Instruction (Wresch, 1984)	47%
Writing On-Line (Collins & Sommers, 1985)	56%
Writing at Century's End (Gerrard, 1987)	46%

Critical Perspectives on Computers and Composition (Hawisher & Selfe, 1989)	67%
Computers and Writing (Holdstein & Selfe, 1990)	70%
Computers and Community (Handa, 1990)	54%
Evolving Perspectives on Computers and Composition Studies (Hawisher & Selfe, 1991)	71%
Re-Imagining Computers and Composition (Hawisher & LeBlanc, 1992)	47%
Literacy and Technology (Selfe & Hilligoss, 1994)	58%

[15] In analyzing research on gender and communication, Daniel J. Canary and Kimberley S. Hause (1993) fault researchers for such bias. Though they believe there are sex differences in communication, Canary and Hause argue that the researchers' tendency to stereotype and polarize men and women clouded their studies.

[16] According to the Southern California survey, of those who used computers at home, 22 percent had a high school education or less, while 57 percent had graduated college. The study also found computer use divided by ethnicity; twice as many non-Latino whites as Latinos reported owning a personal computer (Harmon, 1996).

[17] Carol Hildebrand, in a 1992 study, found that among 301 computer users in administrative and clerical positions, two-thirds were women. Among women computer professionals, Latina and African-American women occupy a higher percentage of low-paying positions (Banks & Ackerman, 1990).

[18] According to one survey, most home computers are purchased for children's education or for keeping track of personal finances, but are actually used for entertainment ("At Play on Home PCs," 1994).

REFERENCES

Abtan, P. (1993). The gender gap. *Computing Canada, 19*(5), 9.

Annas, P. J. (1985). Style as politics: A feminist approach to the teaching of writing. *College English, 47*(4), 360–371.

Ashton-Jones, E. (1995). Collaboration, conversation, and the politics of gender. In L. W. Phelps & J. Emig (Eds.), *Feminine principles and women's experience in American composition and rhetoric.* (pp. 5–26). Pittsburgh, PA: University of Pittsburgh Press.

At play on home PCs. (1994, November, 15). *Wall Street Journal*, p. B1.

Banks, M. E., & Ackerman, R. J. (1990). Ethnic and gender computer employment status. *Social Science Computer Review, 8*(1), 75–82.

Becklund, L. (1996, May 27). Let's talk about a market niche worth billions. *Los Angeles Times*, pp. D1, D4.

Belenky, M. F., Clinchy, B. M., Goldberger, N. R., & Tarule, J. R. (1986). *Women's ways of knowing: The development of self, voice, and mind.* New York: Basic Books.

Benston, M. L. (1984). The myth of computer literacy. *Canadian Women's Studies, 5*(4), 20–22.

Broadhurst, J. (1994, October). On-line sexual advances: How to fend them off. *Glamour*, 101.

Camp, L. J. (1996). We are geeks, and we are not guys: The Systers mailing list. In L. Cherny & E. R. Weise (Eds.), *Wired women: Gender and new realities in cyberspace* (pp. 114–125). Seattle, WA: Seal Press.

Canary, D. J., & Hause, K. S. (1993). Is there any reason to research sex differences in communication? *Communication Quarterly, 41*(2), 129–144.

Castner, J. A. (1997). The clash of social categories: What egalitarianism in networked writing classrooms? *Computers and Composition, 14*, 257–268.

Cayton, M. K. (1990). What happens when things go wrong: Women and writing blocks. *Journal of Advanced Composition, 10*, 322–337.

Chodorow, N. (1978). *The reproduction of mothering: Psychoanalysis and the sociology of gender.* Berkeley, CA: University of California Press.

Clerc, S. (1996). Estrogen brigades and "big tits" threads: Media fandom online and off. In L. Cherny & E. R. Weise (Eds.), *Wired women: Gender and new realities in cyberspace* (pp. 73–87). Seattle, WA: Seal Press.

Colker, D. (1994, June 14). Everything a girl wants in a game—and less. *Los Angeles Times*, pp. E3, E4.

Collins, J. L., & Sommers, E. A. (Eds.). (1985). *Writing on-line: Using computers in the teaching of writing.* Upper Montclair, NJ: Boynton/Cook.

Cooper, M. M., & Selfe, C. L. (1990). Computer conferences and learning: Authority, resistance, and internally persuasive discourse. *College English, 52*(8), 847–869.

Corley, T. (1997, June 9). Her turn. *Los Angeles Times*, pp. D1, D6.

Coyle, K. (1996). How hard can it be? In L. Cherny & E. R. Weise (Eds.), *Wired women: Gender and new realities in cyberspace* (pp. 42–55). Seattle, WA: Seal Press.

Dain, J. (1991). Women and computing: Some responses to falling numbers in higher education. *Women's Studies International Forum, 14*(3), 217–225.

DeBow, Y. (1996). Women's Wire profiles wired women. *Interactive Content, 2*(21), 11.

DeLoughry, T. (1995, February 24). Online. *Chronicle of Higher Education, XLI*, A27.

Dholakia, R., Dholakia, N., & Pedersen, B. (1994, December). Putting a byte in the gender gap. *American Demographics, 16*(2), 20–21.

Dibbell, J. (1993, December 21). A rape in cyberspace. *The Village Voice, 38*(51), 36–42.

Dominus, S. (1994, February). One man's life as a woman. *Glamour*, 72.

Faigley, L. (1990). Subverting the electronic network: Teaching writing using networked computers. In D. A. Daiker & M. Morenberg (Eds.), *The writing teacher as researcher: Essays in the theory and practice of class-based research* (pp. 290–311). Portsmouth, NH: Boynton/Cook.

Flynn, E. A. (1988). Composing as a woman. *College Composition and Communication, 39*(4), 423–435.

Flynn, E. A. (1991). Composition studies from a feminist perspective. In R. Bullock & J. Trimbur (Eds.), *The politics of writing instruction: Postsecondary* (pp. 137–154). Portsmouth, NH: Heinemann.

Frenkel, K. (1990.) Women and computing. *Communications of the ACM, 33*(11), 35–46.

Gannett, C. (1992). *Gender and the journal: Diaries and academic discourse.* Albany, NY: State University of New York Press.

Gerrard, L. (Ed.). (1987). *Writing at century's end: Essays on computer-assisted composition.* New York: Random House.

Gilboa, N. (1996). Elites, lamers, narcs and whores: Exploring the computer underground. In L. Cherny & E. R. Weise (Eds.), *Wired women: Gender and new realities in cyberspace* (pp. 98–113). Seattle, WA: Seal Press.

Gilligan, C. (1982). *In a different voice: Psychological theory and women's development.* Cambridge, MA: Harvard University Press.

Gilligan, C., Ward, J., Taylor, J., & Bardige, B. (1988). *Mapping the moral domain: The contributions of women's thinking to psychological theory and education.* Cambridge, MA: Harvard University Press.

Goff, L. (1990). Is there a computer gender gap? *MIS Week, 11*(14), 29.

Grumet, M. R. (1988). *Bitter milk: Women and teaching.* Amherst, MA: University of Massachusetts Press.

Handa, C. (Ed.). (1990). *Computers and community: Teaching composition in the twenty-first century.* Portsmouth, NH: Boynton/Cook.

Harding, S. (1986). *The science question in feminism.* Ithaca, NY: Cornell University Press.

Harmon, A. (1996, October 7). Computing in the '90's: The great divide. *Los Angeles Times*, pp. D1, D4.

Hawisher, G., & LeBlanc, P. (Eds.). (1992). *Re-imagining computers and composition: Teaching and research in the virtual age.* Portsmouth, NH: Boynton/Cook.

Hawisher, G., & Selfe, C. L. (Eds.). (1989). *Critical perspectives on computers and composition.* New York: Teacher's College Press.

Hawisher, G., & Selfe, C. L. (Eds.). (1991). *Evolving perspectives on computers and composition instruction studies: Questions for the 1990s.* Urbana, IL: National Council of Teachers of English.

Herring, S. (1992). *Gender and participation in computer-mediated linguistics discourse.* Washington, DC: ERIC Clearinghouse on Languages and Linguistics. (ERIC Document Reproduction Service No. ED345552)

Herring, S. (1993). Gender and democracy in computer-mediated communication. *Electronic Journal of Communication* [Online], *3*(2). Available: http://www.cios.org/www/ejc/v3n293.htm

Hess, R. D., & Miura, I. T. (1985). Gender differences in enrollment in computer camps and classes. *Sex Roles, 13*, 193–203.

Hildebrand, C. (1992). Desktop division: Study finds gender roles differ. *Computerworld, 26*, 37.

Holdstein, D. H., & Selfe, C. L. (Eds.). (1990). *Computers and writing: Theory, research, practice.* New York: Modern Language Association.

Hornig, L. S. (1984). Women in science and engineering: Why so few? *Technology Review*, 31–41.

Huff, C., & Cooper, J. (1987). Sex bias in educational software: The effect of designers' stereotypes on the software they design. *Journal of Applied Social Psychology, 17*(6), 519–532.

It's the education, stupid; forget the gender gap: Schooling drives the market. (1995, April). *Marketing Computers, 15*(4), 8.

Jacobs, K. (1994, May/June). RoboBabes: Why girls don't play videogames. *I. D.: The International Design Magazine, 41*(3), 38–45.

Jessup, E. (1991). Feminism and computers in composition instruction. In G. E. Hawisher & C. L. Selfe (Eds.), *Evolving perspectives on computers and composition studies: Questions for the 1990s* (pp. 336–355). Urbana, IL: National Council of Teachers of English.

Kantrowitz, B. (1994, May 16). Men, women, and computers. *Newsweek*, 48–55.

Keller, E. F. (1984). *Reflections on gender and science.* New Haven, CT: Yale University Press.

Kendall, L. (1996). MUDder? I hardly know'er! Adventures of a feminist MUDder. In L. Cherny & E. R. Weise (Eds.), *Wired women: Gender and new realities in cyberspace* (pp. 207–223). Seattle, WA: Seal Press.

Kondo, A. (1995). The gender trap. *Marketing Computers, 15*(4), 37–42.

Kramarae, C., & Taylor, H. J. (1993). Women and men on electronic networks: A conversation or a monologue? In H. J. Taylor, C. Kramarae, & M. Ebben (Eds.), *Women information technology and scholarship* (pp. 52–61). Urbana, IL: Center for Advanced Study, University of Illinois.

Levin, T., & Gordon, C. (1989). Effect of gender and computer experience on attitudes toward computers. *Journal of Educational Computing Research, 5*, 69–88.

Lewis, L. H. (1985). New technologies, old patterns: Changing the paradigm. *Educational Horizons*, 129–132.

Maier, F. (1995, February 19). Cyberspace: Where the women aren't. *San Francisco Examiner*, pp. B5–B6.

Marshall, J. C., & Bannon, S. (1988). Race and sex equity in computer advertising. *Journal of Research on Computing in Education, 2*, 115–127.

McCormick, K. (1994). "On a topic of your own choosing...." In J. Clifford & J. Schilb (Eds.), *Writing theory and critical theory* (pp. 33–52). New York: Modern Language Association.

Miller, S. (1991). The feminization of composition. In R. Bullock & J. Trimbur (Eds.), *The politics of writing instruction: Postsecondary* (pp. 39–53). Portsmouth, NH: Heinemann.

Missingham, R. (1994). *Cyberspace: No women need apply; librarians and the Internet.* Unpublished manuscript.

Ness, C. (1994, November 27). Computer network puts women online. *San Francisco Examiner*, p. A4.

Newton, J. (1995). What is feminist pedagogy anyway?: Distinctions in content and process. In B. Bradbury (Ed.), *Teaching women's history: Challenges and solutions* (pp. 135–145). Athabasca, Alberta, Canada: Athabasca Press.

On line. (1996, June 21). *Chronicle of Higher Education, XLII*, A17.

Payne, D. (1987). Computer-extended audiences for student writers: Some theoretical and practical implications. In L. Gerrard (Ed.), *Writing at century's end: Essays on computer-assisted instruction* (pp. 21–26). New York: Random House.

Pereira, J. (March 16, 1994). A toy for men: Video games help boys get a head start. *Wall Street Journal*, p. B1.

Perenson, M. J., Ehrenman, G. C., & Brown, E. (1994, November 8). What do women want? Software for women and girls. *PC Magazine, 13*(19), 437.

Perry, T. S., & Adam, J. A. (1992). E-mail: Pervasive and persuasive. *IEEE Spectrum, 29*(10), 22–23.

Pine, D. (1996). A chat room of one's own: Women in cyberspace. *Home PC, 3*(5), 143–146.

Rich, A. (1979). *On lies, secrets, and silences: Selected prose, 1966–1978.* New York: W. W. Norton.

Rigdon, J. E. (1994, March 18). Now women in cyberspace can be themselves. *Wall Street Journal*, p. B1.

Romano, S. (1993). The egalitarianism narrative: Whose story? Which yardstick? *Computers and Composition, 10*(3), 5–28.

Romero, D. (1995, December 1). A new force lurks amid the cyber shadows. *Los Angeles Times*, pp. E1, E6.

Sanborn, J. (1992). The academic essay: A feminist view in student voices. In N M. McCracken & B. Appleby (Eds.), *Gender issues in the teaching of English* (pp. 142–160). Portsmouth, NH: Boynton/Cook-Heinemann.

Selfe, C. L. (1990). Technology in the English classroom: Computers through the lens of feminist theory. In C. Handa (Ed.), *Computers and community: Teaching composition in the twenty-first century* (pp. 118–139). Portsmouth, NH: Boynton.

Selfe, C. L., & Hilligoss, S. (Eds.). (1994). *Literacy and technology: The complications of teaching and learning with technology.* New York: Modern Language Association.

Selfe, C. L., & Meyer, P. (1991). Testing claims for on-line conferences. *Written Communication, 8*(2), 162–192.

Selfe, C. L, & Selfe, R. L., Jr. (1994). The politics of the interface: Power and its exercise in electronic contact zones. *College Composition and Communication, 45*(4), 480–504.

Shade, L. (1993, August 17). *Gender issues in computer networking.* Paper presented at Community Networking: The International Free-net Conference, Ottawa, ON, Canada.

Sinclair, C. (1996). *Net chick: A smart-girl guide to the wired world.* New York: Henry Holt.

Spender, D. (1980). *Man made language.* London: Routledge and Kegan Paul.

Spitzer, M. (1986). Writing style in computer conferences. *IEEE Transactions on Professional Communications, 29,* 19–22.

Sutton, L. A. (1996). Cocktails and thumbtacks in the old west: What would Emily Post say? In L. Cherny & E. R. Weise (Eds.), *Wired women: Gender and new realities in cyberspace* (pp. 169–187). Seattle, WA: Seal Press.

Tamosaitis, N. (1995). Why don't women log on? Cyberspace shouldn't be just where the boys are. *Computer Life, 2*(2), 139–140.

Tannen, D. (1990). *You just don't understand.* New York: Ballantine Books.

Technology jobs fail to end gender gap: Study finds occupational segregation. (1993, February 7). *San Jose Mercury News,* p. 2PC.

Tuell, C. (1993). Composition teaching as "women's work": Daughters, handmaids, whores, and mothers. In S. I. Fontaine & S. Hunter (Eds.), *Writing ourselves into the story: Unheard voices from composition studies,* (pp. 123–139). Carbondale, IL: Southern Illinois University Press.

Turkle, S., & Papert, S. (1990). Epistemological pluralism: Styles and voices within the computer culture. *Signs, 16,* 128–157.

Underwood, G., McCaffrey, M., & Underwood, J. (1990). Gender differences in a cooperative computer-based language task. *Educational Research, 32*(1), 44–49.

Wajcman, J. (1995). Feminist theories of technology. In S. Jasanoff, G. E. Markle, J. C. Petersen, & T. Pinch (Eds.), *Handbook of science and technology studies* (pp. 189–204). London: Sage.

Weiler, K. (1991). Freire and a feminist pedagogy of difference. *Harvard Educational Review, 61*(4), 449–474.

West, C., & Zimmerman, D. H. (1975). Sex roles, interruption and silences in conversation. In B. Thorne & N. Henley (Eds.), *Language and sex: Difference and dominance* (pp. 102–117). Rowley, MA: Newberry House.

Wilkinson, S. (1995, November 6). What's a fast car to some is just a tool for others. *PC Week, 12,* 22.

Wresch, W. (Ed.). (1984). *The computer in composition instruction: A writer's tool.* Urbana, IL: National Council of Teachers of English.

Wylie, M. (1995). No place for women: Internet is flawed model for the infobahn. *Digital Media, 4*(8), 3.

An Online Dialogue with the Contributors*

Kristine Blair
Bowling Green State University

Pamela Takayoshi
University of Louisville

On May 28, 1997, a number of the contributors to *Feminist Cyberscapes* met online at Lingua MOO in a special room, "The CyberParlor," designed to promote a dialogue among us about the impact of various technologies in the professional and personal lives of women, particularly women in composition. As part of this dialogue, we addressed issues such as the social construction of technology as a male-dominated enterprise, the limited potential of the Internet for women who have had little to no technological access, and the need for women to extend their professional lives within online forums. While the MOO was an excellent way to foster a multiplicity of voices, our resulting conversation had its technological limits for several contributors, who encouraged us not to forget the importance of face-to-face dialogue among women. As Shannon Wilson put it:

> Any time that I participate in conversations my tendency is to listen very carefully, process, and respond after the dust settles a bit. This didn't seem possible in the MOO. There is also, I believe, a big difference in listening face-

* Voices in this dialogue include Joanne Addison, Kristine Blair, Margaret Daisley, Lisa Gerrard, Morgan Gresham, Sibylle Gruber, Cecilia Hartley, Paula Gillespie, Frances Johnson, Susan Romano, Pamela Takayoshi, and Kathleen Blake Yancey.

> to-face to many different voices and trying to read a real-time manuscript of many voices. For one thing, you are completely dependent upon one sense—vision—as opposed to being about to process sight, sound, touch—all of the things that contribute to the group conversations that take place around kitchen tables. (personal communication, June 2, 1997)

Shannon's comment after the dialogue reflects both the technical and logistical constraints of establishing a space for dialogue and communication, as a number of participants were either disconnected or less able to orient themselves to the conversation because of software and networking problems with their respective machines. Even those able to maintain a technical connection stressed the need to establish a social connection within the dialogue itself, since a number of the participants had never met in face-to-face forums, such as the Computers and Writing Conference or the Conference on College Composition and Communication (CCCC). Regardless of these difficulties, there is clearly an attempt to create both an open and playful space as various participants simultaneously craft a sense of self and togetherness, whether it be talking about real-time regional weather conditions, or even clothing, strategies that suggest a mapping of social space online, to replicate the positive and important connections between women that Shannon reminds us of in her message. In order to maintain the integrity of that mapping process, we have done little rearranging of actual text and have often kept the layers of synchronous conversation between participants in tact.

Still, other contributors questioned the assumption that this online dialogue was somehow less linear and ultimately more dialogic, a common presumption about many online forums. Picking up on a thread initially started by Kathy Yancey, Paula Gillespie contends "Kathi's plea for a little linearity on the MOO made me see how much [mooing] resembles the stereotypical male discourse, where you get pre-empted, ignored, silenced, not because of anyone's intent to co-opt the discourse, but because of its multilevel nature" (personal communication, May 29, 1997). For Paula, as well as other scholars as Stabile (1995) and Hawisher and Sullivan (1998), there are limits in harnessing virtual space for our own political agendas. Borrowing from Foucault's metaphor of the garden in which all vegetation can share space, thrive, and grow, Hawisher and Sullivan assert that "Ideally we would like e-spaces to be cultivated as gardens are cultivated—through mediation, persuasion, and acts of kindness—to create a rich and fertile ground for collective feminist action" (p. 195). Although the MOO dialogue relies more on the metaphor of a private parlor in which the participants were encouraged to kick up their heels and dance, our goals were similar to the goals of Hawisher and Sullivan's all-women listserv women@waytoofast, in that we were attempting to give the participants in this collection an opportunity "to act and gain presence" in a way that extends their perspectives on the status of women and technology beyond the limits of more linear, print-based processes.

Yet as Margaret Daisley concluded, for many women, including academic women, there are material conditions that prohibit both access to and comfort with such online forums, regardless of the safe space they can be designed to provide:

> I was surprised at myself that I was even able to manage getting on the MOO and participating—I'm terrified of these venues, partially because of the antiquated system I use for access, partially because of lack of experience, and partially because of what Paula brings up-the freewheeling polyvocality.... It's like being at what we used to call a "cocktail party" or a "mixer"—unless you hole up in a corner with one or two people, you just spend the evening making small talk or skimming the surface of any real issue. So, yes, I'm looking forward to reading the transcript here, and maybe continuing the discussion at a more leisurely pace. (personal communication, May 29, 1997)

Although such concerns about MOOs and other online forums sometimes inhibit women's participation within them, the opportunity to share ideas and bring a sense of community to *Feminist Cyberscapes* was worth some of the technical difficulties some of us experienced as we tried to find the time to talk with each other online about the issues that comprise the book and to share our concerns about the continuing role of technology in women's lives. Despite Kathi's call for a little linearity, we have attempted to maintain both the intertextual and hypertextual spirit of the conversation. Ultimately, such a conversation chronicles the multiplicity of ways in which the possibilities and constraints of online communication manifest themselves in our daily experiences as women and compositionists, attempting to integrate these newest technologies of literacy into our classrooms and our scholarship and facing similar obstacles to institutional access and support. While this MOO transcript is part of our more nontraditional conclusion to *Feminist Cyberscapes*, it is by no means meant to represent a sense of closure, but rather a more open space in which to question the future possibilities for personal, professional, and political empowerment in both the virtual and material terrain. In this sense, we hope the MOO conversation reflects both caution and optimism for what several participants see as the ability of our lives to "transcend scripts," including the one that follows.

cyberparlor

a small cozy room possessing an ethereal glow as the smell of freshly brewed coffee wafts through the air. There are several comfortable overstuffed chairs calling you to relax and converse with your cybercolleagues about life in the virtual world, particularly those of you associated with Kris and Pam's Feminist Cyberscapes project. A small table with brightly colored coffee mugs suggests that all are welcome to have a drink and stay awhile. A green brocade loveseat beckons as a fireplace embraces you in its warmth.

You see coffee, fireplace, tea, wall, pastries, and recorder here.

PamT, Cissy, and Sibylle are here.

Obvious exits: [west] to MOOLoquium and [out] to Courtyard

morgan arrives.

PamT says, "Miss Morgan, welcome!"
Sibylle asks "Does anybody know if I can get my typing window bigger on that Surf&Turf client. It's only about a line right now."
morgan says, "hi folks!"
Kris-B says, "Oh, I wish I did, Sibylle, but I've never used S&T; I'm using MacMoose."
PamT says, "Can't help, either, Sibylle. I'm telnetting."
Paula arrives.
Cissy says, "I'm telnetting too, Sibylle."
Cissy says, "Hi, Paula."
kathi arrives.
kathi says, "hi everyone."
PamT says, "Hi, Paula and Kathi!"
Sibylle laughs "ok you telnetters, I'll not mention it again."
kathi says, "is this the fun part?"
Cissy says, "There's a fun part?"
morgan says, "so how many are we expecting tonight?"
kathi says, "isn't that why we're here, for fun?"
Sibylle wonders "kathi, maybe it's the 'getting used to it all part?"
Kris-B says, "actually, quite a few people said they'd show up, so let's hope so."
Sibylle asks "and are we going to have tea? or chocolate would be fine too :-)"
Lisa arrives.
kathi says, "will someone introduce all of us to each other?"
PamT says, "We thought we'd play for about ten minutes or so until everyone got on and got comfortable."
kathi says, "oh, this is the get-comfortable part. so the fun part is next?"
Kris-B, "Hi Lisa, how are you doing?"
Sibylle asks "comfortable, Pam? That might take a while longer!"
Cissy says, "Somebody be sure to tell Kathi when the fun part starts :-)"
PamT says, "And Kathi is director of fun. (You've all seen how she can dance at *CCCC*!)"
kathi says, "Thanks, Cissy. Yes, I do love fun. And dancing, you bet!"
Paula says, "If kathi is here, fun is happening."
Lisa says, "hi, everyone"
kathi says, "this is already fun. I'm laughing out loud."
Sibylle says, "Kathi, I missed the dancing part. What kinds of dances?"
kathi says, "You name it, I dance it. I *love* to dance."
Kris-B whips out a disco ball and puts some Donna Summer on a beat-up turntable in the corner. "Flashback, anyone?"
kathi says, "oh baby"
PamT says, "Morgan—disco baby?"
Cissy says, "Oh dear"
Lisa says, "LOVE disco"
Kris-B, "where are the Bee-Gees when you need them?"
PamT says, "I wanna request Spice Girls!"
Paula grabs kathi and they start dancing.
morgan says, "oh god. disco is back!"
Cissy says, "AHHHHHHHHHHHH BeeGees. I was in LOVE with Barry Gibb"

kathi says, "they're coming back, the BeeGees."
Shannon arrives.
kathi says, "hi Shannon"
PamT says, "Be warned Shannon, things are already getting out of hand!"
Cissy says, "Hi, Shannon"
Shannon says, "hi"
morgan says, "hey, is there a way to keep your lines from getting interrupted by new lines?"
margaret arrives.
kathi says, "Hi margaret"
Cissy says, "Just keep typing. It'll come out okay when you hit enter."
Kris-B says, "Hi margaret"
Shannon says, "hi"
Paula says, "We don't see your lines interrupted. Only you see that."
Lisa says, "Hi Shannon. Hi Margaret. Join the dance."
kathi says, "what other music we got here?"
Cissy tosses out a Gloria Gaynor 45.
Kris-B says, "well, we had this request for the Spice Girls..."
kathi says, "no, but I could. Whatcha want??"
PamT says, "Just tell me what you want, what you really really want..."
margaret says, "Hi everyone...is my presence already knowns@who"
Cissy says, "That could be dangerous, Pam"
PamT says, "That's me, Danger Spice"
Sibylle says, "Morgan, I am using this Surf and Turf client, and I can type without being interrupted. You have to start it from Netscape 3.0..."
Paula says, "Hey, what's everybody wearing?"
margaret says, "paula—jeans, and black top...typical NY dress. Cyberwear?"
kathi says, "Jeans, one of my fav Liz Claiborne bulk sweaters, blue, tenny pumps"
Cissy says, "Jeans, top, no socks, cold toes"
margaret says, "So, what is the agenda for the evening? Hmmmmmmmm?"
Paula says, "Jeans, purple T, navy sweater"
Kris-B, "jean dress, blue loafers."
kathi says, "Doncha love jeans?"
Lisa says, "tank top, shorts, bare feet. It's 90 degrees today and I'm home. This is fun."
Shannon says, "Stretch pants, big ugly green plaid shirt...I'm seven months pregnant...terminally cranky."
Paula says, "Somebody's going to show up in shorts and I'll be jealous that they're warm enough for that."
Cissy says, "Okay Lisa, I hate you. Where is it 90 degrees?"
PamT says, "were wanting to talk about cyberspace"
margaret says, "OK, re jeans: Story: I still remember seeing one of my mom's friends at 80 or something, wearing jeans, me thinking, I hope that's the way I'll be when I'm..."
Joanne arrives.
kathi says, "It's supposed to be 90 degrees here, but it's only 60 and gray and ugly."
Sibylle also asks "yeah, what's the agenda? Hey, Margaret, maybe we'll set our own..:-)"

Cissy says, "Hi, Joanne"
Kris-B, "[to Shannon] ooh a surfer girl on the way, congratulations!"
PamT says, "what I was trying to write...we want to sort of talk about stuff you've been thinking about technology since you wrote your articles. What's happening now?"
Joanne says, "Hi!"
Kris-B says, "hiya joanne"
Lisa says, "90 degrees in Santa Mo, CA; 100 degrees in the valley. Too hot for me. I like cool and damp."
Joanne walks to the coffee.

```
                          ______________________
                         |                      |
Kris-B holds up a BIG sign: | is it time to have fun? |
                         |______________________|
```

margaret says, "oh, yeah. Etiquette... Hello, everyone. Margaret here. Ready to join the conversation."
Cissy says, "Well, I know my mind is moving far more toward connecting my students OUTWARD...outside the academy than before."
PamT says, "One thing we realized in reading the articles recently is that there's not much about the Web in them, for example, because that happened so recently."
Lisa says, "that was meant to be Santa Monica, CA. My screen is scrolling SO FAST!"
margaret says, "Well, maybe web-schmeb??"
kathi says, "is that a problem, the absence of the web?"
Sibylle thinks about all the new technological advances that will allow the Americans to move into a wired community—or as Bill Clinton says...A computer for every child in every school...
PamT says, "No, not exactly, just something to think about—what's not in the collection."
Cissy says, "Pam, of course the web is just facilitating a lot of what we were talking about in terms of connections, don't you think?"
margaret says, "...and a chicken in every pot?"
Kris-B says, "yes, what do you all think about all the techno-hype about the web?"
kathi says, "Oh let's not drag Billy Bob in here; that's hype if you ask me."
kathi says, "he's also going to test every school child in America. Now that's a road to..."
frances arrives.
Sibylle responds to Kris, "Hype is a good word here. Some of the things going on don't seem to facilitate teaching or communication at all but are just 'hyping' everybody to think so..."
margaret says, "yes... what's IN, and what's out?"
PamT says, "Hi, Frances!"
kathi says, "IMPROVEMENT. Sorry. I'll hush now."
Cissy says, "Kris, I think the web makes connections like this more accessible and easier for people, but isn't really adding anything new"
Paula says, "Hi, Frances"
kathi says, "I think the web will add something new; is in some ways, but it's not clear"

morgan says, "Cissy, I dunno. Seems like there are some good things for webs—portfolios?"

PamT says, "I told Emily, my twelve year old step daughter what I was doing (so she wouldn't pick up the phone)—her response. Cool."

Kris-B says, "After looking at articles in total, many of them focus on classroom use of e-mail or women's experiences on listservs, given where we are were when we started the collection. Any new perspectives?"

Paula says, "My daughter's response would have been to pick up the phone. I'm at work."

Cissy says, "Morgan...yes, but aren't portfolios something different? Presentational? I was speaking mainly in terms of connecting people"

kathi says, "E-mail is less a universal good."

Paula says, "e-mail is less a universal good, Kathi? explain?"

Cissy says, "My perspective on listserv has changed quite a bit, I think"

Sibylle wonders "maybe the 'new part' is the ability to include visuals, sound, and all that. That might be very useful for students who are multisensory learners."

kathi says, "I think portfolios can be done off line and on; depends on the purpose."

Kris-B says, "We titled this collection Feminist Cyberscapes; has the web changed what our definition of a cyberscape would be?"

morgan says, "i guess i'm wondering how we define 'connecting'?"

margaret says, "E-mail less a universal good???!!! My family, and extended family, is just now discovering it (and think, of course, that I'm some kind of a maven.... Let's not fall into that "new is good" trap, please!"

Cissy says, "Hmmm...good question, Morgan."

Kris-B says, "Does connecting online presume empowerment?"

kathi says, "I think lots of us have seen e-mail as benign at worst, ideal at best."

margaret says, "Connecting... good focal point"

Paula says, "Kathi, has that changed?"

Lisa says, "I think women are getting louder and louder on the net, and it's great. Has anyone heard about the flap over Bill Gates' Technology Summit? He invited 103 guests, including Al Gore, but only one woman. Several women's groups are retaliating by organizing a summit that will invite female leaders in the tech. industry."

Cissy says, "Not empowerment per se. But a potential for voice"

PamT says, "Technology gets used to support existing power formations, doesn't it? What are the alternatives we know about?"

kathi says, "we're bouncing around here. Can we work a little more linearly, she asks."

Sibylle says, "Pam, it might support existing power structures and also add new ones that we haven't experienced yet. I definitely don't think it'll even out the playing field..."

margaret says, "... and just like existing power formations, we can use them to move along our own ends... which I see as being (at the very least) being included in the picture."

Cissy says, "I think this medium resists linearity, kathi. What do you think?"

PamT says, "So then what else is there to say? (being a little cynical tonight...)"

Kris-B says, "The Gates Summit is Bad. The coolest thing just happened. A class just came into the lab I'm in by myself. There are learning how to do web pages, and the majority of the students in the class are women. The other cool thing is that the instructor is letting me stay."
kathi says, "I think we could use this in a more linear way if we chose."
PamT says, "There's a slogan for us, Kris (we were trying to think of slogans earlier)—The Gates Summit is Bad!"
Sibylle thinks (and it takes her a long time) "I don't know what else we can say.... Maybe we can talk about how we have used e-mail, the web, or whatever since we have written out articles"

```
                              __________
                             |          |
Kris-B holds up a BIG sign:  | Bill is Bad! |
                             |__________|
```

kathi says, "bill is a jerk"
morgan says, "Kris—how'd you do those signs?"
PamT says, "Yeah, I guess I'm just feeling practically challenged.... I've been thinking about this for a while and now I want action."
margaret says, "Bill's Summit is Sexist?"

Kris-B says, "I like that idea, Sibylle. Has our use of cyberscapes changed, increased, diminished? Are we doing more with our classes?"
kathi says, "I want a web that allows lots of directions of all kinds."
Paula says, "Since we finished our article (kathi, Laura Julier and I) I joined a Webmaster's guild and have seen a lot of cool stuff that people in other departments here are doing with websites. Stuff that's good for learning."
Kris-B says, "Morgan, to do a sign you type bb and your message."
PamT says, "What do you mean, lots of directions?"
kathi says, "I don't particularly like linearity myself, but I know those who do."

```
                            ____
                           |    |
Cissy holds up a BIG sign: | test |
                           |____|
```

Lisa says, "Love those signs. The women's groups organizing the summit say their goal is to discuss the future of tech. for those who aren't white male millionaires."

```
                           ________________________
                          |                        |
PamT holds up a BIG sign: | Put that sign down, Cissy! |
                          |________________________|
```

Kris-B says, "the attack of the sign-women!"
kathi says, "Lots of directions means lots of ways of knowing, lots of ways of moving"
Cissy says, "Kathi, I think there will always be an element of linearity, even in cyberspace. It's tough to get rid of it."

kathi says, "yes, exactly."
PamT says, "I wonder what they'll find. Seems to me that we could make educated guesses."

Cissy says, "Ahh...it should be interesting to find out."
morgan says, "that depends on who they invite—academics or industry"
kathi says, "the summit is in Sept, yes?"
Cissy says, "Pam, you and Kris have read all the articles in this collection. Do you see any emerging themes coming from our group?"
margaret says, "make that: academics AND industry AND...."
frances says, "how do we get in the summit?"
Sibylle is listening to NPR
kathi says, "could you intro us?"

```
                                 __________
                                |          |
margaret holds up a BIG sign:   | AGENDA?  |
                                |__________|
```

frances says, "margins exist on the web"
Sibylle says, "and just think of all the people who DO NOT have access at all, kathi."
PamT says, "Why don't we introduce ourselves? We can pause after we enter one so someone else can post an intro and not overlap too much?"
Lisa says, "The summit is scheduled fall for Los Angeles or San Francisco."
margaret says, "intersections exist on the web..."
Kris-B says, "Cissy, many of the articles leave us with the sense that while there is much potential to online networks, it doesn't just happen by sheer virtue of the technology or the desire itself. There's a long way to go."
frances says, "each year some of my kids know the web well, others not at all"
Kris-B says, "I agree, introductions would be good."
kathi says, "tell us about the long way, after we intro ourselves?"
Shannon says, "I have to say something here or mutt will disconnect me."
Cissy says, "Absolutely, Kris"
Cissy says, "Wanna introduce yourself Shannon? :-)"
PamT says, "I'm Pam, you all know me. I'm leaving town for a month this week, returning in July and moving houses. Aaagh....I'm tired."
Kris-B says, "yes, Shannon. Please do."
PamT says, "Who's next?"
kathi says, "shannon"
Shannon says, "I am a mutt-challenged graduate student at Miami of Ohio. Currently working on my diss."
frances says, "im Frances i teach at rowan, mostly I work w engineers who presume a lot about technology and the WWW"
kathi says, "and Paula?"
Paula says, "I'm Paula Gillespie. I'm just about to leave for Ireland for the summer. I teach at Marquette U."
Shannon says, "Sorry, this system is not agreeing with me and I am having trouble reading and typing at the same time! Duh."
kathi says, "and Joanne?"
frances says, "me too shannon"
Joanne says, "I'm an asst prof at CU-Denver looking forward to a backpacking trip in Alaska this summer."

Paula says, "kathi?"

kathi says, "I'm kathi/kathleen yancey, at UNC Charlotte"

Sibylle introduces herself. "I am Sibylle. I teach at Northern Arizona University and am also the Writing Center Director and Computer lab director. It's fun, and the town is beautiful. There are lots of hiking trails around here."

Cissy says, "I'm at University of Louisville. Middle of Ph.D. coursework."

Paula says, "Sibylle, that was elegant."

Sibylle smiles "Thank you, Paula :-)"

PamT says, "Morgan?"

kathi says, "and Kris?"

Kris-B says, "I'm Kris—currently at Bowling Green State, have to miss C&W this year because I'll be in California instead. Right now, the weather, after a long winter, is finally beauty-ful. Green and lush, cool breezes. In some way, that makes mooing somewhat difficult."

morgan says, "oh—that's me. Morgan—a PHD student at UofL"

PamT says, "lisa?"

kathi says, "oh morgan, you're the one who did the piece in Kairos?"

morgan says, "yep."

kathi says, "nice piece: I told that to your partner. I hope he told you."

Lisa says, "I'm Lisa Gerrard. I teach at UCLA, in the Writing Programs. I'm hoping to meet at least some of you in Honolulu next week."

PamT says, "Who else is out there?"

morgan says, "Kathi—he did. thanks!"

Cissy says, "I was wondering about a Honolulu get together for the group. Who all will be there?"

kathi says, "that was nicely linear. Thank you, all"

PamT says, "breakfast, Cissy?"

Lisa says, "Thank you for organizing that little intro. Very smooth."

frances says, "when pressed, we all try to be linear"

Kris-B says, "linear can be a good thing, as Martha Stewart would say."

Paula says, "Are you still dancing, kathi?"

kathi says, "I love this, the connection b/t pressed and linear. Hmm. Tactile."

PamT says, "So, again, back to the question of technology and women NOW (as in this current historical moment)"

kathi says, "what is the question?"

PamT says, "Where are you headed with this issue as scholars?"

kathi says, "ok."

Paula says, "Our techies used to be all men; now it's about 50-50, with lots of women as experts to consult when we have questions or problems."

kathi says, "to figuring out how e-mail works in class to do what I want it to do"

PamT says, "I'm finding my desire for concrete action is leading me to work with girls."

Kris-B says, "where are you at with technology, in terms of seeing possibilities and constraints for women online? How are the current technologies impacting your professional and personal lives?"

frances says, "i'm trying to link my classes with others using the web in the fall"

Cissy says, "Well, practically speaking, there's a lot going on. I did some part time work in the IS (Informations Systems) department of a major corporation this year. The male/female ratio was really even. The head of web design team was a female. That's a different issue from empowerment and community, tho."

PamT says, "Because by the time girls are women, they've got so many hangups about technology that they don't think technology is a good avenue for them professionally. That's frustrating."

Joanne says, "I'm not sure if this is a direction my future research will go in, but one area I'm increasingly concerned with is distance education and the ways it works to limit women geographically."

kathi says, "I'm looking to rewrite Lanham. Or thinking about it."

Cissy says, "Like the workshop we talked about, Pam."

Lisa says, "I have been discovering so many terrific listservs and web sites for women—really supportive informative stuff."

PamT says, "What do you mean, Joanne?"

Shannon says, "I have been using listservs with classes and have lots of things that I want to try. I haven't been teaching lately so I have nothing going right now."

kathi says, "someone pointed out to me that the major theoreticians are male. Is that so?"

frances says, "I hope that my female engineers will find other female engineers to talk to and i want to get some money for a system that stays on"

PamT says, "Yes, when are we going to do that, Cissy and Morgan?"

Joanne says, "'What I mean is that while distance ed may open up some virtual possibilities for women, it often does so by keeping them confined to the home."

Kris-B says, "This year, I got involved in a computer/community literacy project in a junior high school, helping instructors to use even the most basic of word processing technologies in their language arts classes and observing what kids do with technology."

Cissy says, "Pam, I think if we get to work quickly, we can get one planned for the end of the summer."

PamT says, "Yeah, Joanne, the way electronic cottages allow women to work and take full time care of their kids."

kathi says, "I'm writing an article on tutoring with 4 female grad students here."

kathi says, "they say that the computer was the major socializing force."

Paula says, "I got our tutors here in the writing center their first taste of online tutorials with a rural high school AP English class. The HS has only one computer."

Joanne says, "For example, in much of the advertising our university is doing, we state that distance ed is a great alternative for women with children. I'm not sure that it's much of an alternative if it works to keep women in traditional home/child care roles."

Lisa says, "I wonder, Kathi, if what *counts* as theory is what men produce. Women tend to write more concretely (don't yell at me for the generalization!!) Sometimes I think that there's lots of theory in all the pedagogy that women write about, but it isn't perceived as such because it hasn't invented a new nomenclature, and it's comprehensible. Just a thought."

Kris-B says, "Yes, Joanne. The rhetoric of distance education is all-empowering, and it certainly does have its benefits, though I get the sense that the powers that be see dollar signs rather than community and social change."

kathi says, "I agree with what you're saying, Lisa. But then I want it translated so"

Joanne says, "What's really scary is that there are all of these fly-by-night companies setting up shop and convincing schools to outsource their distance ed programs."

Cissy says, "Lisa, good point. If the theory is couched in terms of practical classroom experience, it's not seen as theory?"

kathi says, "you have to be able to theorize the practice: it's Foucault."

Paula says, "My daughter Leigh took a distance ed. class as part of her MBA. She has a small baby and a full time job, and she found it great not to have to ride the BART every night in to San Francisco."

Sibylle agrees partly with Joanne but has some reservations. "I taught a distance ed course this semester, and my students were from 600 miles away. The women in my class were grade school teachers, a college teacher, and an administrative secretary. We also have many reservation schools hooked up to our nets. They wouldn't be able to make it at all otherwise."

Joanne says, "Yes, I don't mean to suggest that there aren't some great benefits."

Kris-B says, "to what extent does the technology of listservs, completely online composition courses, etc., inhibit that sense of community. I wish Barbara Monroe were here—her article really gets at his in that she compares the face to face interactions of her students after they've been online."

Lisa says, "Yes, Cissy, and if the language used to talk about it is concrete, easily graspable, I think people don't accord the ideas the value they deserve. It reminds me of the way my students are afraid to say something directly in their papers because they're afraid it will sound simplistic. I think people assume that if they can't understand something, it must be profound, subtle."

kathi says, "I'm not endorsing Foucault per se. But he has a point worth considering."

frances says, "that's a good point Lisa."

Cissy says, "Kris, what are you defining as community? The classroom only? Or the links students can make to communities outside the classrooms."

kathi says, "Let me push this further. Even theorists like Harkin are finding ways to endorse lore, to theorize it."

PamT says, "I had an article sent back to me to revise, and the editor said "Your point about women and technology is like x and y; it doesn't seem new." The articles cited (X and Y) were not about WOMEN, though. There's this other attitude that if its about women, it's been said better from some other perspective, I think, sometimes."

kathi says, "the timing on this is right. I just would like to be part of it is all, and one thing I think is that this project and ones like it are helping us see new ways to work. Paula, can you talk about the web version of our text?"

Kris-B says, "good point, Cissy. Community is a buzz-word, but I like to define it broadly, the idea of connecting classroom practice to people's lives in ways that help them, not just to get a job, or take a class, but use the new technologies of literacy to speak out, to ultimately create social change. Of course, this is very idealistic of me, I know."

Cissy says, "I think so, but I see it the same way you do. I'm really moving toward wanting my students to connect to many different communities."

PamT says, "Speaking of ideals, what is the ideal future for women and technology?"

PamT says, "What is it we're shooting for?"

morgan says, "cissy, ...and to look at those communities critically."

Cissy says, "A place to be heard."

Joanne says, "Kris, Michelle Comstock and I have been doing work on the emergence of a lesbigay youth cyberculture that focuses on the ways that technology is allowing this group of youth to influence social change in ways they couldn't without the technology."

daisley says, "that we're right in there, in the throes of it all...assumed to be in the CENTER, not the margins."

Cissy says, "A place to be heard, Pam? To make change?"

kathi says, "a place to develop a woman's expression a la Rich."

Cissy says, "Yes, Morgan. That's a very important part of it. Maybe the most important."

PamT says, "Make change in what ways?"

Paula says, "Kathi, Laura (where is Laura?), and I wrote an article together for this collection. It's set up in columns and different margins to sort of indicate levels of text and metatext. Laura and I were speaking on the phone last weekend and decided we needed our article to be on a website so there could be links, pictures. Laura wanted us all to go to photo booths and have strips of pictures made, happy, sad, bemused, and we wanted images of some of the metaphors in the text."

Joanne says, "The links between the potential for social change and technology are not hard to see when you're watching these young people."

Kris-B says, "Yes, Joanne, Michelle has talked to me about your work. The technology gives them solidarity, the power of a multiple voice?"

kathi says, "Thanks, Paula."

Kris-B says, "Paula, is your article online yet? I want to see."

PamT says, "I love the idea of emoticons using your real faces!"

Joanne says, "Yes, but perhaps most importantly it allows them to distribute information and life stories."

Cissy says, "The only answer I can think of is "real" change. A cop out. But change that allows women to become a part of the existing structures and then shift them. Kind of like what happens to discourse communities over time."

kathi says, "so woman's expression—images, emoticons, metaphors, associative connections."

Lisa says, "Ideally, tech. would be seamlessly available to all women, not just rich ones and those affiliated with institutions who give them them access. If poor women could be heard, we might actually see some social change."

kathi says, "distribute information and life stories to what end?"

Paula says, "the article is far from online. We still need (ahem) a reference from kathi, who is now dancing..."

PamT says, "That's why we don't hear from poor women more often."

Shannon says, "I don't want to be a wet blanket, but to me it seems important we also talk about access...in schools and homes...and it still seems that that we're talking about women in ways that are too monolithic"

kathi says, "dancing to get the reference."

frances says, "life stories are valuable just as giving voice to life stories."

daisley says, "I think women's perspectives (should be in quotes) seem to allow for the idea of multiple perspectives. i.e. we assume that we do not speak in on, but many tongues...?"

Cissy says, "two really good points, Shannon."

Sibylle agrees with Lisa. "Yes, isn't it amazing that we can talk about "women" but leave out 1/2 of the female population (or more)?"

Shannon says, "So I guess I am agreeing with/repeating what Lisa is saying"

Kris-B says, "Yes, our infatuation with technology is very class-based, Lisa. I would rather see Internet stations in women's shelters rather than my local coffeehouse, a virtual extension of the cappuccino lifestyle."

Joanne [to explain]: "strategies for dealing with homophobic peers, proved information on safe sex and aids, to let each other know that there are other lesbigay youth going through similar experiences."

kathi says, "well, but change comes slowly, and not all women want this change, right?"

Paula says, "today i took a woman colleague upstairs from a workshop we were attending and showed her how to access her e-mail from the computer center. She'd moved and couldn't find her modem, had no idea how else to use the technology."

daisley says, "Shannon, thank you for bringing up the notion of access...jeez-o-pete, talk about access, mine sucks big time..."

PamT says, "That last line goes in the book, Margaret! :-)"

morgan says, "and the gap in access seems to be getting bigger"

Sibylle asks "Kris, do women in women's shelters want to have computers? Or are their needs very different (food, clothes)?"

Shannon says, "yes."

daisley says, "Pam...and so it goes..."

kathi says, "not here. We really do have a fair amount of access here."

PamT says, "Yeah, this makes me realize what a luxury item this conversation is, although for us it's work."

PamT says, "What we're theorizing is most American's leisure time...cultural studies anyone?"

Lisa- says, "But such FUN work, Pam."

kathi says, "Pollyanna repeats, look at what we are doing to make this real."

Paula says, "this is work?"

Kris-B says, "Very true, Sibylle. To what extent would access to the network help in making connections, to jobs, to technological skills, to each other."

Cissy says, "Yeah, we're only able to have this kind of conversation because we are, in many ways, elite. Poor, but elite. :-)"

daisley says, "It's work... yet it's play? I think that blurring of the lines has a lot to do with what literacy in general is all about."

Joanne says, "why would women in shelters use the computers? having worked in a homeless shelter I can't imagine how I would convince the residents why this technology is important important to their lives."

kathi says, "Distance ed, college ed, reservations, shelters, teacher ed: not a bad start."

Cissy says, "Oh, Margaret. That's a really important point. Morgan and I get into it in our article...the importance of play."

Paula says, "I just visited a men's shelter, and they were concerned about teaching the men word processing so they could get better jobs. All their computers were broken."

PamT says, "Cissy—Have you read Paul Fussell's book, Class? He describes academics as of the X class—not really fitting any categories, as you suggest (elite but poor)."

kathi says, "Jobs: that's what technology can do. And jobs mean independence."

Shannon says, "It seems strange to think of technology as a luxury item that the poor don't want, not a priority, etc. This seems to deny the importance of technology for securing socio-economic privilege."

Lisa says, "Health information, parenting advice, too—much more is available than they cod find at the local public library."

Sibylle says, "yes, Kris, that's the important part? How can computers help those in shelters to get out of their situations? I don't think they would have a lot of fun doing a moo, but they might get a great deal out of finding jobs on the net. That would be a "real" advance..."

Cissy says, "Yeah, Pam. I've read it, but it's been a few years. I should look back at it."

frances says, "word processing used to be an add on for a job, now it's a requirement"

daisley says, "I'm torn: conversations about play; conversations about HOW on-line spaces could be important for shelters...or for anyone..."

Kris-B says, "Yes, Joanne, and to what extent would they find this empowering? What sort of activities could be made to have that type of exigency for women of varying status in our culture. So often the web is touted as a networking schmooze tool for women."

PamT says, "I didn't mean to suggest technology as a luxury item, just this particular conversation. I have the time, the connection, etc. to have this conversation with this group of academic women."

Cissy says, "margaret, I don't think it is so much that online space itself is important for shelters. But the kinds of connections facilitated by online connections are important for women in those situations."

daisley says, "Shelters...I'm thinking that the value of e-space could simply be CONNECTING (there's that word again) with others in the same position?"

frances says, "technology allows me to talk to others each day and to engage in talks like this, its fun and empowering"

kathi says, "suppose we took connecting as the central metaphor: does it work?"

Kris-B says, "And to add to Pam's comment, that our position as academic women has in many cases helped create the opportunity to learn to use the technology, to not feel the same sense of anxiety about it that women with less daily access might feel at walking into a classroom and seeing a room full of computers."

Joanne says, "but if they're in a shelter they're surrounded by people in similar positions. I'm wondering if the types of jobs most people who are in a shelter of some sort would be qualified for are ever advertised on the net."

Shannon says, "I guess I wasn't just talking about this conversation, but also in reference to a lot of material I have been reading about public schooling and funding that argues that the poor just need the basics, not the funds that could put the kind of access that we are talking about in their hands."

PamT says, "One thing I'm thinking...when shelters for battered women were first opened in the 70s, the connection issue became real as women began to realize they weren't the only ones suffering this life...and from that recognition came change."

daisley says, "Connecting ABSOLUTELY works...discourse theorists like Deborah Cameron, etc. have brought such issues to the forefront of discourse theory, under the guise of feminist explorations of discourse."

PamT says, "Yeah, I wonder that too Joanne. There's so much hype about the web that I'm not sure is getting played out for real people yet."

kathi says, "so the connecting that we saw in social activism of the 70s, in"

frances says, "kris, having taught many fearful faculty about computers, working with them to minimize that fear is essential to make any sort of progress."

Sibylle says, "but I don't think "connecting" is "empowering" I can be connected but might be shut down by ongoing conversations, and then I'd feel less empowered than without my connection."

kathi says, "theorizing in the 80s is now online in the 90s?"

Cissy says, "Potentially, kathi. But the same thing is happening that always happens. The net is becoming primarily a commercial endeavor."

Kris-B says, "While the job aspect is a consideration, I would be more interested in helping women to represent their lives online, by sharing stories, but also, connecting to the web, a type of virtual narrative, a history, a re-invention or re-representation of one's life history."

kathi says, "is the net *primarily* commercial?"

daisley says, "the trap is: theorizing that technology itself or connecting itself is empowering...yet, the paradox is that it CAN BE...the options..."

Cissy says, "Connection is getting shoved aside in favor of corporate presence"

kathi says, "yes, exactly, margaret: nothing is guaranteed here. Opportunity is all."

PamT says, "joanne, another thing I'm thinking is that information is the important thing. When i graduated from college, no one I knew could tell me how to find a job short of looking in the newspapers. But I knew somehow that that was not where the good jobs were to be found. But I didn't have the information at my disposal. So I went to graduate school! (just a joke)."

Lisa- says, "I agree with Pam. Just finding other people in the same circumstances can be empowering. There are all kinds of listservs for women with specific health problems, and they allow these women to share the different ways they've dealt with their symptoms, their doctors, including trying nontraditional approaches. There's a whole counter movement to traditional medicine going on online. Women sharing what used to be folk remedies. Women sharing advice on how to get a doctor to listen to you (wear a suit)."

frances says, "everyone has a home page and e-mail and commercials abound its seems like we have exchanged one level of technology for another"

Joanne says, "Yes Kris, this could be very important...it is important to the youth that participate in the internet that I've been working with Michelle"

PamT says, "So access might not be the issue as much as knowledge about what's available.

kathi says, "I think we are creating the knowledge—or there is that potential."

Joanne says, "But sharing this information requires that you have access—again most people do not have access. And if you've ever tried to access the internet from your local library you know that's almost impossible."

kathi says, "My reference to Rich was deliberate. I do think space exists here that is available to us if we use it. And what we develop here—language, attitude."

Lisa- says, "Who is Rich, Kathi?"

kathi says, "knowledge—can be taken offline. Change. Rich: Adrienne. The poet."

PamT says, "Do any of you know of MOOs for women?"

daisley says, "I would say access is the BIGGEST issue...not unlike having access to literacy in more general terms—whether understanding how to "critically" read a newspaper, or having a library card."

frances says, "joanne, access for many in HS and in public education is determined by funding and property taxes, not exactly equal."

Cissy says, "I don't. But there are a ton of listservs. Probably IRC channels as well."

Paula says, "Our public library just got internet service. to use the terminal you have to stand (to keep people from hogging it). Who can get into a community standing in a public library?"

kathi says, "Isn't this a feminist moo? I mean, right now?"

Cissy says, "Paula, anyone who uses that terminal to connect to others"

Kris-B says, "It's clear that we see potential for these new technologies in people's lives, but so much of our actual experiences seem constrained, whether it be in the classroom or in our daily lives. Do we expect too much from these technologies?"

daisley holds up a BIG sign: | CYBORG MOO!! |

kathi says, "The woman doing our library tech is one of our MA's! Change"

Kris-B says, "now that's a slogan, Margaret!"

Joanne says, "We expect too little from those who control the production of technology!"

PamT says, "we have a staff of cybergrrls monitoring the computer lab in the English dept."
Cissy says, "Kris, we probably do. The key is to find ways to use the technology to create opportunities for real change. Shift from idealism to realism."
PamT says, "Men in the dept, have remarked on their presence to me."
morgan says, "Pam, oh really?"
daisley says, "Kris—and the graphics that should surround it would be one of those Ben&Jerry-type dairy cows???"
Lisa says, "Mmm, Ben & Jerry."
morgan says, "I don't think we expect too much from technologies just need to keep up our ideologies."
Paula says, "Lisa, did you say that with a Homer Simpsonesque accent?"
daisley says, "Cissy—PLEASE... not a shift from idealism to realism, but a sustained tension between the two. Isn't that what feminism is all about???"
kathi says, "is there a single feminism?"
Cissy says, "OOps, Margaret, I should have made myself more clear. I don't mean abandon idealism but to show that those ideals *CAN* be accomplished."
PamT says, "I think my idealism is turning me into a cynic. Ask Kris. Or maybe I'm just really tired form a long year."
Lisa says, "I'm not sure, Paula, but I figure any conversation is only 2 degrees of separation from food."
daisley says, "Kathi...NO! it's feminismS...plural."
Kris-B says, "Connections are important between women, particularly women teachers and students. I did a *CCCCs* proposal with two graduate student women in my class on Electronic Discourse about the potential and limits in implementing feminist pedagogies in computerized writing classrooms, because of traditional gendered assumptions about technology as something to be mastered and transmitted by men, rather something to be mentored and shared by women."
kathi says, "ok, but where are we going with this? I mean: is this like African-Americans"
Cissy says, "Kris, you use of verbs is fascinating: mastered/transmitted v. mentored/shared"
PamT says, "What do you mean, kathi?"
kathi says, "who want to be part of the plurality or those who are separatist?"
Kris-B says, "I'm very verbal ;-)"
kathi says, "what's the goal? Will we eventually be working with men? or holding out?"
kathi says, "is your strategy, Kris, short-term for a level playing field?"
frances says, "kathi, I work with men each day. What do you mean?"
kathi says, "and wider participation?"
kathi says, "well, we want more women involved, right?"
daisley says, "c'mon... a 'level playing field'? Isn't it a constant struggle?"
kathi says, "so do we do this by separating or by integrating?"
Cissy says, "Both, kathi."
kathi says, "or some of each? I'm not sure, myself"

Joanne says, "Is separating really an option?"
daisley says, "I agree with Kathi.. it's BOTH, when either is necessary"
kathi says, "isn't that what this book, this moo, is about?"
frances says, "I say both too; we have to integrate if we want to make change."
Cissy says, "Finding community may involve some separation, but change can't occur until we're working inside and outside the system."
Kris-B says, "Good point, kathi. What's that point about having to speak the lingo of the oppressor to effect social change in the first place? I do want to level the playing field; many of the women in my classes are novices with technology."
PamT says, "Sometimes the only way we can withstand the pressures of patriarchy as women are to have our own selective moments with other women alone."
frances says, "right on, Pam"
kathi says, "ok, our own selective moments. I like this. Is that what Gates just had?"
Lisa says, "The way we're having now—a selective moment alone with other women."
Cissy says, "and those selective moments strengthen and solidify us for the rest of the time."
frances says, "yes, we are having more than moments here."
Kris-B says, "that is a cool statement Pam. We need to highlight this somewhere in the book."
kathi says, "I'm with you. I'm looking for the big picture here."
Joanne says, "But even when we are alone with other women there are biases, power struggles, those with authority and those without."
daisley says, "Did Gates have a 'selective' moment? Or, did he assume that his moment was inclusive? That's what I'm suspicious of."
PamT says, "Gates had a public moment which excluded women, and not for the purpose of coalition building (what I was talking about)."
kathi says, "so selective moments are not public? But the book is public?"
Kris-B says, "Yes, Joanne, your article with Susan gets at the power dynamics that reinscribe themselves even in all-women settings that are supposed to be supportive."
PamT says, "But when we're coalition building, we're selective about those differences among women, too."
PamT says, "Or we can be, rather."
kathi says, "I'm not trying to be difficult. But this is a good issue, and we dodge it."
Cissy says, "but is the book a selective moment of community building?"
daisley says, "Joanne—don't you believe that men, in their 'alone' moments, are building their sub-coalitions within their larger coalition?"
Cissy says, "or is it a public message about some of the things we've learned in these communities?"
Joanne says, "I've been in situations (virtual and real) where the claim has been made that we're all women here and feminists on top of it...and yet the discrimination is still apparent."
PamT says, "The kinds of moments I'm thinking of have not been public—they have been behind the scenes exchanges that give me strength to act publicly."

kathi says, "discrimination against?"

kathi says, "I have to gather the ideas. So selective moments that can result in a public."

frances says, "joanne, I think we have all been in situations like that. Sometimes all women groups are worse than dealing with men. But not always of course."

Kris-B says, "I think in many ways, Cissy, the book is our chance to speak about these issues in a focused, overt way. Many of the existing collection have limited discussions of gender, technology, and writing."

kathi says, "message, right?"

daisley says, "PamT—I see what you mean. We need some kind of PUBLIC moment...like a Million Women's March Moment?"

Lisa says, "But surely we've all been in all-women groups that were not supportive. Male-female groups certainly have a different dynamic than all-female groups, but all-female groups can be competitive and nasty as well as friendly and helpful."

Paula says, "Margaret, time to hold up another sign!"

PamT says, "Well, actually, what I was thinking of are the everyday public moments—committee meetings, responding to someone; racist, homophobic comments made in public."

Kris-B says, "Unfortunately, Lisa, that's all too true."

kathi says, "we're all human. Even women:)"

```
                                  ________________________
                                 |                        |
daisley holds up a BIG sign:     | MILLION Women on the 'Net |
                                 |________________________|
```

Paula smiles

PamT says, "Women can be every bit as patriarchal as men—we're all raised in the same culture."

kathi says, "The academy scripts us as patriarchal"

Cissy says, "OOh. Now there's a thought. A site where women can sign in and list a sentence or two about how they use the net. We could try to get one million signs"

```
                                  _________________________________
                                 |                                 |
                                 | I could never be patriarchal, no, no, no |
Kris-B holds up a BIG sign:      |               ;-)               |
                                 |_________________________________|
```

daisley says, "Excuse me, but...F- the academy, and how they try to portray us, or me."

Lisa smiles and cheers.

PamT says, "What about that shampoo commercial, don't hate me because I'm beautiful? Women are encouraged to use patriarchal measures against one another. (I always hated her because she was vacuous...just kidding!)"

kathi says, "It's not how they portray us, Margaret. It's what's required to survive."

susanr arrives.

daisley says, "kathi—ah yes, reality looms."
Kris-B says, "hey, it's susan!"
frances says, "hi susan"
kathi says, "I'm not endorsing academic patriarchy. I'm a product of it. So are we all"
Lisa says, "Ooh, I hate that smug commercial."
PamT says, "Hey, Cissy—sounds like that performance artist Jenny Holzer might be interested in your idea!"
kathi says, "hi susan."
Shannon says, "hi susan."
Lisa says, "Hi, Susan."
Cissy says, "Who's Jenny Holzer?"
daisley says, "Welcome, collaborator-woman!"
PamT says, "A conceptual artist who works a lot with slogans."
susanr says, "hi everyone, sorry to be late. Emergency phonecall."
kathi says, "I do think we can re-script the academy. Again: slowly. It'll happen."
Cissy says, "Ah."
susanr says, "hi daisley cohort."
PamT says, "one of her favorite sayings: Absolute power corrupts absolutely. When the Clint Eastwood movie came out, I cringed."
Joanne says, "At this point, doesn't re-scripting the academy mean re-scripting technology?"
daisley says, "I like that idea...re-script the academy...starring...xxxxx in the role of the cyborg-woman..."
kathi says, "re-scripting technology, you mean in terms of interfacing and all?"
frances says, "joanne, rescripting the academy means rescripting ourselves and the technology."
Joanne says, "Yes, everything."
daisley says, "interfacing, and in-your-facing..."
PamT says, "And that rescripting will fall to us...there are a lot of people who think it's fine just the way it is."
Kris-B says, "The commercial I can't handle is the MCI internet one. You know the one, black and white. There are no genders. There is no race. There are no infirmities. Utopia? No. The internet!"
kathi says, "I think the technology provides a place where we don't have to re-script."
kathi says, "because we can SCRIPT: that's the power of it."
Paula says, "Kathi, say more about the way the academy enforces patriarchy?"
Cissy says, "That commercial kills me! Spoken like people who have never experienced the net!"
PamT says, "Maybe not rescript, but resist the scripts others are carrying into this site."
Joanne says, "What do you mean"
frances says, "I think technology can give a place where we don't have to rescript. But I don't think it does so now"
daisley says, "No, the commercial is spoken like people who are selling the net."

Cissy says, "What scripts are inherent in the technology as it stands?"
kathi says, "the academy rewards hierarchy, conservatism, confidence, aggression."
Joanne says, "Yes, we can script, but we still have to be worried about who's in control of the production of technology and whose interests this production serves."
kathi says, "you want to do well; do these things. But if you are a woman and you do these things, you are a bitch. Gotcha!"
Paula says, "Conservatism?"
PamT says, "So then how do others succeed, kathi?"
Shannon says, "Isn't MCI advertising a nonscripted space?"
frances says, "Amen to that, kathi. women have a hard time finding a place in that mix. My students have great trouble there."
Cissy says, "Maybe. But it's a space that doesn't exist."
Kris-B says, "I like the metaphor of scripting, of coding, to change our image, our online identity. I see that as a potential of the web, from a visual standpoint. Gail Hawisher's talk at *CCCC* was pretty interesting on that, that even as academic we represent ourselves along traditional academic hierarchies."
daisley says, "Good question, Cissy. I think, actually, that many of the 'selling' features of the net revolve around what might be seen as feminist paradigms.. for instance, 'connectivity' (there's that word again)"
Shannon says, "Right. that's what I mean."
kathi says, "I think we play enough by that game to do what we need to do."
PamT says, "Connectivity isn't just feminine—think of old boys networks.
They're really well connected."
kathi says, "Then admitted to the game, we change it."
frances says, "kris, scripting was the metaphor June Haddon Hobbs and I used in our last *CCCC* talk. It went well and we hope to make a book of it."
Kris-B says, "that sounds very cool, Frances."
susanr says, "kris-I didn't hear Gail's talk. Can you elaborate on "traditional academic hierarchies"?"
daisley says, "Tres cool, francis. What will the title be?"
kathi says, "so we don't let the game corrupt us. We align ourselves with likeminded."
kathi says, "folks. We develop new models of the academic. We bring about change."
frances says, "Its called Lives transcending scripts. its about women fighting the good academic fight, winning some and losing some."
kathi says, "Oh I like it. I like the optimism here."
kathi says, "Lives *do* transcend scripts. Put that on a poster, someone."

```
                            ______________________________
                           |                              |
Cissy holds up a BIG sign: | Lives *do* transcend scripts |
                           |______________________________|
```

kathi says, "Thank you Cissy."
daisley says, "I like the idea of...control? power? stepping into the *roles* of those who fight the good fight, or whatever you want to call it..."
frances says, "thanks cissy."

Kris-B says, "Susan, that as female academics, we represent ourselves online according to the traditional academic drill, degrees, dissertation, cv, very little in the way of history, narrative, reinventing ourselves. Some of this, of course, is limited to what freedom university relations departments will let individuals have in web pages—that there might be a canned format for all to follow."

Lisa says, "Let's save these signs. They're giving us slogans to live by. Or are they just like the little titles before every new scene in Fraser."

PamT smiles at Lisa.

Joanne says, "Kathi, is saying "lives do transcend scripts" the same as saying material conditions transcend discourse?"

frances says, "we need a book with some optimism in it. I hate this us and them language we all get so caught up in."

Kris-B says, "we'll have a transcript of the whole thing, Lisa, signs, typos, and all. I can post it to the SCAPES list if everyone wants?"

Cissy says, "Please do, Kris. I was going to ask if we could get a copy."

daisley says, "Joanne—how about actions transcend discourse?"

susanr says, "Did anyone read Ellen Goodman's column on the airforce Kelly Flinn's dismissal. The woman who dismissed her is Sheila Widnall, a woman of firsts (secretary of the Air Force)."

Lisa says, "thanks, Kris."

PamT says, "I took what kathi's sign said to mean that our lives are not scripted out and then followed, but that we can revise as we go?"

kathi says, "Joanne, I'm not sure. I know that if we change the discourse, we change."

frances says, "yes, please do and post to the list. I'd like to print this out and read it at some other time when i can keep track of all these conversations."

kathi says, "the reality, our perception of it, the ways we see things."

kathi says, "we can change our material conditions. Does this make sense? You have to remember that I'm older than a bunch of you, I bet."

Kris-B says, "Can we use the discourse to reinvent ourselves?"

susanr says, "Gee, trouble with typing. Goodman's point is that Widnall had to take the middle road—partially selling out."

Cissy says, "Morgan...Don Juan DeMarco..."

daisley says, "Yes, please do save this *script*, as I've been bumped 3x during the course of conversation."

Kris-B says, "and not just virtually, but like kathi suggests, our material conditions."

Joanne says, "I guess that depends on whether or not you view language as symbolic action ala Burke."

Cissy says, "Re: using discourse to reinvent ourselves."

Lisa says, "I think it's important that books on women's issues do pint out inequities, but sometimes it's so refreshing to read a book like *Wired Women* or *SurferGrrrls* that moves beyond oppression and simply celebrates what women can do and what they're doing. that just gets on with it."

daisley says, "material conditions = access and the means to access (time, money)"

PamT says, "Yes, Lisa. I agree."
kathi says, "idea, not anyone else's. A good idea, as it turns out. I *think*"
PamT says, "I think this is part of my growing cynicism. I just feel weighed down by what I've been doing..."
Joanne says, "Yes, I like that equation."
kathi says, "yes, please post the transcript. Please. I have to think more about this."
Paula says, "Pam, what's got you cynical? You've mentioned that twice now."
Kris-B says, "I do like Wired Women and SurferGrrrls, but my concern with both texts is that their predominant image of women online, with little variation, is that of a young, white female, and from a materialist feminist standpoint of avoiding monolithic definitions of woman, this is very problematic."
daisley says, "Pam—what do you mean about being 'weighted down'—this book thing? the academic career thing? as it relates to technology thing? What?"
kathi says, "Pam, do tell."
frances says, "pam, what have you been doing that has you so cynical?"
susanr says, "I think I'll keep talking to myself. Woman Widnall to cut a deal in real life—i.e. the material world. She had to dismiss the first woman B2 pilot for sleeping with people. Yikes I am having so much trouble typing."
PamT says, "Not the book thing...the academic thing...I'm sort of having a lot of doubts about the value of academic work in the world...the material world."
Kris-B says, "The other book I'm talking about is NetChick by Carla Sinclair."
kathi says, "you mean for the woman on the street?"
kathi says, "Susan, I'm interested in the Flinn thing. But can we finish Pam first?"
frances says, "Pam, I had those doubts when I first stared PHD work and now have them again as a new asst prof. It's hard being at the bottom of the pile again."
PamT says, "Finish me?! aaagh....just what I need!"
Lisa says, "Yes, Kris, it has a real upper-middle-class twenty-something optimism. And as you say, it addresses a narrow audience."
kathi says, "Pam, you laughed. See? It's not so bad!"
PamT says, "That's interesting, Frances—I had the same experience. At some point in graduate school, the whole thing seemed so removed..."
Kris-B says, "Susan, that whole situation is incredible, given that men have received far less punishment, and less public humiliation, for the same 'infractions'."
kathi says, "I do see what you are saying."
kathi says, "And I do think that it's important to believe that we are connected"
kathi says, "there's that word again—to something larger."
PamT says, "I spend so much time in my office, alone, typing, writing, spinning my wheels...maybe this much isolation isn't good for me :-)"
kathi says, "what's the spinning of the wheels part? would you be happier if you were doing program work?"
Cissy says, "Well, when you get moved, walk over. I'll give you coffee or something :-)"

Paula says, "don't you feel sometimes as if you're welded to your computer screens?"

Cissy says, "Paula, yes!"

kathi says, "Yea, Paula, but I like it."

morgan says, "Pam, i know this grad. student you could take to lunch...."

frances says, "I think we all want to move our rhetorics into action and doing that seems isolating, but..."

Paula says, "I like it, too. That worries me from time to time."

Cissy says, "That's funny, morg. I know one too."

PamT says, "No, happier I'm not sure about but sometimes I just don't find it very fulfilling, the emphasis on scholarship."

kathi says, "Yeah, it worries me a little too. But mostly, I think it's ok"

Kris-B says, "Being something other than an academic has been on my mind a lot. Maybe it's because I'm in a field where so much of my time is, as Pam suggests, isolated, and that my self-esteem is so tied to the acceptance of my work in a literal and figurative sense.

kathi says, "so can you do less scholarship?"

kathi says, "the balance, you know, is different for everyone"

Kris-B says, "Hey Susan, we were just getting talking about the Flinn thing."

kathi says, "yes, we're "finishing" Pam, and then we will take up Flinn"

romano says, "Now the self esteem thing is interesting. I hate it when I become vulnerable to criticism."

kathi says, "in the ideal world, Pam, what would you do?"

Paula says, "Pam, do you feel finished?"

PamT says, "I think the technology thing is especially discouraging in some ways—it's an enormous time drain to keep up and current and then it's saddening to see so much of the same happening over and over."

kathi says, "so much of the same?"

romano says, "Pam, what same thing?"

PamT says, "same old power plays."

romano says, "like?"

frances says, "I get very impatient. I'm too old to fight these battles any more and it is depressing, but if i don't fight them and speak up, who will?"

romano says, "I say worriedly, going to my first job."

kathi says, "did you really think that techno would solve this?"

PamT says, "well, susan, funny you should bring that up—actually I was thinking of instances like the one where we were soundly attacked online last year..."

kathi says, "were you, attacked? for what?"

PamT says, "Susan?"

romano says, "Pam, I think what my bad experiences on line have done for me is this: distance from my own words. I had another experience last fall—very weird—but I was able to get less involved emotionally."

Kris-B says, "It's funny. I don't post to lists like ACW and the now dead MBU much at all any more; I don't feel like they fulfill any particular need for community or information. Susan, are you talking about MBU?"

Lisa says, "Susan and Pam, what happened to you? Why were you attacked?"

romano says, "but I'm not sure of the value of getting less emotional. Yes, MBU."

kathi says, "yes, can you fill us in?"

Cissy says, "Kris, same here. It's more like a presentational forum than a community to me."

PamT says, "susan and I were on this listserv and made the argument—quite a simple version, actually—that technology is not such a great place for women all the time. Men online didn't find this a relevant issue to discuss."

Lisa says, "Did the men online change the subject or attack it?"

kathi says, "well, at the risk of sounding cynical, I think many of the listservs we probably frequent are old-boys clubs."

Cissy says, "yes."

Lisa says, "Wow. MBU was hardly the place to be non-ideological. All those academics with all those opinions."

kathi says, "daisley says, "Is it 'nonideological' when you are pulling your ads because of $$$$$?????"

romano says, "two incidents. The one refers to was a fairly civil incident where certain males refused to believe that discourse online might be experienced differently by different people."

Shannon says, "This has been my experience, Kathi."

kathi says, "well, among those in the know, there is a kind of party line, don't you think?"

PamT says, "I'm not on any listservs right now—I didn't have time for the posturing so many people did on MBU and some others."

kathi says, "and isn't it mostly a male party line? Which is why we have small groups of women doing their own thing, and then the women's listservs you all."

PamT says, "What listserv experiences have you had that were empowering?"

kathi says, "mentioned earlier?"

Lisa says, "I think the men on MBU cum ACW think of themselves as liberal, as feminists. They probably couldn't stand the thought that women were challenging their femin. credentials."

PamT nods at Lisa.

Cissy says, "Pam, my empowering experiences have been on all-female lists."

kathi says, "exactly: they think they are us/we. When we challenge that, they feel betrayed."

Shannon says, "This too sounds familiar."

morgan says, "i really havent found listservs empowering—yet anyway."

romano says, "Interesting question Pam. I'm now off most lists because I find they drain me and I get little else done. Never empowered."

Lisa says, "And as for the no sense of humor thing. Make a castration joke. See how hard they laugh;-)"

Cissy says, "Is there a list for women in technology? If not, could we create one?"

kathi says, "I like WCENTER: there are more women there. Now that I think about it."

daisley says, "My 'empower experiences' have also been on all-female lists...but I'm leery in saying so, that we begin to sound like the MBU/ACW message: we're all fems here, open-minded, etc."

Joanne says, "For me a listserv is empowering to the extent that it meets some big need."

kathi says, “yes, margaret, but some lists are perhaps more woman friendly than others?”

romano says, ” Kathi’s WCenter message reminds me to ask this: Do computer lab directors (Pam, you are one, so speak) differ from W Center directors in temperament or am I imagining this?”

Paula says, “Kathi, I like WCENTER, too. Plenty of men and sometimes they show their big, colorful tails, but the discourse doesn’t privilege that kind of grandstanding.”

kathi says, “Paula, exactly. What is it about that listserv that the peacocks don’t play?”

Lisa says, There are a number of women in tech. lists; most of them are populated by women techies, but I’ve enjoyed them all the same. PANDORAZ is one.”

PamT says, “I don’t know much about writing center directors...so I don’t know.”

daisley says, “kathi, yes...but I think the things about lists is that they can become like a lot of real-analog situations: self-perpetuating...there has to be a purpose, as we have here tonight. Some kind of finite existence, if not some moral cause...?”

Paula says, “Maybe it’s the writing center mentality: you have to listen.”

romano says, “I find that one way women empower themselves in online mixed groups is by assuming very techie posture, and then undermining that, once they establish credibility.”

kathi says, “Margaret, yea, I’m with you. I like the structure; it works toward change”

PamT says, “yeah, that’s what Joanne said, too, margaret—this is the thing for me. I’m so busy with so many things at once that things need a focus, an AGENDA, as your sign said earlier.”

kathi says, “see that’s it: assuming (like passing) until you can change things”

romano says, “It’s (to continue myself) like Spivak’s “Can the Subaltern Speak?”—she can talk like the big boys and then say something they wouldn’t say.”

Joanne says, “I need to head out—thanks for the conversation—I look forward to reading the transcript (with all my typos!).”

Paula says, “But why should we talk like big boys?”

kathi says, “Bye, Joanne”

PamT says, “Thanks for coming, Joanne—nice talking with you!”

Shannon says, “bye.”

Joanne has disconnected.

The housekeeper arrives to remove Joanne.

kathi says, “What will you do with this, Kris and Pam?”

PamT says, “Edit it!”

Paula says, “I hope you’ll connect all of Kathi’s fractured messages.”

PamT says, “We’ll shape it up as a conclusion to the book.”

Kris-B says, “it’s the conclusion to the book, in lieu of a more traditional conclusion.”

Lisa says, “i have to leave, too. thank you for organizing this MOO, Pam and Kris. Thanks everyone for the conversation.”

romano says, “Pam’s being too busy is very scary. One piece of advice

received from a friend is this: If you're a woman, be very careful about taking on all the little tasks that people ask you to do. Very careful."
kathi says, "oh lordy, you aren't going to put *this* in the book? can I bowderlize it?"
Cissy says, "Will we be having another discussion here? To add to this?"
Lisa has disconnected.
The housekeeper arrives to remove Lisa.
PamT says, "I think we should do this again! for fun."
Paula says, "this wasn't fun?"
romano says, "P and K will remove typos, I think. Please?"
PamT says, "No, it was fun—but let's have some more!"
kathi says, "Yes, for fun. Not for attribution."
Cissy says, "I think we should have at least one more."
PamT turns off the disco ball.
kathi says, "so hard to dance in the dark."
"Kris-B says, "yes, thanks to everyone. Well, what we can do is we can post to the list, and within reason, if someone says, I can't be saying this in public, we'll edit it out. I can post the "dirty" version to the list asap."
Shannon says, "I agree."
daisley has disconnected.
The housekeeper arrives to remove daisley.
romano says, "Awww , Pam."
Cissy pouts because she never got to do the hustle.
Paula pouts because she never got to be dirty.
kathi says, "ok. I'd appreciate the chance to see what I said. <grimace>"
PamT remembers eighth grade dance lessons in the Catholic school gym, where SHE learned to do the Hustle...
Kris-B quietly retrieves the disco ball and hides it an oversized bag.
kathi pouts cause she has to stop dancing.
PamT says, "Who is going to be in Hawaii?"
kathi says, "I guess I'm signing off. This was fun. Take care, girls."
Cissy raises her hand.
kathi says, "kathi isn't."
Kris-B says, "it was too cool. Turned out so great."
morgan says, "yep—hawaii!"
romano says, "Thank you Pam and Kris. My first enjoyable MOO."
PamT says, "Thanks for coming!"
Paula says, "Mine, too, susan."
Kris-B says, "thanks to you Susan. Glad you could make it!"
Shannon says, "Good night everyone."
romano has disconnected.
The housekeeper arrives to remove romano.
kathi has disconnected.
The housekeeper arrives to remove kathi.
Kris-B says, "Good night, sleep tight, and pleasant dreams to you."
Paula says, "Bye, everyone."
Shannon has disconnected.
Paula has disconnected.
The housekeeper arrives to remove Paula.

PamT says, "I gotta go, I got two girls downstairs who think we're going to the dollar movie, but I don't know what's playing."
Cissy says, "See ya."
morgan says, "bye."
PamT says, "Goodnight everyone!"
morgan says, "goodnight."
morgan has disconnected.
The housekeeper arrives to remove morgan.
Cissy says, "bye all."
Cissy has disconnected.
The housekeeper arrives to remove Cissy.
Kris-B says, "so Pam, we did it."
PamT says, "yeah, that went well, lots of stuff to work with."
The housekeeper arrives to cart Shannon off to bed.
PamT says, "ok...see you."
PamT has disconnected.
The housekeeper arrives to remove PamT.
Kris-B says, "bye."

REFERENCES

Hawisher, G., & Sullivan, P. (1998). Women on the networks: Searching for e-spaces of their own. In S. Jarrett & L. Worsham (Eds.), *Feminism and composition studies: In other words* (pp. 172–197). New York: Modern Language Association.

Stabile, C. (1994). *Feminism and the technological fix*. New York: Manchester University Press.

Mapping the Future: An Interview with Cynthia Selfe

Kristine Blair
Bowling Green State University

Pamela Takayoshi
University of Louisville

In this interview conducted at the 1997 National Council of Teachers of English Convention in Detroit, Michigan, Cynthia Selfe, Professor of Composition and Communication at Michigan Technological University, talks about the ways in which her own concerns as a rhetoric, computers, and composition scholar, have impacted her role as 1998 Chair of the Conference on College Composition and Communication. Selfe also comments on the way in which national future policy decisions regarding instructional technology will impact students and teachers.

Kristine Blair: Perhaps we should start with where you're at in your thinking about technology, particularly within the context of the profession. For example, how might technology issues be connected to your current positions in CCCC and NCTE?

Cynthia Selfe: One of the things that started to change my thinking about technology over time has to do with the scope of what I'm seeing. And it's not that I'm looking at different issues. I've been looking at issues like the intersection of technology, gender, racism, poverty, and literacy, those sorts of overlapping and related sets of issues for me, for the last 7 or 8 years. But I'm starting to look at these overlapping issues in larger ways because I'm dealing with different groups of people and larger groups of people. So in the past year, as I've been preparing for this Chair's address, I've started to think in terms of what I've considered to be a national project to expand technological literacy that our country is undertaking, and that most teachers of English don't recognize as happening right now as a coherent, systematic national project. It's costing us $109 billion over 5 years at the national level. It's sponsored by the Clinton/Gore administration and recognized by the Secretary of Education Richard Riley as a primary literacy project in the country. A project to expand technological literacy, by which they mean to make students aware of how to use technology in a range of ways, but in a very important way, how to communicate in technological environments. How to make every student technologically literate by the beginning of the 21st century, that's their goal.

KB: Do you think English teachers have a problem with that in that technological literacy is seen as an exact knowledge that they don't have mastery of themselves?

CS: I think they have several problems with it. The first problem with it is that they don't recognize it as a literacy project. They separate technology from language studies because it's a convenient and historical separation and also because it's convenient for English teachers not to take on the primary responsibility for planning for technology, designing technology, figuring how to pay for technology, and distributing technology in equitable ways. It's been a very convenient separation for English teachers, and yet in this country, when students are introduced to computers it is very likely to be by an English teacher and not by any other content level teacher because very often we have students using computers in our classes. What English teachers are now doing is training a whole generation of technology consumers without educating them to be critical thinkers about technology.

KB: So the distinction is between technology users but not technology critics.

CS: Well, we're addicting them to technologies, we're even working to get the best, the latest, and the glitziest technologies, we're showing students how to depend on multimedia to communicate, how to communicate in technological environments, we're using technology for every assignment in many cases. And we're never asking, we're never teaching students how to think in critical ways about technology issues like cost, the intersection of technology and patterns of racism, sexism, and poverty issues in our country. And that is a problem.

KB: Do you see it as technology for technology's sake in those extreme instances?

CS: I think of it as English teachers using technology because they realize students are going to have to communicate in technological environments. It's a very pragmatic choice. They want to prepare students to participate in those environments, and this is a way that they think it can be done, but it is a short-sighted focus on functional literacies skills rather than a deep understanding between the intersection of literacy practices and social issues.

KB: That's a really interesting perspective, because I think of the emphasis in the secondary schools on proficiency, a functional definition as opposed to a cultural and critical understanding of literacy and language issues.

CS: Absolutely. The other thing that's disturbing is that I think we're talking about looking at these things on a macro-level perspective, and the thing that bothers me most about this and what I'm going to try and talk about at the CCCCs is that this literacy project is motivated by the economic and political agenda and not by an educational agenda. And by that I mean that it's motivated by policymakers who saw America's leadership potential sliding in the international scene because the Cold War was over. Our manufacturing edge was gone; Japan was threatening to become an economic leader. In the domestic scene, we had high unemployment, we had a lot of unrest and poverty in our country, continuing patterns of poverty and racism in our country. Our educational system wasn't doing what people were hoping it would do. So policymakers in the Clinton/Gore administration had to find key features of the culture that would drive a domestic recovery and international program of increasingly effective leadership, and they chose technology as that key. And they saw in technology at the international level that it would provide focus of specialization for America in a global market where people needed specialization for the U.S. so we could move into global markets for a specialization for goods and services again, which we desperately needed to do to maintain our leadership economically. It would also give us leadership in terms of forward movement in the world because we would be the people who would be offering to set up information infrastructures. On the domestic scene, it would serve as an economic engine, a fuel for recovery of the economy because in order to produce this expanded program of technology you have to have a workforce trained in technology. In order to have a workforce trained in technological use and development, it has to happen in the schools. So we teach people in the schools how to be technologically sophisticated. They go into the workforce and they produce more sophisticated technology.

KB: To run the capitalist machine!

CS: And at home they want to consume more sophisticated technology. They become addicted or adapted, they learn the habit of using technology at school and technology at work, so they buy more computers at home, they consume more computers and their appetite for sophisticated computers is whetted and so at work, they create more sophisticated computers. It's a cycle in that schools have more pressure to get sophisticated equipment, more sophisticated workers to enter the system. One of the things I'm trying to trace in this whole talk is the role of the government in this project, the role of parents in supporting this project, the role of the corporate sector, and the role of the educational system. We're all entering into this project, we're all contributing to this project, and it feeds on itself, fuels itself. It's both the engine and the fuel.

KB: Do you think English teachers are particularly resistant to this whole process and should they be?

CS: I don't think they're resistant at all. Right now, I think they've adopted a strange brand of enthusiasm and inattention. I think English teachers now have gone beyond the stage where they have to be convinced to use computers. They're using computers very readily, and it's in their own classes that they're using those computers. But computers have gotten to the point to which they can be very easily integrated into curricula. And so when teachers have students use those computers; they have become almost invisible in the curriculum. It's not as if computers are strange anymore.

KB: They're almost transparent?

CS: They're almost transparent, but not quite. So teachers are using them, and it's become a natural thing to expect technological support and to educate students in terms of the technological environments that they're going to have to communicate in once they leave the academy. Teachers are doing that, but what they're not doing is teaching people in critical terms about what that means. What does it mean now when we look at schools that the ratio of students to computers is lower than ever, 10 to 1, that's nationally, it's lower than it's ever been, which is very positive. There are more computers in the schools than ever before, and there are more multimedia computers in the hands of rich students and white students than poor students and students of color, and there are schools with higher populations of poorer students and students of color are having a harder time finding the discretionary funds to support a hookup to the infrastructure for those students. So it's a continuing pattern with technology distribution along the axis of race, socioeconomic status, and class.

KB: And it seems when those "disadvantaged" schools, programs, and students get that kind of technology, it's almost tokenized. Because I've been involved in this community literacy project in Toledo, where Bowling Green State University gave a middle school what the vice-principal referred to as "junk" computers—they took the junk because the junk was all they could get at the time. So now they do have a relationship with Ohio State, where they were given some better computers. But all we were able to give was old, obsolete Mac Classics, where all they could run on these machines were drill and practice grammar software that certainly promoted that more functional as opposed to cultural/critical literacy. And it was tough talking about those issues, because in some ways, we at the university had been critiquing the teachers and administrators for using drill and skill, that they supposedly wanted to do that to teach to proficiency. The vice-principal's remark made me realize that we didn't really equip them with the tools to do much more than that.

CS: Yes, we're all implicated in this in strange ways. We're implicated as parents too. The largest growth in the computer market is in the home computer area because enormous numbers of parents are buying computers to support their children at school. But these are the parents who can afford to buy the computers to support their children at school. And there are kids that are not getting the support at home, so we're getting a replication of a privileged group and a group that lacks privilege with regard to technology. So these are the kinds of issues I try to bring forward in NCTE meetings, or in the CCCCs. These are the issues that I feel I need to talk about and need to deal with and at least sketch out in my work.

KB: Especially for new teachers, too. I work with a lot of pre-service English teachers, and all my classes are in the lab, but all of my students are from the some homogenous white, middle-class background basically, and it's not like when I was in Texas and there were a variety of multicultural students and as a result cultural conflicts. And when I did computer literacy narratives there these conflicts really came into play. At BG, they've mostly grown up on their Commodore 64s, and they have all evolved into a mindset of bigger is better. But it is really interesting for those who are now doing their student teaching and their methods, and going out into the schools and seeing the types of cultural disadvantages various schools might have based on race, class, but also urban and rural, especially in a place like Northwest Ohio. And I think they're starting to recognize that there are inequities in terms of technology because they would like to teach with technology. There's a selfish perspective in that they want to teach with technology, they like it, but they're not going to be able to do it because they're going into a program or a school where there's no money to do it. So how do we give them the tools to think about what it means to bring technology into the classroom and to do things that can equalize that knowledge base? It's a tough, but important issue in that we sort of reinscribe our own students as they go through this process if we don't give them a chance to think about these issues.

CS: I think one of the things that happens at the department level is that we end up dealing with the same issues whether you're a national professional organization or an individual teacher, like you were just talking about the pre-service teachers or a small academic unit, like a department. The sets of issues we deal with at Michigan Tech—how do you make sure students are educated to think in those critical terms especially if they're going to be managers of technology, or teachers about technology, and that's another interesting set of sites to enact; it's where theory and scholarship is put to the test of practice. And you have to instantiate your theoretical and scholarly understanding with a daily administrative practice that you're not ashamed of. Where you spend the money, who has the machines, how you create a place like the Center for Computer-Assisted Language Instruction, that actually promotes students' conscious awareness of issues in connection with technology and actually demands and requires that they become involved in decision making. How do you, in a program like that, provide an education for GTAs so that they don't simply hold classes that reinscribe students into this cycle of technological consumerism? Then how do you educate colleagues so that's not their only goal to have the best and latest personal computer on their desk without understanding what those issues are?

KB: It's ironic that the new teachers tend to come in with some of the most traditional values. I taught a class in electronic discourse last semester, and some people wanted to focus more on helping students distinguish between online treasure and online trash, from a scholarly standpoint, not from a political standpoint, and how to help students understand the difference. And I admit that these are issues, how to determine what's reliable, what's valid on the web as opposed to what's in the library.

CS: But they all still presume the use of computers. Rather than even questioning where computers are appropriate, if they're appropriate, and when they're not appropriate.

KB: Yes. And what's lost?

CS: And also we've not been asking the questions, who benefits, who is reaping money from this process. Cui bono is a real good question to always ask about computers, who benefits, who gains from this? Asking that gets you back to some of the more critical issues too.

KB: Well, it's even part of the ideology of things like software—when I was in Texas we used Daedalus and now in Ohio I use Aspects. Presumably they do the same sorts of things, but the Daedalus chats could be saved and retrieved, they could be treated as important dialogues that we could go back to and reflect upon. In Aspects, unless you save it to a clipboard yourself, it's over with, it's gone.

CS: That's an interesting example because Daedalus as you know was developed and designed by teachers of English and Aspects was not. Well, at least Aspects has had much more commercial input.

KB: It seems like the whole process/product paradigm. What does that say about how an online conversation should be valued, if you can't easily save and retrieve it as a function of the program, archival, and from a rhetorical function, invention.

CS: Then there's always the way in which these issues come into play in our editorial work, Gail and I. We've talked about the national professional organizations, and the department and program level, and the site of computer facility. We're trying to do the same thing in our editorial work and in our books. We have a new book on international or global literacies and technology that's going to be an interesting collection. It's challenging the myth that World Wide Web provides a global, almost a neutral global environment for literacy practice. That it's a great big web that will bring all of the peoples of the world together in some sort of harmony. And so we have writing teams of people who are looking at specific cultural literacy practices in a setting of culture on the Web. And trying to determine how culture really influences the work that gets done on the Web and how that environment is far from neutral, that it's imbricated with cultural values, and those cultural practices determine whether or not that environment is useful for writers.

KB: It's very interesting to listen to you talk about this, because what occurs to me is whether you ever actually saw yourself, saw your own role as a scholar in computers in composition becoming such a political and activist role, and that's what you've become. And I think that what that's done for the profession or for the subfield is that we have also made that shift, that we went through our own mini-paradigm shift, from everything is beautiful, not to everything is bad, but that things should be questioned. How "pretty" is it really? Did you expect that, do you think that this is sort of a logical progression, given the connection between technology and capitalism and literacy?

CS: No, I think it's a indication of how much my own thinking is shaped by and influenced by the good work of other people, that the profession as a whole is becoming more aware of the social and political implications surrounding language. And we're waking up to the fact that we're not alone in the world, we're one of many world English's for instance, that our economic actions take place in a whole global context as well as in an environmental context. So the kinds of actions we're engaged in make a difference in this world, and it's become evident in composition studies. And because that's evident in composition studies, my own work has benefited in that way.

KB: The whole issue of educational equity, and the presumption that it's there.

CS: It's a very odd situation, isn't it, when we wake up to those things. I was at a meeting about future directions of the NCTE the other day. And there was some longtime members, Sheila Fitzgerald, who is a past president of the council, and Yetta Goodman, who is also a longtime leader of the council, and they were all talking about these kinds of issues as well. They see things in a different perspective being around as long as they have. And I think in part it's being around long enough to see patterns, seeing incidents as patterns rather than as individual incidents. I think that's a possibility.

KB: I'm thinking that because this collection is a book about gender and I'm wondering about how your work has been influenced by others, if you could talk about how this process comes about as part of your collaborative relationships with people, Gail, for example?

CS: Particularly Gail, our collaboration has made it possible for my work to exist. I don't think I could, I know I would not be able to do the work I'm doing today without that collaboration because it multiplies my own efforts by more than a hundred percent. The sum of our collaboration is greater than its individual parts. I think that's a tribute to her and to the notion of collaboration because it brings multiple perspectives to the study of any topic, and when you can do that, you have a very different kind of study. You don't have a single vision. You have a stereovision. And it's one of the things I like the most about working with Gail, and she is such a good collaborator. I am so dependent on her in terms of her work habits and her equanimity in the face of setbacks and challenges and also her insight in terms of human beings. Gail is absolutely stunning in that respect.

KB: She's a people person.

CS: She knows every person she's ever met. She can remember everybody and is absolutely terrific. So in all those respects, in her scholarly and her intellectual respect and in her other skills she brings to the collaboration, I am absolutely dependent on her, and have been as you know for a decade. So collaboration is very important. And not just with Gail. Gail and I find collaboration to be an entrée, an excuse to be connected, a strategy of being connected to other people in the field who are doing great work, especially women.

KB: It's a collaboration that has helped to create a community, *Computers and Composition*, for example, beginning with Kate Kiefer.

CS: That's right. Kate Kiefer was the mother of invention with regard to *Computers and Composition.* It's funny when you look at it, women have done a lot of that. There were women who started computers and composition in our field, there are women who are major editors in the field, there were women who were the moving force behind the first computers and writing conferences in our field, and I think because so often women were in positions where they had very little to lose in those early days of computers. I'm talking about the 1980s, when women did much of the experimentation with computers and might have been in part-time jobs and in writing center jobs.

KB: Helen Schwartz talked a lot about that in her interview. It was either women who were in low status positions and didn't have tenure or men who came to it after not getting tenure.

CS: I would want not to slight the involvement of men. They were actually in similar positions, but men are culturally expected to take to technology, so in that sense it is not surprising to me. Women are not culturally expected to take to technology, and so the role of women within this subdiscipline, as you have identified it, is unusual, unexpected, and gratifying. That's what I really liked about Gail and Pat's project, the women@waytoofast project, that was so cool because it brought together so many women in so many ways. And our online conversations of various kinds, including Megabyte [University], have done the same.

KB: Within that there are still conflicts because here I'm thinking of the Addison and Hilligoss article in the book that talks about the presumption of community and empowerment on a group like woman@waytoofast so that while it's there, it may not be at the same level and the same intensity for everybody.

CS: Absolutely, and that's another thing that women bring to computers and writing as a subdiscipline, being aware of difference at the same time honoring connection. They honor both; they engage in difference and engage in connection simultaneously.

KB: Well, it's a very difficult process, because when Pam and I were working on the introduction to the collection, at one point in the introduction we make the statement that from our own position as white, middle-class, heterosexual, academic women, there's no way this project, and the compilation that we've done here, meets the needs and encompasses the experiences of all women online. And definitely, if you look at the book it is all white women, there are no women of color in the book.

CS: That's a shortcoming of our field, and of the subdiscipline in particular. Involving people of color in the subdiscipline is very tough because we've inherited a lot of the baggage of a racist society. In dealing with that, we know that people of color have less access to technology, and less sophisticated technology, And we get to the point where we are now, where we look around in our subdiscipline and we should not be surprised. That's the case in public schools. When students of color get less access to less sophisticated technology and less often, we shouldn't be suprised that we have fewer colleagues of color who are participating in our discussions about technology.

KB: So that the technology is a lifelong learning process.

CS: And we're killing ourselves. I mean we're the ones who are responsible for having so few colleagues of color. Unless we can really work to change the distribution of wealth and technology in this country and the involvement of people of color, our obligation is on two fronts. On the more immediate and personal front: every time we do a collection or collaboration to seek out as best we can difference to involve in our projects, difference in sexual orientation and difference in race and work to honor people who represent that difference by involving them, and asking them to be involved in that project. In the long term, we have to put in our scholarly focus an emphasis on pushing the realization that technology is not equitably distributed in this country and in this world and work on programs that would make that distribution more equitable.

KB: So more school/college collaboration as well? I think the thing that I would ask is from a teacher's standpoint, is what can I do. To put myself in that role not just of technological critic, but also of technological activist, because I think that's what we've become, and what we should become. As educators we're not just focusing on what this means for our scholarship, whether or not somebody's writing skills are improved, that sort of self-justification scholarship that we no longer do.

CS: Activism takes place on a number of levels, and one of the levels is on the level of scholarship. It's no small feat, as Paulo Freire said, to make people conscious. That's always the first step. But it can always take place on other levels, and needs to. In the public schools, one of the things that I would be absolutely in favor of is parents of students insisting that more money in school districts go to those schools that have high populations of students of color. That is where the technology money should go, and in absolute direct proportion, that the higher these populations, the more money for technology.

KB: But many parents don't do that.

CS: Well, parents need to insist that it's done in the school district. Within particular classrooms, the same way, teachers need to pay particular attention to students of color and involve them as actively as possible in not only using technology, but in thinking critically about technology and making decisions about technology. And in leading others in connection with technology. In assignments, it has to be the same thing. Assignments in first-year English classrooms have to focus on issues connected with technology, issues of power, the gendered nature of technology, technology and power, technology, poverty, and race. These are all social issues we have to have students reading about and being aware of if this is ever going to change. So if we can enact that activism at all those different levels simultaneously and make some dent. It's micropolitics, a lot of people, a lot of little change, at a lot of different sites. Sometimes creates a tangential force that makes a larger-scale change.

KB: Well, and there are small steps. I'm thinking of this whole Toledo project. It was an entirely African-American school, and what they would do with the junkie Macs that we gave them. They could presumably do things like community newsletters that they could then distribute, that it wasn't just a virtual community and it wasn't just a classroom community. It was something that extended beyond the classroom and into the larger cultural community that surrounded this population, their families, their friends. One of the women on our panel about this project talked about other types of literacy practices within African-American culture, church bulletins for example, and how technology could be used to create such texts, and with more advanced technology distribute them. So that you could have online bulletins.

CS: Absolutely, and even in that summer workshop that Gail and I do up in Houghton.

KB: Which I'd love to come to.

CS: You should come up someday, because that's another site where we need to enact difference. One of the things that I've started doing there is offering a scholarship to any person of color who will come to it. That's a small step but at least it provides some incentive. It starts at a very individual level.

KB: It's very endemic to our field. I'm thinking of our own graduate students at Bowling Green, and Pam's students at Louisville and graduate programs across the country, that there are very few people of color, not just within technology, but within the field of rhetoric and composition still.

CS: One of the things that I worry about is that we all start feeling so guilty that we're paralyzed by this type of situation. So many people are becoming aware of these inequities that it's become a positive force. So when you're aware of this, and when students are aware of it, we've got to change the way that we look at it in the long run. Even starting with that awareness, that's good, that's positive, but it's not enough.

KB: It's interesting how uncomfortable it makes people.

CS: It makes me very uncomfortable. There's only so many hours a day I can reflect on this, and there's got to be a time where you can't allow the guilt to paralyze you. It's not enough to know those inequities exist. You've got to have enough heart to keep going on, to do this day after day, and you can't keep beating yourself up. You've got to take some joy and pleasure in your job, even when things are not as you would have them, I think.

KB: In wrapping this up, we need to do more than scratching the surface, that we still have a rhetoric of empowerment. That oh yeah, now you can get online and go to the White House.

CS: As if that's the answer.

KB: You can e-mail a White House staffer and what does that do? You have technological capability and that still doesn't give you access to the political process, and even for the groups we're talking about, access to the technology to even do that. So what that the White House is online?

CS: And you don't only want to make it possible for people to enter a system and replicate that system. I think that what you do for the students we're working with and the culture at large is to reveal for yourself and for other people the system of relationships that exist in a culture between technology and these other factors that we've talked about. You reveal that system of relations and then trust that the natural inventiveness and coping strategies of other human beings are going to come up strategies for dealing with that system of relations. Anthony Giddens says that people's understanding of the social systems in which they work is very potent, so we know that individual cultural understandings can lead to change. We know this. We've seen that in the past. In laying out that series of relations, that's our hope, that other groups, large groups, small groups, individuals are going to be able to carry forward change once they see the system of relations.

KB: And our goal as writing teachers in part is that the technology can make that process visible and not transparent. That you can use something like the Web, that you can use something like online discourse as a medium for this type of critique.

CS: Both a medium for it and a focus of the critique itself.

KB: In some ways, it's a very self-reflexive process, that move toward critical literacy and not functional literacy. Thanks very much, Cindy.

Author Index

Subject Index

About the Editors

Kristine Blair is Assistant Professor of English at Bowling Green State University, where she teaches computer-mediated writing courses and graduate level courses in rhetorical theory, composition pedagogy, and electronic discourse. Her most recent work on technology appears in the journal *Computers and Composition* and in the book *Situating Portfolios: Four Perspectives* (1997; with Pamela Takayoshi). Her current research includes multimedia literacy and the application of cultural studies pedagogy to the electronic writing classroom.

Pamela Takayoshi is Assistant Professor of English and Director of Computer-Assisted Writing Instruction at the University of Louisville, where she teaches courses in rhetoric and women's studies. Her work on technology has appeared in the journals *Computers and Composition* and *Teaching English in the Two-Year College,* as well as the book *Situating Portfolios: Four Perspectives* (1997). Her scholarly interests revolve around the intersections between feminisms, cultural studies, writing theories, pedagogy, and technology. She is currently involved in several research projects aimed at understanding the ways girls negotiate their relationships with technologies such as e-mail and the World Wide Web.

About the Contributors

Joanne Addison is an Assistant Professor at the University of Colorado-Denver where she teaches undergraduate and graduate courses in rhetorical theory, cultural studies, and computers and writing. Her work has recently been published in the journals *Computers and Composition* and *Written Communication.* Joanne is currently co-editing a collection with Sharon James McGee titled *Feminist Empirical Research: Emerging Perspectives* (forthcoming).

Christine Boese is Assistant Professor of English at Clemson University. A graduate in Rhetoric and Communication from Rensselaer Polytechnic Institute, her work focuses on communication technologies and the Internet in terms of feminist theory and cultural rhetoric. She completed the first hypertextual dissertation to be accepted at Rensselaer, titled "The Ballad of the Internet Nutball: The Xenaverse in Cyberspace," accessible online at http://www.nutball.com.

Margaret Daisley is a Ph.D. candidate in composition and rhetoric at the University of Massachusetts, Amherst, whose studies have focused on themeaning of computer technologies in literacy narratives. Currently on leave of absence from her graduate program, Daisley is working as a freelance editor. She is pleased to report that, since completing the co-writing of this collage, she has finally upgraded to a bigger, faster, AV-equipped computer with point-and-click access to the Net.

Lisa Gerrard holds a Ph.D. in comparative literature from the University of California, Berkeley, and is a lecturer in the UCLA Writing Programs. Her publications include books and articles on computers and writing, foreign language composition, and feminist literary criticism. She co-authored the software *HBJ Writer* (Harcourt Brace Jovanovich, 1986), the *Prewriting Stacks* (Chariot Software, 1992), and *La Preescritura* (Chariot Software, 1992) and is currently developing a computer program that explores issues of language and gender.

Paula Gillespie discovered e-mail on her way to Marquette University's electronic card catalogue; her first modem was intended to help students find research sources, but it and its successors have led her to new friendships and new ways of looking at connectedness. She directs the Ott Memorial Writing Center and has been published on such topics as writing center research, on voice, and on James Joyce.

Morgan Gresham is a doctoral student in rhetoric and composition at the University of Louisville. She is currently working on her dissertation on feminist theory and CAI/CMC administration and will begin a position as an assistant professor at Texas Woman's University in the Fall of 1999.

Dene Grigar is an Assistant Professor of English at Texas Woman's University, where she teaches composition (in electronic classrooms), Greek literature and language, English education, and women's studies. Her most recent work has appeared in the journal *Kairos* and in *The Dialogic Classroom: Integrating Computer Technology, Pedagogy, and Research* (1998).

Sibylle Gruber is an Assistant Professor in Rhetoric and Composition at Northern Arizona University. Her research focuses on the acquisition of academic literacy of nontraditional students in online environments. Her publications include articles in the journals *Computers and Composition, Computer Supported Cooperative Work,* and *Journal of the Assembly on Computers in English.* She is also the editor of *Weaving a Virtual Web: Practical Approaches to New Information Technologies* (forthcoming).

Cecilia Hartley is completing her Ph.D. in rhetoric and composition at the University of Louisville. Her research focus is computer-mediated conversation and the roles it plays in students' negotiations between and among discourse communities.

Susan Hilligoss is Associate Professor of English at Clemson University,where she teaches in the professional communication program. She has published a study of Robert Coles and, with Cynthia L. Selfe, co-edited *Literacy and Computers: The Complications of Teaching and Learning with Technology.*

Mary Hocks is Assistant Professor of English at Georgia State University. She is the co-director, with Anne Balsamo, of Women of the World Talk Back, a multimedia exhibit that they originally designed for the Fourth World Conference on Women in Beijing, China, in 1995. Her research includes hypertext theory, multimedia development, and writing in multimedia environments.

Laura Julier is an Associate Professor of American Thought and Language at Michigan State University, where she teaches American literature, writing, and women's studies. Currently, she is involved in investigating the connections between service-learning and writing pedagogies, and is co-editor (with David D. Cooper) of

Writing in the Public Interest: Service-Learning and the Writing Classroom (1997) for the Curriculum in the Academy and the World monograph series. Among her other publications are articles on the rhetoric of the Clothesline Project, and the essayist Joan Didion.

Donna LeCourt is an assistant professor at Colorado State University, where she teaches courses in literacy, gender and writing, and theories of writing. Her most recent publications appeared in the *Journal of Advanced Composition*, the *International Journal of Education*, and *Computers and Composition.*

Barbara Monroe's research and practice both center on the politics of technological contact zones—the cultural collisions in virtual environments, when women, minorities, and the working class get online. She is especially interested in how African-American expressive culture will be colonized and transformed by technology. Monroe is the Project Director of the Murray-Wright High School/University of Michigan Connection, a 3-year distance-learning literacy program. The project has become the model for the University of Michigan's outreach to other high schools in Detroit and around the state.

Susan Romano is Assistant Professor of English at the University of Texas at San Antonio. She is interested in the newly developing pedagogies of online writing instruction, and her recent research examines the rhetorical means by which student participants in electronic conferences establish and reject discussion topics and social identities. She has published articles about ethnicity and gender in online teaching environments, about writing program administration in the electronic age, and about composition research on the World Wide Web. Her 1993 *Computers and Composition* article "Egalitarianism Narrative" won the Ellen Nold Award for best article in computers and composition studies.

S. J. Sloane is Associate Professor of English at the University of Puget Sound, where she also directs the program in women's studies. She has published book reviews, poetry, an article on 18th-century rhetoric, and several articles on gender, computers, and composition. She is working toward publishing her first book, *Computing Fictions: Reading and Writing in a Material World*, with Ablex Publishing in this same series. She has a Ph.D. from Ohio State, an M.F.A from the University of Massachusetts, Amherst, and an M.A. from Carnegie Mellon University.

Shannon L. Wilson is a doctoral candidate in rhetoric and composition at Miami University of Ohio. Her research interests include feminist pedagogy, narrative theory, and cultural studies. Her dissertation, "Educating the 'Individual': College Composition, Narrative Theory, and the Politics of Public Discourse," is a feminist rhetorical analysis of the ways subjects and public policy are constructed through the dominant narrative of the autonomous individual.

Kathleen Blake Yancey is Associate Professor of English at the University of North Carolina at Charlotte, where she teaches undergraduate courses in first-year and advanced writing, and graduate courses in rhetorical theory and writing assessment. Her work includes the edited collections *Portfolios in the Writing Classroom: An Introduction* (1992) and *Voices on Voice: Perspectives, Definitions, Inquiry* (1994), *Situating Portfolios: Four Perspectives*, with Irwin Weiser (1997), and her book *Reflection in the Writing Classroom* (1998).